1082

The Press
and
America

FOURTH EDITION

The Press and America

An Interpretative History of the Mass Media

EDWIN EMERY

Professor of Journalism and Mass Communication
University of Minnesota

MICHAEL EMERY

Professor of Journalism
California State University, Northridge

Prentice-Hall, Inc., Englewood Cliffs, New Jersey 07632

Library of Congress Cataloging in Publication Data

EMERY, EDWIN.
  The press and America.

  Includes bibliographies and index.
    1. Press—United States. 2. American newspapers.
I. Emery, Michael C., joint author. II. Title.
PN4855.E6 1978   071'.3   77-25474
ISBN 0-13-697979-3

PRENTICE-HALL INTERNATIONAL, INC., *London*
PRENTICE-HALL OF AUSTRALIA PTY. LIMITED, *Sydney*
PRENTICE-HALL OF CANADA, LTD., *Toronto*
PRENTICE-HALL OF INDIA PRIVATE LIMITED, *New Delhi*
PRENTICE-HALL OF JAPAN, INC., *Tokyo*
PRENTICE-HALL OF SOUTHEAST ASIA PTE. LTD., *Singapore*
WHITEHALL BOOKS LIMITED, *Wellington, New Zealand*

The first edition of *The Press and America* won the coveted Sigma Delta Chi national research award, the highest in the field of journalism.

Edwin Emery, Ph.D., is Professor of Journalism and Mass Communication at the University of Minnesota. He has been president of the Association for Education in Journalism and editor of its research journal, *Journalism Quarterly*. Author or editor of seven books, Professor Emery also won the Sigma Delta Chi national award for his *History of the American Newspaper Publishers Association* and has been a Guggenheim Fellow. He is a former United Press bureau manager.

Michael Emery, Ph.D., is Professor of Journalism at California State University, Northridge. He is co-editor of *Readings in Mass Communication: Concepts and Issues in the Mass Media,* which won a Kappa Tau Alpha special research award, and of *America's Front Page News, 1690–1970.* He has been associate editor of *Journalism History,* chairman of the West Coast Journalism Historians Conference, and a United Press International correspondent.

Contents

Illustrations

Foreword

Journalism history is the story of humanity's long struggle to communicate freely with each other—to dig out and interpret news and to offer intelligent opinion in the market place of ideas. Part of the story has as its theme the continuing efforts by men and women to break down the barriers that have been erected to prevent the flow of information and ideas, upon which public opinion is so largely dependent. Another aspect of the story is concerned with the means, or media, by which this essential news and opinion reaches the public, from the days of the handwritten ''newes letter'' to the printed page, radio, and television. Just as important to this story are the heroes and villains, as well as the bit actors, who made the press (meaning all media of communication) what it is today. Finally, all this becomes more meaningful when the development of America's journalistic tradition is related to the political, economic, and social progress of its people.

The title, *The Press and America,* reflects the emphasis placed upon correlation of journalism history with political, economic, and social trends. In this interaction, the press has had its influence upon the course taken by the United States. Conversely, the conditions and influences present in each historical era have cumulatively determined the shape of the press. Within this framework emerges the story of the men and women of journalism and of the institutions and traditions they created. Thus, the story ranges from newspaper editor James Franklin, critic of 1721 authorities, to television reporter Dan Rather, critic of 1974 authorities; from newspaper publisher Mary Katherine Goddard to Katharine Graham; from opinion-molder Horace Greeley to Edward R. Murrow; from radical publicist Sam Adams to I. F. Stone; from talented writer Tom Paine to Tom Wolfe.

In the opening chapters, beginning with the European roots of American journalism and covering the long time-span ending with the Civil War, the primary concern is with an exposition of the principles upon which the American Fourth Estate was founded. The modern mass media—newspapers, television, radio, magazines, press associations—are then extensively examined as they play their roles in an increasingly complex society. At the same time, the book surveys landmark events in journalism history, probing significant issues, personalities, and institutions and tracing how major events in American history were covered and interpreted by reporters, editors, and broadcasters.

The electronic media have been given increased emphasis in this edition, reflecting the impact of television in political campaigns, the Watergate era, and the Vietnam war and television's controversial social role in the 1960s and 1970s. New material is incorporated on minorities and alternative journalism, investigative reporting, women journalists, media law, and technology. Media economics are updated and condensed into one comprehensive chapter, and a chapter on media responses to current criticism has been added. Extensive editing and writing revisions have been made throughout the book, particularly in concluding chapters, and chapter bibliographies and illustrations have been updated.

ACKNOWLEDGMENTS   Thanks are due to many persons who have aided in this venture during three decades. For this edition, comprehensive criticisms of the manuscript came from Professor William H. Taft of the University of Missouri and Professor Bruce H. Westley of the University of Kentucky. Extending manuscript aid in special areas were Sam Kuczun, University of Colorado; Tom Reilly, California State University, Northridge; and Peter Donaghue and Judith Sobel, University of Minnesota. Making information available to us generously were Paul Jess, University of Kansas; Ralph E. Kliesch, Ohio University; Maurine Beasley and Joseph P. McKerns, University of Maryland; Marion Marzolf, University of Michigan; Félix Gutiérrez, California State University, Northridge; Sharon Murphy, University of Wisconsin, Milwaukee; and Harvey Saalberg, Angelo State University. Richard Kielbowicz, Minnesota, assisted in bibliographical search. Our special thanks go to William H. Oliver, journalism editor, and Lynda Heideman, production editor, of Prentice-Hall, Inc.

The debts for aid with earlier editions can be acknowledged here only in part. Very substantial acknowledgments are due Henry Ladd Smith, then at Wisconsin, co-author for the first edition, particularly for graceful writing in the early chapters; first edition manuscript readers Ralph D. Casey, University of Minnesota, Frederick B. Marbut, Pennsylvania State University, and Kenneth E. Olson, Northwestern University; third edition manuscript critic Richard A. Schwarzlose of Northwestern; and journalism bibliographers Warren C. Price, University of Oregon, and Calder M. Pickett, University of Kansas. Harold L. Nelson, University of Wisconsin, gave invaluable assistance during the preparation of the original index and has offered many suggestions for text revisions, particularly for the colonial period. Co-author Michael Emery began his association with the book during the third edition revision.

Mention must be made of past aid by journalism professors Ralph O. Nafziger and William A. Hachten, Wisconsin; Quintus C. Wilson, Northern Illinois; Robert W. Desmond, California; Roland E. Wolseley, Syracuse; Henry G. La Brie III, Maine; John D. Stevens, Michigan; William E. Ames, Washington; Donald L. Shaw, North Carolina; Randall L. Murray, California Polytechnic, San Luis Obispo; Paul V. Peterson, Ohio State; Robert V. Hudson, Michigan State; and R. Smith Schuneman, Raymond B. Nixon, Edwin H. Ford, J. Edward Gerald, Minnesota. We also wish to thank the many others whose encouraged us. To Mary M. Emery and Suzanne S. Emery for assistance and patient support.

Finally, we acknowledge our debt to the many sch contributions to journalism history are listed in the footnote

The Press
and
America

The Daily Courant.

Wednefday, March 11. 1702.

From the Harlem Courant, Dated March 18. N. S.

Naples, Feb. 22.

ON Wednefday laft, our New Viceroy, the Duke of Efcalona, arriv'd here with a Squadron of the Galleys of Sicily. He made his Entrance dreft in a French habit; and to give us the greater Hopes of the King's coming hither, went to Lodge in one of the little Palaces, leaving the Royal one for his Majefty. The Marquis of Grigni is alfo arriv'd here with a Regiment of French.

Rome, Feb.25. In a Military Congregation of State that was held here, it was Refolv'd to draw a Line from Afcoli to the Borders of the Ecclefiaftical State, thereby to hinder the Incurfions of the Tranfalpine Troops. Orders are fent to Civita Vecchia to fit out the Galleys, and to ftrengthen the Garrifon of that Place. Signior Cafali is made Governor of Perugia. The Marquis del Vafto, and the Prince de Caferta continue ftill in the Imperial Embaffador's Palace; where his Excellency has a Guard of 50 Men every Night in Arms. The King of Portugal has defir'd the Arch-Bifhoprick of Lisbon, vacant by the Death of Cardinal Soufa, for the Infante his fecond Son, who is about 11 Years old.

Vienna, Mar. 4. Orders are fent to the 4 Regiments of Foot, the 2 of Cuiraffiers, and to that of Dragoons, which are broke up from Hungary, and are on their way to Italy, and which confift of about 14 or 15000 Men, to haften their March thither with all Expedition. The 6 new Regiments of Huffars that are now raifing, are in fo great a forwardnefs, that they will be compleat, and in a Condition to march by the middle of May. Prince Lewis of Baden has written to Court, to excufe himfelf from coming thither, his Prefence being fo very neceffary, and fo much defir'd on the Upper-Rhine.

Francfort, Mar. 12. The Marquifs d' Uxelles is come to Strasburg, and is to draw together a Body of fome Regiments of Horfe and Foot from the Garifons of Alface; but will not leffen thofe of Strasburg and Landau, which are already very weak. On the other hand, the Troops of His Imperial Majefty, and his Allies, are going to form a Body near Germefhein in the Palatinate, of which Place, as well as of the Lines at Spires, Prince Lewis of Baden is expected to take a View, in three or four days. The Englifh and Dutch Minifters, the Count of Frife, and the Baron Vander Meer; and likewife the Imperial Envoy Count Lowenftein, are gone to Nordlingen, and it is hop'd that in a fhort time we fhall hear from thence of fome favourable Refolutions for the Security of the Empire.

Liege, Mar. 14. The French have taken the Cannon de Longie, who was Secretary to the Dean de Mean, out of our Caftle, where he has been for fome time a Prifoner, and have deliver'd him to the Provoft of Maubeuge, who has carry'd him from hence, but we do not know whither.

Paris, Mar. 13. Our Letters from Italy fay, That moft of our Reinforcements were Landed there; that the Imperial and Ecclefiaftical Troops feem to live very peaceably with one another in the Country of Parma, and that the Duke of Vendome, as he was vifiting feveral Pofts, was within 100 Paces of falling into the Hands of the Germans. The Duke of Chartres, the Prince of Conti, and feveral other Princes of the Blood, are to make the Campaign in Flanders under the Duke of Burgundy; and the Duke of Maine is to Command upon the Rhine.

From the Amfterdam Courant, Dated Mar. 18.

Rome, Feb. 25. We are taking here all poffible Precautions for the Security of the Ecclefiaftical State in this prefent Conjuncture, and have defir'd to raife 3000 Men in the Cantons of Switzerland. The Pope has appointed the Duke of Berwick to be his Lieutenant-General, and he is to Command 6000 Men on the Frontiers of Naples: He has alfo fettled upon him a Penfion of 6000 Crowns a year during Life.

From the Paris Gazette, Dated Mar. 18. 1702.

Naples, Febr. 19. 600 French Soldiers are arrived here, and are expected to be follow'd by 3400 more. A Courier that came hither on the 14th. has brought Letters by which we are affur'd that the King of Spain defigns to be here towards the end of March; and accordingly Orders are given to make the neceffary Preparations againft his Arrival. The two Troops of Horfe that were Commanded to the Abruzzo are pofted at Pefcara with a Body of Spanifh Foot, and others in the Fort of Montorio.

Paris, March. 18. We have Advice from Toulon of the 5th inftant, that the Wind having long ftood favourable, 22000 Men were already fail'd for Italy, that 2560 more were Embarking, and that by the 15th it was hoped they might all get thither. The Count d' Eftrees arriv'd there on the Third inftant, and fet all hands at work to fit out the Squadron of 9 Men of War and fome Fregats, that are appointed to carry the King of Spain to Naples. His Catholick Majefty will go on Board the Thunderer, of 110 Guns.

We have Advice by an Exprefs from Rome of the 18th of February, That notwithftanding the preffing Inftances of the Imperial Embaffadour, the Pope had Condemn'd the Marquis del Vafto to lofe his Head and his Eftate to be confifcated, for not appearing to Anfwer the Charge againft him of Publickly Scandalizing Cardinal Janfon.

ADVERTISEMENT.

IT will be found from the Foreign Prints, which from time to time, as Occafion offers, will be mention'd in this Paper, that the Author has taken Care to be duly furnifh'd with all that comes from Abroad in any Language. And for an Affurance that He will not, under Pretence of having Private Intelligence, impofe any Additions of feign'd Circumftances to an Action, but give his Extracts fairly and Impartially; at the beginning of each Article he will quote the Foreign Paper from whence 'tis taken, that the Publick, feeing from what Country a piece of News comes with the Allowance of that Government, may be better able to Judge of the Credibility and Fairnefs of the Relation: Nor will he take upon him to give any Comments or Conjectures of his own, but will relate only Matter of Fact, fuppofing other People to have Senfe enough to make Reflections for themfelves.

This Courant (as the Title fhews) will be Publifh'd Daily: being defign'd to give all the Material News as foon as every Poft arrives; and is confin'd to half the Compafs, to fave the Publick at leaft half the Impertinences, of ordinary News-Papers.

LONDON. Sold by E. Mallet, next Door to the King's-Arms Tavern at Fleet-Bridge.

Facsimile of the first daily newspaper in the English language.

1

The Heritage of the American Press

Give me but the liberty of the press and I will give to the minister a venal House of Peers ... and servile House of Commons ... I will give him all the power that place can confer upon him to purchase up submission and overawe resistance—And yet, armed with liberty of the press ... I will attack the mighty fabric he has reared ... and bury it amidst the ruins of the abuses it was meant to shelter.

—Richard Brinsley Sheridan

We might begin our story with the appearance of the first newspaper in colonial America; that would appear to be the beginning of American journalism. The colonial newspaper, however, was so closely patterned after the British product that to understand the function of the press at that time, it is necessary to explain a little about the English influence. Many able writers, including Bleyer and Shaaber, have started their histories of the American press with the appearance of corantos, or primitive newspapers printing foreign news, in the early seventeenth century. The English coranto was, in turn, traceable to similar publications on the continent. It is now generally conceded that the modern press is the gift of no one nation and that it was already in the process of development in other parts of the world long before the corantos began to be read in London.

THE EARLIEST   The oldest known and preserved copies of a primitive newspaper were
NEWSPAPERS   published in Germany in 1609, but the existing copies do not indicate the
city, printer, or publisher. From an analysis of paper, type, printing technique, political content, and religious coloring, experts deduced that the site of this earliest known newspaper had to be in North Germany. According to Dr. Ralph O. Nafziger, who made a lengthy study of the evidence produced by German researchers, the 1609 *Aviso* appeared in Wolfenbüttel rather than in Bremen as earlier thought.

Painstaking research has established other early newspaper publication in Strasbourg, also in 1609, and in Cologne in 1610. By 1620 it had spread to Frankfurt, Berlin, Hamburg, Basel, Vienna, Amsterdam, and Antwerp. Amsterdam printers were publishing papers in the English and French languages in 1620, but the first London publication appeared in 1621, and the first Paris paper in 1631. A court newspaper begun in Stockholm in 1645 still appears and is the world's oldest known continuously published newspaper.[1]

Other countries also contributed to the development of the press. In 1566 the Venetian Magistracy ordered accounts of the war in Dalmatia to be read and posted in public places. Persons interested in this news paid a small coin, called a *gazetta,* for the privilege of obtaining it. Thirty volumes of these "Gazettes" have been preserved in the Maggliabecchi Library in Florence.[2] Even before this, the Italian peninsula was noted for its advances in the publication of current events; as far back as 59 B.C., news sheets known as *Acta Diurna* were posted in public places in Rome. These were filed each succeeding day in a special building housing records, where they were available to anyone wishing to make use of them.

During the European Middle Ages, the Chinese made important contributions to the art of printing. In A.D. 868, Wang Chieh published a book printed from blocks. Copies of it survive as man's oldest printed book. The first known use of movable type was by another Chinese, Pi Shêng, around 1045. Although the influence of the Chinese craftsmen on Western pioneers would be difficult to establish, it is known that Marco Polo described Chinese printing methods when he returned to Venice from the East in 1295. It was in the same area that paper was first used in printing. The court gazette at Peking set a record for continuous publication by appearing for more than 1,000 years, but disappeared in 1911.

THE CONCEPT OF NEWS

The point to all this is that England had no special claim as the home of the modern press, even though it advanced beyond all other countries journalistically. In England, as in other lands, news was exchanged long before there was even the most primitive form of newspaper. One of the great attractions at the country fairs of the Middle Ages was the opportunity to exchange gossip and information. Countrymen and gentry traveled annually to Bartholomew, Donnybrook, or Stourbridge as much to swap news as to buy yearly supplies of staples. Newspapers did not create news; news created newspapers.

It has been said that the true newspaper must meet the following qualifications: (1) it must be published at least once a week; (2) it must be produced by mechanical means (to distinguish it from the handwritten "newes letters"); (3) it must be available to anyone willing to pay the price, regardless of class or special interests; (4) it must print anything of interest to a general public, as contrasted with some of the religious and business publications; (5) it must have an appeal to a public of ordinary literary skill; (6) it must be timely, or at least relatively so in light of technical development; and (7) it must have stability.[3]

Any publication that could meet all these qualifications was indeed an innovation. It might even be said that the newspaper was the most significant contribution of the printing press. There were extensive libraries of books long before there was a printing press. The so-called cradle books, produced immediately after Johann Gutenberg introduced movable type to Europe around 1440 at Mainz and printed his famous Bible in the 1450s, were not essentially different from the handwritten volumes common before that date. The newspaper, on the other hand, was something new. Not until movable type had been perfected was it possible to produce literature and printed reports cheap enough to reach the masses. The revolution was not so much in the medium, perhaps, as in the audience. At any rate, the newspaper was the most novel product of the printing press.

With a publication of this type, there was some incentive for gathering and processing information of interest to the general public—news. News thereupon became a commodity, like food or merchandise, produced for profit to meet a demand. Up to about 1500, "Tydings" was the usual word to describe reports of current events. The word "news" was coined to differentiate between the casual dissemination of information and the deliberate attempt to gather and process the latest intelligence.[4]

It is significant that the newspaper first flourished in areas where authority was weak, as in Germany, at that time divided into a patchwork of small principalities; or where rulers were more tolerant, as in the low countries. This explains why the development of the press lagged in England. True, William Caxton set up the first press in England in 1476, but nearly two centuries elapsed before the country had a genuine newspaper.

Caxton learned about printing on the continent, where it had been a craft since the middle of the fifteenth century. He had been governor of a chartered association of "adventurers," or merchants interested in foreign enterprise. Caxton was a learned man, the author and translator of several volumes, and a collector of fine books. He believed that it was his mission to bring the culture of the continent to his countrymen. His king, Edward IV, encouraged these ideas. Edward had just come to power, following a long civil war that had split the country. Not until 1471 was he safely in control of his government.[5] At once he began to repair the ravages of the internal conflict. Edward was responsible for progress in law, industry, and culture. It was under such circumstances that Caxton set up his tiny press "at the Sign of the Red Pale" in the almonry of the abbey at Westminster in 1476.[6]

THE TUDOR REIGN: LICENSING
The Battle of Bosworth Field in 1485 brought a new dynasty into being. Henry Tudor, the victor, ended the long feud between the royal houses of York and Lancaster, thereby bringing the country back to the stability it so desperately needed. A Lancastrian by blood and a Yorkist by marriage, he emerged from the Wars of the Roses, as the civil strife was called, with powers that were eventually to make the Tudors as nearly absolute in power as English monarchs could be. The nobility, which had previously restrained the powers of the English kings, was decimated by the long years of fighting. The Tudor monarchs took full advantage of the situation. Most of them were brilliant and able administrators. Under Tudor leadership England experienced a golden age. It was not conducive to the progress of the press, however.

Caxton enjoyed relative freedom from royal interference, mostly because he never tried to test his status. Printing was not a social force for about 50 years after its establishment in England. Under the Tudors, however, the press became a matter of kingly concern, for that strong dynasty was noted for its attempts to grasp all possible power. Henry VIII started the control of the press with a list of prohibited books. This was in 1529, and the purpose was to set up a bulwark against the rising tide of Protestantism. The first licensing system under government control was established a year later, and by a proclamation on Christmas day 1534, Henry VIII required printers to have royal permission before setting up shop. Thus the concept of "prior restraint" became law.

During this period the powers of the Privy Council were also increased, at the expense of Parliament and the older courts but to the advantage of the crown. The Council supervised the administration of laws, regulated trade, kept an eye on the courts, and controlled the press. Beginning in 1542 the records of the Council show a continuous report of proceedings against individuals for "unfitting worddes," seditious utterances, and the like. As early as 1540 the Council made arrests for the printing of street ballads about political matters. The proclamation (ordinance) was the tool employed by the king or his Council to give legality and force to the regulation of the press. By later standards there was no legality to such royal ordinances, but they were enforced as law by the strong Tudors.[7]

Despite these repressive measures, a kind of literary black market supplied the forbidden information and entertainment. We know, for example, that Henry VIII was angered in the thirty-sixth year of his reign by accounts of a battle in Scotland. The news was peddled by London "broadsheet" vendors, a broadsheet being a paper printed specifically to describe a certain event. The king's complaint was not so much that the reports were false but that the news had been printed without his permission. Apparently, even the absolute powers of the king could not throttle the press, but the climate was not healthy for the steady growth of journalism.

THE STATIONERS COMPANY

One way to control an industry is to make it a monopoly and then to hold the directors of it responsible for abuses. The Tudors did that with the printing industry in 1557 when Queen Mary established the Stationers Company. This organization had existed since 1357 as a society of court and text writers, to which the "limners," or illustrators, were admitted after 1404. By 1500 the printers had also been admitted, but by Mary's time the word "stationer" was applied to the publishers and dealers in books, as distinct from the printers.[8] It was a kind of printing trust, and it made it easier for authorities to run down rebel printers not members of the elite group or sanctioned by it. Queen Elizabeth supplemented this control by her "Injunctions," which gave the religious hierarchy a measure of control over printing. Until the upheavals of the mid-seventeenth century the Stationers Company exerted one of the most powerful controls over the press. In 1576, for example, the Stationers adopted an order for weekly search of London printing houses (where almost all printing was concentrated). Pairs of searchers reported on work in progress, the number of orders on hand, identity of customers, number of employees, and wages paid. That was an effective check on extensive bootleg printing.

THE STAR CHAMBER

The infamous Star Chamber court, originally set up to protect the public but later the symbol of repression, was another barrier to free expression during the long period preceding the appearance of the English newspaper. By edict of the Privy Council in 1566 and of the Star Chamber in 1586, the pattern of restrictions for the next hundred years was outlined. Severe penalties were prescribed for printers foolish enough to defy the authorities. Strange as it may seem, there were printers willing to run that risk. There was William Carter, who was hanged for printing pamphlets favorable to the Catholic cause. Arrested and tortured in 1580, he was executed in 1584.[9] Puritan rebels against the Established Church included Hugh Singleton, Robert Waldegrave, John Stroud, and John Hodgkins. The attack on the monopoly control was led by John Wolfe, Roger Ward, William Holmes, and John Charlewood. Waldegrave was the printer of the first "Martin Marprelate" tracts, the Puritan arguments published surreptitiously against the Established Church. Hodgkins carried on when Waldegrave was hounded from the country.

The Tudor control of the press was maintained in the interest of public safety. From Henry VIII to Elizabeth I, the Crown acted on the principle that peace demanded the suppression of unwarranted dissent. The Tudors were able, and even brilliant, administrators on the whole. Sensitive to public opinion, they understood their people so well that they knew just how far to push their arbitrary rule. Ruthless and erratic as they were at times, their subjects admired them (with some exceptions, of course). Under the Tudors the country had developed great national pride. The Tudors "had the feel" of the country and more often than not were interested in the general welfare. Resistance to them was negligible, therefore, at least from the journalistic standpoint.

THE STUARTS AND TURMOIL   The upheaval came when a new dynasty came to power. James I (he was James VI of Scotland) was sincere and well-meaning, but he was never in tune with the times, or with his subjects. He was the son of the unfortunate Mary Queen of Scots, whose life had been marked by scandal and violence. As the son of Mary, he was early suspected of "Papist" sympathies in a day when that was religious jargon for treason. It was also his misfortune to succeed one of England's great rulers, Elizabeth I—"Good Queen Bess." He suffered badly in comparison with that astute and able monarch. Under the Stuarts, beginning with James, the opposing factions formed battle lines. And since the press thrives in such a climate, if restraints break down, perhaps this partially explains the rapid development of journalism during the seventeenth century.

During the early part of that century news became of great importance to the English people. The religious disputes, the rise of England as a maritime power, the struggles between king and Parliament, and the changing social conditions made the public more interested in events beyond its local sphere. The balladeers and broadsheet vendors could not meet the demand. Prose pamphlets were much more effective, as evidenced by the success of the Marprelate tracts, but such publications were not regular enough. The news letter writers, or "intelligencers " as the publishers of handwritten sheets were called, were capable journalists, but the average person could not afford their products.[10] The time was ripe for a new type of publication.

FIRST ENGLISH CORANTOS   In the summer of 1621, nearly a century and a half after Caxton introduced printing to England, the very rudimentary prototypes of the modern newspaper appeared on the streets of London. These primitive news sheets were called corantos. They lacked the regularity that is a necessity of the true newspaper, and they were too specialized in content, but they did fulfill a need.

In 1620 the English were interested in continental developments. The popular Princess Elizabeth had married Frederick, Elector of the Palatinate, in 1613. He was a Protestant, highly favored by nonconformists both on the Continent and in England. When he decided to accept the crown of Bohemia against the wishes of the Holy Roman Emperor, he precipitated the Thirty Years' War.

Printers in the Netherlands were quick to capitalize on this interest. At least 25 English-language corantos reporting war news were produced, nearly all at Amsterdam, by George Veseler and Broer Jonson. These single sheets, now in the British Museum, were dated December 2, 1620, to September 18, 1621. Nathaniel Butter, a bookseller, was the English distributor. Sales were so brisk that in the summer of 1621 Butter decided to do the publishing himself, pirating his news from Dutch news sheets. Thomas Archer, a printer, was probably his partner. Copies of their sheets printed in the summer of 1621 do not survive. Six similar corantos,[11] dated September 24 to October 22, do. But by that time printer Archer had run afoul of the law.

When Frederick, the newly elected king of Bohemia, led his forces to defeat in revolt against the Hapsburgs at a battle near Prague, English sentiment favored intercession by James I for his son-in-law. James could not make up his mind, however. The corantos were critical of his foreign policy, and in retaliation the king cracked down on the editors, using the old rules of the Tudors. In December of 1620 and again in July of 1621 the king issued proclamations against "the great liberty of discourse concerning matters of state." He followed this up with an order suppressing corantos, but apparently some of the printers flouted his orders, for there is a record of the Stationers Company calling up Archer for a hearing in August. He was imprisoned.

Nicholas Bourne now enters the picture. He was a respected member of his craft, and it is possible that Butter teamed up with him because of his prestige. Their first coranto was authorized in September of 1621 and undoubtedly bore the legend "Published With Authority" at the top of the page, as did later issues. The earliest surviving coranto of this press is dated May 23, 1622. Archer, now out of prison, was the printer. Butter was probably the editor and Bourne was the publisher, or responsible promoter. The paper was printed on one side only, and the sheet was somewhat smaller than a page of modern typewriter paper.

It was not until 1624 that the corantos began to be identified by name, thus supplying something of the continuity required of a true newspaper. The earliest known coranto published by title was *The Continuation of Our Weekly Newes,* from the office of Bourne and Butter. Because this title appeared on at least 23 consecutive issues, the offering marks another step in the development of the newspaper.

The earliest corantos printed nothing but foreign news. The first domestic reports can be traced back to the publication by the Westminster clerks of Parliamentary proceedings dated about 1628. Out of these accounts developed the "diurnals," or daily reports of local events. The diurnals flourished during the struggle between king and Parliament, when it was safe to comment on local news because neither side was strong enough to take punitive measures and when both factions were seeking public support. Many of the restrictions on the press were modified by the Long Parliament, and after 1640 diurnals appeared by the score. Oldest known paper of this type is John Thomas's *Diurnall Occurrences,* which first appeared November 29, 1641.

MILTON'S   The interim of the first decade of the revolution beginning in 1640 was
AREOPAGITICA   a period of great development for the press. The Long Parliament
                                 abolished the dreaded Star Chamber in 1641. Voices began to be raised
in favor of a greater freedom of expression. On November 24, 1644, the poet John Milton published his famous *Areopagitica,* probably the best known of the great pleas for a free press.[12] Milton spoke eloquently for the right of discussion and declared that

... though all the winds of doctrine were let loose to play upon the earth, so truth be in the field, we do injuriously by licensing and prohibiting to misdoubt her strength. Let her [truth] and falsehood grapple; who ever knew truth put to the worse, in a free and open encounter?[13]

Milton gave the most perfect expression to the idea of a free press, but just as courageous and articulate were such journalistic heroes as William Walwyn, who argued for liberty of the press following his studies on religious toleration; Henry Robinson, who based his theory of a free press on economic principles and free enterprise; Richard Overton, the Tom Paine of his day, who expanded his Separatist views on religion into principles of democracy; and John Lilburne, who did more than any of his compatriots to make his countrymen conscious of their right of discussion.[14] As a matter of fact, Milton had very little effect in bringing about any improvement. His words were not widely disseminated at the time. The ideas expressed in *Areopagitica* were picked up nearly a hundred years later by people all over the world, notably in America, struggling to obtain even greater freedom than they already enjoyed.

With the execution of Charles I in 1649 and the rise of the Commonwealth under Oliver Cromwell, the press again fell upon evil days. Cromwell's "Roundheads" had taken over the royal prerogatives, which had at times so restricted Puritan writers and publishers, but the new regime was no more tolerant of the press than the Crown had been. Cromwell permitted only administration organs to be published, such as *Mercurius Politicus,* censored by the great Milton, *A Perfect Diurnall,* also controlled for a time through Milton, and later the *Publick Intelligencer* (1655). All unauthorized publications were treated roughly.

The restoration of Charles II in 1660 resulted in the establishment of an exclusive patent, or monopoly, system under Henry Muddiman and Roger L'Estrange. For a time the ancient, handwritten news letters were the only means of disseminating information with any degree of freedom. Printed newspapers could be liquidated by confiscating presses, whereas news letters could be produced as long as scribes could find a hideaway or were willing to defy authorities. During this period ultimate control was divided between Crown and Parliament. Regulations and restrictions were fewer, but they were clearly stated and enforcement was effective under the Surveyor of the Press.

It was under Charles that a new era of journalism was ushered in with the publication of the *Oxford Gazette* in 1665. Edited by Muddiman while the royal court was fleeing from the London plague, it was, strictly speaking, the first periodical to meet all the qualifications of a true newspaper. It was printed twice a week, by royal authority. After 24 issues, the publication became the *London Gazette* when the court moved back to the capital. It continued to be published right on up through the twentieth century as the official court organ.

LICENSING ENDS   The old licensing powers appeared to be crumbling as the Restoration period drew to a close. This was not through choice of the authorities but more likely a result of the growing tendency for class and political alignments. In 1679 Parliament allowed the Licensing Act of 1662 to lapse. It was revived from time to time, but with the increasing tension between Crown and Parliament, each side sought to protect its own spokesmen. The so-called Regulation of Printing, or Licensing, Act expired in 1694, not because authorities were convinced as to the injustice of licensing but because it was politically unsound. From 1694 to the passage of the first Stamp Act of 1712, the only controls were the laws of treason and seditious libel and regulations against reporting proceedings of Parliament. Prior restraint had ended.

One last victim under Charles was Benjamin Harris, a brash and somewhat reckless journalist. Harris was convicted of violating the king's laws. He was fined and pilloried. Unable to pay the fine, he spent two years in prison. When his office was again raided in 1686, Harris fled to Bristol with his family and took passage for America. He appears again soon in these pages as the publisher of one of the first newspapers in America.

After the Revolution of 1688, which brought a change in the monarchical institution, journalists were accorded considerable freedom. William and Mary were rulers by right of public opinion, and they had the common sense not to antagonize printers and publishers, who were factors in the development of public opinion. There are no serious persecutions in their reign. By 1694 the old Licensing Act died of senility and neglect. With the rise of the two-party system during the reign of William and Mary, it was difficult to maintain licensing. Without the decisive action of the old monarchs, it was impossible to continue such an archaic system. The attack on the Act in Commons centered around the commercial unfairness of the monopoly system, the restrictions on the printing industry, the tendency of suspected violators to use bribery, and the inadequacy of censorship. But as Macaulay declared in his *History of England,* "on the great question of principle, on the question whether the liberty of unlicensed printing be, on the whole, a blessing or a curse to society, not a word is said."[15]

RISE
OF A MIDDLE CLASS

Journalistic progress was speeded up by the development of the party system of government. It is significant that parties emerged at the very time that the newspaper began to be a force in the political and social affairs of a people interested more and more in government. The corantos were printed during the death throes of an outworn social system. England was moving steadily from feudalism, whose economic manifestation was production for use, to capitalism, translated economically into production for profit. The change brought social strains as power was grasped by one class at the expense of another.

A new type of citizen began to assert himself. He was the commercial man—the trader, the merchant, and (later) the manufacturer. A great middle class was arising. Standing between the producer and the consumer, it profited from the processing and distribution of goods. In doing so, it helped to raise living standards to the highest level. And the wealth accumulated during this process was inevitably translated into power. The emerging middle class could win recognition and influence only by acquiring some of the feudal privileges and powers of the traditional classes.

Three groups struggled for power. One was largely Anglican in religion, Tory in politics, and aristocratic as a class. The second was likely to be Presbyterian, Whig, and middle class. The third was made up of religious dissenters, radicals, and people of more lowly station. All three classes produced newspapers and journalists; perhaps inevitably the Whig middle class would provide the capital and the printing equipment for writers and editors emerging from the working class, dissenters or radicals though they might be.

EIGHTEENTH-CENTURY
JOURNALISM

The popularity of the newspaper was so great that publishers were encouraged to print daily issues. On March 11, 1702, the *Daily Courant* appeared on the streets of London. It was the first daily newspaper printed in the English language. It was produced and "sold by E. Mallet," and authorities differ on the sex of the founder—Elizabeth or Edward? Whichever, the initial venture lasted only a few days.

The real hero of the *Daily Courant* was Samuel Buckley, who revived the daily and made it into a remarkable newspaper. Buckley insisted on a standard of journalism quite unheard of at the time.[16] It was a *news* paper, not a rumor-mill. He insisted upon reporting factual news, rather than opinion. He was impartial in his publication of these facts. He was careful to dateline the articles, ". . . that the Publick, seeing from what Country a piece of News comes with the Allowance of that Government, may be better able to Judge of the Credibility and Fairness of the Relation. . . ."[17] He practiced what he preached. Although Buckley was a Whig, he did not manipulate news of that party to its favor, even when the Whigs were engaged in desperate struggle for power. Printing on a single sheet of paper, with the reverse largely devoted to profitable advertising, except on exceptional news days, he had little opportunity for experimentation in makeup. Occasionally, however, Buckley used maps and tabulated figures to clarify his reports. Much of the advertising was spurious by modern standards, but

Buckley made money from it. Undoubtedly this revenue made possible his excellent coverage of foreign news.

The high literary quality of eighteenth-century journalism is indicated by the "essay papers," read by students on both sides of the Atlantic even today. The *Tatler* (1709–11) and the *Spectator* (1711–12, 1714) were the products of, first, Richard Steele and then of Steele and Joseph Addison. Printed on one side of a sheet and selling for a penny, this type of paper was enormously popular. The *Spectator* was issued daily and at one time reached 60,000 readers, its promoters boasted. Moreover, its literary form was widely imitated, even in America.

Greatest English journalist of the period was Daniel Defoe, who edited *Mist's Journal* from 1717 through 1720. Steele probably got the idea for his *Tatler* series from reading Defoe's brilliant offerings in earlier papers. Some authorities go so far as to hold that Defoe was the father of the modern editorial. He discussed all manner of topics in a most charming and persuasive style. He, too, was widely copied by American journalists. But Defoe, like all other editors, was always in danger of arrest for seditious libel, especially for reporting news of Parliament. News letter writers like John Dyer, the Tory adherent, smuggled handwritten reports to select readers.

CATO'S LETTERS   In the great controversy between Tories and Whigs, Dean Swift wrote some of his greatest satire. That was while he was editing the *Examiner* (1710). The conflict brought out other great writers whose ideas were conveyed to the masses mostly through the newspapers. Influential both in England and America were the so-called "Cato Letters," written by John Trenchard and Thomas Gordon over the pen name "Cato." The series appeared between 1720 and 1723 in the *London Journal,* later called the *British Journal.*[18] In convincing, readable form they discussed theories of liberty, representative government, and freedom of expression. In 1724 this series was collected and published in four volumes. Copies were in great demand in the colonies, where the first stirrings of revolution were beginning to be felt. Through American newspapers and pamphlets, the influence of "Cato" can be seen right up to the signing of the Declaration of Independence.

Such progress came at great cost, however. Although party conflict raised the voices of free expression, a reactionary government in control was able to force new restrictions. In 1712 the Tories succeeded in imposing a tax on newspapers and advertisements. These "taxes on knowledge" tended to curb the press by economic sanction. Even worse, they kept the price of papers high, so that the masses did not have ready access to such publications—which was certainly one of the intentions of the authorities. Advertisement taxes and the stamp tax on news sheets were not fully removed for another 140 years. The British newspaper, as a result, was low in circulation and small in size until the 1850s. Thanks to the satire of Dr. Samuel Johnson and the courage of newspaper publisher John Wilkes, whose jailing for sedition in the 1760s aroused widespread public reaction, the ban on reporting proceedings of the Commons was dropped in 1771. But threat of trial for seditious libel still hung over those who defied authority.

It is clear from a study of this period that modern journalists can learn much from the experiences of the past. The progress of press freedom shows that the press belongs to those who rule. If power is concentrated in the hands of a monarch, or an elite group, there is no need for the public to receive information and ideas pertaining to political or social matters. Indeed, providing the public with intelligence (news) may actually constitute a threat to national security and stability, and hence the press must be confined strictly to entertainment or innocuous comment under such a system. On the other hand, if the public participates in government it must have access to information in direct ratio to its place in the political scheme.

Another lesson to be learned from this period is that the more secure a government is, the less it fears undermining, and the more freedom it accords its press. This is true right up to the present moment. During and after wars when political leaders and their followers are apprehensive about national safety, liberty of speech and press is in danger of restrictions. Henry VIII's insecurity after his establishment of the English church resulted in strict enforcement of press regulations. Elizabeth cracked down on the press when her claim to the throne was in some doubt. On the other hand, the stability of the government from the end of the seventeenth century was accompanied by press freedom such as the world had never before seen. As Siebert says, "It is axiomatic that government does not exert itself in its own protection unless it is attacked, or believes itself to be seriously threatened."[19]

In the next chapter we shall see the process carried over to America, where the concept of a free press was eventually to prevail as it had in no other country. The philosophy providing the stimulus for this progress developed from the English spokesmen, however, and the American debt to English press traditions is incalculable.

NOTES

1. Folke Dahl, ed., *The Birth of the European Press* (Stockholm: The Royal Library, 1960), summarizes much of this research. Dahl found local news emphasized in a Viennese paper of 1629—an unusual development. The oldest known Swedish paper was printed at Strängnäs in 1624.

2. Venice and Florence were early news centers in Italy, but Genoa is credited with the first continuously titled paper, begun in 1645.

3. Eric W. Allen, "International Origins of the Newspapers: The Establishment of Periodicity in Print," *Journalism Quarterly,* VII (December 1930), 314; quoting from Otto Groth, *Ein System der Zeitungskunde (Journalistik)* (Mannheim: J. Bensheimer, 1928), V. I, pp. 21 ff.

4. One example was the widespread collection of news by the great commercial house of Fugger, whose sixteenth-century news letters are famous.

5. Relatively speaking, that is. The wars continued after his death in 1483, when his heir was pushed aside by Richard of Gloucester. Gloucester was ultimately defeated by young Henry Tudor at Bosworth Field. There was a period under Edward IV when England was peaceful, however, and it is to this time that the passage refers.

6. It is not absolutely established where Caxton set up his press, but the consensus is that it was in the abbey. In 1660, one Richard Atkyns, a Stuart supporter, tried to prove that the first press was established by royal grant in 1468. Atkyns was trying to show precedent for royal control of printing. Caxton apparently began printing on his own initiative and without sanction. Most authorities on the subject now agree there is no validity to the Atkyns claims. See Fredrick Seaton Siebert, *Freedom of the Press in England, 1476-1776* (Urbana. University of Illinois Press, 1952), pp. 22-24.

7. Siebert, *Freedom of the Press in England,* chapter 1, describes the situation admirably.

8. Ibid., chapter 3, for a detailed discussion of the Stationers Company. Siebert has found that some of these dates have been incorrectly reported.

9. It was the only execution of this type under the Tudors, however.

10. As Siebert points out, the first real English reporters were the "intelligencers" John Chamberlain, John Pory, William Locke, and the Reverends Larkin and Mead.

11. These six corantos, bearing only the initials "N.B." as publisher, have perplexed English historians. They probably were issued by Nicholas Bourne (discussed next), but they could have been a continuation of Nathaniel Butter's summer series. The account here of the first London corantos is based upon Siebert, who found evidence in records and correspondence going beyond that offered by the surviving corantos. See also Matthias A. Shaaber, *Some Forerunners of the Newspaper in England, 1476-1622* (Philadelphia: University of Pennsylvania Press, 1929), pp. 314-18.

12. His ideas and even some of his phrases had already been expressed by Peter Wentworth, who made a

speech in Parliament in 1571 on freedom of discussion. Milton's Parliament speech, later published as *Areopagitica,* arose out of his difficulties with the Stationers Company after Milton published a series of licensed and unlicensed pamphlets on divorce.

13. Quoted from Rufus Wilmot Griswold, ed., *The Prose Works of John Milton,* Vol. I (Philadelphia: J. W. Moore, 1856), p. 189. Milton's glory is dimmed somewhat by the fact that he himself was serving as licenser and censor only seven years later.

14. The Separatists, one of many dissenting sects, were strong believers in the separation of church and state. The Lilburne thesis was that Englishmen had a birthright in speaking out fearlessly on all measures and that restrictions were usurpation of power.

15. Siebert, *Freedom of the Press in England,* p. 262, from T. B. Macaulay, *History of England* (London: J. M. Dent and Sons, Ltd., 1906), III, 328.

16. An excellent description of the paper is given by Marvin Rosenberg, "The Rise of England's First Daily Newspaper," *Journalism Quarterly,* XXX (Winter 1953), 3–14.

17. Ibid., p. 4.

18. The first series appeared in the *Independent Whig* between January 20, 1720, and January 4, 1721. Much of the text in the 53 essays was concerned with religious liberty. After the financial crash known as the "South Sea Bubble," the authors wrote 144 more letters on the responsibilities of government in protecting citizens. These appeared in the *London Journal* and the succeeding *British Journal* between November 12, 1720, and December 7, 1723.

19. Siebert, *Freedom of the Press in England,* p. 10. For a scholarly proof of Siebert's proposition ("The area of freedom contracts and the enforcement of restraints increases as the stresses on the stability of the government and of the structure of society increase") see Donald L. Shaw and Stephen W. Brauer, "Press Freedom and War Constraints: Case Testing Siebert's Proposition II," *Journalism Quarterly,* XLVI (Summer 1969), 243, an analysis of the threats against a North Carolina Civil War editor.

ANNOTATED BIBLIOGRAPHY

Bibliographies

Indispensable references for students of American journalism are Warren C. Price, *The Literature of Journalism: An Annotated Bibliography* (Minneapolis: University of Minnesota Press, 1959), with 3,147 entries, and Warren C. Price and Calder M. Pickett, *An Annotated Journalism Bibliography 1958–1968* (Minneapolis: University of Minnesota Press, 1970), with 2,172 entries including some from pre-1958. Entries are particularly full in the areas of general journalism histories, specialized and individual histories, biographies, and narratives of journalists at work. Other sections cover press appraisals, press law, international communication, magazines, radio and television, public opinion and propaganda, communication theory, techniques of journalism, journalism education, periodicals of the press, bibliographies, and directories. British and Canadian journalism is well covered. Also useful is Eleanor Blum, *Basic Books in the Mass Media* (Urbana: University of Illinois Press, 1972), a selected book list.

For listings of American newspapers, Clarence S. Brigham's *History and Bibliography of American Newspapers, 1690–1820* (Worcester, Mass.: American Antiquarian Society, 1947) is the guide to surviving early newsprint. Winifred Gregory's *American Newspapers, 1821–1936: A Union List of Files Available in the United States and Canada* (New York: Wilson, 1936) has diminished usefulness since libraries began to discard their more recent bound volumes in favor of microfilm. The Library of Congress publishes *Newspapers on Microfilm,* updating periodically, listing microfilm holdings of libraries newspaper by newspaper. The largest single newspaper collection for the entire period of American history is at the Library of Congress; the largest for the colonial period at the American Antiquarian Society. Ranking high in overall strength are the libraries of the Wisconsin State Historical Society and Harvard University, with the Bancroft Library of the University of California famous for its western collections as well. Strong in importance for their regions are the New York Historical Society, New York Public Library, Chicago Historical Society, University of Chicago, Pennsylvania Historical Society, and Boston Public Library. Noteworthy for general collections are University of Missouri, University of Minnesota, Yale University, University of Washington, and UCLA.

Two major bibliographies for the study of American history are *A Guide to the Study of the*

United States of America (Washington: Library of Congress, 1960) and the *Harvard Guide to American History* (Cambridge, Mass.: Harvard University Press, 1974). The first named, while less voluminous, carries extensive annotations lacking in the second.

For well-balanced discussions of recent trends in American historiography—involving the progressive, consensus, and New Left schools—see Richard Hofstadter, *The Progressive Historians: Turner, Beard, Parrington* (New York: Knopf, 1968), by a onetime consensus advocate; John Higham, *Writing American History* (Bloomington: Indiana University Press, 1970), by a critic of the newer schools; and C. Vann Woodward, ed., *The Comparative Approach in American History* (New York: Basic Books, 1968). Bibliographies in this volume will identify leading exponents of these various approaches to American history.

For historiography in journalism and mass communications, see Ronald T. Farrar and John D. Stevens, eds., *Mass Media and the National Experience* (New York: Harper & Row, 1971). Essays on communications history techniques and subject areas are written by the editors and by William E. Ames, Dwight L. Teeter, Donald L. Shaw, Richard F. Hixson, John M. Harrison, R. Smith Schuneman, Richard C. Burke, William H. Taft, and Robert K. Thorp. A good discussion linking newspaper history and public affairs is William H. Taft's *Newspapers as Tools for Historians* (Columbia, Mo.: Lucas Brothers, 1970). Also see "Seeking New Paths in Research," a symposium with essays by Garth S. Jowett, Richard A. Schwarzlose, John E. Erickson, Marion Marzolf, and David H. Weaver in *Journalism History,* II (Summer 1975).

Books

BLAGDEN, CYPRIAN, *The Stationers Company*. London: Allen & Unwin, 1960. A scholarly account of licensing and control of printing.

BLEYER, WILLARD GROSVENOR, *Main Currents in the History of American Journalism*. Boston: Houghton Mifflin, 1927. Chapter 1 is a good description of early English journalism, to about 1750.

BOND, DONOVAN H., AND W. REYNOLDS MCLEOD, eds., *Newsletters to Newspapers: Eighteenth-Century Journalism*. Morgantown, W.Va.: West Virginia University, 1977. Symposium papers covering England and colonies.

BOND, RICHMOND P., *The Tatler: The Making of a Literary Journal*. Cambridge, Mass.: Harvard University Press, 1971. Addison and Steele's London paper.

CLYDE, WILLIAM M., *The Struggle for the Freedom of the Press from Caxton to Cromwell*. New York: Oxford University Press, 1934. This excellent study is now largely superseded by Siebert (see below).

CRANFIELD, G. A., *The Development of the Provincial Newspaper, 1700–1760*. London: Oxford University Press, 1962. Researched story of British printers.

DAHL, FOLKE, ed., *The Birth of the European Press*. Stockholm: The Royal Library, 1960. A 36-page brochure cataloging an exhibition of early papers from the library's famous collection.

DESMOND, ROBERT W., *The Information Process: World News Reporting to the Twentieth Century*. Iowa City, Iowa: University of Iowa Press, 1977. Scholarly, comprehensive survey from invention of the alphabet to 1900 integrates worldwide data.

FORD, EDWIN H., AND EDWIN EMERY, eds., *Highlights in the History of the American Press: A Book of Readings*. Minneapolis: University of Minnesota Press, 1954. Selected articles from magazines; the first four discuss sixteenth-century ballads, journalism of the Civil War (1640) period, the eighteenth-century British press, and Daniel Defoe.

FRANK, JOSEPH, *The Beginnings of the English Newspaper*. Cambridge, Mass.: Harvard University Press, 1961. Carries the story through the Restoration of 1660.

HART, JIM ALLEE, *Views on the News: The Developing Editorial Syndrome, 1500–1800*. Carbondale: Southern Illinois University Press, 1970. An overview of the origins of the newspaper editorial and development of the opinion-giving function.

HERD, HAROLD, *The March of Journalism: The Story of the British Press from 1622 to the Present Day*. London: Allen & Unwin, 1952. A condensed, readable history of British newspapers and magazines.

KUNZLE, DAVID, *The Early Comic Strip: Narrative Strips and Picture Stories in the European Broadsheet from c. 1450 to 1825.* Berkeley: University of California Press, 1973. A 471-page study, with artistic analysis.

McMURTRIE, DOUGLAS C., *The Book: The Story of Printing and Bookmaking.* New York: Oxford University Press, 1943. Tells the Gutenberg story, and traces the spread of printing in Europe and the New World.

MOORE, JOHN ROBERT, *Daniel Defoe: Citizen of the Modern World.* Chicago: University of Chicago Press, 1958. Defoe's ideas and role in early press development.

MORAN, JAMES, *Printing Presses: History and Development from the Fifteenth Century to Modern Times.* Berkeley: University of California Press, 1973. Detailed and illustrated.

MORISON, STANLEY, *The English Newspaper: Some Account of the Physical Development of Journals Printed in London between 1622 and the Present Day.* Cambridge, England: Cambridge University Press, 1932. One of the recognized histories in its field, well illustrated.

SHAABER, MATTHIAS A., *Some Forerunners of the Newspaper in England, 1476–1622.* Philadelphia: University of Pennsylvania Press, 1929. Authoritative, detailed.

SIEBERT, FREDRICK SEATON, *Freedom of the Press in England, 1476–1776.* Urbana: University of Illinois Press, 1952. The outstanding study of the subject. Corrects many inaccuracies of older histories.

STEINBERG, S. H., *Five Hundred Years of Printing.* Baltimore: Penguin, 1974. A brief account of the history of printing, emphasizing the relationships of technical developments and ideas.

STRAUSS, VICTOR, *The Printing Industry.* New York: R. R. Bowker, 1967. A history of printing from Gutenberg to computers.

The Tatler and The Spectator. London: G. A. Aitken, ed., 1898–99. The complete file of the famous Addison and Steele literary papers.

VON KLARWILL, VICTOR, ed., *The Fugger News Letters,* first series. New York: G. P. Putnam's Sons, 1924. Second series, 1926. An interesting study of the content of news before the days of newspapers.

WERKMEISTER, LUCYLE, *The London Daily Press, 1772–1792.* Lincoln: University of Nebraska Press, 1963. Only detailed history of late eighteenth-century press.

WILLIAMS, FRANCIS, *Dangerous Estate: The Anatomy of Newspapers.* New York: Macmillan, 1958. History of the British press since 1702 with emphasis on the press as a social institution.

Periodicals and Monographs

ALLEN, ERIC W., "International Origins of the Newspapers: The Establishment of Periodicity in Print," *Journalism Quarterly,* VII (December 1930), 307. Discusses qualifications of the true newspaper.

BAKER, HARRY T., "Early English Journalism," *Sewanee Review,* XXV (October 1917), 396. Nathaniel Butter and Sir Roger L'Estrange are highlighted in this detailed account.

BLEYER, WILLARD G., "The Beginnings of English Journalism," *Journalism Quarterly,* VIII (September 1931), 317. A study of foreign news in early English corantos, showing ties with the continent.

GIFFARD, C. A., "Ancient Rome's Daily Gazette," *Journalism History,* II (Winter 1975), 106. Begun in 59 B.C. by Julius Caesar, known as *Acta Diurna.*

LOWENTHAL, LEO, AND MARJORIE FISKE, "Reaction to Mass Media Growth in 18th-Century England," *Journalism Quarterly,* XXXIII (Fall 1956), 442. How literary tastes were lowered by mass consumption.

MOORADIAN, KARLEN, "The Dawn of Printing," *Journalism Monographs,* 23 (May 1972). First steps of printing—stamp and cylinder seals—found in Mesopotamia and Crete; movable type in Crete dates 2,000 years before use in China.

ROSENBERG, MARVIN, "The Rise of England's First Daily Newspaper," *Journalism Quarterly,* XXX (Winter 1953), 3. An excellent description of the *Courant.*

The first effort at a colonial newspaper, and the order banning it.

2

The Birth
of the American
Newspaper

The way to get at the nature of an institution, as of anything else that is alive, is to see how it has grown.[1]

—A. G. Keller

New England was the birthplace of the American newspaper, but it was not until 1704, or 84 years after the establishment of the first successful colony in that area, that a publication meeting all the qualifications of a true newspaper appeared. Printers were available from the very beginning. William Brewster and Edward Winslow, two of the "elders," or leaders, of the Pilgrims who came to Plymouth in December of 1620, were printers. They had published religious tracts for the Separatists, the more radical offshoot of English Protestantism, and they had lived for a time near George Veseler, who was printing the first English coranto in the Netherlands while the Pilgrims were on the way to the New World in the *Mayflower*. Despite this background, the Plymouth colony existed nearly a century before it enjoyed a newspaper or popular periodical.

Ten years after the arrival of the Pilgrims, another group of religious exiles settled around Boston, a day's sail to the north of Plymouth. This Massachusetts Bay Colony, as it was then known, was to be the cradle of American journalism. Many of its members were prosperous. The educational level was high, and some of the settlers were respected scholars. Unlike the Plymouth settlement, which grew slowly, the Massachusetts Bay Colony increased rapidly in population and area of influence. From the beginning it had a high degree of self-government. The charter of the organization had been brought to America, where it served as a kind of constitution beyond the tampering of jealous officials in the home government. In effect the colony had a form of autonomy, or at least of participating home rule, that was to be of great significance in the political development of New England.

17

THE NEW ENGLAND ENVIRONMENT These colonists were concerned about the education of their children. Having enjoyed educational advantages themselves, they wished to pass on the heritage to succeeding generations. Six years after the founding of the settlement, they established Harvard College (1636). In the larger towns there were "grammar schools," which prepared boys for Harvard. As part of this educational process, the authorities established the first press in the English colonies at Cambridge in 1638. Its function was to produce the religious texts needed in school and college. Other presses were set up not long after. Later, these presses printed cultural material, including the first history of the colony and some poetry.

It was this interest in education and cultural dissemination that made Boston famous as the intellectual capital of the New World. Here were all the ingredients for the development of a newspaper—high literacy, interest in community matters, self-government, prosperity, and cultural leadership—yet no successful newspaper appeared until the fourth generation.

There was good reason for the lag. At first, the wilderness absorbed the energies of the colonists. Any demand for news was satisfied well enough by the English papers, which arrived on every ship from home. The colonists had few ties with other communities in the New World. Years after they arrived, the settlers were still oriented toward the homeland, not toward their neighbors.

So there was no demand for the type of news that had fostered early newspapers in Europe. Nor was there any visible means of supporting a popular press. There was little to sell and little to advertise. Yet during this period the area was producing a breed of citizen that was to expand the frontiers of social and political freedom in America, aided by an aggressive and powerful press. It took time, that is all.

The New Englander was a product of glaciation, rugged climate, and Calvinism. Glaciers had scored the country into a land of narrow valleys, swiftly flowing streams, and thin soil. The endless field stone fences of New England are evidences of the toil involved in scratching a living from such a land. It was difficult for one family to care for many backbreaking acres, and so the individual farms tended to be small. The narrow valleys and the small farms brought people closer together. This suited the New Englanders, who preferred to live in towns where they could attend church and the meetinghouse. In the South, where broad rivers drained the wide savannahs, people lived more spaciously. It is significant that here the gatherings were more in the nature of social events. Southerners met to enjoy themselves. New Englanders met to improve themselves—and others.

It was fortunate for later generations of Americans that the New England settlers had great appreciation for property, especially in the form of land. Land had been the symbol of prestige and standing in England. The decline of feudalism and the emergence of the capitalist class brought many dispossessed British farmers to America. Driven from the land by the manor lord who had turned from subsistence farming to wool raising and required much less help; sick of the stinking slums that were the only refuge of the dispossessed; and unwanted, large numbers of these ex-plowmen fled to America. The country needed them, and that alone is enough to start strong loyalties. In America they could not only work the land they loved, but they could also acquire property, the mark of a superior person.[2]

The New England woman was another significant factor in the development of the region. Women came over with the original settlers. They reared large families, and the group kept its identity. In South America and to some extent in French Canada, colonists tended to be absorbed by the native populations, because Europeans in those regions did not generally bring women along with them. The New England pioneer preserved the traditions of an old race and the characteristics of a great culture. This solidarity was even more secure in New England than in other American colonies because of the rejection of Negro slavery there. In the South, slavery was to be disruptive of homogeneity in years to come. The New Englander was saved from the curse of slavery not just because he was opposed to the system, but because it was uneconomical.

COMMERCE: FORERUNNER OF THE PRESS   The commercial stimulation that encourages the development of a popular press was brought to New England in a curious way. Because farming paid such a small return on the energy invested in it, the New England Yankee early turned to fishing as an easier way of earning a living. Surrounding waters teemed with fish. Soon Yankee fishermen were the main suppliers of fish to the Mediterranean basin, where a combination of religions and diet provided a ready market. The South might just as well have developed a fishing industry, but plantation life was more satisfactory to the southerner than spending cold weeks in pitching vessels on the Grand Banks fishing grounds.

Fishing made New Englanders into great seafarers. Soon they were building their own vessels, designed for special purposes and superior to anything under sail up to then. The forests provided the raw material for a thriving industry. The region abounded in excellent harbors. Shipbuilding and ocean commerce stimulated the growth of lumbering, wood manufacture, and other small industries, for which there was abundant water power. As a result, a class of shrewd, tough, independent businessmen began to win renown for New England. Many of them became wealthy and were ready to help support a publication that could advertise wares and spread pertinent information.

For a time the coffeehouses had sufficed as a news medium, even as the market places and fairs had served Europe in previous centuries. Here men of congenial interests met to exchange gossip and useful information. Buyers, as well as retailers, were interested in the arrival and departure of ships. Businessmen were curious about conditions in areas largely ignored by the British papers. Commerce along the American coast was slowly increasing, for example, and there was a thriving trade with the West Indies. What was being done to disperse local pirates? Was it true that a new postal system was about to be established by His Majesty's Government? Finally, as rivalry spurred trade in the growing communities, the merchant discovered he could move his goods to the local customer faster if he printed notices, or advertisements, in a publication read by his customers. The emphasis on this aspect of journalism is indicated by the number of early newspapers with the word "Advertiser" in the name plate. The development of commerce, then, had an important bearing on the establishment of the first newspaper, and all the early publications appeared in commercial centers.

Commerce and Calvinism, the religion of the Yankee, fitted well together. The New Englander was usually a believer in the doctrine of John Calvin, the sixteenth-century reformer who had set up a theocratic government in Geneva. The essence of Calvinism is "predestination." The Calvinist believed that the world and its people followed a plan of God. Man's salvation or damnation was thus already predetermined according to this pattern. Prosperity was a sign that God had looked upon a man with favor. A successful businessman could think of himself as having passed through the eye of the needle into the circle of the elect. So, of course, every good Calvinist tried to look prosperous to show the world that he had been marked by God for salvation.

THE SOUTHERN
AND MIDDLE COLONIES
The New England "Puritan" made many important contributions to the culture and society that were to prepare the way for the American experiment in self-rule and eventual independence. Other areas fortunately infused some of the more human qualities into the product, however. The South, for example, was in strong contrast to New England. Life was easier and more relaxed on the wide plantations. The general viewpoint remained agrarian, rather than commercial. Communications develop slowly in such a society. Although Virginia, the "Old Dominion," was settled 13 years before the Pilgrims landed at Plymouth, it lagged far behind in press progress. But the South contributed great ideas and spokesmen, essential to the development of democracy, with which the press was to be so closely integrated. The graciousness of the South was a fortunate leavening for the tough-mindedness of the Yankee, when the time came for the colonies to cooperate.

The South could even teach a few lessons on democracy in the earliest days of colonization. The New England Puritan was not noted for tolerance. Intellectual misfits, such as Anne Hutchinson, the first great American feminist, and Roger Williams, were driven into exile by the intransigent theocrats of Massachusetts because of ideas unacceptable to the leaders. It took a little while for Americans to learn the lesson that it takes ideas to keep democracy dynamic—that is, adjustable to changing conditions. The institutions of the South were not necessarily more democratic, but the areas of intolerance were different. At least the southerner appeared to have a more human outlook on life.

The Middle Atlantic, or "bread," colonies helped to fuse the regional characteristics of the colonies. Philadelphia and New York were the great commercial centers. In this respect the middle colonies resembled the New England of Boston, Salem, and Providence in this first century of colonial history. But the inhabitants tended to live more spaciously, like the southerner. Young Ben Franklin, hiding out in Philadelphia, found it to be as bustling as Boston but more congenial to one of his inquisitive nature. And it is significant that Philadelphia was the second American city to support a successful newspaper.

The middle colonies attracted settlers of various national and religious backgrounds. Along the Delaware river the Swedes had established communities dating from the early seventeenth century. The Dutch West India Company in 1621 established New Netherland colony, later to be renamed "New York" by the English successors. Later many other groups moved into the area. Areas in Pennsylvania became almost as Germanic as the cities in the Palatinate whence the "Pennsylvania Dutch" (Deutsch) had come. The region also absorbed religious expatriates, such as Catholics, Lutherans, Quakers, and Dutch Reformers.

By the end of the seventeenth century there were about 250,000 inhabitants of European extraction in the American colonies. Massachusetts had grown from about 100 in 1620 to 45,000 by 1700. Virginia had a white population of about 50,000. Maryland was next, with 20,000. The others were much smaller but were growing fast. A few families had accumulated respectable fortunes by this time, but the general income level was relatively low.

POLITICAL UNREST
The colonies reflected the religious and political troubles of the mother country. Many Americans had emigrated because of differences in beliefs, and they brought their problems with them. The restoration of Charles II after the revolution of 1640 was a period of political reaction. Once again the king exerted his old powers—or tried to. James II, who succeeded Charles, should

have learned that it was dangerous to flout the good will of his subjects, but James was even more unpopular than his predecessors. Under James, revolt seethed. The unrest was reflected in the colonies.

In 1664 the British conquered the Dutch and took as one of the spoils of war the New Netherland colony. In the next few years the king tried to strengthen his power in England. It is not surprising that the same process was apparent in the colonies. The General Court of Massachusetts, for example, passed the first formal act restricting the press in 1662. The only printing plant in the colony at the time was the one at Harvard, consisting of two presses, but the authorities were taking no chances with possible subversive literature, and the law provided for rigorous censorship.[3]

One of the governors sent out to the colonies about this time was Sir Edmund Andros. He first took over the seat of government in New York in 1674. It was his understanding that his commission gave him jurisdiction over the area between the Delaware and Connecticut rivers. This was interpreted by colonial leaders as proof that the Crown wished to establish a more effective control of this area by means of centralization of authority. The charters of the New England colonies were declared invalid, and Andros believed he had a mandate to take over this region, too. By 1686 he was in control of most of the populated and prosperous colonies.

Two years later (1688) Parliament deposed James II in the "Glorious Revolution." The crown was then offered jointly to his eldest daughter, Mary, and her husband, William of Orange. William and Mary were wise rulers. Aware of the circumstances under which they had been offered the crowns, they tended to be conciliatory. The counterpart of these events in America was the revolt against royal authority in the guise of Andros. He was sent back to England in 1689 for trial.[4]

BENJAMIN HARRIS, PRINTER　　It was at this very time that an ex-London bookseller and publisher decided to offer a periodical that the ordinary person could afford and could understand. Boston then had a population of nearly 7,000 and was the largest city in America. It offered sufficient sales potential for the type of publication the promoter had in mind. Cultural and literacy levels were sufficient to warrant the financial risk. There was a demand by the commercial interests for such an organ, and they could offer the essential support. The situation was made to order for a newspaper, and the man of the hour was at hand, although he never did quite achieve the honor of producing the first American newspaper.

The hero of this episode was the exiled printer, Benjamin Harris, who was last seen fleeing from the law. Harris arrived in Boston in 1686. Already he had had considerable experience in the London publishing business. Unfortunately, Harris was a troublemaker, and shortly after he had started his London newspaper in 1679, he was arrested for having seditious literature in his possession. He was sentenced to the pillory, which was erected in front of his own office. Friends kept passersby from throwing refuse at the prisoner, but they could not help him pay the stiff fine imposed, and Harris had to go to jail. From his cell he continued to edit his paper. In 1686 his shop was again raided. Officers seized a quantity of pamphlets connecting Harris with subversive organizations, and a warrant was issued for his arrest. Warned of the danger, Harris fled with his family to America. In the fall of 1686 he opened a combined coffee and book shop in Boston at the corner of State and Washington streets.

The shop was a favorite meeting place for some of Boston's most interesting citizens. Judge Sewall, chronicler of his times and a former publisher, was a regular customer. Most of the local wits and writers made the shop their headquarters. The progressive views of the proprietor are indicated by the fact that his was the only coffee shop in the city where respectable women were welcome.

Harris was a shrewd businessman. He succeeded against formidable opposition. There were seven booksellers in the neighborhood when Harris set up shop. He sat down and wrote a spelling book that was a best seller in the country for many years. He published books for a distinguished clientele and thus acquired a respect and prestige that some of his rivals lacked. He was not a printer at this time, but rather the promoter of literary works. The downfall of Andros gave Harris the opportunity to go back to his first love, the publication of a newspaper.

PUBLICK OCCURRENCES, 1690

On September 25, 1690, the printing shop of R. Pierce issued a four-page newspaper. It was printed on only three sides. The fourth page was blank so the reader could add his own news items before passing it on. The pages measured only 6 × 10¼ inches. There was very little attempt at makeup. This was Harris's *Publick Occurrences, Both Foreign and Domestick,* called by some authorities the first American newspaper. It might very well have been, except that it was banned after the first issue, and one of the qualifications of a newspaper is periodicity, or continuity. If continuity is ignored, a publication printed the year before might just as logically be called the first American newspaper. This was *The Present State of the New-English Affairs,* printed in 1689 as a report from the Reverend Increase Mather to Governor Broadstreet of Massachusetts. The Reverend Mr. Mather was representing the colony in London, and the publication was designed to let the public know what progress had been made in colonial problems. This was certainly news and was printed as such. There are even earlier examples of broadsheets and reprints of big new events. The characteristic that set *Publick Occurrences* apart was that it looked like a newspaper, it read like a newspaper, and it was intended as a permanent news organ, unlike the others.[5] Harris was a good reporter for his time. His style was concise—"punchy," the modern editor would call it. The paper included both foreign and local news—another distinction from earlier news publications. Indeed, his "occurrences" covered a multitude of interests. Thus, we find at the bottom of the outside column on page one:

> The *Small-pox* which has been raging in *Boston,* after a manner very Extraordinary is now very much abated. It is thought that far more have been sick of it than were visited with it, when it raged so much twelve years ago, nevertheless it has not been so Mortal. The number of them that have dyed in *Boston* by this last Visitation is about three hundred and twenty, which is not perhaps half so many as fell by the former. . . .[6]

Harris knew what would interest his readers. He included intelligent comment, but he knew that most of his readers would be attracted more by appeals to basic emotions and by reference to familiar persons and places. Conflict and fear were two such emotions emphasized in his paper. The pattern has been used successfully right up to today, which is not to say that this is the *only* means for winning subscribers.

Harris got into trouble with the local authorities, not because he printed libels, but because he printed the truth as he saw it. He had also violated licensing restrictions first imposed in 1662. One of Harris's items reported that Indian allies of the "English Colonies & Provinces of the West" had forced an army under General Winthrop to postpone an attack on the French. The Indians, Harris wrote, had failed to provide "canoo's" for the transportation of the forces into enemy territory. War chiefs had explained that the redmen were too weakened from smallpox to fulfill their commitments, and that was probably true. They were not too weak to make individual raids, however. From one of these raids, Harris reported, they "brought home several *Prisoners,* whom they used in a manner too barbarous for any English to approve." The journalist referred to these Indian allies as "miserable savages, in whom we have too much confided."

All these remarks could be taken as criticism of colonial policy, which at that moment was concerned with winning, not alienating, Indian neighbors. Harris was also accused of bad taste. He had spiced up his paper by reporting that the French king had been taking immoral liberties with the prince's wife, for which reason the prince had revolted. Judge Sewall wrote in his diary that the Puritan clergy was scandalized by this account in a publication reaching the Boston public.

It was the Massachusetts licensing act that ended Harris's career as an American newspaper publisher, however. How he expected to get around that restriction is not at all clear. Harris eventually returned to England, where he fades out of the scene as the penurious vendor of quack medicines.

Not for another 14 years was there a newspaper in the American colonies, and when one did appear, it operated alone for 15 years. The example of *Publick Occurrences* may have warned away any journalistic promoters during this interim. When the next newspapers did appear, they were inclined to be stodgy and dull, partly because the publishers lacked Harris's color and boldness and partly because all news had to be "safe" to pass the licensers. Each of the successful Boston publishers in the next 30 years was careful to notify his public that he printed "by authority." More important, they had the protection of an important office—for the journalists who followed immediately after Harris were all postmasters.

In Europe there had been a long tradition of affiliation between the postal service and journalism. Many of the early continental newspapers had been published by postmasters. There was good reason for this. Postmasters were especially interested in disseminating information. That was their principal business. They had access to most of the intelligence available to the community. They broke the seals of official pouches and delivered important dispatches. Postmasters then, as today, heard much of the local gossip. They were "in the know." And in colonial times, as in modern times, the postmaster was likely to be an important political figure. That was how he usually earned his office.

But such advantages do not necessarily produce good newspapers. Softness and safety never beget great journalism—then or now. Newspapers have progressed farthest in times of strife. Yet the early postmaster-publishers contributed much to American journalism. At least they understood that the main problem was survival, which is more than could be said of Harris. It was the ability to adjust to conditions that enabled a postmaster to produce the first genuine newspaper in America. And if he lagged 14 years behind Harris, the fault was not all his. Until 1692 there had been no official postal service in the colonies. In that year the British government authorized an intercolonial mail system—an indication that the respective colonies were beginning to take note of each other.

JOHN CAMPBELL'S   One of the postmasters appointed by the Crown for the new
NEWS-LETTER, 1704   intercolonial service was John Campbell. He took over the Boston
post office in 1700. From the very beginning he made use of the postal service to supply information to special correspondents in other colonies. He issued this intelligence in the form of a news letter—the primitive, handwritten report that had been the common medium of communication in Europe before the invention of printing. Most of the information sent out by Campbell was concerned with

The Boston News-Letter.

B. C.   Numb. 3.

Publiſhed by Authority.

From **Monday** May 1. to **Monday** May 8. 1704.

London Gazette, from *Novemb.* 8 to 11. 1703.

Weſtminſter, *Novemb.* 9.

THE Parliament met here this day, and Her Majeſty being come to the Houſe of Peers, and ſeated on the Throne in Her Royal Robes, with the uſual Solemnity, the Gentleman Uſher of the Black Rod, was ſent with a Meſſage to the Houſe of Commons, requiring their Attendance in the Houſe of Peers, whither they came accordingly, and Her Majeſty was pleaſed to make a moſt Gracious Speech to both Houſes, which follows.

My Lords and Gentlemen,

I Have Called you together aſſoon as I thought you could conveniently Come out of your Countries, that no Time may be loſt in making Our Preparations for Carrying on the Preſent War, in which I do not Doubt of your Cheerful Concurrence, ſince you can't but be ſenſible, that on the Succeſs of it depends Our Own Safety and Happineſs and that of all *Europe.*

I Hope I have Improved the Confidence you Repoſed in Me laſt Year, to your Satisfaction and the Advantage of Us and Our Allies, by the Treaty with the King of *Portugal,* and the Declaration of the Duke of *Savoy,* which in great Meaſure may be Imputed to the Cheerfulneſs with which you Supported Me in this War, and the Aſſurance with which you Truſted Me in the Conduct of it : And We cannot ſufficiently Acknowledge the Goodneſs of Almighty God, who is pleaſed to Afford Us ſo far a Proſpect as We now have, of bringing it to a Glorious and Speedy Concluſion.

I muſt therefore Deſire you, *Gentlemen of the Houſe of Commons,* to Grant Me ſuch Supplies as ſhall be requiſite to Defray the Neceſſary Charge of the War in the next Year, with regard, not only to all Our former Engagements, but particularly to Our Alliance lately made with the King of *Portugal* for recovering the Monarchy of *Spain* from the Houſe of *Bourbon,* and Reſtoring it to the Houſe of *Auſtria,* which Treaty being in it ſelf of the higheſt Importance imaginable, and requiring all poſſible Diſpatch in the Execution of it, has Neceſſarily Occaſion'd a great Expence even in this preſent Year, tho' not ſo much as it will Require, and for which, I hope, We ſhall be amply Recompenſed in the next.

The Subſidies which will now be immediately Required for the Aſſiſtance of the Duke of *Savoy,* will likewiſe Occaſion a further Neceſſary Charge.

I muſt take Notice to you, That tho' no particular Proviſion was made in the laſt Seſſion, either for the Charge of Our preſent Expedition to *Portugal,* or for that of the Augmentation Troops deſired by the *States General,* yet the Fonds given by Parliament have held out ſo well, and the Produce of the Prizes has Prov'd ſo Conſiderable, that you will find the Publick will not be in Debt by Reaſon of either of theſe Additional Services.

I may further obſerve to you, That tho' the Fonds for the Civil Government are diminiſht by the War I have, in Conjunction with the *States General,* Contributed out of My Own Revenue towards ſome Publick Services, and particularly the Support of the Circle of *Suabia,* whoſe firm Adherence to the Intereſt of the Allies under the greateſt Preſſures, did very well Deſerve our Seaſonable Aſſiſtance : And I ſhall ſtill be Careful not to engage My Self in any Unneceſſary Expence of My Own, that I may have the more to Spare towards the Eaſe of My Subjects.

My Lords and Gentlemen,

I Heartily Wiſh ſome eaſe and leſs chargeable Method could be found for the Speedy and Effectual Manning of the Fleet.

I muſt alſo Recommend to you to make ſome Regulation for Preventing the Exceſſive Price of Coals, I have Examined this Matter, and taken particular Care to appoint Convoys for that Service ; but the Price has not been in the leaſt Abated notwithſtanding a very conſiderable quantity has been Imported ſince that time ; This gives great ground of Suſpicion there may be a Combination of ſome Perſons to Enrich themſelves by a general Oppreſſion of others, and particularly the Poor : 'Twill deſerve your Conſideration how to Remedy this great Inconvenience.

And in all your Affairs, I muſt Recommend to you as much Diſpatch as the Nature of them will admit ; This is Neceſſary to make Our Preparations early, on which in great Meaſure Depends the good Succeſs of all Our Enterprizes.

I want Words to Expreſs to you My earneſt Deſires of Seeing all My Subjects in perfect Peace and Union among themſelves : I have nothing ſo much at Heart as their general Welfare and Happineſs ; Let Me therefore Deſire you all That you would Carefully Avoid any Heats or Diviſions that may Diſappoint Me of that Satisfaction, and Give Encouragement to the Common Enemies of Our Church and State.

London, December 9.

ON Monday the Marqueiſe *de Hencourt,* a French Proteſtant Refugee, departed this Life, in the 72 year of his Age, leaving behind him a very good Name, for his great Piety and other Vertues, truly becoming a Noble-man. As he had cheerfully made a Sacrifice of a great Eſtate to his Religion, he lived in his Exile after ſo Exemplary a manner, that juſtly gained him the eſteem of all that knew him.

By His Excellency *JOSEPH DUDLEY* Eſq. Captain General and Governour in Chief, in and over Her Majeſties Province of the *Maſſachuſetts-Bay* in *New-England.*

A PROCLAMATION for a General FAST.

UPon Conſideration of the troubleſome State of *Europe,* by reaſon of the Calamitous Wars wherein theſe Nations are Engaged amongſt themſelves, and of Her Majeſties Great and Juſt Intereſt therein : As alſo the preſent

The first successful newspaper to be printed in America, by John Campbell.

commercial and governmental matters. Boston was the most important city in the colonies then, and the postmaster's information was therefore highly pertinent all along the Atlantic seaboard. Meetings, proclamations, complaints, legal notices, actions in court, available cargo space, and the arrivals of Very Important Persons provided the grist for Campbell's news mill. There was such a demand for his news letter that Campbell began to look around for some way of relieving the pressure upon his time and energy. He got his brother, Duncan, to help, but even together they could not supply the demand for news. They just could not write longhand fast enough. A shrewd Scotsman, Campbell decided there must be an easier way to earn a living. He set out one afternoon to make a call on Bartholomew Green. Green was one of the few printers in the area. That day the two struck a bargain.

In Green's shop on Newbury Street there was printed on the morning of April 24, 1704, the first genuine American newspaper. It was called the *Boston News-Letter,* an appropriate title, since it was merely a continuation of the publication the Campbells had been producing since 1700. The *News-Letter* was printed on both sides of a sheet just a little larger than the dimensions of Harris's paper—that is, slightly larger than a sheet of typewriter paper.

The news in the first issue was not very startling. The publisher-editor-postmaster had simply clipped the incoming London newspapers, already weeks old, and had inserted the items as foreign exchanges. Since he did not have space for all the European dispatches, he put aside excess information for future use. As a result, some of his news was months old before it reached the reader. On the other hand, local news was fairly timely. It was terse, but surprisingly informative. For example:

Boston, April 18. Arrived Capt. Sill from Jamaica, about four Weeks Passage, says, they continue there very sickly.
Mr. Nathaniel Oliver, a principal Merchant of this place dyed April 15 & was decently inter'd. April 18, Aetatis 53. . . .
The 20 the R'd Mr. Pemberton Preached an Excellent Sermon on 1 Thes. 4:11. "And do your own business"; Exhorting all Ranks & Degrees of Persons to do their own work, in order to a REFORMATION; which His Excellency has ordered to be printed.
The 21 His Excellency Dissolved the Gen. Assembly. . . .[7]

But it was savorless journalism, after Harris's reports on bloodthirsty savages and lustful kings. Campbell cleared all the copy with the governor, or with his secretary. That made his paper libel-proof, censor-proof, and well-nigh reader-proof. Though we have noted that it was the only newspaper in the colonies for 15 years, Campbell never had enough subscribers to make his venture profitable. The first advertisement in an American newspaper was concerned with this problem of circulation. It was what the trade would call a "blind ad," or piece of promotion. Campbell discovered, as many another editor-publisher was to find out later, that the public is never willing to pay the full price for the information it must have to exert its rights. The postmaster was frantic on several occasions because so many subscribers were in arrears. His circulation seldom exceeded 300. Twice Campbell was saved from bankruptcy by a government subsidy. The paper was valuable for the publication of official notices, which could be reproduced cheaper in the *News-Letter* than by private printing. Despite this support, the publisher had to suspend publication for eight months at one critical period for lack of funds.

Even Campbell's embryonic journal contributed to the traditions of an honorable craft. He had a strong sense of responsibility to his public. That is proved by his determination to print the news in spite of public apathy and financial distress. It was also evidenced by his sincere policy of printing "for a Publick Good, to give a true Account of all Foreign & Domestick Occurrences, and to prevent a great many false reports of the same"—a policy still respected by honest publishers.

Despite his clumsiness at news gathering and news writing, Campbell tried his best to be fair and accurate. In one issue he apologized for misplacing a comma in a preceding number, although this was only a drop in the sea of other errors. An uninspired minor bureaucrat in an unpopular administration, he still had the good editor's sense of decency and kindness for his fellow men. Of a suicide involving a poor woman, he wrote that "he hoped the Inserting of such an awful Providence here may not be offensive, but rather a Warning to all others to watch against the Wiles of our Grand Adversary." He obviously regretted having to print the account of a prisoner's whipping, but the culprit had cheated the public by selling tar mixed with dirt. The news, Campbell explained sadly, "is here only Inserted to be a caveat to others, of doing the like, least a worse thing befal them." Clearly, Campbell deserves better of history.

Unimpressive as it was, the *Boston News-Letter* was like the Biblical mustard seed. From it stemmed the mighty American Fourth Estate, a force no one could ignore.

NOTES

1. Famous in his time as a great teacher and lecturer on sociology at Yale University.
2. True, the farm colonist might have settled in other areas, but New England had its share, along with its middle-class émigrés.
3. One of the best discussions of this period will be found in Clyde A. Duniway, *The Development of Freedom of the Press in Massachusetts* (New York: Longmans, Green & Company, 1906).
4. He was never tried. Indeed, he was soon returned to favor and came back to America as governor of Virginia.
5. Even on this count it would fail to qualify technically as a newspaper, according to the criteria listed on page 4, because Harris intended to issue the paper only once a month, unless an "unusual glut of occurrences" made greater frequency of publication practicable.
6. From a facsimile filed in the London Public Office (1845), as reprinted in Willard G. Bleyer, *Main Currents in the History of American Journalism* (Boston: Houghton Mifflin, 1927), p. 45.
7. From a fascimile in the Wisconsin State Historical Society Library.

ANNOTATED BIBLIOGRAPHY

Books

The most useful books for the general reader from among histories of American journalism earlier than this volume are those by Mott, Bleyer, A. M. Lee, and Payne, listed below. The earliest attempt at a general account was that by Isaiah Thomas in 1810 (see bibliography for chapter 3). Next were those by Frederic Hudson in 1873 and by S. N. D. North in 1884 (see bibliographies for chapters 11 and 15, respectively). These three books remain of special use to journalism historians. Other general histories have been those by James Melvin Lee, *History of American Journalism* (Boston: Houghton Mifflin, 1917); Robert W. Jones, *Journalism in the United States* (New York: Dutton, 1947); Edith M. Bartow, *News and These United States* (New York: Funk & Wagnalls, 1952); John W. Tebbel, *The Compact History of the American Newspaper* (New York: Hawthorn, 1963), a readable but quick survey of high points; Sidney Kobre, *Development of American Journalism* (Dubuque, Iowa: Wm. C. Brown Company, 1969), a compiling of earlier works that adds details about many regional papers; Robert A. Rutland, *The Newsmongers* (New York: Dial Press, 1973), a readable popular supplement to basic journalism history books; and John W. Tebbel, *The Media in America* (New York: Thomas Y. Crowell, 1974), a popular account emphasizing the nineteenth century. For analysis of the subject see the annotations in Price, *The Literature of Journalism,* pp. 3–7; and Allan Nevins, "American Journalism and Its Historical Treatment," *Journalism Quarterly,* XXXVI (Fall 1959), 411. For documentary sources, see citation below for Pickett.

For historical accounts of the roles of women in United States journalism, see the citation for Marion Marzolf, below, and others in bibliographies for succeeding chapters, especially 6, 11, 16, and 22. Extensive unannotated bibliographies were published in two issues of *Journalism History* devoted to women in journalism: Marion Marzolf, Ramona R. Rush, and Darlene Stern, eds., "The Literature of Women in Journalism History," *Journalism History,* I (Winter 1974), 117; and a supplement edited by Marzolf, *Journalism History,* III (Winter 1976), 116. For documentary sources, see citation below for Beasley and Silver.

Especially recommended for background reading in American history are the interpretative histories by the Beards and Boorstin and the studies of American thought and society by Curti, Furnas, Parrington, and Williams, listed below. Other excellent general histories include John D. Hicks and George E. Mowry, *A History of American Democracy,* 4th ed. (Boston: Houghton Mifflin, 1970); Richard Hofstadter, William Miller, and Daniel Aaron, *The United States: The History of a Republic,* 3rd ed. (Englewood Cliffs, N.J.: Prentice-Hall, 1972); Samuel Eliot Morison and Henry Steele Commager, *The Growth of the American Republic,* 6th ed. (New York: Oxford University Press, 1969); Henry Bamford Parkes, *The United States of America, a History* (New York: Knopf, 1968); and Bernard Bailyn et al., *The Great Republic: A History of the American People* (Boston: Little, Brown, 1977).

BEARD, CHARLES A., AND MARY R. BEARD, *The Rise of American Civilization.* New York: Macmillan, 1930. A provocative history of the United States, with much socioeconomic and intellectual detail woven into a general narrative. Brilliantly presents a progressive history theme of economic class conflict. While the images of conflict for the Constitutional Convention and Jacksonian era proved to be overdrawn, Beards' accounts of revolutionary aspects of 1776 and the Civil War, and of racial, ethnic, and religious conflict, stand tests.

BEASLEY, MAURINE, AND SHEILA SILVER, *Women in Media: A Documentary Source Book.* Washington, D.C.: Women's Institute for Freedom of the Press, 1977. Thirty documents from Mary Katherine Goddard to *Ms.* magazine.

BLEYER, WILLARD GROSVENOR, *Main Currents in the History of American Journalism.* Boston: Houghton Mifflin, 1927. One of the standard histories of journalism—reliable and detailed. Places emphasis on leading editors after the 1830s.

BOORSTIN, DANIEL J., *The Americans: The Colonial Experience.* New York: Random House, 1958. A major voice of the consensus school of historians, stressing "togetherness" and continuity, rather than conflict. First of three volumes that feature group action themes, minimize impact of individuals' ideas. Thus Sam Adams is a "local hero," Andrew Jackson a western "booster," and Alexander Hamilton is ignored. To put Boorstin's imaginative thematic essays into perspective, the reader needs the background of a conventional narrative.

CHANNING, EDWARD, *History of the United States,* Vol. II. New York: Macmillan, 1927. A learned and readable summary of events and forces significant in colonial social and political development.

CURTI, MERLE, *The Growth of American Thought,* 3rd ed. New York: Harper & Row, 1964. One of the most scholarly studies of the American social and literary heritage by a Pulitzer Prize historian.

DUNIWAY, CLYDE A., *The Development of Freedom of the Press in Massachusetts.* New York: Longmans, Green & Company, 1906. A detailed and invaluable contribution to the history of early American journalism.

EMERY, MICHAEL C., R. SMITH SCHUNEMAN, AND EDWIN EMERY, eds., *America's Front Page*

News 1690–1970. New York: Doubleday, 1971. Some 300 newspaper pages reproduced to trace main themes of United States political history, wars, popular movements, triumphs and tragedies. See also Edwin Emery's *The Story of America as Reported by Its Newspapers 1690–1965* (New York: Simon & Schuster, 1965).

FURNAS, J. C., *The Americans: A Social History of the United States, 1587–1914*. New York: G. P. Putnam's Sons, 1971. A fresh approach, consensus-oriented.

LEE, ALFRED MCCLUNG, *The Daily Newspaper in America*. New York: Macmillan, 1937. A topical history with a sociological approach, especially useful for its discussions of economic factors.

MARZOLF, MARION, *Up from the Footnote: A History of Women Journalists*. New York: Hastings House, 1977. A study from colonial days to the present. See also her "The Woman Journalist: Colonial Printer to City Desk," *Journalism History*, I–II (Winter 1974–Spring 1975), a two-part article.

MILLER, PERRY, *The New England Mind: The Seventeenth Century*. New York: Macmillan, 1939; and *The New England Mind: From Colony to Province*. Cambridge, Mass.: Harvard University Press, 1953. The first volume, covering to 1660, is a readable interpretation of the Puritan character. The second volume discusses society and thought to 1730.

MOTT, FRANK LUTHER, *American Journalism*. New York: Macmillan, 1941, rev. eds. 1950, 1962. The most detailed general reference book by an outstanding scholar of American journalism. The revisions add sections for the 1940s and 1950s.

NETTELS, CURTIS P., *The Roots of American Civilization*. New York: Appleton-Century-Crofts, 1938. Study of economic factors leading to colonial self-development and conflict with Britain.

PARRINGTON, VERNON LOUIS, *Main Currents in American Thought*, Vol. I, "The Colonial Mind." New York: Harcourt Brace Jovanovich, 1927. A Pulitzer Prize winning study of the social, economic, and political backgrounds of American literature, in three volumes, which ranks as a classic of the progressive historians.

PAYNE, GEORGE H., *History of Journalism in the United States*. New York: Appleton-Century-Crofts, 1920. An old history, but accurate and detailed, particularly useful for the period up to 1800.

PICKETT, CALDER M., *Voices of the Past: Key Documents in the History of American Journalism*. Columbus, Ohio: Grid Publishing, 1977. A storehouse of first-hand materials.

TEBBEL, JOHN W., *A History of Book Publishing in the United States*, Vols. I, II. New York: Bowker, 1972, 1975. Vol. I covers to 1865, Vol. II to 1919.

WERTENBAKER, THOMAS JEFFERSON, *The Founding of American Civilization: The Middle Colonies*. New York: Scribner's, 1938. Describes contributions of the region to the cultural development of the country.

WILLIAMS, WILLIAM APPLEMAN, *The Contours of American History*. Cleveland, Ohio: World Publishing Company, 1961. A ground-breaking reinterpretation of moral, social, and economic development since colonial times, in New Left outlook by a major spokesman.

WISH, HARVEY, *Society and Thought in Early America*. New York: Longmans, Green & Company, 1950. An excellent background study of the period under discussion. First of a two-volume work (Vol. 2, New York: McKay, 1962).

WRIGHT, LOUIS B., *The Cultural Life of the American Colonies, 1607–1763*. New York: Harper & Row, 1957. A study focusing on the aristocracies of the plantations and the trade centers.

Periodicals and Monographs

"The First American Newspaper and the 'New England Primer,'" *Bookman*, LXXVI (January 1933), 103. A brief account of the life of Benjamin Harris.

KOBRE, SIDNEY, "The First American Newspaper: A Product of Environment," *Journalism Quarterly*, XVII (December 1940), 335. Social and economic factors leading to the founding of the press.

PARKES, H. B., "New England in the Seventeen-Thirties," *New England Quarterly*, III (July

1930), 397. A valuable appraisal of the Puritan traditions, which also discusses the effect of British essay papers.

SHAABER, MATTHIAS A., "Forerunners of the Newspaper in America," *Journalism Quarterly,* XI (December 1934), 339. Describes predecessors of *Publick Occurrences.* Reprinted in Ford and Emery, *Highlights in the History of the American Press.*

THE

New-England Courant.

[Nº 58

From MONDAY September 3. to MONDAY September 10. 1 7 2 2.

Quod est in corde sobrii, est in ore ebrii.

To the Author of the New-England Courant.

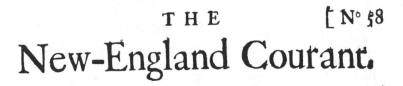

SIR, [No XII.

IT is no unprofitable tho' unpleasant Pursuit, diligently to inspect and consider the Manners & Conversation of Men, who, insensible of the greatest Enjoyments of humane Life, abandon themselves to Vice from a false Notion of *Pleasure* and *good Fellowship.* A true and natural Representation of any Enormity, is often the best Argument against it and Means of removing it, when the most severe Reprehensions alone, are found ineffectual.

I WOULD in this Letter improve the little Observation I have made on the Vice of *Drunkenness,* the better to reclaim the *good Fellows* who usually pay the Devotions of the Evening to *Bacchus.*

I DOUBT not but *moderate Drinking* has been improv'd for the Diffusion of Knowledge among the ingenious Part of Mankind, who want the Talent of a ready Utterance, in order to discover the Conceptions of their Minds in an entertaining and intelligible Manner. 'Tis true, drinking does not *improve our Faculties,* but it enables us to *use* them; and therefore I conclude, that much Study and Experience, and a little Liquor, are of absolute Necessity for some Tempers, in order to make them accomplish'd Orators. *Dic. Ponder* discovers an excellent Judgment when he is inspir'd with a Glass or two of *Claret,* but he passes for a Fool without those of small Observation, who never saw him the better for Drink. And here it will not be improper to observe, That the moderate Use of Liquor, and a well plac'd and well regulated Anger, often produce this same Effect; and some who cannot ordinarily talk but in broken Sentences and false Grammar, do in the Heat of Passion express themselves with as much Eloquence as Warmth. Hence it is that my own Sex are generally the most eloquent, because the most passionate. " It has been said in the Praise of some Men, " (says an ingenious Author,) that they could talk " whole Hours together upon any thing ; but it " must be owned to the Honour of the other Sex, " that there are many among them who can talk " whole Hours together upon Nothing. I have " known a Woman branch out into a long extempo- " rie Dissertation on the Edging of a Petticoat, and " chide her Servant for breaking a China Cup, in all " the Figures of Rhetorick. "

BUT after all it must be consider'd, that no Pleasure can give Satisfaction or prove advantageous to a reasonable Mind, which is not attended with the Restraints of Reason. Enjoyment is not to be found by Excess in any sensual Gratification ; but on the contrary, the immoderate Cravings of the Voluptuary, are always succeeded with Loathing and a palled Appetite. What Pleasure can the Drunkard have in the Reflection, that, while in his Cups, he retain'd only the Shape of a Man, and acted the Part of a Beast ; or that from reasonable Discourse a few Minutes before, he descended to Impertinence and Nonsense?

I CANNOT pretend to account for the different Effects of Liquor on Persons of different Dispositions, who are guilty of Excess in the Use of it. 'Tis strange to see Men of a regular Conversation become rakish and profane when intoxicated with Drink, and yet more surprizing to observe, that some who appear to be the most profligate Wretches when sober, become mighty religious in their Cups, and will then, and at no other Time address their Maker, but when they are destitute of Reason, and actually affronting him. Some shrink in the Wetting, and others swell to such an unusual Bulk in their Imaginations, that they can in an Instant understand all Arts and Sciences, by the liberal Education of a little vivifying *Punch,* or a sufficient Quantity of other exhilerating Liquor.

AND as the Effects of Liquor are various, so are the Characters given to its Devourers. It argues some Shame in the Drunkards themselves, in that they have invented numberless Words and Phrases to cover their Folly, whose proper Significations are harmless, or have no Signification at all. They are seldom known to be *drunk,* tho they are very often *boozey, cogey, tipsey, fox'd, merry, mellow, fuddl'd, groatable, Confoundedly cut, See two Moons,* are *Among the Philistines, In a very good Humour, See the Sun,* or, *The Sun has shone upon them* ; they *Clip the King's English, are Almost froze, Feavourish, In their Altitudes, Pretty well enter'd,* &c. In short, every Day produces some new Word or Phrase which might be added to the Vocabulary of the *Tiplers* : But I have chose to mention these few, because if at any Time a Man of Sobriety and Temperance happens to *cut himself confoundedly,* or is *almost froze,* or *feavourish,* or accidentally *sees the Sun,* &c. he may escape the Imputation of being *drunk,* when his Misfortune comes to be related.

I am SIR,
Your Humble Servant,

SILENCE DOGOOD.

FOREIGN AFFAIRS.

Berlin, May 8. Twelve Prussian Batallions are sent to Mecklenburg, but for what Reason is not known. 'Tis said, the Emperor, suspecting the Designs of the Czar, will secure all the Domains of the Duke of Mecklenburg. His Prussian Majesty, to promote the intended Union of the Reformed and Lutherans in his Dominions, has charged the Ministers of those two Communions, not to make the least mention in the Pulpits of the religious Differences about some abstruser Points, particularly the Doctrine of Predestination, and to forbear all contumelious Expressions against one another.

Hamburg, May 8. The Imperial Court has order'd the Circles of Lower Saxony, to keep in Rea-

Ben Franklin's "Silence Dogood" essay on drunkenness, in the *New England Courant.*

3

The Press Wins
a Beachhead

They that can give up essential liberty to obtain a little temporary safety deserve neither liberty nor safety.

—Benjamin Franklin

Colonial readers had a choice of newspapers for the first time after December 21, 1719, when Campbell fell from political favor. William Brooker won the appointment as postmaster. He was encouraged by his sponsors to continue publication of a semiofficial newspaper. Campbell refused to relinquish the *News-Letter,* however, so Brooker had to start a new publication. And so, after 15 years of monopoly, the pioneer American newspaper faced "opposition." The new rival was the *Boston Gazette.*

Competition did not noticeably improve either the semiofficial *Gazette* or the free-enterprise *News-Letter.* The *Gazette* started out as an imitator, and a stodgy one at that. Except for a market page, it offered nothing that Campbell had not given his readers. Brooker had one great advantage, however. As postmaster, he could distribute his publication at lower cost.

Five successive postmasters continued the *Gazette* until 1741, when it was merged with another rival that had appeared in the meantime—the *New England Weekly Journal.* The merger was only noteworthy as the first such transaction in the history of American journalism, since these early newspapers were all rather dull. Campbell, Brooker, and their successors, as minor bureaucrats, were careful not to offend officials upon whom they were dependent for privileges and subsidies. Every issue of the papers was approved by a government representative before publication, even though formal licensing laws had lapsed before 1700 in the mother country. The line "published by authority" also provided an aura of credibility to the contents in a time when it was difficult for the printer to indicate the sources of his news and verify the reliability of specific items.

THE *NEW ENGLAND* COURANT, 1721   This safe policy was brought to an abrupt end with the establishment in 1721 of the *New England Courant*. This vigorous little sheet was published by James Franklin, elder brother of the more famous Benjamin, but a notable American in his own right. James had been printer of the *Gazette* when Brooker was postmaster. When the publisher lost his appointment, and the *Gazette* passed on to the succeeding postmaster, the paper was printed in another shop. Franklin was irked by this turn of events, and when a group of leading citizens opposed to the governing group encouraged him to start another paper, he agreed to the proposal.

The spirit of rebellion was manifest in the *Courant* from the start. Although it lasted only five years, it exerted a great influence upon the American press. It was a fresh breeze in the stale journalistic atmosphere of Boston. The *Courant* was the first American newspaper to supply readers with what they liked and needed, rather than with information controlled by self-interested officials. Its style was bold and its literary quality high. James Franklin had one of the best libraries in the city. He was also familiar with the best of the London literary publications. Here was a publisher who knew how to interest readers. He lightened his pages by poking fun at rivals. His personality sketches appealed to local interests.

James Franklin was also the first to use a device that was almost an essential of the newspaper at a much later date. This was the "crusade" type of journalism, involving an editorial campaign planned to produce results by presenting news in dramatic form. A crusading editor is not content with the mere reporting of events but knows how to generate stories of interest to the public. Franklin was an expert in the use of this device.

James Franklin was much more than just a tough and independent newspaperman. The *Courant* also filled a great literary vacuum. Literature of a high standard for popular consumption was rare in colonial America in the first quarter of the eighteenth century. Now and then a peddler sold a copy of some such classic as Hakluyt's *Voyages,* but most of the available reading of that day was heavily larded with moral lessons and religious doctrine. James Franklin was a cultured man, for his day and society, and while learning the printing trade in England he had enjoyed the essay papers that were then so popular.

Franklin, and many editors who followed him, offered a starved reading public something new in literary fare. Most of the *Spectator* and *Guardian* essays were reprinted in colonial newspapers. Addison and Steele were introduced to hundreds of Americans through such papers as the *Courant*. Such writers were imitated in the colonies, and some of this local material was very good. The young Benjamin Franklin, apprenticed to his brother James at an early age, secretly authored such essays for publication in his brother's newspaper. Indeed, Ben Franklin's "Silence Dogood" essays rank as about the best of the American imitations, even though he was just 16.

The literature in the *Courant* was witty, pertinent, and even brilliant at times. But the colonial press after the appearance of the *Courant* also offered more solid cultural contributions. Daniel Defoe's great book, *Robinson Crusoe,* was printed serially in many colonial papers as fast as installments could be pirated from abroad. Not every reader could discern the significance of Defoe's work, which expressed in the novel form his criticism of the existing social structure. Those who missed the social message could still enjoy the excellent narrative, and indeed it is still read for this purpose alone, as any youth can testify. In thus broadcasting the new literature, the American newspaper made another contribution to the culture of a new society.

JAMES FRANKLIN, REBEL

But the most important contribution of James Franklin was his unshackling of the American press from the licenser. All the other publishers had bowed to official pressures to print "by authority" despite the end of actual licensing.[1] Franklin printed his paper not "by authority" but in spite of it. He thus helped establish the tradition of editorial independence, without which no press can be called free. Nor was Franklin cautious in the use of this new power. The pompous and restrictive religious and political leaders of the community were the particular targets of his editorial shafts.

The restrictive authorities were both spiritual and temporal. Censorship was supervised by government officials, of course, but the influence of the church leaders was nearly as great, if less direct. Puritan thought dominated the region, and the hierarchy was directed by two brilliant and strong-willed clergymen, Increase Mather and his son, Cotton. Many citizens of the region secretly detested the stern discipline imposed by the Mathers and their followers, but few dared challenge the dominant theocrats. This situation changed when Franklin began to publish the *Courant*.

A man of James Franklin's intellectual independence was certain to be irked by the type of restraint imposed by the Mathers. He began his attack at once. One wishes that Franklin might have selected some other issue to contest with the Mathers, however, because in this case he actually obstructed medical progress.

The issue was smallpox inoculation. The disease took an enormous toll of life in those days and sometimes reached the proportions of a plague. Around 1720, Dr. Zabdiel Boylston of Boston injected blood from recovered smallpox patients into the bodies of other persons. There was no doubt that an immunity could be achieved this way, but the risks were great and most physicians of the period frowned on the practice. It was almost 80 years before the great scientist, Edward Jenner, introduced the safer vaccination method.

Cotton Mather encouraged Dr. Boylston in his researches. There was considerable controversy over the subject, and because of the positions of the protagonists, the issue became political and social, as well as medical. James Franklin used the inoculation quarrel as a means of attacking the Mathers. What he did, although he did not know it at the time, was to launch the first newspaper crusade in America. He developed an issue by dramatic treatment until everyone in the area was aware of the fight. Around Franklin gathered the rebels against Increase and Cotton Mather. They contributed articles to the *Courant,* some of them so vindictive as to be libelous. The insufferable Mathers[2] discovered that the tide of public opinion was strong against them. They defended themselves in vain in the rival *Gazette* and *News-Letter*. The governing authorities, even, welcomed their discomfort.

But when the spunky journalist turned around and fired a fusillade at the administration, the authorities believed it was time to swat this gadfly. Franklin accused the government of ineffective defense against pirates in the vicinity. Called before the Council in 1722 on a charge of contempt, Franklin was as outspoken as he had been in the columns of his paper. For such impertinence the editor-publisher was thrown into jail.

BENJAMIN FRANKLIN, APPRENTICE

James showed not the slightest remorse for his rude appraisal of the administration, and jail had no effect upon him in this way. Once free, he stepped up his criticism of authorities—both religious and political. By the end of the year both factions agreed on one thing, at least: James Franklin was too troublesome to be allowed in the community without restriction. At this point the General Court declared that "James Franklin be strictly forbidden . . . to print or publish the *New-England Courant* or any Pamphlet or paper of the like Nature, Except it be first Supervised, by the Secretary of this Province."[3] This, of course, was a reaffirmation of the old licensing power.

James evaded the order by making his brother, Ben, the official publisher of the paper. No such restriction had been imposed upon the younger Franklin. But in carrying out this evasion, James eventually lost the services of his essential brother. James ostensibly canceled Ben's apprenticeship in order to name the boy as publisher. At the same time, he made Ben sign secret articles of reapprenticeship. This was the chance Ben had been awaiting. True, the secret articles were binding, and under the law James could return his brother if Ben tried to run away. But if James did so, he would thereby acknowledge that he had flouted the Court's order. Young Ben was clever enough to size up the situation. The next time we meet him is as a printer in his own right in Philadelphia.

The *Courant* declined in popularity and influence after that. Five and a half years after he had established the paper, James abandoned it. Later he accepted the position of government printer for Rhode Island. At Newport, in 1732, he founded the *Rhode Island Gazette,* first newspaper in that colony. It survived only a short time, and James never did achieve his former eminence in journalism.[4] If he did nothing else but establish the principle in America of printing "without authority," he would deserve a high place in America's journalistic hall of fame. He had accomplished much more, however. He had shown that when a newspaper is aggressive and readable in serving the public cause, it will elicit support sufficient to protect it from powerful foes.

PHILADELPHIA'S JOURNALISM BEGINS

The second largest city in the colonies at this time was Philadelphia. Two years after the founding of that city in 1683, William Bradford set up the first printing press in the colony. At first he printed only pamphlets and religious tracts for Quaker patrons, but because he had the only press in the region, he was also useful to the administration. Soon he was devoting much of his time to the printing of government documents. Unfortunately, he quarreled with his Quaker superiors, and in 1693 he moved his printing shop to New York, where he established the first newspaper in that city many years later, in 1725. We shall meet him again in the next chapter.

William Bradford's son, Andrew, published the first newspaper in Philadelphia. It was also the first newspaper outside Boston. His *American Weekly Mercury* first appeared on December 22, 1719, the day after Brooker published the first issue of the *Gazette,* Boston's first rival to the *News-Letter.* The *Mercury* was another postmaster paper, but it was a little more outspoken than the usual safe, semiofficial publications of that type that were to appear in the next two decades. On occasion the *Mercury* criticized the administration. It defended James Franklin when the Boston journalist was jailed by angry authorities. It printed the controversial "Cato Letters," which had first appeared in London as arguments for civil and religious liberties. But Bradford was overshadowed in Philadelphia by the greatest printer-journalist of the period.

BENJAMIN FRANKLIN'S *PENNSYLVANIA GAZETTE*

He was Benjamin Franklin, who arrived almost penniless in the City of Brotherly Love after running away from his apprenticeship to brother James. Within five years he was a successful and prosperous citizen of the town. Ben Franklin's whole career was one of success, color, and usefulness. There has never been another American quite like him. He was "the complete man," like DaVinci, Michelangelo, or Roger Bacon. First of all a printer and journalist, he was also an inventor, scientist, politician, diplomat, statesman, pioneer sociologist, businessman, educator, and world citizen.

Franklin took over the management of the *Pennsylvania Gazette* in October 1729 from its founder, Samuel Keimer. Keimer had employed Franklin when he first arrived in Philadelphia, but Ben outgrew that role after traveling to London to learn printing and engraving from England's best. With a friend, Hugh Meredith, he opened his own shop in the spring of 1728 and planned a paper to rival Andrew Bradford's *Mercury*. Keimer, learning of Franklin's project, issued the *Pennsylvania Gazette* in December 1728. It attracted some readership until a new feature began to appear in the rival *Mercury*. A series of clever essays in the Addison and Steele style soon brought delighted patrons to Bradford's shop for copies of the *Mercury*. The series came to be known as the "Busy-Body Papers." The anonymous author was actually Benjamin Franklin, and his most frequent target of satire was none other than Samuel Keimer. With his sales down to fewer than 100 copies, Keimer gave up the struggle. On October 2, 1729, Ben Franklin took over as publisher.

Franklin had little difficulty winning public acceptance, and with it came a volume of profitable advertising. In addition to being a readable paper, it was a bold one. Franklin's experience in Boston, plus his innate common sense, kept him from getting into serious trouble with the authorities. But he took a stand on issues, just the same. Men have many opinions, he explained to his readers, and printers publish these opinions as part of their business.

"They are educated in the belief," he added, "that when men differ in opinion, both sides ought equally to have the advantage of being heard by the public; and that when truth and error have fair play, the former is always an overmatch for the latter [shades of Milton and his *Areopagitica*]. . . . If all printers were determined not to print anything till they were sure it would offend nobody," said he, "there would be very little printed."[5]

With Keimer out of the way, Andrew Bradford remained as Franklin's only serious rival. He had what amounted to a government subsidy through his contract for official printing. Franklin met that challenge by writing up an important legislative address, which he then sent to every member of the Assembly at his own expense. The same report appeared in the *Mercury,* but the *Gazette* story was so much better that Franklin made a great impression on the lawmakers. He continued this reporting, and within a year had won away the government printing contract.

He now bought out his partner, Meredith, with money loaned to him by influential businessmen he had cultivated in his short career in Philadelphia. Thus, at the age of 24, we see him as the sole proprietor of the best newspaper in the American colonies. It soon had the largest circulation, most pages, highest advertising revenue, most literate columns, and liveliest comment of any paper in the area. Retiring from publishing 18 years later, he had made a fortune in a business that usually offered a bare subsistence to its promoters.

Franklin excelled as a printer, engraver, and type founder. He is regarded as a patron saint not only of printers but also of the advertising world, in recognition of his own advertising copywriting and business skill. Franklin's shop made 60 percent of its money on the *Gazette* and 40 percent on other printing, including the fabulously successful *Poor Richard's Almanack* begun in 1732. Franklin also tried to issue a magazine in 1741, as did his rival Bradford, but both failed. It was Franklin, too, who helped establish the first foreign-language paper at Germantown, near Philadelphia. When he retired from the active management of the *Gazette* at 42, he busied himself helping young men set up newspapers in other colonies. He became deputy postmaster general for the colonies and employed postriders to carry newspapers between colonies. His role as diplomat and statesman lay ahead.

But Franklin's greatest contribution to American journalism was that he made it respectable. Campbell, Brooker, the Bradfords, and Keimer were dull fellows, on the whole. Some, like Campbell, lived and died in their communities without achieving more than casual recognition. James Franklin was too tactless to win the respect of "solid" citizens. Most of the printer-journalists had trouble meeting expenses, as their frequent pleas to delinquent subscribers indicate. Franklin showed that a good journalist and businessman could make money in the publishing field. That was, and is, an effective way of making any business respectable. When intelligent and industrious youths saw the possibilities of journalism, as developed by the grand old man of the press, they began to turn more often to this calling. Getting this improved type of personnel into the craft was the best possible tonic for American journalism.

PAPERS IN OTHER COLONIES

After 1725, newspapers sprouted all over the colonies. In Boston, Samuel Kneeland established the *New England Weekly Journal* on March 20, 1727. It is worth a mention because it was the first newspaper to have correspondents in nearby communities whose duty it was to send in pertinent information about the neighborhood, a practice still followed by newspaper publishers. Another important Boston paper was the *Weekly Rehearsal,* founded in 1731 by Jeremy Gridley, a lawyer. A year later he turned over the publication to Thomas Fleet, James Franklin's old printer. Fleet changed the name to the *Evening Post* a few years later. Under him, it became the best and most popular paper in Boston. It lasted until Revolutionary War times. Gridley went on to become editor of Boston's *American Magazine* (1743–46).

Maryland was the fourth colony to have a newspaper.* William Parks, a former English editor, set up the *Maryland Gazette* at Annapolis in 1727. His paper reflected good taste, literary skill, and pride in the craft he had learned so well under the best English masters. Later, in 1736, he founded the *Virginia Gazette,* first newspaper in Virginia, at Williamsburg. That little shop has been restored and is now one of the interesting exhibits at the old colonial capital. Because it tells us what the printing business must have been like in colonial days, it might be worth a moment to look into this quaint building.

THE ENGLISH COMMON PRESS

The office is on the ground floor of a small brick building. In the center stands the English Common Press, shipped over in pieces from the mother country, for no presses were to be had in America until Isaac Doolittle of Connecticut began turning them out in 1769. Close at hand are the accessories: the imposing stones, upon which the type is gathered; the "horse" and "bank" tables, from which the paper is fed to the press; the wetting trough, for the preparation of the paper; an ink grinding stand; and the matrix punches, made in England by William Caslon himself, for cutting the beautiful type that bears his name. The press stands seven feet high and weighs about 1,500 pounds. It is firmly braced to

*The other colonies were Massachusetts, Pennsylvania, and New York. Other firsts in their respective colonies were *Rhode Island Gazette* and *South Carolina Gazette,* 1732; *North Carolina Gazette,* 1751; *Connecticut Gazette,* 1755; *New Hampshire Gazette,* 1756; *Georgia Gazette,* 1763; *New Jersey Gazette,* 1777; *Vermont Gazette,* 1780; and *Delaware Gazette,* 1785. James Parker, one of Ben Franklin's protégés, founded the Connecticut paper. Another of Franklin's "boys" established the South Carolina paper, although there is some doubt as to which one of two has the more valid claim.

Drawing of a colonial wooden hand press.

floor and ceiling by heavy oak beams to insure rigidity when heavy pressure is applied to the type forms.

From this clumsy apparatus colonial printers such as the Bradfords, Greens, Sowers, Parks, and Franklins produced letterpress work of the highest quality.* There was much bad printing during this period too, but that was often the fault of poor craftsmanship and worn equipment. There is abundant proof that the colonial printing press was capable of turning out superb work, under the supervision of a skilled printer. He had to know his business, however. A single impression, or "token," required 13 distinct operations. Two expert craftsmen and an apprentice might turn out about 200 tokens an hour.

Let us watch the colonial printer as he works. The bed of the press is rolled out by means of a wheel and pulley arrangement. The type, all set by hand, is locked tight in the form and placed on the bed. A young apprentice, or "devil," applies the homemade ink to the type, using a doeskin dauber on a stick for this purpose. The paper is then moistened in a trough so that it will take a better impression. It is placed carefully over the type. The bed is rolled back under the press. The "platen," or upper pressure plate, is then pressed against the type by means of a screw or lever device. The platen is released; the bed is wheeled out; the sheet is hung on a wire to dry before it is ready for its second "run" for the reverse side.

The usual colonial paper consisted of four pages, often about ten by fifteen inches in dimension. The paper was rough foolscap. There were no headlines, as we know them, until after 1750, and even then they were uncommon. The only illustrations were the colophons, or printers' trademarks, on the title page, and an occasional woodcut to embellish an advertisement. The Greens and Sowers made their own paper, but most of it was imported from England. It was made of rags and was of surprising durability,

*There were two great Bradford printing families. William Bradford was founder of the Pennsylvania line and was a pioneer printer in Philadelphia and New York. His son, Andrew, established the first newspaper in Philadelphia. William Bradford III was the famous soldier-editor of the Revolution and publisher of the *Pennsylvania Journal* in Philadelphia. His son, Thomas, succeeded the father as editor. John Bradford, no relative of the Pennsylvania clan, was a surveyor who founded the first paper in Kentucky, at Lexington. His brother, Fielding, was also active in journalism. James, another member of this branch, founded the first newspaper in Louisiana and may have been the first American war correspondent, according to Mott (p. 196). The Greens were prominent in New England. Bartholomew and Samuel were pioneers in the Boston-Cambridge area, the former as printer of the first successful newspaper in America. From Samuel Green of Cambridge descended a long line of printer-journalists. Timothy Jr. founded the New London, Conn., *Summary* in 1758. His son, Timothy III, changed the name to the *Gazette* after the death of the father. Samuel and Thomas founded the first paper in New Haven in 1767. Thomas, the brother of Timothy III, founded the *Connecticut* (now *Hartford*) *Courant* in 1764. Timothy IV was co-founder of the first Vermont paper. The fourth printing family were the Sowers, Germans who settled near Philadelphia. First in the printing dynasty was Christopher, who, with the encouragement of Benjamin Franklin, established one of the earliest foreign language newspapers, the Germantown *Zeitung*. A mechanical genius, he constructed his own press and made his own ink and paper. His sons carried on the business, but Christopher III was a Tory during the Revolution and his journalistic career was ruined by the American victory. The Franklin influence in Massachusetts, Rhode Island, and Pennsylvania has been described.

despite its mottled appearance. With this primitive equipment the printer-journalist not only produced fine graphic art, but he also had at hand an implement that was soon to make the press truly a Fourth Estate.

NOTES

1. This thesis is emphasized by Daniel Boorstin in *The Americans: The Colonial Experience* (New York: Random House, 1958), who saw the early printer as a "government man" acceptable to the ruling group in his colony (p. 335).

2. The Mathers were insufferable in the sense that their righteousness made them too sure of themselves, but that does not detract from their important place in colonial history. Increase was licenser of the press after 1674, in addition to his duties as the leading minister of the dominant Puritans. He was president of Harvard and was a respected agent of Massachusetts in London. Cotton opposed the arrogant Sir Edward Andros, ousted from New England after the Revolution of 1688. The Mathers were prolific writers of considerable merit. They were also outstanding historians. In later life they became more tolerant. In all, they contributed much to the development of their community.

3. As quoted in Frank Luther Mott, *American Journalism* (New York: Macmillan, 1950), p. 20. Colonial writing style called for use of many hyphens, such as in New-England, which are not used here for reasons of simplicity in identifying newspapers.

4. His widow, two daughters, and a son carried on the printing business in Newport. In 1758, James, Jr., with the help of his rich uncle Benjamin, established the *Newport Mercury,* which survived until 1934. Its name was then retained in a small weekly edition of the *Newport News*.

5. As quoted in Carl Van Doren, *Benjamin Franklin* (New York: Viking, 1938), p. 100.

ANNOTATED BIBLIOGRAPHY

Books

BOWEN, CATHERINE D., *The Most Dangerous Man in America: Scenes from the Life of Benjamin Franklin*. Boston: Little, Brown, 1974. Franklin the man, the utilitarian, the philosopher.

BRIGHAM, CLARENCE S., *History and Bibliography of American Newspapers, 1690–1820,* 2 vols. Worcester, Mass.: American Antiquarian Society, 1947. Gives brief descriptions of all newspapers up to 1820. An indispensable tool of the colonial press historian.

———, *Journals and Journeymen*. Philadelphia: University of Pennsylvania Press, 1950. Fifteen essays on the colonial press; one particularly interesting one on advertising.

Cambridge History of American Literature, I. New York: G. P. Putnam's Sons, 1917–21. Volume I of this four-volume work discusses Franklin (pp. 90–110) and colonial newspapers and magazines (pp. 111–23).

COOK, ELIZABETH C., *Literary Influences in Colonial Newspapers, 1704–1750*. New York: Columbia University Press, 1912. Describes the role of the press in supplying the craving for popular literature.

DE ARMOND, ANNA JANNEY, *Andrew Bradford: Colonial Journalist*. Newark, Del.: University of Delaware Press, 1949. Well-documented.

FRANKLIN, BENJAMIN, *The Autobiography of Benjamin Franklin,* edited by Leonard W. Labaree. New Haven: Yale University Press, 1964. A new text, restored to Franklin's original.

KOBRE, SIDNEY, *The Development of the Colonial Newspaper*. Pittsburgh: The Colonial Press, Inc., 1944. A short, but classic, study of the integration of political, social, and economic forces in the development of the American press.

The Papers of Benjamin Franklin, Vol. I. New Haven: Yale University Press, 1959. Covers period to 1734, including Silence Dogood and Busy-Body letters. Extensive introduction by editor Leonard W. Labaree.

THOMAS, ISAIAH, *History of Printing in America,* 2 vols. Worcester, Mass.: Isaiah Thomas, Jr.

(first printing), 1810; Albany, N.Y.: Joel Munsell, 1874. The standard authority on colonial journalism; contains biographies of printers and accounts of newspapers in all colonies and in some states after independence.

Van Doren, Carl, *Benjamin Franklin*. New York: Viking, 1938. The most readable account of a great printer-journalist by a prize-winning biographer.

Wroth, Lawrence C., *The Colonial Printer*. Portland, Me.: Southworth-Anthoensen Press, 1938. An excellent study of the printing craft.

Periodicals and Monographs

Fogel, Howard H., "Colonial Theocracy and a Secular Press," *Journalism Quarterly*, XXXVII (Autumn 1960), 525. A study of how the colonial press won its freedom from interference by religious authorities.

Ford, Edwin H., "Colonial Pamphleteers," *Journalism Quarterly*, XIII (March 1936), 24. A scholarly discussion of the journalistic contributions of such colonial leaders as Increase and Cotton Mather and Samuel Sewall. Reprinted in Ford and Emery, *Highlights in the History of the American Press*.

Hudson, Robert V., "The English Roots of Benjamin Franklin's Journalism," *Journalism History*, III (Autumn 1976), 76. Influence of British essayists.

King, Marion Reynolds, "One Link in the First Newspaper Chain, the South Carolina Gazette," *Journalism Quarterly*, IX (September 1932), 257. Describes the arrangement by which Franklin financed his apprentices.

Lipper, Mark, "Comic Caricatures in Early American Newspapers as Representations of the National Character." Ph.D. thesis, Southern Illinois University, 1973. Concludes they were primarily vehicles for satire.

Mott, Frank Luther, "What Is the Oldest U.S. Newspaper?" *Journalism Quarterly*, XL (Winter 1963), 95. Title goes to *Hartford Courant*, founded as the weekly *Connecticut Courant* in 1764 and a daily since 1837.

THE
Pennsylvania GAZETTE.

Containing the freſheſt Advices Foreign and Domeſtick.

From July 24. to July 31. 1735.

TO BE SOLD,
At the Houſe of the Widow Richardſon in Front-Street, near the North-Eaſt Corner of Market-Street.

A LIKELY Negroe Wench about 16 or 18 Years old. ſingle and double refin'd Loaf-Sugar, Barbadoes white and muſcovado Sugar. Alſo Choice Barbadoes Limes in Barrels at reaſonable Rates.

Juſt Imported from London and Briſtol,
And to be SOLD by JOHN INGLIS, at his Store below the Draw-Bridge, in Front-Street, Philadelphia :

B Road-Cloths, Kerſeys and Plains, Ruggs, Blankets, Ornabrigs, Cheeks, London Shalloons, Tammies, Calimandoes, ſeven eighths and yard wide Garlix, Men and Womens worſted Stockings, Men and Womens Shammy Gloves, Pinns, Baladine Silk, ſilk Laces, faſhionable Fans, Paduaſoys, Ribbons, ſilk Ferrits, Gartering, Caddis, Buttons and Mohair, cotton Romals, linnen Handerchiefs, Chiloes, Mens worſted Caps, Bunts, fine Bed-Ticks made up in Suits, India Taſſities, Damasks and Perſians, ſix quarter Muſlins, Suits of ſuper fine Broad-Cloth, with Lining and Trimmings, London double refin'd Sugar, Bird, Pidgeon, Duck, Gooſe and Swan Shot, Bar Lead, 8, 10 and 20 penny Nails, Window Glaſs, Patterns of Chintz for Beds, ſarſnet Handkerchiefs, Briſtol quart Bottles ; and ſundry other Goods, for ready Money, or the uſual Credit.

W Hereas George Carter, a thick ſhort Man, with light buſhy Hair, about 40 Years old, born in White Pariſh, ſix Miles from New-Sarum, in Wiltſhire, by Trade a Baker, went on board a Ship at Briſtol, bonnd to Penſilvania, about the Year 1722 : Theſe are to deſire the ſaid George Carter (if living) to return to his native Country, or to give Notice where he lives to John Atkinſon, at the White Lyon Tavern, on Cornhil, London, or to Iſrael Pemberton, jun. of Philadelphia, who can inform him of ſomething conſiderable to his Advantage : 'If he be deceas'd, Information is deſir'd when and where he died. And if any of his Children be living they may have the ſame Advantage, by applying as aforeſaid.

TO BE SOLD,

B Y James Oſwald in Front-Street, at the Houſe of Mr. Joſeph Turner, and by William Wallace, at the Upper-End of Second-Street, Sugar Bakers, Choice double refin'd LOAF-SUGAR at Eighteen-pence the Pound, ſingle refin'd, Sugar Candy, Mollaſſes, &c. at reaſonable Prices.

R U N away from the Subſcriber, the 4th Day of November laſt, a Servant Woman, aged about 28 Years, fair Hair'd, wants ſome of her Teeth before, a little deafiſh, named Suſannah Wells, born near Biddeford, in England : She had on when ſhe went away, a Callico Gown, with red Flowers, blue Stockings, with Clocks, new Shoes, a quilted Petticoat, Plat Hat. Whoever ſecures ſaid Servant, and delivers her to ſaid Subſcriber at Wilmington, or to Robert Dixon in Philadelphia, ſhall have Twenty-five Shillings Reward, and reaſonable Charges paid by Robert Dixon, or   Thomas Downing.
Philad. December 4. 1740.
N. B. It's believed the ſaid Servant was carried from New-Caſtle in the Ship commanded by Capt. Lawrence Dent, now lying at Philadelphia.

Juſt Publiſhed.

P OOR Richard's ALMANACKS, for the Year 1741. Alſo, Jerman's Almanacks, and Pocket and Sheet Almanacks. Printed and Sold by B. Franklin.

A LL Perſons are hereby deſired to take Notice, That the Bills of Credit of the Province of Pennſylvania, bearing Date any time before the Year 1739, are by an Act of Aſſembly of the ſaid Province, made in the Year aforeſaid, declared to be null and void, ſince the tenth Day of the Month called Auguſt laſt paſt: And that the ſame ſhould be no longer the current Bills of the ſaid Province. Therefore all Perſons who are poſſeſſed of any of the ſaid Bills, are deſired forthwith to bring them in to the General Loan-Office of the ſaid Province at Philadelphia, where Attendance will be given to Exchange them for New-Bills.   J. KINSEY.

R U N away from the Subſcriber the 3d Inſt. a Servant Man named Thomas Wenn, by trade a Barber, appears by his looks to be at leaſt 40 Years old, but pretends he is not 30, middle Stature, well ſet, ſore ey'd, and near ſighted : Had on when he went away, a ſmall Hat but good, a ſmall black Wig, but may have taken another of ſome other colour, a kerſey Coat almoſt new of a mixt colour rediſh and white, lin'd through with a red half thick or ſerge, large flat metal Buttons, old white dimity Jacket, a pair of ſtout buckſkin Breeches almoſt new with braſs Buttons, a pair of new thick mill'd Stockings of a bluiſh colour, Shoes about half worn. Whoever ſecures the ſaid Servant ſo that he may be had again, ſhall have if twenty Miles off this City Twenty Shillings, if thirty, thirty Shilings, and if forty, forty Shillings Reward, paid by
Philad. January 5. 1740.   William Crofthwaite.

TO BE SOLD

By ELIZABETH COMBS, at her Houſe over the Draw-Bridge,

A LL kinds of white and check Linnens, Dimities, Callimancoes, Friſes, Hankerchiefs, Cotton Gowns, ſortable Shot, Sail Cloth, and ſeveral other Goods, for ready Money or ſhort Credit.

For SOUTH-CAROLINA directly,
The Ship Loyal-Judith, LOVELL PAYNTER, Commander,

W ILL Sail when the Weather permits. For Freight or Paſſage agree with the ſaid Maſter on board the ſaid Ship, now lying at Mr. Samuel Auſtin's Wharff ; or with Benjamin Shoemaker, Merchant, in High-Street Philadelphia.

Juſt Imported,

A Parcel of likely Negro Men, Women, and Children : As alſo, choice London double and ſingle refin'd, clay'd and Muſcovado SUGARS, and GINGER ; to be ſold by Joſeph Marks, at the Corner of Walnut and Second-Street, Philadelphia.

Juſt Imported,
And to be Sold very reaſonably by Peter Turner, at his Store over againſt the Poſt-Office in Market-Street, Philadelphia ;

A Large Sortment of Kerſeys, napt and fine Drab Kerſeys, Broad-Cloths, London Shalloons, Embro'd Flannens, Womens Shoes and Cloggs, Hat Lineings, fine Gulic and Hingham Holland, Seven-eights Garlix, Callicoes, Writing Paper, crimſon, blue and green haratteens for Beds, fine half Ell crimſon, blue and green worſted Damasks, 3, 4, 8 penny Nails, London Steel, Scythe, Wool-Cards, Shot and Lead, fine and coarſe Bolting Cloths, Hungary Water, fine Green Tea, fine lackeed Sconces, ell wide Perſians, black and coloured Taſſitye, with ſundry other Goods.

PHILADELPHIA: Printed by B. FRANKLIN, POST-MASTER, the NEW PRINTING-OFFICE, near the Market. Price 10 s. a Year.

The *Pennsylvania Gazette* advertises sales of Negroes, *Poor Richard's Almanack*.

4

Rise
of the Fourth Estate

The question before the court... is not [just] the cause of the poor printer.... No! It may in its consequence affect every freeman... on the main of America. It is the best cause; it is the cause of Liberty... the liberty both of exposing and opposing arbitrary power... by speaking and writing Truth.

—Andrew Hamilton's defense in the Zenger trial

In the second quarter of the eighteenth century the newspaper became a force to be feared by arrogant administrators. True, the infant newspaper mortality rate was high, usually as a result of financial malnutrition. For example, more than half of the 2,120 newspapers established between 1690 and 1820 expired before they were two years old.[1] Only 34 lasted a generation. Nevertheless, by 1750 most literate Americans had access to some journal of information. In that year there were 14 weekly newspapers in the six most populous colonies, and soon the increase in such publications was to be rapid, as we shall see in the next chapter.

The product was better, too. Semiweekly and even triweekly newspapers were available after the mid-century and had first appeared even earlier. Circulation was rising. A few publishers had won fame and fortune in the business. Rapid increase in population, better transportation and communication facilities, and rising political tensions partly explain the growth of the press. Many colonials had become prosperous and were looking around for ways of investing capital. Ports, such as New York, began to achieve world importance. About a third of the ships in the British merchant fleet were launched by New England shipwrights. There were 360 whalers operating from American ports. There were skillful artisans in the towns. The famous "Pennsylvania Rifle," one of the great weapons of the time, was a product of such craftsmen, for example. Despite the restrictions of the mother country, manufacture of finished articles continued to furnish employment for many hands. In one year alone during this period New Englanders shipped out 13,000 pairs of shoes.[2]

The press was useful to the ambitious trader and businessman. Advertising was the cheapest way to move goods offered for sale by the rising commercial class.

Business intercourse between the colonies increased, and accordingly there was need for information only American journalists could provide quickly and cheaply.

Better roads led to better communications. Early editor-postmasters had a double reason for improving roads. Benjamin Franklin, who reversed the process by being appointed postmaster *after* taking up journalism, was named as deputy postmaster of all the colonies, along with William Hunter of Virginia, another printer-journalist. When Franklin took office in 1753, it required six weeks to bring the posts from Boston to Philadelphia by land, and there was a mail pickup only fortnightly. Franklin, who took over most of the postal responsibility because of Hunter's ill-health, cut the travel time in half and established weekly service.

There was also improvement in education, always a factor in developing publics favorable to the newspaper. Many parents could now afford to send their children to school, and seminaries and academies were available in the urban centers. Colleges in many colonies produced not only teachers and ministers, effective foes of illiteracy, but also writers and political spokesmen.

The great technical advances in printing were far in the future, but better type was available during this period. About 1720 William Caslon began modifying Nicolas Jenson's fifteenth-century type into a more readable form. Caslon type was adopted by American printers soon after, and it is still popular. The best standard press was the invention of Willem Janszon Blaeu, a Dutch craftsman of the seventeenth century. Not until around 1800, when Adam Ramage and the Earl of Stanhope came out with the iron press, was there any great improvement in this essential equipment.

THE FIRST ADVERTISING MESSAGES The development of commerce led to progress in the advertising field. Advertising and printing had been closely associated almost from the beginning. William Caxton, who set up the first press in England, issued a broadside advertising his service (religious) book, *The Pyes of Salisbury Use,* in 1480. Number 62 of the *London Gazette,* first complete newspaper in the English language, included an announcement of a special advertising supplement in June 1666. An interesting use of advertising is shown in Number 94 of the same paper. After the great fire of London in the fall of 1666 the paper opened its columns to those seeking word of missing loved ones. There were also advertisements concerning salvaged furniture, addresses of scattered families, and houses offering shelter to the homeless.

Presbrey calls John Houghton the father of modern advertising.[3] Houghton was an apothecary; merchant of coffee, tea, and chocolate; book critic; Fellow of the Royal Society; and publisher. He established a newspaper for commercial readers in 1692. This prototype of the *Wall Street Journal* was the first newspaper to emphasize the role of advertising. Houghton had an appreciation of advertising ethics in an age when the margin between quackery and professional knowledge was narrower than it is today. He was willing to advertise almost any product, but he would not give his seventeenth-century "seal of approval" to statements he believed to be dangerously dishonest. That advertising was a topic for debate and criticism two hundred years ago, as it is today, is implied by a comment of that famous pundit, Dr. Samuel Johnson, in the *Idler* of January 20, 1758:

... Advertisements are now so numerous that they are very negligently perused, and it is therefore become necessary to gain attention by magnificence of promises and by eloquence sometimes sublime and sometimes pathetick. Promise—large promise—is the soul of advertising. . . . The trade of advertising is now so near perfection that it is not easy to propose any improvement.[4]

The advertiser could teach the journalist some important lessons on the subject of reader response. For example, the advertiser quickly discovered that his message must be simply stated to reach the most people. It took the news writer a long time to learn this lesson. Advertisers also understood the value of attractive presentation. They led the way in experimentation with type, illustrations, makeup, and legibility. The press owes much to these practical psychologists and literary showmen.

RISING POLITICAL TENSION
The greatest stimulus to the development of the American press of this period was the rising political tension that was to culminate in the War of Independence. The press had an essential role in the drama about to unfold. The newspaper thrives on controversy, provided it is able to take part in the discussions with any degree of freedom. The great development of the press during the first half of the eighteenth century was its victory over the forces that would have restricted that liberty. This victory made the press the most powerful weapon of the American revolutionaries. Almost forgotten today are the battles and sacrifices by which this concept won general acceptance.

In 1692, before the first successful newspaper had yet been born in America, a Philadelphia printer boldly stated one of the cardinal principles of a free press. He was William Bradford, founder of a remarkable printing dynasty. Bradford had to placate both a jealous government and a sensitive Quaker hierarchy when he set up his little shop. Every now and then he was threatened by one or the other because of ideas expressed in pamphlets he turned out at regular intervals. Arrested in 1692 for a minor infraction, Bradford declared he was tired of such interference and notified the authorities he was taking his press to a more congenial community. Officials were alarmed by this threat, for they depended upon Bradford for the dissemination of governmental, religious, and commercial information. The General Assembly therefore quashed the charge and induced Bradford to remain by granting him a yearly retainer of 40 pounds and all the printing he could handle by himself.

Because of the disposition of this case, Bradford's defense was not widely known, but it is worth a mention here because it brought up an issue that was hotly debated a generation later. For the printer had insisted that the jury in such cases was responsible for judging both the *law* and the *fact*. Now courts had held that when seditious libel (criticism of government) was charged, it was the duty of the jury only to establish the authorship of the statement. This was a point of *fact*. It was up to the judges to determine whether the statement was punishable. This was a point of *law*. Bradford objected to this. Some 40 years later, the issue that Bradford had successfully pressed in 1692 was to become a principal point in the trial of John Peter Zenger.

THE ZENGER CASE: BACKGROUND
The most celebrated case involving freedom of the press was the Zenger trial of 1734–35. It has been much overrated for its effect on legal reform, and it settled nothing because of the dubious circumstances under which it was conducted. Its inspirational impact was tremendous, however.

At this point we meet again William Bradford, late of Philadelphia. The senior Bradford had moved to New York when he was offered the position of government printer there. As a subsidized businessman, Bradford printed nothing that would antagonize his patrons. On November 8, 1725, he printed the first newspaper in the colony—the *New York Gazette*. Of course it favored the administration on all issues. Like many an editor who followed, Bradford rebelled when persecuted, as in Philadelphia, but conformed when offered special privileges and inducements by the same group he might have fought under different circumstances.

By 1733, New York was experiencing a mild revolution. A group of wealthy merchants and landowners insisted upon a greater share of control in the colony's affairs. But it had no way of communicating its ideas. Bradford had the only newspaper, and he was firmly committed to the royal faction. However, Bradford's former apprentice and partner had opened his own print shop. He was John Peter Zenger, an immigrant from the German Palatinate, who had been apprenticed at the age of 13. In the fall of 1733, a delegation of the commercial faction asked Zenger if he would be willing to edit a paper that would be a medium for expressing their news and views.

The situation that prompted this request was complex. The colonial governor died in 1731, and it was 13 months before his replacement, Sir William Cosby, arrived from London. Rip Van Dam, member of the governor's council for 30 years and a colonial Dutch leader, served as acting governor. Cosby demanded half the fees Van Dam had collected for his services; the Dutchman refused. Money cases were to be heard in regular courts, but Cosby moved his case to a court of chancery that he controlled. In the ensuing struggle, Chief Justice Lewis Morris sided with Van Dam and was removed by the governor. Van Dam and Morris now sought to have Cosby recalled by London. The anti-administration forces had other grievances close to their pocket-books: Cosby was accused of demanding one-third of the sale of all public lands sold under his jurisdiction; there was suspected illegal acquisition of land around what is now Utica; and Cosby was seeking to juggle the council membership so that it would approve his new chief justice, young James Delancey.[5]

The leaders of the anti-administration forces were articulate and able citizens. They included men like Van Dam; Justice Morris; James Alexander, a member of the council and also surveyor general for the colonies of New York and New Jersey; and William Smith, noted for his *History of the Colony of New York From Its Founding to 1762* and a well-known public figure at the time of the trial. They, and other important citizens, were interested in having Zenger start a newspaper that would express their views.

The first issue of Zenger's *New York Weekly Journal* appeared on November 5, 1733. From the very first day, the *Journal* clashed with the administration. Bradford at the *Gazette* was no match for Zenger and the brains behind his venture. The main voice was that of lawyer Alexander, who with his friends had successfully put up Lewis Morris for an Assembly seat in a by-election. The first *Journal* issue reported Morris's election despite what was called harassments of voters over their qualifications. On December 3 a story appeared in Zenger's paper attacking Governor Cosby for permitting French warships to spy on lower bay defenses. In the same issue, an irate New Jersey settler (who wrote very much like Alexander) denounced the colonial bureaucracy for incompetence, referring to the Van Dam-Morris controversy.

The public enjoyed this show, and Zenger had to run off extra copies to satisfy customers. The governor was not so enthusiastic about such journalistic enterprise. Charging Zenger with "Scandalous, Virulent and Seditious Reflections upon the Government," Cosby ordered his handpicked chief justice, Delancey, to obtain an indictment against the brash editor. But the grand jury refused to return a true bill. The Assembly likewise balked at filing any charges. Finally, a selected group of the governor's council agreed to start an action against Zenger. On a Sunday afternoon, November 17, 1734, Zenger was arrested on a charge of "raising sedition."

ZENGER'S TRIAL, 1735   The trial did not begin until August 4, 1735. Richard Bradley, Cosby's attorney general, filed an "information" that held Zenger in jail. The *Journal* continued to appear, with Zenger's wife, Anna, running the shop and Alexander filling the editor's role. When Alexander and Smith disputed the validity of the prosecution, they were disbarred. John Chambers, appointed to the case, asked for a postponement until August. The Zenger defense then prevailed on an 80-year-old Philadelphia lawyer, famed for his courtroom presence, to risk traveling to New York for the trial. He was Andrew Hamilton. With him, the stage is set for a drama.

Chambers makes a plea to Justice Delancey, then Hamilton arises, his white hair falling to his shoulders. His first words are a bombshell: "I cannot think it proper to deny the Publication of a Complaint which I think is the right of every free born Subject to make," he declares, "and therefore I'll save Mr. Attorney the trouble of examining his Witness to that point; and I do confess (for my Client) that he both printed and published the two Papers set forth in the Information. I do hope in so doing he has committed no Crime."

Bradley, delighted at this apparent easy victory, says that since publication of the offending articles has been admitted by the defense, there is nothing more for the jury to do but bring in a verdict of guilty. To this Hamilton replies calmly, but firmly: "Not so, neither, Mr. Attorney. There are two Sides to that Bargain. I hope it is not our bare printing or publishing a Paper that will make it a Libel. You will have something more to do before you make my client a libeller. For the Words themselves must be libelous—that is, *False, Malicious, and Seditious*—or else we are not guilty."

Bradley approaches the bench and renews his arguments. One by one Hamilton demolishes them. He goes back to the Magna Carta and to the abolishing of the Star Chamber to prove that the concept he upholds—freedom to express justifiable truth—has long been accepted in the older courts and that colonial New York is behind the times. His arguments are worded in decisive language, but his manner is so courtly, and his voice so mild, that the fascinated crowd listens as though hypnotized. When the spectators begin to cheer during a lull, however, the prosecution objects to Hamilton's statements, and when Hamilton insists that "the *Falsehood* makes the *Scandal*, and both the *Libel*," and then offers to "prove these very Papers that are called Libel to be *True*," Justice Delancey remonstrates.

"You cannot be admitted, Mr. Hamilton," says the judge sternly, "to give the Truth of a Libel in evidence . . . The Court is of the Opinion you ought not to be permitted to prove the Facts in the Papers," and he cites a long list of supporting authorities.

"These are Star Chamber Cases," answers Hamilton patiently, "and I was in hopes that Practice had been dead with that Court."

Angered by this veiled criticism of his legal knowledge, the youthful Delancey cries out angrily: "The Court have delivered their Opinion, and we expect you will use us with good Manners. You are not permitted to argue against this Court."

ANDREW HAMILTON'S GREAT PLEA

Hamilton pauses a moment. He looks at the jury, then at the audience, and then at Zenger, like a great actor sensing the mood of his public. Now he turns to the judge and bows courteously.

"I thank you," he replies without a trace of rancor. Then, turning his back upon the bench, he acknowledges the jury with a courtly flourish. He speaks to the jurymen directly, in a voice loud enough to carry to all parts of the room.

"Then it is to you, Gentlemen, we must now appeal for Witnesses to the Truth of the Facts we have offered, and are denied the Liberty to prove. . . ."

Now Hamilton is talking as though Delancey were not even in the room. He exhorts the jury to act like freemen and to follow their own consciences, without fear of official reprisals, as guaranteed under the English system of law. He ends:

". . . old and weak as I am, I should think it my Duty if required, to go to the utmost Part of the Land, where my Service could be of any Use in assisting to quench the Flame of Prosecutions upon Informations, set on Foot by the Government, to deprive a People of the Right of Remonstrating (and complaining too), of the arbitrary Attempts of Men in Power. *Men who injure and oppress the People under their Administration provoke them to cry out and complain; and then make that very Complaint the Foundation for new Oppressions and Prosecutions.*

". . . But to conclude; the Question before the Court and you Gentlemen of the Jury, is not of small nor private Concern. It is not the Cause of the poor Printer, nor of *New York* alone, which you are now trying; No! It may in its Consequence affect every Freeman that lives under a British Government on the main of *America*. It is the best Cause. It is the Cause of Liberty; and I make no Doubt but your upright Conduct, this Day, will not only entitle you to the Love and Esteem of your Fellow-Citizens; but every Man who prefers Freedom to a Life of slavery will bless and honour You, as Men who have baffled the Attempt of Tyranny; and by an impartial and uncorrupt Verdict, have laid a Noble Foundation for securing to ourselves, our Posterity and our Neighbors, That, to which Nature and the Laws of our Country have given us a Right—the Liberty—both of exposing and opposing arbitrary Power (in these Parts of the World, at least) by speaking and writing—Truth."

On that note, Hamilton won his case. The jury returned a verdict of "not guilty," and Zenger was freed. He has now become a hero of American journalism. Less known, but equally heroic, was Andrew Hamilton, who argued the cause of liberty so ably.

THE ZENGER TRIAL ANALYZED

But there are some negative aspects of the case. The verdict had no effect on libel law for more than half a century. Pennsylvania was the first state to recognize the principles of truth as a defense and the right of the jury to decide both the law and the fact, by including them in its 1790 constitution. New York accepted them in 1805. It was 1792 in England before Fox's Libel Act gave the jury power of decision, and it was 1843 before Lord Campbell's Act recognized truth as a defense.

It is very possible that expediency, rather than principle, guided the authorities after trial. They admitted no new legal precedent in the Zenger case. It is quite probable that Zenger would have been rearrested for his very next offense, except for circumstances. Governor Cosby was cautious for a time after the trial ended, because Justice Morris was in England arguing for Cosby's dismissal, and the governor had no wish to achieve any further notoriety for himself. Then he fell desperately ill during the winter of 1735–36 and died the following March. Had he lived, he might not have accepted defeat so easily.

Again, all the reports of the trial are one-sided. The only complete account of the trial is in Zenger's own newspaper. The Crown never did issue a report giving its side of the verdict. Since the accused had good reason to paint the picture in black and white, the Crown arguments and principles have been largely ignored. O'Callaghan's *Documents Relative to the Colonial History of New York* (Albany, 1849, V) include statements of Governor Cosby to the Lords of Trade, and they are the nearest thing to a presentation of the other side of the argument.

Justice Delancey, who has always been portrayed as an arrogant judge, showed great restraint in refusing to set aside the verdict and in not overruling Hamilton. He might even have had the old lawyer arrested for his contempt of the bench. The British government in this case, as in many others, including the Stamp Act of 1765, did not use its powers to curb opinion but backed down in the face of overwhelming public dissatisfaction.

This is an important point. The courts as much as the press guard the freedom so jealously maintained by a democratic people. To flout the law for the sake of expediency in a press case is a dangerous precedent. When defendants are acquitted because of political feelings, rather than a calm appraisal of the known law, that is a threat to a system every bit as important to our freedom as the liberty of the press.

Justice Delancey appears somewhat ridiculous today in his opinion that truth could not be offered as a defense in this type of libel action. The fact is, he had considerable precedent to back him up. For the principle recognized by the courts of that day was "the greater the truth, the greater the libel." The logic behind this doctrine was this: public accusations, or criticisms of those in authority, might upset the entire community and cause a serious breach of the public peace. In Zenger's case, popular opinion was behind him, but this did not sway colonial writers on the subject of seditious libel. Almost all of them remained agreed that government could be libeled and that to do so was properly to be considered a crime. And many responsible citizens agreed with them. The threat of punishment—under the common law of seditious libel or under the power of a legislature to punish for contempt—for those who criticized officials remained strong until the close of the eighteenth century when the struggle over the Sedition Act of 1798 brought the issue to a climax.[6]

These negative aspects of the case are counteracted by the inspirational contributions of Zenger and Hamilton and the psychological effects of the trial. For the trial did enunciate a principle—even if it did not establish legal precedent—and this principle is vital to our libertarian philosophy of today in matters of free speech and press. The right to criticize officials is one of the main pillars of press freedom.[7] Psychologically, the Zenger trial advanced this goal, for no other colonial court trial of a printer for seditious libel after 1735 has come to light. Some were found to be in contempt by their own colonial legislatures or governor's councils, but none was tried by the Crown.[8] Popular opinion had proved its power. The Zenger case thus merits its place in history, as a forerunner of what was to follow.

NOTES

1. Clarence S. Brigham, *History and Bibliography of American Newspapers, 1690–1820* (Worcester, Mass.: American Antiquarian Society, 1947), p. x (Intro.).

2. These aspects of development are admirably presented in Sidney Kobre, "The Revolutionary Colonial Press—A Social Interpretation," *Journalism Quarterly,* XX (September 1943), 193–97.

3. Frank Presbrey, *The History and Development of Advertising* (Garden City, N.Y.: Doubleday, 1929), p. 56.

4. Ibid., p. 70.

5. Warren C. Price, "Reflections on the Trial of John Peter Zenger," *Journalism Quarterly,* XXXII (Spring 1955), 161, provides much new data on the Zenger case and points to the land-grabbing episode as one reason why public opinion swung to the Zenger-Morris side so heavily. "Cosby Manor" at Utica, 20 miles by 10 miles in extent, was an example of the governor's greed.

6. Leonard W. Levy, *Legacy of Suppression* (Cambridge: Harvard University Press, 1960), develops this thesis of colonial adherence to the concept of seditious libel except as it could be turned against one's own faction. Levy traces this attitude as prevailing as late as the 1790s.

7. The others: (1) the right to publish without official license, established in America by James Franklin; (2) the right to report matters of public interest, a right not widely recognized until well into the nineteenth century and still contested by reluctant public officials.

8. Harold L. Nelson, "Seditious Libel in Colonial America," *American Journal of Legal History, III* (April 1959), 160–72. Professor Nelson finds the colonial assembly more effective than the courts in disciplining printers and cites available evidence that Zenger's trial was the last. The most exhaustive study of the subject by an outstanding scholar.

ANNOTATED BIBLIOGRAPHY

Books

ADAMS, JAMES TRUSLOW, *Provincial Society, 1690–1763,* A History of American Life, Vol. III. New York: Macmillan, 1927. This series was the first large-scale attempt at social history and remains highly usable. Other volumes will be cited later. The series was edited by Arthur M. Schlesinger and Dixon Ryan Fox.

ALEXANDER, JAMES, *A Brief Narrative of the Case and Trial of John Peter Zenger, Printer of the New York "Weekly Journal,"* ed. Stanley N. Katz. Cambridge, Mass.: Harvard University Press, 1963. Scholarly reprint with annotations of document by Zenger's lawyer.

BRIDENBAUGH, CARL, *Cities in the Wilderness: the First Century of Urban Life in America, 1625–1742* and *Cities in Revolt: Urban Life in America, 1743–1776.* New York: Knopf, 1955. Cities studied are Boston, Newport, New York, Philadelphia, and Charleston.

BURANELLI, VINCENT, ed., *The Trial of Peter Zenger.* New York: New York University Press, 1957. Reprint of the text of the trial, with biographical information about participants and an analysis of its meaning.

DUNIWAY, CLYDE A., *The Development of Freedom of the Press in Massachusetts.* New York: Longmans, Green & Company, 1906. An early and scholarly study.

LEVY, LEONARD W., ed., *Freedom of the Press from Zenger to Jefferson.* Indianapolis: Bobbs-Merrill, 1966. A collection of documents tracing theories of freedom of the press from Zenger trial to Jeffersonian period and rise of libertarianism.

——, *Legacy of Suppression.* Cambridge, Mass.: Harvard University Press, 1960. A prize-winning study of the English and colonial roots of freedom of expression that documents a thesis that only a narrow concept of such freedom was held before 1800.

MACCRACKEN, HENRY NOBLE, *Prologue to Independence: The Trials of James Alexander, 1715–1756.* New York: Heineman, 1964. The lawyer who edited Zenger's paper.

MOTT, FRANK L., ed., *The Case and Tryal of John Peter Zenger.* Columbia, Mo.: Press of the Crippled Turtle, 1954. An exact reprint of Zenger's original pamphlet.

OSGOOD, HERBERT L., *The American Colonies in the Eighteenth Century,* Vol. II. New York: Columbia University Press, 1924. Pages 443–82 give the political background for the Zenger trial, examining the Cosby administration.

OULD, HARMON, ed., *Freedom of Expression.* London: Hutchinson International Authors, Ltd., 1945. A memoriam on the tercentenary of Milton's *Areopagitica.* Contributors are important British and foreign writers, journalists, and lawyers.

PRESBREY, FRANK, *The History and Development of Advertising.* Garden City: Doubleday,

1929. The best known and most complete history of advertising. Especially useful because of its numerous illustrations.

RUTHERFURD, LIVINGSTON, *John Peter Zenger*. New York: Peter Smith, 1941. Reprints the text of the trial, with a biographical study of Zenger and an analysis of the political setting. The above edition is a reprint from a 1904 edition published by Dodd, Mead and Company.

SCHUYLER, LIVINGSTON R., *The Liberty of the Press in the American Colonies Before the Revolutionary War*. New York: Thomas Whittaker, 1905. A short history of an important period in press development.

WOOD, JAMES PLAYSTED, *The Story of Advertising*. New York: Ronald Press, 1958. Less extensive but more readable than Presbrey. Relatively brief in its coverage of the period before 1850.

Periodicals and Monographs

COVERT, CATHY, " 'Passion Is Ye Prevailing Motive': the Feud Behind the Zenger Case," *Journalism Quarterly,* L (Spring 1973), 3. Zenger was the printer of James Alexander's ideas.

KOBRE, SIDNEY, "The Revolutionary Colonial Press—A Social Interpretation," *Journalism Quarterly,* XX (September 1943), 193. A digest of a more detailed study by the same author. Especially useful for its background information.

NELSON, HAROLD L., "Seditious Libel in Colonial America," *American Journal of Legal History,* III (April 1959), 160. Establishes thesis that after the Zenger trial, printers were disciplined by legislatures or governor's councils, rather than by trial courts. The colonial assembly became the major force in limiting press freedom. Exhaustive study by legal scholar.

PRICE, WARREN C., "Reflections on the Trial of John Peter Zenger," *Journalism Quarterly,* XXXII (Spring 1955), 161. Deals with the negative aspects of Hamilton's appeal insofar as legal status was concerned, and examines Cosby's land-grabbing operations.

STEINER, BERNARD C., "Andrew Hamilton and John Peter Zenger," *Pennsylvania Magazine,* XX (Summer 1896), 405. Since Hamilton is as much a hero of this period as is Zenger, this description of the lawyer's place in history is very useful.

Pennsylvania Magazine of History and Biography

John Dickinson, the Colonial Whig

Magazine of American History

James Rivington, leading Tory editor

Bettmann Archive

Samuel Adams, the Radical propagandist

C. K. Shipman and American Antiquarian Society

Isaiah Thomas, Patriot editor

5

The Seeds
of Revolution

The United Voice of all His Majesty's free *and* loyal *Subjects in
America—Liberty and Property, and no Stamps.*
—Motto of various colonial newspapers

Many believe today that the American Revolution was strictly a struggle by freedom-loving people for independence from a tyrannical British king. Actually, the reasons for the Revolution were much more complex. The clash of debtor and creditor was a factor. The weakness of British policy, inept leadership, and overemphasis of the mercantile system (by which Europeans exploited colonies) were all involved in the dispute. Colonists resented restraints on American development of commerce and industry. They complained that their frontier was being denied to them after the hard-won victory over the French, which they had expected to open up vast new areas to expansion. Refusal of the British to grant home rule was another point of dispute.

But these are not sufficient *reasons* for the war. All the above disputes might have been settled peaceably, some historians say. Other British colonies had similar grievances at the time, yet they did not have to resort to war. Nor can it be held that the issue was confined to Britain and her colonies. In other parts of the world the same issues were being raised. France and South America were soon to be embroiled in revolution, indicating that the War of Independence was a regional manifestation of world unrest.

Many students of the period maintain that the war was unnecessary. The American shipper might quarrel over British denial of certain markets, but he knew that the British navy made it possible for him to sail the high seas with reasonable safety from seizure. Certainly the little Atlantic seaboard communities in America could not have provided such essential protection—not by themselves, at least. Merchants resented the trade restrictions, but they knew full well that they also enjoyed great benefits through monopolies and bounties that only a great trading nation, such as

Great Britain, could make possible. Frontiersmen might curse such measures as the Quebec Act, which limited westward expansion, but the same complainants were aware that the motherland provided the roads by which the frontier was developed and tamed. They knew, also, that British troops garrisoning forts up and down the colonies were the main bulwarks against Indian retaliation.

CAUSES OF THE REVOLUTION

How, then, did the American colonies find themselves at war with the homeland in 1775? Perhaps it can be explained that the war was as much a class struggle—a domestic rebellion, even—as it was a struggle for political separation. The fight for freedom was both internal and external, if we see it as a class conflict. This class struggle was directed by an able and articulate group of "agitators"—one of the best proofs, indeed, of the nature of the conflict. It is even possible that there might have been no shooting war, had it not been for these class leaders. Sam Adams was a typical leader of this movement. He was a spokesman for a class insisting upon a greater share of control. Having aroused his public, he proceeded to win his goals. For that reason, it is pertinent to study this period in terms of public opinion and through the eyes of those who manipulated public support leading to war.

It is significant that the Stamp Act of 1765 alienated two very influential groups—the lawyers and the journalists. The new law placed a heavy duty on paper used in publishing newspapers. There was also a heavy tax on all legal documents. Thus, the lawyer, who swayed people by the spoken word, and the journalist, who had an even wider influence through the written word, were both turned against those who favored the unpopular act.

Yet one can scarcely blame the British for proposing some such law. After the Seven Years' War, which saw the British triumphant over the French in North America and India, Great Britain emerged as a great empire—one of the greatest of all time. On the other hand, victory found the British nearly bankrupt. Some way had to be found to pay the cost of defending the wide frontiers. Since the Americans had gained so much from the victory over the French, they should be willing to pay a small share of the defense costs, the statesmen in London insisted.

The colonists were indeed willing to offer help—in their own fashions. Colonial legislatures were ready to raise levies, but they did not raise enough, and they did not exert themselves enough to turn over such funds when needed. Since the legislatures controlled the colonial purse strings, not much could be done when levies were in arrears. Empire leaders believed the solution was the imposition of special taxes that could be collected more effectively for this purpose. The Stamp Act was one such attempt. The British themselves paid such a tax. George Grenville, sponsor of the hated measure, pointed out that even Massachusetts had imposed a similar tax in 1755. A little later New York did the same.

The colonists replied that the local stamp acts were imposed by the people paying the tax. As Sam Adams brought out in his resolutions of 1765, the colonies had no direct representation in Parliament. He recognized that this would be impracticable, considering the distance apart of the two areas. That was why he insisted that the colonies be given home rule under a common king.[1] But that was no solution to the immediate problem.

The opposition of the editors took many forms. Some suspended publication. Some publications appeared without title or masthead, which technically took them out of the newspaper classification. A few appeared without the required stamp but with the notice that none could be procured, which may have been true since mobs prevented the sale of stamps in every colony. Several publications satirized the event. On the day before the tax was to be enforced, the *Pennsylvania Journal and Weekly Advertiser* appeared with heavy black column margins, or "turned rules," the traditional symbol of journalistic mourning but this time in the shape of a tombstone.

The Stamp Act agitation was actually only an episode in a long conflict between Great Britain and her colonies. The British were leading exponents of the "mercantile system." Under this program, colonies were to be developed for raw materials and again as markets for finished products. Essential to the system was a favorable balance of trade for Great Britain, meaning that the value of exports must exceed that of imports. This policy was fostered by whatever party gained control. That was why the British Government had imposed restrictions on trade, industry, and finances in the colonies beginning in 1651. Scarcity of money in the colonies became a serious matter, for example, but the refusal of British creditors to ease the debt burden embittered many a colonial.[2] An Act of 1751, specifically, denied the printing of paper money secured by land, which would have made money less dear. Sam Adams, often called "The Father of the Revolution," never forgot that his father had been ruined by these restrictive laws and that he had been cheated of his patrimony thereby.

The colonists did not make violent objection, however, until after the victory over the French. Smuggling went on openly, engaged in by respected citizens as a legitimate way around measures believed to be unsound by local consensus. But after 1763, the British began to enforce old laws and to impose new ones. A royal proclamation closed all the frontier west of the mountains to settlement and expansion, thereby raising land values in the older areas. Smuggling was reduced by an effective amendment to an old law of 1733. Currency restrictions were tightened. Commodities never before taxed were now enumerated. And just to rub it in, the home government asserted the right of Parliament to make all laws for the colonies.

The reaction to the trend is seen in the colonial attempts to present their grievances peaceably at first and then by more direct action when this policy failed. The Stamp Act Congress, which succeeded in bringing about the repeal of the hated law, showed the colonies what could be accomplished by united, decisive action. Granted all this, one must still conclude that economics were only a factor in the coming revolution. For ideas were stirring men, too. Indeed, it can be said that the revolution was completed by 1775, if ideas are the criteria; in which case the war was only the means of defending them against those who could not subscribe to the new thought.

Here is where the press of the time played such an important part. In newspaper and pamphlet (often reprints of weekly journals) appeared the literature of the Revolution. Here it was that the passions and arguments of the revolutionaries found expression. As Beard has said:

... Unlike France of the Old Regime, provincial America did not produce, long before the struggle commenced, great treatises such as the *Encyclopedia* or the ringing calls for revolt such as Rousseau's *Social Contract*.

The reasons were not difficult to find: the colonists already had textbooks of revolution in the writings of Englishmen who defended and justified the proceedings of the seventeenth century—above all, John Locke's writings, wherein was set forth the right of citizens to overthrow governments that took their money or their property without their consent.... All that editors and publicists had to do was to paraphrase, decorate, and repeat....[3]

Thursday, October 31, 1765.　　NUMB. 1195.

THE
PENNSYLVANIA JOURNAL;
AND
WEEKLY ADVERTISER.

EXPIRING: In Hopes of a Resurrection to LIFE again.

I AM sorry to be obliged to acquaint my Readers, that as The STAMP ACT, is fear'd to be obligatory upon us after the *First of November* ensuing, (the *fatal To-morrow*) the Publisher of this Paper unable to bear the Burthen, has thought it expedient to *STOP a while,* in order to deliberate, whether any Methods can be found to elude the chains forged for us, and escape the insupportable Slavery; which it is hoped, from the just Representations now made against that Act, may be effected. Mean while, I must earnestly Request every Individual of my Subscribers, many of whom have been long behind Hand, (that I may be immediately Discharge their respective Arrears, that I may be able, not only to support myself during the Interval, but be better prepared to proceed again with this Paper, whenever an opening for that Purpose appears, which I hope will be soon.
WILLIAM BRADFORD.

Facsimile of the famed "Tombstone Edition" protesting the 1765 Stamp Act.

The conflicting ideas as the Revolution progressed can be followed conveniently by studying the products of three journalists who represented their respective classes or groups. They were James Rivington, the Tory spokesman; John Dickinson, "the penman of the Revolution," representing the Whig philosophy; and Samuel Adams, evangelist of democracy and leader of the "agitators" or Radicals.

JAMES RIVINGTON, THE TORY SPOKESMAN

We are likely to think of the American Tory as something of a traitor because of his refusal to bear arms against his king in the War of Independence. Actually, it was the Tory who remained loyal to his country when others rebelled. Only defeat in war made the Tory a traitor. Readers of Kenneth Roberts's historical novel, *Oliver Wiswell,* can understand that there were many sincere and honest Americans who believed in the Tory cause in the middle of the eighteenth century. About 20 percent were Tories in 1776.

The goal of the Tory, apparently, was to retain the basic structure of colonial society. He wished to continue governing by right of property, heredity, position, and tradition—which would appear to be the attributes of a nobility. This seems a strange and distasteful desideratum, by democratic standards, but it had its persuasive proponents. Such a one was Rivington.

"Jemmy" Rivington came to the colonies in 1762, after he had lost his fortune at the race track—not the last newspaperman to suffer in this way, it might be added. Despite this preoccupation with the sport of kings, Rivington was a credit to journalism and to his class. One can hardly blame him for his Tory views. For generations his family had been official publishers of religious books for the Church of England—the Established Church, and therefore the one that had the most general appeal to most good Tories. King and Bishop represented authority, by which order could be maintained most effectively, the Tory argued. Thus, an attack on the authority of the state was also a threat to the authority of the church, men like Rivington insisted, and history of revolution has shown that this is indeed the usual consequence. It was the duty of all citizens, therefore, to help the forces of law and order against anarchistic elements.

Rivington was influential in America and could do much for the Tory cause. He was proprietor of the first chain of bookstores in America, with branches in Boston, New York, and Philadelphia. He had been so successful in this venture that he decided to publish a newspaper. In 1773, on the eve of the revolt in the colonies, he founded *Rivington's New York Gazetteer or the Connecticut, New Jersey, Hudson's River and Quebec Weekly Advertiser,* a local paper, despite its impressive, regional title. The paper was well edited and skillfully printed. It was also very profitable, as shown by the fact that it averaged about 55 percent advertising.

Rivington merited respect for his venture because he was willing to discuss both sides of political questions—an objectivity that was not the standard in his era. Such objectivity was just what the "Patriot" rivals resented, however. They were not interested in fair and accurate reports. That was no way to fight for a cause, they believed, and so we find Rivington complaining in his issue of April 20, 1775:

> The Printer is bold to affirm that his press has been open to publication from ALL PARTIES. . . . He has considered his press in the light of a public office, to which every man has a right to have recourse. But the moment he ventured to publish sentiments which were opposed to the dangerous views and designs of certain demagogues, he found himself held up as an enemy of his country.

Rivington's complaint was a common one for Tories in the decade preceding outbreak of war. Power was slipping away from the English authorities into the hands of the colonial assemblies. In their eyes, criticism of the Crown was no longer seditious libel. But criticism of the assemblies, or of the Patriot cause, might well be seditious or contemptuous. Freedom of expression meant largely freedom for your side—and the Tory was on the losing side.

The troubles of the Tory printers came largely from public pressures generated by such Radical "agitators" as Sam Adams rather than from official actions. An organized campaign of threats and economic coercion was reinforced at times by mob action against printers who were not all-out for the Radical cause. The Tories, or Loyalists, were nearly all hounded out of business; those who tried to be neutral were either forced into the Radical camp or into suspension.[4]

In Boston, for example, the well-organized Radical group used threats to persuade some reluctant printers to use their propaganda and to mute Tory voices. When John Mein's stoutly Tory *Chronicle* refused to cower, but instead attacked the Radical leaders, Mein was hanged in effigy, attacked on the street, and finally mobbed. He had to flee to England, and his paper was suspended in 1770. Thomas Fleet's *Evening Post* which tried to print both sides of the argument, closed down in 1775, as did the Tory *Post-Boy*. The last Tory voice, the *News-Letter,* died early in 1776. In Philadelphia, Patriot William Goddard was roughed up for publishing pro-Crown materials in his *Pennsylvania Chronicle*. Rivington thus could complain about the experiences of others, as well as his own, in opposing the Radical-generated tide of public opinion.

After Lexington and Concord, Rivington ceased to be objective. During the war he was as partisan as his Patriot rivals. His wartime paper, renamed the *Royal Gazette,* reeked with unfounded charges against American leaders. He appeared to relish vicious rumors that might harm the rebels—but this was in time of war, whose first casualty is objectivity. And he had little reason to feel charitable toward his political and social enemies. He had been burned in effigy by mobs for expressing his views. Twice his shop had been raided—the type destroyed on one occasion. He had been forced to sign a humiliating public apology for merely voicing his opinions. He had even been driven back to England in 1776, to return as king's printer in 1777. When in 1781 the news of Yorktown reached the *Royal Gazette,* Rivington became conciliatory. He objectively reported the scene in which General Washington bade farewell to his officers in New York City, after the British had departed. But the Radicals, led by Isaac Sears, were unrelenting; the same mob that had burned him out in 1775 came back New Year's Eve 1783 to close him down. Rivington did not leave with other Tories; he died in New York in 1802.

JOHN DICKINSON, THE WHIG PHILOSOPHER   Spokesmen for other groups disputed Tory views—some mildly, and some violently. The American Tory was opposed by a rising capitalist faction—it could not as yet be called a party—often referred to as the Colonial Whigs. An articulate Whig was John Dickinson of Pennsylvania, sometimes called "The Penman of the Revolution."

Although not a publisher or printer, Dickinson deserves to be ranked with the great journalists of the period. By newspaper and pamphlet he spread the gospel of his political faith. The gist of his philosophy appeared in a series of articles entitled "Letters From a Farmer In Pennsylvania." The first such letter was printed in the *Pennsylvania Chronicle* in 1767. Eleven others followed on into 1768. They were widely reprinted up and down the seaboard.

Two 1767 events had alarmed Dickinson: the imposition of the Townshend Acts as direct taxes by Parliament, and the suspension of the New York Assembly for not granting tax money to the governor. The Colonial Whig, to be safe in his property, had to control taxes in his own assembly, argued Dickinson. This emphasis upon property was the hallmark of sound government.

Dickinson had no wish to bring on a war for independence, but he, more than any other writer except Sam Adams, prepared public opinion for the Revolution, since he stated basic principles that Colonial Whigs came to feel they must defend. Ironically, this mild Quaker became the author of the *Declaration of Rights of the Stamp Act Congress* and two *Petitions to the King* and coauthor of the Articles of Confederation.

Dickinson was as contemptuous of rabble-rousers as were Rivington and the rest of the Tories. For the Whig had rather narrow ideas of liberty. The great battle cry of the Whig, for example, was "no taxation without representation," which is strictly an economic aspect of the struggle. The Whig had no great interest in the rise of the common man. He had only the vaguest of ideas regarding the "natural rights" philosophy of social reform, for he thought more in terms of property than of human rights. Yet he, too, was fighting for a principle, and in the conflict he brought liberties to others less able to fight on fair terms. The curious twist to all this was that the worst enemy of the American Whig was his counterpart in England. The British Whig imposed commercial restrictions that were considered harmful to American business interests. The American argued that if British businessmen in control of the government both at home and abroad could impose taxes arbitrarily without colonial representation, then American business rivals could be driven into oblivion.

When the Revolution had to be defended by arms, the American Whig had to choose between loyalty to the Crown, which provided the law and order he so prized, or loyalty to his local government, which held the promise of the unrestricted enterprise he coveted. The dilemma forced the Whig into becoming either a Loyalist or a Patriot during the shooting war, for there was by that time no place for the compromiser. Dickinson himself had to make this choice. He could not bring himself to stand for outright independence from his beloved motherland, and he refused to sign the Declaration of Independence. But he carried a musket in defense of his home.

Dickinson was influential because he was respected by the propertied class—a group generally regarded as hardheaded, practical, and unemotional. Once convinced, the businessman could do more than anyone else in swinging his neighbors in favor of a cause. For his neighbors reasoned that if a "sound" businessman believed in proposed changes, there must be good reason for his attitude. Dickinson reached this group by articles geared to their interests. His letters were brilliant, convincing, and readable. They were widely printed. All but three of the newspapers of the period carried the complete series by the "Pennsylvania Farmer." Ideas expressed in these contributions were reflected in the press for weeks, and even for years.

SAMUEL ADAMS, THE RADICAL PROPAGANDIST The weakest group at the beginning of the struggle, and the most important at the end of the conflict, was the so-called "Radical" or "Patriot"—words not at all synonymous at a later date. The Tory had great interest in hereditary rights; the Whig was preoccupied with economic issues; but the Radical carried on into a very different field. The Radicals were the only ones seriously interested in social change. They might have been overcome, as they had been in England, however, had it not been for the very effective leadership in America. Probably the best example of the Radical leader was Samuel Adams, one of the most prolific journalists of his time.

As a propagandist, Adams was without peer. He understood that to win the inevitable conflict, he and his cohorts must achieve five main objectives. They must justify the course they advocated. They must advertise the advantages of victory. They must arouse the masses—the real shock troops—by instilling hatred of enemies. They must neutralize any logical and reasonable arguments proposed by the opposition. And finally, they must phrase all the issues in black and white, so that the purposes might be clear even to the common laborer. Adams was able to do all this, and his principal tool was the colonial newspaper.

Adams believed that the American colonies were justified in repudiating the mother country because Parliament continued to ignore basic rights. It was the British who broke the contract, he argued, and hence the obligations of the colonials no longer applied. (The theory of the law of contracts was, and still is, that violation by one party releases all other contractors from obligations.) Adams made it appear as though his class and party fought for the traditional rights, now ignored by the British Parliament. Technically, then, it was the British who were in revolt—the colonists were the people maintaining the traditional ways.

Sam Adams was not the only propagandist of the revolution, but he was the greatest of them all. He was truly the "master of the puppets," as his enemies dubbed him. He was perfectly fitted for the role. Adams had turned away from the ministry, from law, and from teaching, although he was familiar with all these professions. As a young Radical, Adams met regularly with the Caucus Club, founded by his father and other aggressive Boston spirits. The club sponsored a newspaper, the *Independent Advertiser,* and in 1748, at the age of 26, Sam Adams became editor of that publication. Later, he was a regular contributor to the *Boston Gazette and Country Journal,* descendant of the second newspaper published in the colonies.

Adams made a strike for liberty in May 1764, when he was appointed one of a committee of five to instruct his town's representative to the legislature. Included was a denial of Parliament's right to impose Grenville's hated Stamp Act. A final paragraph of the document also suggested a union of all the colonies for the most effective expression of grievances.[5] These instructions were printed by the *Gazette,* and since this paper was closely followed as the mouthpiece of the "Patriot" element, the stirring message was broadcast up and down the seaboard.

EDES AND GILL'S At once Adams was recognized as leader of a small but vociferous
BOSTON GAZETTE group. Two of this band were Benjamin Edes and John Gill, boyhood
friends and now proprietors of the *Gazette.* By the end of 1764 the newspaper was the nerve center of the Boston Radicals. Many famous Americans wrote for the paper, especially after the passage of the obnoxious Townshend Acts of 1767 levying new duties on colonial imports, but none was more effective than Sam Adams.

He was more than a writer; he was an expert news gatherer. His Committees of Correspondence, organized in 1772, kept him alert to every movement and sentiment throughout the colonies. His agents "covered" every important meeting as ably as modern reporters gather information for the press services today. In a remarkably short time all such news reached Adams's local committee, which then processed it for effective dissemination where such information was needed. This primitive news service was highly efficient, yet no one in the colonies had thought of such a device until Adams came along.

He was just as successful at instilling his enthusiasm for the cause into the hearts of useful helpers. Since a man's greatness can be measured by the caliber of his associates, we must assume that Adams was a great man indeed. Cousin John, who later became second president of the United States, sometimes disappointed Sam, as in John's defense of the British soldiers involved in the "Boston Massacre," but on the whole the two respected each other, as indicated by the fact that Sam used his influence in John's behalf even while the two argued. They were both honest men. John was useful in enlisting the more dignified members of the community, especially the legal fraternity, disdainful of Sam's noisier methods.

Another associate was Josiah Quincy, who understood what some organizers now refer to as "solidarity." Quincy argued that to think justly was not enough; citizens must also think *alike* before there could be a united force of public opinion strong enough to make warriors of the cause invincible. Still another great co-worker was Joseph Warren, the charming and kindly physician, who spoke with great logic for the Patriot cause. Warren insisted upon taking direct action when the shooting began. He lost his life as a high-ranking officer in the first pitched battle of the war at Breed's (Bunker) Hill. James Otis was the spellbinder of the group—one of the great orators of his day. The British feared Otis most of all, because of his persuasive powers.

THE SONS OF LIBERTY   The Boston Radicals who gathered about Sam Adams at the *Gazette* office were the core of the revolutionary movement. But they needed a way to win the support of other colonies for the hard line toward the British they were developing in Massachusetts. This was supplied by the Sons of Liberty, whose chapters sprang into being during the spontaneous popular uprising over the Stamp Act of 1765. Adams, printer Benjamin Edes, and engraver Paul Revere were among the key Boston members, from the *Gazette* group. Other printers rated as strong activists in the Sons of Liberty propaganda network were fellow Bostonian Isaiah Thomas of the *Massachusetts Spy;* John Holt of the *New York Journal;* Peter Timothy of Charleston's *South Carolina Gazette;* William Goddard of Philadelphia's *Pennsylvania Chronicle* and Baltimore's *Maryland Journal;* and Solomon Southwick of the *Newport Mercury.* William Bradford III was a Sons of Liberty officer in Philadelphia but did not fully commit his *Pennsylvania Journal* to the Radical line.

The Townshend Acts of 1767 permitted the Radicals to develop their Non-Importation Agreements, which bound merchants not to import British goods and citizens not to use them. Dickinson's letters had given support to the Boston group, and James Otis and Joseph Warren made bitter attacks on Governor Francis Bernard in the *Gazette.* Bernard played into their hands by persuading London to send two additional regiments of redcoats to Boston to ensure his control. The Boston press and public greeted these troops with indignation and hostility.

Adams and the Sons of Liberty decided to cash in with an intensive campaign of intercolonial propaganda communications that has been called "the most sustained effort to spread ideas through news items that was made in the entire twenty years (1763-83)."[6] This was the "Journal of Occurrences" of 1768-69, which began with the arrival of the new British troops and ended when Governor Bernard was replaced by Thomas Hutchinson.

The still unidentified authors of the "Journal of Occurrences," working under Adams's direction, compiled a record of alleged events involving the British troops and sent it to John Holt to publish in his *New York Journal.* Other papers from New England to Georgia picked up items. The writers chronicled misdeeds of the British troops in garrisoned Boston, ranging from insults and indignities to assault and attempted rape. Since the events were reported in the Boston papers approximately two months after Holt printed the "Journal of Occurrences" in New York, rather than concurrently, researchers have concluded that Tory complaints of falseness were probably justified. What the ''Journal of Occurrences'' did was foster the public feeling that an occupying military force treated people badly and that London was thus punishing Patriots in Boston.

John Holt was the major conduit for this activity of the Sons of Liberty and the most important Radical printer outside Boston. He worked with Franklin's associate James Parker before launching his *New York Journal* in late 1766 as a Whig paper. He became increasingly activist as events occurred that fed the Sons of Liberty movement: the ''Boston Massacre'' of 1770; the Tea Act of 1773, which precipitated the Boston Tea Party in December; the passage of the Intolerable Acts and closing of the port of Boston in 1774 in retaliation. Holt ran stories from the Boston papers, funneling the Radical arguments to Timothy in Charleston, Goddard in Baltimore, and others.

This helped keep intercolonial support for the hard line the Boston Radicals were proposing. When tempers flared in Massachusetts in September 1774, Joseph Warren wrote the Suffolk Resolves, which were carried by Paul Revere on horseback to Philadelphia. There the Continental Congress, barely organized, adopted them at the urging of Sam Adams. The action pledged support for the Massachusetts rebels who soon were to be facing British rifles. Not everyone who voted that day realized what Adams had accomplished.

ADAMS'S KEY ROLE

Sam Adams could sense victory in 1774. Behind him lay twenty years of propagandizing, organizing, and using every device to forward his aims. Day after day Adams had pressed his foes through newspaper and through pamphlet. He emphasized the need for a realignment of class power. Tory doctrine, which was made to sound so noble by newspaper editors such as Rivington, was only window dressing, said Adams. It could fool only the gullible. He appealed to the self interest of every type of American, shifting his style with his quill. At least 25 pen names have been recognized as in his hand. Late at night passersby looked up at the lighted window of the Adams home, and they knew the veteran revolutionary was still at work, writing a piece for the *Gazette,* perhaps, making it hot for the Tories. His neighbors could not help but be impressed. Many of his loyal followers may not have known just what all the furor was about, but they knew that Adams spoke for them, and they were certain that ''whatever the old man wanted'' must be all right.

Granted all this, is a public writer justified in smearing men's characters, even for a cause? The question is pertinent right on up to modern times. Adams believed that his technique was essential to victory. For years the laborer and clerk had shown inordinate deference to aristocratic ''superiors.'' This attitude was less marked in America than in England, but the attitude had to be completely changed if the masses were to make the big push for liberty and popular sovereignty. For if one class were to be treated with special deference, then the words and ideas of these ''superior'' persons would have weight all out of proportion to merit and numbers. Somehow, Adams had to whittle the aristocrat down to size. Until the common man was raised and the aristocrat was brought down to a common level, the majority of workers was clearly at a disadvantage. Adams knew how to find the soft spots in the Tory shell.

The ways of the idol wrecker may not be pretty. Governor Hutchinson was correct when he called Adams an assassin of reputations. The governor knew whereof he spoke, for the last British administrator was a favorite target for the caustic rebel journalist. In the end, Hutchinson, who traced his ancestry back to the illustrious and independent Anne (first outstanding woman in American public life), was forced to leave his native land for England. No wonder Hutchinson was so bitter. But Adams was playing a desperate game. His smear attacks were one way of helping to bring down the odds.

The "Master of the Puppets" did his work well. No one had more to do with the outcome than Adams. On the morning of April 19, 1775, the "shot heard 'round the world" was fired at the battle of Lexington and Concord. From then on, the country was in arms, fighting for the ultimate victory that Adams had helped to engineer.

NOTES

1. "Resolutions of the House of Representatives of Massachusetts, October 29, 1765," in Harry R. Warfel, Ralph H. Gabriel, and Stanley Williams, eds., *The American Mind* (New York: American Book, 1937), p. 138.
2. Curtis P. Nettels, "The Money Supply of the American Colonies Before 1720," *University of Wisconsin Studies* No. 20 (1934), pp. 279–83.
3. Charles A. and Mary R. Beard, *The Rise of American Civilization,* Vol. I (New York: Macmillan, 1930), p. 187.
4. See Arthur M. Schlesinger, *Prelude to Independence: The Newspaper War on Britain, 1764–1776* (New York: Knopf, 1958), for the story of the use of the press by the Radical propagandists.
5. William V. Wells, *The Life and Public Services of Samuel Adams,* Vol. I (Boston: Little, Brown, 1865), p. 48.
6. Philip Davidson, *Propaganda and the American Revolution 1763–1783* (Chapel Hill: University of North Carolina Press, 1941), quoted from the Norton Library edition (New York, 1973), p. 237.

ANNOTATED BIBLIOGRAPHY

Books

BAILYN, BERNARD, *The Ordeal of Thomas Hutchinson.* Cambridge, Mass.: Harvard University Press, 1974. Sam Adams's conservative victim.

———, *The Ideological Origins of the American Revolution.* Cambridge, Mass.: Harvard University Press, 1967. A structured study, utilizing the Harvard Library pamphlet collection, that exhibits feeling for the radical nature of the Revolution. See also his *Origins of American Politics* (1968).

BECKER, CARL L., *The Eve of the Revolution.* New Haven: Yale University Press, 1918. An excellent one-volume summary of this period by an eminent authority.

BEER, GEORGE L., *British Colonial Policy.* New York: Macmillan, 1907. Presents the British point of view in a way that may not be familiar to the reader.

BOWEN, CATHERINE D., *John Adams and the American Revolution.* New York: Little, Brown, 1950. Follows the school of historical writing that allows the author to describe the feelings of her subjects.

CALHOON, ROBERT M., *The Loyalists in Revolutionary America, 1760–1781.* New York: Harcourt Brace Jovanovich, 1973. Traces the Loyalists' enunciation of principles, search for accommodation, and final appeal to doctrine.

COMMAGER, HENRY STEELE, *The Empire of Reason.* New York: Anchor Press/Doubleday, 1977. The roots of the American Revolution are traced to the imagination and formulation of the Enlightenment of the Old World.

DAVIDSON, PHILIP, *Propaganda and the American Revolution.* Chapel Hill: University of North Carolina Press, 1941. Reveals the tremendous impact of pamphlets, broadsides, newspapers, and books in conditioning the public to rebellion.

GIPSON, LAWRENCE H., *The Coming of the Revolution, 1763–1775.* New York: Harper & Row, 1954. Stresses colonial resistance to more efficient English administration. Part of the New American Nation series.

GREENE, EVARTS B., *The Revolutionary Generation, 1763–1790*. A History of American Life, Vol. IV. New York: Macmillan, 1943. Source for social history.

MILLER, JOHN C., *Sam Adams: Pioneer in Propaganda*. Boston: Little, Brown, 1936. A "debunking" treatment of Adams; sometimes vague, but useful. See also Miller's *Origins of the American Revolution* (Boston: Little, Brown, 1943).

MINER, WARD L., *William Goddard, Newspaperman*. Durham, N.C.: Duke University Press, 1962. Detailed study; also covers his mother and sister.

MORGAN, EDMUND S., AND HELEN M. MORGAN, *The Stamp Act Crisis*. Chapel Hill: University of North Carolina Press, 1953. A scholarly study of the 1765 crisis as a "prologue to revolution."

ROSSITER, CLINTON, *The Political Thought of the American Revolution*. New York: Harcourt Brace Jovanovich, 1963. Written with consensus theory approach, emphasizing unity and continuity in U.S. experience.

SCHLESINGER, ARTHUR M., *Prelude to Independence: The Newspaper War on Britain, 1764–1776*. New York: Knopf, 1958. An excellent detailed study of the role of the newspaper in promoting revolution, and a history of the press for the period.

WALETT, FRANCIS G., *Patriots, Loyalists, and Printers*. Worcester, Mass.: American Antiquarian Society, 1976. Bicentennial booklet containing many reprints. See also his *Massachusetts Newspapers and the Revolutionary Crisis, 1763–1776* (Boston: Massachusetts Bicentennial Commission, 1974).

WOOD, GORDON S., *The Creation of the American Republic, 1776–1787*. Chapel Hill: University of North Carolina Press, 1969. An analysis of political and social thought and the institutions shaping it.

Periodicals and Monographs

CULLEN, MAURICE R., JR., "Benjamin Edes: Scourge of Tories," *Journalism Quarterly*, LI (Summer 1974), 213. Traces Edes's life and role in Sons of Liberty.

———, "The Boston Gazette: a Community Newspaper," *Journalism Quarterly*, XXXVI (Spring 1959), 204. Tells how the *Gazette* reflected Boston life in the 1760s and 1770s.

"The Father of the Revolution," *Harper's New Monthly Magazine*, LIII (July 1876), 185. A good summary of the influence of Adams.

HIXSON, RICHARD F., "Literature for Trying Times: Some Pamphlet Writers and the Revolution," *Journalism History*, III (Spring 1976), 7. A survey.

LAWSON, JOHN L., "The 'Remarkable Mystery' of James Rivington, 'Spy,'" *Journalism Quarterly*, XXXV (Summer 1958), 317. Disposes of myth that Rivington was a secret spy for George Washington.

SCHLESINGER, ARTHUR M., "The Colonial Newspaper and the Stamp Act," *New England Quarterly*, VIII (March 1935), 63. An outstanding Harvard historian describes the influence of the newspaper medium.

TEETER, DWIGHT L., "'King' Sears, the Mob and Freedom of the Press in New York, 1765–76," *Journalism Quarterly*, XLI (Autumn 1964), 539. The mob, disrespectful of freedom of ideas, drove James Rivington out of business.

YODELIS, MARY ANN, "Who Paid the Piper? Publishing Economics in Boston, 1763–1775," *Journalism Monographs*, 38 (February 1975). Based on Ph.D. thesis, University of Wisconsin, 1971. See also her "Courts, Counting House and Streets: Attempts at Press Control, 1763–1775," *Journalism History*, I (Spring 1974), 11, and "Advertising in the Boston Press," *Journalism History*, III (Summer 1976), 40. Depth studies by colonial journalism scholar.

Facsimile from *Pennsylvania Gazette,* 1754.

THE Massachusetts Spy

Or, Thomas's Boston Journal.

"Do thou Great LIBERTY inspire our Souls—And make our Lives in thy Possession happy—Or, our Deaths glorious in thy just Defence."

VOL. IV.)   THURSDAY, JULY 7, 1774.   (NUMB. 179.

JOIN   OR   DIE

WORCESTER, MAY 3.

AMERICANS! forever bear in mind the BATTLE of LEXINGTON!—where British Troops, unmolested and unprovoked, wantonly, and in a most inhuman manner fired upon and killed a number of our countrymen, then robbed them of their provisions, ransacked, plundered and burnt their houses! not could the tears of defenceless women, some of whom were in the pains of childbirth, the cries of helpless babes, nor the prayers of old age, confined to beds of sickness, appease their thirst for blood!—or divert them from their DESIGN of MURDER and ROBBERY!

The particulars of this alarming event will, we are credibly informed be soon published by authority, as a Committee of the Provincial Congress have been appointed to make special enquiry, and to take the depositions, on oath, of such as are knowing to the matter. In the mean time, to satisfy the expectation of our readers, we have collected from those whose veracity is unquestioned the following account, viz.

A few days before the battle, the Grenadier and Light-Infantry companies were all drafted from the several regiments in Boston, and put under the command of an officer, and it was observed that most of the transports and other boats were put together, and fitted for immediate service. This manoeuvre gave rise to a suspicion that some formidable expedition was intended by the soldiery, but what or where the inhabitants could not determine—however, the town watches in Boston, Charlestown, Cambridge, &c. were ordered to look well to the landing-places. About 10 o'clock on the night of the 18th of April, the troops in Boston were discovered to be on the move in a very secret manner, and it was found they were embarking in boats (which they privately brought to the place in the evening) at the bottom of the Common; expresses set off immediately to alarm the country, that they might be on their guard. When the expresses got about a mile beyond Lexington, they were stopped by about fourteen officers on horseback, who came out of Boston in the afternoon of that day, and were seen lurking in bye-places in the country till after dark. One of the expresses immediately fled, and was pursued two miles by an officer, who when he had got up with him presented a pistol, and told him he was a dead man if he did not stop, but he rode on until he came up to a house, when stopping of a sudden his horse threw him off; having the presence of mind to hollow to the people in the house, "Turn out! Turn out! I have got one of them!" the officer immediately retreated as fast as he had pursued; The other express after passing through a strict examination, by some means got clear. The body of the troops in the mean time, under the command of Lieut. Colonel Smith had crossed the river, and landed at Phipp's Farm: They immediately to the number of 1000 proceeded to Lexington, 6 miles below Concord, with great silence: A company of militia, of about 80 men, mustered near the meeting-house; the troops came in sight of them just before sun-rise; the militia upon seeing the troops began to disperse; the troops then set out upon the run, hallooing and huzzaing, and coming within a few rods of them, the commanding officer accosted the militia in words to this effect, "Disperse you damn'd rebels!—damn you disperse!" Upon which the troops again huzzaed, and immediately one or two officers discharged their pistols, which were instantaneously followed by the firing of four or five of the soldiers, and then there seemed to be a general discharge from the whole body; It is to be noticed they fired upon our people as they were dispersing, agreeable to their command, and that we did not even return the fire: Eight of our men were killed and nine wounded;—The troops then laughed, and damned the Yankees, and said they could not bear the smell of gun-powder. A little after this the troops renewed their march to Concord, where, when they arrived, they divided into parties, and went directly to several places where the province stores were deposited. Each party was supposed to have a tory pilot. One party went into the goal yard, and spiked up and otherways damaged two cannon belonging to the province, and broke and set fire to the carriages—They then entered a store and rolled out about an 100 barrels of flour, which they unheaded, and emptied about 40 into the river; at the same time others were entering houses and shops, and unheading barrels, chests, &c. the property of private persons; some took possession of the town-house, to which they set fire, but was extinguished by our people without much hurt. Another party of the troops went and took possession of the North-bridge. About 150 provincials who mustered upon the alarm, coming towards the bridge, the troops fired upon them without ceremony, and killed two upon the spot!——(Thus did the troops of Britain's king fire FIRST at two several times upon his loyal American subjects, and put a period to ten lives before one gun was fired upon them.)—Our people THEN returned the fire, and obliged the troops to retreat, who were soon joined by their other parties, but finding they were still pursued, the whole body retreated back to Lexington, both provincials and troops firing as they went. During this time an express from the troops was sent to General Gage, who thereupon sent out a reinforcement of above 1400 men, under the command of Earl Piercy, with two field pieces. Upon the arrival of this reinforcement at Lexington, just as the retreating party had got there, they made a stand, picked up their dead and took all the carriages they could find and put their wounded thereon; others of them to their eternal disgrace be it spoken, were robbing and setting houses on fire, and discharging their cannon at the meeting-house. Whilst this was transacting a few of our men at Menotomy, a few miles distant, attacked a party of twelve of the enemy, (carrying stores and provisions to the troops) killed one of them, and took possession of their arms, stores, provisions, &c. without any loss on our side, The enemy having halted above an hour at Lexington, found it necessary to make a second retreat, carrying with them many of their dead and wounded. They continued their retreat from Lexington to Charlestown with great precipitation; our people continued the pursuit, firing till they got to Charlestown Neck, (which they reached a little after sun-set) over which the enemy passed, proceeded up Bunker's Hill, and the next day went into Boston under the protection of the Somerset man of war of 64 guns.

A young man, unarmed, who was taken prisoner by the enemy, and made to assist in carrying off their wounded, says, that he saw a barber who lives in Boston, thought to be one Warden, with the troops, and that he heard them say, he was one of their pilots; he likewise saw the said barber fire twice upon our people, and heard Earl Piercy order the troops to fire the houses: He also informs, that several officers were among the wounded who were carried to Boston, were our informant was dismissed. They took two of our men prisoners in battle who are now confined in barracks.

Immediately upon the return of the troops to Boston, all communication to and from the town was stopped by Gen. Gage. The provincials who flew to the assistance of their distressed countrymen, are posted in Cambridge, Charlestown, Roxbury, Watertown, &c. and have placed guards on Roxbury neck within gun-shot of the enemy; guards are also placed every where in view of the town to observe the motion of the King's troops: The Council of War, and the different Committees of Safety and Supplies set at Cambridge, and the Provincial Congress at Watertown. The troops in Boston are fortifying the place on all sides, and a frigate of war is stationed up Cambridge river, and a sixty-four gun ship between Boston and Charlestown.

Deacon Joseph Loring's house and barn, Mrs. Mulliken's house and shop, and Mr. Joshua Bond's house and shop, in Lexington were all consumed. They also set fire to several other houses, but our people extinguished the flames. They pillaged almost every house they passed by, breaking and destroying doors, windows, glasses, &c. and carrying off cloathing and other valuable effects. It appeared to be their design to burn and destroy all before them; and nothing but our vigorous pursuit prevented their infernal purposes from being put in execution. But the savage barbarity exercised upon the bodies of our unfortunate brethren who fell, is almost incredible: Not content with shooting down the unarmed, aged and infirm, they disregarded the cries of the wounded, killing them without mercy, and mangling their bodies in the most shocking manner.

We have the pleasure to say, that notwithstanding the highest provocations given by the enemy, not one instance of cruelty, that we have heard of, was committed by our Militia; but, listening to the merciful dictates of the Christian religion, they "breathed higher sentiments of humanity."

Isaiah Thomas arouses hatred in his famed *Massachusetts Spy*.

6

The Press and Revolution

Should the liberty of the press be once destroyed, farewell the remainder of our invaluable rights and privileges! We may next expect padlocks on our lips, fetters on our legs, and only our hands at liberty to slave for our worse than EGYPTIAN TASKMASTERS, OR—FIGHT OUR WAY TO CONSTITUTIONAL FREEDOM.

—Isaiah Thomas

Printers, publishers, and editors were important influences in preparing the public for revolution and in maintaining the fighting spirit during the War of Independence. Edes and Gill, mentioned in the previous chapter as proprietors of the Radical *Boston Gazette,* were examples of the patriot-journalist. William Bradford III, grandson of the founder of a famous printing dynasty, wielded both the pen and the sword during the war. His *Pennsylvania Journal* was faithful to the Patriot ideology. But the greatest journalist of the period was Isaiah Thomas, one of the important pioneers of the American Fourth Estate.

ISAIAH THOMAS, PATRIOT EDITOR Thomas began his career when he was only six, as an apprentice printer. He had to help support his widowed mother and therefore missed the advantages of formal education. Later, he became a great scholar, owner of one of the finest private libraries in the country, first president of the learned Antiquarian Society, and historian of the colonial press.

Thomas once wrote that he owed his education to the type case over which he worked so long as a lad. He learned to spell from setting type. He broadened his knowledge from studying galley proof. Zechariah Fowle, Thomas's master, was an inconsiderate employer who turned over much of the actual operation of the shop to his apprentice without appropriate recognition of the young man's worth. The resentful Thomas ran away to Halifax. In 1766, at the age of 17, Thomas was aroused by the agitation over the Stamp Act. He was so outspoken in his views that his new master had to discharge him. After a time as an itinerant printer's-helper, Thomas returned to Boston in 1770. Fowle welcomed his runaway apprentice and offered to take him into partnership. Together they founded the *Massachusetts Spy,* a newspaper that lived until 1904.

THE *MASSACHUSETTS SPY,* 1770

Thomas soon bought out his shiftless partner. Under his proprietorship the *Spy* became one of the most successful newspapers in the colonies. It was nominally nonpartisan, but it followed the Whig philosophy for the most part in its early days. Thomas tried to be fair, however. A line under the name plate advertised that the *Spy* was "A Weekly Political and Commercial Paper—Open to All Parties, but *influenced* by None." Until hostilities began this was a successful formula, for at 21 the handsome publisher owned a paper exceeded only by Rivington's in circulation and bulk.

Thomas began to shift his Whig doctrine as it became apparent that conciliationists like Dickinson were ineffective. Eventually he had to make the choice all Whigs had to make—to remain loyal, or to side with the Radicals. Thomas chose the latter course. Soon he was the acknowledged spokesman for the Independence group in his area. When British troops arrived in Boston to enforce laws formerly flouted by the colonials, Thomas became a leader of the underground movement. It was they who flashed the signal light from the steeple of Old North Church warning the Minutemen couriers of the impending British raid on Lexington and Concord.[1]

Next day Thomas was an eyewitness of the first battle in the War of Independence. If he did not hear "the shot heard 'round the world," he at least understood its significance. His report of the encounter remains today as the most notable war reporting of that conflict. He would have been the first to deny that his "story" of the fight was objective. By that time he was committed to the use of his press as an instrument of war, and his report is therefore highly colored with propaganda favorable to his compatriots. Even so, his word picture of the event was probably accurate in its main theme, and there is so much color and vigor in his writing that the account deserves mention here. According to Thomas's report:

About ten o'clock on the night of the eighteenth of April, the troops in Boston were discovered to be on the move in a very secret manner, and it was found they were embarking in boats (which they privately brought to the place in the evening) at the bottom of the Common; expresses set off immediately to alarm the country, that they might be on their guard. When the expresses got about a mile beyond Lexington, they were stopped by about fourteen officers on horseback, who came out of Boston in the afternoon of that day, and were seen lurking in by-places in the country till after dark. One of the expresses immediately fled, [this was probably Dr. Samuel Prescott] and was pursued two miles by an officer, who, when he had got up with him presented a pistol, and told him he was a dead man if he did not stop, but he rode on till he came up to a house, when stopping of a sudden his horse threw him off, having the presence of mind to halloo [the rider, of course, not the horse] to the people in the house,

"Turn out. Turn out. I have got one of them."

The officer immediately retreated and fled as fast as he had pursued. The other express, [Paul Revere] after passing through a strict examination, by some means got clear.

The body of troops in the meantime, under the command of Lieutenant Colonel Smith, had crossed the river and landed at Phipp's Farm. They immediately, to the number of 1000, proceeded to Lexington, about six miles below Concord, with great silence. A company of militia, of about eighty men, mustered near the meeting house; the troops came in sight of them just before sunrise. The militia, upon seeing the troops, began to disperse. The troops then set out upon the run, hallooing and hussaing, and coming within a few rods of them, the commanding officer accosted the militia, in words to this effect,

"Disperse, you damn'd rebels—Damn you, disperse."

Upon which the troops again hussaed and immediately one or two officers discharged their pistols, which were instantaneously followed by the firing of four or five of the soldiers; and then there seemed to be a general discharge from the whole body. Eight of our men were killed and nine wounded. . . .[2]

The war was hard on Patriot editors and publishers. They had committed themselves to the cause so wholeheartedly that it was impossible to stay in business under British occupation. Both the *Gazette* and the *Spy* printing plants had to be smuggled out of Boston, if these two Patriot organs were to continue beating the drums for the American cause. The *Gazette* was moved at night across the Charles river to Watertown, where it was published until the British were forced out of Boston in 1776. Thomas had his press sent by trusted employees to Worcester on the eve of the Lexington battle, and he made that city his permanent home thereafter.

Once firmly established in Worcester, Thomas again began to thrive as a journalist and publisher. By the time his fellow Patriots emerged from war triumphant, he was the leading publisher of his day. Seven presses and 150 employees kept his shop in Worcester humming. Under his imprint appeared more than 400 books on law, medicine, agriculture, and science. He was the first American to publish Blackstone's *Commentaries,* a Greek grammar, printed music, and a novel by a native author—William Hill Brown's *Power of Sympathy.* The first American dictionary, by William Perry, was brought out by Thomas and sold 50,000 copies. Later Thomas also published Perry's speller, sales of various editions totaling 300,000 copies. Among his hundred children's books were the first American versions of *Mother Goose* and *Little Goody Two-Shoes.* Thomas had something for everyone. When he retired from business in 1802, he wrote his two-volume *History of Printing in America* (1810), a classic, and founded the American Antiquarian Society, whose Worcester building today houses the leading collection of colonial printing.

TOM PAINE,
THE RADICAL WRITER

Thomas did much to *prepare* the public for the conflict. Another effective journalist of the war was a penniless and somewhat disreputable stranger to these shores.[3] He was Tom Paine, the Thetford Quaker, who arrived on the eve of the war. He was then 37 years old, and his life up to that point had been anything but inspiring. His mother, whom the boy disliked, belonged to the Established Church. Apparently there was philosophical friction between parents and son from the beginning. After an unsuccessful attempt to work in the corset-making business, young Tom Paine was appointed an exciseman. He was soon accused of incompetency and neglect of duty. Reinstated, he was discharged again for what we would now call "unionization." He had been chosen by the excisemen of his district to represent them in their agitation for higher pay, and it was partly because of his failure as an agitator that he left his homeland.

By a fortunate coincidence, he met Benjamin Franklin, then at the height of his career as our spokesman in Europe. Franklin, a shrewd judge of men, saw enough in Paine to write a letter of recommendation. Paine was advised to go to America, where Franklin's son-in-law, Richard Bache, would offer helpful advice. Paine arrived in Philadelphia sick in mind and body. He later said that the very air of America was his tonic. With every breath of freedom he grew stronger. He spoke wonderingly of being able to sit in the same coffeehouses with the "gentry." Paine's first contributions were to Robert Aitken's *Pennsylvania Magazine,* one of several such periodical ventures that flowered and withered during this period. Aitken's magazine was one of the better ones. It did not survive, but Paine wrote for it long enough to establish a reputation as a stimulating commentator. Already he was arguing against the institution of Negro slavery and British arrogance and in favor of universal suffrage and education.

PAINE'S PAMPHLET,
COMMON SENSE

His fame as a writer was achieved by means of a pamphlet copied by many of the colonial newspapers of 1776. This was *Common Sense,* which helped to bring the lukewarm Patriots into the revolutionary movement. *Common Sense* appeared in January 1776, just a little more than a year after the arrival of the uncouth English immigrant. Its popularity was instantaneous and amazing. More than 120,000 copies were sold in the first three months. "I challenge the warmest advocate for reconciliation to show a single advantage that this continent can reap by being connected with Great Britain," he wrote. This challenge was hurled at the Dickinsonian Whigs, who shuddered at the word "independence," and they replied in the local newspapers with condemnation of this upstart. In a matter of weeks, however, Paine's views in *Common Sense* were known to virtually every literate American, and it is significant that only six months later, the Declaration of Independence committed the former colonies to this doctrine. Although *Common Sense* was a "best seller," Paine would accept no remuneration for his writing. His work was strictly for the cause.

After the fighting broke out Paine offered to serve in what amounted to a foreign legion. When the unit was cut to pieces by the British at Amboy, Paine made his way to Washington's headquarters at Fort Lee, where the defeated Americans were licking their wounds preparatory to withdrawal to the Delaware River line. His curious status as a foreigner, which was neither that of an officer nor of an enlisted man, gave him access to both groups. He talked with all types of Americans as he marched along the wintry roads. Actually, the season was unusually mild, but for the ill-clad troops the nightly bivouac brought only misery. The tattered companies were breaking up fast. In 1776 the ideology of the conflict was still vague. Many of the soldiers had only a hazy notion of what the shooting was all about.

PAINE'S *CRISIS* PAPERS

At this crucial moment, Paine wrote his first *Crisis* paper. Whether or not he wrote it at Washington's direction, by candlelight on a drum head, is inconsequential. There is no doubt, however, that it was written from the heart and under pressure. There was nothing new in what he said, but like a poet, he expressed what others could only feel. His work was rough, but that made it all the more appealing to the common man for whom it was written. The foot-slogging militiamen understood that one of their own was speaking.

The *American* CRISIS,
N U M B E R   I.
By the Author of COMMON SENSE.
Will be published in a Hand-Bill this evening.

Advertisement for first *Crisis* paper in *Pennsylvania Packet.*

And who can overestimate the power of words in arousing the will to fight? Down through history hopeless wars and battles have been won when words have doubled the force of arms. So it was with Paine's *Crisis*. His style had a kind of Biblical resonance and rhythm. Like Winston Churchill's "We shall fight them on the beaches" speech of World War II, the words rallied weary men by that most potent of spiritual tonics—dedication to a cause. They are words that have lived through the generations. In the bleak days of World War II, when there were no victories to report, the conquered peoples, despairing of freedom, listened with kindling hope as these words, written December 19, 1776, came through the ether to their secret radio receivers:

These are the times that try men's souls. The summer soldier and the sunshine patriot will, in this crisis, shrink from the service of his country; but he that stands it NOW, deserves the love and thanks of man and woman. Tyranny, like hell, is not easily conquered; yet we have this consolation with us, that the harder the conflict the more glorious the triumph. What we obtain too cheap, we esteem too lightly—Tis dearness only that gives every thing its value. Heaven knows how to put a proper price upon its goods; and it would be strange indeed if so celestial an article as FREEDOM should not be highly rated.

The first *Crisis* paper exceeded *Common Sense* in popularity. Printed first in John Dunlap's *Pennsylvania Packet* on December 27, the clarion call was echoed from Patriot newspapers throughout the colonies. Washington had the *Crisis* papers read to his numb troops as the words emerged fresh from Paine's pen. It is significant that the week after Paine made his first plea to the dejected, they turned on the foe and won a needed victory at Trenton.

Other *Crisis* papers appeared as the need demanded. More than any other writer of the war, Paine caught the significance of the American Revolution. While others presented political and economic arguments, Paine advocated social revolt as well. But his adopted country rejected him for his radicalism. The author of the *Rights of Man* and *Age of Reason,* a participant in both the American and French revolutions, died ignored in 1809, listing as his most important contribution to democracy his pamphlet *Common Sense*.

THE REVOLUTIONARY PRESS

Only 20 of the 35 newspapers being published at the beginning of the war survived. Considering the vicissitudes of the times, that was not a bad record. Many would have disappeared had there been no war. And 35 new papers were established during the six years of fighting. Enough of these survived to bring the total number of papers at the end of the war up to the prewar figure. All were weeklies, and most of them were Patriot in sentiment.

Revolutionary newspapers went into about 40,000 homes, but each issue had a larger number of readers per copy than would be true in modern times. Every word was read, even to the small "liners" and advertisements. Many an American first learned of the Declaration of Independence through his newspaper. It first appeared publicly in the *Pennsylvania Evening Post* of July 6, 1776, but others soon published the document.

Such enterprise is impressive. On the other hand, any student of the times becomes aware very soon of the primitive communications facilities of the period. It took six weeks for the account of Lexington and Concord to reach Savannah. Often the reporting of war events was of the most haphazard type. "The Hartford Post tells us," Hugh Gaine, the turncoat Patriot editor wrote in the February 2, 1778, issue of his *New*

York Gazette and Mercury, ''That he saw a Gentleman in Springfield, who informed him that he (the Gentleman) saw a letter from an Officer in Gen. Howe's Army to another in Gen. Burgoyne's, giving him to understand, war was declared on the sides of France and Spain against the MIGHTY Kingdom of Britain.'' The news had actually come from a Boston paper already a month old, and the story was not true, in any case.[4] Some of the news was high in reporting quality, however. Often it was printed verbatim, which added to its charm and authenticity. That was how the details of the battle of Yorktown reached the office of the *Freeman's Journal* in Philadelphia:

BE IT REMEMBERED

That on the 17th day of October, 1781, Lieut. Gen. Charles Earl Cornwallis, with about 5,000 British troops, surrendered themselves prisoners of war to His Excellency, Gen. George Washington, Commander-in-Chief of the allied forces of France and America. LAUS DEO.[5]

That was all the paper had to tell of the greatest, and final, victory of the war. The account should have been authentic, because the reporter was none other than General Washington. The editor had printed verbatim the dispatch sent out by the general.

A serious problem was the shortage of printing supplies. Paper, ink, and type had come from Europe before the war, for the most part. Not until 1769 was an American press sold commercially. American paper mills could not begin to supply the demand for stock. Paper at that time was made of linen, and cloth of any kind was scarce, especially in wartime. That was why Washington did not put it beneath his dignity to issue a plea, asking Patriot women to save all available material that might be converted into printing paper, showing how important the Commander-in-Chief considered the press to be. In this connection, it is interesting to note that he contributed his prestige to encourage the founding by the Quaker printer Isaac Collins of the *New Jersey Gazette,* which for a time served as a kind of army newspaper.

An example of journalistic prosperity in wartime was the *Connecticut Courant.* By 1781 it had the then amazing circulation of 8,000 subscribers each issue. It was full of advertising. Few London papers could boast of such success. The *Courant* printed on paper from its own mill. It was one of the best-printed papers in America. On the other hand, Patriot John Holt had to leave his *New York Journal's* printing equipment behind in New York in 1776 when the British came, settled down in Kingston only to be routed again by British troops, finally reestablished the *Journal* in Poughkeepsie, and returned to New York in 1783—only to die the following year a worn-out man.

COLONIAL WOMEN PRINTERS

Recent research has shown that women played significant roles in the story of colonial journalism. Most of the 14 known colonial women newspaper printers took up and carried on the trade after the death of their printer husbands, a common colonial practice. Two notable exceptions were Sarah and Mary Katherine Goddard, the mother and eldest sister of printer William Goddard.[6]

The Goddards lived in Providence, Rhode Island, when the widowed Sarah apprenticed William to James Parker in 1755. He came back in 1762 and with his mother and Mary Katherine founded a print shop and the *Providence Gazette.* William soon disappeared to follow up connections his work for Parker had given him in New York and Philadelphia and founded the *Pennsylvania Chronicle* in 1767. Sarah and

Mary Katherine Goddard

Mary Katherine put the nearly defunct *Gazette* back in order and also offered Providence a print shop, bookstore, and post office. Their paper was first staunchly Whig, then increasingly Patriot.

Their success in Providence was interrupted when William called on them for help with his *Pennsylvania Chronicle,* in the wake of difficulties caused by his erratic and quarrelsome conduct. Both went to work in the Philadelphia shop in late 1768; Sarah died two years later. Mary Katherine managed the print shop and made it one of the largest in the colonies by 1774. Again, William's wanderlust brought a change. He had founded the *Maryland Journal* in Baltimore in 1773 and needed his sister to manage it while he worked to establish a colonial postal system independent of British control. So Mary Katherine directed the *Maryland Journal* and its print shop for the next ten years. Returning it to William after a quarrel, she ran her bookstore until 1802. She was called "a woman of extraordinary judgment, energy, nerve, and strong, good sense." Isaiah Thomas, the colonial press historian, found she met his exacting standards as an "expert and correct compositor."

So did Elizabeth Timothy of South Carolina and two daughters of James Franklin. Mrs. Timothy was the first colonial woman newspaper publisher, for the *South Carolina Gazette* (1738–46), and mother of Sons of Liberty hero Peter Timothy. Anne Franklin and her daughters took over husband James's printshop in Rhode Island in 1735, and Mrs. Franklin her son's *Newport Mercury* (1762–63). Margaret Draper, last printer of the *Boston News-Letter* (1774–76), did battle against the Radicals and left with the British. From Dinah Nuthead, first woman printer (Maryland, 1696), to the present, women did and continue to do their jobs.*

*The other colonial women printers: Anna Catherine Zenger, *New York Journal,* 1746–48; Cornelia Bradford, *American Weekly Mercury,* Philadelphia, 1742–52; Anne Green, *Maryland Gazette,* 1767–75; Clementina Rind, *Virginia Gazette,* 1773–74; Mary Crouch, *Charleston Gazette,* 1778–80, and *Salem Gazette,* 1781; Hannah Watson, *Connecticut Courant,* 1778–79; Elizabeth Boden, *South Carolina Weekly Advertiser,* 1783; Ann Timothy, *Gazette of South Carolina,* 1783–92; and Elizabeth Holt, *New York Journal,* 1784–85. (Widows of John Peter Zenger, Andrew Bradford, Peter Timothy, John Holt.)

NOTES

1. Rider Paul Revere was an influential member of the Patriot group and made engravings for their publications. A major mission of the riders was to warn Samuel Adams and John Hancock that General Gage had ordered their arrests.
2. *Massachusetts Spy,* May 3, 1775. This appeared on the inside (page 3) of the paper under a Worcester dateline. After moving to Worcester, Thomas described his paper in a page-one skyline as "THE MASSACHUSETTS SPY, or American ORACLE of Liberty."
3. Paine is usually identified as a writer or political philosopher. In this book the journalist is defined as one

who acts as the transmission belt carrying ideas, information, and inspiration to the general public, dependent upon such resources for rational opinion. This was Paine's prime function during the American Revolution. His work for Aitken on the *Pennsylvania Magazine,* often ignored in sketches about him, also qualifies him for consideration as a journalist, in the broad sense.

4. Frank Luther Mott, *American Journalism,* rev. ed. (New York: Macmillan, 1962), p. 100.

5. From *America Goes to Press,* by Laurence Greene, copyright 1936, used by special permission of the publishers, Bobbs-Merrill.

6. Marion Marzolf, "The Woman Journalist: Colonial Printer to City Desk," *Journalism History,* I (Winter 1974), 100. See bibliographies for chapter 2 and this chapter.

ANNOTATED BIBLIOGRAPHY

Books

ALDRIDGE, ALFRED O., *Man of Reason: The Life of Thomas Paine.* Philadelphia: Lippincott, 1959. The best study of Paine since Moncure D. Conway's two-volume *Life of Thomas Paine* (London: Putnam's, 1892). See also Mary A. Best, *Thomas Paine* (New York: Harcourt Brace Jovanovich, 1927).

CHANNING, EDWARD, *History of the United States,* Vol. III. New York: Macmillan, 1927. The high literary quality and thoughtful comments make this volume of Channing particularly useful as background reading of the period.

COMMAGER, HENRY STEELE, ed., *Documents of American History.* New York: Appleton-Century-Crofts, 1934; Hawthorn Books, 1969. Contains writings of Dickinson, the Adamses, Madison, Jefferson, etc. Very useful in checking the original sources.

EAST, ROBERT, *Business Enterprise in the American Revolutionary Era.* New York: Columbia University Press, 1938. A scholarly review of the capitalistic development during this period.

FONER, ERIC, *Tom Paine and Revolutionary America.* New York: Oxford University Press, 1976. Places Paine in American setting, as a radical contributing to a new society.

GREENE, LAURENCE, *America Goes to Press.* Indianapolis: Bobbs-Merrill, 1936. Goes to source materials to describe how the news of important events reached the people through the press.

HIXSON, RICHARD F., *Isaac Collins: A Quaker Printer in 18th Century America.* New Brunswick, N.J.: Rutgers University Press, 1968. The scholarly biography of a Patriot printer-editor.

JENSEN, MERRILL, *Founding of the New Nation: A History of the American Revolution.* New York: Oxford University Press, 1968. A major study.

JONES, MICHAEL WYNN, *Cartoon History of the American Revolution.* New York: G. P. Putnam's Sons, 1975. Both an illustrated history of the period and a collection of drawings.

LORENZ, ALFRED L., *Hugh Gaine: A Colonial Printer-Editor's Odyssey to Loyalism.* Carbondale: Southern Illinois University Press, 1972. Business conservatism led to his moderate politics. His "turncoat" *New York Gazette and Mercury* did not survive.

MARBLE, ANNIE R., *From 'Prentice to Patron—The Life Story of Isaiah Thomas.* New York: Appleton-Century-Crofts, 1935. The standard biography.

MONTROSS, LYNN, *Rag, Tag and Bobtail.* New York: Harper & Row, 1952. Demonstrates that the people's army and government operated remarkably effectively.

PAINE, THOMAS, *The Life and Major Writings of Thomas Paine,* ed. Philip S. Foner. New York: Citadel Press, 1961. Annotated texts of Paine's major works.

SMITH, PAGE, *A New Age Now Begins: A People's History of the American Revolution.* New York: McGraw-Hill, 1976. A two-volume narrative of the revolutionary era. Newspapers were used extensively to provide precise details for its 1,900 pages.

SNYDER, LOUIS L., AND RICHARD B. MORRIS, eds., *A Treasury of Great Reporting.* New York: Simon & Schuster, 1962. This book contains excerpts from outstanding journalistic writings between colonial times and post-World War II.

TREVELYAN, SIR GEORGE OTTO, *The American Revolution,* Part III. New York: Longmans, Green & Company, 1907. The epoch viewed from the standpoint of a great British historian.

VAN TYNE, CLAUDE H., *The War of Independence: American Phase.* Boston: Houghton Mifflin, 1929. Volume two of a study by a leading authority.

Periodicals and Monographs

GARCIA, HAZEL, "Of Punctilios Among the Fair Sex: Colonial American Magazines, 1741–1776," *Journalism History,* III (Summer 1976), 48. Bulk of material printed about or for women came from men.

HENRY, SUSAN, "Colonial Woman Printer as Prototype: Toward a Model for the Study of Minorities," *Journalism History,* III (Summer 1976), 20. Argues for use of social, biographical, economic, and local history sources.

HOOPER, LEONARD J., "Women Printers in Colonial Times," *Journalism Educator,* XXIX (April 1974), 24. A factual survey. See also Susan Henry, "Margaret Draper: Colonial Printer Who Challenged the Patriots," *Journalism History,* I (Winter 1974), 141; and Norma Schneider, "Clementina Rind: 'Editor, Mother, Wife'," *Journalism History,* I (Winter 1974), 137, for sketches of Massachusetts and Virginia women printers.

JENSEN, MERRILL, "The American People and the American Revolution," *Journal of American History,* LVI (June 1970), 5. Excellent example of newspaper, pamphlet, broadside use.

MOTT, FRANK LUTHER, "The Newspaper Coverage of Lexington and Concord," *New England Quarterly,* XVII (December 1944), 489. A day-by-day analysis of how the news was spread. Reprinted in Ford and Emery, *Highlights in the History of the American Press.*

PARKER, PETER J., "The Philadelphia Printer: A Study of an 18th Century Businessman," *Business History Review,* XL (Spring 1966), 24. The colonial artisan becomes a fledgling capitalist.

STEIRER, WILLIAM F., JR., "A Study in Prudence: Philadelphia's 'Revolutionary' Journalists," *Journalism History,* III (Spring 1976), 16. They shied away from social and political issues. Uses stand on slavery as basis for judgment.

TEETER, DWIGHT L., "A Legacy of Expression: Philadelphia Newspapers and Congress During the War for Independence, 1775–1783," Ph.D. thesis, University of Wisconsin, 1966. A perceptive and scholarly study; the existence of contending factions enabled press to freely criticize. See also his "Press Freedom and the Public Printing: Pennsylvania, 1775–1783." *Journalism Quarterly,* XLV (Autumn 1968), 445.

"Tom Paine's First Appearance in America," *Atlantic Monthly,* IV (November 1859), 565. Describes Paine's propaganda activities and journalistic contributions. Reprinted in Ford and Emery, *Highlights in the History of the American Press.*

YODELIS, MARY ANN, "The Press in Wartime: Portable and Penurious." *Journalism History,* III (Spring 1976), 2. Apparently subscriptions and advertising paid for newspaper printing costs, with profits coming from other printing. General and religious customers were major sources of that income, rather than government and political.

Philip Freneau

Benjamin Russell

William Cobbett

Philip Freneau, as an Anti-Federalist editor, helped stimulate the "Second Revolution" that put Thomas Jefferson into the White House. Benjamin Russell, editor of the *Columbian Centinel,* was a pillar of the Federalist party and a noted journalist of his time. William Cobbett, better known as "Peter Porcupine," came from Britain to become a rabid Federalist editor who perhaps has never been exceeded in the art of invective. *(Magazine of American History)*

7

The Press
and the Second Revolution

Men who distrust the people and the future may overwhelm us with their learning, but they do not impress us with their wisdom—thank God.

—Gerald Johnson

During the war the Tory had disappeared as a political factor in America, but two other groups now struggled for control of the government. One of the elements was conservative in tone. It consisted, for the most part, of citizens engaged in commerce, banking, manufacturing, and property management. Generally, this group was more interested in preserving and extending its economic advantages than in risking social experiments. The other element was largely made up of the agrarian, small-farmer class, increasingly strengthened by the city wage-earner, or "mechanic " as he was called then, but with a significant leavening of intellectuals and political philosophers interested in social reform.

At the end of the American Revolution, the people of the United States had a choice to make. They might continue to experiment with social change, endorsing the ideas that had been their battle cries. Or they might consolidate strength by making right of property the fundamental consideration. Or they might work out some arrangement completely satisfactory to neither but warranting mutual support. The record of the Confederation gave the conservatives hope that public opinion might be swung to their side. The opportunity was the proposal to draft a new national charter.

State legislatures sent the delegates to the Constitutional Convention at Philadelphia, and state assemblies were dominated by the property group. This was because the big commercial centers were strongholds of the conservatives, where land ownership and voting qualifications disfranchised many "mechanics," or laborers. It was therefore the men of means and community standing who brought about the fundamental change in government under the Constitution. They succeeded in placing financial power in the hands of a strong, central government and otherwise protecting the position of property against attacks within individual states. But they could not have their way entirely. They could not have obtained acceptance of the new charter by the people unless the authors had made concessions. The document they produced is a marvel of balanced forces.

THE BILL OF RIGHTS AND PRESS FREEDOM One of the concessions offered by the conservatives was the Bill of Rights. Offered as the first ten amendments, these articles have since been considered part of the Constitution in the sense that they were the price paid by the authors for the liberal consent that made the document practicable. The first article of the Bill of Rights is of special interest to journalists. It provides that ''Congress shall make no law . . . abridging the freedom of speech or of the press.'' This is the cornerstone of our press liberty, but there is evidence that the authors of the Constitution spent little time discussing this issue. Madison's careful minutes of the convention show only casual and infrequent mention of the press.

But there was long precedent for the protection that finally was provided the press. British Common Law, as used in the various states, provided great freedom of expression for the times, even though it still recognized seditious libel laws. The same basic principles were stated in the Declaration of Rights written by John Dickinson when the First Continental Congress convened in 1774. Nine of the 13 states had already provided such constitutional protection by 1787. The Virginia Bill of Rights, of 1776, stated: ''That freedom of the press is one of the great bulwarks of liberty, and can never be restrained but by despotick governments. . . .'' Article XVI of the Massachusetts Bill of Rights, of 1780, expressed similar sentiments, and other states used variations of this theme to establish the principle.[1]

This probably explains why the authors of the new national charter ignored the press issue. They assumed that full protection was already granted under the states. Charles Pinckney of South Carolina did present a draft of a constitution with a clause similar to the one eventually adopted, but apparently little attention was paid to his suggestion at that time.

It soon was clear, however, that the Constitution could not possibly succeed without concessions to public sentiment. Delegates from Massachusetts reported it would be impossible to win ratification of the Constitution in that state without a clause concerning freedom of expression. Virginia could not muster enough votes for ratification until Governor Edmund Randolph called upon the framers to add the Bill of Rights. A constitutional committee was appointed to draft such a bill. The resolution was a modification of the Virginia document. Delegates were then told to return to their respective states and to use all influence available in mustering support for ratification of the main document on the promise that the Rights clauses would be included in the charter. It was on this understanding that New York finally approved the Constitution, but even so, it was not an easy victory for the Federalists.

Because of promises given, the Bill of Rights was an important issue in the first session of Congress. Madison headed the committee charged with drafting the amendments. When his first draft was read out of committee, it stated: ''. . . no state shall violate the equal rights of conscience or of freedom of speech. . . .'' The select committee to which the report was referred added ''. . . or of the press.'' Modified by House and Senate, the clause became the first amendment, as ratified in 1791.

It should be noted that freedom of the press is part of our fundamental law, regardless of how it came to be included. In Great Britain, Parliament provides the protection granted by our Constitution, and presumably, Parliament could also take away that right. In the United States, such freedom could not be restricted legally without submitting the question to Constitutional amendment. Neither the president nor Congress could abridge freedom of the press without running into resistance from the courts. In Great Britain, the courts have no such check. Furthermore, the specific mention of press freedom in our Constitution *in addition* to our recognition of the common law on the subject, which the British have depended upon as a safeguard, showed that liberty of the press was more advanced on this side of the Atlantic in 1791 than it was in the freest state in Europe.

THE FEDERALIST SERIES   Curiously, the press, which had to be protected as a concession to the public sentiment, was the most effective weapon of the conservatives in winning support for the charter they grudgingly admitted was the best document they could obtain in favor of their interests. The best exposition of the conservative doctrine was a series of articles that first appeared in the semiweekly *New York Independent Journal* from October 1787 to April 1788. Reprinted throughout the country and later published in pamphlet and (with six new essays) book form, these articles are known collectively as *The Federalist*.

They were written for mass consumption, and they were so effective that they gave their name to the party that was actually nationalist in doctrine, rather than federalist. The Federalists, as they came to be known during the publication of the 85 offerings, won their fight with this journalistic effort. Written hastily, much as daily editorials were written later on, these are still read, not only as revealing political studies but also as good literature. Alexander Hamilton wrote the largest number of *Federalist* articles over the pen name "Publius." James Madison is believed to have written 29, some of which are the best in the series. John Jay, a noted New York state political leader, probably wrote a half-dozen. In clear, concise style, *The Federalist* explained the philosophy of the Constitutional party. The gist of this doctrine is described in the tenth, supposedly written by Madison. Madison stood somewhere between the two opposing leaders. He disapproved of Hamilton's financial and autocratic ideas, but he veered from his mentor, Jefferson, in sponsoring a stronger national government. Madison had attended all the meetings of the constitutional committee and had engineered many of the modifications in the document. Said he, in describing the form of government prescribed by the framers of the national charter: ". . . justice must prevail [even] over a majority " to prevent the whims of an unstable public from wrecking the ship of state. This control would be accomplished through a republican form of government, offering protection to the masses, without direct control by them, as under the true "democratic" system.

ALEXANDER HAMILTON,   *The Federalist* firmly established Alexander Hamilton as
LEADER   leader of the party that took the title of the series as its label.
OF THE FEDERALISTS   He saw himself as the St. George of the anarchist dragon, fostered, he felt, by the radicalism and disorganization of the liberals. "We should be rescued from democracy," Hamilton insisted, and he looked forward to a restoration of an aristocracy, according to at least one of his biographers.[2] It has been suggested that Hamilton's respect for the aristocracy, and his continual seeking of recognition by those who valued heredity most highly, may have depended on the uncertainty of his paternity. Why was he a Patriot in the Revolution, instead of a Tory then? Born and reared to young manhood in the British West Indies, Hamilton became an American not so much out of hatred of the British social and political structure as out of contempt for British corruption and mismanagement.

That is why he fought for home rule, and there can be no doubt that he had strong feelings on the subject before the cause of revolution was generally endorsed. His war record was excellent. General Washington, who recognized Hamilton's virtues and who understood the youngster's faults (he was 18 at the time of Lexington and Concord), had a hard time keeping the fiery Patriot out of battle and behind the ledgers, where he was much more useful.

This was the man who led the Federalists. One cannot speak of him without indicating bias, one way or the other. In his day he was one of the most respected and reviled men in government. He had little knowledge of social forces. Never having lived the life of toil, he tended to dismiss the problems of the working people. He was quick to see that a government of fine phrases and glittering shibboleths was certain to be ineffective. He believed that the way to make government work was to let those with special interests in it control it, since they had most to lose by inept rule. Let those qualified take command, insisted Hamilton, who always imagined himself as the ideal soldier, ruling by command rather than by consultation.

Hamilton believed it his duty to establish the credit of the country by drastic financial measures, regardless of the luckless victims of an inadequate monetary system. He had no compassion for popular leaders such as Daniel Shays, the Massachusetts war veteran who led a hopeless revolt in 1786 against a taxation and hard money policy that threatened the very livelihood, to say nothing of the freedoms, of the small farmer. Hamilton saw the danger in such uprisings of the common man, and that was one reason he wished to rush through the Constitution, which he correctly predicted would solve many problems. But he would have taken care of the Shayses by force, rather than by placating the aggrieved. He admired military efficiency. Yet his life was to prove his genius not as a soldier but as a writer and political thinker. As Bowers says:

He was a natural journalist and pamphleteer—one of the fathers of the American editorial. His perspicacity, penetration, powers of condensation, and clarity of expression were those of a premier editorial writer. These same qualities made him a pamphleteer without peer. That he would have shone with equal luster in the reportorial room of a modern paper is shown in his description of the hurricane and in his letter to Laurens picturing vividly the closing hours of Major Andre. From the moment he created a sensation with "A Farmer Refuted" in his eighteenth year, until in the closing months of his life he was meeting Coleman surreptitiously in the night to dictate vigorous editorials for the New York *Evening Post* he had established, he recognized his power. No man ever complained more bitterly of the attacks of the press; none ever used the press more liberally and relentlessly to attack ... Nowhere in the literature of invective is there anything more vitriolic than the attack on a war speculator and profiteer, under the signature of "Publius." ... But usually he appealed to reason, and then he was at his best.... It will be impossible to comprehend the genius of Hamilton, his domination of his party, and his power, despite his unpopularity with the masses, without a foreknowledge of his force with the pen. It was his scepter and his sword.[3]

That was how the biographer, Bowers, answered those who underestimated Hamilton's journalistic role. This was the man who led the forces working for the ratification of the Constitution. Curiously, Hamilton did not like the document. It was a ''shilly-shally thing of milk and water which could not last and was good only as a step to something better,'' he once said.[4] Although the Constitution was supposedly the product of the conservatives, it was all too liberal for an admirer of aristocracy, such as Hamilton. He sponsored it, however, by facing what he believed to be the facts. The document offered a means of drawing together the types of persons Hamilton believed should control government. And although he disapproved of its populist concessions, he was shrewd enough to see that such compromise was essential, if any protection of property were to be imposed. When, on a summer day, he drifted slowly down the Hudson River on the New York packet and thereupon decided to subordinate his personal preferences in writing the first of *The Federalist* papers, he reached the height of his greatness. Had he accomplished nothing else in his lifetime, his services as a journalist that day would have justified his niche in the memory of his countrymen.

THE FEDERALIST EDITORS: FENNO, WEBSTER, COBBETT, RUSSELL

The outstanding Federalist newspaper in the lush days of the party was the *Gazette of the United States.* Sponsored and supported by Hamilton, it was edited by John Fenno, who issued the first edition at the national capital, then in New York, April 15, 1789. Fenno had been a school teacher, and it is noteworthy that we are already beginning to see the development of the specialized journalist. Most of the previous editors and publishers had come up through the print shop. Fenno established his reputation as a journalist without benefit of mechanical apprenticeship. Soon his paper was the acknowledged mouthpiece of the Federalist party and it moved with the government when Philadelphia became the national capital in 1791.

Another powerful Federalist voice was that of Noah Webster, remembered for his dictionary but a man of many parts. Lawyer, pioneer weatherman, translator, historian, economist, and scientific farmer, Webster was recognized in his day as a great editor. He started out as a lawyer and teacher. He was fascinated by words. His avocation resulted in a three-part *Grammatical Institute of the English Language.* The first part, the speller, appeared in 1784 and enjoyed a phenomenal sale—eventually 60 million copies were sold (not all within the author's lifetime, of course). Webster came back to New York in 1793 to edit the daily *Minerva* and the semiweekly *Herald* (after 1797 the *Commercial Advertiser* and *Spectator,* respectively), as a supporter of Hamilton.

Webster was an articulate and intelligent interpreter of the Federalist program. He defended President Washington against the smear tactics of such editors as Freneau and Bache and stood firm for the party against opposition attacks. Webster was no mere party hack, however. He resented what he called the "betrayal" of President Adams by Hamilton, the circumstances of which will be described later. At any rate, the *Minerva* was an important organ in the Federalist attempt to regain control. Eventually Webster tired of politics, however, and returned to his old love—linguistics. He is remembered now for his dictionary, which appeared in preliminary form in 1803 and as a great contribution to lexicography in 1828.

Another great Federalist editor was William Cobbett, who never was an American at all but who offered severe criticism of the (Jeffersonian) Republicans and defended the Federalists between 1794 and 1800. Cobbett was a refugee in this country after exposing graft and corruption in the British army. He first showed his writing abilities in an attack on Joseph Priestley, whose scientific views were curiously related to his political views, which were leftist. Encouraged by the success of his writing and sponsored by friends of the Federalist party, Cobbett gave up his modest tutoring position in 1797 to edit *Porcupine's Gazette and Daily Advertiser* in Philadelphia. He timed its appearance with the inauguration of John Adams.

In the short span of three years, Cobbett made a name for himself throughout the new country. He made no pretense of objectivity. His purpose was to expose his enemies, and his weapon was his vitriolic pen. Few editors in history have surpassed the British exile in sustained vituperation. His general theme was alliance with Britain, war against France, and perdition for Republicans. Tom Paine was his special target, and his biography of the Revolution's penman was all the more readable because Cobbett never let himself be restrained by the facts. In short, he had a marvelous time lampooning his enemies and their ideas. His pseudonym, "Peter Porcupine," appeared regularly after he "told off" a magazine editor in a pamphlet entitled *A Kick for a Bite*. A reviewer of the piece likened Cobbett to a porcupine, a creature with bristles erect against those who sought to manhandle it. That was just the creature Cobbett fancied himself as being, and he gloried in the name.

The oldest Federalist paper was Major Benjamin Russell's *Massachusetts* (later *Columbian*) *Centinel,* published at Boston. Russell fought at Lexington as a lad of 13. He learned the printing trade under Isaiah Thomas and after serving his time as a journeyman founded his paper in 1784. His first big crusade was his attempt to push his state toward ratification of the Constitution. That put him in the forefront of the forces that eventually rallied under the Federalist banner. Russell was pro-British, anti-French, an advocate of an American nobility, and later a hater of Jefferson. His paper followed the Federalist line 100 percent, but in addition, it had excellent news coverage, and it enjoyed great prosperity.

THE FRENCH   With such journalistic big guns trained upon their hapless opponents, the
REVOLUTION   Federalists rapidly consolidated their power. Had it not been for the French
Revolution, they might have annihilated the ideas for which many an American had fought. As Colonel Thomas W. Higginson wrote in his voluminous notes of the period, the French Revolution "drew a red hot plow share through the history of America."[5] Whereas America had triggered the French upheaval after its own fight for freedom, the French were now repaying in kind—and just in time. The French influence stopped the American monarchists in their tracks. It destroyed the last hope of the aristocrats and it changed the trend toward realliance with the British. It also provided the literature and philosophy needed as ammunition against the skillful journalistic batteries defending the Federalist citadel. All that was needed was a great leader. As usual in such emergencies, a great one emerged.

THOMAS JEFFERSON,   He was Thomas Jefferson, then Secretary of State in Washing-
ANTI-FEDERALIST   ton's cabinet. Jefferson was the antithesis of his colleague,
Hamilton, both in temperament and in ideology. The American yeoman, rather than the commercial man, was Jefferson's ideal of the sovereign citizen. He was convinced that no other people of the world were so well off as the independent, rural landowners of the United States. Having seen the wretchedness of European cities, he was all the more certain that the benefits of the American yeoman must be maintained. It should be pointed out, however, that Jefferson did not stand as tribune for all the groups made up of the common man. He distrusted the proletariat—the workers in the cities. The slum was his measurement of a sick society.

It is commonly believed that Jefferson was an idealist, as opposed to Hamilton, the hardfisted realist. Actually, an argument could be presented to show that just the reverse was true. If we assume that a realist is one who would make the best of the situation facing him, and the idealist is the proponent of things as they should be, then Jefferson emerges more and more as the realist. Jefferson and Hamilton lived before the age of great industrial development in this country. Jefferson based his political philosophy on an existing agrarian economy. He faced conditions as they were and sought to make the best of them. Under the above definition, that would make him a realist. Hamilton did everything he could to gear America for a capitalist, industrial future. He was so far ahead of his time that we can only conclude that he was an idealist.

The two clashed on every point. For Jefferson's purposes, a decentralized, states' rights government was sufficient. Since credit, commerce, and manufacturing were subordinate matters, Jefferson would have been content with no more government than was necessary to preserve internal order. Hamilton stood for exactly the opposite. Thus, the Federalist leader insisted upon a *responsible* government—one that could protect property and aid commerce—whereas Jefferson was much more interested in a *responsive* government and was more concerned with the current needs of the people than with security.

The two champions inevitably clashed openly, as they had privately since their appointments as cabinet officers. The issue came to a head in 1791. Jefferson returned from a tour through New England with Madison to find himself the center of controversy. The two had already been mentioned in the *Maryland Journal* as potential anti-Federalist leaders. At this point, Edmund Burke in England had launched an attack upon those who defended the French Revolution. Paine had replied in his brilliant defense of democracy, *Rights of Man*. The Federalists saw to it that Burke's charges were widely reprinted in America. Paine's reply was slow in coming. Jefferson had obtained a copy from Madison, however, and it elated him; here was the answer to the Federalist gospel. He encouraged the American publication of Paine's book. Unfortunately, Jefferson had to return the only copy of the *Rights of Man* before he had finished it, so that it could be set up in type. To save time, he sent it directly to the printer, and he enclosed a note explaining the reason for the delay: "I am extremely pleased to find it will be reprinted here," he wrote, "and that something is at length to be publicly said against the political heresies which have sprung up among us. I have no doubt our citizens will rally a second time round the standard of *Common Sense*."

Jefferson maintained that he was surprised when he discovered the printer had used this note as a preface to the book. The general reader could only assume that the Secretary of State meant that the "political heresies" applied to such leaders as Vice President John Adams, whose tedious "Discourses of Davilla" were being accepted as holy writ by Federalists as the essays appeared serially in John Fenno's *Gazette of the United States*. This was of course a serious breach of official family etiquette. Cabinet members were not supposed to bicker publicly. As a result, a storm of abuse broke over Jefferson. His friends rose to defend him. Another result was that thousands rushed to buy copies of the Paine book. Thus, the political battle was joined, and Jefferson found himself thrust into the van as leader. He accepted the responsibility.

PHILIP FRENEAU, JEFFERSON'S EDITOR

Philip Freneau, who helped to start the second internal revolution, was a lifelong rebel. It is significant that he was of Huguenot extraction. The Huguenots had suffered for generations in the cause of religious freedom. Freneau was graduated from Princeton in 1771. At that time the college was a hotbed for sedition. Among the students who gathered in the room Freneau shared with James Madison were such "Radicals" as Harry Lee, Aaron Burr, and William Bradford, later a member of Washington's cabinet. Freneau was the most zealous Patriot of the lot. Long before the Revolution he was writing newspaper contributions and fierce poems on liberty. After Lexington and Concord, he took an active part in the conflict—a rather pathetic little man, pitting his feeble efforts uselessly, as it turned out, against the enemy. In disgust, he took to the sea in one of his father's ships.

He was in Bermuda when news arrived of the Declaration of Independence. Here was Revolution he could understand. Freneau hurried home to take an active part in the movement. With Letters of Marque (license for a civilian to wage war) from the Continental Congress, he put his available resources into a privateer, a vessel he called the *Aurora*. The ship had to strike its colors in the first battle, and Freneau spent weary weeks in the notorious British prison hulks anchored in New York harbor—an experience that left him physically shattered and made him an even more implacable hater of the British. At length he was exchanged. Returning to New York sick and penniless, he turned to his last resource—his pen. Freneau's poem, ''The Prison Ship,'' whipped apathetic Patriots into renewed efforts against the enemy. His account of the exploits of John Paul Jones instilled pride into a dejected nation.

By the end of the war he had given his health, his fortune, and all his soul to the cause of liberty. As he saw it, the sacrifice had been in vain. He charged his old leaders—Washington included—with failure to carry out the promises of 1776. He saw Jeffersonian Republicanism as a movement to carry on the original drives of the Revolution over the opposition of the Federalists.

It was Madison, Freneau's classmate, who brought the little rebel to Jefferson's attention. Madison had told the Anti-Federalist leader that Freneau was just the man to engage in journalistic jousting with such champions as Fenno or Russell. Jefferson was always considerate of the ideas of Madison, who was like a son to the master of Monticello. He offered Freneau a small subsidy as State Department translator if he would found an Anti-Federalist paper. It was not money that lured Freneau to the capital at Philadelphia, however. He saw himself as a journalistic crusader.

FRENEAU VS. FENNO: VITUPERATIVE PARTISANSHIP

And so it was that Freneau became editor of the *National Gazette* in 1791. The early editions were mild enough, but there were hints of what was to come. Fenno, his rival, would never have tolerated a phrase like ''public opinion sets the bounds to every government, and is the real sovereign of every free one.''[6] The four short columns of comment on page one of the *National Gazette* looked innocuous in those first few months, but while Fenno was ridiculing the right of plain citizens to complain against government officials, Freneau was telling his readers that ''perpetual jealousy of the government'' was necessary against ''the machinations of ambition,'' and he warned that ''where that jealousy does not exist in a reasonable degree, the saddle is soon prepared for the back of the people.''[7]

Then one day Freneau discharged both barrels at Hamilton over the injustices of debt funding. He used the pen name ''Brutus'' that day, and at once the Federalist leader discovered he had a journalistic foe worthy of his steel. Day by day Freneau sent succeeding volleys after the first one, and his brashness encouraged other articulate voices to sound the call to battle stations. Even the less gifted Anti-Federalist editors could arouse readers now, by picking up *National Gazette* ''exchanges.'' The alarm of the Federalists was indicated by the torrent of abuse flowing from their editorial pens, but this, too, Freneau could return in double measure.

Freneau was so nettlesome that Hamilton made the mistake of joining in the fray personally, writing an unsigned article for Fenno's paper saying that an employee of the government should not be criticizing its policies. Fenno replied that the small stipend paid him in Jefferson's state department did not muzzle him. Hamilton's identity as a writer being already revealed, he now accused Jefferson of being the real author of the *National Gazette*'s vilifications. The quarrel between the two cabinet officers had to be refereed by President Washington, but he found the breach beyond repair. Indeed, Washington was dismayed by "that rascal Freneau," as he called him, when he wrote such items as: "The first magistrate of a country . . . seldom knows the real state of the nation, particularly if he be buoyed up by official importance to think it beneath his dignity to mix occasionally with the people." Freneau considered Washington a fair target because in the editor's opinion the old general had lent his name as "front man" for Federalism.

In the end, it was neither the opposition nor the government that defeated Freneau. The *National Gazette* simply died of financial malnutrition. There were no "angels" to come to the rescue, as there had been for Fenno under Hamilton's sponsorship. Jefferson could offer some help, but when he left the cabinet in 1793, Freneau had virtually no financial support. When yellow fever drove his workmen out of the city, Freneau closed the office. He never reopened it. The paper had lasted only two years, but it is doubtful if any other publication accomplished so much in that time. The end of the paper was just about the end of Freneau as a journalist, too. He tried his hand for a time in New Jersey and New York, but eventually he returned to the sea. Later, he was rediscovered as a poet.

BACHE AND THE *AURORA*

One of the leading journalists who carried the torch of Anti-Federalism dropped by Freneau was Benjamin Franklin Bache, the grandson of Benjamin Franklin. Bache was just 21 in 1790 when he founded the *Philadelphia General Advertiser,* better known as the *Aurora* (the name appeared in small print around the name plate). Bache was a mercurial young man—impetuous, brilliant, and often intemperate in expression. He was influenced by the style of Freneau, and his paper was even more violently partisan than the *National Gazette* had been. Too often he was downright vicious.

Not that the Federalists did not give him cause for his editorial mudslinging. He had seen the statue of his grandfather—one of the great men of the country—desecrated by hoodlums inspired to acts of vandalism by those opposed to the principles so ably enunciated by "Poor Richard" in Franklin's famous *Almanac.* Brought up in France and Switzerland by his doting grandfather, young Bache was sympathetic to the French cause from the beginning of his journalistic career. That put him in opposition to President Washington when the old war hero backed the anti-French party headed by Hamilton and others. Like Freneau, Bache resorted to personal attack in his campaign to wreck the Federalist party. He even tried to besmirch the character of "The Father of His Country."

"If ever a nation was debauched by a man, the American nation has been debauched by Washington," he wrote in the December 23, 1796, issue of the *Aurora.*

Federalists wrecked the *Aurora* office and beat the editor in retaliation. Fenno caned Bache in the street and Cobbett wrote of him in *Porcupine's Gazette:*

This atrocious wretch (worthy descendant of old Ben) knows that all men of any understanding put him down as an abandoned liar, as a tool and a hireling, . . . He is an ill-looking devil. His eyes never get above your knees. He is of a sallow complexion, hollow-cheeked, dead eyed, and has *a toute ensemble,* just like that of a fellow who has been about a week or ten days in a gibbet.[8]

Some historians have called this period the "Dark Ages of Journalism," because of the scurrility of the press. This was a transition period, however, and perhaps violent partisanship, as reflected in the press, was a means of expending some of the venom stored up against the British after the war.[9] Adding to the tension was the war between

Great Britain and Napoleonic France. It was not easy for Americans to take the advice of Washington, who warned against entangling foreign alliances in the last hours of his administration.[10] The new nation had little to gain by taking sides, but unfortunately, the war was forced on the attentions of Americans by the belligerents.

The French and the British were about equally callous regarding American foreign policy. The "paper" blockades imposed by Napoleon violated international precedent, and American shipping interests were infuriated by unlawful seizure of their vessels by the French. But the British were annoying, too. They had fallen back on the "Rule of 1756," which forbade neutrals from trading in wartime with nations not ordinarily regular customers. This made sense to the British, for it was clear to them that the enemy otherwise could supply himself through adjoining neutral countries, despite the blockade. However, the enforcement of this rule threatened the development of American commerce.

THE ISSUE OF FRANCE   But the Federalists saw evil only in France. They were repelled by the excesses of the French Revolution and by the success of Napoleon. Since the Federalists were in firm control of the government, they could manipulate foreign policy to favor the British. The Anti-Federalists argued that America had the duty of siding with France in the name of Rochambeau, Lafayette, and DeGrasse, who had come from France to help us win our war with Britain. Federalists answered that our promises of assistance to France in time of trouble had been made to a government since overthrown by a regime to which we had no binding ties. The fact is, Federalists and Anti-Federalists were in conflict over the issue not because of persuasive logic but because of partisan bitterness.

Both sides found ammunition for their cause in the European issue. There was, for example, the case of "Citizen" Edmond Charles Genêt, minister to the United States from the French Republic. Genêt arrived in Charleston in the spring of 1793. Had he arrived in Boston he might have been sent home packing, but the South was Anti-Federalist territory, and on the Frenchman's month-long trip north, it was roses, roses all the way. By that time he was so certain he had public opinion behind him that when President Washington brushed off suggestions that the French be allowed to use American ports for refitting damaged war vessels, Genêt went right ahead with his plans. Washington was correct in slapping down such a presumptuous guest of the country, and the people, as a whole, approved. The Federalists used the incident to discredit their pro-French opponents.

Even more embarrassing to the Anti-Federalists was the so-called "XYZ Affair," in which it appeared that the unscrupulous French foreign minister, Talleyrand, had informed our diplomats that he would receive them as accredited ministers only after they had paid him a bribe. It was very difficult to defend pro-French sentiment in the face of such raw insults to national pride.

On the other hand, the Anti-Federalists were collecting a few rocks to throw at their enemies, too. Genêt's mistake hurt the Anti-Federalist cause in one way, but it did show how many countrymen were opposed to Federalist policy. Many a timid Republican was thus encouraged to enlist in Jefferson's party. The treaty signed by John Jay in 1794 was also used against the Federalists. "Jay's Treaty" was an attempt to get the British to meet agreements negotiated during the Treaty of Paris, which ended the War of Independence. It did get the British out of the frontier forts that they had promised to evacuate, but nothing was settled about impressment of American seamen, which irritated many Americans, especially those doomed to the harsh life of the British Navy.

Partisan feeling was running high when John Adams took the oath of office as the second president of the United States, after the election of 1796. With the Federalists in firm control, the administration began to prepare for war with France. Congress dutifully authorized an army of 35,000, which was a larger force than Washington had ever had at his disposal during the Revolution. Two new superfrigates, the *United States* and the *Constitution,* were laid down as part of the war program. To pay for these items Congress levied a tax that fell particularly heavily on the small landowner, who was least interested in foreign wars.

The result was a political and journalistic battle that passed all the bounds of decency. Even during the Revolution, when Tory and Patriot clawed at each other, there had never been such a caterwaul. Bache and Fenno carried their personal feud beyond the pages of their papers by engaging in a street brawl. "Peter Porcupine" (William Cobbett) brought invective to finest flower by attacking well-known Anti-Federalists, living and dead.

THE ALIEN AND SEDITION ACTS OF 1798

This was the situation when the administration tried to throttle such violent opposition in the summer of 1798. In June and July of that year, Congress passed the Alien and Sedition Acts. One was a law aimed at troublesome foreigners living in the country; the other concerned the muzzling of irritating editors.

There were then about 25,000 aliens in the United States. Many of them were refugees from stern authorities in their home lands, and they therefore tended to be on the side of the Jeffersonians, who believed in as little government as possible. Others were poor, or at least propertyless, and again such persons were more likely to gravitate into the ranks of the Anti-Federalists. Groups such as the Irish immigrants were by tradition opposed to the British and so could not possibly see any good in the Hamiltonian policy of British appeasement. There were also many intellectuals in this category. Dr. Joseph Priestley, the discoverer of oxygen and seven other gases, was a British expatriate noted for his leftist views. The Du Ponts, at that time aggressive backers of liberalism, brought French ideas into the platform of the Anti-Federalists. And there was Albert Gallatin, destined to be a great secretary of the treasury under Jefferson, who was already making a name for himself in Pennsylvania, despite the difficulty of adjusting to a country so different from his native Switzerland. Men like these were almost certain to be opposed to the administration. The Alien Act, it was hoped, would reduce the ranks of these threatening foreigners.

One provision of the law was an extension of the naturalization period from five to fourteen years. Another clause empowered the president to deport aliens judged by him to be subversive (a power Adams did not actually employ). Some foreign-born Americans, such as John Burk, publisher of the Anti-Federalist *Time Piece* in New York, went underground until the trouble blew over. Anyone could see that the alien section applied only to enemies of the administration. Peter Porcupine (William Cobbett) was not only a foreigner who held Americans in contempt, but he was also becoming obnoxious, even to some Federalist leaders, as the editor of a paper that attacked Vice President Jefferson in almost every issue. But the Sedition Act did not protect the office of vice president against false criticism.

The Sedition Act was an obvious attempt to control the journalistic spokesmen of the Anti-Federalists. It declared: "That if any person shall write, print, utter, or publish . . . any false, scandalous and malicious writing . . . against the government of the United States, or either house of the Congress . . . or the said President . . . or to excite against them the hatred of the good people of the United States . . . or to resist or oppose, or defeat any such law . . . shall be punished by a fine not exceeding two thousand dollars, and by imprisonment not exceeding two years."[11] The laws were to stand for two years.

One of the cornerstones of press freedom is the right to express criticism of government and its administrators freely. The Alien and Sedition laws reversed a process that had made America the envy of the oppressed. And yet there were important contributions in the laws. Nor have the repressive features been properly appraised in many accounts of the period. The original bill called for a declaration of war with France. The clauses that followed imposed penalties on all who gave any aid or comfort to this enemy. At the last minute, the war declaration was defeated by a narrow margin, but the following clauses concerning aliens and the press were allowed to stand. That was why all pro-French sentiment was so ruthlessly attacked by the administration.

And in some ways the Sedition Act can be called a *milestone* on the road to freedom of the press. The law did not forbid criticism of the government. It only attempted to curb malicious and false statements published to defame officials. And it provided a pair of safeguards: truth could be offered as a defense, and the jury could determine both the law and the fact. This was the twin argument made by Andrew Hamilton in the John Peter Zenger trial. Now it was enacted into the law of 1798.[12]

At first glance the Sedition Act may appear to merit support. But experience has shown us time and again that the party in power will inevitably abuse such controls in the interest of expediency. It was so in 1798. Even Alexander Hamilton, the father of the Federalist party, was apprehensive of the measure. The ailing and retired General Washington rose from his bed to warn against the abuses he foresaw. President Adams, an honest man despite his political ineptitude, did what he could to modify the bill. Unfortunately, the leaders who had made the Federalist party dominant in all branches of government no longer had the power to impede the machine they had set in motion. Extremists had taken over control, and they were intent on revenge for all the indignities heaped upon them by opposition editors.

Fearful for their personal safety, Jefferson and his friends gathered at Monticello and planned the Virginia and Kentucky Resolutions, affirming the right of states to nullify federal actions. Missing in 1798 was the far better safety valve of "judicial review," or the right of the United States Supreme Court to declare a legislative act unconstitutional. Not until 1803 did John Marshall establish that court function in *Marbury* v. *Madison*. Having taken the only available course, Jefferson then sat back to await the next step.

SEDITION ACT PROSECUTIONS

The Adams administration played right into his hands. The Federalists abused the new laws so openly that for a time freedom of the press was seriously threatened in America. It was far from being the "reign of terror" charged by the opposition, but the record is not one of which Americans can be proud. Timothy Pickering, the secretary of state, spent half his time reading Anti-Federalist papers so that he could ferret out violators of the law.

One of the victims of the Sedition Act was Matthew Lyon of Vermont. Born in Ireland, Lyon had landed in America as an indentured servant. He had worked his way up to a position of respect and prestige in his community and was representative to Congress from his state. Lyon was one of the famous "Green Mountain Boys" in the War of Independence. Cashiered from the army for an act that should have earned him a medal, he was later reinstated and promoted to the rank of colonel.

One afternoon in the House of Representatives, Roger Griswold, a leading Federalist from that citadel of Federalism, Connecticut, made insulting remarks about Lyon's war record. The Vermonter ignored Griswold at first, but when his colleague grasped his coat and repeated the insult, Lyon replied in the uncouth but effective manner of the frontier—he spat in Griswold's eye. Next day Griswold walked up to Lyon's desk in the House and began beating him with a cane. Lyon grabbed a handy pair of fire tongs and beat back his adversary. The Federalists tried to expel Lyon from the House but failed to muster the needed two-thirds vote.

The Sedition Act was used to settle scores with such persons. The crime charged against Lyon under the Act was the publication of a letter to an editor accusing President Adams of "ridiculous pomp, foolish adulation, and selfish avarice." For such remarks, Lyon was hailed before a Federalist judge, who sentenced the defendant to four months in jail and a fine of a thousand dollars. The vindictiveness of the judge was indicated by the fact that although the trial was held in Rutland, Vermont, where there was a passable jail, Lyon was condemned to a filthy cell at Vergennes, some 40 miles distant. Thousands of local citizens signed a petition requesting parole for the prisoner. It was ignored. When editor Anthony Haswell printed an advertisement in his *Vermont Gazette* announcing a lottery to raise money for paying the fine, he, too, was hustled off to jail for abetting a "criminal."

The Federalists should have heeded the warning. For the public reaction to such injustice was positive and immediate. Lyon was jailed in October 1798, convicted by what he called a packed jury of political opponents. In December he was reelected to the House by a two-to-one vote over his closest opponent. Freed in February 1799, after money had flowed in to pay his fine, the Vermonter returned in triumph to the capital at Philadelphia. At one time the procession behind his carriage was 12 miles long. In 1801 he was to play a crucial role in making Jefferson president.*

Other editors also had felt the lash of the Federalist masters. James Callender was one. He edited the *Richmond Examiner*. For criticizing the president, Callender was brought to trial. He probably deserved what he got, for the man was an unprincipled political opportunist. The Federalists were not attacking him on principle, however, but on technicalities, and his case is just as significant as though he were a man of high character. Callender was defended by William Wirt, the South's leading lawyer and man of letters. The judge was Samuel Chase, who had said before he had even arrived in Virginia that he was going to give the Anti-Federalists a lesson. Just as predicted, Callender was found guilty. He was sentenced to nine months in jail.

A Connecticut editor was imprisoned because he criticized the Army and the military policies of Congress. A New York editor wrote an uncomplimentary article about the president and was promptly jailed. Then the general public began to see through the hypocrisy of the repressive laws. It was noticed that whereas the slightest criticism of President Adams resulted in penalties, violent abuse of Anti-Federalist

---

*The 1800 election brought out a flaw in the political machinery. Jefferson was clearly the popular choice for president, but he and his running mate, Aaron Burr, both received 73 electoral votes under the indirect system of election. This threw the election into the House of Representatives, with 16 states having one vote each. The Federalists, despite Hamilton's opposition, voted for Burr. For 35 ballots Jefferson had eight states, one short of a majority. Burr had six and two state delegations were split. One was Vermont. On the final ballot the Federalist from Vermont abstained, thus allowing Lyon to cast the decisive vote. Lyon had not run again in 1800, but he was to serve in the House from 1803 to 1811 as congressman from Kentucky.

officials passed unpunished. Bache, for example, was indicted for criticism of Adams and others, while Fenno, who was just as violent, went unscathed.

The persecutions under the Alien and Sedition Acts have sometimes been described as insignificant. In all, there were 14 indictments under the Sedition Act. Eleven trials resulted, with 10 convictions. During the same time span there were at least five other convictions for seditious libel under the provisions of British Common Law in state or federal courts. Eight of the convictions involved newspapers.[13] Whatever the numbers, the uproar over the prosecutions was enough to make it clear that the states had erred in enacting laws during the Revolution perpetuating the concept of seditious libel. What caught a Tory then caught a Republican now. There were a few more seditious libel cases after 1800 but the example of the Sedition Act proved conclusive. People saw that the test of tyranny is not necessarily the number of prosecutions but the number of men and women restrained from speaking freely because of fear.

THE END
OF THE BATTLE
By 1800 the battle was over. Fenno and Bache both died in the terrible yellow fever epidemic that scourged Philadelphia in the summer of 1798 while Bache was still under indictment. Freneau, driven out by the fever, never reestablished his *Gazette*. Cobbett had left the country, following a libel suit that forced him into bankruptcy.

On the whole, the press improved after the outstanding character assassins were silenced in one way or the other. The widow Bache married her husband's assistant, William Duane, whose wife had died of the fever. Duane made a decent woman of the *Aurora*. The *Aurora* continued to back Jefferson and his party, but it was much more reasonable in tone under Duane. He was as courageous as Freneau, without Freneau's shrillness and bad taste. He was as colorful in his writing as Cobbett, but without the Englishman's recklessness. Duane suffered for the cause, along with other Anti-Federalists. He was beaten by hoodlums. He also was arrested under the Sedition Act.

The party battle in the House over the Sedition Act continued after the close 44–41 passage vote in 1798. Attempts were made to amend or repeal it in 1799 and again in 1800. In February 1801, a Federalist effort to extend it two more years was defeated 53–49, with 6 Federalists from the South deserting the party to join all 47 supporters of the new President Jefferson. The law expired March 3, 1801, under its own terms and was the last federal sedition law until the wartime law of 1917. Jefferson promptly pardoned all those in jail and cancelled remaining trials.[14]

The removal of the national capital from Philadelphia to Washington ended an epoch and began a new one. There had been a complete change in party and administration control, too. In the election year of 1800, Federalists were dominant in the House, the Senate, the presidency, the cabinet, the courts, the churches, business, and education. Up to four-fifths of the newspapers opposed Jefferson and his party. Yet Jefferson won.

As the historian Arthur M. Schlesinger, Jr., has written: "When a party starts out by deceiving the people, it is likely to finish by deceiving itself."[15] Since there is good evidence that this statement is true, the press, as demonstrated in this chapter, is more than ever essential in its role of disclosing party deceptions, for without such disclosures the vast majority of the public would not long remain free. Unfortunately, men had to suffer before this was generally understood—men like Lyon, Bache, Duane, and Thomas Adams of the *Boston Independent Chronicle*. Adams and his brother, Abijah, refused to be intimidated by their Federalist persecutors, although prison and worse confronted them. Sick and near death, they answered their detractors in double-space, double-measure Caslon bold type: "The Chronicle is destined to persecution. . . . It will stand or fall with the liberties of America, and nothing shall silence its clarion but the extinction of every principle which leads to the achievement of our independence."[16]

NOTES

1. Henry Steele Commager, ed., *Documents of American History* (New York: Appleton-Century-Crofts, 1934), p. 104, Article XII, and p. 109, Article XVI.
2. Claude G. Bowers, *Jefferson and Hamilton* (Boston: Houghton Mifflin, 1925), p. 31.
3. Ibid. p. 26. Bowers, it should be pointed out, is a respecter, but no admirer of Hamilton.
4. As quoted in Wilfred E. Binkley, *American Political Parties: Their Natural History* (New York: Knopf, 1943), p. 32.
5. Quoted from Vernon L. Parrington, *Main Currents in American Thought,* I (New York: Harcourt Brace Jovanovich, 1927), p. 321.
6. *National Gazette,* December 19, 1791.
7. *National Gazette,* February 9, 1792.
8. *Porcupine's Gazette,* November 16, 1797.
9. See, for example, B. E. Martin, "Transition Period of the American Press," *Magazine of American History,* XVII (April 1887), 273–94.
10. It is remarkable all during these critical years how all roads to safety eventually led right back to Washington. He was not a political genius, but he appeared to know instinctively the policies that would offer the greatest security to the nation he had saved in wartime.
11. *U.S. Statutes at Large,* "The Sedition Act," I, Sec. 2, p. 596.
12. The key votes in the House of Representatives on the Sedition Act were almost entirely on party lines. There were 47 Federalists, 39 Anti-Federalists. The bill passed 44–41, with 43 Federalist votes. Six Federalists joined in the modifications involving truth as a defense. The jury provision, however, was backed by all 39 Anti-Federalists and 28 Federalists. See John D. Stevens, "Constitutional History of the 1798 Sedition Law," *Journalism Quarterly,* XLIII (Summer 1966), 247.
13. James M. Smith, *Freedom's Fetters: The Alien and Sedition Laws and American Civil Liberties* (Ithaca, N.Y.: Cornell University Press, 1956), verifies 14 indictments under the Sedition Act. Other totals are from Mott, *American Journalism,* p. 149.
14. Stevens, "Constitutional History," p. 254.
15. *The Age of Jackson* (Boston: Little, Brown, 1945), p. 282.
16. Thomas Adams was the first important editor to be indicted under the Sedition Act. Before he could be tried, he was indicted under the common law for criticizing the Massachusetts legislature. He was too sick to stand trial, but his brother, Abijah, was convicted and jailed for a month, although he too was ailing. The defiant Thomas, faced with both federal and state sedition trials, sold the *Chronicle* in May 1799, two weeks before he died.

ANNOTATED BIBLIOGRAPHY

Books

Axelrad, Jacob, *Philip Freneau: Champion of Democracy*. Austin: University of Texas Press, 1967. Carefully researched biography.

Bailey, Thomas A., *A Diplomatic History of the American People*. New York: Appleton-Century-Crofts, 1969. Eighth edition of a leading account of foreign policy.

Binkley, Wilfred E., *American Political Parties: Their Natural History*. New York: Knopf, 1963. A clear and thoughtful study of the topic. The chapters on the early party era are good background reading.

Boorstin, Daniel, *The Americans: The National Experience*. New York: Random House,

1965. Consensus history; traces social history to the Civil War, minimizing political conflicts, clashes of ideas.

BOWERS, CLAUDE G., *Jefferson and Hamilton*. Boston: Houghton Mifflin, 1925. This book is particularly interesting to the student of journalism because the author draws heavily on newspaper sources for much of his documentation. Strongly Anti-Federalist.

COBBETT, WILLIAM, *Selections*. Oxford: Clarendon Press, 1923. These excerpts from the journalist's detailed *Works* demonstrate the style and content of Cobbett's best contributions.

FAŸ, BERNARD, *The Two Franklins*. Boston: Little, Brown, 1933. A contrast between Benjamin Franklin and his grandson, Benjamin Franklin Bache.

HARTZ, LOUIS, *The Liberal Tradition in America*. New York: Harcourt Brace Jovanovich, 1955. An interpretation of political thought since the Revolution; leading effort to generalize the idea of an American consensus—a liberal community which developed no proletariat but a victorious middle class.

JENSEN, MERRILL, *The New Nation*. New York: Knopf, 1950. A brilliant refutation of the dreary picture of the confederation period, as painted by such classic historians as John Fiske.

KROUT, JOHN ALLEN, AND DIXON RYAN FOX, *The Completion of Independence, 1790–1830,* A History of American Life, Vol. V. New York: Macmillan, 1944. Social history.

LEARY, LEWIS, *That Rascal Freneau*. New Brunswick: Rutgers University Press, 1941. The standard "life" of the Anti-Federalist editor.

LEVY, LEONARD W., ed., *Freedom of the Press from Zenger to Jefferson*. Indianapolis: Bobbs-Merrill, 1966. Contains documents and essays related to the Sedition Act, the rise of a Libertarian outlook toward the press, and Jefferson's philosophy.

LIPSET, SEYMOUR, *The First New Nation: The United States in Historical and Comparative Perspective*. New York: Basic Books, 1963. Application of the comparative approach to U.S. history.

McMASTER, JOHN BACH, *A History of the People of the United States from the Revolution to the Civil War*. 8 vols. New York: Appleton-Century-Crofts, 1883–1913. McMaster is chosen from among some of the best historians who wrote of this period, because he depended on newspaper sources to bring out the flavor and the temper of the times.

MILLER, JOHN C., *Crisis in Freedom: The Alien and Sedition Acts*. Boston: Little, Brown, 1951. A relatively brief account of passage of the laws and details of the trials.

NEVINS, ALLAN, *American Press Opinion, Washington to Coolidge*. Boston: Heath, 1928. An excellent selection of the partisan editorials of the period is included.

OSBORNE, JOHN W., *William Cobbett: His Thought and His Times*. New Brunswick, N.J.: Rutgers University Press, 1966. Biography of the Federalist editor of *Porcupine's Gazette*.

POLLARD, JAMES E., *The Presidents and the Press*. New York: Macmillan, 1947. The attitude of the Chief Executive regarding the press is an indicator of journalistic prestige and power, decade by decade. This book is useful as a supplementary text.

RUTLAND, ROBERT ALLEN, *The Birth of the Bill of Rights, 1776–1791*. Chapel Hill: University of North Carolina Press, 1955. A documented study of the origins and passage of the ten amendments.

SCHACHNER, NATHAN, *Alexander Hamilton*. New York: Appleton-Century-Crofts, 1946. A middle-of-the-road interpretation.

SCUDDER, H. E., *Noah Webster*. Boston: Houghton Mifflin, 1882. An adequate, concise biography of a versatile and interesting personality, who, among his other accomplishments, was a noted journalist.

SMITH, JAMES, M., *Freedom's Fetters: The Alien and Sedition Laws and American Civil Liberties*. Ithaca, N.Y.: Cornell University Press, 1956. Detailed and documented analysis of the laws and court cases.

STEWART, DONALD H., *The Opposition Press of the Federalist Period*. Albany: State University of New York Press, 1969. A scholarly study of the partisan press with much new detail.

VAN DOREN, CARL, ed., *The Federalist*. New York: Heritage Press, 1945. An annotated edition of the famous series of political editorials.

BALDASTY, GERALD J., "Toward an Understanding of the First Amendment: Boston Newspapers, 1782–1791," *Journalism History,* III (Spring 1976), 25. Revises Levy by focusing on common law of defamation rather than seditious libel.

BOSTON, RAY, "The Impact of 'Foreign Liars' on the American Press (1790–1800)," *Journalism Quarterly,* L (Winter 1973), 722. Political refugees from Britain spearheaded press attack on Federalists.

"Cobbett," *Fraser's Magazine,* XII (August 1835), 207. A personality sketch that brings out the journalist's wit and pugnacity.

COLL, GARY, "Noah Webster: Journalist, 1783–1803," Ph.D. thesis, Southern Illinois University, 1971. Assesses his contributions to both form and content of the newspaper and magazine.

DOWLING, RUTH N., "William Cobbett, His Trials and Tribulations as an Alien Journalist, 1794–1800." Ph.D. thesis, Southern Illinois University, 1972. Seven libel charges, some unfairly made, prompted him to leave for England.

GOLDSMITH, ADOLPH O., "The Roaring Lyon of Vermont," *Journalism Quarterly,* XXXIX (Spring 1962), 179. The stormy career of the congressman reelected while in jail for Sedition Act conviction.

GROTTA, GERALD L., "Philip Freneau's Crusade for Open Sessions of the U.S. Senate," *Journalism Quarterly,* XLVIII (Winter 1971), 667. The editor wins out.

KNUDSON, JERRY W., "Political Journalism in the Age of Jefferson," *Journalism History,* I (Spring 1974), 20. Summarizes his Ph.D. thesis, University of Virginia, 1974. Jefferson faced criticism of a predominantly Federal press.

PADOVER, SAUL K., "Wave of the Past," *New Republic,* CXVI (April 21, 1947), 14. A concise description of the effect of the Alien and Sedition laws on the Federalist defeat of 1800.

PRINCE, CARL E., "The Federalist Party and Creation of a Court Press, 1789–1801," *Journalism Quarterly,* LIII (Summer 1976), 238. Political rivalries and favors account for transformation of press system.

REITZEL, WILLIAM, "William Cobbett and Philadelphia Journalism," *Pennsylvania Magazine,* LIX (July 1935), 223. An excellent interpretation of the journalist. Reprinted in Ford and Emery, *Highlights in the History of the American Press.*

STEVENS, JOHN D., "Congressional History of the 1798 Sedition Law," *Journalism Quarterly,* XLIII (Summer 1966), 247. A detailed report of the partisan battle in the House, with analysis of votes.

"William Cobbett," *Littell's Living Age,* XLI (Spring 1854), 61. A short but surprisingly complete biographical sketch, with an interesting section on Cobbett's career in America.

National Intelligencer.

IN SENATE.

WASHINGTON.

Friday, March 3.

THE QUESTION SETTLED.

SUPREME COURT.

POSTSCRIPT.

NEW YORK, MARCH 7.

FROM SOUTH AMERICA.

FURTHER FROM CADIZ.

MARRIED.

PUBLIC SALE.

The *National Intelligencer* reports the passage of the 1820 Missouri Compromise.

8

The Press
and the Expanding Nation

I have lent myself willingly as the subject of a great experiment . . . to demonstrate the falsehood of the pretext that freedom of the press is incompatible with orderly government.

— Jefferson to Seymour

Jefferson's victory in 1800 made his party subject to the same type of attack that had so recently been launched against the Federalists while they were in power. The Jeffersonian "Republicans" had gained control of the administration, but the president estimated that up to three-fifths of the editors continued to support Federalist policies. In some areas Federalist newspapers outnumbered their political rivals by as much as five to one. The rank and file voter was not impressed by this "one-party" press, apparently, for he continued to return to office a long succession of candidates representing the Republican party (as the Anti-Federalists became known before eventually adopting the name Democratic party).

The disparity between public and editorial opinion in the periods of Jefferson, Jackson, and since the administration of Franklin D. Roosevelt has concerned students of our press. They point to the occasions when overwhelming popular mandates coincided with preponderant press opposition to the popular cause, and critics sometimes wonder if the American press is the power the journalists say it is. This history will indicate that the power of the press is not in its persuasion by opinion, but in its dissemination of information and its arousal of interest in important issues hitherto submerged in public apathy.

THE *NEW YORK EVENING POST,* 1801   One of the important Federalist organs was founded by Alexander Hamilton a year after the defeat of his party in 1800. The Federalist leader believed that a reputable party paper was needed more than ever to stem the tide of Republican popularity. This was the *New York Evening Post,* destined to become the city's oldest newspaper. Hamilton chose William Coleman as the first editor. Coleman was a lawyer and former court reporter, again indicating the trend of journalism since the days when the printer-editor was the rule. He was an able editor, but while "The General," as Hamilton liked to be called, was around, it was plain to all that Coleman was subordinate in the office.

Coleman was a writer of some literary pretensions. He could express his convictions in a slashing style that often cut down wavering opposition within and without the party. He also had great personal charm and courage. Eventually, he broke with Hamilton because of Coleman's loyalty to Aaron Burr,[1] but in the founding days of the *Post,* Coleman did not make an editorial move without consulting his sponsor. It is significant that Coleman was a shorthand expert, and that was one reason he had been selected by Hamilton. Late at night Coleman could have been seen in the empty streets hurrying to the home of the Federalists' great leader to take dictation for the next day's editorial. These editorials needed no reworking. They were the work of Hamilton at his journalistic best. Picked up by Federalist editors around the country, they exerted an important party influence.

The victorious party in 1800 needed opposition, as does any party in power. Jefferson had committed himself frequently as a believer in press freedom. His party had fought against the Alien and Sedition Acts in accordance with this doctrine. He had sponsored and encouraged the Virginia and Kentucky Resolutions as an attack on press restrictions by the Federalists. He had helped Freneau and Thomas Ritchie establish newspapers to help stem the tide of Federalist dominance.[2] Now he found himself after the party victory accused of press restrictions by the Federalists. This is a pattern commonly found in the history of American journalism—the reversal of free expression policies once a group wins power.

JEFFERSON'S VIEW OF THE PRESS   Jefferson appears to have been sincere in his defense of a free press. Even when the press humiliated him, he defended its freedom. Wrote Jefferson to his friend Carrington in 1787:

> I am persuaded that the good sense of the people will always be found to be the best army. They may be led astray for a moment, but will soon correct themselves. The people are the only censors of their governors; and even their errors will tend to keep these to the true principles of their institution. To punish these errors too severely would be to suppress the only safeguard of the public liberty. The way to prevent these irregular interpositions of the people, is to give them full information of their affairs through the channel of the public papers, and to contrive that those papers should penetrate the whole mass of the people. The basis of our government being the opinion of the people, the very first object should be to keep that right; and were it left to me to decide whether we should have a government without newspapers, or newspapers without a government, I should not hesitate a moment to prefer the latter.

This part of Jefferson's letter to Carrington is widely quoted. It is bandied about particularly when press moguls fear various degrees of restriction or inconvenience from any quarter. But the second part of Jefferson's letter is not so well known, though it is a qualification essential to the above statement. The great statesman went on to say:

> But I should mean that every man should receive those papers, and be capable of reading them.

Later, when the Federalist editors had made life miserable for him, he wrote in exasperation to a friend:

> The newspapers of our country by their abandoned spirit of falsehood, have more effectually destroyed the utility of the press than all the shackles devised by Bonaparte.[3]

But that was in 1813, when he was very tired. His more considered views of the vicious opposition press are better summed up in the following 1802 letter:

> They [Federalists] fill their newspapers with falsehoods, calumnies, and audacities. . . . We are going fairly through the experiment of whether freedom of discussion, unaided by coercion, is not sufficient for the propagation and protection of truth, and for the maintenance of an administration pure and upright in its actions and views. No one ought to feel under this experiment, more than myself. Nero wished all the necks of Rome united in one, that he might sever them at a blow. So our ex-federalists, wishing to have a single representative of all the objects of their hatred, honor me with that post and exhibit against me such atrocities as no nation has ever before heard or endured. I shall protect them in the right of lying and calumniating, and still go on to merit the continuance of it, by pursuing steadily my object of proving that a people, easy in their circumstances as ours are, are capable of conducting themselves under a government founded not in the fears and follies of man, but on his reason, on the predominance of his social over his dissocial passions, so free as to restrain him in no moral right, and so firm as to protect him from every moral wrong, which shall leave him, in short, in possession of all his natural rights.[4]

But although Jefferson's views on the press were well known to his followers, and although he wielded strong control over his party, he could not keep his subordinates from trying to impose restrictions on opposition editors, now that the Jeffersonians were in power.

An example of this vindictiveness was the prosecution of Joseph Dennie for remarks deemed by Republican party leaders to be seditious. Dennie, a grandson of Bartholomew Green, Jr., onetime printer of the *Boston News-Letter,* was one of the ablest editors of his day. His *Farmer's Weekly Museum,* published at Walpole, New Hampshire, was so popular that it achieved national recognition. Later, Dennie took over the editorial direction of the *Port Folio,* an outspoken Federalist magazine published in Philadelphia. Shortly after Jefferson moved into the unfinished White House, Dennie wrote a series of editorials pointing out the weaknesses of popular rule. Although he did not attack the American government specifically, he made it clear that he believed democracy to be futile. These remarks were declared by government officials to be seditious, and the editor was indicted on that charge. After all that Jefferson had written about the press as a rightful censor of its government, the administration action appeared to be highly hypocritical. The jury must have thought so, too, for after a brilliant defense by Joseph Hopkinson, composer of the Patriot song, "Hail, Columbia," Dennie was acquitted.

THE CROSWELL SEDITIOUS LIBEL CASE   The most celebrated case involving the press during this period was prosecuted under a state law, as recommended by the president. The defendant was Harry Croswell, editor of a Federalist paper at Hudson, New York. Croswell called his little weekly *The Wasp,* and it was an appropriate name. It was so vicious and annoying that respectable Federalists disdained it. *The Wasp* stung political opponents in every column. One day Croswell printed an "exchange" from the *New York Evening Post,* Hamilton's personal mouthpiece. The article reported that Jefferson had paid James Callender, the Richmond editor, to spread the word that George Washington had been a robber, traitor, and perjurer and that other Federalist leaders were equally reprehensible. This was a serious charge against Jefferson and the dignity of his office. *The Wasp,* rather than the *Post,* was prosecuted because Croswell's paper was the type of scandal sheet

Jefferson had in mind when he suggested smoking out the worst of the Federalist editors under state law.

Croswell was indicted in 1804. He was found guilty, but appealed the case. When the trial was called, a titan arose to argue for the defense. He was Alexander Hamilton, Jefferson's arch rival. The four judges listened with obvious respect as the brilliant pleader stated a principle as applicable today as it was in 1804. The press, Hamilton argued, had "the right to publish with impunity truth, with good motives, for justifiable ends, though reflecting on Government, Magistracy, or individuals." Since the "good motives" and "justifiable ends" would have to be disproved by the complainant, Hamilton was essentially saying that truth, and truth alone, was a defense in a libel action. In his arguments against the need for a Bill of Rights covering press freedom, Hamilton had not appeared as very sympathetic to the cause of liberty of written expression. But when he stood up at the Croswell trial and insisted upon the "right" of submitting truth as a full defense, Hamilton won his place alongside the great fighters for press freedom.

It so happened that Hamilton lost the case, when the four judges were evenly divided in their opinions. The New York state laws still adhered to the old policy, "the greater the truth, the greater the libel." Truth had been recognized as a defense in the Sedition Act, but the law had lapsed four years before, and the precedent had not been accepted in the courts. Hamilton also insisted on the right of a jury to determine both the law and the fact. Both issues had been raised in the Zenger case, but only in Pennsylvania had they been recognized in law (in 1790).

The significance of the Croswell trial can be seen in legislation immediately following Hamilton's plea. Even before the judges had handed down the verdict, a bill was introduced in the New York Legislature providing that truth thereafter was to be admitted in defense. The same bill gave the jury the right to determine both the law and the fact. By 1805, these principles had become law in New York—70 years after Zenger's trial. Soon other states followed suit and the shadow of the British Common Law of seditious libel was lifted. In 1812 the Supreme Court held that the federal government could not prosecute under the old law.

The great pioneer in press freedom did not live to see his eventual triumph; ironically, it was another libel episode that brought about Hamilton's violent death. A remark attributed to Hamilton that appeared in an Albany newspaper while the Croswell case was being tried angered New York's second most imposing political figure—Aaron Burr. Burr's prestige was by this time slipping, which probably made him especially sensitive to insults, real or imagined. He challenged Hamilton to a duel. Hamilton might have declined with no great blackening of his honor, but he accepted the gage. On July 11, 1804, his seconds rowed him across the Hudson river to the grassy bank near Weehawken where his son had been killed in a duel several months before. Burr was an expert marksman, and in the exchange of shots he wounded Hamilton so critically that the great leader died the next day.

GROWTH OF THE PRESS: FIRST DAILIES

The first daily newspaper in America was established by Benjamin Towne at Philadelphia in 1783. His *Pennsylvania Evening Post* was as characterless as its publisher. Towne was a Patriot in 1776 and was one of the first to print the Declaration of Independence for the public. Later, he became a Tory. After the surrender he confessed his sins and resumed a partial state of grace in his community. However, this shoddy little daily lasted only 17 months.

It was succeeded by a very good daily, the *Pennsylvania Packet and Daily Advertiser,* published by the partnership of John Dunlap and David C. Claypoole. Like the *Evening Post* owned by Towne, the *Packet* was originally a weekly publication that had been founded by Dunlap in 1771. Switching from triweekly to daily status in 1784, the Dunlap and Claypoole venture was successful from the beginning.

By 1800, most big ports and commercial centers were supporting daily papers. Philadelphia had six; New York, five; Baltimore, three; and Charleston, two. But for some curious reason Boston, the home of the American newspaper, had no daily paper at this time. Many of these publications had been forced into the daily field to meet the competition of the coffeehouses, where the London papers were available and where news was freely exchanged. The American journalists met the challenge by issuing first semiweekly, then triweekly, and finally daily editions.

Philadelphia even had an all-day newspaper for a time. It was the *New World,* published by Samuel Harrison Smith in morning and evening editions. It was not successful, but it indicated the growing interest in fresh news presentation. Of 512 papers being printed in 1820, 24 were dailies, 66 were semiweeklies or triweeklies, and 422 were weeklies. They were still generally slanted toward the more prosperous citizen, for the price was more than the average man could afford. Circulations were not impressive, either, by present standards. A circulation of 1,500 was considered adequate in all but the largest centers. But because the bulk of circulation was among the prosperous class who tended to gravitate to the conservative political party, most editors patterned their products accordingly. With the rising pressure of the masses for greater political recognition, the pages of these papers began to be filled more and more with political information and opinion.

In the hinterlands the press was also booming. The number of newspapers beyond the urban fringe increased sixfold during this period.[5] Advertising helped to support this newspaper boom. For although most families tended to buy their supplies in wholesale lots for seasonal storage, there was already some development of the retail trade that was to sustain the press in later years. The development of the postal system also accounted for some of this expansion. By postal acts of 1782 and 1792, educational and informational matter could be mailed at very low rates.

THE PRESS MOVES WESTWARD   The expansion of the press reflected the spirit of the country. It had taken 150 years to settle the seaboard colonies, and on the basis of the past record, it should have taken another 200 years to push the frontier to the Mississippi river. But once the Appalachian mountains were conquered, the lands to the west were rapidly taken up. Jefferson, who had always opposed national imperialism, had a chance in 1803 to purchase the vast Louisiana territory, and the bargain was too good to turn down out of principle. When this domain was added to the United States as a vast territory for exploitation, settlers poured in from the East. The lust for western lands is indicated by the numerous petitions for statehood during this period. Between 1790 and 1820, nine new states were admitted to the Union.

The waterways were the highways into these frontier regions. Along the Ohio, the Kanawha, and the Cumberland, tiny communities began to appear that would some day become teeming cities. By present standards they were mere hamlets, but each served a wide trading area. They were thus far more important as markets and social centers than their populations would indicate. If they were county seats, with courts, law enforcing agencies, and land offices, they were even more important. And usually one of the first to set up shop in such communities was the frontier printer-editor. He was the enthusiastic promoter of the village that he was certain would one day rival London. He was a leading businessman. But most of all he was the man who, more than anyone else, knit the community into an organization that could begin to bring civilization to the remote areas.

The first newspaper in this new West was John Scull's venture of 1786, the *Pittsburgh Gazette,* still thriving as the *Post-Gazette.* A year later, John Bradford, who bore a name well known in the printing industry, although he was only indirectly related to the famous Philadelphia publishing family, set up his shop in Lexington, Kentucky. His *Kentucky Gazette* might have been the first paper in the West, had his equipment not been wrecked in transit the year before the establishment of the Pittsburgh enterprise. By 1800, 21 newspapers had been started west of the mountains. The Ohio river was the most important artery of commerce in this early period, but there were also important settlements, and newspapers, along the Wabash and lesser streams, such as the Muskingum, Scioto, Maumee, and Cuyahoga.

Advertising was rarely adequate to support the news business, but fortunately there needed to be some means of publishing legal information in this new area, and that was often sufficient inducement to start up a paper. Elihu Stout, for example, himself poled up the Wabash with his press to found the *Indiana Gazette* at Vincennes in 1804. He had been induced to give up his business in Frankfort, Kentucky, on the promise that he would be awarded the territorial legal printing contract—enough of a stake for him to establish a paper.

The northern route to the frontier was along the Mohawk valley, straight across New York state from the Hudson river. This was the route of the Erie Canal, which was soon to make New York City the largest metropolis in the land, but even before that, it was an important highway. At the end of the valley, the Great Lakes served as transportation and communication routes between the vast wilderness and the East. Detroit, one of the outer bastions of the frontier then, had a newspaper, the *Gazette,* by 1817. Soon other communities in the area could boast the same. A Congressional Act of 1814 provided that all federal laws must be printed in two (later, three) newspapers in each state and territory. This was a logical way of letting electors know what their representatives were doing, but it also encouraged the founding of pioneer papers in communities not quite ready to support such ventures.[6]

| THE FRONTIER NEWSPAPER | The flimsy little weeklies of the isolated villages and booming river towns had much to do with the crystallization of public opinion that made the West a new factor in American politics. What were they like, |

these newspapers that exerted such influence in the West? They were small, hand-set, scrubby publications, on the whole. It is apparent that there was no place on them for large staffs, regular correspondents, or columnists furnishing opinions for readers too busy to form their own. There was plenty of opinion, of course, but most of it was contributed by readers. Usually there was a column or two of local news, printed sometimes as scattered items without benefit of headlines. There might be half a column of exchanges, or news gleaned from other newspapers arrived by the last post. The remaining material, exclusive of the notices, or advertisements, was very likely submitted by readers. Every subscriber who could wield a pen sooner or later appeared in the columns. All the aggrieved wrote out their pet complaints for the pages of the local mercury. Even government officials participated in this exchange, not always openly, true, but with sufficient identity to warrant spirited replies. Often this material was strident and in bad taste. ''Straight news'' tended toward distortion, flamboyance, and vindictiveness. But whatever its faults, it was a robust, colorful press. The great French observer, de Tocqueville, described the institution at a somewhat later period, but his remarks then were pertinent to this decade. He was impressed by the virility of the American press even while repelled by its provincialism. Western crudeness shocked him, but he was amazed at the success of the democratic experiment, and he conceded that the press had been an important implement in this development. De Tocqueville found a close relationship between the press and its public, fostered, no doubt, by the active participation of readers in the local journalistic effort. The public appeared to respect the Fourth Estate, he reported, and this was manifest in the great freedom accorded the institution.

By the end of the first decade of the nineteenth century, the western press was lusty and influential. Editors and politicians who understood their constituencies saw that the region had its special problems. They tended to side with the Jeffersonians on the rights of the common man, but their dependence on the federal government for defense of their sparse settlements against the Indian threat made them favor strong, centralized administration.

THE INFLUENCE OF THE FRONTIER

The new states also turned to the federal government for the development of transportation, so essential to their growth and prosperity. Again, the great land companies, organized to promote colonization at a profit, were dependent on the national administrations, rather than the territorial or parent-state politicians. There was a tendency, then, for the westerner to demand local and statewide autonomy to work out the destiny he believed to be peculiar to his region, but he was less touchy about state sovereignty because of his need of strong, centralized government. He insisted on solid representation in the administration of that government, as indicated by the impatience of territories for statehood. But he visualized that government as a kind of public service corporation, not a dispenser of privileges for the wealthy and powerful. Under the Northwest Ordinances, land was set aside to be sold for educational revenue, and the pattern was generally followed in other areas. Suffrage was likely to be broader than in the more settled regions; property might be a voting requisite, but it was easy to acquire.

The West was to have a profound influence on the development of the new nation. The importance of that influence has been disputed since Professor Frederick Jackson Turner suggested that the frontier was a political and social laboratory that had produced a distinctive American character.[7] His studies had convinced him that climate alone had as much to do with political traditions as established philosophies. He argued that regions, rather than boundaries, identified peoples. Weather might be responsible for great social change. A severe drought in a wheat area might cause a migration to more prosperous communities. Turner pointed out that the poor and underprivileged were more interested in popular rule than were the wealthy, because it gave them a chance to even up the opportunities. Carried to its conclusion, the Turner theory would hold that "radicalism" is only the political expression of economic maladjustment. Those who are satisfied do not desire change or experimentation. But the men and women who moved across the mountains usually accepted the perils and discomforts of pioneer life because they were dissatisfied with the older community life.[8] On the frontier these pioneers lived roughly and dangerously. When people suffer and face dangers together, they tend to act together, regardless of past background, customs, privileges, or attitudes. Such people begin to make demands. They blame those in control for failing to consider their problems. When they become strong enough politically and economically, they tend to force the older society to adopt measures that have proved to be effective under the exacting tests of the wilderness. Thus, the Turner school maintains, the frontier has been responsible for much of the social and political experimentation that helped to distinguish the American character and organization.

"Historians have debated so long and hard whether the frontier thesis is profoundly valuable or fundamentally misleading that there has been a danger of losing sight of the paradox that it can be both," historian Richard Hofstadter writes, adding that Turner's sharpest critics have rarely failed to concede the core of merit to his thesis—the obvious influence of the frontier on American life.[9] Critics have most often quarreled with his views concerning the effects of the frontier on democracy and individualism and its role as a "safety valve" for eastern discontent. Of the Turner themes, the supposed role of the West in forcing democratization in the East proved most vulnerable. Turner's vagueness in defining the term "individualism" has led to unresolved debates in that area. As Daniel Boorstin points out, because of the danger, "Westward-moving pioneers everywhere found group travel and group living normal," becoming what he calls Joiners and Organizers.[10]

THE WAR OF 1812

The War of 1812 will serve as an example of how the frontier had come to influence American thought and politics. This disgraceful conflict reflects little on either of the belligerents. We do not like to be reminded of General William Hull's abject surrender to an inferior British and Indian force at Detroit or the burning of our national capitol. There were heroic episodes, too, such as Commodore Oliver Hazard Perry's useless naval victory on Lake Erie;[11] the courageous, but futile, sea battles of American naval vessels and privateersmen against the world's greatest sea power; and General Andrew Jackson's victory at New Orleans, two weeks after the peace had been signed at Ghent.[12] But for better or for worse, the force of public opinion in the West was largely responsible for that war.

Generations of Americans believed that the War of 1812 resulted from American resentment over British abuses of free transit on the high seas and the "impressment," or forcible return, of former British naval ratings by methods insulting to our national pride. If these were major causes for war, then New England should have been preponderantly in favor of the conflict. The big shipping interests were centered in that area, and the commercial interests there suffered most from British naval arrogance. The fact is, New Englanders emphatically voiced disapproval of the war. It was the West that forced military action. Western newspapers offer the evidence on this point.

In 1810 the Indians went on the warpath under the great leader and statesman, Tecumseh, and his brother, Teuskwatawa, "The Prophet." Frontiersmen discovered that the Indians were killing Americans with weapons supplied by the British through Canada. The leaders of the West were in favor of war to settle the dispute. These were the men who became known as the "War Hawks." They were not interested in the plight of the seamen, or the Napoleonic blockades, or the shipping embargoes imposed by the United States to boycott the arrogant Europeans at such great sacrifice to the commercial interests. It is significant that Henry Clay, perhaps the most vehement of the War Hawks, was elected speaker of the House by the western bloc.

And poor Madison, best known for his constructive contributions to the American experiment, found himself in the role of a war president, thanks to the pressure of western public opinion. Clay controlled enough votes by 1812 to swing the election against Madison, if that great American did not go along with the War Hawks. Madison's opponent, Governor DeWitt Clinton of New York, was opposed to war, so the issue was clear in 1812. It was Madison and war, or Clinton and peace. Thus, it is easy to read the influence of the West by examining the records. The electoral vote of the Northeast, where the shipping and commercial men were important, was unanimous for Clinton and peace. Madison, who was presented to the voters as protector of the shipping interests, received not a single vote from the electors of New England. But the electoral vote of the West was unanimous for Madison and war. The middle and southern states were more evenly divided, but there was enough war sentiment in those areas to endorse the western stand and, from then on, it was "Mr. Madison's War."

As in most wars, the press suffered to some extent in the 1812 period. The most notorious attempt to muzzle an editor was in Baltimore, a shipping center with a strong faction opposed to administration war policies. Especially critical of the president was the *Federal Republican,* published by Jacob Wagner and Alexander Hanson. Some of their statements, made while an enemy was threatening our shores, no doubt merited censorship, but editors and contributors of the paper were charged by the opposition as traitors, although two of the protectors were Generals James Lingan and "Light Horse Harry" Lee, heroes of the War of Independence. When the mob descended on the office, the defenders held out until the irate citizens set up a cannon to blow the building down. At this point cooler heads negotiated a truce, including safe conduct of the besieged to the jail for protection. After the mob destroyed the press and building, its leaders ordered an assault on the jail. Some of the prisoners escaped, but nine were beaten and thrown to the mob. General Lingan was killed. General Lee was maimed for life.

The Federalists, discredited by their Hartford Convention plot, which encouraged New England states to secede from the Union instead of joining the war effort, failed to field a presidential candidate against James Monroe in 1816. On the surface, the country seemed to enjoy peace and prosperity. There was a kind of political truce while the forces realigned themselves. "The era of good feeling," Major Benjamin Russell of the *Columbian Centinel* in Boston called it.[13]

GOVERNMENT REPORTING: THE *NATIONAL INTELLIGENCER*	The most important press development at this time was in government reporting. The right to report meetings of interest to the general public is one of the tests of a free press, by the English-American concept. Reporters had access to the national House of Representatives from April 8, 1789, two days after it was established. For a time the Senate

was more secretive, since it excluded not only reporters but also members of the House from its debates. By December 9, 1795, the Senate had completed a gallery for reporters, however. When the capital was transferred from New York to Philadelphia, the gallery was too far from the rostrum for the reporters to hear clearly, but on January 2, 1802, the Senate (now in Washington) voted the reporters access to the floor. There was some squabbling between reporters and the House over arrangements. In Philadelphia, reporters were assigned "four seats on the window sill," and in Washington, after some agitation, they won the right to report the debates.[14]

One of the most effective reports of government was provided by the *National Intelligencer,* an outstanding newspaper of the period. Its founder was Samuel Harrison Smith, only 28 when Jefferson induced him to give up a promising publishing venture in Philadelphia to start a newspaper in the new capital at Washington. The president was head of the learned American Philosophical Society of Philadelphia (founded by Franklin), and Smith had been secretary of the organization. Jefferson was much impressed with the young man. The *National Intelligencer* soon became the semiofficial organ of the administration, but it served papers of all factions outside Washington with its remarkably objective reporting of Congressional debates.

Smith retired from the paper in 1810, but his work was carried on ably by the partners who succeeded him, Joseph Gales, Jr., and William W. Seaton. One reported proceedings in the House, while the other covered the Senate. Both were experts in a recently perfected shorthand technique, and they were able to offer complete, accurate reports of the debates. Gales and Seaton made the *National Intelligencer* a daily when they assumed control (it had been a triweekly since its founding in 1800).

A patronage system for publishing the acts and journals of the Congress was vital to the development of the *National Intelligencer* and its rivals in the capital. Under this system the House, Senate, and other agencies selected their own printers. John Fenno had held a Senate contract from the Federalists before 1800 and the *Intelligencer* the House contract for 1801–5. Then printing firms got the work on low bids until Congress decided to give the business to the hardworking newspapermen covering the debates and providing the country's press with the only immediately available accounts. Gales and Seaton held the Senate contract for 1819–26 and the House award for 1819–29. As political fortunes tilted to the Democrats, Duff Green's *United States Telegraph* won the contracts in voting battles on the floor, later sharing with Francis P. Blair's *Washington Globe*. Congress ended the patronage plan for newspapers in 1846 and established the Government Printing Office in 1860. During 26 years of patronage, the *National Intelligencer* had $1 million in contracts, the *Washington Globe* had $500,000, and the *United States Telegraph* had some $400,000. The system provided financial support for at least two, sometimes three, high quality capital papers.[15]

Gales and Seaton earned another $650,000 for printing the *Annals of Congress* (1789–1824) and the *American State Papers* series. They began the *Register of Debates* in 1824, which was superseded by the *Congressional Globe* in 1834. It was in turn replaced in 1873 by the official *Congressional Record*. The *National Intelligencer* was the voice of the Whig party and briefly became the administration paper when the Whigs elected Harrison in 1840 and Fillmore became president in 1850. Daniel Webster, close friend of Gales and Seaton, was secretary of state in both administrations. The Whig party collapse, and the death of Gales in 1860, reduced the once-great *National Intelligencer* to a minor role, but it survived until the close of the Civil War.

MAGAZINES GAIN A FOOTHOLD

But the *National Intelligencer* was not typical of the press of the "era of good feeling." Few other newspapers won historical recognition at this time. On the other hand, there was an interesting development in the magazine field during the period. Efforts to publish magazines had been made occasionally since 1741, when Benjamin Franklin was thwarted in his plans by Andrew Bradford, who published the first periodical three days before Franklin's magazine appeared.

Five magazines were established in the revolutionary period. By that time there was some indication that the magazine might one day be self-supporting. It was the *Pennsylvania Magazine,* published in Philadelphia by Robert Aitken, that offered the American public its first taste of Tom Paine. This periodical was well edited. It was full of interesting political information, literary contributions of good quality, and discussions of important issues. Eventually it failed, but it showed that the magazine had possibilities.

An interesting publication started in the period of the party press was the *Farmer's Weekly Museum,* printed at Walpole, on the New Hampshire side of the Connecticut river. Founded by Isaiah Thomas, who retained his interest in it, it gained its greatest fame under the same Joseph Dennie who later got into trouble for his attacks on democracy printed in the *Port Folio* during Jefferson's first administration. Dennie was so witty, critical, and readable that his paper was in demand all over the nation. It was actually a forerunner of the news magazine.

Other magazines at the end of the eighteenth century are now valuable sources of information for the historian. The *Columbian Magazine,* founded in 1786, was elaborately illustrated (with copperplate engravings), thus pointing the way to the picture magazine. Mathew Carey's *American Museum,* founded a year later, was the best-edited periodical of its day, according to Frank Luther Mott, the leading authority on magazine history in this country. It has been a mine of information on political, social, and economic history for students of the period. Some issues ran to more than a hundred pages.

The war with Britain ended in 1815, but magazines of that period continued to present views both favorable and unfavorable to the British. One of the anti-British publications was the *North American Review,* founded in 1815 under the auspices of the Anthology Club of Boston. It became a quarterly after three years as a bimonthly magazine and was published until 1914. After its first few years it became closely associated with Harvard. Jared Sparks and Edward Everett, foremost scholars of the day, were regular contributors. Although circulation was small, the magazine was read by thoughtful men and women who wielded influence in their communities.

NILES' WEEKLY
REGISTER

Mott estimates that several hundred quarterly, monthly, and weekly magazines were printed at one time or another in the first third of the nineteenth century. Most of them have long since been forgotten. One that deserves special mention, however, was *Niles' Weekly Register.* Edited by Hezekiah Niles, a printer with common sense, integrity, and a flare for concise reporting on current trends, the *Register* is known to every historian of the period. It was published in Baltimore, but was read in every state in the Union. The *Register* was the early nineteenth-century equivalent of the modern news magazine. Niles started his publication in 1811. There was a minimum of opinion in it at first. Most of the material was a weekly roundup of speeches, important documents, and statements of leaders everywhere concerning current problems. Niles was an objective journalist. He was conservative in his views but he was also honest in his evaluation of events. Thus, both sides of a controversy found space in the *Register,* and the material was indexed for ready reference, much to the delight of the later researchers. Its files were so important to historians that the entire publication has been reprinted, issue by issue, for libraries all over the world needing an authoritative chronicle of the first half of the nineteenth century (to 1849). Probably no day passes without some researcher digging into the information supplied with so much care and responsibility by Hezekiah Niles, a journalist who deserves the honorable recognition of his craft.

NOTES

1. Coleman was a great admirer of Burr and remained loyal even after Hamilton was killed by Burr in a duel in 1804. By that time the editor of the *Post* was expressing himself independently.

2. In 1804 the president helped Thomas Ritchie found the *Richmond Enquirer,* soon the most influential paper in Virginia. Ritchie was political boss of his state, and his views were therefore of significance throughout the South and were widely reprinted there.

3. From the *Letters.* The above is quoted from Saul K. Padover, *Thomas Jefferson on Democracy* (New York: Penguin, 1939), pp. 92–93. Copyright 1939, D. Appleton-Century Company, Inc. By permission of the publishers, Appleton-Century-Crofts, New York.

4. To Volney, 1802. New York Public Library, Manuscript II, 199, in Padover, *Jefferson,* p. 95.

5. Most of the newspaper figures and comments in this section are based on Clarence S. Brigham, *History and Bibliography of American Newspapers, 1690–1820,* 2 vols. (Worcester, Mass.: American Antiquarian Society, 1947).

6. Regulations such as this and the law requiring publication at state cost of letters uncalled for at the post office were also a means of rewarding pro-administration editors. As administrations changed, political rivals found ready-made organs of expression.

7. The Turner theory, first suggested by the Wisconsin historian in 1893 and elaborated by him and an entire school of historians, is explained in his own *The Significance of Sections in American History* (New York: Holt, Rinehart & Winston, 1933), in Walter Prescott Webb's *The Great Plains* (Boston: Ginn, 1931), and with a modified updating in Ray Billington's *America's Frontier Heritage* (New York: Holt, Rinehart & Winston, 1967). It is opposed in Henry Nash Smith's *The Virgin Land* (Cambridge, Mass.: Harvard University Press, 1950), by Fred A. Shannon in "Critiques of Research in the Social Sciences," *Social Science Research Council Bulletin,* No. 46 (New York: The Council, 1940), and by Louis M. Hacker in "Sections or Classes," *Nation,* CXXXVII (July 26, 1933), 108. For two well-balanced discussions of Turner's influence on American historiography see Richard Hofstadter, *The Progressive Historians: Turner, Beard, Parrington* (New York: Knopf, 1968) and John Higham, *Writing American History* (Bloomington: Indiana University Press, 1970). For a biography, see Ray A. Billington, *Frederick Jackson Turner* (New York: Oxford University Press, 1973).

8. Studies have shown that by no means all of the pioneers were of this type. It took some capital to head west, otherwise the slums would have been the reservoirs of the frontier society, which they were not. But dissatisfaction can take many forms, and the statement would appear to be true, in general.

9. Hofstadter, *The Progressive Historians,* p. 119.

10. Daniel J. Boorstin, *The Americans: The National Experience* (New York: Vintage Books, 1965), p. 54.

11. A useless victory, because the armies to be supplied by the Great Lakes route, such as Hull's command, were ineffective by the time Commodore Perry cleared the enemy from the lake.

12. The treaty was signed December 24, 1814. Jackson won his remarkable victory January 8, 1815. News of the battle reached Washington January 28; news of the treaty reached New York by ship February 11. As a result, many Americans believed that Jackson's victory had much to do with the successful negotiations.

13. One of Russell's many colorful phrases, which were widely quoted. Another had its birth in 1812, when a man named Gerry was governor. The Republican legislature of Massachusetts had divided a political district into a weird shape in order to gain voting power. According to one account, Gilbert Stuart called Russell's attention to the new district's resemblance to a salamander. "Better say a Gerrymander!" replied the Federalist editor, although in truth the governor had had no part in the original "gerrymandering."

14. See Elizabeth Gregory McPherson, "Reporting the Debates of Congress," *Quarterly Journal of Speech,* XXVIII (April 1942) pp. 141–48.

15. William E. Ames, "Federal Patronage and the Washington, D.C. Press," *Journalism Quarterly,* XLIX (Spring 1972), 22. See also his *History of the National Intelligencer* (Chapel Hill: University of North Carolina Press, 1972).

ANNOTATED BIBLIOGRAPHY

Books

ADAMS, HENRY, *History of the United States of America During the Administration of Thomas Jefferson.* New York: A. & C. Boni, 1930. The first two volumes of Adams' brilliant history; the next two cover the Madison administration. Adams' first six chapters magnificently portray the United States of 1800. The nine-volume work first appeared in 1889–91.

AMES, WILLIAM E., *A History of the National Intelligencer.* Chapel Hill: University of North Carolina Press, 1972. Intensive use of files, other documentary materials; covers Smith, Gales, Seaton, other editors of the outstanding paper. See also his "Samuel Harrison Smith Founds the *National Intelligencer,*" *Journalism Quarterly,* XLII (Summer 1965), 389, and "Federal Patronage and the Washington, D.C. Press," *Journalism Quarterly,* XLIX (Spring 1972), 22.

BARTLETT, RICHARD A., *The New Country: A Social History of the American Frontier, 1776–1890.* New York: Oxford University Press, 1974. Most recent work.

BOWERS, CLAUDE G., *Jefferson in Power.* Boston: Houghton Mifflin, 1936. A continuation of the author's *Jefferson and Hamilton.* Bowers uses newspaper sources heavily.

FORD, WORTHINGTON C., *Jefferson and the Newspaper, 1785–1830*. New York: Columbia University Press, 1936. Gives examples of how the great statesman regarded the journalists and their media.

LUXON, NORVAL NEIL, *Niles' Weekly Register*. Baton Rouge: Louisiana State University Press, 1947. This doctoral dissertation is the best available information on this influential publication.

MALONE, DUMAS, *Jefferson and His Time*. 5 vols. Boston: Little, Brown, 1962–75. Volume three, *Jefferson and the Ordeal of Liberty*, is followed by two on his presidential terms. Most ambitious of the Jefferson biographies.

MOTT, FRANK LUTHER, *History of American Magazines, 1741–1850*. New York: Macmillan, 1930. Volume one of a series by the outstanding authority on the subject. The author won a Pulitzer award for his study.

———, *Jefferson and the Press*. Baton Rouge: Louisiana State University Press, 1943. An excellent monograph.

NELSON, HAROLD L., ed., *Freedom of the Press from Hamilton to the Warren Court*. Indianapolis: Bobbs-Merrill, 1967. A collection of documents, cases, essays, with a lucid introduction by the editor summarizing press freedom trends since 1800.

PADOVER, SAUL K., *Thomas Jefferson on Democracy*. New York: Penguin, 1939. Excerpts from his letters and speeches. One section is concerned with the press.

PETERSON, MERRILL D., *Thomas Jefferson and the New Nation*. New York: Oxford University Press, 1970. Biography by a leading Jeffersonian scholar covering his entire life.

POLLARD, JAMES E., *The Presidents and the Press*. New York: Macmillan, 1947. Describes relationships of Jefferson, Madison, and Monroe with the press during this period.

William Winston Seaton. Boston: James R. Osgood and Company, 1871. The biography of the great Washington editor of the *National Intelligencer*, with notes of family and friends.

WOOD, JAMES PLAYSTED, *Magazines in the United States*. New York: Ronald Press, 1956. A study of the influence of magazines on American society.

Periodicals and Monographs

CLARK, CARLISLE, "The Old Corner Printing House," *Granite Monthly*, XXX (August 1901), 91. Describes the *Farmer's Weekly Museum*, started by Isaiah Thomas, and later a pioneer national magazine.

GLICKSBERG, CHARLES, "Bryant and the United States Review," *New England Quarterly*, VII (December 1934), 687. Describes early nineteenth-century periodicals.

LEE, ALFRED MCCLUNG, "Dunlap and Claypoole: Printers and News-Merchants of the Revolution," *Journalism Quarterly*, XI (June 1934), 160. The story of the men who founded the first successful American daily.

LYLE, CORNELIUS R., II, "New Hampshire's *Sentinel:* The Editorial Life of John Prentiss, 1799–1846," Ph.D. thesis, Northwestern University, 1972. The story of a weekly editor, first a Federalist, then a Whig.

MARTIN, BENJAMIN ELLIS, "Transition Period of the American Press—Leading Editors in This Century," *Magazine of American History*, XVII (April 1887), 273. Describes battles between Federalist and Republican journalists. Includes interesting facsimile examples of papers.

MURPHY, LAWRENCE W., "John Dunlap's 'Packet' and Its Competitors," *Journalism Quarterly*, XXVIII (Winter 1951), 58. The story of the struggle for survival among the first dailies.

PLASTERER, NICHOLAS N., "The Croswell Case: Paradox of History," *Journalism Quarterly*, XLIV (Spring 1967), 125. Argues that Croswell case deserves more attention than Zenger's.

TEETER, DWIGHT L., JR., "John Dunlap: The Political Economy of a Printer's Success," *Journalism Quarterly*, LII (Spring 1975), 3. Making of a fortune by the publisher of the *Pennsylvania Packet*.

ARGUS OF WESTERN AMERICA.

[Number 39.] FRANKFORT, KENTUCKY, WEDNESDAY, NOVEMBER 17, 1824. [Volume XVII.]

This pro-Jackson frontier paper was edited by Amos Kendall
and Francis P. Blair.

9

Coonskin Democracy and the Press

A country, like an individual, has dignity and power only in proportion as it is self-informed.

—William Ellery Channing

America in the 1820s was still largely rural, but industry was beginning to exert the influence that was to be so profoundly felt by society in the near future. All the new states followed the Vermont pattern in providing suffrage for all white males. After 1810, state after state in the East dropped restrictive voting qualifications, though not always peaceably. The enfranchisement of the common man was to bring about what amounted to a bloodless revolution, but in the 1820s the so-called "common man" was not yet fully aware of the new power he had won. Until 1828, federal administration of government was still largely by "gentlemen," like Madison, Monroe, and John Quincy Adams. Yet it was in this period that the pressures for popular sovereignty began to be exerted, and the press was to play an important role in this drama.

AN EXPANSION OF THE PRINTED WORD Indeed, the press was more and more counted on to supply the information, inspiration, agitation, and education of a society often unable to keep up with its need for schools. Newspapers, books, and magazines increased so fast in this period that presses could not meet the craving for such material. There were 375 printing offices in 1810. By 1825 there were three times as many. Between 1820 and 1830, publication of books alone increased 10 percent and still did not supply the need, for Americans continued to buy 70 percent of their books from European publishers. Despite this literary dependence on the Old World, Americans were offering every encouragement to journalist promoters. It is significant that by 1820 more than 50,000 titles, including books, magazines, and newspapers, were listed as American. Sale of such products increased by more than a million dollars in the decade beginning in 1820, when publications grossed about $2.5 million.[1]

True, much of this American material was extremely shallow and provincial. The *Port Folio,* one of the most literate of the magazines, rarely exceeded 2,000 subscribers. The authoritative *North American Review* had a normal circulation of about 3,000 copies. The biggest New York newspapers printed up to 4,000 copies an issue, but 1,500 to 2,500 was much more common. Only in the religious field was circulation impressive. The Methodist *Christian Journal and Advocate,* for example, had about 25,000 subscribers by its own estimate in 1826. But although circulations were small, popular publications were reaching more and more citizens, and their numbers increased yearly.

Unfortunately, most ordinary citizens could not afford to pay five or ten dollars a year in advance for such publications. The prevailing wage scale gave many workers only about eight dollars a week, which put virtually all magazines, and most newspapers, out of their reach. Even so, enough circulation reached the common man to give the United States the highest per capita newspaper readership in the world. In 1826, newspaper circulation in America exceeded that of Great Britain by more than three million annually. In 1810 there were 376 newspapers in the United States. By 1828, at the time of Jackson's election, there were nearly 900 (mainly weeklies). Nevertheless, what the nation needed was a newspaper press that could reach deeper into the population—first into the middle class, then to the workers.

In many communities, newspapers were the only literature available for the bulk of the citizenry. They served as the main educational device until other cultural institutions could take up the slack caused by rapid migrations. European visitors often did not realize the obstacles to cultural progress in such a new land. They sometimes failed to see that the United States was at a stage where rudimentary education fulfilled the needs of much of the population. What had Americans, other than Franklin, contributed to science, literature, the arts, or philosophy, Reverend Sydney Smith asked rhetorically in an article from the *Edinburgh Review* reprinted in an American newspaper. Actually, the United States was beginning to fill this vacuum. In the field of letters the country could offer Washington Irving, James Fenimore Cooper, William Cullen Bryant, Margaret Fuller, Nathaniel Hawthorne, and Ralph Waldo Emerson, all of whom would soon be recognized even in Europe.

JOHN MARSHALL'S COURT DECISIONS The trend toward a more enlightened age was noticeable by the end of the 1820s. By that time there were 49 colleges in the United States. The increase in endowed institutions of learning was appreciable after the decision of the Supreme Court in the Dartmouth College case of 1819. Until then, the trend had been toward state control of such educational establishments. The apathy of the philanthropist in supporting universities is therefore understandable. The Court held in the Dartmouth College case that a state had no right to change contracts, specifically, to make a private institution into a state university. Potential patrons of endowed education had hesitated to make donations to educational institutions threatened by state control.

The Dartmouth College decision was one of a series by which Chief Justice John Marshall guided the Supreme Court in establishing a philosophy of government. Two famous decisions, *McCulloch* v. *Maryland* (1819) and *Gibbons* v. *Ogden* (1824), asserted the supremacy of the national government over the states. Other decisions limited the states in their restriction of the rights of property-holders. They were indicative of the general attitude regarding the superiority of private controls. This was the heyday of unrestricted enterprise. The attitude on this subject is also reflected in the philosophies of Justice Joseph Story of Massachusetts, author of *Commentaries on the Constitution,* and of James (Chancellor) Kent of New York, who wrote *Commentaries on American Law*. The two eminent and influential jurists interpreted laws so as to make them fit the needs of an increasingly commercial nation. They had no sympathy for an extension of government regulation that might curb the individual businessman, but they were willing to let the government come to the help of the commercial interests when such aid was convenient.

This was what Senator Thomas Hart Benton of Missouri had in mind when he argued at the end of the decade that the "East," the symbol of business and banking, saw to it that western demands for the homestead laws were obstructed in order to maintain a cheap labor supply for the eastern businessman. Another instance of this philosophy in action was the passage of the tariff of 1828—the "tariff of abominations"—which protected the business promoter at the expense of other interests.

AMERICA OF THE 1820s   But this turn to the right had brought social and political strains. As the businessman assumed a more dominant place in federal control, and as he began to exert his influence to his own advantage, there was an equal and opposite reaction. It is significant that labor unions and a labor press emerge about this time. The cries of anguish over the "tariff of abominations," especially in the agrarian areas, were a prelude to the battle cries of the War Between the States. And yet, curiously, American writers had little to say about the forces shaping the destiny of our country at this time. We can learn more by reading the reports of foreign observers who visited our shores during the first 30 years of the century.

Many, such as Basil Hall and Mrs. Frances Trollope, were devastating in their contempt for American culture and materialism. Others, such as Harriet Martineau, a trained journalist with an understanding heart, saw through the American veneer. In between were reporters, such as Charles Dickens, who were generally severe but reasonably accurate.[2] They were appalled, for the most part, by American provincialism, unmindful that the American was preoccupied with hacking a nation from a wilderness. This complete absorption in the development of our own resources had resulted in a strong nationalism obnoxious to the foreign observer. Earlier visitors had confined their observations to the more sophisticated East, but the European reporters of the 1820-30s were more interested in the western regions. They were disgusted by the boastfulness, the smugness, superior attitudes, and ill-mannered ignorance of the type of American about to step into control of the government. Most of these observers carried home a great disdain for the American concept of popular rule. One who did not was the French observer, Alexis de Tocqueville, whose *Democracy in America* reflects his observations of 1831–32.

The full consequence of the industrial revolution in America was not apparent until a later date, but the trend was already started in the 1820s. The opening of the Erie Canal in 1825 was to make New York truly the "Empire State" and its metropolis one of the world's great commercial centers. In 1830, only about 7 percent of the people lived in cities, but the influence of industry was manifested by the obsession of political leaders with such problems as tariffs and the recognition of the working man's vote.

On the whole, the new class emerging out of the industrial revolution was at first inarticulate. The so-called "common man" appeared to be unaware of his new power.

But as early as 1820 there was the beginning of populist revolt in Massachusetts, where workers were insisting upon a greater voice in government. New York experienced the same thing in 1821. In Rhode Island, where the worker was less successful at first, pressure built up into actual violence (Dorr's Rebellion), although the denouement dragged out into a later period. The issue was the rights of property versus the rights of the individual. The mechanic, as the urban worker was called at that time, resented exploitation by what he believed to be a privileged class. He resented being paid in wildcat banknotes that sometimes depreciated to less than half of his contracted wage. It is significant that in 1829 about 75,000 men were jailed for debt. More than half of these victims owed less than $20. Conditions of labor, especially for women and children, brought out a long line of social reformers who insisted on protective legislation.

Slowly the common man began to realize his power at the polls. In 1824, only six states still chose presidential electors through the legislators, heretofore the frequent tools of the property group. By 1832, only South Carolina maintained this system, and it was in that year that the party convention took at least some of the power away from "King Caucus"—the selection of candidates by secret conclave of political leaders.

THE JACKSONIAN REVOLUTION   By 1824 a realignment in American politics was well under way. A financial panic in 1819 had brought distress to speculators and debtors in the South and West, where the Bank of the United States became a great absentee landlord through foreclosures. Those affected saw politics as a way out, if they could get relief laws and new public land and tariff policies and make war on the older money interests of the East, typified by the national bank. But presidential politics were fragmented in 1824, and party lines were blurred. Andrew Jackson, military hero and westerner, led in the small popular vote and had the largest electoral total, but not a majority. John Quincy Adams, typifying the Federalist elitist tradition, ran a strong second. Henry Clay threw his support to Adams in the balloting in the House of Representatives; when Adams named Clay as secretary of state, Jackson labeled it a "deal" and began campaigning as a Democrat for 1828.

In his strongholds in the South and West, Jackson appeared to be one of their kind: a militant nationalist who could handle the Indian, a natural enemy of the older eastern money power, and a champion of egalitarianism, particularly a symbol of equal access to office. As Richard Hofstadter puts it, "So far as he can be said to have had a popular mandate, it was to be different from what the people imagined Adams had been and to give expression to their unformulated wishes and aspirations."[3] Like all victors in political revolutions, Jackson was bound to disappoint some of the groups who supported him. The growing support for the Jacksonian Democratic party in the East included many of the workers and immigrants, but it also counted some of the skilled craftsmen and small and large tradesmen and merchants who were more immediate beneficiaries of the democratization of politics. Shifting trends in transportation and manufacturing had also created a democratization of business; the new entrepreneurs and capitalists were sometimes alienated by the older money power and its symbolic political strength in Federalism and Adams. The unfortunate Adams was painted as an intellectual snob, aristocrat, and defender of the old order—images that won votes both West and East for Jackson.

But Jackson clearly began as the candidate of the South and West; only later did the Jacksonian Democrats make a temporary inroad in the East. In 1828 Jackson won 56 percent of the popular vote and defeated Adams 178 to 83 in the electoral college. But Jackson won only Pennsylvania and New York in the East, while Adams won only

Maryland and Delaware in the South and West. In 1832 Jackson added Maine, New Hampshire, and New Jersey to his eastern total while holding onto 54 percent of the popular vote against a weak Whig candidate, Henry Clay—who carried only his home state of Kentucky in the West. Martin Van Buren, Jackson's astute political manager from the East, won all that area except Massachusetts and New Jersey as the 1836 Democratic candidate against three Whig rivals. But when the Whigs united behind a western military hero, William Henry Harrison, in 1840, against a depression-plagued Van Buren, the Jacksonian party coalition was shattered. Van Buren held onto only New Hampshire and Illinois in the East and West and five southern states. Polk in 1844 and Pierce in 1852 won the East as Democrats but against extremely weak Whig opponents.

The Whigs had three problems to face, Louis Hartz points out: the absence of an aristocracy to fight, the absence of an aristocracy to ally with, and the absence of a mob to denounce (although they tried this when Jackson's western friends trod White House floors in muddy boots). The capitalist Whiggery of Hamilton was frightened of democracy, and the democratic tradition of Jackson was therefore able to destroy it, thereby seeming to deny its faith in capitalism. In reality, Hartz believes, Jacksonian democracy promoted a democratic-based capitalism and the Jacksonian revolution was a middle class revolution insofar as political impact was concerned.[4]

Amos Kendall, the West's contribution to the Jacksonian leadership, saw the conflict differently. He described it as a fight between the "producing" classes of farmers, laborers, and craftsmen and the "nonproducing" capitalist, middleman, and landlord. Although outnumbered, this nonproducing class remained dominant through control of banks, education, most of the churches, and the bulk of the press. Thus, Kendall pointed out, "those who produce all the wealth are themselves left poor."[5] This was "radical" thinking, well to the left of that of Van Buren, the East's leader in the Jackson camp.

The Whig party was just as far to the right in its thinking. The sanctity of property was explained very comfortably by the ultra-Whig *American Quarterly Review,* published in Philadelphia, which reported just after the end of the decade: "The lowest orders of society ordinarily mean the poorest—and the highest the richest. Sensual excess, want of intelligence, and moral debasement distinguish the former—knowledge, intellectual superiority, and refined, social and domestic affections the latter." As the Pulitzer Prize historian of this period remarks: "Property, in [Whig] reflexes, became almost identified with character." Nicholas Biddle, who as head of the powerful Second Bank of the United States, believed he was the leader of a class too strong for any attempted restraint by the Jacksonians, smugly summed up the opposition Democrats as a party made up of "men with no property to assess and no character to lose."[6]

The pompous Biddle was utterly astounded when, in the summer of 1832, Jackson vetoed a bill for rechartering the Bank of the United States. "Biddled, diddled, and undone," Charles Gordon Greene of the *Boston Post* wrote of Jackson's veto. In his veto message Jackson paid respects to the farmers, mechanics, and laborers who were seeking protection against governmental injustices, but he also declared that government should provide equal protection for both high and low, rich and poor—something with which the new entrepreneurs could agree. Unfortunately for Jackson and his party, the destruction of Biddle's bank opened the door to poor fiscal policies, wildcat banking, and inflation. By 1837 both rich and poor were victims of a "panic" of major proportions. Van Buren, rather than Old Hickory, caught the blame. But, all told, Jackson deserves having his name attached to an "era" of political reform, expanded economic opportunity, better schools, a growing literature, and a popular press. Its keynote was faith in the common man.

FIRST LABOR PAPERS   A direct result of the industrial revolution and the growing need for recognition of a new type of citizen was the development of the labor press. A depression during the icy winter of 1828–29 and the rising cost of living fostered the beginning of a labor revolt long overdue. The appearance of the first labor paper in 1827—the *Journeyman Mechanic's Advocate* of Philadelphia—was a clear signal that the laboring man intended to fight for his advantage, as the property man had long fought for his. The first labor paper lasted only a year. The times were too difficult for workers to provide sufficient support. It was a significant "first," however, for in conjunction with the success of the populists at the polls in 1828, the attempt of labor to express itself was prophetic. Two months before Jackson's election, the first working man's party was organized. It was sponsored by the Mechanic's Union of Trade Associations. In the same year the *Mechanic's Free Press* was established as the first successful labor newspaper. Until the depression of 1837 killed it, the *Free Press* had an average weekly circulation of around 1,500—very good for a period when even the biggest New York dailies rarely exceeded 4,000.

In many ways, the early labor papers were superior to modern labor organs. Their functions were primarily to counteract prejudices against the working man, to supply labor information that the commercial press ignored, and to offer inspiration to the dispirited. The *Free Press* actually had much less propaganda and biased reporting

The militant Fanny Wright is denounced by the conservative *Courier and Enquirer*.

than would be found in the typical modern labor paper. It offered thoughtful articles on pertinent legislation. The reports were concise, reasonably factual for the times, and well written.

This agitation led to the organization of the first national labor association—the National Trades Union, founded in 1834. A strong supporter of the labor organization movement was the *Working Man's Advocate,* founded in New York in 1829 by George H. Evans, an English printer. Another important publication supporting labor's cause (along with other social issues) was the *Free Enquirer,* edited in New York by the charming and talented Frances "Fanny" Wright. Fanny Wright, who came to the United States from Scotland in 1818, became a power in the New Harmony utopian experiment conducted by Robert Dale Owen. She had helped put out the *New Harmony Gazette,* published in New York from 1829 as the *Free Enquirer.* Among Miss Wright's many admirers was a young carpenter who was a great believer in democracy, and whose poems began to sing of the people. The poet was Walt Whitman, himself a journalist a little later.

Most of the standard newspapers had scant regard for this labor movement, but one or two helped the cause. William Cullen Bryant, the poet and editor of the *New York Evening Post,* pleaded the case of the working man. The stand of the *Post* indicated how far it had veered since its establishment by the father of Federalism, Alexander Hamilton. Bryant had been employed in 1825 by Coleman, the militant Federalist editor of the paper. Four years later Bryant was in full charge of the *Post,* and remained with the paper, except for a few lapses, for half a century. Under Bryant, the *Post* cast off much of its Federalist tradition. On many issues the paper sided with the Jacksonian Democrats. Thus, denouncing what it believed to be an unjust verdict against a "criminal conspiracy" (strike) by the Society of Journeyman Tailors, the *Post* said:

> They were condemned because they determined not to work for the wages offered them . . . If this is not SLAVERY, we have forgotten its definition. Strike the right of associating for the sale of labour from the privileges of a freeman, and you may as well at once bind him to a master.[7]

William Leggett, part owner of the *Post,* and interim editor after Bryant went abroad in 1834, was even more pro-labor than was Bryant. He was so outspoken, indeed, that the more temperate Bryant had to cool him down on occasion. Later, as we shall see, the cause of the working man was taken up by another famous editor, Horace Greeley. There were magazines, too, fighting for labor during this period. One was the *Democratic Review,* edited by the fiery John L. O'Sullivan. Despite these editorial champions of the underprivileged, the press in general took a dim view of the labor movement.

KENDALL AND BLAIR: THE *WASHINGTON GLOBE*   Equally obnoxious to the Whigs was the "Kitchen Cabinet" of the president. Some of the most influential members of this inner circle were journalists. Duff Green, the editor of the party paper in Washington, was one of the cronies until his endorsement of Calhoun lost him Jackson's support. Isaac Hill, the crippled, rebellious, and vituperative New Hampshire editor, was another intimate of the president. The two most important powers behind the party, however, were Amos Kendall and Francis Preston Blair.

Amos Kendall was the most important member of the group. Reared on a New England farm, he was too frail for such rugged work. He had a passion for scholarship, and his family recognized this bent. After he was graduated from Dartmouth College, Kendall headed for the frontier, where opportunities were better for inexperienced lawyers. He hung out his shingle in Kentucky.

As a lawyer, Kendall easily turned his energies to politics. He was a protégé of a regional political chieftain, Colonel Richard M. Johnson, who insisted that the erudite New Englander take over the editorship of the Democratic party organ. The newspaper was the *Argus of Western America,* published at Frankfort. Kendall made it the party voice of the entire region. His position was achieved not without great risk, politically as well as physically. For a time he carried a pistol and a bowie knife for protection against those he had scorched in his *Argus* articles. An able, honest, and articulate journalist, his fame as a party spokesman eventually came to the attention of the party's supreme commander, General Jackson. Kendall fought courageously for the debtor's relief system that split Kentucky wide open during Adams's administration. After the voters of Kentucky were cheated of their victory in the "Relief War," he put all his energies into the election of Jackson and came to Washington.

Perhaps their physical ills gave them a common bond. The president was old and full of the miseries. Kendall was something of a hypochondriac, but he had always been frail, so perhaps his attitude was justified. At any rate, there was a strong bond between the two men. Jackson was not a polished writer, and he was happy to have Kendall edit his important statements. Time and again Kendall took down the dictation of the wan warrior. Jackson would lie on a faded sofa beneath the portrait of his beloved Rachel, while Kendall skillfully interpreted his chief's rough ideas and put them into presentable form. Jackson spoke forcefully, but there was too much of the western uncouthness in his diction. Kendall would smooth away the crudeness and read back the paragraph to the president. Perhaps they would have to try again, but eventually the old general would nod approval. Kendall was often surprised at the effectiveness of the speech as it appeared in print.

When Jackson first moved into the White House, the administration organ at Washington was the *United States Telegraph,* founded in 1826.[8] Duff Green was editor of the paper. He had worked hard to elect Jackson, but his other hero was John C. Calhoun, Jackson's party rival. The split in loyalty cost Green the support of the president. The Jacksonian faction decided to make Francis P. Blair Green's successor. Blair had taken over the editorship of the *Argus* after Kendall went to Washington. He had proved to be a very able journalist, but he had to be cleared of $40,000 in debts before he could accept the Washington proposal.

Blair's paper, the *Washington Globe,* appeared at the end of 1830. By that time Jackson and Blair were on the best of terms. "Give it to Bla-ar," the president used to say when he had a particularly trenchant statement requiring journalistic finesse. From Blair's pencil, on scraps of paper held on his knee, came the fighting editorials that helped to knit the party even closer. In 1832, John C. Rives became Blair's assistant. Rives, a shaggy giant, quite in contrast to his colorless associates, also came to enjoy the confidences of the inner guard.

But Kendall was the most important of them all. As one of Jackson's rivals put it, Kendall was ". . . the President's *thinking* machine, and his *writing* machine—ay, and his *lying* machine. . . . He was chief overseer, chief reporter, amanuensis, scribe, accountant general, man of all work—nothing was well done without the aid of his diabolical genius."[9] And ex-President Adams, not given to exaggeration, once stated of Van Buren and Jackson, "Both . . . have been for twelve years the tool of Amos Kendall, the ruling mind of their dominion." Kendall became postmaster general in 1835.

INVENTIONS
FOR A PEOPLE'S PRESS

But where were the publications for the masses? Surely all this democratic ferment must have had its consequences in developing a newspaper the man in the street could afford and enjoy. As a matter of fact, the same forces that brought about the emergence of the common man also accounted for the establishment of a people's press. The industrial revolution, which resulted in cheaper goods, also made it possible to produce a cheaper paper. All the social pressures mentioned in the preceding pages shared in making possible the newspaper for the masses. There was a vast, untapped public tempting the promoter, if only the product could be made attractive. And by 1833, the technical progress had reached the point where this was possible.

In 1822, Peter Smith, connected with R. Hoe and Company, printing-press makers, invented a hand press with a much faster lever action. Five years later Samuel Rust of New York put out the Washington hand press, still seen in some offices. It had many automatic devices—a platen raised and lowered by springs; an ingenious toggle device for quick impressions; a faster-moving bed; and later, automatic ink rollers.

The next step was to harness power to the press. This was the Age of Steam, and at once inventors set themselves to the problem. Daniel Treadwell of Boston had partial success in 1822. A steam book press was developed by Isaac Adams of Boston in 1830 and was popular for many years, but it was a European who perfected the process for speedy power printing. He was Friedrich Koenig of Saxony, who after many delays produced the first of his presses in London in 1811. It had a movable bed

An American adaptation of Koenig's power press.

that carried the type back and forth to be inked after each impression. Paper was fed into the top of a cylinder. Three years later Koenig invented a two-cylinder press that printed both sides of the paper—the so-called "perfecting press." The *Times* of London was the first to use this press for newspaper work late in 1814. The paper proudly stated that it could outstrip all rivals by printing papers at the unbelievable rate of 1,100 an hour.

In 1830 David Napier of England perfected the Koenig steam press and tripled the speed of printing. America's R. Hoe and Company, which was to become a by-word in newspaper plants, chose the Napier press as the prototype of a new product for American printers. The new Hoe was actually a great improvement over the Napier, and it was able to produce 4,000 double impressions an hour. Such technical progress was essential to the production of a cheap paper that the masses could afford to buy.

By 1833 all the ingredients were available for the establishment of such a venture. It was possible to print a paper that would sell for one cent, in contrast to the six cents charged by the average commercial dailies. To a workman, six cents was the equivalent of a quarter-pound of bacon or a pint of local whisky. In England, Henry Hetherington had published two periodicals for the masses. He failed, not because of the price he charged but because he was caught evading the so-called "taxes on knowledge," which kept the price of British newspapers out of the hands of the common man, as intended. John Wight, the Bow Street police reporter, had also demonstrated by 1820 the type of news that would make the presses for the masses successful.

In 1829, Seba Smith founded a daily paper at Portland, Maine, that was smaller than a standard newspaper but cheaper by half than the usual daily. It cost four dollars a year, payable in advance. A year later, Lynde M. Walter, a Boston brahmin, bought an existing paper and made it into the daily *Transcript,* offered at four dollars a year. More popular because it offered spicier items, perhaps, was the *Boston Morning Post,* founded as a four-dollar daily by Charles G. Greene in 1831. Two years later Captain John S. Sleeper founded the *Boston Mercantile Journal,* offered at the same price. All were successful, but they were sold by subscription, which took them out of the reach of the usual worker, who could not pay a lump sum in advance.

In Philadelphia, Dr. Christopher Columbus Conwell established a penny paper, *The Cent,* in 1830. Although interesting as a forerunner of the press for the masses, it survived such a short time that it is of little significance to the present summary. A serious and nearly successful attempt to put out a genuine penny paper for the masses, to be sold by the issue and not entirely by subscription, was made by Horace Greeley in partnership with Dr. H. D. Shepard, a dentist, in January 1833. This was the *New York Morning Post.* A violent snow storm kept so many citizens indoors the first few days of its appearance that the promoters had to give up the venture.

The time was ripe for a successful penny paper, however. Indeed, the next attempt to produce a penny paper was to bring such a significant change to American journalism as to warrant the description "revolutionary."

NOTES

1. Merle Curti, *The Growth of American Thought* (New York: Harper & Row, 1943). p. 215.
2. See Godfrey T. Vique, "Six Months in America"; Thomas Hamilton, "Men and Manners in America"; Harriet Martineau, "Society in America"; reprinted in Allan Nevins, ed., *American Social History* (New York: Holt, Rinehart & Winston, 1923).

3. Richard Hofstadter, *The American Political Tradition* (New York: Vintage Books, 1948), p. 55.
4. Louis Hartz, *The Liberal Tradition in America* (New York: Harcourt Brace Jovanovich, 1955), p. 89.
5. Arthur M. Schlesinger, Jr., *The Age of Jackson* (Boston: Little, Brown, 1945), p. 306.
6. All quoted from ibid., p. 14.
7. *New York Evening Post,* June 13, 1836.
8. The *electric* telegraph had not been invented at that time. The name probably derived from the semaphore signal.
9. Schlesinger, *The Age of Jackson,* p. 73.

ANNOTATED BIBLIOGRAPHY

Books

BROOKS, VAN WYCK, *The World of Washington Irving.* New York: Dutton, 1944. An interpretation of the period through the literary contributions of American writers.

BROWN, CHARLES H., *William Cullen Bryant.* New York: Scribner's, 1971. A comprehensive study of the editor of the *New York Evening Post.*

Cambridge History of American Literature, II. New York: G. P. Putnam's Sons, 1917–21. Pages 160–75 describe magazines during 1783–1850; pages 176–95 describe the general newspaper picture from 1775 to 1860. Book publishing is surveyed in Volume 4 (pp. 533–53).

FISH, CARL RUSSELL, *The Rise of the Common Man, 1830–1850,* A History of American Life, Vol. VI. New York: Macmillan, 1927. Social history.

FORSYTH, DAVID P., *The Business Press in America, 1760–1865.* Philadelphia: Chilton, 1964. A prize-winning history of business journalism.

GABRIEL, RALPH H., *The Course of American Democratic Thought.* New York: Ronald Press, 1956. Intellectual history since 1815.

SCHLESINGER, ARTHUR M., JR., *The Age of Jackson.* Boston: Little, Brown, 1945. A penetrating study of the political background by a Pulitzer Prize winner. Includes a chapter on the press. See also Glyndon G. Van Deusen, *The Jacksonian Era.* New York: Harper & Row, 1959; and Edward Pessen, *Jacksonian America* (New York: Dorsey, 1969), whose revisionist study counters Schlesinger.

TOCQUEVILLE, ALEXIS DE, *Democracy in America.* New York: Doubleday, 1969. Editions have been appearing since 1835 of this famous French observer's study of American democracy and its effect on the social system.

TYLER, ALICE FELT, *Freedom's Ferment: Phases of American Social History to 1860.* Minneapolis: University of Minnesota Press, 1944. Emphasizes effects of religious and reform movements.

WELTER, RUSH, *The Mind of America, 1820–1860.* New York: Columbia University Press, 1975. Emphasis is on commonly shared attitudes. See also Russel B. Nye, *Society and Culture in the United States, 1830–1860* (New York: Harper & Row-Torch, 1974).

Periodicals and Monographs

HAGE, GEORGE S., "Anti-Intellectualism in Press Comment: 1828 and 1952," *Journalism Quarterly,* XXXVI (Fall 1959), 439. Comparison of newspaper content in two presidential elections. A full study is in his doctoral dissertation, "Anti-Intellectualism in Newspaper Comment in the Elections of 1828 and 1952," University of Minnesota, 1957.

MILLER, ALAN R., "America's First Political Satirist: Seba Smith of Maine," *Journalism Quarterly,* XLVII (Autumn 1970), 488. The creator of Major Jack Downing at the *Portland Courier.*

SINGLETARY, MICHAEL W., "The New Editorial Voice for Andrew Jackson: Happenstance or Plan?," *Journalism Quarterly,* LIII (Winter 1976), 672. Blair.

SMITH, WILLIAM E., "Francis P. Blair, Pen-Executive of Andrew Jackson," *Mississippi Valley Historical Review,* XVII (March 1931). 459. A vivid portrait of the *Washington Globe* and its editor. Reprinted in Ford and Emery, *Highlights in the History of the American Press.*

James Gordon Bennett of the *Herald*

Horace Greeley of the *Tribune*

10
A Press for the Masses

But the world does move, and its motive power under God is the fearless thought and speech of those who dare to be in advance of their time—who are sneered at and shunned through their days of struggle as lunatics, dreamers, impracticables, and visionaries; men of crotchets, vagaries, and isms. They are the masts and sails of the ship to which conservatism answers as ballast. The ballast is important —at times indispensable—but it would be of no account if the ship were not bound to go ahead.

—Horace Greeley

Whenever a mass of people has been neglected too long by the established organs of communication, agencies eventually have been devised to supply that want. Invariably this press of the masses is greeted with scorn by the sophisticated reader because the content of such a press is likely to be elemental and emotional. Such scorn is not always deserved. Just as the child ordinarily starts his reading with Mother Goose and fairy stories before graduating to more serious study, so the public first reached by a new agency is likely to prefer what the critics like to call "sensationalism," which is the emphasis on emotion for its own sake. This pattern can be seen in the periods when the most noteworthy developments in popular journalism were apparent. In 1620, 1833, the 1890s, or 1920, this tapping of a new, much-neglected public started with a wave of sensationalism.

The phenomenon is clearly exhibited in the period of the 1830s and 1840s covered by this chapter. For it was in 1833 that the first successful penny newspaper tapped a reservoir of readers collectively designated "the common man." The first offerings of this poor man's newspaper tended to be highly sensational. This was only a developmental phase, however. Very quickly the penny newspapers began to attract readers from other social and economic brackets. And the common man, as his literacy skill improved, also demanded a better product. Within a decade after the appearance of the first penny paper, the press of the common man included respectable publications that offered significant information and leadership.

Before the appearance of the penny papers, publishers charged from six to ten dollars a year in advance for a newspaper subscription. That was more than most skilled workmen earned in a week, and in any case, the man of limited means could not

119

pay that much in a lump sum. The standard newspapers usually were edited for people of means, and that partially accounted for the preponderance of conservatism in the press. It also was a factor in keeping circulations small, although mechanical limitations certainly had a similar effect. In 1833 the largest dailies in New York were the morning *Courier and Enquirer,* published by the colorful and irascible Colonel James Watson Webb, and the *Journal of Commerce,* founded by Arthur Tappan in 1827 but soon taken over by Gerard Hallock and David Hale.[1] The largest afternoon paper was William Cullen Bryant's *Post.* These and the other eight city papers sold for six cents a copy, and most of them were distributed by subscription, rather than by the street sale that was to characterize the penny press.

DAY'S *NEW YORK SUN,* 1833   Journalism began a new epoch on September 3, 1833, with the appearance of a strange little newspaper, the *New York Sun* ("It Shines for ALL"). Its founder was Benjamin H. Day, who arrived in New York as a lad of 20 after an apprenticeship on Massachusetts' excellent *Springfield Republican.* That was in 1831. For two years he operated a printing shop without much success; there were financial disturbances, and in 1832 a plague further cut into the city's prosperity. In desperation, Day decided to publish a paper in an effort to take up some of the slack in his declining job-printing business. He had watched the early attempts to establish penny papers in Boston, Philadelphia, and New York, and it appeared to him that such a publication would be successful if it could be sold and financed on a per-issue basis. He discussed the proposal with two friends, Arunah S. Abell and William M. Swain. They warned him against the undertaking, a bit of advice they had to eat sometime later when they founded their own successful penny papers in Philadelphia and Baltimore. Day went ahead with his plans anyway.

The appearance of the *Sun* that September day did not give the impression that it would soon outshine all rivals in circulation.[2] It was printed on four pages, each about two-thirds the area of the modern tabloid page. The front page was three columns wide and devoid of any display devices. Emphasis was on local happenings and news of violence. Most of the material was trivial, flippant—but highly readable. Most important, it was cheap. Within six months the *Sun* had a circulation of around 8,000, nearly twice that of its nearest rival.

The reporting of George Wisner accounted for some of this success. Remembering the popularity of the Bow Street police-station news in the London forerunners of the penny press, Day hired Wisner, a Bow Street veteran, to write for the *Sun.* He was an instant success. Wisner received four dollars a week for covering the courts, plus a share of the profits of the paper. Within a year he had become co-owner of the paper.

"Human interest" news was a specialty of the *Sun.* Here is a sample of the *Sun* technique taken from a typical issue after the paper was firmly established:

Some six years ago a young gentleman, the oldest son of a distinguished baronet in England, after completing his course in education, returned home to pay his respects to his parents, and to participate in the pleasures of their social circle.[3]

The account goes on to describe how the handsome youth fell in love with a girl his father had adopted as a ward. Eventually the couple ran off together because such marriages were forbidden, and the scion was disinherited by the angry baron. On the death of the father, however, the son was declared heir to the title. A younger son tried to wrest the estate by charging his elder brother with incest. This part of the story fills all of the *Sun's* first page for that day. No names are used. It could have been complete fabrication, except that the word "recent" is used to give a news flavor to the piece. The fate of the heir is never determined, although the account is embellished:

> ... And while our hero was unsuspiciously reposing on the soft bosom of his bride, a brother's hand, impelled by a brother's hate, was uplifted with fratricidal fierceness for destruction.

A half column on the following page headed "Shocking Accident" described how a 19-year-old New Hampshire youth had been buried alive in a well cave-in. This had been picked out of the exchanges, apparently because of the twist to the story. It seems the poor chap was to have been wed the following week, which was the type of tear-jerker the *Sun* editors loved. There was humor of a sort mixed up in all this rubbish. Under a standing head, "Police Office—Yesterday," there was an item about the night watch being called to foil a desperate jail break, only to find that a pet squirrel in a cage was the source of the suspicious riot sounds. A Negro woman before the police magistrate made a whimsical remark based on the confusion of the words "prosecute" and "prostitute." All good, rich fare for the sensation-hungry *Sun* reader.

The only concession to the commercial interests of the community in this typical issue was a column of shipping news on the third page. Obviously, the paper was not printed for the property class. And yet anyone could see that the paper was bringing in plenty of advertising revenue. The back page was solid advertising, and about half the third page was devoted to classified notices, including "Want Ads." Even page one contained advertising, such as the one about Robert Hoe and Son, the printing-press maker at 29 Gold Street, who had just installed a new cylinder press for the *Sun* that was the fastest in the city—1,500 complete papers an hour.

A PENNY PRESS FOR THE COMMON MAN

The appearance of the penny press and the rise of the common man were closely integrated. The newspaper for the masses arrived just as the labor class began to win recognition under the Jacksonian democracy. Politics for the masses had some of the flaws corresponding to the faults of the factory system. Too often majority rule encouraged the spoils system, bossism, and mediocrity in government. Too often the early penny papers provoked criticism in striving to reach the public by lowering standards. The *Sun,* for example, was ready to sacrifice truth if that would bring in more customers. The fact is, it nearly trebled in circulation in 1835 when one of its reporters, a descendant of John Locke, the political philosopher, wrote a series of articles purporting to describe life on the moon. The so-called "moon hoax" of Richard Adams Locke may not have increased public confidence in the paper, but readers did not appear to resent the journalistic trick that had been played on them.

And yet there was much that was revealed as good in the sunrise of a new journalism, despite all the vulgarity, cheapness, and spuriousness of the first penny paper. The *Sun* was a recognition of the common man on the communications level. The working man had already won the right to vote. Now the penny papers could reach out to him as no other medium could. It did not take the politician long to discover this fact. The student of journalism will look in vain for any profound expressions of political philosophy in the early editions of the penny press, but after the first wave of sensationalism, the editors of these publications began to offer information of a more significant type. At the same time, readers began to show a little more interest in the government they had the power to control.

But of course it took a little time to win them away from the outright emotionalism with which they had been lured into the journalistic fold. Even in later stages of his development the common man showed little interest in the complicated and erudite opinions comprising the main fare of the orthodox press. The newly recognized public was more interested in *news* than in *views*. The penny papers concentrated on supplying this type of intelligence in readable form. The *Sun* and its galaxy of imitators proved that news was a valuable commodity, if delivered in a sprightly manner.

Another person began to take a special interest in the newspaper for the masses. This was the advertiser, who was impressed by the amazing circulations of the new medium. Putting an ad in every publication bought by small splinter groups was expensive and ineffective sales promotion. The large circulations of the penny papers now made it feasible to publicize articles for sale that formerly would not have warranted advertising expense. The first advertising agency man, Volney B. Palmer, who opened shop in 1849 as middleman between the papers and businessmen, soon had offices in several cities.

On the other hand, advertising revenue made it possible for editors and publishers to expand and to experiment with new methods of news gathering. Since advertising flowed to the circulation leaders, and since news appeared to be the most popular type of literature, publishers began to invest heavily in various devices for improving news coverage. The full scope of this development will be described in the next chapter, but the relation between advertising and the penny press deserves mention at this point. As publishers began to understand the technique of obtaining mass circulations, they had to have better presses. Moses Y. Beach, Ben Day's brother-in-law, who took over the *Sun* in 1837, used part of his profits to buy a new steam-driven Hoe cylinder press capable of producing 4,000 papers an hour. It was the most advanced printing equipment of its day.

The penny papers also brought changes in distribution methods. Commercial and standard newspapers had been sold on the subscription basis. Workmen not only could not pay a large sum in advance, but many also moved around too much to subscribe regularly. There were times when the worker could not read at all because of his job, or because of his poverty. The penny papers reached such readers by depending primarily on street sales, under the so-called "London Plan." Vendors bought the papers from the publisher at the rate of a hundred copies for 67 cents, to be sold for one cent each. This put a premium on individual initiative, as indicated by the shrill cries of the vendors on street corners. The distribution system also inevitably changed the appearance of the paper, as editors tried to lure readers from rival publications through the use of better makeup and more readable type.

The raw product of the press was also changed by the newspaper of the masses. When the *views*paper became a *news*paper, the style of the writer also changed. Editors were less interested in opinion and were more concerned with reporting straight news. This was less a development toward objectivity than it was a shift away from political partisanship.

BENNETT'S *NEW YORK HERALD*, 1835   One of the most successful promoters of a newspaper cutting through the partisanship of the times was James Gordon Bennett.[4] Bennett was strictly a reporter and editor, in contrast to the printer-publishers who have figured so prominently in this history. He had gained valuable experience as a Washington correspondent, which was to stand him in good stead when he began to develop national news as a commodity. As editor for Colonel James Watson Webb, he had engineered the 1829 merger of the *Courier* and the *Enquirer,* to make it the largest newspaper in New York. Twice he had tried to found a paper of his own, but without success. The newspaper he produced on the morning of May 6, 1835, changed this picture.

Bennett was 40 years old, disillusioned, and deep in debt when he founded the *New York Morning Herald.* His capital was only $500; he also had some credit from his printers. His office was a cellar in the basement of a building at 20 Wall Street. Equipment consisted of a desk made from a plank spanning two dry goods boxes, a secondhand chair, and a box for files. His entire staff consisted of himself. On this basis Bennett built one of the most profitable newspaper properties of his time.

There was a month's delay after the first appearance of the *Herald,* but from June 1835, the paper boomed. The *Herald* was an imitator of the *Sun* in using sensational material, but Bennett added many tricks of his own. When it came to crime reporting the *Herald* knew no equal. The issue of June 4, 1836, a year after regular publication of the paper, showed the typical *Herald* treatment of such news. The whole front page, unrelieved by headlines, was devoted to the Robinson-Jewett case. This involved the murder of a prostitute in a brothel by a notorious man-about-town, and Bennett gave the sordid murder all the resources of his paper. He stirred up so much interest in the case that the court could not continue hearing testimony when the defendant was up for trial. The tone of *Herald* reporting is indicated by this "precede" to the main story of the trial and the disturbances in the court room:

> The mayor—the sheriff, all endeavored to restore order—all in vain. A terrible rain storm raged out doors—a mob storm indoors. The Judges and the Officers left the hall. Robinson was carried out of court, and the Public Authorities were trying to clear the hall of the mob, when this extra went to press.
> Why is not the militia called?
> We give the additional testimony up to the latest hour. . . . The mystery of the bloody drama increases—increases—increases.[5]

The "extra" feature of this news coverage (an "extra" is a special edition) was typical of Bennett's aggressive style of journalism. Soon this type of news treatment gave way to an increasing interest in more significant news. Bennett himself had no qualms about using violent news, for he was certain his paper was getting better every day. He got out of the penny-paper category in the summer of 1836 and defended his policy by stating that his readers were getting more for their money—the new price was two cents—than they could get anywhere else.

Year by year the *Herald* branched out into other fields of journalism. The paper appealed to the business class by developing the best financial section of any standard journal. Bennett, a former teacher of economics, wrote what he called the "money page." He had had experience in such reporting, and he took a special interest in this phase of journalism. When administrative duties at last forced him to give up this work, he saw to it that his best staff men were assigned to the Wall Street run. In the meantime, he was offering more serious background material than his rivals on the *Sun.* His editorial comment was seldom profound, but it was decisive, reasoned, and informative. The *Herald* led the pack in hounding news from all areas, local, foreign, and national, as we shall see in the next chapter. Bennett built up an interesting "letters" column, where readers could comment on the paper as well as events. He helped develop the critical review column and society news. Long before other editors recognized the appeal of the subject, Bennett was offering sports news. Thus it was all along. The great contribution of the *Herald* was as an innovator and perfecter.

One of Bennett's most famous front pages, using 1845 woodcuts.

This aggressive policy paid big dividends. The *Herald* was full of advertising and was on its way to circulation leadership. It had 20,000 readers in 1836 and would be the world's largest daily, at 77,000, by 1860. Such success for a disliked rival brought a movement to boycott the *Herald*. The attack by Bennett's critics was started in May 1840 by Park Benjamin of the *New York Signal*. Colonel James Watson Webb, Bennett's onetime employer, joined in the fray (he once administered a caning to the editor of the *Herald*), and soon all the opposition papers joined the "moral war" against the upstart journalist. Bennett was accused of blasphemy (he had carried his saucy style into the coverage of religious news) and some of the leading clergymen used their influence to make the boycott effective. Advertisers who feared to offend the moral experts withdrew their accounts. There is no doubt that Bennett offended decent members of the community with his bad taste, quackery, and sensationalism, but the real cause of the moral war was resentment over Bennett's amazing success. He had made his rivals appear stuffy and outdated.

Bennett solved the problem confronting the *Herald* in characteristic manner. He sent his best reporters out to cover the church beats, including all religious meetings of any consequence. A man of little religious feeling, he had the news sense to understand that here was another neglected public worth cultivating. He also toned down some of the obvious charlatanism that had made the *Herald* the symbol of publicized wickedness. The result was victory for Bennett.

Bennett put some needed ingredients into American journalism. He added spice and enterprise and aggressive news coverage. He proved that a publisher devoted to the continual improvement of his product could expect rich rewards. It cost a large fortune to provide all the machinery and personnel that put the *Herald* ahead of its rivals, but the investment paid huge dividends. Bennett left a valuable property to his son, and he died a rich man. But the *Herald* was remembered not so much for *what* it said as for *how* it said it. Bennett's contributions were largely technical.

PENNY-PRESS EXPANSION: PHILADELPHIA, BALTIMORE   Other publishers spread the gospel of penny-press journalism to other cities. Benjamin Day's printer friends, William M. Swain and Arunah S. Abell, saw the *Sun* thrive despite the pessimistic advice they had offered, but they fully admitted their errors when they founded the *Philadelphia Public Ledger* in March 1836, with Azariah H. Simmons as partner. Philadelphia had already been introduced to penny-press journalism by Dr. Christopher Columbus Conwell, who had experimented unsuccessfully with a penny paper, *The Cent,* in 1830. In 1835 William L. Drane founded the *Daily Transcript* and was operating successfully when the three partners founded the *Public Ledger*. But the new paper was soon to become one of the great American dailies. It was a cleaned up version of the *Herald*—full of sensational news but without the extreme bad taste of the New York paper. It was an effective policy. Within two years after its founding, the *Public Ledger* had absorbed its rival, the *Transcript,* and was printing more than 20,000 copies a day. Like the *Herald,* the *Public Ledger* made full use of the most modern technical and news coverage developments.

Swain was the dominant figure on the *Public Ledger,* and after an interval, Abell decided to strike out for himself. He selected Baltimore as a likely city. It was second only to New York as a trade center and was then third in population. Swain and Simmons were not enthusiastic about the undertaking at first. Eventually they underwrote the investment, but Abell promoted the Baltimore publication pretty much by himself. The *Baltimore Sun* first rose May 17, 1837. Its appearance coincided with a depression that had already closed the banks. The first issue of the paper played up the story of a city council meeting the day before, at which $100,000 worth of fractional currency ("shinplasters") was authorized to meet the financial crisis. This was scarcely the appropriate time to found a new paper, it would seem, but the *Sun* prospered, like its New York namesake, and appeared to be safely established at the end of the first year with a circulation of 12,000. Like its Philadelphia affiliate, the *Sun* was always noted for its enterprise and technical progress. It was a pioneer in the development of telegraph news. Both the Baltimore and Philadelphia penny papers worked with the *New York Herald* in exchanging the latest news. The arrangement accounted for numerous scoops, especially during the Mexican war. But the *Baltimore Sun* made a contribution of its own. It developed the Washington bureau of correspondence in its first year of operation. Soon other papers came to value the Baltimore publication for complete and accurate coverage of national news. Government officials also began to follow the paper closely for trends in political development.

The success of the penny-paper pioneers encouraged other publishers to follow the pattern. There were 35 penny papers started in New York in the 1830s. All but the *Sun* and *Herald* succumbed, but in other cities the promoters fared better. By 1840, the four largest American cities had penny papers. Most of them had similar news policies: much local news, great attention to human interest stories, and a fat budget for entertainment material. But more and more significant news was creeping into the columns, and the penny papers led in aggressive news gathering.

GREELEY'S *NEW YORK TRIBUNE,* 1841

The maturing of the press for the masses was best indicated by the newspaper founded at the very beginning of the fifth decade of the century. The paper was the *New York Tribune,* and its founder was Horace Greeley, soon to become one of the most influential editors in the history of American journalism. More books have been written about him than about any other American of the period, except Lincoln.

Horace Greeley was like a character from a Dickens novel—so real that he appeared to be a caricature. He had the angularity of the Vermonter (which he was), a stiff, homespun personality, coupled with the shyness that makes the New England breed so difficult for others to understand. His inconsistencies were legendary. A professed Whig (the party opposed to popular rule), he worked all his life to bring a greater share of material and political benefits to the common man. A leader of the group standing for a continuance of the status quo, he was one of the most "radical" men of his age. At a time when the democratic process was under great stress, Greeley "put his faith in the unshackled mind."

He saw the ample resources of the United States, and he was certain that every American could enjoy the abundant life, if only simple justice could be made to prevail. He believed in what he called "beneficent capitalism." The practical application of this theory was the American System, sponsored by Henry Clay. Clay was Greeley's great hero. Until death ended the career of the Great Compromiser, Greeley devoted a column of his paper to discussions of current issues under the standing headline, "Henry Clay." Greeley, like Clay, honestly believed that if the proceeds of the protective tariff could be used to develop markets for the farmers, all the workers of the country would be prosperous. Because Greeley advocated the high tariff, he was sometimes suspected by the masses of opposing their interests. Because he had scant regard for agrarian dominance in an age of expanding industrialism, he was accused by the farmer of hypocrisy. Because he believed in the organization of unions to prevent exploitation by the privileged, he was frequently attacked by the property interests.

Actually, his idea was to direct the forces of capitalism so that industry, labor, and agriculture could complement each other in improving the common lot. The day Greeley had in mind was one in which opportunity, work, and education would be available to all. Women would be paid at the same rate as men, for similar services, and would have equal civil rights. Temperance would prevail in all things. Labor would be well organized for its own protection. Capital would reap the benefits of a prosperous community, but would feel responsible for better living standards. Slavery and imprisonment for debt would be abolished. John R. Commons, the great authority on the labor movement, called the *Tribune* "the first and only great vehicle this country has known for the ideas and experiments of constructive democracy."[6]

The man who proposed these revolutionary ideas was hardly messianic in appearance. He looked as though he had stepped out of a modern comic strip. He walked with a shambling, uncertain gait, as though he were feeling his way in the dark. His usual garb was a light-gray "duster," or gown, which he had purchased from an immigrant for three dollars and wore winter and summer over his ill-fitting, nondescript suits. His guileless, baby-blue eyes were set in a moonlike face fringed with wispy whiskers sprouting out of his collar like reeds around a mossy stone. A high-pitched, whiny voice added nothing to this unimpressive ensemble. Yet this was the man who was to capture the loyalties of newspaper readers as few editors have in the history of American journalism.

Greeley began his career at the age of 15 as an apprentice to a printer whose business soon failed. He traveled around New York State as a tramp printer for five years, reading voraciously all the while. When he arrived in New York in 1831 he had just ten dollars to his name. After part-time work as a compositor, he finally landed a permanent position on the *Evening Post*.

Soon he and a partner, Francis Story, set up a shop of their own. They printed a small weekly on contract, but the main revenue was from lottery advertising, a circumstance his foes and rivals never let him forget later on. The attempt of the partners to found a penny paper in the winter of 1833 has already been described. In 1834, Greeley founded the *New Yorker,* a stimulating and well-edited publication mainly devoted to literary fare. While publishing this paper he wrote editorials for the *Daily Whig* and had entire charge of a political paper published at Albany by the Whig party leaders. For six months during the presidential campaign of 1840 he edited and published a campaign paper, the *Log Cabin*. He was an experienced journalist, therefore, when he announced in the *Log Cabin* that beginning April 10, 1841, he would publish a daily penny paper, the *New York Tribune*.

His political activities had made Greeley one of the New York Whig triumvirate, which included state party boss Thurlow Weed, the Albany journalist, and Governor William H. Seward. Now was the time to found a newspaper that could carry the Whig message to the common man. It is significant that the *Tribune* appeared just a month after President William Henry Harrison's inauguration following the Whig victory of 1840. Greeley must have been aware that the climate was right for his undertaking. His influence in state and federal political circles must certainly have been a factor in the establishment of the paper. It should be pointed out, too, that Henry Clay, Greeley's hero, expected to be a key figure in the new administration and was confident that the

American System, also promoted by Greeley, would be pushed through at once. But the president died a month after his inauguration, and many ambitions were cut short thereby. Not Greeley's, however.[7]

With $1,000 of borrowed money and about that much money of his own, plus a mortgage on his shop—a total capitalization of not more than $3,000—Greeley issued the first *New York Tribune* as a penny paper. It was not much to look at. Its four pages were five columns wide and about the dimensions of a modern tabloid. The printing was good, however, and so was the content, apparently. At least it attracted readers, for Greeley boasted of a circulation in excess of 11,000 after the second month. This was about one-fourth the print order of the *Sun,* then the most popular paper in America, but it was enough to establish the *Tribune* firmly. Greeley was a good editor but a poor manager. He himself never shared in the fortune that his paper was to make for others. Indeed, the paper might have failed had not the very able Thomas McElrath purchased a half interest for $2,000. The paper was then losing money. At the end of the second year the price was raised to two cents (weekly subscribers paid 1½ cents an issue) and the *Tribune* began to make money.

The *Tribune* always trailed both the *Sun* and the *Herald* in daily circulation, but part of its great reputation was to rest on its weekly edition, which was a phenomenal success. It first appeared September 2, 1841. Offered at two dollars a year or one dollar a year when "clubs" of 20 members bought it (which was very common) the weekly *Tribune* largely established Greeley's reputation as the greatest editor of his day. It was said to have been read in the midwestern states' areas "next to the Bible."

The early issues of Greeley's *Tribune* offer no clue as to his greatness. The three pages of fine print describing the details of the president's funeral contain none of the stimulation and challenge for which Greeley was to become famous. And yet the very first issue indicates the significance of the *New York Tribune*. It sold for one cent, in competition with the other penny papers, and therefore was plainly intended for mass readership. But instead of pandering to emotionalism, the entire issue was devoted to serious discussion and reportage. The *Tribune* could offer its public murder stories just as sensational as those of its rivals, but that type of journalism was not the hallmark of the paper. Greeley had the curious faith that the masses could be attracted by reason as well as by emotionalism. He did not insult the common man by trying to "write down" to him. There is nothing that can raise the dignity of the scorned more effectively than honest recognition, and this appeal undoubtedly was a factor in the *Tribune*'s success.

GREELEY'S ROLE IN OPINION LEADERSHIP AND SOCIAL CHANGE

Admittedly, much of the *Tribune*'s later content was rational only in the broad sense. Any crackpot social philosopher could express himself in the paper, if he wrote forcefully. The common criticism of Greeley, indeed, was that he was utterly irrational. But some of his "idealism" was founded on sound reasoning. He saw that Jeffersonian ideas, based on an agrarian society, were not applicable to a nation fast becoming an industrial power. He also realized the dangers of unrestricted industrialism. The slums of Europe warned of that. Allowing selfish business interests and rugged individualism to dominate American society could only lead to anarchy, Greeley reasoned. The duty of the statesman, as he understood it, was to reduce social friction between classes and economic interests. That could be done only when the state had strong regulatory powers.

So Greeley groped for the way out. Lacking formal education, he knew little about social and political philosophers. He preferred to learn by experimentation. That is why he allowed Albert Brisbane the use of his columns. Brisbane was the American prophet of Fourierism, a scheme for curing the ills of capitalism by a form of collective living he called "associationism." In the 1850s the *Tribune* spent many pages explaining Socialism, and Greeley himself debated the issue publicly with brilliant opponents, including Henry Raymond of the *New York Times*. For a decade one of the London correspondents for the *Tribune* was Karl Marx, co-founder of Communism. Greeley fought steadily for agrarian reforms, including the Homestead Bill offering land in the West that immigrants could afford to develop. All this completely violated Whig doctrine, and yet Greeley was one of the leaders of the party. No wonder his critics were confused.

But it should be clear that Greeley did not endorse all the opinions expressed in the *Tribune*. He was aware that most of the suggestions were impractical. But he was also aware that America was still groping toward a goal and that it would have to continue experimenting if democracy were to be kept dynamic. His readers appeared to understand. They saw Greeley was intent on producing a better world—and a better press. If his experiments were ineffectual, they were no more so than those of a scientist who keeps working with test tubes to find solutions.

Despite all criticism, Greeley was read by all types of persons. Whether he wrote on politics, farming, labor, education, the horror of debt, the rights of women, temperance, marriage, the frontier, or slavery, all classes of society took note of the *Tribune*. He upbraided a nation for its whisky consumption—and the liquor-loving public kept right on reading the *Tribune*. He denounced the tobacco smokers and chewers—they, too, remained regular readers. He criticized the speculator and financier—they fumed and fussed and read on.

Why should such persons, many of whom resented all this "radicalism," not only have tolerated the paper but also have supported it loyally? There was no doubt of its success. It was full of advertising—its front page was usually solid with commercial notices—universally read, and highly respectable. The weekly edition had more readers than any other publication of the period. Many of its 200,000 subscribers were farmers in the Middle West, who had no sympathy with many of Greeley's ideas on industrial society. The daily lagged behind the *Sun* and the *Herald,* but the circulation was always high. Could such a paper succeed today? It had more inflammatory material in it than even the labor papers of the time. Was it popular because the reader trusted the sincerity of its editor?

The secret of Greeley's popularity was his consciousness of responsibility to the reader. His flights into socialistic fancy were erratic and irresponsible, perhaps, but the average reader appeared to understand that the motives were sincere. That was why the farmers, who often disagreed violently with Greeley's views, read the "Try-bune," as they usually called it, "next to the Bible." How could anyone doubt the sincerity of a man who advocated a fairer distribution of wealth and who lived up to his advice by giving away to his employees all but a few shares of the gold mine he had made out of the *Tribune?* He changed the press of the masses from the vulgar level of sensationalism to a promoter of culture and stimulating ideas, and made it pay dividends. His protégés also raised the standards of the Fourth Estate. For many years Charles A. Dana, who will appear again in these pages, was Greeley's assistant, and much of the early success of the *Tribune* has been ascribed to Dana. Henry J. Raymond, soon to establish the *New York Times,* started out under Greeley. Margaret Fuller, one of the truly great literary figures of the period, wrote regularly for the

Tribune. Carl Schurz, John Hay, Whitelaw Reid, Henry James, William Dean Howells, George Ripley, and Richard Hildreth, who made names for themselves in various fields of literature, journalism, and history, served under "Uncle Horace."

The identification of Greeley with his paper is brought out by an anecdote told by Joseph Bishop in his *Notes,* written after Bishop had left the editorship of the *Post.* The editor was in Vermont a year of so after Greeley's death in 1872 and made some remark about an article that had recently appeared in the *Tribune.* "Does the Try-bune still print?" asked a farmer in the audience. "Why, I thought Greeley was dead."[8]

RAYMOND'S *NEW YORK TIMES,* 1851

A thesis was advanced at the beginning of this chapter that when a new public is first tapped by the mass media, the appeal is invariably on an emotional plane. The result is a "sensational" vehicle of communication. Readers of the *Sun* first bought it primarily for its police reports. Many of these readers matured with the years, however, for as time went on, cheap papers competing successfully with the *Sun* offered more nourishing fare. Greeley proved that a publisher could reach the masses without resorting to sensationalism. Even the *Sun* and the *Herald* offered more substantial material as time went on. They had to, to keep up with the increasing skills of their readers. Eventually, such papers left the semiliterate public behind, and another wave of sensational papers had to be established (as in the 1890s) to take up the slack. The completion of this cycle is exemplified by Henry J. Raymond of the *New York Times.*

From early boyhood, Raymond showed promise as a thinker, and he was graduated from the University of Vermont in 1840 with the highest honors. "Like most of his honors," one of his biographers has said, "they cost more than they were worth."[9] His studies almost ruined his health, and the habit of overwork established in college may have contributed to his early death.

As a college student, Raymond contributed to Greeley's *New Yorker,* which the youth admired greatly. After a visit to the New York editor, Raymond became Greeley's chief assistant in 1841, the year the *Tribune* was founded. George Jones was a colleague in the business office of the *Tribune.* Together they planned to put out the "ideal daily." Neither had sufficient money, however, for already it was impossible to establish a New York paper with $500 and a few packing-box desks, as Bennett had.

Raymond and Greeley were naturally incompatible. The younger man could never appreciate the erratic mental behavior of his employer, and soon Raymond left to work for Colonel James Watson Webb on the *Courier and Enquirer.* During this interim he established a reputation as an orator and budding politician. He was elected to the State Assembly in 1849 and became speaker in 1851. At this point he broke with Webb on the Free Soil Party issue. He took a position as an editor of *Harper's New Monthly Magazine* (established in June 1850), where he remained until 1856 as part-time editor.

It was in 1851 that Raymond and Jones realized their old ambition of publishing a New York newspaper of their own. The first issue of the *New York Daily Times* appeared September 18, 1851. It sold for one cent, and thus showed its intention of being a paper for the masses, but it eschewed the sensationalism of the *Sun* and *Herald,* and the whimsy of the *Tribune,* as described in the policy expressed the first day: ". . . we do not mean to write as if we were in a passion [a slap at Greeley, who was regularly the butt of Raymond's jibes]—unless that shall really be the case; and we shall make it a point to get into a passion as rarely as possible."[10] One of the *Times'* strong points was the interpreting of foreign news. Raymond sought to excel in reporting European events.

Raymond soon established a reputation as a reasonable and objective editor.

Actually, compromise, rather than objectivity, was Raymond's chief characteristic. "The great temporizer," Maverick, one of his biographers, called the *Times* editor, adding that this quality ruined him as a politician and eventually as a leader.[11] He appealed to readers who liked the *Herald'*s aggressiveness but resented its bad taste, who admired the *Tribune* but suspected Greeley's fanaticism, or who had confidence in the solidness of the *Courier and Enquirer* but were bored by its pompousness.

From the very beginning Raymond used every opportunity to plague his old mentor, Greeley. By 1852 Raymond was up to his neck in politics, despite the promise he had made to his partner after Jones warned that politics and editorships did not mix. At that time the prohibition of liquor was a big issue. It was one of Greeley's pet subjects, and he expected to be elected governor of New York because of his editorial stand on temperance. But Thurlow Weed, the Albany editor who controlled the state convention that year, needed an upstate man to hold the party together on the dry issue. That meant that the lieutenant governor had to be a big city "wet" in order to hold the party together on other issues. Weed selected Raymond, rather than his old teammate, Greeley. As Greeley once said of the episode: ". . . no other name could have been . . . so bitterly humbling to me."[12]

Indeed, from this time on, Raymond was as much a politician as he was an editor. As we shall see, the *Times* editor became a power in Republican circles. Greeley was to see his rival badly mauled in the postwar political arena, but in the 1850s Raymond rode the crest of the wave. Within two years after the founding of the *Times,* even Greeley admitted that it outsold the *Tribune* within the city limits. Raymond left a reputation as one of the great journalists of the century.

Raymond's contribution was the development of reasonable decency in public reporting. There was a minimum of personal invective in the *Times.* It seldom presented issues in the black and white patterns favored by Greeley. It was invariably fair in tone, if not in content, and no rival equaled it in developing the technique of careful reporting. It substituted accuracy for wishful thinking, even when Raymond was deep in politics. Curiously, Raymond, who was addicted to politics, stood for a strangely objective nonpartisanship in his paper. It was as though the man had two completely different personalities.

THURLOW WEED, PARTY BOSS

Two other journalists of the period deserve passing mention. One was Thurlow Weed, better known as a political boss, and the other was Samuel Bowles III.

Thurlow Weed began a career of influence as an apprentice printer in upstate New York. For a time (1808–17) he worked as a journeyman, became interested in politics as a follower of DeWitt Clinton, and worked on the *Rochester Telegraph.* By 1825 he had become a political power. He purchased the *Telegraph* that year and used it to promote his candidates. Weed had strong anti-Masonic principles in a day when Masonry was a burning political issue. The Anti-Masonic party raised funds to establish a paper at Albany, and Weed was made editor while he was still serving as a leader in the Assembly. The *Evening Journal* appeared in February 1830, and under Weed it became virtually the official organ of the Whigs. Weed was given much of the credit for electing William H. Seward governor in 1838, and the two, plus Greeley, were instrumental in putting Harrison into the White House in 1840.

Weed was the typical party boss. It was said that Seward had the principles and Weed had the votes. Greeley was the sounding board for new ideas. The big boss was Weed, however. He had the knack of making all acquaintances believe he was a special friend. The secret of his popularity was that he sincerely liked people—all kinds of people. During his heyday he was one of the important Americans of the period, and his paper was therefore influential.

Weed's power waned after Seward's defeat in 1842. He recouped his political fortunes somewhat when he backed General Zachary Taylor for president in 1848 and sent Seward to the Senate. The Whigs were doomed by 1850, however, and Weed went to Europe defeated and dejected. He accepted the new Republican party reluctantly, but was unsuccessful in promoting Seward within it. From then on, Weed's fortunes declined. He gave up the editorship of his paper in 1863. He tried to make a comeback as a journalist in 1867 by taking over the editorship of the *New York Commercial Advertiser,* but he had to give up the position because of poor health. He died in retirement in 1882.

BOWLES AND THE *SPRINGFIELD REPUBLICAN*

Another outstanding paper at this time was Massachusetts' *Springfield Republican.* Its founder was Samuel Bowles II, although his son, Samuel Bowles III, is more important to this history. The father was reared in Connecticut, where the family had been driven by depression. He was apprenticed to a printer at the age of 15, after the first Samuel Bowles, a grocer, died and bequeathed to the boy his entire worldly possessions—a Bible and a watch. Bowles grew up as a poor boy, but from an early age he was interested in cultural development, as evidenced by the literary club he established.

His first regular job was with the *New Haven Register.* In 1819 he joined with John Francis of Wethersfield as a partner in the *Hartford Times,* a weekly that soon failed under the adverse conditions of the time. He and his wife and family loaded their household possessions and the *Times* press on a flatboat and poled up the Connecticut River to Springfield, Massachusetts. There, a group of Anti-Federalists helped him relocate as a publisher. First copies of the *Springfield Republican* appeared September 8, 1824. It was a weekly, and its 250 subscribers paid two dollars a year for it. Bowles ran the paper by himself; it grew slowly, but outlasted five rivals, and by 1840 Bowles had established a reputation as a reliable publisher. By that time Springfield was beginning to boom as a railroad center, and circulation was up to 1,200. The original publisher died in 1851, but by that time the paper was largely the product of the son.

Samuel Bowles III made the most of the excellent opportunities presented to him by his father, and it was the son who established the national reputation of the *Republican.* It was he who argued his father into "going daily" in March 1844 (it was an evening paper then but became morning a year later). Bowles made the paper successful by skillful organization of regional correspondence, so that every little community in the upper Connecticut Valley had reason to take the paper. Young Bowles was educated for the role he was to take in journalism. As a boy he shared his room with his father's three apprentices. He grew up in the back shop. He delivered papers and personally knew all the local subscribers and their interests. At 18 he was ready to assume his place as a peer in the Fourth Estate. It was at this time that he persuaded his father to let him try a daily. It was hard going at first. He worked as much as 40 hours at a stretch without sleep. His health began to fail. The paper almost foundered financially. But in the end, Bowles produced one of the great newspapers of the nineteenth century.

Partly responsible for the success of the paper were William B. Calhoun, who wrote many of the editorials credited by readers to Bowles; Josiah Gilbert Holland, a fluent and articulate writer; and George Ashmun, friend of Abraham Lincoln and a noted politician. But the main emphasis of the *Republican* was news, and Bowles made that his special department.

He took over full control after the death of his father in 1851 (Holland had an interest in the paper but not enough to control it). Actually, it is not until the late 1850s and the 1860s that the *Republican* exerted its greatest influence, so that this discussion must be reserved for a later chapter. But the foundations of success were laid in the period covered in this section. Bowles was a sponsor of the new Republican party. By 1860 his weekly edition was a national institution, with a circulation of about 12,000, but with a reputation throughout the country exceeded only by that of the *Tribune*. The daily hovered around 6,000, but that, too, was good for a provincial paper.

Its reporters and editors were craftsmen, proud of their product, and absorbed in their work. Young men from all over the United States tried to get on the *Republican* staff. A tour with the Springfield paper was a kind of advanced degree in journalism. A "*Republican* man" was welcome on the biggest papers in the country.

NOTES

1. The paper had strong religious undertones, but it was aggressive in its news policies and business coverage. It will receive more attention in a later discussion on the development of cooperative news gathering.
2. By 1837 the *Sun* was printing 30,000 copies a day, which was more than the total of all New York daily newspapers combined when the *Sun* had first appeared.
3. *New York Sun,* January 3, 1835.
4. It would be ridiculous to maintain that the penny press avoided partisanship. Papers like the *Herald* took up issues every day, and often fought for them as violently as in the old partisan-press days. But that was not the purpose of these papers, as it had been when papers reflected factions and parties. The newspaper was a little more impersonal than the viewspaper, but the development of objectivity had barely started, and the goal had not been reached more than a hundred years later. All such progress must be measured relatively.
5. *New York Herald,* June 4, 1836 ("Morning" was dropped from the nameplate in 1835).
6. John R. Commons, "Horace Greeley and the Working Class Origins of the Republican Party," *Political Science Quarterly,* XXIV (September 1909), 472.
7. Harrison's running mate, John Tyler of Virginia, proved as president to be more southern than Whig and vetoed Clay's pet bills. In the 1844 presidential year the Whigs ditched Tyler for Clay, but Democrat James K. Polk won.
8. H. L. Stoddard, *Horace Greeley* (New York: G. P. Putnam's Sons, 1946), p. 322.
9. *Dictionary of American Biography,* XV, p. 408.
10. Willard G. Bleyer, *Main Currents in the History of American Journalism* (Boston: Houghton Mifflin, 1927), p. 240.
11. Augustus Maverick, *Henry J. Raymond and the New York Press* (Hartford: A. S. Hale and Company, 1870), p. 170.
12. Letter to Governor Seward, dated New York, November 11, 1854, in Thurlow Weed Barnes and Harriet Weed, eds., *Life of Thurlow Weed,* Vol. II (Boston: Houghton Mifflin, 1884), p. 280.

ANNOTATED BIBLIOGRAPHY

Books

BARNES, THURLOW WEED, AND HARRIET WEED, eds., *Life of Thurlow Weed.* 2 vols. Boston: Houghton Mifflin, 1883–84. The first volume is the politician's autobiography, edited by his daughter, Harriet. The second volume comprises the memoirs, documents, and letters compiled by Weed's grandson.
BIGELOW, JOHN, *Retrospections of an Active Life,* IV. New York: The Baker and Taylor

Company, 1909–13. The journalistic field of the period described by a well-known *Post* executive.

BROWN, FRANCIS, *Raymond of the Times*. New York: Norton, 1951. A first-rate biography of a great editor.

CARLSON, OLIVER, *The Man Who Made News*. New York: Duell, Sloan & Pearce, 1942. The best biography of James Gordon Bennett, Sr.

CROUTHAMEL, JAMES L., *James Watson Webb, A Biography*. Middletown, Conn.: Wesleyan University Press, 1969. Carefully documented study of a leader in news gathering.

DAVIS, ELMER, *History of the New York Times, 1851–1921*. New York: The New York Times Company, 1921. Valuable for the early period of the great newspaper.

GREELEY, HORACE, *Recollections of a Busy Life*. New York: J. B. Ford and Company, 1868. The editor's own version of his career.

HALE, WILLIAM H., *Horace Greeley: Voice of the People*. New York: Harper & Row, 1950. A good modern biography.

HOOKER, RICHARD, *The Story of an Independent Newspaper: One Hundred Years of the Springfield Republican, 1824–1924*. New York: Macmillan, 1924.

ISELY, JETER ALLEN, *Horace Greeley and the Republican Party, 1853–1861*. Princeton: Princeton University Press, 1947. An examination of Greeley's writings for the eight years.

MAVERICK, AUGUSTUS, *Henry J. Raymond and the New York Press*. Hartford: A. S. Hale and Company, 1870. An outstanding authority, this book contains many valuable documents.

MERRIAM, GEORGE S., *Life and Times of Samuel Bowles*. New York: Appleton-Century-Crofts, 1885. More complete than the Hooker study, above, and full of interesting letters and documents.

O'BRIEN, FRANK M., *The Story of The Sun*. New York: George H. Doran Company, 1918. Revised ed., New York: Appleton-Century-Crofts, 1928. The standard history of the first successful penny newspaper.

PARRINGTON, VERNON L., *Main Currents in American Thought*, Vol. II. New York: Harcourt Brace Jovanovich, 1927. Greeley, Margaret Fuller, and Bryant are discussed.

PARTON, JAMES, *Life of Horace Greeley*. New York: Mason Brothers, 1855. The standard reference, written by a contemporary.

STODDARD, HENRY L., *Horace Greeley: Printer, Editor, Crusader*. New York: G. P. Putnam's Sons, 1946. Not as deep as some of the other biographies of the editor, but much more human, readable, and convincing than the earlier studies.

VAN DEUSEN, GLYNDON GARLOCK, *Horace Greeley: Nineteenth Century Crusader*. Philadelphia: University of Pennsylvania Press, 1953. This is the best, and most detailed, of the Greeley biographies. The same author is the biographer of Thurlow Weed and Henry Clay, who were so closely associated with Greeley.

Periodicals and Monographs

ABBOTT, LYMAN, "Reminiscences," *Outlook,* CVI (April 25, 1914), 897. Sidelights on Raymond's brush with the courts on a contempt citation.

BORDEN, MORTON, "Some Notes on Horace Greeley, Charles Dana and Karl Marx," *Journalism Quarterly,* XXXIV (Fall 1957), 457. It was Dana who kept Marx on the *Tribune*'s payroll. See also Summer 1959 issue for texts of five letters from Dana to Marx (p. 314).

BRADFORD, GAMALIEL, "Samuel Bowles," *Atlantic Monthly,* CXVI (October 1915), 487. An excellent character study. Reprinted in Ford and Emery, *Highlights in the History of the American Press.*

BROWNE, JUNIUS HENRI, "Horace Greeley," *Harper's New Monthly Magazine,* XLVI (April 1873), 734. Describes Greeley's idiosyncrasies.

COLEMAN, ALBERT E., "New and Authentic History of the Herald of the Bennetts," *Editor & Publisher,* LVI–LVIII (March 29, 1924 to June 13, 1925).

COMMONS, JOHN R., "Horace Greeley and the Working Class Origins of the Republican

Party," *Political Science Quarterly,* XXIV (September 1909), 468. A significant article by a great authority and writer on American Labor.

EBERHARD, WALLACE B., "Mr. Bennett Covers a Murder Trial," *Journalism Quarterly,* XLVII (Autumn 1970), 457. The 1830 trial of a sea captain, covered for the *Courier and Enquirer* in a style foreshadowing his *Herald* days.

HERBERT, WILLIAM, "Jackson, the Bank, and the Press," Ph.D. thesis, University of Missouri, 1975. Newspapers overlooked changing economics in debate on the Second Bank of the United States.

HOLLAND, DONALD R., "Volney B. Palmer (1799–1864): The Nation's First Advertising Agency Man," *Journalism Monographs,* 44 (May 1976). Palmer began offering his services to businessmen to reach newspapers in 1842, had agency by 1849.

NILSSON, NILS G., "The Origin of the Interview," *Journalism Quarterly,* XLVIII (Winter 1971), 707. Police and court reporting of 1830s was the progenitor of the interview.

PEEBLES, PAUL, "James Gordon Bennett's Scintillations," *Galaxy,* XIV (August 1872), 258. A revealing and rewarding study of the editor. Reprinted in Ford and Emery, *Highlights in the History of the American Press.*

"Personal Reminiscences of Horace Greeley," *Bookman,* XIII (April 1901), 126. Sympathetic and readable anecdotes.

SAALBERG, HARVEY, "Bennett and Greeley, Professional Rivals, Had Much in Common," *Journalism Quarterly,* XLIX (Autumn 1972), 538. Pioneers in developing news and editorial leadership are reviewed on hundredth anniversary of deaths.

"Sketches of the Life and Labors of Horace Greeley," *National Quarterly Review,* XXVI (December 1872), 153. Strong posthumous defense of the editor's character.

"The *Herald*—Onward," *Democratic Review,* XXXI (November 1852), 409. A favorable appraisal of a maligned newspaper.

TURNBULL, GEORGE, "Some Notes on the History of the Interview," *Journalism Quarterly,* XIII (September 1936), 272. An authority on journalism history holds that Greeley was the father of the modern interview.

CALIFORNIAN.

SAN FRANCISCO, AUGUST 14, 1848.

The "Californian" again appears before its patrons this morning, as it will continue to do occasionally in these "golden times," during the temporary suspension of business. As soon as a re-action takes place, and business resumes its wonted channels, and our thoroughfares again wear their usual business-like and bustling appearance, we will issue the paper regularly, as heretofore.

To Correspondents.— "Soldado" is inadmissible. Reason why—we do not wish to conflict in any manner with military proceedings, especially during the absence of the proprietors.

"One of the People" is crowded out to make room for the Peace intelligence.

Our Sonoma friend "O'C" we hope will continue his favors.

All correspondents should be aware when writing for this paper, that they are responsible, and if public or private character should, inadvertently on our part, get maliciously assailed in its columns, and it should become requisite, their names will be freely given; otherwise we preserve them as an inviolable secret.

For the matter which appears as editorial, during the absence of the legitimate editor, Benjamin Franklin Foster is solely responsible.

GLORIOUS NEWS.

RATIFICATION OF THE TREATY
OF PEACE.

END OF THE
WAR.

We have received by a Courier from Monterey, bringing dispatches for the military department here, the glorious intelligence of the ratification of the treaty of peace made between the United States and Mexico, as amended and ratified by the Senate of the United States.

There is now no longer a doubt about the treaty being concluded. We get the news officially. The mail left Col. Burton, at La Paz, on the 27th June, and reached Monterey on the 6th inst.

We have not the exact terms of the treaty, but the most important points are as follows: the boundary is to commence at the mouth of the Rio Grande, up that river to the parallel of latitude which will strike the head of the Gila, down that river to its junction with the Rio Colorado, and with that to the parallel which will strike the Pacific one league south of San Diego.

It is said that in consideration of the cession of territory by Mexico, that the United States pay their own expenses of the war, pay Mexico in cash fifteen millions of dollars, and assume the payment of the claims of the citizens of the United States against the Mexican government to the amount of three millions of dollars.

We have no disposition to speculate upon the terms of this treaty, as to its general bearing upon the two nations, nor have we the means of forming a proper judgment, but of one thing we feel satisfied: that the citizens of all the territory acquired by the United States, will be greatly benefited by the change, and so far as California is concerned, she will be elevated in the scale of human advancement beyond all possible calculation. Half a century has passed away since the first settlement of California, and although the mountains and the plains were covered with cattle and horses, yet the lands remained almost entirely uncultivated, the inexhaustible and unparalleled mineral wealth lay untouched in the bowels of the earth. The Indians made their houses literally of gold, without knowing that it was more valuable than other yellow dirt.

THE GOLD MINE.

A few months ago we were in the habit of speaking of the agricultural resources and the commercial qualities of California, as being the source of her greatest wealth; and although now they are not inferior to any portions of the world, the soil constitutes but a small part of her wealth, all interests having been absorbed in the working of the mines.

The present number of the "Californian" is intended for circulation abroad as well as at home, and will, by going a minute and general view of the all absorbing topic, the gold mine, be found useful to persons to send to their distant friends. The information which we shall give, has been gathered from actual observation, and from persons who have been engaged at the mines, and from the most authentic sources, as it is desirable that the facts be correctly known through other countries, and especially through the United States.

Some time in the spring, Messrs. Marshall and Bennet, in opening a ditch for a tail race for a saw-mill, which had been built on the American Fork of the Sacramento, found some gold, which the current had collected in the bottom of the race, which, after being examined, was found to be very pure. It soon began to attract attention, and some persons discovered the gold in the river below and for some distance above. In large quantities, so much so that persons who only gave credit to one third of what was said about it left their homes and went to work in the mines. Thus the work of but a few weeks, to bring almost the entire population of the territory together to pick up the precious metal. The result has been, that in less than four months, a total revolution has been effected in the prospects and the late of Alta California. Then, the capital was in the hands of a few individuals engaged in trade and speculation, now labor has got the upper hands of capital, and the laboring men hold the great mass of the wealth of the country—the gold.

There are now about four thousand persons, besides a number of...

engaged at the mines, and from the fact, that no capital is required, they are working in companies on equal shares or alone with their basket. In one part of the mine called the "dry diggins," no other implements are necessary than an ordinary sheath knife, to pick the gold from the rocks. In other parts, where the gold is washed out, the machinery is very simple, being an ordinary trough made of plank, and two feet wide at the top, with a riddle or sieve at one end to catch the larger gravel, and three or four small bars across the bottom, about half an inch high to keep the gold from going out with the dirt and water at the lower end. This machine is set upon rockers, which gives it a half rotary motion to the water and dirt inside. But far the largest number use nothing but a large tin pan or an Indian basket, into which they place the dirt and shake it until the gold gets to the bottom and the dirt is carried over the side in the shape of muddy water. It is necessary in some cases, to have a crowbar, pick and shovel, but a great deal is taken up with large horns, shapen upon fashion at the large end.

From the fact that no capital is necessary, a fair competition in labor without the influence of capital, men who were only able to procure one month's provisions, have now thousands of dollars of the precious metal. The laboring class have now become the capitalists of the country.

As to the richness of the mine, were we to set down half the truth, it would be looked upon in other countries as a "Sinbad" story, or the history of "Aladdin's Lamp," which required that its possessor should but wish, and his wishes should be accomplished. Many persons have collected in one day, of the finest grade gold, from three to eight hundred dollars, and for many days together averaged from 75 to $150. Although this is not universal, yet the general average is so well settled, that when a man with his pan or basket does not easily gather 30 to 40 dollars in a day, he moves to another place, so that taking the general average, including the time spent in moving from place to place and in looking for better "diggins," we are of the opinion that we may safely set down an ounce of pure gold or $16 per day to the man. Suppose there are 4000 persons at work, they will add to the aggregate wealth of the territory about 4000 ounces, or about 64,000 dollars a day.

The value of the gold, like all things else, is regulated by the demand. Four months ago, flour was sold in the market for four dollars per hundred, now sixteen; beef cattle six, now thirty; ready made clothing, grocer's and other good have not risen in the same proportion, but are at least double their original cost. If we make bread and meat the standard by which to determine the value of the gold, then it is only worth one fourth of what it is elsewhere. But if gold and silver be the standard, then the bread and meat is worth four times what it was. But the relative value of the grain gold, compared with gold and silver coin, can only be changed by the action of government, for, however abundant the gold may be, it must produce its relative value in coin, and while a five dollar gold piece will be received in the treasury as five dollars, so long must an ounce of gold be worth sixteen dollars.

As to the future hopes of California, her course is onward, with a rapidity which will astonish the world. Her unparalleled gold mines, silver mines, iron ore and lead, with the best climate in the world, and the richest soil, will make it the garden spot of creation.

We call the attention of our readers to the Proclamation of Gov. Mason, on first page.

Laws.—Governor Mason has had printed both in the English and Spanish languages, a code of laws for the better government of the territory of California—the preservation of order, and the protection of the rights of the inhabitants, during the military occupancy of the country by the U. S. forces.

Appointment.—His Excellency Governor Mason has appointed Charles V. Gillespie, to be Notary Public in and for the district of San Francisco.

We acknowledge, with pleasure, our indebtedness for news, to several citizen gentlemen and military officers, all of whom will please accept our humble thanks.

The second Alcalde of the district of San Francisco, Dr. Leavenworth, we understand, will remain for the present in the discharge of the duties of his office.

ILLUMINATION MEETING.

At a large and respectable meeting of the citizens of this town, held at the City Hotel on Thursday evening, at 8 o'clock, for the purpose of making suitable arrangements to celebrate the glorious news of peace having been made between the United States and Mexico, the following gentlemen were elected officers, viz:

His Honor Judge Hyde was called upon to preside.

W. D. M. Howard, Esq., Lieut. T. J. Roach, Capt. S. E. Woodworth, and E. H. Harrison, Esq., were elected Vice Presidents, and Jas. G. Leighton, Esq., Secretary.

The Chairman briefly stated the object of the meeting, after which the following resolutions were proposed:

Resolved, That in consequence of the arrival of the glorious news of a permanent peace between the United States and Mexico, that the citizens of San Francisco give a general illumination on Friday evening, Aug 11, at 8 o'clock.

Resolved, That all the citizens of the town be called upon to lend their hearty cooperation in throwing light upon the patriotic movement.

Resolved, That the masters of the vessels in the harbor be requested to hoist their colors at sunrise and make every other demonstration of joy that may be possible to aid in making a suitable response to the movement on shore.

Resolved, That a Committee of six be appointed to carry these resolutions into effect. The following gentlemen were appointed as the Committee:

Robt. Semple, Esq. of Benecia; Capt. S. Peny; Wm H Davis, Esq.; Jas. G. Ward, Esq.; C V Gillespie, Esq.; Robt A Parker, Esq.

Wm M Smith, Esq. being called upon to address the meeting, stated that he was about leaving town to make an excursion to the "Gold Regions," and regretted that he would not be able to join with us in celebrating so glorious an event; still he would, he said, spread the news far and wide.

Dr Semple was then called upon to address the meeting, when he arose and said that he had not expected to be called upon for a speech, but upon an occasion like the present, he did not feel himself at liberty to decline. It was an event in which California was more interested and more benefited than any other portion of the United States or of Mexico. Whatever may be the terms of the treaty, it was enough for us to know that Upper California was left in the United States. Give us equal privileges with citizens of that glorious Republic, and the industry, enterprise and intelligence of the "universal Yankee Nation" will soon develope the inexhaustible mineral wealth of this beautiful country to an extent hitherto unparalleled in the known world. Let us have peace with all Nations and ten years would make us one of the richest States in the Union. Every man here was directly interested in this question, and he asserted that the desire for peace on any terms which might be agreed on was unanimous in California. He thanked Providence that his feet were again firmly on the U. States and that the "Star Spangled Banner" should continue to wave o'er the adopted land. Loud cheering.

Lt. Roach, of the New York Volunteers, was then called on for the patriotic song the "Star Spangled Banner"—which was sung by several gentlemen in chorus with great warmth of feeling.

Dr Leavenworth, Alcalde of San Francisco, was then called upon, and after making a few penciable remarks, sat down amidst tremendous applause.

Ex-Gov Boggs of Sonoma was then called upon, and addressed the meeting in his usual happy style.

The meeting then adjourned.

Agreeably to the resolutions, on Friday the 11th, the ships in the harbor hoisted their flags and fired salutes, the merchants closed their doors, and citizens and soldiers one and all entered into the spirit of universal rejoicing. In the course of the day several gentlemen formed a cavalcade and passed through our principal streets in handsome order under the command of Lieut. Gilbert. In the evening, the Californian office, the hotels, and almost every dwelling house in town was brilliantly illuminated, some of them beautifully. Tar barrels were brought into requisition and bonfires blazed in every part of the town. A number of ladies and gentlemen promenaded the streets in social parties, while others followed the bent of their own inclinations, and the whole town presented one universal scene of rejoicing. Some were so much rejoiced with the news of peace that they first made war upon brandy, then upon each other, that they might have the pleasure of making a treaty of peace in which they alone were personally interested.

The *Californian*, first state paper, reports on the Gold Rush and the Mexican War.

11

The Race
for News

Journalism is literature in a hurry. . . .
—Matthew Arnold

The pioneers of the penny press probably did not realize what a profound change they were to bring about in American journalism. As the historian-journalist Gerald W. Johnson once pointed out, editors like Day, Bennett, Greeley, and Abell lived in a period of great change—change so profound that by comparison the modifications after the War of Independence were slight.[1] Many institutions were to be drastically altered after 1830, but none more than the press.

Three factors control the development of the newspaper. They are (1) the reading public, (2) the system of communications, and (3) improvements in production. In the second quarter of the nineteenth century, all three factors exerted great influence on the press. The public was more discerning as it acquired a greater literacy skill and as more and more publications of various types were offered. The system of communications was developed beyond the wildest dreams of its promoters. The steam press, the beginning of automatic printing, and the perfection of paper making also helped to change the character of the press. The pioneers of the penny press thus found themselves engaged in a game, all the rules of which had been cancelled, while the new regulations were still in the process of formulation. As Johnson says, "To survive, it was necessary to guess what the new rules would be, and to guess correctly most of the time. Conditions demanded alert and supple intelligence, backed by sturdy common sense; for policies whose necessity is as plain as day now were then wrapped in obscurity."[2]

The race for news reflected American zeal in promoting technological progress. The communications revolution to be described in this chapter evolved out of this expansionism. Its effect on the press has been measured in a study of 1820–60 newsgathering undertaken at the University of North Carolina. Its early findings showed that the average time lag on publication of stories of news events in papers of the Lower South dropped from 29 days in the 1820s to 10 days in the 1850s. Increased ability to use telegraphic news would further decrease the lag. It would give the papers more dependable news sources, at the price of increasing conformity in news sources and appearance. Part of the improvement in time lag was due to an increase from 30 to 70 percent in news items actively gathered by a reporter, editor, or correspondent of the sampled papers.[3] This meant a big drop in clipped items, contributions, and other general fare.

FIRST WASHINGTON REPORTERS

One of the first news sources to be tapped methodically was Congress. The beginning of a Washington press corps can be traced to the establishment by Nathaniel Carter of a capital service for his paper, the *New York Statesman,* in December 1822. His paper used the phrase "Washington Correspondence" from then until 1824. Next on the scene, when Congress convened in December 1827, were three correspondents: James Gordon Bennett of the *New York Enquirer;* Joseph I. Buckingham, *Boston Courier;* and Samuel L. Knapp, *Charleston Courier.* They inaugurated what has been continuous press coverage of Congress ever since. Buckingham left after the session; Knapp stayed into the 1830s. Bennett later became the correspondent of the *Courier and Enquirer* and most famous of the early Washington press corps.[4]

Eliab Kingman was the first long-term Washington correspondent, running a stringer service for various clients, including the *Journal of Commerce,* from 1830–61. Matthew L. Davis worked from 1832–40 for the *Times* of London and the *Courier and Enquirer* (who called him "The Spy in Washington"). James and Erastus Brooks, founders of the *New York Express,* reported in the 1830s.

Washington's first important woman journalist was Anne Royall, an unconventional but competent writer and editor who at age 61, in 1831, founded a four-page paper, *Paul Pry.* From 1836–54 she printed *The Huntress,* standing for Jacksonian principles, free public education, free speech, and justice to immigrants and Indians. Holding the honor of being the first woman to sit in a congressional press gallery was Jane Grey Swisshelm, editor of the anti-slavery *Saturday Visitor* in Pittsburgh. She came to Washington to send her columns to Horace Greeley's *New York Tribune,* at five dollars a week. April 17, 1850, she sat in the Senate press gallery, then decided not to return. Nationally known as a crusader and feminist, she became a Minnesota editor.[5] Margaret Fuller of *Dial* fame came to Washington while a *New York Tribune* staff member, 1844–46. She became editor of *Dial,* journal of transcendental philosophy, in 1840 at the age of 30. Known for her intellectual leadership and literary skill, she lived in Italy from 1846 to 1850, sending back articles to Greeley. She died in an 1850 shipwreck, an acknowledged feminist leader. First woman editor of a major daily was Cornelia Walter, who ran the family-owned *Boston Transcript* from 1842–47.

By 1860 the Senate listed 23 correspondents, the House 51. Lawrence A. Gobright became Associated Press agent after 1853. Ben:Perley Poore of the *Boston Journal* arrived in 1854 for a 33-year career. John Nugent, *New York Herald,* and James W. Simonton, *New York Times,* had pre-Civil War brushes with Congress. Noah Brooks, *Sacramento Union,* and Samuel Wilkeson, *New York Tribune,* were among leaders of the wartime press corps.

Foreign news, taken from European papers, had always been presented in

Margaret Fuller (*left*) and Jane Grey Swisshelm, leading women journalists.

American newspapers. But not until 1811 was there much concern shown in offering foreign news reports while they were still fresh. British naval vessels were then searching American ships at sea for British deserters. War was imminent, and every message from Europe told of new threats to American commerce. To satisfy the craving of his customers for such information, Samuel Gilbert had provided a reading room in his seven-story Exchange Coffee House, which dominated the Boston waterfront as the tallest building in America. The reading room was typical in that it supplied available foreign newspapers, as was the custom of coffeehouses. Gilbert's special contribution was a Marine News Book, which offered much more current and local intelligence for the edification of his merchant and shipping office clientele. When the preparation of the news books began to take too much time, Gilbert hired an assistant to carry on this work. On November 20, 1811, he announced in the *Columbian Centinel* that young Samuel Topliff, Jr., would henceforth be in charge of the "Marine and General News Books." Topliff began to meet incoming ships in his rowboat, so that he could return sooner with important news. It was the first systematic attempt in this country to gather foreign news. Later, Topliff hired correspondents in Europe to prepare the dispatches he received from incoming ship captains.

Other cities perfected similar services. The *Charleston Courier* was first in America with news of the peace with Great Britain in 1814, its ship-news reporter having learned of the event only seven weeks after its occurrence. By 1828 New York had taken the lead in such news gathering. The most enterprising news merchant in that fast-growing city was David Hale, manager of the *Journal of Commerce,* published by Arthur Tappan. The paper was the newest of the ten dailies then being published in New York. Hale soon found that the older publications had combined to run him out of business. They had established a service for obtaining news from incoming ships, and they used rough tactics to keep Hale's boats from threatening the monopoly. In desperation, Hale purchased a fast sloop, which met the European packets as they were trimmed off Sandy Hook for the run up the bay. He was able to return with news hours before the merchantmen hove into view from Battery Place.

Not long after this Hale and his partner, Gerard Hallock, purchased the *Journal of Commerce* and made it into the most aggressive of the six-penny papers. Like the penny-press editors, the partners understood the value of news as a commodity. They sometimes put out extras when there were important stories to offer the public. They made the front page the show window, as in modern newspaper practice. But above all, they promoted any system that would speed the gathering and dissemination of news. It was Hale and Hallock who inaugurated the pony express service between Washington and New York. The *Courier and Enquirer* offered stiff competition, but until Bennett came along and outperformed the partners, Hale and Hallock led the New York pack in sniffing out the news.

PONIES, PIGEONS, TRAINS, STEAMBOATS Bennett was of course not content with anything short of the best in news gathering. When Daniel Craig began using carrier pigeons to fly news reports from distant points, Bennett subscribed to the service and even provided his own pigeons. When the steamship, the railroad, and the magnetic telegraph superseded sailing ships, ponies, and pigeons, Bennett was quick to use the new means of communication, but so were his competitors.

The United States government had a hand in developing the rapid processing of news during this period. Following the lead of the newspapermen, Postmaster General Amos Kendall established regular pony express service between Philadelphia and New York, taking over a route from the *Courier and Enquirer* in 1835.[6] By 1836 this express service had been extended across the main routes, cutting the travel time between New York and New Orleans to less than seven days. Express riders did not carry the full newspapers but rather proof sheets of important stories. These "slips," as they were called, preceded the regular papers by as much as a week on such long routes as the New Orleans system. The arrangement enabled newspapers around the country to work out cooperative exchange systems for beating rivals to big news.

In the 1830s and 1840s, railroads gradually began to replace the pony expresses. From 23 miles of track in 1830, construction went up to 9,000 miles by 1850. The railroad was a great boon to the newspapers. It not only provided fast distribution but served also as a communications agency. In May 1837, the *Baltimore Sun* rushed President Van Buren's message from Washington in less than two hours by way of the Baltimore & Ohio Railroad. Previously, Abell and his associates would have had to wait until the following morning to obtain such news from the Washington papers.

In 1841, Bennett, Swain (*Philadelphia Public Ledger*), and Abell (*Baltimore Sun*) together hired a special locomotive to carry President Harrison's inaugural address from Washington to Baltimore, Philadelphia, and New York. The *Baltimore Sun* was able to put out an early afternoon extra covering the noonday speech. Proofs of the speech were mailed to the paper's exchanges, which thereby scored a 24-hour scoop over rivals.

The steamship also contributed to the development of fast news gathering. Travel across the Atlantic was reduced from weeks to days. In 1845, when the Oregon question brought a threat of war with England, leading papers cooperated in meeting fast ships at Halifax, the first port of call for the Atlantic steamers. Horses brought the news across the Nova Scotia peninsula to the Bay of Fundy, where a fast steamer relayed the information to Portland, Maine. A railroad train brought the news to Washington less than 50 hours after it had been received in Halifax.

reported the American victories with a mixture of pride, jingoism, and business sense, some also worried about the moral consequences of the conflict. To Horace Greeley it was a war "in which Heaven must take part against us."[14] James Gordon Bennett, meanwhile, was an adamant supporter of the conflict, arguing, "We are on the verge of vast and unknown changes in the destiny of nations."[15]

The penny press leaders threw their editorial support behind the war and at the same time established the New York to New Orleans express system to deliver the news from the battle zones. The express system "is a creature of modern times," Bennett explained to his readers, "and is characteristic of the American people."[16] If not characteristic of the people, the system clearly was characteristic of the American press in the 1840s. Led by the New York morning dailies, a number of papers participated, including the *Philadelphia North American* and *Public Ledger,* the energetic *Baltimore Sun,* the *Charleston Courier* and the *New Orleans Picayune.* During the final six months of the war these papers pooled their efforts to operate the delivery system on a daily basis.

The New Orleans press, closest to the war zones, led the coverage of the conflict.[17] Because newspapers of the day depended heavily on news from their "exchanges"—free copies they received of other newspapers—the reporting of the New Orleans correspondents with the armies was widely reprinted throughout the United States.

Star reporter of the Mexican War was George Wilkins Kendall, editor-publisher of the *New Orleans Picayune.* He covered all the major battles from Monterrey to Chapultepec and gave accurate accounts of the military strategy involved. At least ten other "special correspondents" followed Kendall into the field: Christopher Mason Haile, Francis A. Lumsden, Daniel Scully, Charles Callahan, and John E. Durivage of the *Picayune;* James L. Freaner and George Tobin of the *New Orleans Delta;* John Peoples for the *Delta, Bee,* and *Crescent;* William C. Tobey ("John of York") of the *Philadelphia North American;* and John Warland of the *Boston Atlas.* Haile, a West Point dropout, matched Kendall's reporting ability and added the innovation of providing readers detailed lists of battle casualties. Freaner and Peoples, former New Orleans printers, became accomplished writers, gaining national reputations under their respective pseudonyms of "Mustang" and "Chaparral." Freaner capped his successful career as an army correspondent by personally delivering the peace treaty from Mexico City to Washington in a then-record 17 days.

In addition to the special correspondents, papers received reports from "occasional correspondents," usually former printers or reporters who initially joined the army as volunteers and later had time to write to the editors at home on an informal basis. Enterprising American printers also followed in the wake of the occupation forces, establishing "war newspapers." Before the fighting ended the Americans established 25 such publications in Mexican territory, including two dailies in Mexico City. Serving both the troops at the front and the public at home, these papers became an important source of news about the war.

The reports from the correspondents at the front often supported America's involvement in the war and the idea of Manifest Destiny. They also empathized with the plight of the invading American forces, which were isolated in the interior of Mexico; reflected attitudes of distrust and bias against the Mexicans; and promoted and reinforced the popular war hero images of generals Zachary Taylor and Winfield Scott. Taylor, benefiting from a wave of favorable newspaper publicity resulting from his battlefield exploits, captured the White House in 1848.

A quixotic chapter in the war was provided by the colorful publisher of the *New York Sun,* Moses Yale Beach. Accompanied by Jane McManus Storms, an editorial writer for his paper, Beach went to Mexico City in 1847 on a secret peace mission for the American government. The effort failed and Beach, suspected of assisting anti-war forces in Mexico, barely escaped capture by Santa Anna. Storms, a strong advocate of Manifest Destiny, wrote commentaries about the war to the *Sun* and *New York Tribune* from Havana, Vera Cruz and the Mexican capital under her pseudonym "Montgomery."[18]

The war also witnessed incidents of military interference with the press coverage. The army, spread thin over hundreds of miles of occupied territory, often could only maintain order through the strict use of martial law. These strained conditions led to at least ten cases of newspaper suppression (five American and five Mexican), occasional uses of censorship and other forms of press harassment. Overall, the American press enjoyed wide latitude of freedom in its coverage of the two-year conflict, but its freedom was not absolute.

PRESSES FOR MASS CIRCULATION

This brings us to the final factor in developing the press. Mass circulation, and all the changes it brought about, could not have been accomplished unless papers could be produced cheaply, quickly, and in general bulk. This problem had to be solved by the technical expert, especially the builder of printing presses.

The improvement in presses and the need for fast printing are indicated by the experience of the *Philadelphia Public Ledger.* It was founded in 1836 as a penny paper dependent on circulation for success, but its printing equipment consisted of the usual hand press, seen in a majority of newspaper shops. In six months the paper acquired a circulation of nearly 8,000, and it was no longer possible to meet the demands of the public with the cumbersome Clymer press. Swain therefore installed the finest equipment obtainable at the time—a Napier single-cylinder press powered by steam. A year later the publisher had to order another press, this time a double-cylinder machine. Bennett's progress was even more amazing. Ten years after he founded his paper without even a press of his own, he was using four double-cylinder presses with four men to each unit in order to get out enough papers.

The first cylinder presses merely rolled back and forth over the flat typebed—like some of the proof presses seen in printing shops today. Speed could be doubled by using two cylinders at a time. But even these presses were not fast enough to keep up to the circulations developed by the penny papers. The problem was solved for the time by Richard Hoe's type-revolving press, first installed in the *Public Ledger* shop in 1846. Hoe substituted a horizontal cylinder for the flat bed. Countersunk in these cylinders were curved iron beds, one for each page in the paper. Type matter was locked in these beds by an ingenious system of wedge-shaped rules to keep the type from flying out as the cylinders revolved at high speed. In 1849 the *New York Herald* installed one of these "lightning" presses with six cylinders capable of printing 12,000 impressions an hour. By the outbreak of the Civil War it was possible for an enterprising publisher to print up to 20,000 impressions an hour.

The type-revolving press speeded up the processing of news, but it also imposed limitations on the editor and publisher. On such a press it was difficult to print anything except one-column headlines. It was not practicable to hold type matter in place on the whirling cylinder when it was set in two- or three-column measure, because the wedges did not have enough pressure on the curved sides of the cylinder. Thus, as long as the

This ingenious Hoe type-revolving press of 1855 printed 20,000 sheets an hour.

type-revolving press was standard equipment, we find very few multiple-column headlines.

Another improvement in the technical process was the use of stereotype plates. James Dellagana, a London printer, produced curved, solid plates by making an impression of the type forms in a soft mold, curving this mold to fit the cylinder, and then pouring hot lead onto the mold or "matrix" to make a type plate. Stereotyping made it possible to make duplicates of pages so that several presses could run off an edition at the same time, thereby speeding the printing to a point limited only by the amount of equipment a publisher could afford. Bennett, for example, had five presses printing from duplicate stereotype cylinders at the same time, during the Civil War demand for papers. Stereotyping made possible bigger headlines, appropriate for war news, and advertising display devices.

NEWSPAPERS MOVE WEST

The small city newspapers changed much less radically than did their big city rivals, but even in the hinterland the press was experiencing the impact of the communications revolution. The telegraph lines reached Portland, Maine, by 1846, Charleston in the South the next year, as well as St. Louis in the Middle West, and were extended to Chicago and Milwaukee in 1848. Pony expresses continued to operate beyond the ends of the lines—notably the overland pony express from St. Joseph, Missouri, to Sacramento, California, which opened in 1860 and continued until the telegraph reached the Pacific in October 1861. By that time there were more than 50,000 miles of wires.

Newspapers in the interior did the best they could. While local news was a leading commodity, they scrambled to get the Washington and foreign news from proof slips, exchange papers, and meager telegrams. Cincinnati and St. Louis, particularly, were major publishing centers and both had several daily newspapers by the 1850s. The leaders in Cincinnati were the *Gazette,* founded in 1815 as a weekly and transformed into a daily in 1827, and the *Commercial,* begun in 1843. St. Louis had as its top dailies the *Missouri Republican,* founded as the *Gazette* in 1808, and the *Missouri*

Democrat in 1852. Secondhand presses, printing equipment, ink, and paper moved out from these centers to smaller towns as the newspaper followed the lines of settlement.

Population was booming in the Great Lakes area, where Chicago and Milwaukee became prominent. Chicago's first paper was the *Weekly Democrat,* begun in 1833 and made into a daily in 1840. The *Chicago Tribune* appeared in 1847, and after its purchase by Joseph Medill and his partners in 1855, it became the leading daily, absorbing the *Democrat* in 1861. Milwaukee's initial weekly was the *Advertiser,* which was founded in 1836 and lived to become the *Wisconsin News.* The *Milwaukee Sentinel,* started in 1837, became the city's first daily in 1844. The transformation from weekly to daily publication was repeated elsewhere; the *Minnesota Pioneer* of 1849, the state's first paper, became a daily in 1854 and had several competitors in St. Paul.

Establishment of rival papers as spokesmen for political groups accounted for some of the growth. Some of the western papers were founded as means of promoting settlement and sale of lands, like the *Oregon Spectator,* begun in Oregon City in 1846 as the first Pacific Coast publication. Others were missionary papers, like the first publications in Kansas and the Oklahoma region. Army posts also contributed papers. The weeklies typically carried a good deal of literary material, in addition to local news. The dailies, too, attempted to satisfy the hunger for reading matter as well as news. The *Alta California,* which began in San Francisco in 1849 and became the city's first daily in 1850, later achieved fame for publishing the writings of Bret Harte and Samuel Clemens, better known as Mark Twain. Nevada's *Territorial Enterprise,* founded in 1858, boasted Mark Twain as city editor in the early 1860s.

The push into the Far West and into the mining country produced other early newspapers: the *Oregonian* in Portland in 1850; the *Sacramento Union* (1851), *Los Angeles Star* (1851), and *San Francisco Bulletin* (1855) and *San Francisco Call* (1856); the Mormon Church's *Deseret News* in Salt Lake City in 1850; and the *Rocky Mountain News* in the Denver mining area in 1859. Easterners who flocked to the California gold fields and to the Nevada and Colorado mining towns wanted more news than the local papers offered, however. New York papers, particularly the *Herald* and the *Tribune,* issued California editions that were sent by steamer around the Horn, or by overland stage. Papers in other eastern cities soon followed suit. For wherever an American went in the expanding nation, he or she wanted the news that an aggressive press corps was providing.

NOTES

1. Gerald W. Johnson et al., *The Sunpapers of Baltimore* (New York: Knopf, 1937), p. 50.
2. Ibid., p. 51.
3. The North Carolina-based study directed by Donald L. Shaw was reported in part by Professor Shaw and Mary E. Junck in *Research Previews,* April 1971, and by Shaw in "Technology and Conformity: A Study of Newsgathering in the American Press, 1820–60," an unpublished paper presented at the Association for Education in Journalism meeting, 1972, using three leading New York papers as a case study. Papers presented to the AEJ in 1976 by David H. Weaver, "U.S. Newspaper Content from 1820 to 1860: A Mirror of the Times?" and by Gerald J. Baldasty, "The South Carolina Press and National News, 1807–47," reflect similar interest. Weaver, in a random sample study of North Carolina-collected data, found that papers in all sections of the country emphasized general community, general political, and intellectual and cultural news; paid attention to economic news and science and technology, but little to education; gave little emphasis to the conflict issues of slavery, abolition, expansionism, and sectional differences, except in the Lower South. The sample, of course, could not measure news play at exact moments of major sectional

conflict events. Baldasty found the South Carolina press depended heavily on the Washington press, particularly the *National Intelligencer,* through the 1830s, then reflected more diversity as technological change occurred.

4. Frederick B. Marbut, *News from the Capital: The Story of Washington Reporting* (Carbondale: Southern Illinois University Press, 1971), pp. 29–37.

5. Maurine Beasley, *The First Women Washington Correspondents* (Washington: GW Washington Studies, No. 4, 1976), pp. 3–9.

6. The *Courier and Enquirer* had found the cost of maintaining a pony route too great. But the *Journal of Commerce* continued its private express, extending it to Washington so as to gain a day over rival New York papers depending on the government's Philadelphia-New York express. Other papers were showing similar news enterprise, particularly those in Boston, the *Providence Journal,* and the *Charleston Courier.*.

7. Frederic Hudson, *Journalism in the United States* (New York: Harper & Row, 1873), pp. 366–67. Oliver Gramling, in his *AP: The Story of News* (New York: Farrar, Straus & Giroux, 1940), presents a dramatic account of the beginnings of the Associated Press, but the historical basis for the details he relates has never been established.

8. Richard A. Schwarzlose, "Early Telegraphic News Dispatches: Forerunner of the AP," *Journalism Quarterly,* LI (Winter 1974), 595. The *Courier and Enquirer,* also studied, ran the identical story on July 7. The study's depth forbade reading of more than three files. Schwarzlose was unable to determine who was running the news service in 1846.

9. Victor Rosewater, *History of Cooperative News-Gathering in the United States* (New York: Appleton-Century-Crofts, 1930), pp. 64–66.

10. The document was uncovered by Richard A. Schwarzlose, a leading researcher in the history and operations of the press associations. See his "Harbor News Association: The Formal Origin of the AP," *Journalism Quarterly,* XLV (Summer 1968), 253, in which he reviews all the evidence concerning the genesis of the AP.

11. Reprinted in Rosewater, *History of Cooperative News-Gathering,* pp. 381–88.

12. *Baltimore Sun,* April 12, 1847.

13. *New York Herald,* May 15, 1846.

14. *New York Tribune,* May 12, 1846.

15. *New York Herald,* May 12, 1846.

16. *New York Herald,* February 26, 1846.

17. The best known of these papers were the *Picayune, Delta, Crescent, Tropic, Commercial Times,* and the *Bee.*

18. *New York Sun,* January 20, April 15, 19, 1847. For a detailed study see Thomas W. Reilly, "American Reporters and the Mexican War, 1846–1848," Ph.D. thesis, University of Minnesota, 1975.

ANNOTATED BIBLIOGRAPHY

Books

BAUER, K. JACK, *The Mexican War: 1846–48.* New York: Macmillan, 1974. Good military account.

CHEVIGNY, BELL GALE, *The Woman and the Myth: Margaret Fuller's Life and Writings.* Old Westbury, N.Y.: Feminist Press, 1976. Biography of famed intellectual leader and writer of 1840s.

COPELAND, FAYETTE, *Kendall of the Picayune.* Norman: University of Oklahoma Press, 1943. An interesting account of the life and times of a pioneer New Orleans editor and Mexican War correspondent.

DABNEY, THOMAS E., *One Hundred Great Years.* Baton Rouge: Louisiana State University Press, 1944. The centennial history of the *New Orleans Times-Picayune.*

GRAMLING, OLIVER, *AP: The Story of News.* New York: Farrar, Straus & Giroux, 1940. A colorful account of the rise of the Associated Press. Its content cannot always be substantiated by document and evidence, however.

GREELEY, HORACE, *Overland Journey from New York to San Francisco in the Summer of 1859,* edited with notes by Charles T. Duncan. New York: Knopf, 1963. Valuable biographical material as well as Greeley's view of the West.

HAGE, GEORGE S., *Newspapers on the Minnesota Frontier, 1849–1860*. St. Paul: Minnesota Historical Society, 1967. What frontier journalism was like, carefully researched and well written.

HARLOW, ALVIN F., *Old Wires and New Waves: The History of the Telegraph, Telephone, and Wireless*. New York: Appleton-Century-Crofts, 1936. First half of the book covers the pre-Civil War period.

HOE, ROBERT, *Short History of the Printing Press*. New York: R. Hoe and Company, 1902. Obviously a promotional venture, but valuable in describing presses.

HUDSON, FREDERIC, *Journalism in the United States, 1690–1872*. New York: Harper & Row, 1873. One of the oldest journalism histories, but especially useful in the description of the mid-nineteenth century period because the author knew many of the persons he discusses.

JOHNSON, GERALD, ET AL., *The Sunpapers of Baltimore*. New York: Knopf, 1937. An excellent case history of the penny press outside New York.

McMURTRIE, DOUGLAS C., AND ALBERT H. ALLEN, *Early Printing in Colorado*. Denver: Hirschfeld Press, 1935. McMurtrie also wrote articles about the journalism of other western states, for *Journalism Quarterly* and other periodicals.

MARBUT, FREDERICK B., *News from the Capital: The Story of Washington Reporting*. Carbondale: Southern Illinois University Press, 1971. History of reporting, both print and broadcast, by a longtime student of the Washington press corps.

ROSEWATER, VICTOR, *History of Cooperative News-Gathering in the United States*. New York: Appleton-Century-Crofts, 1930. Standard source for origins.

SWISSHELM, JANE GREY, *Half a Century*. Chicago: Jansen, McClurg and Co., 1880. Autobiography of first woman Washington correspondent, crusader.

Periodicals and Monographs

BEASLEY, MAURINE, *The First Women Washington Correspondents*. Washington: GW Washington Studies, No. 4, 1976. Report on seven nineteenth century newswomen. See also her "Pens and Petticoats: Early Women Washington Correspondents," *Journalism History*, I (Winter 1974), 112, and "The Curious Case of Anne Royall," *Journalism History*, III (Winter 1976), 98.

CARTER, JOHN D., *The San Francisco Bulletin, 1855–1865*. Ph.D. thesis, University of California, 1941. A study in the beginnings of Pacific Coast journalism.

ENDRES, KATHLEEN, "Jane Grey Swisshelm: 19th-Century Journalist and Feminist," *Journalism History*, II (Winter 1975), 128. Early Washington correspondent.

FIREBAUGH, DOROTHY GILE, "The Sacramento Union: Voice of California, 1851–75," *Journalism Quarterly*, XXX (Summer 1953), 321. The story of a dominant paper.

HALL, MARK W., "1831–49: The Pioneer Period for Newspapers in California," *Journalism Quarterly*, XLIX (Winter 1972), 648. Mexican War brought Yanks.

LORENZ, ALFRED L., " 'Out of Sorts and Out of Cash': Problems of Publishing in Wisconsin Territory, 1833-1848," *Journalism History*, III (Summer 1976), 34. See also his "Hamilton Reed: An Editor's Trials on the Wisconsin Frontier," *Journalism Quarterly*, LIII (Autumn 1976), 417.

MARBUT, FREDERICK B., "Early Washington Correspondents: Some Neglected Pioneers," *Journalism Quarterly*, XXV (December 1948), 369. See also his "The United States Senate and the Press, 1838–41," *Journalism Quarterly*, XXVIII (Summer 1951), 342.

McINTYRE, JERILYN, "Communication on a Western Frontier—Some Questions About Context," *Journalism History*, III (Summer 1976), 53. News use patterns.

NELSON, ANNA KASTEN. "Mission to Mexico—Moses Y. Beach, Secret Agent." *The New York State Historical Society Quarterly* LIX (July 1975), 227.

NELSON, JACK A., "The Pioneer Press of the Great Basin," Ph.D. thesis, University of Missouri, 1971. Nevada and Utah editors lacked news ethics.

PICKETT, CALDER M., "Technology and the New York Press in the 19th Century," *Journalism Quarterly*, XXXVII (Summer 1960), 398. Based on "Six New York Newspapers and Their

Response to Technology in the 19th Century,'' Ph.D. thesis, University of Minnesota, 1959.

REILLY, TOM, "Newspaper Suppression During the Mexican War," *Journalism Quarterly,* LIV (Summer 1977), 262.

REILLY, THOMAS W., "American Reporters and the Mexican War, 1846–1848," Ph.D. thesis, University of Minnesota, 1975. Coverage of war was extensive and reinforced the American belief in Manifest Destiny. Much new material presented interestingly.

SCHWARZLOSE, RICHARD A., "Early Telegraphic News Dispatches: Forerunner of the AP," *Journalism Quarterly,* LI (Winter 1974), 595. Pinpoints AP birth.

———, "Harbor News Association: Formal Origin of the AP," *Journalism Quarterly,* XLV (Summer 1968), 253. Legal date of AP predecessor's founding is January 11, 1849, document discloses.

WEIGLE, CLIFFORD F., "San Francisco Journalism, 1847–1851," *Journalism Quarterly,* XIV (June 1937), 151. The beginnings of a colorful journalistic tradition.

FREEDOM'S JOURNAL.

"*RIGHTEOUSNESS EXALTETH A NATION.*"

CORNISH & RUSSWURM,
Editors & Proprietors.

NEW-YORK, FRIDAY, MARCH 16, 1827.

VOL. I. NO. 1.

TO OUR PATRONS.

IN presenting our first number to our Patrons, we feel all the diffidence of persons entering upon a new and untried line of business. But a moment's reflection upon the noble objects, which we have in view by the publication of this Journal; the expediency of its appearance at this time, when so many schemes are in action concerning our people —encourage us to come boldly before an enlightened publick. For we believe, that a paper devoted to the dissemination of useful knowledge among our brethren, and to their moral and religious improvement, must meet with the cordial approbation of every friend to humanity.

The peculiarities of this Journal, render it important that we should advertise to the world the motives by which we are actuated, and the objects which we contemplate.

We wish to plead our own cause. Too long have others spoken for us. Too long has the publick been deceived by misrepresentations, in things which concern us dearly, though in the estimation of some mere trifles; for though there are many in society who exercise towards us benevolent feelings; still (with sorrow we confess it) there are others who make it their business to enlarge upon the least trifle, which tends to the discredit of any person of colour; and pronounce anathemas and denounce our whole body for the misconduct of this guilty one. We are aware that there are many instances of vice among us, but we avow that it is because no one has taught its subjects to be virtuous; many instances of poverty, because no sufficient efforts accommodated to minds contracted by slavery, and deprived of early education have been made, to teach them how to husband their hard earnings, and to secure to themselves comforts.

Education being an object of the highest importance to the welfare of society, we shall endeavour to present just and adequate views of it, and to urge upon our brethren the necessity and expediency of training their children, while young, to habits of industry, and thus forming them for becoming useful members of society. It is surely time that we should awake from this lethargy of years, and make a concentrated effort for the education of our youth. We form a spoke in the human wheel, and it is necessary that we should understand our pendence on the different parts, and theirs on us, in order to perform our part with propriety.

Though not desirous of dictating, we shall feel it our incumbent duty to dwell occasionally upon the general principles and rules of economy. The world has grown too enlightened, to estimate any man's character by his personal appearance. Though all men acknowledge the excellency of Franklin's maxims, yet comparatively few practise upon them. We may deplore when it is too late, the neglect of these self-evident truths, but it avails little to mourn. Ours will be the task of admonishing our brethren on these points.

The civil rights of a people being of the greatest value, it shall ever be our duty to vindicate our brethren, when oppressed; and to lay the case before the publick. We shall also urge upon our brethren, (who are qualified by the laws of the different states,) the expediency of using their elective franchise; and of making an independent use of the same. We wish them not to become the tools of party.

And as much time is frequently lost, and wrong principles instilled, by the perusal of works of trivial importance, we shall consider it a part of our duty to recommend to our young readers, such authors as will not only enlarge their stock of useful knowledge, but such as will also serve to stimulate them to higher attainments in science.

We trust also, that through the columns of the FREEDOM'S JOURNAL, many practical pieces, having for their bases, the improvement of our brethren, will be presented to them, from the pens of many of our respected friends, who have kindly promised their assistance.

It is our earnest wish to make our Journal a medium of intercourse between our brethren in the different states of this great confederacy: that through its columns an expression of our sentiments, on many interesting subjects which concern us, may be offered to the publick: that plans which apparently are beneficial may be candidly discussed and properly weighed; if worthy, receive our cordial approbation; if not, our marked disapprobation.

Useful knowledge of every kind, and every thing that relates to Africa, shall find a ready admission into our columns; and as that vast continent becomes daily more known, we trust that many things will come to light, proving that the natives of it are neither so ignorant nor stupid as they have generally been supposed to be.

And while these important subjects shall occupy the columns of the FREEDOM'S JOURNAL; we would not be unmindful of our brethren who are still in the iron fetters of bondage. They are our kindred by all the ties of nature; and though but little can be effected by us, still let our sympathies be poured forth, and our prayers in their behalf, ascend to Him who is able to succour them.

From the press and the pulpit we have suffered much by being incorrectly represented. Men, whom we equally love and admire have not hesitated to represent us disadvantageously, without becoming personally acquainted with the true state of things, nor discerning between virtue and vice among us. The virtuous part of our people feel themselves sorely aggrieved under the existing state of things—they are not appreciated.

Our vices and our degradation are ever arrayed against us, but our virtues are passed by unnoticed. And what is still more lamentable, our friends, to whom we concede all the principles of humanity and religion, from those very causes seem to have fallen into the current of popular feeling and are imperceptibly floating on the stream—actually living in the practice of prejudice, while they abjure it in theory, and feel it not in their hearts. Is it not very desirable that such should know more of our actual condition, and of our efforts and feelings, that in forming or advocating plans for our amelioration, they may do it more understandingly? In the spirit of candor and humility we intend by a simple representation of facts to lay our case before the publick, with a view to arrest the progress of prejudice, and to shield ourselves against the consequent evils. We wish to conciliate all and to irritate none, yet we must be firm and unwavering in our principles, and persevering in our efforts.

If ignorance, poverty and degradation have hitherto been our unhappy lot; has the Eternal decree gone forth, that our race alone, are to remain in this state, while knowledge and civilization are shedding their enlivening rays over the rest of the human family? The recent travels of Denham and Clapperton in the interior of Africa, and the interesting narrative which they have published; the establishment of the republic of Hayti after years of sanguinary warfare; its subsequent progress in all the arts of civilization; and the advancement of liberal ideas in South America, where despotism has given place to free governments, and where many of our brethren now fill important civil and military stations, prove the contrary.

The interesting fact that there are FIVE HUNDRED THOUSAND free persons of colour, one half of whom might peruse, and the whole be benefitted by the publication of the Journal; that no publication, as yet, has been devoted exclusively to their improvement—that many selections from approved standard authors, which are within the reach of few, may occasionally be made—and more important still, that this large body of our citizens have no public channel—all serve to prove the real necessity, at present, for the appearance of the FREEDOM'S JOURNAL.

It shall ever be our desire so to conduct the editorial department of our paper as to give offence to none of our patrons; as nothing is farther from us than to make it the advocate of any partial views, either in politics or religion. What few days we can number, have been devoted to the improvement of our brethren; and it is our earnest wish that the remainder may be spent in the same delightful service.

In conclusion, whatever concerns us as a people, will ever find a ready admission into the FREEDOM'S JOURNAL, interwoven with all the principal news of the day.

And while every thing in our power shall be performed to support the character of our Journal, we would respectfully invite our numerous friends to assist by their communications, and our coloured brethren to strengthen our hands by their subscriptions, as our labour is one of common cause, and worthy of their consideration and support. And we do most earnestly solicit the latter, that if at any time we should seem to be zealous, or too pointed in the inculcation of any important lesson, they will remember, that they are equally interested in the cause in which we are engaged, and attribute our zeal to the peculiarities of our situation, and our earnest engagedness in their well-being.

THE EDITORS.

From the Liverpool Mercury.
MEMOIRS OF CAPT. PAUL CUFFEE.

"On the first of the present month of August, 1811, a vessel arrived at Liverpool, with a cargo from Sierra Leone; the owner, master, mate, and whole crew of which are free blacks. The master, who is also owner, is the son of an American slave, and is said to be very well skilled both in trade and navigation, as well as to be of a very pious and moral character. It must have been a strange and an animating spectacle to see this free and enlightened African, entering as an independent trader with his black crew into that port, which was so lately the *nidus* of the slave trade.—*Edinburgh Review for August,* 1811."

We are happy in having an opportunity of confirming the above account, and at the same time of laying before our readers an authentic memoir of Capt. *Paul Cuffee,* the master and owner of the vessel above alluded to, who sailed from this port on the 20th ult. with a licence from the British Government, to prosecute his intended voyage to Sierra Leone.—The father of Paul Cuffee was a native of Africa,—whence he was brought as a slave into Massachusetts. He was there purchased by a person named Slocum, and remained in slavery a very considerable portion of his life. He was named Cuffee, but as it is usual in those parts, took the name of Slocum, as expressing to whom he belonged. Like many of his countrymen he possessed a mind far superior to his condition; although he was diligent in the business of his master, and faithful to his interest, yet by great industry and economy he was enabled to purchase his personal liberty. At the time the remains of several Indian tribes, who originally possessed the right of soil, resided in Massachusetts. Cuffee became acquainted with a woman descended from one of those tribes, named Ruth Moses, and married her. He continued in habits of industry and frugality, and soon afterwards purchased a farm of 100 acres at the point in Massachusetts.

Cuffee and Ruth had a family of ten children. The three eldest sons, David, Jonathan, and John, are farmers in the neighbourhood of West Point; filling respectable situations in society, and endowed with good intellectual capacities. They are all married, and have families to whom they are giving good educations. Of six daughters four are respectably married, while two remain single. Paul was born on the Island of Cutterhumpker, one of the Elizabeth Islands, near New-Bedford, in the year 1759—he was about fourteen years of age, his father died, leaving a considerable property in land, but which being at that time unproductive, afforded but little provision for his numerous family, and thus the care of supporting his mother and sisters devolved upon his brothers and himself. At this time Paul conceived that commerce furnished to industry more ample rewards than agriculture, and he was conscious that he possessed qualities which under the proper culture, would enable him to pursue commercial employments with prospects of success—he therefore entered at the age of sixteen, as a common hand on board of a vessel destined to the bay of Mexico, on a whaling voyage. His second voyage was to the West Indies, but on his third he was captured by a British ship during the American war, about the year 1776—after three months detention as a prisoner, at New-York, he was permitted to return home to Westport, where owing to the unfortunate continuance of hostilities he spent about two years in his agricultural pursuits. During this interval Paul and his brother John Cuffee, were called on by the collector of the district, in which they resided, for the payment of a personal tax. It appeared to them, that by the laws and constitution of Massachusetts, taxation and the whole rights of citizenship were united. If the laws demanded of them the payment of the personal taxes, the same laws must necessarily and constitutionally invest them with the right of representing and being represented in the state legislature. But they had never been considered as entitled to the privilege of voting at elections, nor of being elected to places of trust and honor. Under these circumstances they refused payment of the demands. The collector resorted to the force of the laws, and after many delays and detentions, Paul and his brother deemed it most prudent to silence them by paying the demands; but they resolved, if it were possible to obtain the rights which they believed to be connected with taxation. They presented a respectful petition to the state legislature. From some individuals it met with a warm, and almost indignant opposition. A considerable majority was, however, favorable to their object. They perceived the propriety and justice of the petition, and with an honorable magnanimity, in defiance of the prejudice of the times, they passed a law rendering all free persons of color liable to taxation, according to the established ratio, for white men, and granting them all the privileges, belonging to the other citizens. This was a day equally honorable to the petitioners and the legislature—a day which ought to be gratefully remembered by every person of color, within the boundaries of Massachusetts, and the names of John and Paul Cuffee, should always be united with its recollection.

To be Continued.

COMMON SCHOOLS IN NEW-YORK.—It appears from the report of the Superintendent of Common Schools in the state of New-York, presented last week to the House of Assembly, that of the 723 towns and wards in the State, 721 have made returns according to law: That in these towns there are 8114 school districts, and of course the same number of schools; from 7544 of which returns have been received: That 441 new school dis-

12

The Press
and the Rise
of Sectionalism

He who opposes the public liberty overthrows his own.
—William Lloyd Garrison

The Jacksonian era brought out clearly the increasing absorption in sectional differences. The beginning of the "irrepressible conflict," as one historian has called the War Between the States, can be traced back to colonial times.[1] The petitions to the king long before 1776; the arguments over the Constitution at the Philadelphia convention; the drafting of the Kentucky and Virginia Resolutions after the Alien and Sedition Acts were passed; and the debates over the tariff of 1828 are some of the evidences of the fault line along which the country would one day split. By 1848, people were no longer voting by party but by section.

Up to about 1820 there was no great southern unit with the regional cohesion that was apparent a decade later. The South actually was more torn apart by dissension than any other section up to 1820. The upland communities had fought against the tidewater elite in the Revolution, largely as a result of social strains. Large areas of the South had more in common with the West. And the Negro added another source of social friction.

There is a tendency to think of the South as turning away from American traditions when it seceded in 1861. But it was the North, meaning the industrial Northeast, not the South, that developed a different way of life after 1820. Generally speaking, the South was about the same in 1861 as it had been in 1761. On the eve of the War Between the States, the South retained the impress of the eighteenth century. Life centered in the plantation, and so commercial cities did not assume the importance they had in the Northeast. Lacking such centers, the South had only a small middle class and virtually no white proletariat. But it abounded in great orators, great statesmen, and great literary spokesmen. British cotton and tobacco buyers took the South's main crops, and the southerner bought as well as sold abroad.

151

From this environment came a governing group with a high sense of honor and morals. Family and land counted for more than money in the South, because money was not so essential to the agrarian as it was to the northern capitalist and wage earner. Money was the sign of success in the North. Land was the criterion in the South. But land values declined in the South some time after 1800, as the staple crops exhausted the soil. Little was known of fertilization of soil then, and so immigrants moved to fresh land, thereby reducing the demand for, and consequently the value of, the older lands. Since there was no profit to be made in land speculation, trade, or industry, the capitalist tended to leave the agrarian in full control. The South thus had reason to fear for its future. The industrial North was growing much faster than the South. Population pressure would inevitably give the North political dominance. Already the "tariff of abominations" of 1828 had disclosed what the North would impose upon the South if given free rein.

Both sections turned to the West as an ally, when it became clear that the frontier region would determine the outcome of the conflict. The West was agrarian, like the South. It also suffered from high tariffs. Westerners had natural antipathies to the industrial North. They resented the northern sabotage of every legislative attempt to ease the debt of the farmer and to open up free lands. On the other hand, the westerner was not as dependent on world markets as was the southerner. The westerner was interested in reaching local or regional markets. His problem was to get his produce to these markets cheaply and easily, and here he found an ally in the northern capitalist. Roads, canals, steamboat subsidies, and railroads were the prices paid by the North for the temporary allegiance of the West against the South.

The westerner also demanded the opening up of the frontier to homesteaders. Both the North and South were opposed to this. Southerners feared the opening of new lands would lead to a preponderance of free states, which would add to the overwhelming weight against the South. Northerners, on the other hand, tended to block westward expansion because it depressed property values in their section and because free land kept wages higher than they would otherwise have been, or else reduced the reservoir of cheap labor in the industrial areas. The point here is that western victory on this issue was a kind of bribe paid by the North for the support of the West. One evidence of this was the Homestead Act, passed on the eve of the war after years of northern objection. Once the West had committed itself, the South had only two choices. It could admit defeat and modify its way of life to suit the North, or it could cast off from an alien system and go its own way—secede.

So far, nothing has been said about slavery as a main cause of the Civil War. If slavery had been such an important issue, time alone would have solved the problem. For slavery was already doomed. World opinion was against it. Already it had proved itself to be uneconomical in the upper tier of slave states. By 1860 these states were unloading surplus slave labor as fast as planters in the deep South could absorb it. The capitalist of the North had demonstrated that it was cheaper to pay a man only while he was useful than to support him as a slave throughout the unproductive years of his life.

Slavery was not a primary cause of the conflict, but it became important as the means for joining the battle, and here the journalist played his big role. There would probably have been sectional strife with or without slavery. But slavery, like the religious double talk of two centuries earlier, was the basket in which all the differences of peoples, regions, and ideologies could be carried. The slavery shibboleth was the rallying standard for all the various belligerents. It was the simplification of complex problems and summed up the attitudes of those who had to do the dying in battle.

It is unfortunate that slavery had to be the issue on which the concept of the American union had to be tested. When the South seceded, it did so on the principle that the minority had the right to protect itself from the tyranny of a majority. Slavery lifted the doctrines of North and South onto a plane that made them more discernible to the average man. Few would be willing to die for economic principles. But slavery could supply the hate transference that could make a John Brown, for example, die for such a cause at Harper's Ferry in 1859. To Ralph Waldo Emerson, "Old Ossawatomie" Brown had "made the gallows glorious like the cross." And Walt Whitman, poet and sometime journalist, wrote of Brown's execution:

I would sing how an old man, with white hair, mounted the scaffold in Virginia,
(I was at hand, silent I stood with teeth shut close, I watch'd,
I stood very near you old man when cool and indifferent, but trembling with age and your
    unheal'd wounds, you mounted the scaffold . . .)[2]

This indicates what the slavery issue meant to men of lofty sentiment. It took some time to sweep the masses into the movement, but eventually the people of the North and South made slavery a fighting issue, and the press was effective in bringing this about. Advocates of the campaigns against slavery were known as "abolitionists." An outstanding abolitionist editor was William Lloyd Garrison. He makes an excellent case study of how the press became such an important factor in the struggle.

GARRISON AND THE *LIBERATOR*

Garrison was born in Newburyport, Massachusetts, of English and Irish stock. The father was a drunkard who abused his family, and the boy must have been influenced by these circumstances when he took up the temperance issue while still a youth. He was a jack-of-all-trades until he became a printer. That appeared to be his proper niche. Like Benjamin Russell and Isaiah Thomas, Garrison received most of his education at the type case. It was an education that made him literate rather than learned.

He was in his twenties when he met Benjamin Lundy, the gentle Quaker who had started out as a temperance missionary but who had since carried this reforming zeal over into the anti-slavery movement. It is significant that Quakers had been important in the successful anti-slavery movement in Great Britain. At any rate, Garrison became one of Lundy's recruits. Soon Garrison had been satisfactorily persecuted—an essential step in the progress of any effective zealot. He emerged from seven months in jail a confirmed abolitionist, and with that supreme gift—a cause so absorbing that life itself is not too great a price for it. He moved to Boston, and on January 1, 1831, he issued there the first copy of the *Liberator*.

It was not very impressive, this voice of the abolitionist. Garrison said in 1837 that his publication had never exceeded 3,000 subscribers. Much of the time it hovered around 1,500, and about one-fourth of the circulation was in Negro areas, where the readers were either disfranchised or had little political influence. The editor was always losing entire blocks of readers because of his tactless scorn of men, institutions, or traditions sacred to certain publics. And yet this was part of the medium that was to rouse the North to battle.

Garrison had one weapon, his press, but it was to make him invincible. Through this press he spread his creed far and wide, until the abolitionist movement began to work on the minds of the apathetic. He reached such persons with words like these:

He who opposes the public liberty overthrows his own. . . .
There is no safety where there is no strength; no strength without Union; no Union

without justice; no justice where faith and truth are wanting. The right to be free is a truth planted in the hearts of men. . . .[3]

This describes Garrison, a man of courage and determination, imbued with righteousness, narrow and fanatical. What he said was bad for business. Most of the country was prosperous at this time. When people are comfortable, conscience is often half asleep. Garrison jerked consciences awake—always an unpopular move. Even the religious leaders resented the man, particularly his self-righteousness. One clergyman complained that abolitionists like Garrison did not do their work like "Christian gentlemen." To which Garrison replied:

These are your men of "caution" and "prudence" and "judiciousness." Sir, I have learned to hate those words. Whenever we attempt to imitate our Great Exemplar, and press the truth of God in all its plainness upon the conscience, why, we are imprudent; because, forsooth, a great excitement will ensue. Sir, slavery will not be overthrown without excitement—a most tremendous excitement.[4]

Garrison caused the most violent public reaction since Tom Paine drew his red hot plowshare through American history. Amos Kendall, himself a great journalist and a leader of Jacksonian democracy, believed that Garrison should be gagged. As postmaster general he allowed abolitionist papers to be rifled from the official mail sacks by southern "committees" charged with that task.[5] The state of Massachusetts was ready to forbid the export of the *Liberator,* and in many states, distributors of the paper were intimidated. without redress.

ABOLITIONISTS AND "FIRE-EATERS"   James G. Birney, one of the more reasonable abolitionists, was mobbed when he began printing his paper, the *Philanthropist,* at Cincinnati. Note that this was a city in a northern, not a southern, state. From that day on, Birney began to devote his energy to fighting for a free press along with his fight for freeing slaves. The abolitionists saw very clearly that the slavery issue would sooner or later affect all the freedoms in both the North and the South. One of the most stirring messages on this subject, "Free Speech and Free Inquiry," appears in the April 2, 1847, issue of the *Liberator.*

At least one abolitionist died for this cause. He was Elijah Lovejoy, editor of the *St. Louis Observer,* a strident abolitionist weekly founded in 1835. A mass meeting of irate citizens resulted in a resolution informing Lovejoy that free expression as guaranteed in the Bill of Rights did not extend to editors such as Lovejoy who threatened the peace of the community. Lovejoy replied that public resolutions could not fetter an editor.

As an act of good faith, however, Lovejoy moved his press across the river to Alton, Illinois. His office was at once wrecked by a mob. He appealed nationally for support and received enough help to set up another press. This was also demolished. Again he appealed for assistance, and again there was a quick and positive response. The climax came in 1837 while he was setting up his third press in Alton. A group of citizens decided that the Lovejoy nuisance should be abated. They called a mass meeting to devise plans. Lovejoy refused to be intimidated and boldly attended the meeting to present his side. He promised to suspend publication if his readers requested him to, but he declared he would not be ruled by mob hysteria. He said he would return to his office and would defend his right to publish with his life, if need be. When the mob marched down the street after the meeting, it was motivated not by the desire to destroy a press but to destroy a man who refused to renounce his right to think and to express himself. Lovejoy was killed by the mob.

Garrison's *Liberator* reports the murder of abolitionist Elijah Lovejoy.

The southern counterpart of the abolitionist was the "fire-eater." Outstanding fire-eaters were William Lowndes Yancey, Edmund Ruffin, and Robert Barnwell Rhett. Yancey was one of the great orators of his era. It was Yancey who led the South from the Democratic convention of 1860. Ruffin was an agricultural writer, who introduced marl as a fertilizer to restore exhausted tobacco land. He was a tireless and indomitable southern patriot. When more timid souls hesitated to fire upon Fort Sumter in 1861, it was Ruffin who snatched the lanyard of the nearest cannon and sent the first ball screaming its message of war. And it was Ruffin who committed suicide rather than take the oath of allegiance after Appomattox. But of all the fire-eaters, Rhett was most effective.

Rhett, sometimes called the "father of secession," was editor of the *Charleston Mercury,* which he made into one of the leading papers of the deep South. By 1832 he was declaring openly that the only safety for the South was for it to go its own way. No one paid much attention to Rhett at first. He was treated about as coldly in the South as Garrison had been in the North. But after such magnificent propaganda successes as *Uncle Tom's Cabin,* the South began to depend on its Rhetts, Yanceys, and Ruffins for justification. By 1848, Rhett was once again powerful politically. In 1851 he succeeded to the Senate seat of the great Calhoun.

Ironically, Rhett had no intention of involving his section in a war. He had aroused the South to fighting pitch, but he had assumed all along that the North would not dare fight. On the day Sumter was fired upon, Rhett was still reassuring readers of the *Mercury* that the South would secede peaceably. He should have known better. Lincoln's refusal to evacuate the fort peacefully was proof that this time the North meant business.

BLACK JOURNALISTS   Abolitionists like Garrison and fire-eaters like Rhett attracted
AS ABOLITIONISTS   both immediate and continuing attention because they represen-
                          ted the extremes of white America's reaction to Negro slavery,
whose emotional clash eventually produced a civil war. Nothing the Negro could do or
say for himself seemed important to a society that viewed him as an economic,
political, and educational nonequal. In 1850 there were about a half-million free
Negroes in the American population, half of them in the North and half in the South.
But in the South, state laws prohibited Negroes from receiving any formal education,
and chances to make decent incomes were few. In the North, state laws restricted
Negro voting rights, and the uneven availability of public schools weighed quickly on
children of disfranchised, poor, and illiterate blacks. There was a chance, however, to
"get ahead," and some Negroes succeeded. A handful of freedmen won sufficient
education to become writers, lawyers, physicians, businessmen in the era before the
Civil War. To them, and to their friends in the white population, 40 struggling black
newspapers were addressed between 1827 and 1865.[6]

These were virtually all dedicated contributions to the anti-slavery, abolitionist
movement. And as such, they rank high in the regard of today's students of the black
experience in America. It should not be startling to discover that there were blacks who
spoke out for themselves; what is startling is that they could succeed as well as they did
in the face of poverty and illiteracy among most of their audience, as well as in the face
of almost total rejection by a white society that ignored their existence.

Slavery was not abolished everywhere north of the Mason-Dixon line until 1804,
and early leadership among slaves seeking their freedom is found in Massachusetts and
Pennsylvania before 1800. By 1830 there were some 50 Negro anti-slavery societies,
with the most active located in New York, Philadelphia, Boston, and New Haven.
Negro self-expression had long been centered in the folk songs and spirituals of the
black slaves. Now a few freedmen had become adept at oratory, at poetry, at
autobiographical writing that had produced moving accounts in book form of what it
meant to live as a slave. Some freedmen had seen their articles or letters published by
white editors in the regular press; some had worked with Garrison and his *Liberator*
group or the other white abolitionists. A particularly vicious attack on these Negro
leaders by Mordecai M. Noah, editor of the *New York Enquirer,* is credited with
spurring the founding of the first black-published newspaper in the United States.[7]

Freedom's Journal was its name and in its first issue on March 16, 1827, it
printed this simple explanation of the venture: "We wish to plead our own cause. Too
long have others spoken for us." Its editors were John B. Russwurm, first Negro to
graduate from a college in the United States (Bowdoin in 1826), and Reverend Samuel
Cornish, a Presbyterian who edited three different weeklies in New York City in this
period. A four-page paper, 10 by 15 inches in size, *Freedom's Journal* agitated
ruthlessly against the inhumanity of slavery but also ran newsy items, sermons,
poetry, and other literary fare. Russwurm left in 1828 to undertake a career as editor
and government official in Liberia, and Cornish continued the paper under the name
Rights of All. The known file ceases in October 1829.[8]

It was in 1829 that David Walker issued his *Appeal* out of Boston, advocating
violent measures to eliminate slavery, and George Moses Horton protested in Raleigh
through the columns of his *Hope of Liberty*. During the racial turmoil in 1965 Walker's
call for militant resistance was republished in paperback book form.

Another major effort at a black paper in New York City came in 1837 when Phillip
A. Bell founded *The Weekly Advocate*. Renamed two months later as *The Colored
American,* it appeared until 1842. Its first editor was Reverend Samuel Cornish and the

publisher was a Canadian, Robert Sears of Toronto. Cornish and Bell retired from the paper in May 1839 and Dr. Charles Bennet Ray became the guiding force of the spirited little paper. He made it not only an anti-slavery organ but also a "paper devoted primarily to the interests of the colored population, and . . . a first-rate family paper." Circulation reached 2,000 in an area from Maine to Michigan.[9]

When the regular dailies in Pittsburgh refused to run contributions by Negroes in 1843, Dr. Martin R. Delaney, first of his race to graduate from Harvard, founded *The Mystery*. William Wells Brown, the black writer and novelist of the period, described the physician as "decided and energetic in conversation, unadulterated in race, and proud of his complexion."[10] Delaney got in a libel suit but managed to keep his paper going until 1848 when it was purchased by the African Methodist Episcopal Church. Renamed the *Christian Herald,* then moved to Philadelphia in 1852 as the *Christian Recorder,* it was surviving in 1970 as oldest of the Negro religious weeklies.[11]

There were other notable efforts. One was the *Alienated American,* published from 1852 to 1856 in Cleveland by W. H. Day, a graduate of Oberlin College. Another was the *New Orleans Daily Creole,* an 1856 effort that was the first black-owned paper in the South and the first Negro daily. Bell, founder of the *Advocate* in New York, migrated to San Francisco and in 1865 began publishing *The Elevator,* which survived until 1889, an unusual feat for black papers. But the most famous of the pre-Civil War black papers were edited by the dynamic leader of the freed slaves and inspiration of his race, Frederick Douglass.

FREDERICK DOUGLASS, EDITOR

By the 1970s, Frederick Douglass had become a symbol of black achievement and inspiration—his home in Washington had become a national shrine, his autobiographical writings enjoyed fresh printings, his face was on a postage stamp, young black males spelled their names with a double "s" if they were named Douglas. All of which was merited, for this son of a Negro slave woman and a white man ran away from a Maryland plantation to make himself a leader of those of the black race who needed his skill at writing and oratory to assert their cause.

Born in 1817, he escaped slavery in 1838 and went to New England to work and gain additional education with the encouragement of William Lloyd Garrison, the abolitionist. He began to write for the newspapers and to speak as an eyewitness to the tragedy of the slavery system. In 1845 he went to England where friends raised enough money to buy his freedom from his Maryland owner. Back in the United States and known for the first of his autobiographical books (*Narrative of the Life of Frederick Douglass*), he was named an editor of *The Ram's Horn*. The paper was started in January 1847 by Willis A. Hodges as a black protest to such practices as that of the *New York Sun,* which had printed a letter from him and then sent him a bill for $15. Hodges's venture failed the next year but its columns carried this announcement in late 1847:

PROSPECTUS for an anti-slavery paper; to be entitled *North Star*. Frederick Douglass proposes to publish in Rochester a weekly Anti-slavery paper, with the above title. The object of the *North Star* will be to Attack Slavery in all its forms and aspects: Advocate Universal Emancipation; exalt the standard of Public Morality; promote the Moral and Intellectual improvement of the COLORED PEOPLE; and hasten the day of FREEDOM to the Three Millions of our Enslaved Fellow Countrymen.[12]

Publication of *The North Star* began November 1, 1847. It quickly rose to a circulation of some 3,000 and both was read in and received contributions from Europe

Bettmann Archive

Frederick Douglass

and the West Indies as well as much of the United States. In addition to articles about slavery and blacks, it carried a good cross section of national and world news. The masthead proclaimed: "Right is of no Sex—Truth is of no Color—God is the Father of us all, and we are all Brethren." Not everyone in Rochester thought so; just as the white abolitionists were terrorized, Douglass saw his house burned and his papers destroyed. But the spunky character of the paper and its literary quality were both so high that it survived financial difficulties and racial antagonism. Renamed *Frederick Douglass' Paper* in 1851 after a merger with a weaker sheet, the paper was symbolic of its editor's position as the recognized leader of the Negro population.

By mid-1860, with the issue of slavery clearly bringing the country to the verge of civil war, Douglass found the financial struggle too great and suspended his weekly. For the next three years he put out *Douglass' Monthly,* an abolitionist magazine aimed at a British audience, to aid the Northern war cause. In 1870 he became contributing editor of a Washington weekly, the *New Era,* that sought to aid the now-freed black people. The paper was no more popular than the cause; Douglass invested money in it, renamed it the *New National Era,* and became its fighting editor before admitting defeat (and a $10,000 loss) in 1875.[13] His second autobiographical effort, *My Bondage and My Freedom,* had appeared in 1855; now the final volume, *Life and Times of Frederick Douglass,* appeared in 1878. The remarkable ex-slave, skillful editor, polished orator, and inspirational fellow citizen died in 1895 at the age of 78.

THE NORTHERN PRESS AND THE SLAVERY ISSUE

The important standard papers of the day picked up the slavery issue presented to them by the black editors, the abolitionists, and the fire-eaters. By 1852 Horace Greeley's weekly *Tribune* had a circulation of more than 200,000, much of it in the crucial West. It was the acknowledged leader of those opposed to slavery. Greeley felt so strongly on the subject that he was willing to cast off the lifetime allegiances of the Whig to help organize a new party that brought Abraham Lincoln to the White House in 1860.

In January 1861, Greeley published the first of his "stand firm" editorials—accepted by readers, at least, as Lincoln's own commandments. In February he called for unity against the South by a slogan in large type at the head of the editorial column: "NO COMPROMISE/ NO CONCESSIONS TO TRAITORS/ THE CONSTITUTION AS IT IS." When the first shot of the war was fired April 12, 1861, Greeley wrote: "Sumter is temporarily lost, but Freedom is saved! It is hard to lose Sumter, but in losing it we have gained a united people. Long live the Republic." He asked for patience when critics, including Raymond, offered unreasonable suggestions, but by summer, he, too, was demanding action. On June 26 appeared the memorable editorial: "The Nation's War Cry: 'Forward to Richmond! The Rebel Congress must not be allowed to meet there on July 20. By that date the place must be held by the National Army.'" This was repeated in subsequent issues. After all this pressure, Greeley had a heavy conscience following the rout of the Union Army at the first battle of Bull Run. Managing editor Charles A. Dana had been in charge of the paper while Greeley was traveling, and Fitz-Henry Warren, the *Tribune's* Washington correspondent, had actually written the editorials.

All this time the "reasonableness" of Henry Raymond's *New York Times* had made the paper and its editor important journalistically and politically. When Greeley broke with Governor Seward and Thurlow Weed, Raymond largely succeeded as the mouthpiece of the old group. When the Whigs foundered on the free soil issue, Raymond threw in his lot with the new Republican party. He wrote the statement of principles at the Pittsburgh convention in 1856. It is noteworthy that he was lukewarm on abolitionism, however, until after Sumter. An early critic of Lincoln (possibly because his rival, Greeley, had helped nominate the rail-splitter) Raymond quickly adjusted to circumstance, as usual. Once the fighting began, Raymond was a staunch defender of the president.

Samuel Bowles III, who took over the *Springfield Republican* in 1851 after the death of his father, was faithful to the obsolete Whig party up to the eve of its death. He attacked the abolitionists at every opportunity, on the presumption that they were more interested in causing trouble than in solving problems. His concern over the growing quarrel between the two sections was shown in his approval of the Fugitive Slave law. He did not approve of slavery certainly, but neither did he approve of the agitation over it that might wreck the nation. His conversion came after passage of the Kansas-Nebraska bill in 1854, which junked the old compromises and once more opened up the question of slavery in the West.

The *New York Herald,* on the other hand, was mostly opposed to the abolitionist movement. It endorsed the Kansas-Nebraska Act, which the South looked upon as a victory for slavery. Bennett wrote on February 28, 1854: ". . . for twenty odd years, through good and evil report, the *New York Herald* has been the only Northern journal that has unfailingly vindicated the constitutional rights of the South." Naturally, the *Herald* was popular with southern leaders, who quoted it often. The *Herald* was the most popular American newspaper in Great Britain, and because the British were inclined to favor the South, through the close relationship of their textile industry and the cotton growers, it was widely reprinted. As a result, many British readers had a very false notion of the temper of the North on the eve of the war. Bennett gave grudging support to Lincoln, once the fighting began, but continued an annoyance.

The *New York Evening Post* under the guiding hand of William Cullen Bryant continued to offer enlightened editorial leadership to its readers. It was Bryant who first put the more responsible elements of the standard press on the side of such men as James G. Birney, whose paper, the *Philanthropist,* was wrecked by anti-abolitionists at Cincinnati. Birney had asked if freedom of the press were possible when slavery had to be protected from its critics. If freedom of expression were to be repudiated permanently by such measures as the southern gag laws, could democracy continue to exist? he asked. Bryant picked up these arguments and made them respectable.

In the West, Joseph Medill's *Chicago Tribune* was a thunderer against slavery. Founded in 1847, the paper made rapid progress after Medill and five partners took it over in 1855. Medill was one of the western leaders of the Republican party and was said to have suggested the name of the new political organization. The *Tribune* was an early supporter of Lincoln. Medill was largely responsible for the Lincoln boom. He enthusiastically followed the future president, reporting the speeches that are now history. Usually Medill followed his reports with a lively editorial on the subject. Lincoln often came to the *Tribune* office for conferences with the West's leading spokesman. Medill's intimacy with Lincoln is indicated by the crude familiarity with which he conversed with the rising politician. "Dammit, Abe, git yore feet off my desk," Medill is said to have told the lanky backwoodsman on one occasion.

By 1860, the newspaper press of the United States was highly developed. The typical daily was likely to be drab, by modern standards, but the makeup and readability had improved since the advent of the first penny papers. The standard paper was six columns wide. Eight pages usually sufficed, although Raymond's *Times* often ran to ten pages. There were few pictures or graphic illustrations. Many of the penny papers actually sold for twice that by the end of the period, and the *Times* was up to three. Headlines were mostly confined by the column rules to one-column labels, and the great development in display headlines was still waiting on the war. Advertising was increasing steadily. Three of the eight pages of the conservative-looking weekly edition of the *Springfield Republican* usually were devoted to classified notices, and this was common throughout the country.

As a whole, the press was strong and prosperous. It was well that the publishing industry was so healthy, for it was about to be tested as it never had been before. The test began on the day Edmund Ruffin sent the first shot of the Civil War toward Fort Sumter, April 12, 1861.

NOTES

1. Arthur Charles Cole, *The Irrepressible Conflict* (New York: Macmillan, 1934). See also Avery Craven, *The Repressible Conflict* (Baton Rouge: Louisiana State University Press, 1939).
2. Both quotations are reprinted in Louis L. Snyder and Richard B. Morris, eds., *A Treasury of Great Reporting* (New York: Simon & Schuster, 1949), pp. 124–25.
3. Wendell Phillips Garrison and Francis Jackson Garrison, *William Lloyd Garrison: The Story of His Life Told By His Children,* Vol. I (New York: Appleton-Century-Crofts, 1885), p. 200.
4. Vernon L. Parrington, *Main Currents in American Thought* (New York: Harcourt Brace Jovanovich, 1927), II, p. 356. Parrington's fascinating analysis of the abolitionist leader quotes many such statements of Garrison.
5. Kendall justified his action by holding that each issue of the *Liberator* reaching a southern state was a criminal libel, that is, a threat to public peace. He tried to explain the situation in his annual report for 1835, when he asked Congress for an official banning of "obnoxious" literature in southern states. This would have taken the responsibility out of the hands of the postmaster general and indicates that Kendall knew his past actions had been arbitrary. It is interesting to see the South's great leader, John C. Calhoun, challenge the constitutionality of Kendall's request. Calhoun's alternative was a recommendation for states with appropriate laws to ban such literature at the source.
6. Carter R. Bryan, "Negro Journalism in America Before Emancipation," *Journalism Monographs,* No. 12 (September 1969), 1, 30–33.
7. I. Garland Penn, *The Afro-American Press and Its Editors* (Springfield, Mass.: Wiley, 1891), p. 28.
8. Armistead S. Pride, *A Register and History of Negro Newspapers in the United States* (Ph.D. thesis, Northwestern University, 1950), p. 4.
9. Bryan, "Negro Journalism," pp. 11–14.
10. Ibid., p. 17.
11. Roland E. Wolseley, *The Black Press, U.S.A.* (Ames: Iowa State University Press, 1971), pp. 24–25.
12. As quoted in Bryan, "Negro Journalism," p. 19, from *The Ram's Horn,* November 5, 1847, p. 4.
13. Wolseley, *The Black Press,* pp. 22–23.

ANNOTATED BIBLIOGRAPHY

Books

Many of the references cited at the end of chapter 10 will be found to be useful in a study of the period covered by this chapter, including the biographies of Greeley, Raymond, Bennett, and Weed and the histories of the *New York Times* and *Springfield Republican*.

COLE, ARTHUR CHARLES, *The Irrepressible Conflict,* A History of American Life, Vol. VII. New York: Macmillan, 1934.

CRAVEN, AVERY, *The Repressible Conflict.* Baton Rouge: Louisiana State University Press, 1939.
Both of these books present the debatable issues leading up to the war in a frame of reference still being investigated by historians.

DANN, MARTIN E., ed., *The Black Press: 1827–1890.* New York: G. P. Putnam's Sons, 1971. A collection of articles from black newspapers with theme of quest for national identity.

DETWEILER, FREDERICK G., *The Negro Press in the United States.* Chicago: University of Chicago Press, 1922. Quotes extensively from the papers.

DILLON, MERTON L., *The Abolitionists: The Growth of a Dissenting Minority,* DeKalb, Ill.: Northern Illinois University Press, 1974. Unravels abolitionist ideologies and strategies, places them in historical context.

———, *Elijah P. Lovejoy, Abolitionist Editor.* Urbana: University of Illinois Press, 1961. Used primary sources.

DOUGLASS, FREDERICK, *My Bondage and My Freedom.* Chicago: Johnson Publishing Company, 1970. Second of three autobiographical chronicles, originally published in 1855. Others: *Narrative of the Life of Frederick Douglass* (1845), *Life and Times of Frederick Douglass* (1878). Douglass lived from 1817 to 1895 as a slave, freeman, politician, reformer, editor, and orator.

FONER, PHILIP S., *Frederick Douglass.* New York: Citadel Press, 1963. By the author of the outstanding four-volume *Life and Writings of Frederick Douglass.*

GARRISON, WENDELL PHILLIPS, AND FRANCIS J., *William Lloyd Garrison.* 4 vols. New York: Appleton-Century-Crofts, 1885–89. The life story of the famous abolitionist, told by his children.

GARRISON, WILLIAM LLOYD, *Selections.* Boston: R. F. Wallcut, 1852. Excerpts from speeches and writings of the famous abolitionist.

GENOVESE, EUGENE D., *The Political Economy of Slavery.* New York: Pantheon, 1965. A New Left historian uses the comparative approach. See also *Roll, Jordan, Roll* (New York: Pantheon, 1975), story of the world slaves made.

GILL, JOHN, *Tide without Turning: Elijah P. Lovejoy and Freedom of the Press.* Boston: Beacon Press, 1958. A well-documented biography of the martyr.

ISELY, JETER ALLEN, *Horace Greeley and the Republican Party, 1853–1861.* Princeton: Princeton University Press, 1947. Analysis of Greeley's writings in the *Tribune* about slavery.

NEVINS, ALLAN, *The Evening Post: A Century of Journalism.* New York: Boni and Liveright, 1922. See especially chapters 4, 5, 6, and 7.

———, *Ordeal of the Union* (2 vols., 1847–57), *The Emergence of Lincoln* (2 vols., 1857–61), *The War for the Union* (4 vols., 1861–65). New York: Scribner's, 1947–71. The culminating work of a famous American historian.

NYE, RUSSEL B., *Fettered Freedom: Civil Liberties and the Slavery Controversy, 1830–1860.* East Lansing: Michigan State College Press, 1963. How the abolitionists finally won popular support.

PENN, I. GARLAND, *The Afro-American Press and Its Editors.* Springfield, Mass.: Wiley Company, 1891. The source book for the nineteenth-century black press.

POTTER, DAVID M., *The Impending Crisis, 1848–1861*. New York: Harper & Row, Publisher, 1976. Political study; winner of 1977 Pulitzer Prize for history.

QUARLES, BENJAMIN, ed., *Frederick Douglass*. Englewood Cliffs, N.J.: Prentice-Hall, 1968. Negro editor presented in own and peers' words.

SNYDER, LOUIS L., AND RICHARD B. MORRIS, eds., *A Treasury of Great Reporting*. New York: Simon & Schuster, 1962. Outstanding newspaper articles of the period.

THOMAS, JOHN L., *The Liberator: William Lloyd Garrison, a Biography*. Boston: Little, Brown, 1963. Excellent biography, but focuses on political activities.

WHITE, LAURA A., *Robert Barnwell Rhett*. New York: Appleton-Century-Crofts, 1931. Describes the southern "fire-eater" and his part in the slavery issue.

WOLSELEY, ROLAND E., *The Black Press, U.S.A.* Ames: Iowa State University Press, 1971. Chapter 2 deals with nineteenth-century black papers.

Periodicals and Monographs

BRYAN, CARTER R., "Negro Journalism in America Before Emancipation," *Journalism Monographs*, No. 12 (September 1969). Careful study of early black press.

CHU, JAMES C. Y., "Horace White: His Association with Abraham Lincoln, 1854–60," *Journalism Quarterly*, XLIX (Spring 1972), 51. Was reporter, adviser.

CULLEN, MAURICE R., JR., "William Gilmore Simms, Southern Journalist," *Journalism Quarterly*, XXXVIII (Summer 1961), 298. A South Carolina editor first opposes secession, then defies the invading Union army.

EATON, CLEMENT, "The Freedom of the Press in the Upper South," *Mississippi Valley Historical Review*, XVIII (March 1932), 479. A study of the muzzling of press freedom prior to the Civil War.

KENNEDY, FRONDE, "Russell's Magazine," *South Atlantic Quarterly*, XVIII (April 1919), 125. Analysis of the periodical published at Charleston, which argued the pro-slavery viewpoint.

MARTIN, ASA EARL, "Pioneer Anti-Slavery Press," *Mississippi Valley Historical Review*, II (March 1916), 509. Describes the *Philanthropist*, an early abolitionist paper, and discusses other such publications of the early period.

NYE, RUSSEL B., "Freedom of the Press and the Antislavery Controversy," *Journalism Quarterly*, XXII (March 1945), 1. Discusses one of the main considerations of this chapter.

PRIDE, ARMISTEAD S., "A Register and History of Negro Newspapers in the United States," Ph.D. thesis, Northwestern University, 1950. Most scholarly effort to identify black newspapers.

SAALBERG, HARVEY, "Martyrs to the Press," *Editor & Publisher*, CIX (June 19, 1976), 7. First of a series of six articles on deaths of six United States newsmen.

Advertisements from *National Intelligencer* (1823) and *Western America* (1836).

HARPER'S WEEKLY.
A JOURNAL OF CIVILIZATION

Vol. V.—No. 218.]　　　NEW YORK, SATURDAY, MARCH 2, 1861.　　　[Price Five Cents.

Entered according to Act of Congress, in the Year 1861, by Harper & Brothers, in the Clerk's Office of the District Court for the Southern District of New York.

The country looks to Lincoln as he prepares to take office.

13

The Irrepressible Conflict

Come with a sword or musket in your hand, prepared to share with us our fate in sunshine and storm . . . and I will welcome you as a brother and associate; but come as you now do, expecting me to ally the reputation and honor of my country and my fellow soldiers with you, as the representative of the press, which you yourself say makes so slight a difference between truth and falsehood, and my answer is, NEVER.

—General Sherman to Knox, of the *Herald*

The War Between the States affected all aspects of journalism. Reporting, editing, circulation, printing, advertising, and illustration were all modified during the conflict. Relations between press and government also changed during this period. One of the serious problems of the war was how to keep the public properly informed without giving aid and comfort to the enemy. This was the world's first modern rehearsal of mass warfare—involving both armies and civilians. It was one of the costliest wars, in terms of men and money, ever fought up to that period. And because large elements of the populations opposed the bloody strife on both sides of the lines, there was continuous and outspoken criticism of both administrations. The most usual medium for this expression was the newspaper.

In contrast with World Wars I and II, reporters in the War Between the States were much more irresponsible. But it should be pointed out that the communications lessons of 1861–65 were of invaluable assistance in working out later policies. For experience has shown that when a country with a free press tradition mobilizes, leaders must adjust themselves to a dilemma.

A few voices still answered the roll call of the once-great legion of progress. Greeley did not change but he, too, was overwhelmed by the war. He lived to see all his illusions shattered on the rock of postwar public cynicism, but at least he stuck to his principles. His regard for mankind made Greeley abhor war. At one time he favored letting the South secede peacefully. But once the shooting began, Greeley concluded that the most humane course for the Unionists was to end the war quickly.

By the close of 1861 the *Tribune* was engaged in a campaign to free slaves in conquered areas. The president had already discussed the issue with his cabinet, and he had definite plans for accomplishing emancipation. The climax of the *Tribune* crusade was Greeley's famous "Prayer of Twenty Millions" editorial of August 20, 1862, which was a call for action on the slavery issue. Lincoln replied by a personal letter to Greeley, which he also gave to the *National Intelligencer* for publication on August 23. The letter included the paragraph now so familiar to students of the period:

My paramount object in this struggle *is* to save the Union, and is *not* either to save or destroy Slavery. If I could save the Union without freeing *any* slave, I would do it; and if I could save it by freeing *all* the slaves, I would do it; and if I could do it by freeing some and leaving others alone, I would also do that.

Greeley wrote another open letter to the president urging more concern with the issue. When Lincoln announced his preliminary Emancipation Proclamation a month later, to be effective January 1, 1863, many readers of the *Tribune* assumed that "Uncle Horace" had done it again. "It is the beginning of the new life of the nation," Greeley exulted in his September 23 issue. The president and his cabinet had worked out the details without any help from the editor, but surely a man so sensitive to public feelings as Lincoln must have been aware of the popular pressure.

By the time of the election of 1864, Lincoln and Greeley appear to have tired of each other. "You complain of me—what have I done, or omitted to do, that has provoked the hostility of the *Tribune*?" asked the president.[1] But eventually Greeley swung around behind his old friend again. Of the 17 New York daily newspapers, only five were solid supporters of the administration. They were the *Tribune, Times, Evening Post, Sun,* and *Commercial Advertiser.* Greeley did not hesitate to take unpopular stands when wartime passions made such outspokenness highly dangerous. When Greeley supported the president's draft call of 1863, the *Tribune* was stoned.

War was the golden age for Henry J. Raymond, who had made the *New York Times* one of the outstanding dailies of its time. The paper offered reasonable, penetrating, and thorough reportage. The feeling for objectivity on the part of *Times* writers is indicated by the four open letters Raymond wrote to Yancey, the southern fire-eater. They were able and dispassionate antisecession arguments that showed an understanding of the southern viewpoint. But on essential issues, the *Times* gave Lincoln strong support.

Raymond was an expert correspondent and writer, and his partner, George Jones, had wisely urged him to confine his energy to journalism rather than politics. The temptation was too great, however. By 1863, he was chairman of the Republican National Committee, one of the key political positions in the nation. He managed the 1864 campaign in which Lincoln and his "union" ticket partner, Andrew Johnson of Tennes-

Harper's Weekly

Henry J. Raymond

see, defeated General George B. McClellan, the Democratic candidate, thanks to solid Union Army victories in the fall. Raymond also wrote the party platform and was elected to the House of Representatives.

When Congress convened in 1865, it was assumed Raymond represented the administration. He proved to be no match, however, for Thaddeus Stevens and other advocates of punishment for the South. Lincoln's assassination removed his party sponsor. He lost his national committee seat and declined to run again for Congress in 1866. He then bolted the party, ending his political career. "Shocking Cruelty to a Fugitive Slave," Greeley headlined the account of the episode in the *Tribune*. Later, Raymond and the *Times* returned to solid ground with the Republicans, but the paper's founder died of a cerebral hemorrhage in 1869 while waging an editorial fight against the infamous Tweed ring of political corruptionists that was looting the city treasury.

Bennett and his *Herald* caused the Lincoln administration considerable annoyance. The paper was politically independent, but it was definitely "soft" toward the South, where it had great influence. Because of its extensive news coverage, particularly of business and commerce, the *Herald* was the most popular American newspaper in Europe. The British government at this time was making friendly overtures to the South, which provided British mills with cotton in normal times. The attitude of the widely read *Herald* was therefore of concern to Lincoln and his cabinet, for it was important that European neutrals have a fair evaluation of the American issues.

After the first battle of Bull Run, Bennett gave his full, but somewhat grudging, support to the Lincoln administration and the war. Even so, it was necessary from time to time for the president to "sweeten up"—as Lincoln put it—the aggressive editor of the *Herald*. "I write this to assure you that the Administration will not discriminate against the *Herald,* especially while it sustains us so generously. . . ." Lincoln wrote to Bennett after personally interceding for a *Herald* reporter who had been refused a pass to go down the Potomac river with a military detachment.[2] As a former pro-southern newspaper, the *Herald* continued to attack specific issues of the Republican party, but its intentions were not subversive.

There were other instances in which *Herald* reporters tangled with authorities. Actually, the aggressiveness of the *Herald* could have caused it much more trouble, if military officials had exerted their authority. At any rate, the editorial tactics paid off, for the *Herald* climbed to a circulation of more than 100,000 soon after the beginning of the war. It was then the most popular newspaper in the United States.[3]

Few presidents suffered more from editorial abuse than Lincoln. Opposition editors and disappointed favor-seekers accused him in print of vicious deeds, which the patient president usually ignored. He was falsely accused of drawing his salary in gold bars, while his soldiers were paid in deflated greenbacks. He was charged with drunkenness while making crucial decisions, with granting pardons to secure votes, and with needless butchering of armies as a result of his lust for victories. Once he was accused of outright treason. Typical of his press detractors was the *La Crosse Democrat,* a Wisconsin weekly, which said of the draft: "Lincoln has called for 500,000 more victims."

Continuous and unlicensed criticism was voiced by political opponents. Democrats actually polled a larger vote than Republicans in 1860.[4] They were so split by sectional differences, however, that they could not agree on a candidate. The Republicans were aware that they had won by default.

Most northern Democrats were loyal during the war, although they tended to welcome peace overtures short of total victory for Lincoln's aims. There were some who served as a kind of fifth column for the South, however. They were called Copperheads, after the dangerous reptile that gives no warning of its attack. Some formed underground groups engaged in treasonable acts; others were vocal above-ground Copperheads.

Clement Laird Vallandigham, an Ohio editor and politician, was a well-known Copperhead. He became co-owner in 1847 of the *Dayton Empire,* an anti-abolitionist magazine, and won a seat in Congress in 1858. As secretary of the Democratic National Committee in 1860, he sought to avoid war. By 1863 he was one of the Copperheads arrested by order of General Ambrose E. Burnside. Sentenced to prison, he was banished behind the Confederate lines by Lincoln's order.

MILITARY CENSORSHIP   No war had ever been so fully and freely reported before.
IN THE NORTH   New York newspapers usually devoted at least a third of their space to war news. But sooner or later the press had to work out an understanding with military authorities in the interests of public security. There is no record in War Department files of military censorship prior to the Civil War. Although there had been some censorship during the Mexican War, a system had to be developed by trial and error. As a result, both the press and the government made many mistakes in working out the problems, and criticism from all sides was often bitter. Yet many valuable lessons were learned in the Civil War about controls of communication agencies, which set the tone for wartime in this century.

The problem was aggravated by the fact that the American press had become so prosperous, aggressive, and independent in the years preceding the war that it was sensitive to any form of restriction. The telegraph and the railway posts were other factors to be considered. They made it possible to disseminate news much faster than before. The potential danger of information useful to the enemy was therefore all the greater. On the other hand, this was the first of the all-out wars involving civilian populations, and since public morale was now a much more important factor in prosecuting the war, the channels of information had to be kept open.[5]

There were three stages in the development of Civil War military censorship. The first period of fumbling began with the denial by the Post Office of messages sent to enemy areas. The high command in Washington began to realize that the enemy was obtaining valuable military intelligence through the free flow of information to the press and to persons in private life. Then, on July 8, 1861, General Winfield Scott, commander of the Union armies, issued an order, backed up by Secretary of War Simon Cameron, forbidding the telegraph companies from sending any information of a military nature. This was illegal, but it served the purpose until Congress gave the president such control in January 1862.

The first drastic use of the telegraph censorship was after the first battle of Bull Run, July 21, 1861. Raymond, who had turned in a bulletin to the *Times* announcing a Union victory and was thereby put to shame by the reports of his rivals, maintained that his follow-up story had been blocked by the censors. The same thing happened to Lawrence A. Gobright of the New York Associated Press. Already it was clear that if the government had to restrict certain types of information, it was just as necessary to provide the news to which reporters were entitled.

Since honest journalists and military planners both recognized the problem, it was natural that they should try to work out some agreement. On August 2, 1861, General George B. McClellan, commanding the Army of the Potomac, called an historic press conference of Washington correspondents. Each of the delegates to the conference signed a document binding him to transmit no information of military value to the enemy. On the other hand, the general agreed to use all his considerable influence to facilitate the gathering of news that was of interest to the public. The men who left the meeting that day congratulated themselves on the wisdom of the voluntary plan.

Unfortunately, the program was unsuccessful, not because of any serious flaw in the agreement but because of division of authority. The official censor was H. E. Thayer, who understood nothing about the problem. He was not under the supervision of the War Department but was under the direction of the secretary of state. The jealousy of the War and State Departments resulted in a complete breakdown of the voluntary censorship plan less than three months after it was proposed. For on October 22, Secretary of State Seward instructed Thayer to prohibit telegraphic dispatches from Washington that related to military *and civil* operations of the government. Since this violated the very spirit of the McClellan agreement, the press reverted to its old system of getting news as best it could.[6]

The second phase of censorship began when the censor was taken from the State Department and put under the direction of the secretary of war, Edwin M. Stanton. He quickly brought order out of chaos. By an order of February 25, 1862, Stanton clarified the triple set of restrictions under which correspondents had been bound by voluntary, State Department, and War Department censorship. By the Stanton order, correspondents were to submit copy to provost marshals for approval before transmission, but it was understood that deletions would apply only to military matters. Now the reporters knew just about how far they could go in reporting battles, and the press was able to serve much more effectively.

General William T. Sherman also helped to clarify censorship rules. The general had been bedeviled by reporters, who were irked by his press relations. Sherman was certain much military failure could be blamed on information leaks. The issue came to a showdown after Thomas E. Knox, a correspondent for the *Herald,* transmitted information that clearly violated military regulations of censorship. Sherman had the reporter arrested and held as a spy. He had no intention of shooting the man, as he had every right to do, but he was convinced that this was a good test case. In the end, the president intervened, Knox got out of his predicament, and Sherman got what he wanted—the understanding that all correspondents must be *accredited,* or recognized, journalists and that they must be *acceptable* to commanders in the field. Thus was established a precedent followed ever since by military correspondents.

From 1864 to the end of the war, censorship entered its third and successful phase. General Sherman marched all the way to the sea in hostile country without once having his plans disclosed by the press. On the whole, the press was cooperating by the end of the war.

SUSPENSIONS OF NORTHERN NEWSPAPERS In the main, the northern press enjoyed great freedom throughout the war. The great power of the president after his suspension of habeas corpus was used sparingly. Most of the punitive actions were taken by military commanders. In June 1863, the *Chicago Times* was suspended for three days by order of General Ambrose Burnside, commanding the Department of Ohio, which included the military districts in Illinois. This was one of the so-called "Burnside Decrees," based on the right of a commander to silence public expression of ideas and information deemed harmful to the military effort. The general appears to have had plenty of provocation for his action. Wilbur F. Storey, publisher of the *Times,* lacked both conscience and principle. He used the most violent language in attacking Lincoln after the Emancipation Proclamation was issued. He repeatedly ignored military warnings to stop fomenting Copperhead dissatisfaction in the area. Pushed beyond endurance by the anti-Federal sentiments of the *Times,* General Burnside ordered the newspaper padlocked. Lincoln's reaction was typical. He wished to back up his own general, and he knew Burnside had much to complain about, but the president also had definite ideas about freedom of expression. After three days he rescinded the military order.

Other newspapers ran afoul of the censor. One was the *New York World,* established in 1860 as a penny paper with religious overtones. At first it was a supporter of the Lincoln administration. It lost money and continued to fail even after it absorbed the assets of the famous old *Courier and Enquirer.* Eventually it was taken over by Manton Marble, an able editor who increased circulation by espousing the cause of the "Peace Democrats." After the Emancipation Proclamation, the *World* was openly hostile to the administration. It became the focus of Copperhead infection in an area where the war was already unpopular. In May 1864, the military authorities had a chance to strike back.

The *World* and the *Journal of Commerce* published a forged presidential proclamation purporting to order another draft of 400,000 men. The document was actually the product of Joseph Howard, Jr., city editor of the *Brooklyn Eagle.* He had hoped to make a profit in the stock market by this hoax, although this was the least of his crimes. Such a story in the tense metropolis was almost certain to cause bloodshed and probably death by rioting. Other editors refused to carry the story, after checking the facts, but the *World* and *Journal of Commerce* appeared with the article prominently displayed. General John A. Dix promptly suppressed them. After a lapse of two days, during which the editors were severely reprimanded, they were allowed to resume publication.

One of the most celebrated suspension cases outside New York was that of Samuel Medary, editor of the *Crisis* and of the *Ohio Statesman* at Columbus. The *Crisis* was a special organ of the Copperheads, and it supported C. L. Vallandigham, the Copperhead candidate for governor. In 1864 Medary was indicted by a federal grand jury as the spokesman for a group then declared to be subversive. He was released from jail on bond furnished by the editor of the *Cincinnati Enquirer,* who wished to test the wartime freedom of the press. Medary died before the case was tried in court.

THE NORTH REPORTS THE WAR

Indeed, when it came to the reporting of military actions, Civil War correspondents, or "specials," as they were then called, enjoyed a freedom that would not be tolerated in modern times. Many of the battles were fought in remote areas, and the struggle to get back firsthand accounts often was heroic. Some of the best reporting in American journalism was offered the public by the hundreds of correspondents during this test of a nation.

Newsmen were everywhere. They roamed the South long after their detection might have resulted in their execution as spies. Some of them were famous already, including Raymond of the *Times,* who was at Bull Run, and William Howard Russell, the world-renowned British war correspondent fresh from his triumphs in the Crimea.

Some of the best war reporters earned their spurs after the conflict began, however. One of these was B. S. Osbon, a minister's son who had embarked on a life of seafaring and adventure. He was working for the *New York World* at nine dollars a week on that April morning in 1861 when the curtain went up on one of the great

American tragedies. From the deck of a naval cutter, Osbon watched the bombardment of Fort Sumter. The lead of the story he sent back was a prototype of the news style developed during the war:

CHARLESTON, APRIL 12—*The ball is opened. War is inaugurated.*
The batteries of Sullivan's Island, Morris Island, and other points were opened on Fort Sumter at four o'clock this morning. Fort Sumter has returned the fire, and a brisk cannonading has been kept up.[7]

Later Osbon shipped back on the U.S.S. *Baltic,* carrying the exhausted Major Robert Anderson, commander of the fort's garrison. It was Osbon who disclosed in a published interview that a junior officer had raised the flag of surrender after Anderson had ordered the last round to be fired and further resistance appeared to be hopeless.

Not long after, Bennett hired Osbon to report for the *Herald* at $25 a week. He was on the quarterdeck with Admiral Farragut at the siege of New Orleans. He seemed to be wherever a good story was about to break.

But there were other stars, too. Albert D. Richardson of the *Tribune* sent reports from the deep South through the line by transmitting his stories in cipher by way of the New York banks. He watched the great battle of Fort Henry from a treetop observation post. He saw Island Number Ten at the Vicksburg approaches reduced to rubble as he stood with Commodore Foote on the hurricane deck of a Union ironclad. He ran the blockade of Vicksburg; was knocked from the deck by the shock of a cannon ball that nearly struck him; and then was picked from the water and imprisoned by the Confederates. His escape through the lines was one of the exciting journalistic feats of the time.

George W. Smalley, later one of the pioneer foreign correspondents, first gained fame while covering the war for the *Tribune.* At the battle of Antietam, where he served as a dispatch rider for General Hooker, he lost two horses by gunfire. It was Smalley who first got the news of the battle to Washington, where Lincoln was anxiously waiting for some encouraging report before announcing his plans for emancipation.

Many of the correspondents wrote under a pen name. There was "Agate," for example, who was actually Whitelaw Reid, the successor to Greeley on the *Tribune* in the early 1870s. He was already famous for his report on the battle of Shiloh when he sent a dispatch one day from Gettysburg. His story, datelined "Field of Battle, Near Gettysburg, July 2," took up 14 of the 48 columns of the *Cincinnati Gazette.* It remains as a classic of Civil War reporting. Standing on Cemetery Hill, the point most exposed to rebel fire, Reid turned in an eyewitness account of the decisive battle, of which the following is an excerpt:

Hancock was wounded; Gibbon succeeded to command—approved soldier, and ready for the crisis. As the tempest of fire approached its height, he walked along the line, and renewed his orders to the men to reserve their fire. The rebels—three lines deep—came steadily up. They were in pointblank range.
At last the order came! From thrice six thousand guns there came a sheet of smoky flame, a crash of leaden death. The line literally melted away; but there came a second, resistless still. It had been our supreme effort—on the instant we were not equal to another.
Up to the rifle pits, across them, over the barricades—the momentum of their charge, the mere machine strength of their combined action swept them on. Our thin line

The *New York Herald,* leader in war correspondence, records the South's surrender.

could fight, but it had not weight enough to oppose this momentum. It was pushed behind the guns. Right on came the rebels. They were upon the guns, were bayoneting the gunners, were waving their flags above our pieces.

But they had penetrated to the fatal point. . . .[8]

In the Confederate camp near Hagerstown, Maryland, the reporter for the *Richmond Enquirer,* retreating with Lee's army, sent back this eloquent version of the same battle to soften the blow to the bereaved at home:

Though many a Virginia home will mourn the loss of some noble spirit, yet at the name of Pickett's division and the battle of Gettysburg, how the eye will glisten and the blood course quicker, and the heart beat warm, as among its noble dead is recalled the name of some cherished one. They bore themselves worthy of their lineage and their state. Who would recall them from their bed of glory? Each sleeps in a hero's grave. . . .[9]

The *New York Herald,* true to its tradition, exceeded its rivals in aggressive war coverage. It had more than 40 specials in the field at any given time. One of its foremost reporters was a young Bavarian immigrant, Henry Hilgard, who soon changed his name to Villard after his arrival in 1853. While learning the language, he edited the *Volksblatt,* a German paper published at Racine, Wisconsin. Later he covered the Lincoln-Douglas debates for the *Staats-Zeitung* of New York. His account of Lincoln's departure from Springfield for Washington, and of the long ride under increasing national tension, established Villard as one of the best correspondents of his day. He was only 25 when he began reporting the war for the *Herald.* He is best remembered for two great reporting "scoops." The first was his account of the first battle of Bull Run, the first accurate one to reach New York. The second exclusive account was his report of the battle of Fredericksburg.

THE SOUTH REPORTS THE WAR

Not much has been said about the southern press up to this point, although it played an important part in the fortunes of the Confederacy. In many ways editorial reactions were the same in the North and South. Southern editors were highly critical of military strategy, and journalists such as Rhett, for example, attacked the Confederate administration just as violently as Lincoln was being attacked in the North. War aims were not as much an issue as they were in the North, however, nor was there anything quite corresponding to the Copperhead press.

Most of the news of the battles was supplied to southern editors by the Press Association of the Confederate States of America, better known as "PA," which, appropriately enough, was just the reversed logotype of the biggest northern news agency, the AP.[10] When the war began, the South had no system for preparing or transmitting news of public interest to replace the severed connection with the New York AP. An Augusta editor began sending out a brief daily summary by telegraph to a few papers willing to pay for the service, but this was never widely used. In 1862, the combined newspapers of Richmond tried to establish a more effective organization. Publishers realized that to meet the enormous expense of covering a war, they would have to work together. They also saw that in order to place correspondents where they were needed, they would have to pool resources. It was soon evident that the Richmond papers could not achieve these results by themselves.

Following a series of conferences, Joseph Clisby of the *Macon Telegraph* summoned the editor of every daily in the South to attend a meeting at Augusta on February 4, 1862. The Association of the Richmond Press had just been organized, and the plan was to expand the idea by organizing the PA. A board of directors hired a superintendent, J. S. Thrasher, "at a salary not to exceed $3,000," and the organization was ready to function.

The value of the association was at once apparent in the signing of contracts with telegraph agencies and the abolishing of onerous postal regulations. On May 15, 1863, the directors passed a resolution defending Thrasher for his stand against unwarranted military censorship.

On the whole, PA served its clients well. When General P. G. T. Beauregard began to hold up dispatches, Thrasher called on him personally and told the general that the aim of the press association was to obtain accurate reports for the good of the public, consistent with military security. The general was impressed. He told Thrasher that the PA reporters "should have every facility for early access to intelligence compatible with the public interests," and he wrote letters to high military authorities recommending similar cooperation. Thrasher won the confidence of other leaders. In return, he instructed PA correspondents to send no opinions or comments on events—the procedure that had so irritated northern commanders. They were warned to sift rumors and to offer no information that would aid the enemy. The objectivity of the PA stories has been regarded as constituting a "complete revolution" in journalistic writing.[11]

The superintendent, in return, was jealous of arrogant commanders who held up legitimate copy, and he used the power of his office to enforce cooperation from the military. Correspondents were ordered to send to the home office copies of dispatches unreasonably censored at the telegraph office. These reports were to include the name and rank of the responsible censor, and these documents were then used to pry greater concessions from those in higher authority.

The development of PA was a big step in the progress of southern journalism. The surviving 43 daily papers in the South were all members of the association. The editorial weight of this group was impressive. Dispatches were transmitted over the Military Telegraph Lines, the army system, at half rates. There was also a satisfactory arrangement with the private South-Western Telegraph Company. Newspapers that had seldom had access to regular wire news budgets were now able to keep readers up to date on the war. Short, but complete, reports supplanted the rambling, confused accounts of prewar days. Reporters with the armies were paid $25 a week, which was good for that time, and the writing was of good quality. On the whole PA gave a good account of itself until the crumbling Confederacy saw a collapse of restraints and organization. As in the northern armies, reporters were sometimes ejected for releasing information believed useful to the enemy. But Thrasher appears to have perfected a great news gathering agency. He offered relatively high objectivity. He kept the press as free as possible, considering the circumstances.

There were perhaps 800 newspapers being published in the 11 states of the Confederacy in 1861, of which about 10 per cent were dailies. Hand presses were in use in most of these newspaper offices and circulations were small. The *Richmond Dispatch,* with 18,000 subscribers when war broke out, was outranked only by the largest New Orleans dailies. And as important as the Richmond papers were in the journalism of the Confederacy, the *Dispatch* had more readers than the *Enquirer, Whig,* and *Democrat* combined. The *Enquirer* was the organ of the Jefferson Davis administration until 1863 when the *Sentinel* was established for that purpose. Richmond also spawned a *Southern Illustrated News* in 1862 to fill the void left by the disappearance of *Harper's Weekly;* it soon had 20,000 readers.[12]

Southern publishers were harassed by a shortage of print paper; they were reduced eventually to single sheets, to extras printed on galley proof slips, even to printing on the back of old wallpaper. They also ran out of ink, type, and men to man their shops. After 1863, when New Orleans fell, their cities were overrun by federal troops. Only about 20 of the dailies were still printing when Lee surrendered. But they had compiled a journalistic record of the Confederate arms, and had sent, all told, more than 100 correspondents to cover the Southern armies.

The historian of Civil War correspondents, J. Cutler Andrews, ranks two of these men as head and shoulders above the others.[13] One was Felix Gregory de Fontaine, who signed himself "Personne" in his dispatches to the *Charleston Courier*. The other was Peter W. Alexander, primarily identified with the *Savannah Republican,* but whose "P.W.A." signature was also found in the *Atlanta Confederacy,* the *Columbus Sun,* the *Mobile Advertiser,* the *Richmond Dispatch,* and the *Times* of London. Ranking behind them were such versatile war reporters as Samuel C. Reid, Jr., of the *New Orleans Picayune* and other papers; James B. Sener and William G. Shepardson of the *Richmond Dispatch;* Albert J. Street of the *Mobile Register;* John H. Linebaugh of the *Memphis Appeal;* and an unidentified "Shadow" who covered the Battle of Atlanta and who may have been Henry Watterson of future Louisville fame.

De Fontaine and Alexander crossed paths as "regulars" in the major campaigns; both were at Antietam in September 1862 when Lee was repulsed in his invasion of the North, escaping a vastly superior McClellan. De Fontaine wrote a seven-column story of more than 8,000 words about the campaign, in what Andrews calls his greatest story of the war. It appeared in the *Charleston Courier* first. At one point the young but war-weary correspondent described the scene in front of the Confederate center along a sunken road called "Bloody Lane":

From twenty different standpoints great volumes of smoke were every instant leaping from the muzzles of angry guns. The air was filled with the white fantastic shapes that floated away from bursted shells. Men were leaping to and fro, loading, firing and handling the artillery, and now and then a hearty yell would reach the ear, amid the tumult, that spoke of death or disaster from some well aimed ball. Before us were the enemy. A regiment or two had crossed the river, and, running in squads from the woods along its banks, were trying to form a line. Suddenly a shell falls among them, and another and another, until thousands scatter like a swarm of flies, and disappear in the woods. A second time the effort is made, and there is a second failure. Then there is a diversion. The batteries of the Federals open afresh; their infantry try another point, and finally they succeed in effecting a lodgement on this side. Our troops, under D. H. Hill, meet them, and a fierce battle ensues in the centre. Backwards, forwards, surging and swaying like a ship in a storm, the various columns are seen in motion. It is a hot place for us, but is hotter still for the enemy. They are directly under our guns, and we mow them down like grass. The raw levies, sustained by the veterans, come up to the work well, and fight for a short time with an excitement incident to their novel experiences of a battle; but soon a portion of their line gives way in confusion. Their reserves come up, and endeavor to retrieve the fortunes of the day. Our centre, however, stands firm as adamant, and they fall back.[14]

This was at noon; by two o'clock Hill was out of men to defend the center—but McClellan failed to mount a breakthrough and settled for less than an overwhelming victory. More soldiers died in a single day at Antietam than in any other battle in American history—23,000 in all.

Alexander was at Antietam also and composed his battle account for the *Mobile Advertiser* in the midst of the wounded and dying in an army hospital. "There is a smell of death in the air," he wrote, "and the laboring surgeons are literally covered from head to foot with the blood of the sufferers." It was Alexander who wrote the most penetrating southern account of the Battle of Gettysburg, questioning Lee's wisdom in committing himself to full-scale assault the second day and wondering if Lee and his staff had not exhibited too much confidence in the ability of their troops to win against any odds. Most of the southern press reprinted his story.[15]

ARTISTS AND PHOTOGRAPHERS: MATHEW BRADY

A small army of artists covered the war, describing the events in almost photolike drawings. These were printed only by a laborious process of engraving by hand on a wooden block. Such woodcuts were not new, but they were used in newspapers much more regularly after 1861 to depict battle scenes and the likenesses of leading wartime figures. In another development, some of the metropolitan papers printed large maps to illustrate campaigns, thereby leading the way to new makeup no longer limited by column rules.[16] The *Herald* of September 12, 1863, is a good example of this technique. The paper was a little smaller than a modern standard daily and ran to eight pages, six columns wide. About a quarter of page one of this particular issue was devoted to a map accompanying a story on the Arkansas campaign. On page three a huge map of the Morris Island success in Charleston harbor filled all but two columns of the page from top to bottom.

Illustrations were also the touchstone for success in magazine publishing. Two forerunners of twentieth-century news and picture weeklies were *Frank Leslie's Illustrated Newspaper,* a 16-page ten cent weekly founded in 1855, and *Harper's Weekly,* begun in 1857. Their superb artists' drawings for woodcuts brought the war visually to 100,000 or more subscribers. They also covered sports, crime, and disasters. *Harper's Monthly,* an 1850 entry from the same publishing house, won a record 200,000 circulation before the war by featuring woodcut illustrations along with its fiction in issues double the usual size. Hand-colored engravings of fashionable clothing for ladies and gentlemen were one of the secrets of *Godey's Lady's Book,* founded in 1830 by Louis A. Godey and edited from 1836 to 1877 by Sarah J. Hale. The illustrations and copious fiction and poetry brought a 150,000 circulation in the 1850s. A rival in fashion illustration was *Peterson's Magazine,* begun in 1842 by Charles J. Peterson with Ann Stephens as associate editor and fiction writer. It exceeded Godey's book in circulation during the war, indicating the growing recognition of women in the economic picture.

The most notable contribution to pictorial journalism in the 1860s was the photograph. Pioneer war photographer was a lovable Irishman, Mathew Brady. True, his photographs could not be used in newspapers of the time, since a practical method for transferring light and shade in the printing process was not perfected for another decade. But Brady was famous for his war pictures, and his photographic record of the conflict comes down to us as one of the finest examples of reporting.

Brady was everywhere during the war, apparently. He recorded on his clumsy plates the scene at Fort Sumter. His photographic interpretations of famous battles and war leaders could not be matched in mood and accuracy by the printed word. It is surprising how many of the great men of the period posed for Brady.[17] And because he was so successful in using this new medium of reporting, he is worthy of recognition at this point.

Brady was born about 1823, either in Cork, Ireland, or more probably in upper New York state. As a youth he worked for A. T. Stewart, the pioneer New York department store owner. Stewart took an interest in the bright lad. When Brady took up the study of photography, the wealthy merchant brought his protégé to the attention of Samuel F. B. Morse, famed as the inventor of the telegraph but equally interested in the science of optics. Morse made Brady his understudy. Together they worked with Professor J. W. Draper of New York University, who was to make the first instantaneous photographic exposure in America.[18] In 1839, Morse took Brady to Europe, where they met Louis Jacque Mandé Daguerre, inventor of the "daguerreotype," a photograph on metal.

Brady returned to America and set up a daguerreotype shop at the corner of Broadway and Fulton Street, opposite Barnum's museum. That was about 1842. Soon he was famed as a photographer of the great and near-great.[19] Five years in a row he won the American Institute award for his contributions to photography. He was famous and prosperous.

But Brady was not satisfied with this success. The daguerreotype was too slow to be adaptable to anything but portrait work, and he sought a faster process. In 1855 he went to Scotland to learn about a new and faster "wet plate" developed by the scientist, Scott-Archer. Brady returned with Alexander Gardner, Scott-Archer's associate, and they set up offices in Washington as semiofficial government photographers. When the war loomed, Brady gave up this lucrative business.

He persuaded his friends President Lincoln and Allan Pinkerton of the Secret Service to let him make a photographic record of the war with Gardner. They were permitted to go anywhere, protected by the Secret Service. Soon Brady's little black wagon, which was his portable dark room, was a familiar sight on the active fronts. He had an uncanny knack of knowing where the fighting would start. Soldiers dreaded the sight of Brady arriving on the scene, for they knew that soon thereafter the shooting would begin. He was often under sniper fire as he set up his camera at exposed vantage points. By the end of the war he had collected about 3,500 photographs.[20]

These pictures give us an entirely different impression than the usual reports of people and events. Although Brady's equipment was inferior to the simplest box cameras of three generations later, he produced amazing pictures. Somehow he was able to capture through his lens the hysteria, horror, and occasional glory of war.

WARTIME BRINGS TECHNICAL ADVANCES

War brought important technical changes to the press. Dependence on the telegraph led to modification in news writing, as correspondents tried to save tolls by striving to be more concise. One way to compress stories was to omit opinion and coloration. By modern standards, Civil War reporting was rambling and colored, but compared with the journalism of an earlier day it was much more readable. Some of the copy, such as that transmitted out of Washington by the New York Associated Press and out of Richmond by the Confederate Press Association, would not be much out of place in a modern newspaper.

The summary lead, which put the main feature of the story in the first paragraph, was developed during the war by reporters in the field who feared that their complete dispatches might not get through. Bennett once said that the cable, rather than the telegraph, was responsible for this, but the cable was not in successful operation until 1866, and the summary lead was fairly common by that time. Here is the way the *New*

York Times started off one of its important front page articles of April 16, 1865, for example:

WASHINGTON, Saturday, April 15–12 A.M. Andrew Johnson was sworn into office as President of the United States by Chief Justice Chase today, at eleven o'clock....

Because vital news streamed from the telegraph by the hour, metropolitan papers began to bulletin the highlights, and soon the smallest papers were imitating this procedure. These bulletins led to the modern newspaper headline, which summarizes the story in a few lines.

Most of the newspapers continued to use the eight-page, six-column makeup carried over from before the war. By modern standards they were likely to be drab, with their small type, lack of pictures, and the dreadful uniformity of one-column makeup limitations. But the use of huge maps was breaking down the confines of the column rule, and the experimentation with headlines indicates the contrast with the page dress of only a decade earlier.

Presses had to be fast to keep up with other developments in journalism. On the Sunday following the fall of Fort Sumter, the *Herald* printed 135,000 newspapers—a record press run up to that date. In 1863, William Bullock brought out the web perfecting press, which printed both sides of a continuous roll of paper on a rotary press. Although it was not until 1871 that R. Hoe and Company produced such presses as standard equipment, the stimulus of the war is nevertheless apparent.

It was indeed an exciting era that came to a close on the evening of April 14, 1865. Lawrence A. Gobright of the New York Associated Press was working late in his office. He had already sent out dispatches about President Lincoln's theater party, reporting that General Grant had declined an invitation to see the play, "Our American Cousin," in order to go to New Jersey with Mrs. Grant. The door burst open and an excited friend rushed in with news of the tragedy at Ford's Theater. Gobright quickly wrote out a bulletin before going to work on an extended account of the evening's development. No modern reporter could have broken the news more succinctly. The lead said:

WASHINGTON, FRIDAY, APRIL 14, 1865—The President was shot in a theater tonight, and perhaps mortally wounded.

NOTES

1. For relations of Lincoln and the press see James E. Pollard, *The Presidents and the Press* (New York: Macmillan, 1947), pp. 312–97.
2. Ibid., p. 360.
3. The *New York Times* climbed from 45,000 to about 75,000 in the same period. The daily *Tribune* trailed behind, but the weekly edition, largely responsible for Greeley's national reputation, reached more than 200,000. This was the largest circulation of any single American paper. The *New York Ledger* had almost twice that many subscribers, but it was not a newspaper, as its nameplate would indicate, but a weekly story periodical.
4. Lincoln had only 40 percent of the popular vote in 1860, and he won by only 400,000 votes in 1864, when none of the southern Democrats had any voice in the elections. This was a serious consideration for Republican leaders contemplating the postwar political problem.
5. The outstanding study of this problem is Quintus Wilson, "A Study and Evaluation of the Military Censorship in the Civil War" (Master's thesis, University of Minnesota, 1945).

6. Ibid., p. 50.

7. Louis L. Snyder, and Richard B. Morris, eds., *A Treasury of Great Reporting* (New York: Simon & Schuster, 1949), p. 130.

8. Ibid., p. 146.

9. Ibid., p. 149.

10. This subject is presented in detail by Quintus C. Wilson, "The Confederate Press Association: A Pioneer News Agency," *Journalism Quarterly,* XXVI (June 1949), 160–66.

11. Ibid., p. 162.

12. J. Cutler Andrews, *The South Reports the Civil War* (Princeton: Princeton University Press, 1970), pp. 26–33.

13. Ibid., p. 50.

14. *Charleston Daily Courier,* September 29, 1862.

15. Andrews, *The South Reports the Civil War,* pp. 316–17.

16. It was not impossible to print spread headlines and large maps on the earlier type-revolving presses, but it was hazardous and inconvenient, because the column rules had to be locked tight to keep the metal type from flying out as the presses revolved. It was accomplished now and then, however. Big maps were printed by the newspapers in the Mexican War period and after.

17. As must happen to all news photographers, Brady missed some great picture opportunities. He had his camera trained on President Lincoln at the time the immortal Gettysburg Address was delivered. Edward Everett, famous orator and main speaker at the memorial, talked so long that Brady had to keep changing his plates, which had to be exposed while still wet with sensitizing solution. He was in the midst of removing a dried-out plate when the president arose to speak. The inspiring message was so short that Brady's assistant could not fetch a fresh plate from the portable dark room in time to photograph Lincoln before he bowed and retired. One of the great "news shots" of American history was thereby lost to posterity.

18. The word "instantaneous" had a much broader meaning then than now. It could mean anything up to several minutes.

19. This period is well described in Robert Taft, *Photography and the American Scene: A Social History, 1839–1889* (New York: Macmillan, 1938).

20. Some of the best of these are available in a single volume, Roy Meredith, *Mr. Lincoln's Camera Man, Mathew S. Brady* (New York: Scribner's, 1946).

ANNOTATED BIBLIOGRAPHY

Books

ANDREWS, J. CUTLER, *The North Reports the Civil War*. Pittsburgh: University of Pittsburgh Press, 1955. Most extensive (813 pages) of histories of Civil War reporting, and thoroughly documented. Lists several hundred northern reporters.

————, *The South Reports the Civil War*. Princeton: Princeton University Press, 1970. Like his *The North Reports the Civil War,* a prize-winning job of research and writing.

CATTON, BRUCE, *Mr. Lincoln's Army*. Garden City, N.Y.: Doubleday, 1951. Includes many instances of military-press relations.

CROZIER, EMMET, *Yankee Reporters, 1861–65*. New York: Oxford University Press, 1956. A readable account of correspondents' work.

FAHRNEY, RALPH RAY, *Horace Greeley and the Tribune in the Civil War*. Chicago: University of Chicago Press, 1929. Documented.

GOBRIGHT, LAWRENCE A., *Recollections of Men and Things at Washington during a Third of a Century*. Philadelphia: Claxton, Remsen, and Haffelfinger, 1869. By the Associated Press correspondent.

HARPER, ROBERT S., *Lincoln and the Press*. New York: McGraw-Hill, 1951. Readable and detailed account of Lincoln's press relations after 1858, written from newspaper sources.

HORAN, JAMES D., *Mathew Brady: Historian with a Camera*. New York: Crown, 1955. A good biography, with 453 pictures.

KLEMENT, FRANK L., *The Copperheads in the Middle West*. Chicago: University of Chicago Press, 1960. Wilbur Storey, C. L. Vallandigham, and Samuel Medary are among those covered.

MATHEWS, JOSEPH J., *Reporting the Wars*. Minneapolis: University of Minnesota Press, 1957. History of war news reporting since the mid-eighteenth century. See also F. L. Bullard, *Famous War Correspondents* (Boston: Little, Brown, 1914).

MEREDITH, ROY, *Mr. Lincoln's Camera Man, Mathew S. Brady*. New York: Scribner's, 1946. A colorful account of the pioneer war photographer, with some of the best of his reproductions.

Photographic History of the Civil War. New York: Review of Reviews Company, 1911. 10 vols. A very complete collection of Brady's pictures, with explanatory material in chronological order.

POLLARD, JAMES E., *The Presidents and the Press*. New York: Macmillan, 1947. The chapter on Lincoln and the press is very useful for those wishing to read a concise discussion of the problem.

REYNOLDS, DONALD E., *Editors Make War: Southern Newspapers in the Secession Crisis*. Nashville, Tenn.: Vanderbilt University Press, 1970. Research in the files proved most Southern editors were in forefront of secession movement.

SALMON, LUCY B., *The Newspaper and Authority*. New York: Oxford University Press, 1923. The chapters on Civil War threats to a free press offer stimulating ideas on the subject.

SANDBURG, CARL, *Abraham Lincoln: The War Years*. New York: Harcourt Brace Jovanovich, 1939. 4 vols. Contains excellent portraits of leading Civil War editors and newspapers.

SNYDER, LOUIS L., AND RICHARD B. MORRIS, eds., *A Treasury of Great Reporting*. New York: Simon & Schuster, 1962. Examples, with pertinent comment, of Civil War news stories are included.

STARR, LOUIS M., *Bohemian Brigade: Civil War Newsmen in Action*. New York: Knopf, 1954. One of the best studies; considers all aspects of the newspaper in wartime, including reporting, editing, censorship.

WEISBERGER, BERNARD A., *Reporters for the Union*. Boston: Little, Brown, 1953. Mainly a study of correspondents' political biases and criticisms of the military; least useful of such books.

Periodicals and Monographs

BLACKMON, ROBERT E., "Noah Brooks: Reporter in the White House," *Journalism Quarterly*, XXXII (Summer 1955), 301. Brooks was the Washington correspondent of the *Sacramento Union* in wartime.

GOLDSMITH, ADOLPH O., "Reporting the Civil War: Union Army Press Relations," *Journalism Quarterly*, XXXIII (Fall 1956), 478. A good summary of the problem.

GUBACK, THOMAS H., "General Sherman's War on the Press," *Journalism Quarterly*, XXXVI (Spring 1959), 171. A well-done account, featuring Sherman's famous clash with the *Herald's* Knox.

PETERSON, DONALD CHRISTIAN, "Two Pioneer American Picture Magazines." Master's thesis, University of Wisconsin, 1953. A detailed study of *Harper's Weekly* and *Frank Leslie's Illustrated Newspaper*.

RANDALL, JAMES G., "The Newspaper Problem and Its Bearing Upon Military Secrecy During the Civil War," *American Historical Review*, XXIII (January 1918), 303. Long the main authority for a discussion of Civil War censorship, by a leading historian of the period.

REILLY, THOMAS W., "Early Coverage of a President-Elect: Lincoln at Springfield 1860," *Journalism Quarterly*, XLIX (Autumn 1972), 469. Henry Villard reports for the *New York Herald*. Taken from "Henry Villard: Civil War Journalist," Master's thesis, University of Oregon, 1970. A discerning, carefully researched study of early news reporting.

WILSON, QUINTUS C., "A Study and Evaluation of the Military Censorship in the Civil War." Master's thesis, University of Minnesota, 1945. This is the most complete and best documented study of the subject. and largely supersedes Randall's monograph.

———, "The Confederate Press Association: A Pioneer News Agency," *Journalism Quarterly*, XXVI (June 1949), 160. A digest of a chapter in Wilson's censorship study.

SAMUEL BOWLES.

THE death of SAMUEL BOWLES, who breathed his last on the evening of January 16, has deprived American journalism of one of its most noteworthy representatives. The Springfield *Republican*, of which he was the editor, has for many years exercised a national influence in politics. Although published in a comparatively small New England town, half-way between New York and Boston, and overshadowed by the press of both cities, it has held its own for half a century, and is more prosperous and more widely quoted at this moment than ever it was before. It is altogether an exceptional journalistic outgrowth. Impersonal at least in the theory of his treatment of public affairs, it has derived a distinctive personality from its editor. Provincial in its professions and aims, seeking to represent the provincial life by which it is surrounded, it is regarded as a power in the land by the politicians of all parties.

An anomaly of this sort could be produced only in America, for the reason, perhaps, that we have no recognized centre of thought and action, no London or Paris, so that the newspapers of every section are enabled to display whatever is in them with the certainty of adequate consideration. Thus the *Republican*, in spite of its geographical situation, has built up a reputation as solid as that of any of its contemporaries which happen to be issued from cities of ten and twenty times the population of Springfield.

SAMUEL BOWLES, to whom the greater achievements of the *Republican* belong, was the son of the founder of the paper. SAMUEL BOWLES the elder was a Hartford printer, who went to Springfield in 1824, and began the publication of the *Weekly Republican*. SAMUEL BOWLES the second, or rather the third—for his grandfather bore the same name—was born in 1826. He grew up about his father's office. There is a tradition that he got the rudiments of a sound academic education in the schools of Springfield; but as he entered the service of the *Republican* before he was seventeen years of age, it is likely that he evolved the strong and simple writing which marked his editorial style out of an inner consciousness sharpened by contact with types, and purified by the free and early use of printers' ink. Certain it is that he was born, as he was raised, a journalist, owing his success, like so many eminent members of his profession, to the practical tuition of the composing-room.

In 1844 he prevailed upon his father to issue the *Daily Republican*, and from the outset had very much the charge of it. The years 1846–48 brought with them the Mexican war and the telegraph, and, of consequence, a revolution in journalistic practice. At this time " SAM" BOWLES, as his friends always called him, was just of age, full of ambition and ardor, with plenty of work in him; and here he laid the beginnings of the substantial fame and fortune he has enjoyed ever since. He did every thing—edited and made up the paper, helped work it off on an old ADAMS press, acted as mailing clerk, cashier, and reporter—eating, working, and sleeping in the office. The *Daily* became a passion with him. The *Republican* was SAM BOWLES, and SAM BOWLES was the *Republican*. It owed its character entirely to

the features impressed upon it by its editor. Its rugged independence of the politicians, its tolerance and entertainment of new and original ideas, its shrewd every-day sense, its extraordinary compilation of news adapted to a certain peculiar audience, whose wants it studies and serves in the minutest way, its racy good nature, varied just enough by an occasional ugly streak or angry flash to give it the needful quantum of snap—all were characteristic of Mr. BOWLES.

In 1857 Mr. BOWLES was induced to go to Boston as editor of a paper made by the fusion of some half a dozen journals, under the title of

SAMUEL BOWLES.—[PHOTOGRAPHED BY SARONY.]

The Boston Daily Traveller. It was an eight-page paper, modelled on the style of the New York daily journals. It did not take, however, and at the end of about six months Mr. BOWLES resumed the editorship of the Springfield *Republican*, of which he was still the owner. He gave a stanch and vigorous support to the Republican party until 1872, when he opposed the renomination of General GRANT, and in the Liberal Convention at Cincinnati pressed the name of CHARLES FRANCIS ADAMS as a candidate for the Presidency. Although deeply disappointed by his failure to carry the Convention, he supported Mr.

GREELEY with great warmth and ability. At the same time he disclaimed all party allegiance, and proclaimed the political independence of the *Republican*.

Mr BOWLES at one time incurred the enmity of the late JIM FISK by comments in the *Republican* on his career as a director of the Erie Railway, and FISK brought a libel suit against the editor for $50,000. One evening in December, 1868, while Mr. BOWLES was talking with some friends in the office of the Fifth Avenue Hotel, he was arrested on papers issued by Judge M'CUNN, and taken hastily to the jail, when the jailor denied him the privilege of writing a note to his wife or of receiving the friends who came to aid him. The numerous offers of bail were refused, as the sheriff declined to be annoyed with such matters after business hours. So Mr. BOWLES slept in Ludlow Street Jail. He was bailed out in the morning, and Mr. FISK's contemptible trick afterward formed the subject of a very spicy correspondence between Mr. BOWLES and FISK's lawyer, in which the editor had decidedly the best of the argument.

Mr. BOWLES was fond of travel in his own country and abroad. He visited California several times, and his book, *Across the Continent*, was the first really good picture of the Pacific slope which appeared. He was a singularly agreeable man, and was universally esteemed in society. In his family he was genial and hospitable, and some of the brightest men and women in the country were his warm friends and frequent guests. He was always a hard worker. When he supposed that he was about to die, he said, with a smile, to an old friend, " Nothing is the matter with me but thirty-five years of hard work ;" and he added afterward, " I was never much of a boy ; I had very little boyhood." The immediate cause of his death was paralysis of the brain. He had been ill with congestion of the lungs since the early part of October last, and that malady, combined with a disorder of the heart, caused him acute suffering. Toward the latter part of November he grew worse. On the 1st of December he thought the end had come, and bade his family and friends farewell. During the last two weeks of his life he gradually lost strength, though conscious all the time. He suffered little, was quiet in mind through the afternoon and evening of his last day on earth, and his death was like the peaceful closing of the eyes in sleep.

HEAD-QUARTERS OF MEHEMET ALI.

ON this page we give a picture of the quarters recently occupied by MEHEMET ALI at Kamarli, which is not far south of Orchanieh, on the road between Plevna and Sophia. The Russian advance from the captured stronghold of OSMAN PASHA compelled the abandonment of all the Turkish positions, and the soldiers of the Czar penetrated the passes almost without resistance where they had expected to fight their way step by step. The city of Sophia was hastily evacuated by the Turks, and immediately occupied by the Russians, who thus obtained a footing south of the Balkans, and an excellent base of operations against Adrianople.

The 1878 obituary picture and story for Samuel Bowles in *Harper's Weekly*.

Charles A. Dana, the *New York Sun*

E. L. Godkin, the *Nation* and *Evening Post*

Harvey W. Scott, Portland's *Oregonian*

Henry Watterson, *Louisville Courier-Journal*

14

The Press
at a Watershed

. . . he was the last of those editors who wrote with the power of ownership.

—Arthur Krock, about Watterson

American history in many respects starts afresh at the close of the Civil War. This is not to deny the obvious fact that two and a half centuries of the American experience had produced fundamental guiding forces that would continue to influence the maturing of the nation's economy and the development of its political and social fabric. But great new forces were at work, and between 1865 and 1900 the United States was to pass through a revolution that affected every phase of the national scene. The forces were those of intensive industrialization, mechanization, and urbanization, bringing with them sweeping social, cultural, and political changes. At some point between the Civil War and the turn of the century, the slow maturing process of virtually every aspect of American life was given powerful new impetus or redirection.

So it was with the nation's journalism. The great development of communication and of journalistic techniques that had come in the Jacksonian period of American growth was continuing through the war period. There was a popular press that had appealed to the human interests of its readers, utilized the new communication facilities to develop news enterprise, and sometimes developed editorial force. But the patterns that had emerged, the techniques that had been created, were to be drastically affected by an extensive new effort born of the impact of the new environment.

There was good reason for the development of new approaches to news reporting and editorial expression. The problems the United States faced in the years after the Civil War were heavy ones. The political leadership at hand was not equal to the tasks, and for a generation the talent exhibited in public life was far less than that shown in industry and business. There was no really great president between 1865 and the turn of the century, although Grover Cleveland won considerable recognition, primarily for his honesty and courage. But whatever the shortcomings in presidential leadership, the remainder of the political scene was far more depressing. The effort at political reconstruction of the South degenerated into an ugly battle between a vengeful Congress and an inept president; carpetbaggers and scalawags put in power in the South through arbitrary reconstruction policies gave way in turn to southern home rule without participation by the Negro; scandals rocked the Grant administration and corruption permeated city governments; a "consistent rebellion" flared against economic maladjustments, money supply inequities, and life-squeezing transportation and interest rates assessed against the farmer. In such a setting an independent-thinking editor devoted to presentation of the news was definitely encouraged.

A NEW GROUP OF EDITORS   Emphasizing this change is the passing from the scene of famous figures of the newspaper movement that had begun in the 1830s. Between 1869 and 1878, five leaders of the era of personal journalism died: Henry J. Raymond, founder of the *New York Times*; James Gordon Bennett, Sr., founder of the *New York Herald*; Horace Greeley, founder of the *New York Tribune*; Samuel Bowles III, most famous of his name to edit the *Springfield Republican*; and William Cullen Bryant, for half a century editor of the *New York Evening Post*.

The newspaper builders who followed appeared not only in New York but also from coast to coast as the nation rushed to complete its geographical expansion and began in earnest to consolidate its economy. The new leaders were maturing and refining the processes and practices of their predecessors. Soon, sensing the opportunities presented by the changing environment in which they worked, some were to create what came to be known as the "new journalism."

Among those who replaced the departing leaders of journalism were some editors who represent a middle group, bridging the gap between the old and new: Charles A. Dana of the *New York Sun*, Edwin Lawrence Godkin of the *Nation* and *New York Evening Post*, Henry Watterson of the *Louisville Courier-Journal*, and Harvey W. Scott of the *Oregonian* in Portland. But even while these men and others like them were making their contributions to journalistic advancement as the leaders of a transitional period, the representatives of the new order were appearing. For example, rising in the dozen years between 1876 and 1887 were Melville E. Stone and the *Chicago Daily News*, Edward Wyllis Scripps and the *Cleveland Press*, Joseph Pulitzer and the *St. Louis Post-Dispatch* and *New York World*, William Rockhill Nelson and the *Kansas City Star*, and William Randolph Hearst and the *San Francisco Examiner*. These are among the most famous names of men and newspapers in American journalism, as we shall see later in detail, and their appearance with others of note in such a brief period testifies to the opportunity for journalistic advances that the revolution in American life afforded. By the time Hearst had invaded New York with his *Journal* to do battle with Pulitzer in the late 1890s—at a time when the careers of Dana and Godkin were closing—the transition from the older era to the new had been achieved. American journalism, like American history, is marked by what historian Henry Steele Commager calls "the watershed of the nineties," whose topography is as blurred as those of all watersheds, but whose grand outlines emerge clearly.[1]

POLITICAL AND FINANCIAL CRISES   Before we consider what the editors did, we should examine in more detail the political and socioeconomic situation in which they worked. The Republican party, which had elected Abraham Lincoln as its first president in 1860, found it necessary to run a Union ticket in 1864, pairing Lincoln with a Tennessee Democrat, Andrew Johnson. Even then, Lincoln polled only 400,000 more votes than the Democratic candidate, General

George B. McClellan, with the South excluded from voting. In light of this, many Republicans viewed the immediate return of the South to full voting privileges with real alarm. They feared the result of accepting Lincoln's theory that since the Union was indissoluble, southern states would automatically return to their former status when fighting ceased. Freed from this policy by Lincoln's death, Representative Thaddeus Stevens of Pennsylvania and Senator Charles Sumner of Massachusetts gave leadership to a group that maintained the South had committed "state suicide" and should be considered as conquered territory. They and their followers, who came to dominate the postwar Congresses, were named the "radical Republicans."

In Andrew Johnson, the radical Republicans found an opponent who was made vulnerable by personality weaknesses that obscured his other qualities. When southern states readmitted to the union by Johnson ignored Negro political rights, the radical Republicans moved to handle the South on their own terms. They passed a civil rights bill; they submitted the fourteenth amendment to the Constitution for ratification; they passed over Johnson's veto the reconstruction acts that forced all southern states to again seek re-entry into the Union on radical-Republican terms; and they instituted military rule in the South. Northern carpetbaggers and southern scalawags who took advantage of the unpreparedness of Negro voters for democratic responsibilities disrupted southern life, and home rule was not fully restored until 1877. The contest between the radical Republicans and the president was climaxed by the impeachment of Johnson, who was saved from removal from office by a single vote in the Senate. Thereupon the Republican party turned to General Ulysses S. Grant as its candidate in 1868 and won the election easily.

Political reconstruction thus was a controversial problem, but financial reconstruction was even more so. Commodity prices in the North had doubled during the five years of war. Running of the printing presses to create legal tender paper money, dubbed "greenbacks," had driven coinage into hiding, intensifying the usual wartime inflationary trend. Congress in 1866 therefore voted to retire the greenbacks gradually over an 11-year period. The argument was advanced that retirement of the greenbacks, which constituted a part of the large federal debt, would deflate prices and increase the value of the dollar. Such action would be to the benefit of creditors and of wage earners whose incomes had not kept pace with prices. But farmers, who generally were debtors, would find money dearer and prices for their products lower. Opposition to retirement of the greenbacks from circulation began to develop in the Middle West agricultural areas and of course in the South, whose economy had been prostrated by the collapse of the Confederate currency and the ravages of war. Opponents of paper money forced final retirement of the greenbacks beginning in 1879, further intensifying the problem of an inadequate money supply for the rapidly expanding American economy. Currency supply was not the only complaint of the agricultural West and South. Farmers found interest rates on their borrowed money excessively high and impossible to pay in years of poor crops or low prices. They found the railroads, which were extending their tracks across the country, were basing their rates on the axiom "charge all the traffic will bear."

By the early 1870s a depression was closing in on a country that had fought a costly and devastating war, plunged into a postwar expansion of capital investment at a faster rate than it was producing wealth, and was still borrowing large amounts of money from European investors for its expansion. When the financial crash came in 1873, with declining prices for agricultural products, the farmers were certain that their lot was unbearable. A "consistent rebellion" began as the agricultural West and South sought economic redress. Currency reform, banking reform, regulation of railroad and grain elevator rates, and lowering of interest charges were the major political issues. The Greenback party flourished as a result, to be followed by the rise of the Populists. The Patrons of Husbandry formed their Grange organizations that forced passage of state laws in the Middle West fixing maximum railroad rates, and the United States Supreme Court in a famous decision (*Munn* v. *Illinois,* 1877) upheld the doctrine that the railroads were subject to regulation in the public interest.[2]

GREELEY'S "MUGWUMP" PRESIDENTIAL RACE

In this troubled political and economic setting, the press found much significant news. And as the news principle gained ascendancy, the editorial columns showed definite signs of rebelling against unswerving loyalty to political parties and their beliefs. The way was eased by rebellion within the ranks of the political parties themselves and particularly by the emergence of a "liberal Republican" faction opposing the radical Republicans and their president, General Grant. Independence of editorial expression meant primarily the freedom to criticize the leaders and policies of the party the editor might normally support, but for some it also meant freedom to bolt the party and support a rival. Those who bolted were called "mugwumps" by their opponents.

The mugwumps of 1872 were led by a group of editors. The liberal Republicans, meeting in convention to find a suitable candidate to oppose Grant, included many newspapermen, the most important of whom were Samuel Bowles of the *Springfield Republican,* Horace White of the *Chicago Tribune,* Murat Halstead of the *Cincinnati Commercial,* and Carl Schurz of the St. Louis *Westliche Post.* The convention ended with the selection of a famous editor, Horace Greeley, as the candidate. Greeley also was nominated by the Democrats, and thus an important segment of the Republican-aligned press found itself allied with pro-Democratic papers. But Greeley's bid for the presidency was ill-starred. Many liberals could not find their way clear to support the aging editor, and others commented cruelly on his eccentricities. Thus such critics of the Grant administration as the *New York Evening Post* and *New York Sun,* and the influential magazines *Harper's Weekly* and the *Nation,* shied away from the Greeley cause. And despite growing discontent with the radical Republicans' reconstruction policies, the administrative shortcomings of the Grant regime, and unsolved economic problems, Grant was reelected handily.

Even though the Greeley campaign had failed, the effect of the mugwump rebellion by such influential editors was a substantial gain in journalistic prestige. It added new proof that editors could shift their political positions and survive, and encouraged those newspapers that felt obliged to attack strong political groups.

SCANDALS IN GOVERNMENT

Scandals in government offer a tempting target for any editor, and the political ineptness and moral laxity that characterized the postwar years further stimulated newspapers and magazines to action. The most notorious example of corruption at the city level was in the operations of the Tweed Ring in New York City. Tammany boss William M. Tweed and his Democratic party cohorts, who milked the city of $200 million, had grown so bold and brazen by 1870 that they had listed a plasterer's pay at $50,000 a day for an entire month while constructing a courthouse. The Tweed Ring controlled some newspapers and frightened others into silence, but it met its masters in the *New York Times* and

THE TAMMANY TIGER LOOSE — "What are you going to do about it?"

Thomas Nast's famed Tammany Tiger cartoon in an 1871 *Harper's Weekly.*

Harper's Weekly. The *Times,* published by George Jones and edited by Louis J. Jennings after the death of Raymond in 1869, obtained documentary proof of the Tweed Ring's thefts in 1871 and broke the astounding story. *Harper's Weekly,* ably edited by George William Curtis, provided a gallery for Thomas Nast, the great political cartoonist who used his pen and ink against Tweed in such devastating fashion that he was offered a bribe to halt his attacks. The answer was the driving of the Tweed Ring from power.[3]

The scandals that left the reputation of the Grant administration blackened were being hinted at before the 1872 presidential election, but it was not until the closing days of the campaign that the *New York Sun* publicized what became known as the Crédit Mobilier affair. When the evidence was developed fully after the election, it proved that promoters of the Union Pacific and Central Pacific railroads had developed a simple system for influencing legislators and others whose support was needed in the obtaining of federal land grants for railroad construction. The railroad builders, operating under the name Crédit Mobilier of America, had sold stock to many public men, lending them the money to pay for the stock and then declaring such huge profits that the loans could be repaid in a single year. Exposure of what amounted to gifts from those seeking legislative favor ruined some politicians and cast suspicion on many more, including the prominent Republican leader James G. Blaine of Maine.

Other disclosures of weaknesses of the Grant administration came rapidly: the whiskey tax frauds in the Treasury Department, the bribing of the secretary of war, W. W. Belknap, and the acceptance of improper gifts by Grant's private secretary. The dazed Grant was himself untouched by the scandals, but his party lost control of the House of Representatives to the Democrats in 1874, and politics became a seesaw affair. The country was entering a period of "dead center" government. For 16 of the next 22 years, control of the two houses of Congress and the presidency was split between the two major parties, so closely was the popular vote divided. Little political progress could be made in such a situation, and eventually the protective tariff became the principal issue of frustrated political aspirants who could not cope with the problems that were generating the "consistent rebellion" of the economically discontented West and South.

DANA
AND THE *NEW YORK SUN*

Of the editors who worked in this turbulent postwar period, two in particular stand out as leaders. Their contributions are sharply different. Charles A. Dana in his years as editor of the *New York Sun* taught the journalist world new lessons in the art of news handling and writing. Edwin Lawrence Godkin in his years as editor of the *Nation* and of the *New York Evening Post* provided solid editorial page leadership. With the deaths of the older New York leaders—Bennett, Greeley, Raymond, and Bryant—Dana and Godkin became the strong men who influenced the maturing of the older press.

Dana and his *Sun* in many respects represent the bridge between the older press and the new journalism that was to develop before the end of the century. A New Englander who had been attracted to the Brook Farm socialist experiment in the 1840s along with other intellectuals seeking the answer to the problems created by the industrial revolution, Dana had met Horace Greeley there. He joined Greeley's staff and became managing editor of the *Tribune* in 1849—the first American to hold such a position. When the Dana-Greeley association was broken in the early days of the Civil War as the aftermath of the *Tribune's* mistaken military predictions, Dana entered government service and emerged to struggle for a year as editor of a new Chicago paper, the *Daily Republican* (forerunner of the famous *Inter Ocean*). The newspaper venture was successful, but Dana wearied of Chicago. Returning to New York, he obtained sufficient backing to buy the *Sun,* the original penny newspaper. Its plant and 43,000 circulation were priced at $175,000 by Moses S. Beach whose father had taken over Ben Day's paper. A career with Greeley on the *Tribune* already behind him, Dana in 1868 began a 29-year career as editor of the *Sun.*

Dana's audience consisted mainly of average New Yorkers, workers and small merchants. To them he addressed his first editorial in the *Sun,* which expressed his ideas on newspaper making. The *Sun,* he said, would present "a daily photograph of the whole world's doings in the most luminous and lively manner." Its staff would write simply and clearly as it tried to present that photograph of the life of the people of New York, as well as of the world's doings. The *Sun* would be low-priced and readable, yet it would use enterprise and money to be the best possible newspaper.

Dana insisted that the journalist must be interested in politics, economics, and government, but first of all in people. The average American, Dana knew, was hard at work, yet he loved sentiment and fun and enjoyed stories reflecting a skillful touch of tenderness or wit. As one of the biographers of Dana and the *Sun* put it, Dana had "the indefinable newspaper instinct that knows when a tomcat on the steps of the

City Hall is more important than a crisis in the Balkans."[4] By 1876 his circulation had tripled to 130,000.

Brilliant as the *Sun* was, however, it had serious weaknesses. Since Dana insisted on limiting its size to four pages, comprehensive coverage of significant news suffered. And the editorial page that could originate such ringing phrases as "No king, no clown, to rule this town!" to combat Tweed, and "Turn the rascals out!" to harass Grant, could also be so intellectually "smart" as to approach cynicism. Dana's fondness for wit and levity made for entertaining reading, but his cynical and sometimes perverse comments on public issues greatly weakened the character of his newspaper.

In its discussions of issues, the *Sun* became increasingly conservative, in contrast to Dana's earlier beliefs. The paper detested labor unions. It poked fun at civil service reform advocates and others interested in good government, even though the *Sun* itself crusaded against misconduct in office. And it long advocated imperialistic schemes for the annexation of Canada, Cuba, and other neighboring areas.

GODKIN, THE *NATION*, AND THE *POST*

It remained for an English-born journalist to give the United States the vigorous and intelligent editorial leadership it needed in the postwar period. He was Edwin Lawrence Godkin, the founder of the magazine the *Nation* and successor to William Cullen Bryant as the driving spirit of the *New York Evening Post*.

Of Godkin, historian Allan Nevins has written: "Godkin showed at once a distinctive style, a refreshing penetration, and a skill in ironic analysis never before equalled in American journalism." And because this was so, philosopher William James could write: "To my generation his was certainly the towering influence in all thought concerning public affairs, and indirectly his influence has assuredly been more pervasive than that of any other writer of the generation, for he influenced other writers who never quoted him, and determined the whole current of discussion."[5] President Charles W. Eliot of Harvard University, President Daniel Coit Gilman of Johns Hopkins, James Russell Lowell, James Bryce, Charles Eliot Norton—the intellectual leaders of Godkin's generation—all publicly acknowledged the debt they owed to the pages of the *Nation*. Not, of course, that they always agreed with its editor's viewpoints.

Godkin had been a reporter and editorial writer for English newspapers and had written editorials for Henry J. Raymond's *New York Times* before deciding that the United States needed a high-grade weekly journal of opinion and literary criticism, similar to those in England. In 1865 he found the financial backing for the *Nation* and announced its aims.

The *Nation*, Godkin said, would discuss the political and economic questions of the day "with greater accuracy and moderation than are now to be found in the daily press." It would advocate "whatever in legislation or in manners seems likely to promote a more equal distribution of the fruits of progress and civilization." It would seek to better the conditions of the Negro. It would fix "public attention upon the political importance of education, and the dangers which a system like ours runs from the neglect of it in any portion of our territory." And it would print sound and impartial criticisms of books and works of art.[6]

Godkin was a mid-Victorian English liberal of the John Stuart Mill school of economic thought. Therefore he believed that government should not intervene in economic matters. But unlike many of his time, he did believe that government should take action in social spheres. To a twentieth-century world that has used government as a regulatory force in both economic and social situations, Godkin thus appears at times to be reactionary and at other times liberal.

But in many areas, Godkin was in the forefront of progressive thought. He urged complete reconciliation with the South during the period of military rule; he was one of the earliest advocates of civil service reform to end the spoils system; he believed in women's suffrage when it was an unpopular idea; he was a strong supporter of public education and the new land-grant universities; and, as mentioned above, he wrote in behalf of the Negro. Above all, the *Nation* ceaselessly badgered politicians who were interested more in personal gain than in progressive improvement of government. Its influence ran far beyond its 10,000 circulation.

In 1881, Godkin moved onto a bigger but actually less influential journalistic stage. That year Henry Villard, a Civil War correspondent who later won a fortune building railroads, purchased the *New York Evening Post,* and obtained a trio of outstanding editors for the newspaper. One was Horace White, who had edited the *Chicago Tribune* from 1866 to 1874, taking that newspaper into the liberal Republican camp for a brief period as he advocated tariff reduction, civil service reform, and currency policies favorable to the farmers. A second was Carl Schurz, the former editor of the St. Louis *Westliche Post* who had become Secretary of the Interior in President Hayes' cabinet, and a leading American liberal. The third was Godkin, who sold the *Nation* to Villard but continued to edit it as the weekly edition of the *Evening Post.* Within two years, Schurz and Godkin quarreled over Godkin's antilabor union views, and Schurz resigned, leaving Godkin in control of the *Evening Post* with White as his assistant.

With Godkin, the *Evening Post* and the *Nation* rose to new fame in the presidential election year of 1884. The contest lay between James G. Blaine, the Republican congressional leader from Maine, and Grover Cleveland, Democratic governor of New York. Godkin, declaring that Blaine was unacceptable because of the post-Civil War scandals, fought his election with all his editorial skill. As the campaign progressed, charges of immoral conduct were made against Cleveland, and emotionalism ran high. Some stalwart Republican newspapers in leading cities found themselves opposing Blaine in company with the usual dissenters—the *Evening Post,* the *New York Times, Springfield Republican, Harper's Weekly,* and the *Nation.* Dana of the *Sun,* who would support neither major party candidate, fastened on these papers the name "mugwump," indicating desertion of party regularity. It applied particularly to the *Evening Post,* which had been Republican since the founding of the party in 1856.

The *Evening Post's* particular contribution was Godkin's famous "deadly parallel" column, in which he matched Blaine's campaign statements and congressional record against his personal associations with railroad builders and financiers. The campaign became exceedingly bitter, and it was evident that the New York State vote would decide the election. When Cleveland carried New York by 23,000 votes and became the first Democrat to win the presidency since the Civil War, many explanations were advanced. A Blaine supporter who had described the Democrats as a party of "rum, Romanism, and rebellion" received heavy blame, as did the antilabor *New York Tribune,* whose advocacy of Blaine was judged to be a handicap in the wooing of working men's votes. But Godkin asserted, with some justice, that the victory was proof of the creation of a group of independent voters who would put the public welfare ahead of party loyalty, as had the mugwump newspapers and magazines.

Godkin stood in the early 1880s as New York's leading editor primarily because of his great ability, but also because of the shortcomings of his contemporaries. The *Times,* after the death of Raymond, was slowly going downhill and exhibited spirit and influence only sporadically. Dana's *Sun* was erratic, and the Bennetts' *Herald* had little editorial force. Greeley's *Tribune,* after the founding editor's death in 1872, switched position and became the spokesman for the dominant conservative wing of the Republican party. The *Tribune's* new editor was a famous journalistic figure, Whitelaw Reid, but his editorial stand lacked the qualities of independence shown by an increasing number of editors. While Godkin was urging reconciliation with the South, the *Tribune* was waving the bloody shirt as late as 1880 to preserve Republican supremacy. Godkin was for tariff reform; the *Tribune,* for high tariffs and protection of the industrial interests of the expanding capitalism. Godkin long favored civil service reform, which found favor with the Republican leadership only after the assassination of President James A. Garfield. And the *Tribune* more than matched Godkin's opposition to labor unions, fighting a printers' strike against itself for 15 years.[7] Still, the *Tribune's* standards of news coverage and presentation were such that it was a formidable competitor for the readership of those whom the *Post* called the "gentlemen and scholars."

Unfortunately, Godkin was not a newspaperman despite his editorial genius. He cared little for the news policies of the *Evening Post,* beyond his specialized interests. He disliked sentiment and color in the news, and he would have liked to have kept all news of crime and violence out of the paper's columns. Whatever merit there was to his viewpoints, they put the *Evening Post* at a serious disadvantage in the competition for circulation, and the paper never attained the readership its editorial leadership deserved.

Godkin retired as editor of the *Evening Post* and the *Nation* in 1899. He died in 1902. When Henry Villard died in 1900, his son, Oswald Garrison Villard, became publisher and editorial leader of the two publications. They continued to be fighting liberal organs.[8]

HENRY WATTERSON AND THE *COURIER-JOURNAL*

Other strong editorial voices were raised outside New York during the period of Godkin's dominance. The most notable were those of Henry Watterson of the *Louisville Courier-Journal* and Harvey W. Scott of the *Oregonian* in Portland. Both enjoyed long careers that began at the close of the Civil War and continued until World War I, but both belong primarily in this transitional period of journalism history. Arthur Krock, an associate of Watterson on the *Courier-Journal* staff before becoming a *New York Times* fixture, offers one reason for setting Watterson apart from later editors: ". . . he was the last of those editors who wrote with the power of ownership."[9] The same was true of Scott. Other editors, like Godkin, exercised free rein because of their relationship to owners of their papers, and they have continued to do so since, but admittedly with increasing difficulty as the newspaper became a corporate institution.

Watterson was editor of the *Courier-Journal* for 50 years, and his personality did much to make the newspaper one of the foremost in the country. He was a colorful representative of the era of personal journalism who loved to engage in editorial-page duels with other editors. One of his first foes was Dana and he lived to banter with the editors of another journalistic generation in the twentieth century. He himself said that he belonged to the era of "the personal, one-man papers—rather blatant, but independent."[10]

Watterson had varied youthful ambitions: to be a great historian, a great dramatist, a great novelist, a great musician. He came no closer to those dreams than writing a rejected novel and serving as a music critic in New York, but his catholic interests served in time to make him a versatile and engaging writer of editorials. He was an editorial writer in Washington when the Civil War began, and he cast his lot with the South, editing a Tennessee newspaper named the *Rebel*. After stints on newspapers in Cincinnati, Atlanta, and Nashville, Watterson at the age of 28 found his lifetime work in Louisville.

There Walter N. Haldeman, editor of the *Courier*, was in the process of consolidating the *Journal* and the *Democrat* with his newspaper, and the editorship and part ownership of the new *Courier-Journal* went to Watterson. The year was 1868. Watterson, who despite his work for the southern cause had believed secession to be wrong, raised his voice in behalf of reconciliation of the North and South and gave advice freely to both sections. He told the North that military rule should be relaxed, and he was listened to because he also had sympathy for the Negro. He told the South that Lincoln was a great man and that much of its misery had come about as a result of his assassination. And the South listened, because Watterson was a southerner of good family, not a reforming Yankee. Soon the *Courier-Journal* editorial columns, and particularly its weekly edition, won a position as a leading voice of the new South.

HARVEY SCOTT AND THE *OREGONIAN*

In the Far West, another voice was raised by an editor whose intellectual powers and forceful writing brought him attention as the leading spokesman of his area. He was Harvey W. Scott, who for 45 years edited the *Oregonian* in Portland. The *Oregonian,* founded in 1850 in a village near the junction of the Willamette and Columbia rivers, grew with the community. Scott gave up a law career to become its editor in 1865, and in 1877 he and Henry L. Pittock became the owners.[11]

Like Godkin, Scott was scholarly and forceful in his expression of opinion, but like Godkin, too, he lacked Watterson's human touch. There was one major reason why Scott's editorials were widely read and quoted: he had the ability to grapple with complex problems that many an editor shied away from and to present new viewpoints originating in his own reasoning and analysis. His range of information seemed unlimited, and he used this resource as he thought an editor should, to guide public opinion in the public interest. The *Oregonian* was Republican by choice, but Scott wrote as an independent editor, taking his stand on the basis of his conception of the public good. An editor with Scott's abilities is rare in any period, and his fame spread from the home city in which he was a leading figure as the *Oregonian* won statewide circulation and its editorial voice became nationally recognized.

Dana, Godkin, Watterson, and Scott—particularly the latter two—lived through the enormous changes that were occurring in American life as the industrial revolution hit full stride. They were aware of change, and accepted it, but their journalistic roles were more of the older order than of the new. There were other men among their contemporaries who might well be named, but these were the leaders and the symbols of a transitional era. They and their fellow workers contributed new strengths to American journalism as it approached the "watershed of the nineties."

NOTES

1. Henry Steele Commager, *The American Mind* (New Haven: Yale University Press, 1950), p. 41.
2. This is a brief summary of the farmers' problems, which are given full analysis in such studies as John D. Hicks's *The Populist Revolt* (Minneapolis: University of Minnesota Press, 1931) and Solon J. Buck's *The Granger Movement* (Cambridge, Mass.: Harvard University Press, 1913).
3. Fuller details are given in Gustavus Myers, *The History of Tammany Hall* (New York: Boni and Liveright, 1917).
4. Frank M. O'Brien, *The Story of The Sun* (New York: George H. Doran Company, 1918), p. 231. New edition (Appleton-Century-Crofts, 1928), p. 151.
5. As quoted in Allan Nevins, *American Press Opinion* (New York: Heath, 1928), p. 299.
6. Godkin's full statement of purpose is found in Rollo Ogden, *Life and Letters of Edwin Lawrence Godkin,* I (New York: Macmillan, 1907), pp. 237–38.
7. As previously noted, the *Tribune*'s founder, Horace Greeley, had been the first president of New York City's Typographical Union No. 6, founded in 1850.
8. The younger Villard sold the *Evening Post* in 1918 but remained at the helm of the *Nation* until 1933.
9. Arthur Krock, ed., *The Editorials of Henry Watterson* (New York: Doran, 1923), p. 15.
10. Tom Wallace, "There Were Giants in Those Days," *Saturday Evening Post,* August 6, 1938 (reprinted in John E. Drewry, ed., *Post Biographies of Famous Journalists*).
11. The Scott and Pittock family heirs retained control of the *Oregonian* until 1950, when the 100-year-old paper was sold to Samuel I. Newhouse. See the *Oregonian,* December 11, 1950.

ANNOTATED BIBLIOGRAPHY

Books

BAEHR, HARRY W., JR., *The New York Tribune Since the Civil War*. New York: Dodd, Mead, 1936. One of the better histories of newspapers.

Casual Essays of The Sun. New York: R. G. Cooke, 1905. A collection of *Sun* editorials including "Dear Virginia."

DUNCAN, BINGHAM, *Whitelaw Reid: Journalist, Politician, Diplomat*. Athens, Ga.: University of Georgia Press, 1975. A leading conservative voice at the *New York Tribune*.

FUESS, CLAUDE M., *Carl Schurz*. New York: Dodd, Mead, 1932. A biography of the famous liberal, whose own *Reminiscences* (1907) are rewarding reading.

HICKS, JOHN D., *The American Nation*. Boston: Houghton Mifflin, 1964. A standard text for American history since 1865.

JOSEPHSON, MATTHEW, *The Robber Barons*. New York: Harcourt Brace Jovanovich, 1934. A scathing description of the low state of public morality after the Civil War, focusing particularly on corruption in railroad building. *The Politicos* (1938) is a companion volume.

KELLER, MORTON, *The Art and Politics of Thomas Nast*. New York: Oxford University Press, 1968. A beautifully printed, illustrated, and researched story of the great cartoonist.

KROCK, ARTHUR, ed., *The Editorials of Henry Watterson*. New York: George H. Doran Company, 1923. Excellent preface.

LOGSDON, JOSEPH, *Horace White, Nineteenth Century Liberal*. Westport, Conn.: Greenwood Publishing Corp., 1971. An editor of the *Chicago Tribune* and owner of the *New York Evening Post* and the *Nation*.

NEVINS, ALLAN, *The Emergence of Modern America, 1865–1878,* A History of American Life, Vol. VIII. New York: Macmillan, 1927. A rich social history, whose extensive documentation is accompanied by highly skillful writing.

———, *The Evening Post; A Century of Journalism*. New York: Boni and Liveright, 1922. The Godkin and other eras are presented against a general social and political background.

NYE, RUSSEL B., *Midwestern Progressive Politics; a Historical Study of Its Origins and Development, 1870–1950*. East Lansing: Michigan State College Press, 1951. A comprehensive survey. For more specialized studies, see Solon J. Buck, *The Granger Movement* (Cambridge, Mass.: Harvard University Press, 1913), and John D. Hicks, *The Populist Revolt* (Minneapolis: University of Minnesota Press, 1931).

O'BRIEN, FRANK M., *The Story of The Sun*. New York: George H. Doran Company, 1918. Revised. New York: Appleton-Century-Crofts, 1928. One of the most readable histories of newspapers.

OGDEN, ROLLO, *Life and Letters of Edwin Lawrence Godkin*. New York: Macmillan, 1907. The standard biography.

PAINE, ALBERT BIGELOW, *Th. Nast, His Period and His Pictures*. New York: Macmillan, 1904. Well-illustrated with Nast's famous cartoons.

RHODES, JAMES FORD, *A History of the United States Since the Compromise of 1850*. New York: Macmillan, 1892–1906. A nine-volume political history ending with the turn of the century, written with conspicuous success by a conservative businessman turned scholar.

STAMPP, KENNETH M., *The Era of Reconstruction, 1865–1877*. New York: Knopf, 1965. New points of view admirably presented by consensus school revisionist.

STONE, CANDACE, *Dana and the Sun*. New York: Dodd, Mead, 1938. The top-ranking biography of Dana, critical in tone.

WALL, JOSEPH F., *Henry Watterson: Reconstructed Rebel*. New York: Oxford University Press, 1956. A well-documented study.

WATTERSON, HENRY, *"Marse Henry"; An Autobiography*. New York: George H. Doran Company, 1919. The Louisville editor's own pungent story.

WISH, HARVEY, *Society and Thought in Modern America*. New York: Longmans, Green & Company, 1962. The second volume in Wish's social and intellectual history, beginning with 1865.

WOODWARD, C. VANN, *Origins of the New South, 1877–1913*. Baton Rouge: Louisiana State University Press, 1951. Prize-winning study of the South's emergence from the Civil War.

Periodicals and Monographs

DOWNEY, MATTHEW T., "Horace Greeley and the Politicians," *Journal of American History*, LIII (March 1967), 727. Liberal Republican convention of 1872.

LEITER, KELLY, "U.S. Grant and the *Chicago Tribune*," *Journalism Quarterly*, XLVII (Spring 1970), 71. Based on his Ph.D. thesis, Southern Illinois University, 1969.

MITCHELL, EDWARD P., "The Newspaperman's Newspaper," *Scribner's*, LXXVI (August 1924), 149. A vivid portrait of Dana and his *Sun* by a longtime *Sun* editor.

MURRAY, RANDALL L., "Edwin Lawrence Godkin: Unbending Editor in Times of Change," *Journalism History*, I (Autumn 1974), p. 77. Godkin laments late 1880s social change.

NEVINS, ALLAN, "E. L. Godkin: Victorian Liberal," *Nation*, CLXXI (July 22, 1950), 76. An interpretative essay, followed by a study, written by Lewis Gannett, of Oswald Garrison Villard's editorship.

PLUMMER, L. NIEL, "Henry Watterson's Editorial Style: An Interpretative Analysis," *Journalism Quarterly*, XXIII (March 1946), 58.

PRINGLE, HENRY F., "Godkin of 'The Post,'" *Scribner's*, XCVI (December 1934), 327. A well-balanced article by a newspaperman turned biographer. Reprinted in Ford and Emery, *Highlights in the History of the American Press*.

———, "Kentucky Bourbon—Marse Henry Watterson," *Scribner's*, XCVII (January 1935), 10. Reprinted in Ford and Emery, *Highlights in the History of the American Press*.

Quarterly of the Oregon Historical Society, XIV, No. 2 (June 1913). An issue devoted to Harvey W. Scott, editor of the *Oregonian*.

THORP, ROBERT K., "'Marse Henry' and the Negro: A New Perspective," *Journalism Quarterly*, XLVI (Autumn 1969), 467. It was not as Marse Henry remembered it; he was scarcely their champion.

TURNBULL, GEORGE, "The Schoolmaster of the Oregon Press," *Journalism Quarterly*, XV (December 1938), 359. A study of the influence of Harvey W. Scott by the author of the *History of Oregon Newspapers* (1939).

WALLACE, TOM, "There Were Giants in Those Days," *Saturday Evening Post* (August 6, 1938). The color of the Marse Henry Watterson days is recaptured by another longtime Louisville editor. Reprinted in John E. Drewry, ed., *Post Biographies of Famous Journalists* (Athens: University of Georgia Press, 1942).

WILEY, BONNIE, "History of the Portland *Oregonian,*" Ph.D. thesis, Southern Illinois University, 1965. From Harvey Scott to Samuel Newhouse, 1850 to 1965.

FRANK LESLIE'S
ILLUSTRATED
NEWSPAPER

Entered according to Act of Congress in the year 1857, by FRANK LESLIE, in the Clerk's Office of the District Court for the Southern District of New York. (Copyrighted May 10, 1858.)

No. 128 — VOL. V.] NEW YORK, SATURDAY, MAY 15, 1858. [PRICE 6 CENTS.

OUR EXPOSURE OF THE MILK TRADE OF NEW YORK AND BROOKLYN.

FROM a hundred sources we are receiving, day by day, thanks for our public spirit and fearless exposure of a nefarious and revolting trade, and good wishes and prayers for the ultimate and speedy success of our undertaking.

We feel sincerely gratified and deeply grateful for the outside encouragement we receive; it will move us to new exertions, for we feel that we have obtained the ear of the public; that its sympathies and hopes are with us, and armed with this assurance we feel our power equal to the emergency. That our blows have been dealt strongly and truly we have ample evidence. Our exposure has not only broken up all the milk routes we have published, but one whose name we were fortunately enabled to give, is selling off his swill milk cows. His stable is broken up, his swill trade, gone, and mark the consequence—he has contracted with the country dairies for the milk he requires for his customers. Is not the good work begun? May we not hope for the future?

An early crusade was the 1858 "swill milk" campaign in *Leslie's Illustrated Newspaper.*

15

A Revolution
in National Life

The newspaper has a history; but it has, likewise, a natural history. The press, as it exists, is not, as our moralists sometimes seem to assume, the wilful product of any little group of living men. On the contrary, it is the outcome of a historic process....

—Robert E. Park

The journalism of Dana and Godkin was the product of an American society in transition; what was happening to the national life for the first dozen years after the close of the War Between the States could be called a transition. But then, the swelling tide of economic and social change brought not transition but revolution.

In journalism, as in all other aspects of American life, the result was an emergence of new concepts and practices more akin to the twentieth century than to the immediate past. New leaders were to revolutionize the newspaper and the magazine by responding to the abruptly changed environment rather than by clinging to the older patterns. The contrast, by the 1890s, between Dana's cranky, change-resisting journalism and that of the dynamic symbol of the new order—Joseph Pulitzer—was glaring indeed. It was no more glaring, however, than the differences that had developed in literature, in science, in political and economic thought, in business and industry, in the way Americans lived and worked.

AN INDUSTRIAL ECONOMY   What was happening? Industrialization was advancing on a major scale: mechanization of production processes, the rise of the city, vast expansion of communication facilities, the coming of the age of steel, the harnessing of electricity for light and power, and a host of inventions and new businesses.

This was the true nationalization of the United States, the achievement of economic and social interdependence.[1] National growth and increased wealth meant cultural progress in literature, science, and the social sciences. But the wealth was not equally distributed, and there was sharp questioning of the theory of individualism that permitted unrestrained exploitation, enormous concentrations of wealth and economic power, and the many injustices of a materialistic-minded age. Political unrest, the rise of labor unions, and demands for economic and social reform thus were added to the scene.

America was a rich continent for the aggressive and the ingenious to master. Between 1865 and 1880 the national wealth doubled, and by 1900 it had doubled again. The population doubled in those 35 years. The nation's iron ore, its oil, its lumber, and its western agricultural lands were sources of yet untapped wealth. Its people, who by and large admired the successful enterprisers, eagerly provided investment and speculative capital. Only when it became clear that the division of the spoils had been in favor of a few to the detriment of the many, did the protests take effect. In the meantime, the patterns had been set. The dynamic capitalism of an expanding America, seizing on unparalleled natural resources and utilizing the new machines of the industrial revolution, had transformed the national economy.

These are some of the figures that show what was happening to the United States. Total maufacturing production increased sevenfold between the end of the Civil War and 1900: using a base figure of 100 for the years 1909–13, the index figure for 1865 was 8.5; in 1880 it was 27, and by 1900 it was 61.[2] There were 140,000 industries of all types in 1860. By 1880 there were 250,000, and by 1900 the number was over 500,000. The number of persons employed in those industries doubled in each of the 20-year periods. The percentage of the labor force engaged in nonagricultural work was 41 percent in 1860, 50 percent in 1880, and 62 percent in 1900. Estimated national wealth in 1865 was $20 billion. By 1880 it was $43 billion, and by 1900 the figure was $88 billion. Bank deposits tripled between 1865 and 1880, then quadrupled in the next 20 years.

A look at some production figures tells a similar story. The rate of increase was greatest in the twenty years from 1880 to 1900. Coal and pig iron production quadrupled; copper smelters scored a tenfold increase; steel and cement production increased eight times. Petroleum output more than doubled. While the production totals continued to climb steadily after 1900, the rate of increase declined, except in the case of petroleum.

CAPTAINS OF BIG BUSINESS

Familiar symbols of this new economic order are John D. Rockefeller and the oil monopoly, and Andrew Carnegie and the steel combine. But similar concentrations of wealth and business control developed throughout American industry and trade—Cornelius Vanderbilt, Jay Gould, and J. Pierpont Morgan in finance; Leland Stanford, Collis P. Huntington, James J. Hill, and George Pullman in railroading; C. C. Washburn and Charles A. Pillsbury in the milling industry that centered in Minneapolis as the great plains opened; Philip D. Armour and Gustavus F. Swift in the meat packing industry that grew in Chicago and Kansas City as cattle raising became big business; the makers of machine-sewed shoes, ready-made clothes, packaged foods, watches, cameras, farm machinery, and hardware; the lumbermen, the mining kings—all rose to dominate the American scene in the late nineteenth century.

The captains of industry and finance obtained power through a variety of means. Some gained control of large segments of natural resources. A few held patents on basic inventions. Others, of whom Rockefeller was the most noted, won supremacy in part through manipulation of transportation rates and ruthless competitive tactics. Some were lucky in the world of financial speculation. Most important, the

Rockefellers and the Carnegies usually were successful because they had, or could hire, the brains necessary to create a new manufacturing or financial empire.

But, as usual, there was a flaw in the new order. As the machine revolutionized the American economy, it brought with it the threat of overproduction and disastrous competition among the new producers. The dislocation of labor that resulted and the bankrupting of weaker businesses also promoted economic instability. The captains of industry cast about for ways of avoiding the industrial and financial panics that threatened the strong as well as the weak.

One effort to overcome these dangers took the form of the pool agreement. Direct competitors sought by voluntary secret agreement to limit industrywide production, to allocate production quotas, and to stabilize prices. The trouble was that in times of distress the rule quickly became "every man for himself."

A more successful form of industry control was the trust, developed by the Standard Oil group around 1880. By this method the shareholders in the original companies assigned their capital stock to a board of trustees and received trust certificates in return. The trustees thus obtained legal control of the individual units. They could decide production quotas, set selling prices, and eliminate competition.

Hosts of other industries followed the lead of the oilmen before 1890. Sugar, salt, whiskey, rope, lead, tin plate, crackers, matches, newsprint, fence wire and many other products fell under near monopolistic control. The number of producing companies declined sharply in such fields as woolen goods, iron and steel, leather, and farm machinery. Congress passed the Sherman Anti-Trust Act of 1890 in an attempt to restore open competition, but the end result was hardly satisfactory to opponents of industrial monopoly. The sugar trust simply became an incorporated company under the laws of New Jersey, and the Standard Oil group developed the holding-company technique. The amalgamation of many businesses now took the form of a single great corporation, whether in manufacturing, in railroading, or in mining and cattle raising.

THE RISE OF THE CITY   The industrial concentration that was maturing between 1880 and 1900 was of vital significance, but it was only a part of the enormous change in American life. Mechanization, industrialization, and urbanization brought swift and extensive social, cultural, and political developments. People were being uprooted physically and mentally by the effects of the economic revolution, and in the new environment no social institution could remain static. Even a brief examination of the character of this new environment will indicate the basic causes of the tremendous changes that developed in the daily newspapers of American cities by the 1880s.

Arthur M. Schlesinger, Sr., chose the phrase "the rise of the city" to characterize the period from 1878 to 1898.[3] Census figures show that the number of American towns and cities of 8,000 or more population doubled between 1880 and 1900. The total population of those urban places more than doubled, jumping from some 11 million to 25 million. In 1880 there were 50 million Americans, of whom 22.7 percent were living in towns and cities of more than 8,000. By 1900 that figure had risen to 32.9 percent of a total population of 76 million.

The most rapid gain in urbanization occurred during the ten years between 1880 and 1890, which were the years of greatest ferment in the daily newspaper business. The rise of the city was particularly evident in the northeastern industrial states, where urban centers now predominated over declining rural areas, and in the older states of the Middle West. New York City jumped in population from a million to a million and a half during the decade. Chicago, the rail and trade center of inland America, doubled its size, passing the million mark in 1890 to become the nation's second city. Next in line were Philadelphia, at a million; Brooklyn, at 800,000; and Boston, Baltimore, and St. Louis, in the half-million class. Altogether there were 58 cities with more than 50,000 population in 1890: 80 percent of them were in the East and Middle West, and 50 percent of them were in the five states of New York, Pennsylvania, Massachusetts, New Jersey, and Ohio.

Into these cities was pouring an ever-rising tide of immigration, which brought new blood and new problems for American society. Again the decade of 1880–90 stands out, since in those ten years more than five million immigrants came to America, double the number for any preceding decade. All told, approximately nine million foreign-born were added to the population in the 20 years between 1880 and 1900, as many as had come during the 40 years preceding 1880. As a result, the newspapers of New York City in 1890 were serving a population that was 80 percent foreign-born or of foreign parentage, and as might be expected, the character of some of the newspapers changed. Other American cities had from 25 to 40 percent foreign-born residents. To the older Irish, British, and German streams of migration were added great numbers of Scandinavians, Poles, French-Canadians, Italians, Russians, and Hungarians. Of these, the Germans and the Scandinavians particularly migrated to the Middle West, while the other groups tended to remain in the Atlantic states.

The rise of the city meant a quickening of material progress, reflected first in the life of the city dweller and transmitted gradually to the rest of the country. The new American cities hastened the installation of water and sewage systems in the years following the Civil War. They paved their streets with asphalt and bricks, and they bridged their rivers with steel structures patterned after the Roeblings' famed Brooklyn bridge of 1883. A ten-story Chicago building, constructed around a steel and iron skeleton in 1885, heralded the coming of the skyscraper.

Electricity was becoming a great new servant, both as a source of power for industry and transportation and as a source of light. American cities barely had begun to install arc lights in 1879 when Thomas A. Edison invented a practicable incandescent bulb. When the current flowed out from his Pearl Street generating station in 1882 to light the Stock Exchange and the offices of the *New York Times* and *New York Herald,* a new era in living had begun. By 1898 there were nearly 2,800 central electric power stations in the country, as businesses and homes were lighted, electric elevators were installed in the new tall buildings, and electric motors became widely used in industry.

THE COMMUNICATIONS NETWORK

America was being tied together by its industrial revolution, and its communications network kept pace with the sense of urgency that was characteristic of the new order. The telephone, invented by Alexander Graham Bell in the 1870s, already had one user for every thousand persons in 1880. By 1900 there was one telephone for each hundred. Intercity lines multiplied during the 1880s, until by 1900 the Bell System covered the country. Western Union quadrupled its telegraph lines between 1880 and 1900. The railroads, with 93,000 miles of track in 1880, reached a near-saturation point of 193,000 miles by 1900. The federal postal service, still the primary means of communication, greatly extended its free carrier service in cities during the two decades and instituted free rural delivery in 1897. Congress, by clearly defining second-class matter in the Postal Act of 1879 and by providing a one-cent-a-pound rate for newspapers and magazines in 1885, opened the way for cheap delivery of publications. In business offices the invention of the typewriter and adding machine speeded the work pace and simplified the handling of increased correspondence and records.

THE EXPANSION
OF NEWSPAPERS

The most striking evidence of what was happening to the newspaper is to be found in a bare statistical summary. Between 1870 and 1900, the United States doubled its population and tripled the number of its urban residents. During the same 30 years the number of its daily newspapers quadrupled and the number of copies sold each day increased almost sixfold. Both in numbers and in total circulation the daily newspaper was rising even more rapidly than the city that spawned it. The number of English-language, general-circulation dailies increased from 489 in 1870 to 1,967 in 1900. Circulation totals for all daily publications rose from 2.6 million copies in 1870 to 15 million in 1900.[4] A similar advance was being made by weekly newspapers, serving mainly the small towns and rural areas, but also the suburbs and sections of the cities. Between 1870 and 1900, the number of weekly publications tripled, increasing from approximately 4,000 to more than 12,000. The weeklies, however, still represented personal journalistic ventures, and the revolution in newspaper methods was taking place at the big city daily level.

There were many less tangible reasons why the newspaper was making such tremendous strides as an American social institution. The forces of social and economic interdependence, products of industrialization and urbanization, played a leading part in the creation of the lusty "new journalism." The peoples of the cities, being molded together as economic and cultural units, increasingly turned to the daily newspapers for the story of their urban life and their common interests. At the same time the country itself was being rapidly unified by the rush toward economic interdependence. Improved communications facilities were a manifestation of this nationalizing influence that pervaded all American life. And again, the daily newspaper was the chronicler of the national scene, the interpreter of the new environment. The city reader, whether he was seated in new-found comfort on a streetcar or in his better-lighted home, was the eager customer of the publisher who met successfully the new challenge to journalism.

ADVANCES
IN EDUCATION

As American social and economic life became more complex and as the national wealth accumulated, many cultural advances were possible that in turn promoted new interest in the newspaper. The cities, with their concentrated populations and earning capacities, naturally led in expansion of social and intellectual activity. But they also set the pace for a nationalized cultural development. The bookstores, libraries, art galleries, museums, theaters, opera houses, churches, retail stores, schools, and newspapers that brought higher standards in the cities stimulated the interests and the desires of all the country. Progress in education, the result of this general thirst for knowledge and a better life, was particularly important to the expansion of the mass media—newspapers, magazines, books. The percentage of children attending public schools in the United States rose from 57 to 72 percent between 1870 and 1900, while illiteracy declined from 20 to 10.7 percent of the population. The number of high schools jumped from approximately 100 in 1860 to 800 by 1880, and then skyrocketed to 6,000 by 1900.

At higher educational levels, growth of state universities and of private colleges financed by America's new men of wealth resulted in notable advances in the social sciences, as well as progress in the natural and physical sciences and the humanities. Federal land subsidies provided by the Morrill Act of 1862 encouraged the founding and expansion of state universities, particularly in the Middle West and West, where such state-supported universities as Wisconsin, California, Minnesota, and Illinois began to flourish. The private colleges and universities gained in numbers and influence with the founding of Cornell University in 1865 by Ezra Cornell, whose millions came from the electric telegraph; of Johns Hopkins University in 1876 by a Baltimore merchant; of Leland Stanford University in 1885 by a California railroad and business man; of the University of Chicago in 1892 by John D. Rockefeller's benefaction. Johns Hopkins, by emphasizing the role of research in higher education, and Harvard, by giving its students an elective choice of courses, set new patterns for the universities. And university presidents such as Charles W. Eliot of Harvard, Daniel Coit Gilman of Johns Hopkins, and Andrew D. White of Cornell gave effective leadership. No longer was it necessary for Americans interested in scholarly pursuits to go abroad, and the number of graduate students in the United States increased from 400 in 1880 to some 5,600 in 1900. Nor were women ignored in the new spread of education. The state universities became coeducational institutions; Smith College was founded in 1875, soon to be followed by Bryn Mawr and Radcliffe, as fruits of the woman suffrage movement.

NEW SOCIOECONOMIC PHILOSOPHIES

The scholars of the universities and other men and women whose intellectual and cultural achievements were supported by the new wealth of the nation made great advances in the years between 1880 and 1900. Most importantly, they challenged the socioeconomic philosophies that had developed in nineteenth-century society and suggested new concepts better fitted to the revolutionized character of American life. They organized areas of knowledge needed if the country was to understand its problems and cope with them, and in doing so they laid the groundwork for the vast growth of research and interpretation in the twentieth century.[5]

A socioeconomic theory of individualism had been well developed by 1880 to bolster the argument that government should not interfere in economic affairs. The individual, this school of thought declared, supplies the enterprise that makes possible industrial progress, wealth, and national power. Therefore government should do nothing that would adversely affect individual economic enterprise. Government's function, ran the argument, is to provide an orderly society in which the individual is protected as he fulfills his destiny.

Powerful support for the theory of individualism was drawn from the work of the English scientist Charles Darwin, who published his *Origin of Species* in 1859 and his *The Descent of Man* in 1871. Darwin's emphasis on the struggle for individual existence in the process of evolution fitted nicely into the pattern. Another major influence on American thinking came from the writings of the English philosopher, Herbert Spencer. The Spencerian doctrine declared that man's ultimate achievement of a perfect society would be the result of a natural process—an inevitable development that men themselves should not attempt to hasten or to alter. In the United States, sociologist William Graham Sumner, historian John Fiske, and political scientist John W. Burgess shaped their teaching and writing to conform with Social Darwinism and Spencer's ideas of individualism. The influence of this socioeconomic doctrine became so strong, particularly in the rendering of Supreme Court decisions nullifying reform legislation, that Justice Oliver Wendell Holmes was led to protest that Spencer's *Social Statics* was not part of the Constitution.[6]

Those who decried the negativism of this theory of individualism were being heard by the 1880s. They contended that man did have the ability to control his destiny, and to shape his economic and political actions as the general welfare of society might require. Unrestricted exercise of individual power by some only brings misery and poverty to others, and the outcome is not national strength but national weakness, said this school of thought. True progress, they said, depends on cooperation and the use of government's powers in the common good.

A sociologist, Lester Ward, who published the first volume of his *Dynamic Sociology* in 1883, provided logical arguments for the belief that government should be regarded as a positive force and that it should actively seek ways of achieving social improvement. Economist Richard T. Ely attacked the pat theories of the laissez-faire advocates, theories that he and other economics professors pointed out as not conforming to the facts of industrial life. Ely's *Socialism, Its Nature, Strength and Weakness,* published in 1894, made definite proposals for reasonable reform legislation. Economist Thorstein Veblen compared the theories of economic individualists with the actual practices of industrial capitalism and voiced his bitter protest in 1899 with his *Theory of the Leisure Class*. Henry George assailed the unearned increment of wealth through land ownership in his *Progress and Poverty* (1879), and Henry Demarest Lloyd denounced the oil monopoly in *Wealth against Commonwealth* (1894), an effective plea for socioeconomic cooperation.

Newspaper editors Dana, Godkin, and Reid, as we have observed, were supporters of the theory of individualism and opposed government interference in economic spheres. One might expect, in light of what was happening, that other editors would appear who would support the principles of social cooperation and use of governmental power to regulate economic life. And indeed one of the characteristics of the "new journalism" came to be the expression of editorial-page support for the "common man." What publishers and editors like Joseph Pulitzer and E. W. Scripps represented in the field of journalism was only an expression of a larger movement in American thought and life.

**ADVANCES
IN KNOWLEDGE**   Those who thus argued directly with the supporters of individualism were aided by those whose contributions to knowledge widened the country's understanding of its history, its government, and human thought and action. The period of the 1880s and 1890s was one of intense activity in study and publication, and in every field there were major achievements that helped Americans to meet the challenge of economic and social change.

Historians broke new ground by studying and writing about social and economic history, as well as politics. John Bach McMaster pointed the way by using newspapers as source materials for his significantly titled *History of the People of the United States,* begun in 1883. Henry Adams produced his brilliant history of the Jefferson and Madison administrations in 1889, and James Ford Rhodes began publication of his *History of the United States* in 1892. Frederick Jackson Turner's famous essay on the "Significance of the Frontier in American History" appeared in 1893, to father a whole new school of historical interpretation. Colonial history was being rewritten by men with an understanding of economic and social conditions of the early American period.

The landmark for this period in the field of government and political science was James Bryce's *American Commonwealth,* in which the talented Englishman gave to the United States a description of its new environment. The same year, 1888, Frank W. Taussig wrote his *Tariff History of the United States*. Woodrow Wilson's *Congressional Government* appeared in 1885, and by 1903 Charles E. Merriam had completed his *History of American Political Theories*.

The list of men and books could be extended: anthropologist Lewis Henry Morgan's *Ancient Society* (1877); philosopher William James's *Principles of Psychology* (1890); philosopher Josiah Royce's *The Spirit of Modern Philosophy* (1892) and *The World and the Individual* (1900); historian Brooks Adams's *The Law of Civilization and Decay* (1895); educator John Dewey's *School and Society* (1899); Oliver Wendell Holmes's *The Common Law* (1881).

Literature offered Henry James's *Portrait of a Lady* (1881); Samuel Clemens's *Life on the Mississippi* (1883) and *Huckleberry Finn* (1885); and William Dean Howells's *The Rise of Silas Lapham* (1885), an early example of the rise of realism in American literature. In the 1890s, poets Emily Dickinson and Edwin Arlington Robinson and novelists Stephen Crane and Hamlin Garland were making major contributions, while such realistic writers as Theodore Dreiser and Frank Norris were on the verge of fame.

Nor was this great cultural stirring and extension of factual information limited to an intellectual class. Millions shared in the new knowledge through the chautauquas and public study courses that became of major importance toward the close of the century as means of adult education. The world fairs and expositions that caught America's fancy in this period were another means of mass education. At the Philadelphia Centennial of 1876 and Chicago's Columbian Exposition of 1893, millions of Americans viewed the material and artistic achievements of their generation. Free public libraries, spreading across the country after 1880, found their great benefactor in Andrew Carnegie. In these libraries were available the literary triumphs and the popular writings of American and British authors.

INFLUENCE OF MAGAZINES
Magazines came to have increasing influence on American life. Earlier ventures like the *North American Review* (1815) and the *Knickerbocker,* a more popular magazine published from 1833 to 1865, had been eclipsed by *Harper's Monthly,* begun in 1850 by the New York book publishing firm. *Harper's* introduced extensive woodcut illustrations, published the writings of leading English and American authors, and ran up a world record circulation of 200,000 before the Civil War. Two women's magazines, *Godey's Lady's Book* and *Peterson's,* began their careers in 1830 and 1842, respectively, and offered hand-colored engravings of fashions and fiction stories to more than 150,000 readers each by the 1850s.

In 1881, the *Century* joined *Harper's* in the highly literary and artistic class of magazines. *Scribner's* made it a trio in 1886. Unillustrated, but of equal literary quality, was the *Atlantic Monthly,* begun in 1857 and specializing in publishing the writings of the New England authors. In the weekly field were two illustrated periodicals, *Frank Leslie's Illustrated Newspaper* (1855) and *Harper's Weekly* (1857). The latter exercised strong influence in public affairs, along with E. L. Godkin's weekly, the *Nation* (1865). In addition, the *Independent* (1848), the *North American Review,* and such newcomers as the *Forum* (1886), the *Arena* (1889), and the *Outlook* (1893) all discussed the new political and social environment. The *Literary Digest* began summarizing contemporary editorial opinion in 1890.

Coming into the field were publications that depended on humor, cartoons, and political satire. *Puck* (1877) featured Joseph Keppler's dynamic color cartoons. The others were *Judge* (1881) and *Life* (1883), famed for its publication of the "Gibson girl" drawings of Charles Dana Gibson. In the children's magazine competition, *Youth's Companion* (1827) was joined by *St. Nicholas* (1873).

Helped by the cheap postage rates established by Congress under its 1879 act, some new leaders struck out in the 1880s for the mass readership that still awaited American magazine publishers. One was Cyrus H. K. Curtis, who founded the *Ladies'*

Home Journal in 1883 and with Edward W. Bok as his editor soon won a half-million circulation. Curtis bought the *Saturday Evening Post* in 1897 and with editor George Horace Lorimer quickly made it a leader in the low-cost weekly field, which *Collier's* entered in 1888. The older high quality monthlies found stiff competition from three low-priced popular magazines: *Munsey's,* begun in 1889 by Frank Munsey; *McClure's,* started in 1893 by S. S. McClure; and the *Cosmopolitan* (1886). It was these magazines, circulating more extensively than any of their predecessors, that were to open the minds of more readers to social and cultural trends.

THE SOCIETY'S SHORTCOMINGS AND DISCONTENTS   It must be noted, however, that the general level of cultural attainment was still low. Even by 1900 the average American had received only five years of schooling in his lifetime. If the public bought encyclopedias galore from the book publishers because it wanted to know more, it also bought dime novels by the millions. If the chautauqua was a booming institution, so were horse racing, prizefighting, and baseball. Cultural and business organizations were expanding in number, but growing even faster were fraternal and social groups. In the newspaper world Adolph Ochs would be able to find enough serious readers in the metropolis of New York to support the reborn *New York Times,* but the great mass of readers was attracted by the devices of a journalism that sought a popular level as it both entertained and informed.

It should be noted briefly, too, that not everybody was successful or contented in this new economic and social environment, despite the general blessings that industrialization had bestowed on the country. Sharp divisions began to appear between those who had gained wealth in the process of national economic upheaval, and those who had gained only a crowded room in a city tenement, a poverty-stricken tenant farm in the South, or a precarious existence on the dry plains of the West. Falling farm prices in the 1880s spurred the political activities of the discontented in the South and West. There the Grangers, the Greenbackers, the Farmers' Alliance, and the Populists arose to demand economic equality for agriculture and launched third party movements that showed real strength. Not until 1896 did one of the major political parties answer the call of the "consistent rebellion"; at that time, the merging of the forces of free silver coinage, paper money, and general political and economic reform under the Democratic banner of William Jennings Bryan provided America with the greatest political excitement of a generation. But despite the bitter experience of the depression of 1893, the advocates of William McKinley and political and economic conservatism won the decision.

In the cities the rise of the labor movement on a nationally organized scale provided a much sharper clash than that between business and agriculture. Some craft unions, such as those of the bricklayers, railroad engineers, and printers, had become established before the Civil War, and a National Labor Union of some stature was organized in 1866, only to disintegrate during the depression of 1873. The Knights of Labor, carrying on the "one big union" plan under the leadership of Terence V. Powderly, reached a peak membership of 700,000 during the two years of industrial turbulence that followed the panic of 1884. Powderly advocated moderate cooperative action by all working men to better their pay and working conditions and the use of the strike weapon when necessary. Unfortunately for the Knights of Labor, their aggressive action was at its peak in 1886 when anarchists who advocated deeds of violence and terror touched off the Haymarket riot in Chicago. Public reaction coupled Powderly's legitimate labor movement with the troubles caused by the anarchists, and the Knights of Labor movement fell away. As a result the steadier American

Federation of Labor, built in 1881 as a national organization of the various craft unions, became the principal voice of the labor movement. Its nationwide strikes in 1886 for a shortening of the ten-hour workday won a reduction to eight or nine hours for some 200,000 workers out of the 350,000 involved, and newly elected AFL president Samuel Gompers became the individual leader of labor. The reaction in many industries was the formation of employers' associations that raised defense funds to fight the carefully planned demands and strikes of the individual craft unions.

A NEW JOURNALISM EMERGING

In such a swiftly changing and exciting environment, then, the daily newspaper was coming of age. From 850 English-language, general-circulation dailies in 1880 to 1,967 in 1900; from 10 percent of adults as subscribers to 26 percent—these were the statistical evidences of its arrival as a major business. The enormous success of Joseph Pulitizer's *New York World,* which between 1883 and 1887 broke every publishing record in America, was evidence that a ''new journalism'' had been created that would change the character and the appearance of the daily newspaper and enormously increase its mass influence.

But before focusing attention on the *New York World,* whose triumphs caught the attention of even the most unobservant in the newspaper business, we should briefly examine the changes that were occurring in other cities. Certainly Henry W. Grady in Atlanta, Edward W. Scripps in Cleveland and Cincinnati, Melville E. Stone and Victor Lawson in Chicago, and William Rockhill Nelson in Kansas City also were engaged in the creation of the ''new journalism'' in the same years that Joseph Pulitzer was exhibiting his skill, first in St. Louis and then in New York. And in many another city, older newspapers were being challenged by bright-faced newcomers that, in some cases, were destined to take their places among America's best. The new papers were low-priced, aggressive, and easily read. They believed in the news function as the primary obligation of the press; they exhibited independence of editorial opinion; they crusaded actively in the community interest; they appealed to the mass audience through improved writing, better makeup, use of headlines and illustrations, and a popularization of their contents. These were the general characteristics of the ''new journalism''; the individual newspapers, of course, exhibited them in varying degrees.

The rise of evening newspapers was a feature of this growth of the daily. The evening field claimed seven-eighths of the increase in numbers of daily newspapers between 1880 and 1900, and by 1890 two out of three papers were evening editions. The swing toward evening publication was due in part to the changed reading habits of the city populations, and it was strengthened by the discovery that the woman readers to whom retail store advertising was directed favored afternoon-delivered newspapers. Mechanical and news-gathering innovations permitted the evening papers to carry ''today's news today,'' particularly in the Middle West and West, where time differentials aided inclusion of news from the East and from Europe on the same day events occurred. Some morning papers found an answer by publishing afternoon editions under the same nameplate, while others established separate evening papers.

JOURNALISM OF THE EAST

New York remained primarily a morning-paper city, with only the *Evening Post* achieving distinction as an afternoon paper before the Pulitzer invasion. Two additions to the field in 1867 were the *Evening Telegram,* begun by James Gordon Bennett as the afternoon edition of the *Herald,* and the *Evening Mail.* The *Mail* was merged with the older *Express* in 1882 to form the *Mail and Express.* The circulation winner of the period was the *Daily News,* a one-cent evening paper dating back to 1855 for its founding. The *Daily News*, cheap in content as well as in price, circulated in the tenement districts so widely that it challenged the *Sun* and *Herald* throughout the 1870s, and its success suggested to other publishers new ways of reaching the immigrant-crowded tenement sections of the city.

In Philadelphia, two newcomers in the 1870s were the *Record* and the *Times*. The *Record*, begun in 1870, was taken over in 1877 by William M. Singerly, a millionaire railroad builder who cut the paper's price to one cent, brightened its makeup and writing, and engaged in popular crusades against local abuses. By the early 1880s the *Record* was outselling its famous competitor in the morning field, the *Public Ledger*, which had been purchased from the Swain family in 1864 by the able George W. Childs. The *Times* (1875), published by reform-conscious Alexander K. McClure, also pushed into the top circulation bracket, along with the *Evening Item* (1847), which hit its stride in the 1880s as a crusading penny paper, and the *Press* (1857). The *Evening Bulletin* (1847) and the *Inquirer* (1829), ultimately the two survivors in the Philadelphia field, trailed the *Public Ledger* in prestige and the other papers in circulation.

Boston's quiet journalism was upset by the appearance of the *Globe*. Founded in 1872, it had only 8,000 circulation when General Charles H. Taylor became publisher in 1877. Taylor established an evening edition, cut the price to two cents, ran big headlines, emphasized local news, and gave editorial support to the Democratic party. By 1890 the *Globe*, with combined morning and evening circulation of 150,000, ranked among the top ten papers in the country. The staid *Herald* (1846) and the sensationalized *Journal* (1833) kept pace by establishing evening editions. But the morning *Advertiser* (1813) and *Post* (1831), and evening *Transcript* (1830) and *Traveller* (1825), contented themselves with limited circulations. The *Advertiser* did establish an evening edition, the *Record*, in 1884.

The trend was similar in other eastern cities. Baltimore's new entry was the *Evening News* (1872), which in the 1890s under fighting editor Charles H. Grasty rose to challenge the famous *Sun*. The *Evening Penny Press* of Pittsburgh appeared in 1884 as the forerunner of the *Pittsburgh Press* and promptly undertook civic improvement campaigns. The Butler family's *Buffalo News* dates from 1880, and it immediately asserted leadership in the newspaper field as an aggressively run evening paper. Another influential leader in the 1880s was the evening *Brooklyn Eagle*, begun in 1841. In Providence, the *Journal* (1829) saw the trend early and established the *Evening Bulletin* in 1863. The Noyes and Kauffmann families gave Washington a local evening paper in 1852, and by 1890 their *Evening Star* had as its only competitor the morning *Post* (1877).[7]

THE SOUTH: HENRY W. GRADY OF ATLANTA

In the South, Henry Watterson's well-established *Louisville Courier-Journal* started the *Times* as an evening edition in 1884 and soon saw it outsell the parent morning paper. New Orleans' morning leader, the *Picayune* (1837), found new competition from two evening papers, the *Item* (1877) and the *States* (1879). Two other New Orleans morning papers, the *Times* (1863) and the *Democrat* (1875), found the going more difficult and merged in 1881. A famous editor appeared in Raleigh, North Carolina, in 1885 when Josephus Daniels took over the *State Chronicle*, which he soon merged into the *News and Observer*, thereby establishing what became a great Daniels family newspaper.

Most brilliant of the southern newspaper-makers of the period was Henry W.

Henry W. Grady

Grady, who in his brief 39 years demonstrated the qualities of a great reporter and managing editor. Grady's talents were widely exhibited in the dozen years before he became managing editor of the *Atlanta Constitution* in 1880. Indeed, when Grady became editor and one-third owner of the *Atlanta Herald* in 1872, he nearly put the *Constitution,* founded four years before, out of business. But the *Herald,* for all its journalistic superiority, fell victim to the financial depression of 1873 after a four-year struggle. Grady then became a freelance correspondent for such enterprising newspapers as the *Constitution,* the *New York Herald,* the *Louisville Courier-Journal,* the *Philadelphia Times,* and the *Detroit Free Press,* distinguishing himself for his coverage of politics and for his use of the interview technique in reporting and interpreting the news. He traveled widely and his grasp of events and his acquaintanceships increased accordingly.

When the *Constitution,* published by Evan P. Howell after 1876, obtained Grady as a part owner and managing editor, things began to hum. A network of correspondents was built up, and Grady spent lavishly to get all the news coverage possible in every field from politics to baseball. Grady continued to report major news events and political affairs himself. His brilliant story of the Charleston earthquake of 1886 won him national attention as a newsman. The same year his address entitled "The New South," which advocated industrial advancement of the South as a means of reestablishing national solidarity, won him national fame as a spokesman for his area. As a consequence Grady devoted increased attention to the editorial page of the *Constitution* until his death in 1889, and his influence furthered the paper's sharing southern leadership with *Louisville Courier-Journal.*[8]

With Grady's death, Clark Howell, Sr., son of the publisher, became managing editor of the *Constitution.* The other event of the 1880s in Atlanta journalism was the founding in 1883 of the *Journal,* an evening paper that was destined to outmaneuver the Howells' *Constitution* by the 1950s.

NEW DAILIES IN THE WEST   To the West, the newspaper that is now the *Dallas News* was established in 1885, and its future publisher, George B. Dealey, appeared in Dallas that year. The *Los Angeles Times,* begun in 1881, saw Harrison Gray Otis assume its leadership in 1882. In San Francisco, the major event of the period was the sale of the *Examiner* (1865) to George Hearst in 1880 and the turning over of the paper to young William Randolph Hearst in 1887. San Francisco journalism had been lively even before the Hearst entry, with the morning *Chronicle* (1865) leading in civic campaigns and political clean-up movements. Its publisher, Michel H. de Young, one of two brothers who founded the paper, remained in control of the *Chronicle* for 60 years.

A REVOLUTION
IN THE MIDWEST:
E. W. SCRIPPS

What has been described thus far would suffice to prove the point that things were happening to the nation's journalism everywhere. Singerly's *Philadelphia Record,* Taylor's *Boston Globe,* Grady's *Atlanta Herald* and *Constitution* exhibited the major characteristics of the "new journalism." The appearance of the Butler family in Buffalo, of the Noyes family in Washington, of Josephus Daniels in Raleigh, of the Howell family in Atlanta, of Harrison Gray Otis in Los Angeles meant in each case the beginning of the building of a noted American newspaper. But it was in the Midwest of the 1870s and 1880s that the biggest revolution in newspapering was brewing—Detroit, Cleveland, Cincinnati, Chicago, Kansas City, Milwaukee, St. Louis.

The name Scripps is written boldly into the story of midwestern newspaper-making in the 1870s and early 1880s. James E. Scripps, elder half-brother of the famed Edward Wyllis Scripps, started the family on its journalistic mission when, after working on newspapers in Chicago and Detroit, he founded the *Detroit Evening News* in 1873. By the end of 1880, the Scripps family had fostered newspapers in Cleveland, Cincinnati, St. Louis, and Buffalo. The story of the rise of the Scripps newspaper chain belongs later, but the story of the early successes is a part of the general pattern of the rise of the "new journalism." Scripps newspapers were low-priced evening publications; small in size, but well written and tightly edited; hard-hitting in both news and editorial page coverage of the local scene. Above all, they were distinguished for their devotion to the interests of the working man.

When James Scripps needed help to keep his *Detroit News* afloat, he called on his brother George and sister Ellen, and eventually on young Edward, who was the thirteenth child of a thrice-married Englishman now settled on an Illinois farm. Edward helped to build circulation routes for the *News* and reported for it while the struggle to win advertising support was in progress. Detroit had well-established papers, such as the morning *Free Press* (1831), but by the 1880s the *News* emerged as a leading evening paper known for its business operation as well as for its qualities as a newspaper.

Scripps money went into four one-cent evening papers: the short-lived *Buffalo Evening Telegraph,* the ill-fated *St. Louis Chronicle,* and the famous *Cleveland Press* and *Cincinnati Post.* These two latter papers became the products of Edward Wyllis Scripps's own publishing genius and the parent papers of his eventual chain.

Cleveland of 1878 had three going newspapers, the *Leader* (1854), the *Herald* (1835), and the *Plain Dealer* (1842). When the *Penny Press* appeared as a four-page, five-column evening paper, it looked no more permanent than the alley shack in which it was published. But the editor, Edward Wyllis Scripps, paid the top salary to his advertising solicitor and put his own tremendous energy into the venture in a fashion that drove the circulation to 10,000 within a few months and foreshadowed the rise of the Scripps publishing empire.

What happened to Cleveland journalism as a result of the rapid growth of the *Press* can be briefly told. The *Plain Dealer* shifted its emphasis from the evening to the morning field in 1885 as one of the first acts of a new owner, L. E. Holden. Holden bought the plant and morning edition of the *Herald;* the evening editions of the *Leader* and the *Herald* were combined as the *News and Herald.* But the *Press* continued to harass its evening competitors, and in 1905 the other afternoon dailies were combined into a new paper, the *Cleveland News.*

The Scripps opposition in Cincinnati was more formidable. The evening *Times* (1840) and *Star* (1872) were merged in 1880 by Charles P. Taft (half-brother of the later president, William Howard Taft). The *Times-Star* was a two-cent, conservative Republican paper; the Scripps entry that year was one-cent and Democratic. But in the morning field were the *Enquirer* (1841), published by John R. McLean as a Democratic paper that was noted for its adoption of the techniques of sensationalism, and the *Commercial Gazette,* edited by the distinguished liberal Republican supporter, Murat Halstead.[9] The Scripps paper, which became the *Cincinnati Post* after Edward Wyllis Scripps took control in 1883, nevertheless soon gained circulation leadership as the *Press* was doing in Cleveland.

STONE'S *CHICAGO*   Another star that was rising in the Midwest was that of the *Chicago*
DAILY NEWS   *Daily News.* Together with another newcomer, the *Herald,* the
    Daily News quickly won equal prominence with older Chicago papers. The *Tribune* (1847), with Joseph Medill as controlling owner and editor after 1874, was continuing its development as a substantially edited, alert newspaper leader. The *Inter Ocean* (successor to the *Republican* founded in 1865 with Charles A. Dana as first editor) became widely known for its enterprise in news-gathering and in adoption of new journalistic and printing techniques. But the circulation went to the newcomers, the *Daily News* and *Herald.*

Melville E. Stone, the founder of the *Daily News,* was a product both of Chicago journalism and of the new national newspaper environment. Stone became managing editor of the *Republican* in 1872, as an inexperienced young man of 24, and ended up as city editor when the paper became the *Inter Ocean* later that year. In the fall he went on tour for the paper, studying conditions in the South. He records in his autobiography an association with Henry W. Grady and his *Atlanta Herald* partners: "They spent almost every evening with me talking over the profession of journalism. In these discussions we all learned much."[10] On the same trip, Stone studied New Orleans and St. Louis papers, and in St. Louis met a talented young newsman, Eugene Field.

When Stone returned to Chicago he became managing editor of the *Post and Mail,* but almost immediately he left for Washington to serve as correspondent for his and other papers. And in his autobiography, Stone records another major influence; he was watching the successful one-cent *New York Daily News* and deciding that he would try the same price formula in Chicago. He experimented briefly in 1873, then returned to Washington for more seasoning as a correspondent and laid his plans to leave the *Post and Mail.*

In January 1876, the *Daily News* appeared as a four-page, five-column sheet with only a few thousand dollars in capital investment. Stone believed that his first responsibility was to print news; his second responsibility was to guide public opinion; and his third, to provide entertainment. The paper did not reject sensational techniques; Stone's personal favorite was the detection of criminals by the newspaper. Nor did the *Daily News* fail to entertain; Stone brought Eugene Field to Chicago in 1883 from his earlier St. Louis and Kansas City surroundings; and until his death in 1895 Field conducted the famous "Sharps and Flats" column, in which he commented on politics and people in a witty and highly literary style. But the paper won its place by its style of news presentation, by its determination to remain free of political and outside financial pressures, and by its aggressive editorial page policies.

The going was difficult at first, however. There was a chronic shortage of pennies in circulation, so Stone had to import pennies for Chicago banks to handle and promoted "99-cent sales" in stores in order to put a sufficient number of pennies in Chicagoans' pockets to sell his papers. In the first year a young Chicago financier,

Victor F. Lawson, took over the business managership of the paper and two-thirds of the stock. But by 1878 the *Daily News* had bought out the *Post and Mail,* obtaining its Associated Press news rights. A morning edition, eventually named the *Record,* was begun in 1881, and by 1885 the combined circulation had passed the 100,000 mark. When Stone sold his interest to Lawson in 1888 for $350,000, only Pulitzer's *New York World* had a larger circulation among American newspapers than the *Daily News'* 200,000.

The editorial staff Stone had built was a famous one: Eugene Field as a columnist; Slason Thompson as an editorial writer; George Harvey, George Ade, and Finley Peter Dunne (Mr. Dooley) as young reporters; literary figures, scientists, and professors such as Chicago's James Laurence Laughlin and Wisconsin's Richard T. Ely as special contributors. Lawson continued the same type of leadership until his death in 1925; Stone comes into the story again as the general manager and builder of the modern Associated Press.

Rivaling the *Daily News* as an exponent of the new order in journalism was the *Herald,* founded by James W. Scott in 1881 as a low-priced, liberal-independent morning paper. Scott had difficulties providing sufficient capitalization for his expanding paper, but it quickly won the runner-up position to the *Daily News* in circulation. The ambitious Scott followed William M. Singerly of the *Philadelphia Record* as the second president of the newly formed American Newspaper Publishers Association, serving from 1889 to 1895. With his business associates, he founded the *Evening Post* in 1890, and in 1895 he consolidated the older *Times* (1854) with the *Herald* as the *Times-Herald.*[11] At this moment of glory, Scott died and his papers passed into less talented hands.

NELSON'S *KANSAS CITY STAR*

Taking his place with Scripps and Stone as one of the great figures in this midwestern newspaper revolution was William Rockhill Nelson, founder of the *Kansas City Star.* Nelson had been a lawyer and a building contractor before buying into a Fort Wayne, Indiana, newspaper in 1879. But by the time he appeared in Kansas City in the fall of 1880 he was ready to follow the pattern of the times. He and his editors created a small, two-cent evening newspaper, well written and filled with entertaining material as well as news and possessed of the crusading urge. Notably, however, the *Star* shunned sensational treatment of the news in use of headlines and illustrations.

One other difference stands out strongly. Unlike the other great figures of journalism before him, Nelson was not a writer. He believed that the reporter was the heart of the newspaper and had seven of them on his initial staff, and he sought the best news editors and editorial writers. And he was constantly a part of the news, editorial, and business activities of the *Star,* but only as the publisher who guided the actions and writing of his staff. If he had something to say, as he usually did, he told it to others who put the ideas into the printed page. One of Nelson's biographers ascribes the reasons for the development of the *Star*'s sparkling qualities in this fashion:

Next to Nelson, but always through Nelson's triumphant spirit, it was the work of Nelson's editors and their staff of inspired reporters and editorial writers. Possibly Nelson's greatest genius lay in his ability to select editorial talent, to exploit it by giving it freedom, and to cherish its flowering, both by positive encouragement to expression and avoidance of negative rules of suppression.... By adhering to this policy, Nelson succeeded in exploiting the ablest men and gaining their loyalty despite a salary and wage scale which was niggardly.[12]

Melville E. Stone   William Rockhill Nelson

Kansas City was a rough, growing town of little beauty when Nelson came in 1880. It was the gateway to the plains and the receiving point of western cattle. Half-built, cursed with the usual political corruption and vice of the utilitarian America of the 1880s, it offered a great chance for a strong editor. Nelson was that: a big man, with massive face and head, stubborn qualities of independence, and an air of dignity that gave him the title of colonel. William Allen White, writing about him the year he died, commented: "Not that he was ever a colonel of anything; he was just coloneliferous."[13]

Nelson gave Kansas City what he thought it needed through his relentless crusades for big and little things. He fought for cheap and efficient public transportation, bringing cable cars to the city's hills. He battled against politicians and gamblers. He campaigned for years to establish Kansas City's famous parks and boulevards, then himself built model homes along the boulevards and saw that those who lived in them planted trees and flowers. The *Star* helped to inaugurate the commission form of government in the city and by its espousal of progressive reform in government spread the doctrine throughout its circulation area in the Missouri Valley.

Kansas City and the state of Kansas were captured by 1890, and before Nelson's death in 1915 the *Star*'s circulation hit 170,000. The subscription price was ten cents a week at the start, but even after a Sunday edition had been added and the morning *Times* (1868) had sold out to Nelson in 1901, the price for morning, evening, and Sunday editions remained at a dime. A weekly edition, selling for 25 cents a year, climbed to 150,000 circulation. The price formula, plus the *Star*'s intensive coverage of its area and its human interest and literary qualities, made the paper invulnerable to the attacks of competitors who tried to win by using the sensational techniques that Nelson shunned.[14]

In other midwestern cities, changes in newspaper fortunes were
in the air. Milwaukee's several dailies greeted a new competitor
in 1882, Lucius W. Nieman and his *Milwaukee Journal,* which
at once began to show some of the zeal that drove all its competitors, except the
morning *Sentinel* (1837), to cover in the next 60 years. In Minneapolis another *Journal*
began its career as a leading evening newspaper in 1878, while William J. Murphy
gave the morning *Tribune* (1867) new life in the 1890s. St. Paul's *Pioneer Press*
(1849), run by the distinguished team of editor Joseph A. Wheelock and manager
Frederick Driscoll, found competition in the evening *Dispatch* (1868). Another
aggressive evening newspaper was the *Indianapolis News* (1869).

But it was in St. Louis that the climax was reached. The river city long had been a
newspaper center. The *Missouri Republican* (1808), which became the *St. Louis
Republic* in 1888, the *Missouri Democrat* (1852), and Carl Schurz's German-language
Westliche Post (1857) were leading papers. The first shock was the arrival of J. B.
McCullagh from Chicago and his consolidation of the newly founded *Morning Globe*
with the *Missouri Democrat* to start the *Globe-Democrat* on its way in 1875. The great
event was the appearance of Joseph Pulitzer, a penniless immigrant who within ten
years built the *St. Louis Post-Dispatch* and then turned to startle the publishing world
with his *New York World.* All around him in America, a new daily newspaper was
developing in keeping with the changed character of the national life, but Joseph
Pulitzer by his spectacular genius became the recognized leader of the "new
journalism." His story becomes the story of the emergence of the modern newspaper.

NOTES

1. Documented in Allan Nevins, *The Emergence of Modern America, 1865–1878* (New York: Macmillan,
1927), and Ida M. Tarbell, *The Nationalizing of Business, 1878–1898* (New York: Macmillan, 1936). David
M. Potter in *People of Plenty* (Chicago: University of Chicago Press, 1954) argued that economic abundance
provided the touchstone for unified progress, not activists.
2. This and following statistical information is from U.S. Department of Commerce, *Historical Statistics of
the United States, 1789–1945* (Washington: U.S. Government Printing Office, 1949).
3. Schlesinger's *The Rise of the City, 1878–1898* (New York: Macmillan, 1932) is a classic study of the
transformation of American life stemming from the economic revolution. See also Blake McKelvey, *The
Urbanization of America, 1860–1915* (New Brunswick, N.J.: Rutgers University Press, 1969) and its
companion volume, *The Emergence of Metropolitan America, 1915–1966* (1968).
4. The census figures for totals of all types of dailies were 574 in 1870 and 2,226 in 1900. The figures used
above are more comparable to twentieth-century statistics.
5. Well-discussed in Henry Steele Commager, *The American Mind* (New Haven: Yale University Press,
1950).
6. The predominant Social Darwinism theory is attacked, but its influence acknowledged, in Richard
Hofstadter, *Social Darwinism in American Thought, 1860–1915* (Philadelphia: University of Pennsylvania
Press, 1955).
7. Crosby S. Noyes and Samuel H. Kauffmann were leading men in the early years of the *Star;* Noyes' sons,
Frank and Theodore, became active before 1890 and guided the *Star* down to the 1940s.
8. Raymond B. Nixon, "Henry W. Grady, Reporter: A Reinterpretation," *Journalism Quarterly,* XII
(December 1935), p. 343. The full-length biography is Nixon's *Henry W. Grady, Spokesman of the New
South* (New York: Knopf, 1943).
9. The *Commercial Gazette* resulted from an 1883 merger of the *Gazette* (1815) and the *Commercial* (1843),
which Halstead had edited since 1865. After Halstead left Cincinnati in 1890 to go to Brooklyn, the
Commercial Gazette became the *Commercial Tribune* in 1896. It disappeared into the *Enquirer* in 1930.
10. Melville E. Stone, *Fifty Years a Journalist* (Garden City, N.Y.: Doubleday, 1921), p. 44.
11. The *Times,* under editor Wilbur F. Storey, had become known for its shocking sensationalism. Its most
famous headline, over an 1875 story of the hanging of four repentent murderers, read "Jerked to Jesus."

12. Charles E. Rogers, "William Rockhill Nelson and His Editors of the *Star*," *Journalism Quarterly*, XXVI (March 1949), p. 15. The article is based on *William Rockhill Nelson: Independent Editor and Crusading Liberal* (Ph.D. thesis, University of Minnesota, 1948).
13. William Allen White, "The Man Who Made the Star," *Collier's*, LV (June 26, 1915), p. 12.
14. Two of the challengers were Scripps with his *Kansas City World* (1897) and the Denver team of Bonfils and Tammen, who operated the *Kansas City Post* from 1909 to 1922. Neither paper survived.

ANNOTATED BIBLIOGRAPHY

Books

AARON, DANIEL, *Men of Good Hope: A Story of American Progressives*. New York: Oxford University Press, 1951. Studies, among others, Henry George, Edward Bellamy, Henry Demarest Lloyd, Thorstein Veblen, William Dean Howells, and Theodore Roosevelt.

ADAMS, HENRY, *The Education of Henry Adams*. Boston: Houghton Mifflin, 1918. A classic personal reaction to a changing society.

BEARD, CHARLES A., AND MARY R., *The Rise of American Civilization*. New York: Macmillan, 1930. The chapter in Vol. II, "The Second American Revolution," is the best interpretation of the rise of industry in the Civil War and postwar periods.

BOORSTIN, DANIEL J., *The Americans: The Democratic Experience*. New York: Random House, 1973. Prize-winning social history from consensus theory approach.

BROWN, DEE, *Bury My Heart at Wounded Knee*. New York: Holt, Rinehart & Winston, 1971. The history of the West as finally written by the losers, the American Indians.

CLAYTON, CHARLES G., *Little Mack: Joseph B. McCullagh of the St. Louis Globe-Democrat*. Carbondale: Southern Illinois Press, 1969. Helps to illuminate a great figure in newspaper-making of the nineteenth century.

COMMAGER, HENRY STEELE, *The American Mind*. New Haven: Yale University Press, 1950. A provocative and sweeping introduction to intellectual and social trends since the 1880s.

DORFMAN, JOSEPH, *Thorstein Veblen and His America*. New York: Viking, 1934. A study of rebellion against the rugged individualists and their economic thinking.

GOLDMAN, ERIC F., *Rendezvous with Destiny: A History of Modern American Reform*. New York: Knopf, 1952. An interpretative synthesis that traces the tradition of dissent from post-Civil War years to the times of the Fair Deal.

GRAYBAR, LLOYD J., *Albert Shaw of the "Review of Reviews": An Intellectual Biography*. Lexington: University Press of Kentucky, 1974. Account of the birth and death of the *Review of Reviews* and its editor.

HART, JIM ALLEE, *A History of the St. Louis Globe-Democrat*. Columbia: University of Missouri Press, 1961. The story of founder J. B. McCullagh and of the paper, within a social framework.

HARTZ, LOUIS, *The Liberal Tradition in America*. New York: Harcourt Brace Jovanovich, 1955. Major work of the consensus school of historians, based on theme United States was "born free" and had no opposition to liberalism in a land of plenty.

HOFSTADTER, RICHARD, *Social Darwinism in American Thought, 1860–1915*. Philadelphia: University of Pennsylvania Press, 1955. A harshly critical study.

JOHNSON, ICIE F., *William Rockhill Nelson and the Kansas City Star*. Kansas City: Burton Publishing Company, 1935. The best published study of Nelson.

KAROLEVITZ, ROBERT F., *Newspapering in the Old West*. Seattle: Superior Publishing Company, 1965. Pictorial history of "how it was" on the frontier.

McJIMSEY, GEORGE T., *Genteel Partisan: Manton Marble, 1834–1917*. Ames: Iowa State Press, 1971. Editor and publisher of *New York World* in 1860s, with Spencerian social philosophy.

McKELVEY, BLAKE, *The Urbanization of America, 1860–1915*. New Brunswick, N.J.: Rutgers University Press, 1969.

————, *The Emergence of Metropolitan America, 1915–1966.* New Brunswick, N.J.: Rutgers University Press, 1968. Two new studies of the trend.

MOTT, FRANK LUTHER, *A History of American Magazines.* Vol. II, 1850–1865; Vol. III, 1865–1885; Vol. IV, 1885–1905. Cambridge, Mass.: Harvard University Press, 1938–57. The continuation of Professor Mott's authoritative study. Vol. V, 1905–1930 (1968) has a cumulative index.

MYERS, JOHN MYERS, *Print in a Wild Land.* Garden City, N.Y.: Doubleday, 1967. Racy account of newspaperin' in the Old West.

NIXON, RAYMOND B., *Henry W. Grady: Spokesman of the New South.* New York: Knopf, 1943. The definitive biography of a leading southern editor.

NORTH, SIMEON N. D., *History and Present Condition of the Newspaper and Periodical Press of the United States.* Washington, D.C.: U.S. Government Printing Office, 1884. Published as a part of the 1880 census; valuable particularly for its picture of the press in that year.

PAXSON, FREDERIC L., *History of the American Frontier.* Boston: Houghton Mifflin, 1924. Records the passing of the frontier by 1893.

POTTER, DAVID M., *People of Plenty.* Chicago: University of Chicago Press, 1954. American progress has been shaped by the unifying character of economic abundance, not by efforts of radicals, advocates of change.

SCHLESINGER, ARTHUR M., *The Rise of the City, 1878–1898,* A History of American Life, Vol. X. New York: Macmillan, 1932. The best social history of a crucial period. See Ida M. Tarbell, below, for reference to companion volume.

SHARPE, ERNEST, *G. B. Dealey of the Dallas News.* New York: Holt, Rinehart & Winston, 1955. A favorable biography; covers to 1946.

STONE, MELVILLE E., *Fifty Years a Journalist.* Garden City, N.Y.: Doubleday, 1921. The first portion deals with Stone's Chicago newspaper career, the latter with the Associated Press.

TARBELL, IDA M., *The Nationalizing of Business, 1878–1898,* A History of American Life, Vol. IX. New York: Macmillan, 1936.

U.S. DEPARTMENT OF COMMERCE, *Historical Statistics of the United States, 1789–1945.* Washington, D.C.: U.S. Government Printing Office, 1949.

WALSH, JUSTIN E., *To Print the News and Raise Hell.* Chapel Hill: University of North Carolina Press, 1968. Biography of Wilbur F. Storey, controversial editor of the *Chicago Times* in Civil War period.

WARE, NORMAN J., *The Labor Movement in the United States, 1860–1895.* New York: Appleton-Century-Crofts, 1929. More compact than the massive history of labor by John R. Commons and associates, this book emphasizes the Knights of Labor. See also Lloyd Ulman, *The Rise of the National Trade Union* (Cambridge, Mass.: Harvard University Press, 1955).

WIEBE, ROBERT, *The Search for Order, 1877–1920.* New York: Hill and Wang, 1968. Conservative analysis of American society. See also Robert G. McCloskey, *American Conservatism in the Age of Enterprise, 1865–1910.* New York: Harper & Row-Torch, 1971.

YOUNG, JOHN P., *Journalism in California.* San Francisco: Chronicle Publishing Company, 1913. Principally a history of the *San Francisco Chronicle,* consistently one of the West's leading newspapers.

Periodicals and Monographs

BELMAN, LARY S., "Robert Ezra Park: An Intellectual Portrait of a Journalist and Communication Scholar," *Journalism History,* II (Winter 1975), p. 116.

"Fifty Years of Harper's Magazine," *Harper's,* C (May 1900), 947.

HALL, MARK W., "The *San Francisco Chronicle:* Its Fight for the 1879 Constitution," *Journalism Quarterly,* XLVI (Autumn 1969), 505. From M.A. thesis, University of Missouri, 1967.

HEUTERMAN, THOMAS H., "Assessing the 'Press on Wheels': Individualism in Frontier Journalism," *Journalism Quarterly,* LIII (Autumn 1976), p. 423. A study of the *Frontier Index* shows it more accurately reflected its editors than the communities it served.

IRWIN, WILL, "The Power of the Press," *Collier's,* XLVI (January 21, 1911), 15. The first article in Irwin's "The American Newspaper" series, discussing the birth of modern journalism and such publishers as William Rockhill Nelson of the *Kansas City Star* and Harrison Gray Otis of the *Los Angeles Times.*

LENT, JOHN A., "The Press on Wheels: A History of *The Frontier Index,*" *Journal of the West,* X (October 1971), p. 662.

MOTT, FRANK LUTHER, "Fifty Years of Life: The Story of a Satirical Weekly," *Journalism Quarterly,* XXV (September 1948), 224.

NIXON, RAYMOND B., "Henry W. Grady, Reporter: A Reinterpretation," *Journalism Quarterly,* XII (December 1935), 341. Reprinted in Ford and Emery, *Highlights in the History of the American Press.*

PETERSON, PAUL V., "The *Chicago Daily Herald:* Righting the Historical Record," *Journalism Quarterly,* XLVII (Winter 1970), 697. Melville Stone's early Chicago paper appeared in 1873.

ROGERS, CHARLES E., "William Rockhill Nelson and His Editors of the Star," *Journalism Quarterly,* XXVI (March 1949), 15. Based on the author's *William Rockhill Nelson: Independent Editor and Crusading Liberal* (Ph.D. thesis, University of Minnesota, 1948).

STEWART, WALTER H., "The Editorial Paragraph: A Century and More of Development," Ph.D. thesis, Southern Illinois University, 1970. Investigates 14 newspaper editorialists beginning in 1831.

WHITE, WILLIAM ALLEN, "The Man Who Made the Star," *Collier's,* LV (June 26, 1915), 12. A portrait of William Rockhill Nelson by the editor of the *Emporia Gazette.* Reprinted in Ford and Emery, *Highlights in the History of the American Press.*

WHITE, Z. L., "Western Journalism," *Harper's,* LXXVII (October 1888), 678. A contemporary picture of Ohio journalism, including the Scripps enterprises, and journalism farther west.

From *Harper's Monthly Magazine* (1901)

Joseph Pulitzer, from the portrait by John S. Sargent.

16

The New Journalism

... every issue of the paper presents an opportunity and a duty to say something courageous and true; to rise above the mediocre and conventional; to say something that will command the respect of the intelligent, the educated, the independent part of the community; to rise above fear of partisanship and fear of popular prejudice.

—Joseph Pulitzer

Joseph Pulitzer was one of those many immigrants who helped to build the new America of the post-Civil War period. In so doing, he both gave and received: the two great newspapers he established won for him the honor of being named as the leading American editor of modern times,[1] and also built for him a fortune appraised at his death at nearly $20 million, one of the largest ever accumulated in the newspaper field.

The story of Joseph Pulitzer's journalistic success climaxes the story of the new national environment. Pulitzer made his own contributions to the creation of the "new journalism," but more important, he achieved his leadership by being receptive to the ideas of others. His immense energy and his highly developed journalistic sense enabled him to adapt and to develop in his own way the publishing concepts and techniques of his time and to satisfy his passionate desire to win unquestioned recognition as the builder of the brilliant staff and the complex mechanism of a great modern newspaper. This was a notable achievement, but it alone was not enough to win him his reputation as the most useful and worthy American editor in the estimate of his craft. His true greatness lay in his high-minded conception of a newspaper's role, particularly in exercising editorial leadership, and in the way in which he made that conception live in his newspapers.

JOSEPH PULITZER'S EARLY CAREER Pulitzer was born in Hungary in 1847. His father was Magyar-Jewish, his mother Austro-German. At 17, after receiving a good private school education, he ran away from home to join an army. But he had weak eyesight and an unmilitary look that brought rejections from the Austrian army and the French Foreign Legion. Less particular, however, was an American agent who was seeking Europeans who would volunteer for the Union Army in that Civil War year of 1864. The agent enlisted Pulitzer, who became a member of the Lincoln cavalry.

When the war ended, without his seeing any real action, Pulitzer found himself in New York, virtually penniless and handicapped by language difficulties. After a series of short-lived, painful job experiences, which included being a waiter in a St. Louis restaurant, his tremendously inquisitive nature and unbounded energy began to lead him forward. In 1867 he became an American citizen and a year later was hired as a reporter for Carl Schurz's leading German-language daily, the *Westliche Post*. Pulitzer soon surpassed others who laughed at his awkward mannerisms by working endless hours, digging into every type of news.

In rapid order he was elected as a Republican to the Missouri State Assembly from a normally Democratic district, became his paper's legislative correspondent, joined with Schurz in stumping the German-speaking areas of Missouri for Horace Greeley in the 1872 campaign, and became part-owner of the *Post*. Planning for his own future, Pulitzer sold his stock in that paper for $30,000 and earned another $20,000 by buying a mediocre St. Louis daily that happened to have a valuable AP membership. He offered this to Joseph B. McCullagh, a Chicago newspaperman who needed the press association membership to help force a merger between his *Globe* and the rival *Democrat*. Money in his pocket, Pulitzer left St. Louis newspaper work for a few years. He visited Europe four times, was married, and was admitted to the District of Columbia Bar. In the same period he campaigned for Samuel J. Tilden, the 1876 Democratic candidate, and reported for Dana's *New York Sun* on the activities of the electoral commission, which decided that disputed election in favor of Rutherford B. Hayes. By 1878, with a greatly increased knowledge of his adopted country and excellent command of the English language, he returned to St. Louis journalism.

Pulitzer's destiny now was to be fulfilled. The *Dispatch,* founded in 1864, was bankrupt and on the block at a sheriff's sale. Pulitzer won it with a $2,500 bid on December 9, 1878, again obtaining as his principal prize an Associated Press membership. Three days later he effected a combination with the *Post,* started by John Dillon in 1875 (Dillon was a partner for only one year but remained as a Pulitzer associate).

Thus was born one of the country's greatest newspapers, the *Post-Dispatch*. Within four years it was the leading evening paper in St. Louis, netting $45,000 a year and rivaling the morning papers, the influential *Missouri Republican* and McCullagh's powerful *Globe-Democrat*. Behind this achievement lay the talents of the editor-publisher, now in his early thirties. An ambitious and self-contained man, with the artist's love of good music and skilled writing and the scholar's interest in economic, political, and social trends, Pulitzer was driven by his large intellectual capacity and consuming energy.

Pulitzer's flashing eyes expressed his strong will to succeed. Filled with nervous tension, he was not easily approachable, holding even close associates at a distance. But in his own way he showed his appreciation for the work of those who measured up to his exacting standards for newspaper work. Many capable journalists were to serve under the Pulitzer banner in the years ahead, but the most influential was the right-hand man of these early days, John A. Cockerill, who came to the *Post-Dispatch* as managing editor in 1880. A hard-working and pugnacious man capable of carrying out Pulitzer's commands, Cockerill brought with him a keen sense of newspaper methods, which was to serve Pulitzer well for the crucial next 12 years.[2]

But it was Pulitzer who imparted to the *Post-Dispatch* its distinctive spirit. This statement of policies contains memorable words:

The *Post and Dispatch* will serve no party but the people; be no organ of Republicanism, but the organ of truth; will follow no causes but its conclusions; will not support the "Administration," but criticize it; will oppose all frauds and shams wherever and whatever they are; will advocate principles and ideas rather than prejudices and partisanship.[3]

Even more memorable are the words written by a more mature Pulitzer in 1907, near the end of his career, which have become the *Post-Dispatch* platform, printed on the editorial page:

I know that my retirement will make no difference in its cardinal principles; that it will always fight for progress and reform, never tolerate injustice or corruption, always fight demagogues of all parties, never belong to any party, always oppose privileged classes and public plunderers, never lack sympathy with the poor, always remain devoted to the public welfare, never be satisfied with merely printing news, always be drastically independent, never be afraid to attack wrong, whether by predatory plutocracy or predatory poverty.

Not content with reporting the surface news, Pulitzer pushed his staff to "Never drop a thing until you have gone to the bottom of it. Continuity! Continuity! Continuity until the subject is really finished."[4] This resulted in determined crusading in the public interest with an intensity heightened by Pulitzer's personal involvement and Cockerill's techniques in writing and news display. Favorite targets were crooked politicians, wealthy tax-dodgers, a police-protected gambling ring, and a free-wheeling public utility. Pulitzer's day was a loss if his paper did not have one distinctive feature—a crusade, public service, or big exclusive story.

There were serious blemishes on the Pulitzer record during the early St. Louis years. Cockerill had brought with him a reputation for exploiting stories of murder, sin, and sex and for sensationalizing accounts of violence, lynchings, public hangings, and dramatic death. Pulitzer found many of these subjects fitting his "apt to be talked about" definition of news. They delighted in printing bits of gossipy scandal about the "best families" of the St. Louis oligarchy under such headlines as "St. Louis Swells," "An Adulterous Pair," "Loved the Cook," and "Does Rev. Mr. Tudor Tipple?" Tales of sex and sin included "Duped and Deserted" and "A Denver Maiden Taken from a Disreputable House." On the day in 1882 when the assassin of President Garfield was executed, Cockerill, who advocated illustrations, ran a two-column drawing on page one of a condemned man "as he appeared today on the scaffold"—a technical impossibility. The James Boys, outlaws, gave the *Post-Dispatch* a big circulation lift the same year. In these and many other stories, exaggeration, half-truth, and humor at the expense of embarrassed citizens could be found.[5] This was also true, of course, of other papers of the times.

Editorially, Pulitzer's early *Post-Dispatch* hit hard at the wealthy families who monopolized control of the nation's fifth largest city. The crusades it developed, however, were focused not on the problems of the poor and working classes but on those of the middle class and the small businessmen with whom the publisher associated.[6] Everyone benefited, of course, from attacks on monopoly, from battles for cleaner living conditions, from crusades against vice. But the focus on the plight of the oppressed poor that was to be a Pulitzer trademark in New York was not yet present. The paper was also developing its coverage of middle class news interests, such as sports and women's news.

In every field of newspaper publishing, Pulitzer, Cockerill, and their associates on the *Post-Dispatch* were learning the lessons they were soon to apply in New York.

There were many mistakes, many stories and editorials falling short of the Pulitzer goals. But there were successes, for as the *World* commented in 1890, "The foundation of the *New York World* was laid in St. Louis. . . . The battle of new ideas and new theories of journalism was fought there under the banner of the *Post-Dispatch*."[7]

PURCHASE OF THE *NEW YORK WORLD*, 1883

By 1883 Pulitzer was a physical wreck, with eyesight failing and nerves badly impaired by incessant work. Matters had not been helped when Cockerill shot and killed a prominent St. Louis attorney whom the *Post-Dispatch* had attacked in its columns. Cockerill was successful in his self-defense plea but a discouraged Pulitzer headed for what he thought would be a long European vacation. Instead, when passing through New York, he heard that the *World,* founded in 1860 as a morning Democratic newspaper, was for sale. Once well-edited by Manton Marble, the paper had fallen into the hands of the unscrupulous financier, Jay Gould, who wanted $346,000.

The situation was not promising, but Pulitzer, perhaps inspired by his brother Albert's success in starting the breezy one-cent *Morning Journal* the year before with $25,000 capital, closed the deal on May 9. The first installment was paid with profits from the *Post-Dispatch,* but to Gould's surprise, the balance eventually was paid with profits from the *World.*

Pulitzer started with only a 15,000 circulation with his new two-cent, eight-page paper. Its more powerful Park Row rivals were Bennett's *Herald,* running 12 to 16 pages at three cents; Dana's *Sun,* still publishing but four pages at two cents; Whitelaw Reid's *Tribune* and George Jones' *Times,* both selling at four cents for eight pages.

Quickly revamping the *World's* staff and wiring to St. Louis for two good *Post-Dispatch* editors, Pulitzer issued his first edition on May 11. The lead story was an account of a million-dollar storm in New Jersey. Other front page features were an interview with a condemned slayer, the story of a Wall Street plunger, a Pittsburgh hanging, a riot in Haiti, and the sad story of a wronged servant girl. Ordering a press run of 20,000, Pulitzer was matched only by Bennett in sensational coverage. The next day the *World* was the talk of the town.

Exhibiting another important factor in the Pulitzer success formula—aggressive promotion of the newspaper's qualities—Pulitzer used the page one area around the nameplate, the "ears," to plug his paper's circulation and exclusives. His first popular cause was to advocate that the new Brooklyn Bridge, hailed as one of the wonders of the world, be a free bridge for the people who would cross it every day on their way to work.

But mixed in with the sensation and promotion was good news coverage and a new editorial policy. A concise ten-point program appeared on the editorial page: tax luxuries; tax inheritances; tax large incomes; tax monopolies; tax the privileged corporations; institute a tariff for revenue; reform the civil service; punish corrupt officeholders; punish vote-buying; punish employers who coerce their employees in elections. "There is room in this great and growing city for a journal that is not only cheap but bright, not only bright but large, not only large but truly Democratic— dedicated to the cause of the people. . . ,"[8] Pulitzer had said in his first issue.

New Yorkers who resented the flaunted wealth of the moneyed class and believed in economic and social reform found the *World* to be delightful reading; those who worshiped the successful dollar-chasers found the editorial pages filled with heresy. Pushing harder for the poor and the helpless than he had in St. Louis, the immigrant Pulitzer found New York's mass audience different. Well-developed crusades in behalf

The World

VOL. XXIII., NO. 7,947.　　　　　NEW YORK, THURSDAY, MAY 24, 1883.

BUILDING THE BRIDGE.

INCEPTION AND BIRTH OF THE MAMMOTH ENTERPRISE.

To Whom the Honor is Due—The First Passenger—The Finishing Touches—All in Readiness to Wed the Cities.

NEW YORK JOINS HANDS WITH BROOKLYN.

"NUMBER ONE" UNEARTHED

HE HOLDS A RECEPTION AT HIS HOUSE AND MAKES A STATEMENT.

Acknowledging He is the Man Wanted, He Declines to be Interviewed by Advice of Counsel.

SHALL BUTLER BE LL.D.?

The Harvard Overseers Get in a Wrangle Over the Question.

NEW YORK, MONDAY, JULY 9, 1883.

LINES OF LITTLE HEARSES.

BURYING THE BABY VICTIMS OF THE HEATED TENEMENTS.

A Cool Wave Strikes the City and Brings Relief to All but the Sorrowing Families.

Two examples of crusades from Joseph Pulitzer's *New York World* of the 1880s.

of the immigrants, the poor, and the laboring class appeared in his first two years at the *World*. In particular, the injustices of the garment district's sweatshops for immigrant women, the lack of school opportunities, and the inequity of the tax burden were subjects for Pulitzer's pressing editorials and news stories. In July 1883, a heat wave took a terrible toll in the city's teeming slums; the *World* found that of 716 reported deaths the previous week, 392 had been of children under the age of five years. Its reporters went to the scenes of death; its headline writers produced "How Babies Are Baked" and "Line of Little Hearses" in an attempt to shock authorities into concern and action.

The *World*'s liberal political and social stands paid circulation dividends in 1884 when Pulitzer supported Grover Cleveland, the Democratic governor of New York, for the presidency against the conservative Republican champion, James G. Blaine. Some of the gains came from the readership of Dana's *Sun,* which followed an erratic course and endorsed the discredited third party candidate Benjamin Butler. Pulitzer himself was elected to Congress that year but soon abandoned that career.

Meanwhile, Cockerill had arrived from St. Louis to become managing editor. Ever adept in both playing up human interest news and maintaining a solid display of significant local, national, and international stories, he also featured women's and sports news, as he had in St. Louis. Typographically the new *World* was using smaller and lighter type faces than its predecessor, but the words spoke for themselves: "Death Rides the Blast," "Screaming for Mercy," "Little Lotta's Lovers," "Baptized in Blood."[9] Alliteration was frequent; so were sex, conflict, and crime.

Daily circulation at the end of a year was more than 60,000—a fourfold increase that caused other New York papers to cut their prices to meet Pulitzer's threat. The *Herald* even advertised in the *World*'s pages. Four months later the *Sunday World,* effectively using a large number of woodcuts and line drawings,[10] hit the 100,000 mark. Pulitzer's promotion men presented each employee with a tall silk hat and fired a hundred cannon shots in City Hall Park by way of celebration. When in 1887 the 250,000 figure was reached by the *World,* a silver medal was struck off in honor of America's largest newspaper circulation. In addition, by 1884 the *World* had passed the *Herald* in the number of advertising columns printed and had jumped in size to 12 or 14 pages daily and 36 to 44 pages on Sunday. However, as expenses mounted and advertising rates were raised, the price to the attentive public remained at two cents.

REASONS FOR THE *WORLD*'S SUCCESS   What had Pulitzer done? First of all, he had recognized the characteristics of his potential audience. The population of New York City was increasing by 50 percent during the 1880s, and Pulitzer worked to attract the attention of the newcomers to his newspaper. As an immigrant himself, he was alive to the fact that four out of five of the city's residents were either foreign-born or children of foreign-born parents. And as one who was aware of the social and economic trends of his time, he understood the desire of his readers for effective leadership reflecting progressive attitudes, as well as for entertainment.

Therefore he had enlivened the *World*'s significant news coverage to satisfy one set of changing conditions and achieved sensationalism both in news content and in newspaper appearance to satisfy another trend. His critics said Pulitzer had done something else that did not reflect to his credit. He had revived, they said, the sensationalism that had marked the first mass newspapers of the penny-press period of the 1830s. Sensationalism was as old as the newspaper press, but no one had depended on its devices so much in recent years as had Pulitzer. His success encouraged imitation, and this was viewed as a disastrous trend in journalism that made Pulitzer's constructive contributions seem not worth the price.

Pulitzer's answer was that human interest and sensational stories were needed to win a large circulation and that having won the circulation he would create sound public opinion through enticing readers into the editorial columns and news stories about public affairs. He admired the work of the talented Edwin Lawrence Godkin in the *Evening Post,* although he disagreed with Godkin's economic theories, but when he was chided about the contrast between the news policies of the *Post* and the *World* he made his famous retort: "I want to talk to a nation, not to a select committee."[11]

Undoubtedly critics were right in accusing Pulitzer of rationalizing when he presented this defense of the *World*'s revival of coarse sensationalism. But they were not correct if they wrote Pulitzer off as a cynic. This passage from a letter written by Pulitzer to one of his editors in later life reflects his basic high-mindedness and the spirit that won for him recognition as a courageous, worthy, and effective editor:

every issue of the paper presents an opportunity and a duty to say something courageous and true; to rise above the mediocre and conventional; to say something that will command the respect of the intelligent, the educated, the independent part of the community; to rise above fear of partisanship and fear of popular prejudice. I would rather have one article a day of this sort; and these ten or twenty lines might readily represent a whole day's hard work in the way of concentrated, intense thinking and revision, polish of style, weighing of words.[12]

Pulitzer's newspapers on many days fell short of attaining this high goal of journalism, but they approached it often enough to stimulate the efforts of other editors and to win their admiration.[13]

Stunts, as distinguished from useful crusades and promotions, were another *World* specialty. Most ambitious was the sending of Nellie Bly around the world in 1889 to see if she could beat the time suggested by Jules Verne in his fictional *Around the World in Eighty Days*. Nellie Bly was a byline name for Elizabeth Cochrane, a woman reporter who had brightened the pages of the *World* by inviting the attention of mashers and then exposing them and by feigning insanity in order to write about conditions in the New York asylum. As Nellie traveled around the world by ships, trains, horses, and sampans, the *World* ran a guessing contest that drew nearly a million estimates of her elapsed time. Nellie didn't fail her newspaper; a special train brought her from San Francisco to New York with banners flying as the country applauded her time of 72 days.[14]

Expanded size of the *World* permitted its editors to enliven its pages with stunts and features and still maintain coverage of serious and significant news. A large staff of ambitious reporters covered the city in the same manner as Pulitzer had blanketed St. Louis. News editors sought equally hard to get national coverage and cabled news from abroad. Gradually the coarser sensationalism of the first few years of *World* publication under Pulitzer began to disappear, although there was no letup in the demand for well-written human interest stories and for reader-pulling illustrations. The editorial page continued its political support of the Democratic party, backing Cleveland in 1888 and 1892. Yet at the same time it exhibited its independence by opposing the local Tammany Hall machine. Labor found the *World* a solid champion in 1892 when several strikers were killed by Pinkerton guards during the bitter Homestead steel strike in Pittsburgh.

Pulitzer's publishing empire was expanded in 1887 with the establishing of the *Evening World* on the heels of Dana's decision to publish an evening edition of the *Sun*. The evening paper sold for one cent and soon outdid the morning edition in popular appeal. It never attained the distinctive character of the morning edition, however, and to newspapermen the name *World* still meant the original paper.

A new $2.5 million home for the three *Worlds* was the next order of business. It was an impressive building, among the tallest of its time, topped with a gilded dome and filled with the newest machines of the printing arts. But before the building was finished, tragedy struck. Pulitzer had become completely blind. His nerves were shattered as well, and he was under the care of European specialists. In October 1890, he announced his retirement from active editorship of his newspapers, and the *Herald,* thinking that it was bidding him goodby, said "We droop our colors to him."

But Pulitzer was not gone. He was to live until 1911, and he was to continue to build his personality into the newspapers. His affliction left him incapable of bearing even the slightest noise, and he went to incredible lengths to isolate himself from tormenting sounds. His associates found him infuriatingly difficult, but they also found him keenly aware of the progress of the newspapers. No matter where the blinded and bearded Pulitzer was—aboard his yacht; at Bar Harbor, Maine; or on the Mediterranean coast—he was constantly in touch with the *World* staff. Copies of each issue were read to him by young male secretaries and streams of instructions and suggestions came to the offices in the *World*'s gilded dome by cable, mail, and messenger.

There were important editors and managers there in the *World* offices. Some of them in the late eighties and early nineties included Cockerill, who became editor-in-charge; William H. Merrill, who had come from the *Boston Herald* to be chief editorial writer; Ballard Smith, former managing editor of both the *Louisville Courier-Journal* and the *New York Herald,* who served as managing editor; S. S. Carvalho, ex-*Sun* newsman who was city editor of the *Evening World* and later a Pulitzer executive; Colonel Charles H. Jones, a colorful southerner who served as publisher for Pulitzer in both New York and St. Louis; and George Harvey, later to become an important political figure.

Conflicts between strong-willed rivals for authority and for Pulitzer's favor were inevitable under this policy of assembling many men of high talent under the *World*'s dome. But no editor or manager became too powerful or long ignored the wishes of the absent owner. Cockerill lost his place in 1891 during one of the upheavals by which Pulitzer enforced his will on the staff. Jones, who was given complete editorial control of the *Post-Dispatch* in 1895, was forced out two years later when he flouted Pulitzer's wishes. By a constant process of seeking loyal and able assistants from among the country's newsmen, Pulitzer was able to keep the *World* steadily progressing in the manner he had conceived, as the leading exponent of what newspapermen were calling the New Journalism.

THE EDITORIAL STAFF EMERGES

The editorial staff of the metropolitan daily newspaper had taken recognizable modern form by 1890 in numbers and in departmentalized activities. Specialization of duties was necessary as the editing process became more complex and as staffs grew in size. Looking back at the growth of the editorial staff after the founding of the popular press of the 1830s, we can see its evolution from a one-man status to the organization of scores of newsmen who constituted the staff of the *World*.

Regularly employed reporters were rare even after the penny press had become well established in the 1840s. Newspaper editors ran what local news they encountered or had time to cover, used their telegraph news, clipped their exchanges, and printed the contributions of correspondents, such as the group who covered Congress after the mid-1820s. Some owner-editors added chief assistants, notably Horace Greeley, who employed first Henry J. Raymond and then Charles A. Dana to help him handle the news on the *New York Tribune* in the early 1840s. The chief assistants soon became known as managing editors, two of the earliest to hold that title being Dana of the *Tribune* and Frederic Hudson of the *New York Herald.* In the 1850s chief reporters emerged, as forerunners of the city editors. The *Tribune* of 1854 had 14 reporters and 10 editors and had introduced editorial writers, literary editors, and other specialists. But these editorial staff advances were found only on leading newspapers.

Intensified reporting of the Civil War by hundreds of correspondents in the field did much to stimulate the rise of news staffs. Some of the Civil War reporters who thus demonstrated their journalistic skill rose to become editors or owners of newspapers—Murat Halstead, Whitelaw Reid, Henry Villard. Others went on to cover wars in Europe, the Indian wars on the western American plains, and other major news events at home and abroad.

George W. Smalley was an example of the new type of newsman. A graduate of Yale and of the Harvard Law School, he covered the Civil War for the *Tribune,* then reported the Franco-Prussian War and remained in Europe as London correspondent for the paper. Henry M. Stanley of the *New York Herald* covered the Civil War and the Indian wars, went to Asia and Africa as a *Herald* correspondent, and climaxed his career with his expedition to Africa in 1871 to find the missing missionary, David Livingstone. Jerome B. Stillson, another *Herald* reporter, obtained an exclusive interview with the Indian chief Sitting Bull in 1877 that filled 14 columns of the paper. John A. Cockerill, Pulitzer's ace newsman and editor, had covered the Russo-Turkish War. Again, these are examples of a limited activity, but they foreshadow the intensified reportorial achievements of the 1890s.

Emphasis increasingly centered on the reporter. Henry Grady, a free-lance correspondent before becoming managing editor of the *Atlanta Constitution,* had advanced the art of interviewing as a means of both gathering and interpreting the news. Dana and Pulitzer prized their reporting staffs because they themselves had handled news, as had Henry Raymond of the *Times* who covered the Austro-Italian War. Some papers, like the *Sun,* Chicago's *Inter Ocean,* Nelson's *Kansas City Star,* and Stone's *Chicago Daily News*—in addition to the large New York dailies—became known as training grounds for young reporters who later moved on to other staffs.

The *Sun* produced great reporters, among them Julian Ralph, Arthur Brisbane, S.S. Carvalho, Edward W. Townsend, and Richard Harding Davis. Managing editor Amos J. Cummings, an expert in the human interest story, Chester Lord, managing editor after 1880, and other subeditors molded these careers. Ralph later became a prize Hearst reporter; Brisbane was managing editor of the *Evening Sun* before leaving for a fabulous career with both Pulitzer and Hearst; Carvalho was the *Evening World's* first city editor before he too joined Hearst and ended up a top executive; Davis left the *Sun* for Hearst's lure but achieved greatest fame with the *Herald.* The *Sun* and the *Tribune* shared the reporting career of Jacob A. Riis, who wrote with discernment about conditions in the New York City slums and the tragedies they bred.

The upsurge of circulations and competition brought increased specialization within the newsrooms. By the 1870s, leading metropolitan dailies had a chief editor, a managing editor or night editor in charge of the news, a city editor to direct the staff of perhaps two dozen reporters, a telegraph editor to handle the increasing volume of wire and cable news, a financial editor, drama critic, literary editor and editorial writers. As the years passed and reporting staffs grew, the city editor's role took on more importance.

The newsroom operations became more sophisticated with the use of the telephone, typewriter, and the rewrite man. An increased number of editions caused pressure for more rapid handling of local news, and the summary lead gained favor as a means of condensing stories. (But the literary stylists and writers of rambling chronological stories were still numerous.) As Sunday papers became common, additional persons were needed to assist the chief editors. Special Sunday staffs were set up, including cartoonists and artists. Along with this attention to regular news, sports news became increasingly important to the mass audience. Pulitzer realized this and arranged the first separate sports department for his *World*. Specialized writers began to appear in each sports field and several columns of sports news were run in big newspapers by 1890. After the turn of the century regular sports pages began to appear.

WOMEN IN JOURNALISM

Another development was the rapid influx of women staff members. The industrial boom and expansion of business opportunities had meant jobs for women, and this included the newspaper business. There had been women journalists of note dating back to the Revolutionary War days. Before the Civil War Margaret Fuller of the *New York Tribune,* for example, and Jane Grey Swisshelm, a Washington correspondent and Minnesota newspaper editor, gained attention. Victoria Woodhull and her sister, Tennessee Claflin, published their weekly in New York in 1870, championing female emancipation, abortion, and free love. Eliza Jane Poitevant Holbrook was literary editor of the *New Orleans Picayune* in the 1860s, married the publisher, and ran the paper after his death. Ellen Scripps worked with her famous brothers when they started their newspapers in the 1870s and 1880s. Nancy Johnson was the *New York Times'* European travel writer in 1857.

Jennie June Croly—who founded America's first women's club, the New York Press Club and Sorosis—began the first fashion column and set up a duplicate exchange service, the forerunner to later syndicated services. Her professional career spanned 40 years, beginning with the *New York Herald* in 1855. Kate Field wrote editorials for the *Times* of London before joining the *New York Herald* staff as a reporter and critic. In 1891 she established "Kate Field's Washington," a weekly review of books, music, and art. Writing women's news for some of the first women's pages in the 1890s were Fanny Fern of the *Philadelphia Ledger* and Grace Greenwood of the *New York Times*. Florence Finch Kelly, who worked on several papers and helped establish the Women's Press Club in New York in 1889, joined the *New York Times* in 1906 for a 30-year stint in the book review section.

Active writers included Ida M. Tarbell, who was one of the original muckrakers for *McClure's* beginning in 1893; Winifred Black (Annie Laurie), one of Hearst's early stars; Elizabeth Cochrane (Nelly Bly), moral crusader for the *New York World* who circled the world as a promotional stunt; Nixola Greeley-Smith, the granddaughter of Horace Greeley, who was hired by Pulitzer and spent 20 years as a reporter; Sally Joy (Penelope Penfeather), fashion writer of the *Boston Herald* and first president of the New England Women's Press Association in the 1880s. Jessie White Mario was the *Nation's* faithful correspondent from Italy from 1866 to 1904, providing detailed political news.

Women correspondents in Washington multiplied after Jane Swisshelm took her seat in the Senate press gallery in 1850. The 1879 *Congressional Directory* listed

20 women with gallery privileges, among 166 correspondents. Then women were dropped because each paper was limited to three names on the list, and the women correspondents were not breaking-news reporters. In the years 1866 to 1880, the foremost women Washington correspondents were Mary Clemmer Ames, whose column appeared in the weekly *New York Independent,* and Emily Edson Briggs, columnist for the *Philadelphia Press.* Sara Clarke Lippincott did liberal-oriented columns for the *New York Times* in the 1870s (she was also Grace Greenwood by pen name). Mary Abigail Dodge did conservative articles for the 1877–78 *New York Tribune.*

Carrying on the tradition of many earlier women journalists, Miriam Follin Leslie edited *Frank Leslie's Illustrated Newspaper* after her husband's death. Anna Benjamin covered the Spanish-American War for that publication, while that same year Marie Manning was hired by Hearst as a reporter and ended up as Beatrice Fairfax, lovelorn writer for the *New York Journal.* Later Dorothy Dix (Elizabeth Meriweather Gilmore) would write a similar column for the Hearst syndicate. One scholar noted that in 1889 the entire issue of the *Journalist,* a professional periodical, was devoted to profiles of 50 women editors and reporters. Ten of them were black, including Mrs. N. F. Mossell, who edited the women's pages of the *New York Freeman,* and popular columnist Lillian Alberta Lewis, whose pen name was Bert Islew. Her work appeared in the *Boston Advocate* and elsewhere.[15]

The most famous of the feminist newspapers after the Civil War was *The Revolution,* following in the tradition of other women's rights periodicals that had appeared on a steady basis since the 1840s. Elizabeth Stanton and Susan B. Anthony kept it going between 1868 and 1870. In 1869, Lucy Stone and other leaders of the American Woman Suffrage Association founded *The Woman's Journal,* which survived until 1931. The *Business Women's Journal* was popular in the 1890s, describing women in business, sports, and politics and in the home.[16]

Salaries for both men and women on the editorial staff were generally low, except for a few top positions. Principal editors were paid from $25 to $60 a week in 1870; by 1890 managing editors of large papers received up to $125, and city editors and star reporters made from $50 to $100 per week. These were good salaries in 1890 dollars, but many staff members stayed at the same $15 to $25 a week level that had existed for reporters after the Civil War because there was no effective labor organization in the editorial offices as there was in the mechanical departments.

ADVANCES IN COOPERATIVE NEWS GATHERING

Pressure for speedier and more comprehensive coverage of the news, which stemmed both from increasing competition among the dailies and from the needs of the new social environment, brought changes in cooperative news gathering. Railroads and telegraph lines that had been part of the race for news in the 1840s spurted ahead to cover the country. Between 1880 and 1900 the number of railroad tracks doubled and those of telegraph lines quadrupled. Bell Telephone lines joined cities in those years and the federal postal service began free rural delivery in 1897, also improving city carrier service. The Atlantic Cable, which began operating in 1866, linked the United States to London, and another cable stretched eastward to India and the Orient.

The opening of the Atlantic Cable had facilitated reciprocal exchanges of news between the Associated Press of New York (founded by the city's morning papers in 1848) and the press agencies of Europe: Reuters in Britain (1851), Havas in France (1836), Wolff in Germany (1849), and Stefani in Italy (1854). The AP, controlled by the seven charter member New York morning papers, had formed agreements with the Western Union by which preferred treatment and rates could be offered member papers. Regional and local groups that did become members could restrict membership, preventing new competitors from obtaining the basic coverage afforded by the AP. To discourage press service competitors, the New York AP forbade those receiving its service to buy the news of any other agency.

Naturally there were many complaints about this news monopoly. The news report favored morning newspapers. Rates to clients were arbitrarily assessed and papers outside of New York felt they were paying too much of the cost and had too little to say about the operations of the service. Despite the fact that in 1880 only half the morning dailies and a fourth of the evening papers were receiving the service, only the United Press (no relation to the later service of the same name) offered real competition before it was submerged in competition between rival AP factions.[17]

However, some important steps were being taken in cooperative news gathering. A leased wire was set up between New York and Washington in 1875 and carried up to 20,000 words per day. This improved service reached Chicago in 1884, and by 1900 the AP-leased wires were extended to New Orleans, Denver, and Minneapolis. Smaller dailies were given inexpensive service by the making of thin stereotyped plates that could be set directly into the news columns. The prime distributor of thin plates in the 1880s was the American Press Association, which used AP press reports. Feature stories, illustrations, and entertainment material also were available from these syndicates.[18] In addition, some leading papers syndicated proof slips of their exclusive stories by express service, mail, or telegraph. City news services were formally organized in New York and Chicago in the early 1890s. These agencies for the collection of routine city news had taken form during the Civil War.

The new leaders in journalism were willing to spend money for the gathering of news. To supplement their AP coverage they began to send more correspondents to Congress. At the outbreak of the Civil War 45 reporters were in the galleries, but by 1870 this number was 130. The famed Washington Gridiron Club was formed in 1885 by Ben: Perley Poore of the *Boston Journal,* dean of the capital press corps. There were major problems that money could not solve, however. The AP, by its cooperative nature, depended heavily on the news collected by member papers and the foreign press services. Often this was unsatisfactory and Western Union operators had to be called on to supply the coverage of spot news events that AP members could not provide. Those papers outside the AP fold were forced to struggle along, waiting for the day when other press associations would provide competition to the AP.

THE BUSINESS SIDE: ADVERTISING DEVELOPMENTS

The expansion of the editorial staff and its news gathering activities, which thus was heralding the arrival of modern journalism, was made possible by tremendous developments in the business and mechanical departments of the metropolitan daily newspaper. But these developments in turn brought an overshadowing of the figure of the old-time editor and a relative lessening of his influence in the new era of corporate journalism.

This did not mean that editors and news executives were shunted aside, but they no longer could dominate the scene as in the days when an editor-owner stood in command of his less complex enterprise. The achieving of gains in editorial staff efficiency and in comprehensive coverage of the news was to be at the expense of the personal factor in newspaper editing.

Those larger dailies that had become complex business institutions—headed by the *New York World* with its $10 million valuation and its annual $1 million profit in the mid-nineties—were harassed by a host of new problems. It was they who first reflected the corporate nature of the new journalism, although the pressure of the business problems they faced soon came to be felt by an increasing number of middle-sized dailies and to some degree by any newspaper.

The scramble for advertising and circulation supremacy, widespread mechanical innovations and pyramiding capitalization costs, larger payrolls and more difficult labor relations problems, increasing concern over newsprint supply for skyrocketing circulations—these and other problems brought the rise of a managerial corps in newspaper publishing, just as managers were rising as a group in American business generally.

Symbolizing the ascendancy of business problems of the daily newspapers was the establishment of the American Newspaper Publishers Association in 1887 to serve as their trade association. The leaders in the association were representatives of aggressive new papers and of older papers that were alive to the problems of the new journalism. Most of the men taking part in association affairs held managerial posts on their newspapers or were publishers who were primarily interested in business management.

Two of the early presidents were James W. Scott of the *Chicago Herald* and Charles W. Knapp of the *St. Louis Republic,* both news-trained publishers. But men like Colonel Charles H. Jones, S.S. Carvalho, John Norris, and Don C. Seitz—all of whom contended for managerial-side supremacy on Pulitzer's *World* in the 1890s—were more typical leaders of the ANPA. Seitz, who survived as manager of the *World,* and Norris, who became business manager of the *New York Times,* were particularly important leaders of the Publishers Association after the turn of the century. There they spoke for their absent publishers, Pulitzer and Adolph Ochs.

The ANPA was organized at the call of William H. Brearley, advertising manager of the *Detroit Evening News,* James E. Scripps's successful new paper. There were many state editorial associations—17 had been founded between 1853 and 1880—but most of their members published weeklies and small dailies. The National Editorial Association had been organized in 1885 by B.B. Herbert of the *Red Wing Daily Republican* of Minnesota and became the national organization of the weeklies and smallest dailies.

What Brearley and his associates wanted primarily was a daily newspaper trade association that would help its members with the problem of obtaining national advertising. While the ANPA soon became deeply involved in problems of labor relations, newsprint supply, government mail rates, and mechanical developments, it centered much of its attention on the field of advertising.

The first advertising agents had appeared in New York and other eastern cities in the 1840s as middlemen between their advertisers and newspapers. They purchased space for their clients, receiving discounts of from 15 to 30 percent, and sometimes up to 75 percent, on stated advertising rates. This was their profit. While larger papers were able to obtain ads on a steady basis and regulate the agents' commissions, smaller papers sometimes were victimized as agents played one publisher against another and obtained handsome commissions.

There were many attempts to regulate advertising practices and not all agents operated in this manner. The founding around 1870 of the respected agencies of George P. Rowell, N.W. Ayer & Son, and Lord and Thomas helped. Rowell published his *American Newspaper Directory* in 1869, in an effort to locate all of the newly developed newspapers, and Ayer & Son began its continued annual publication in

Two still-famous Chicago department stores advertise in an 1898 *Times-Herald.*

1880.[19] But true circulations were hard to determine, and it was not until 1914 that the Audit Bureau of Circulations was established, solving the problem. Identifying trustworthy agencies was another problem and after years of arguments the ANPA headquarters in New York agreed in 1899 to issue lists of recognized agencies. By common consent the discount figure was determined at 15 percent.

The percentage of newspaper revenue coming from advertising, as compared to circulation income, rose from half in 1880 to 64 percent by 1910. Space given to ads in most dailies rose from 25 percent to a 50–50 ratio with editorial material by World War I. While the amount of advertising was rising, the content was changing. Three pioneers in the department store business, John Wanamaker of Philadelphia, Marshall Field of Chicago, and A.T. Stewart of New York, gave impetus to retail store advertising. Ivory soap and Royal baking powder were leaders in national advertising in the 1880s, and in the 1890s many more products appeared—complete with slogans like "It Floats" and "His Master's Voice" for Ivory soap and Victor phonographs, and others for Eastman Kodak, Wrigley's gum, and foods.

But there was a cloud over the advertising business because the leading clients of newspapers and magazines were the patent medicine makers, pushing Castoria, Scott's Emulsion, and Lydia Pinkham's Female Compound at the unsuspecting public. These misleading, deliberately deceptive, and often outwardly fraudulent advertisements were quickly accepted by most newspaper and magazine representatives because of the great volume of money involved. This practice continued in large scale until Congress began to get involved at the time of World War I. Despite the attempts at governmental regulation, unscrupulous advertisers and dollar-hungry media people continue to the present day to promote useless and sometimes harmful over-the-counter drugs. Television testimonials replaced the crude newspaper pitches, while consumer advocates protested against the overuse of drugs by the American public. The greatest harm came when the cure-alls were accepted for proper medical attention in remote areas and in crowded tenement districts. Many of the drugs were harmless, as some defenders of the practice claimed, but the deception was painful nevertheless, and some of the drugs did contain deadly poisons.[20]

NEW LEADERS FOR MAGAZINES

There were successful new leaders in magazine journalism, just as there were in newspaper making. One was Frank Munsey, a New Englander with a sober and industrious character, who struggled for a decade in the New York magazine publishing field before achieving success with his *Munsey's,* begun in 1889. Another was S.S. McClure, who after establishing a feature syndicate service for newspapers brought out his *McClure's* in 1893. A third was *Cosmopolitan,* founded in 1886 and sold to William Randolph Hearst in 1905.

These well-edited, popularized monthly magazines had found the same answer to the problem of obtaining mass circulation that the daily newspapers had found in the past. The secret was the cutting of the price to first 15 cents, and then a dime, for magazines that competed with older 35 cent publications. The cheap one-cent-a-pound mail rate, in effect from 1885 until zone rates were established during World War I, helped to make this possible. By the turn of the century *Munsey's* had achieved 650,000 circulation to lead by a wide margin, and *McClure's* and *Cosmopolitan* were runners-up. The formula for all three was popular fiction, general articles, and illustrations.

Cyrus H.K. Curtis provided new leadership in the women's magazine field with his *Ladies' Home Journal,* founded in 1883. With Edward W. Bok as editor after 1889, the magazine quickly rose to a half-million circulation at a one dollar annual subscription price. In the weekly five-cent magazine field the *Saturday Evening Post,* bought by Curtis in 1897, and *Collier's,* founded in 1888, pushed to even higher circulations than those of the monthlies.

These new popularly circulated magazines were the ones that made the biggest inroads on available advertising revenue, arising as they did to public notice at the moment when national advertising was expanding. But the general illustrated monthly magazines of high literary and artistic quality—*Harper's, Century,* and *Scribner's*—continued to have major influence, even though outstripped in circulation. Sharing in the competition for reader attention and revenue too were the illustrated weekly periodicals, *Harper's Weekly* and *Leslie's;* the weeklies depending on humor and cartoons, *Puck, Life,* and *Judge;* and the children's magazines, *Youth's Companion* and *St. Nicholas.*

Taking stock of the amount of advertising revenue gained by magazines, newspaper owners formed two business associations, the International Circulation Managers Association in 1898 and the Newspaper Advertising Executives Association in 1900, as well as regional organizations. Beginning in the late 1870s various representatives and associations worked to promote the newspaper as an advertising medium, and in 1913 the American Newspaper Publishers Association was persuaded to sponsor the founding of the Bureau of Advertising. The Bureau, with a paid staff, did an effective job of arguing the case of newspapers. In 1900 magazines were picking up 60 percent or more of national advertising revenue but by the time of World War I they were sharing the money on an equal basis. Because newspapers had local advertising as well, they received a total of roughly 70 percent of all advertising revenues in the early years of the twentieth century.

A REVOLUTION IN PRINTING: PHOTOGRAPHS   The growth of the modern newspaper thus far described went hand in hand with the development of better printing techniques, improvements in presenting illustrations and eventually photographs, and changing relationships between management and labor brought by unionization and battles over the price of newsprint.

As part of the industrial revolution of the late nineteenth century, achievements in printing included the typesetting machine, faster presses, stereotyping, color printing, dry mats, electrotyping, and photoengraving. Ottmar Mergenthaler's Linotype machine first cast a line of type for newspaper use in 1886 in the *New York Tribune* plant. The timesaving performance of the Linotype helped the large evening dailies, which were under pressure to cover more news close to deadline time. Other slugcasting machines were soon developed, and improvements in the type faces themselves began to help readability. The ugly Gothics began to disappear and after 1900 the newly designed Cheltenham family, the graceful Bodoni, and other headline types came into favor. The *New York Tribune* won typographical fame for its early use of the Bodoni upper and lower case headlines.

The press of deadlines and the rush for big circulations led to the development of bigger and faster presses. The leader here was R. Hoe and Company, which earlier had converted the presses of leading papers from hand to steam power and from flatbed to rotary before the Civil War. Next came the adaptation of the stereotyped plate to the newspaper press, which allowed the breaking of column rules for illustrations, headlines, and advertising—a practice not practical for users of type-revolving presses. The use of the curved stereotyped plate permitted a speed-up of the hourly rate of printing and extra stereotypes of the same page could be produced for simultaneous use on two or more presses. Other changes allowed the use of a continuous roll of newsprint, printing on both sides of the sheet in one operation, automatic folders, and in the 1890s, color printing.

By 1890 most of the type-revolving presses had been replaced by presses using stereotyped plates and webs. The finest Hoe press could run off 48,000 12-page papers in an hour and owners of the larger papers were making plans for installing banks of presses to keep up with the skyrocketing circulations. While color inserts printed separately had been used earlier, full-color presses modeled after those being used in Paris were first built for the *Chicago Inter Ocean* in 1892 by Walter Scott. Within a year the *New York World* had color presses and soon the Sunday comics were a regular feature of the newspaper.

More than one newspaper owner had sensed the need for better illustrations. The *New York Herald* had stood out for its early use of woodcuts and, beginning about 1870, the *Evening Telegram,* companion paper for the *Herald,* published a daily political cartoon. Of course *Frank Leslie's Illustrated Newspaper, Harper's Weekly,* and later other periodicals did highly artistic work with woodcuts. Women's magazines used engraved steel fashion plates. But there was a need for something cheaper and faster. In the 1870s Zincographs, line cuts produced by etching on zinc plates, began to appear in United States papers, and illustrators also found they could print photos directly onto woodblocks or zinc plates, where they would form a guide for the artist or etcher who completed the cut.

A major breakthrough came when *New York World* editors began to publish line drawings of prominent local citizens, beginning in 1884. Within a short time a number of other leading papers were arranging for the work of the artist, Valerian Gribayédoff, who estimated in 1891 that there were about 1,000 artists at work supplying illustrations for 5,000 newspapers and magazines.[21] An increasing number of papers began to hire their own artists and to install engraving facilities.

Photoengraving was quickly to curtail this boom for the artists, however. The halftone photoengraving process had been developed in England prior to 1860, but the results were unsatisfactory until Frederic E. Ives went to work on the problem of reproducing photographs in the printing process. Ives was made head of the photographic laboratory at Cornell University in 1876, when he was 20. The next year he produced a photoengraving of a pen drawing, which was published in the student paper at Cornell. In 1878 he made his first halftone. Ives saw that the way to break up masses of dark and light was to lay out a series of prominences on a plate that would transfer the ink to paper point by point. If the points were close together, the mass would be dark; and the more widely they were spaced, the lighter the mass would become. Ives moved to Baltimore, and then after 1879 to Philadelphia, and produced commercially used halftones. He perfected his process in 1886.

There still remained, however, the problem of using the halftones on rotary presses. One of the heroes of the struggle to get pictures into the American newspaper was Stephen H. Horgan. Horgan was the art editor of an illustrated paper called the *New York Daily Graphic,* which began in 1873 and battled bravely until 1889 when it succumbed in the big city competition. It was Horgan who succeeded in publishing a newspaper halftone of good quality in 1880, a picture called "Shantytown." And it was Horgan who first had the idea of how to run halftones on rotary presses. He was rebuffed by doubting pressmen, however, and it was not until 1897 that he perfected the method for the *New York Tribune.* Within a short time other large papers were running halftone reproductions of photographs.

The artists found the news photographers edging into their field in earnest, now that their photos could be reproduced directly. Both groups covered the Spanish-American War. Syndicates quickly added news and feature photographs to their stock in trade, and big city papers began to employ local photographers who carried their heavy, awkward equipment and their flashlight powder out on assignments. Pictorial journalism was on its way, although its full impact would await the tabloids of the 1920s and the documentary films and *Life* magazine of the 1930s.

The sweep of all of these mechanical developments included labor specialization and larger working forces that in turn brought new labor relations problems. The American Federation of Labor had organized printers, pressmen, and engravers, who pressed constantly for shorter working hours and higher pay. The danger of plantwide strikes—suspensions of service that could jeopardize the status of newspapers with their advertisers and the public—was reduced when the International Typographical Union split by specialty into four separate unions. Efforts by the labor unions and publishers, led by the American Newspaper Publishers Association, to have local conciliation and arbitration procedures and the right of appeal to a national arbitration board brought comparative peace to the newspaper industry in 1899 during a time of severe labor disturbances in other industries.

The ANPA also took a leadership role in the campaign to bring cheaper newsprint to its members. The Fourdrinier process introduced from Germany in 1867 allowed low-cost newsprint to be made from wood pulp to which was added a rag content and was a basic factor in the growth of the American newspaper. Prior to this, an expensive, limited industry produced paper by hand from rag stock. During the Civil War newspaper costs ran to $440 a ton for paper. By the 1890s a chemically produced wood pulp, called sulphite pulp, replaced rag stock as the toughening element in newsprint. Prices tumbled rapidly, reaching $42 a ton in 1899 and remaining there for years, except for periods of paper shortage.[22]

One problem remained, however. Domestic newsprint manufacturers had obtained a good-sized tariff on imported newsprint and had effected a virtual monopolistic control over domestic output and sales prices. The ANPA campaigned for years against the tariff, hoping to free the vast Canadian forest resources for American printing use. Finally in 1913 Congress carried out the pledge of the Woodrow Wilson administration to lower the tariff, allowing a flood of Canadian newsprint into the country.

It is evident then, from this survey of changing industrial conditions in the daily newspaper and magazine business, that there was a "watershed of the nineties" for the American newspaper. The advance into the modern era had been accomplished and, for better or for worse, the older era of journalism was no more.

NOTES

1. In a poll of American editors conducted by *Editor & Publisher* in 1934.

2. Cockerill's biographer contends that his experience as managing editor of the *Cincinnati Enquirer* in exploiting local news, and his subsequent exposures to national and international news in Washington and Baltimore and as a war correspondent, made Cockerill a definitely superior newsman to Pulitzer. Much of the imaginative handling of the news, and the sensational approach, is credited to Cockerill. See Homer W. King, *Pulitzer's Prize Editor: A Biography of John A. Cockerill, 1845–1896* (Durham, N.C.: Duke University Press, 1965).

3. As quoted in Don C. Seitz, *Joseph Pulitzer: His Life and Letters* (New York: Simon & Schuster, 1924), p. 101. The name of the paper was soon changed to the *Post-Dispatch*.

4. As quoted in *The Story of the St. Louis Post-Dispatch* (St. Louis: Pulitzer Publishing Company, 1949), p. 3.

5. Documented in the chapter, "A Sensational Newspaper," in Julian Rammelkamp, *Pulitzer's Post-Dispatch 1878–1883* (Princeton, N.J.: Princeton University Press, 1967), pp. 163–206. On the whole Rammelkamp endorses Pulitzer's record.

6. Rammelkamp points out that Pulitzer "mobilized the middle class elements of St. Louis into a dynamic movement of reform" that finally bore fruit early in the twentieth century (ibid., p. 303).

7. As quoted in Willard G. Bleyer, *Main Currents in the History of American Journalism* (Boston: Houghton Mifflin, 1927), p. 325.

8. *New York World,* May 11, 1883.

9. As quoted in Bleyer, *Main Currents in the History of American Journalism,* p. 328.

10. *Journalist,* August 22, 1885.

11. James Creelman, "Joseph Pulitzer—Master Journalist," *Pearson's,* XXI (March 1909), p. 246.

12. As quoted in Seitz, *Joseph Pulitzer,* p. 286.

13. Indicative of that frailty that led to conspicuous failings was Pulitzer's admiration in particular of three publishers whose newspapers utilized sensational techniques but did not measure up to the *World* in high-quality performance. They were William M. Singerly, *Philadelphia Record;* Charles H. Taylor, *Boston Globe;* and the British newspaper popularizer, Alfred Harmsworth, who later became Lord Northcliffe.

14. Three New York newspapers repeated the stunt in 1936. H.R. Ekins of the *World-Telegram* won with a time of 18½ days, defeating Dorothy ("Nellie Bly") Kilgallen of the *Journal* and Leo Kiernan of the *Times.*

15. For a full discussion of these women and dozens more see Marion Marzolf's *Up From the Footnote: A History of Women Journalists* (New York: Hastings House, 1977). Also see her "The Woman Journalist: Colonial Printer to City Desk," *Journalism History,* I–II (Winter 1974–Spring 1975). Also see John Jakes' *Great Women Reporters* (New York: G.P. Putnam's Sons, 1969) and Ishbel Ross' *Ladies of the Press* (New York: Harper & Row, 1936).

16. A thorough treatment of women's publications is found in Anne Mather's "A History of Feminist Periodicals," *Journalism History* I–II (Autumn 1974–Spring 1975), a three-part article.

17. The standard account of this subject is Victor Rosewater, *History of Cooperative News-Gathering in the United States* (New York: Appleton-Century-Crofts, 1930).

18. Alfred M. Lee, *The Daily Newspaper in America* (New York: Macmillan, 1937), p. 511.

19. The detailed story is told in Frank Presbrey, *The History and Development of Advertising* (New York: Doubleday, 1929).

20. William Marz, "Patent Medicine Advertising: Mass Persuasion Techniques and Reform, 1905–1976." M.A. thesis, Calif. State University at Northridge, 1977.

21. *Cosmopolitan,* XI (August 1891).

22. Lee, *The Daily Newspaper in America,* pp. 743–45.

ANNOTATED BIBLIOGRAPHY

Books

The *Union List of Newspapers,* beginning where Brigham's bibliography leaves off in 1820, is supplemented by directories: *Geo. P. Rowell & Co.'s American Newspaper Directory* (1869) and *N. W. Ayer & Son's American Newspaper Annual* (1880), later called the *Directory of Newspapers & Periodicals.* The *Editor & Publisher International Year Book* dates from 1921.

BARRETT, JAMES W., *Joseph Pulitzer and His World.* New York: Vanguard, 1941. A colorful, rambling story of Pulitzer and the *New York World* by the last city editor of the *World.*

CARNES, CECIL, *Jimmy Hare, News Photographer.* New York: Macmillan, 1940. The biography of one of the early leading press photographers.

CONE, FAIRFAX M., *With All Its Faults: A Candid Account of Forty Years in Advertising.* Boston: Little, Brown, 1969. By the head of famed Foote, Cone & Belding agency.

DOWNEY, FAIRFAX D., *Richard Harding Davis: His Day.* New York: Scribner's, 1933. Biography of the glamor-boy of early modern journalism.

ELLIS, L. ETHAN, *Newsprint: Producers, Publishers, Political Pressures.* New Brunswick, N.J.: Rutgers University Press, 1960. The economics of print paper (includes his 1948 study, *Print Paper Pendulum*).

EMERY, EDWIN, *History of the American Newspaper Publishers Association.* Minneapolis: University of Minnesota Press, 1950. Covers the activities of the organized daily newspaper publishers in the fields of labor relations, newsprint, advertising, mailing privileges, mechanical research, and legislative lobbying, from 1887 on.

GUNTHER, JOHN, *Taken at the Flood: The Story of Albert D. Lasker.* New York: Harper & Row, 1960. The career of a pioneer adman at the Lord & Thomas agency.

HOWER, RALPH M., *The History of an Advertising Agency: N. W. Ayer & Son at Work, 1869–1949.* Cambridge, Mass.: Harvard University Press, 1949.

IRWIN, WILL, *The American Newspaper,* edited by Clifford F. Weigle and David G. Clark. Ames: Iowa State University Press, 1969. Reproductions of the original series in *Collier's* of 1911.

——, *The Making of a Reporter.* New York: G.P. Putnam's Sons, 1942. Autobiography of a discerning newspaperman who ranked with the best.

JAKES, JOHN, *Great Women Reporters.* New York: G.P. Putnam's Sons, 1969. The stories of dozens who competed with men for news.

JONES, EDGAR R., *Those Were the Good Old Days: A Happy Look at American Advertising, 1880–1930.* New York: Simon & Schuster, 1959. Illustrations of 50 years of advertising from magazines.

JUERGENS, GEORGE, *Joseph Pulitzer and the New York World.* Princeton, N.J.: Princeton University Press, 1966. A detailed, enthusiastic account of Pulitzer's first four years at the *World,* 1883–87.

KING, HOMER W., *Pulitzer's Prize Editor: A Biography of John A. Cockerill, 1845–1896.* Durham, N.C.: Duke University Press, 1965. Only detailed study of the managing editor, whose biographer contends he overshadowed Pulitzer in handling news.

KNIGHT, OLIVER A., *Following the Indian Wars: The Story of the Newspaper Correspondents among the Indian Campaigners, 1866–1891.* Norman: University of Oklahoma Press, 1960. Well documented.

LOFT, JACOB, *The Printing Trades.* New York: Holt, Rinehart & Winston, 1944. An inclusive account. See also Elizabeth F. Baker, *Printers and Technology: A History of the International Printing Pressmen and Assistants' Union* (New York: Columbia University Press, 1957).

MARZOLF, MARION, *Up From the Footnote: A History of Women Journalists.* New York: Hastings House, 1977. From colonial days to present, by bibliographer for the area. Also see her "The Woman Journalist: Colonial Printer to City Desk," *Journalism History,* I–II (Winter 1974, Spring 1975).

MATHEWS, JOSEPH F., *George Washburn Smalley: Forty Years A Foreign Correspondent.* Chapel Hill: University of North Carolina Press, 1973. Covers the years 1867–1906.

NEWHALL, BEAUMONT, *The History of Photography from 1839 to the Present Day.* New York: Museum of Modern Art, 1964. The standard reference.

POORE, BEN: PERLEY, *Perley's Reminiscences of Sixty Years in the National Metropolis.* Philadelphia: Hubbard, 1886. Two volumes about political, social, and journalistic life in Washington, 1820s to 1880s. Poore was the *Boston Journal's* correspondent.

PRESBREY, FRANK, *The History and Development of Advertising.* New York: Doubleday, 1929. The standard history in its field.

RALPH, JULIAN, *The Making of a Journalist.* New York: Harper & Row, 1903. The autobiography of another top-ranking reporter of the period.

RAMMELKAMP, JULIAN S., *Pulitzer's Post-Dispatch, 1878–1883.* Princeton University Press, 1966. Documented study of evolving journalistic style of Pulitzer, Cockerill, others; restrained approval of Pulitzer's social contributions, criticism of his sensationalized news.

ROSEWATER, VICTOR, *History of Cooperative News-Gathering in the United States.* New York: Appleton-Century-Crofts, 1930. The recognized source for the early history of press associations.

ROSS, ISHBEL, *Ladies of the Press.* New York: Harper & Row, 1936. Valuable for stories of early women journalists.

SEITZ, DON C., *Joseph Pulitzer: His Life and Letters.* New York: Simon & Schuster, 1924. The first Pulitzer study; others draw upon it. Written by Pulitzer's onetime business manager.

SWANBERG, W.A., *Pulitzer.* New York: Scribner's, 1967. Latest and best of the studies of the tempestuous editor-publisher.

TURNER, E.S., *The Shocking History of Advertising.* Harmondsworth, England: Penguin Books, 1965. An updated revision of a good history.

WARE, LOUISE, *Jacob A. Riis.* New York: Appleton-Century-Crofts, 1938. Biography of a socially conscious reporter.

WATKINS, JULIAN L., *The 100 Greatest Advertisements*, 2nd ed. New York: Moore Publishing Company, 1959. Who wrote them and what they did.

WOOD, JAMES PLAYSTED, *The Story of Advertising*. New York: Ronald Press, 1958. Fairly detailed from the 1860s on.

Periodicals and Monographs

The trade journals became available in this period. The leaders were the *Journalist* (1884–1907), the *Fourth Estate* (1894–1927), and *Editor & Publisher* (1901) in the daily newspaper field; the *Publishers' Auxiliary* (1865) in the weekly newspaper field; and *Printers' Ink* (1888) in advertising. The fiftieth anniversary numbers of *Editor & Publisher* (July 21, 1934) and of *Printers' Ink* (July 28, 1938) are particularly valuable sources.

BEASLEY, MAURINE, *The First Women Washington Correspondents*. Washington: GW Washington Studies, No. 4, 1976. Covers six post-Civil War women writers.

BENNION, SHERLYN C., "Fremont Older: Advocate for Women," *Journalism History*, III (Winter 1976–77), p. 124. San Francisco *Bulletin's* women reporters, editors.

BRIDGES, LAMAR W., "Eliza Jane Nicholson of the 'Picayune'," *Journalism History*, II (Winter 1975), p. 110. Owner of the New Orleans paper, 1876–1896.

BRISBANE, ARTHUR, "Joseph Pulitzer," *Cosmopolitan*, XXXIII (May 1902), 51. An intimate contemporary portrait by an editor who jumped from Pulitzer's *World* to Hearst's *Journal*.

BROD, DONALD F., "John A. Cockerill's St. Louis Years," *Bulletin* of Missouri Historical Society, XXVI (April 1970), 227. Study of a political campaign and Cockerill's shooting of a politician to death.

DANIELS, ELIZABETH A., "Jessie White Mario: 19th Century Correspondent," *Journalism History*, II (Summer 1975), p. 54. Correspondent in Italy for the *Nation*, 1866–1904.

EK, RICHARD A., "Victoria Woodhull and the Pharisees," *Journalism Quarterly*, XLIX (Autumn 1972), 453. Exposure of minister's adultery brings reprisals against editor.

HART, JACK R., "Horatio Alger in the Newsroom: Social Origins of American Editors," *Journalism Quarterly*, LIII (Spring 1976), pp. 14–20. Shows editors of 1875 and 1900 are comparable to executives in other major industries.

HUDSON, ROBERT V., "Journeyman Journalist: An Analytical Biography of Will Irwin," Ph.D. thesis, University of Minnesota, 1970. Reportorial career researched in depth.

INGLIS, WILLIAM, "An Intimate View of Joseph Pulitzer," *Harper's Weekly*, LV (November 11, 1911), 7. An article with considerable insight, published at time of Pulitzer's death.

IRWIN, WILL, "The American Newspaper," *Collier's*, XLVI–XLVII (January 21–July 29, 1911). A series of 15 articles that constitutes a history of journalism after the Civil War. One article, "The Fourth Current," which traces the rise of yellow journalism, is reprinted in Ford and Emery, *Highlights in the History of the American Press*.

JONES, DOUGLAS C., "Remington Reports from the Badlands: The Artist as War Correspondent," *Journalism Quarterly*, XLVII (Winter 1970), 702. His drawings were in *Harper's Weekly*.

———, "Teresa Dean: Lady Correspondent Among the Sioux Indians," *Journalism Quarterly*, XLIX (Winter 1972), p. 656.

KAHAN, ROBERT S., "The Antecedents of American Photojournalism," Ph.D. thesis, University of Wisconsin, 1969. The artist vs. the camera.

KNIGHT, OLIVER A., "Reporting a Gold Rush," *Journalism Quarterly*, XXXVIII (Winter 1961), 43. The story of two young reporters from the *Inter Ocean* and *New York Herald* in the Black Hills of 1875.

KNIGHTS, PETER R., "The Press Association War of 1866–1867," *Journalism Monographs*, No. 6 (December 1967). An episode in the story of wire services.

McKERNS, JOSEPH P., "Ben: Perley Poore's Reminiscences: A Reliable Source for Research?" *Journalism History*, II (Winter 1975), p. 125. Poore was an important Washington correspondent, 1854–87.

MASEL-WALTERS, LYNNE, " 'Their Rights and Nothing More': A History of *The Revolution, 1868–70,*" *Journalism Quarterly,* LIII (Summer 1976), pp. 242–51. Details the beginning of women's political journalism and a short-lived national publication. Also see her "A Burning Cloud by Day: The History and Content of the 'Woman's Journal'," *Journalism History,* III (Winter 1976–77), p. 103. Organ of the feminist movement, 1869–1931.

MATHER, ANNE, "A History of Feminist Periodicals," *Journalism History,* I–II (Autumn 1974–Spring 1975). Three-part article.

Outlook, XCIX (November 11, 1911), 603 and 608, contains two estimates of Pulitzer and the *World.*

PIERCE, ROBERT N., "Lord Northcliffe: Trans-Atlantic Influences," *Journalism Monographs,* No. 40 (August 1975).

SAALBERG, HARVEY, "The *Westliche Post* of St. Louis: A Daily Newspaper for German-Americans, 1857–1938," Ph.D. thesis, University of Missouri, 1967. Pulitzer, Schurz, Preetorius figure in the story. See also his "The *Westliche Post* of St. Louis: German Language Daily, 1857–1938," *Journalism Quarterly,* XLV (Autumn 1968), 452.

SCHUNEMAN, R. SMITH, "The Photograph in Print: An Examination of New York Daily Newspapers, 1890–1937," Ph.D. thesis, University of Minnesota, 1966. The rise of photojournalism is developed by extensive research.

———, "Art or Photography: A Question for Newspaper Editors of the 1890s," *Journalism Quarterly,* XLII (Winter 1965), 43. Why the halftone waited until 1897 in big dailies.

SEITZ, DON C., "The Portrait of an Editor," *Atlantic Monthly,* CXXXIV (September 1924), 289. Reprinted in Ford and Emery, *Highlights in the History of the American Press.* Joseph Pulitzer portrayed by biographer.

WARD, HILEY, "A Popular History of the National Newspaper Association," *Publishers' Auxiliary,* CX (July 10, 1975), p. 14. First of a series extending to 1977, substantially researched.

Copyrighted trademarks and brand advertising, 1900–1920.

William Randolph Hearst takes a photo from his yacht during the Spanish-American war.

Hearst at the peak of his career in the 1930s.

17

The Age
of Yellow Journalism

The reason why such journals lie is that it pays to lie; or, in other words, this is the very reason for which they are silly and scandalous and indecent. They supply a want of a demoralized public.

—E. L. Godkin

The American newspaper was making great strides by the mid-nineties, both as an instrument of society and as a business institution. Increased advertising and subscription revenues meant that conscientious publishers and editors could do a better job of telling the news honestly and fully and of demonstrating their community leadership, because they were better able to resist outside pressures. But there were obvious shortcomings. The financial bigness of metropolitan dailies brought a lessening of the personal element in editorial direction and sometimes muffled the voice of the newspaper and dulled its social conscience.

Because mass circulation was achieved by a popularizing of the product, the primary news function sometimes was overshadowed by efforts to entertain. It should be added, however, that corporate journalism did not need to speak in a timid voice. Popularization, while inevitable if mass readership was to be achieved, did not need to become mere sensationalism. Bigger headlines, more readable stories, pictures, and blobs of color might give the newspaper a new face, causing some readers to grimace and wish for the bygone days, but effectively used, these devices could be useful and desirable.

By the same token, these new techniques could be used to emphasize sensationalism at the expense of news. Some editors proceeded in the mid-nineties to do just this, as had been done in earlier periods when new audiences were available. But the difference was that now they had better tools with which to make their sensationalism distinctive and seemingly new—the degrading product of this effort became known as "yellow journalism."

Yellow journalism, at its worst, was the new journalism without a soul. Trumpeting their concern for "the people," yellow journalists at the same time choked up the news channels on which the common man depended with a shrieking, gaudy, sensation-loving, devil-may-care kind of journalism. This turned the high drama of life into a cheap melodrama and led to stories being twisted into the form best suited for sales by the howling newsboy. Worst of all, instead of giving effective leadership, yellow journalism offered a palliative of sin, sex, and violence.

Pulitzer's striking success had demonstrated once again the appeal of the age-old technique of sensation. Other papers, like the *Philadelphia Record* and *Boston Globe*, were playing the same game as the *World*. But it was a mistake to attribute the *World*'s circulation achievements to sensationalism alone, and those who saw the clever promotion and lighter side of the *World* did not see—or disregarded—the solid characteristics of its news coverage and the high qualities of the editorial page. The antics of those who did not make this attempt to balance information and entertainment paid off handsomely in dollars earned. Their competitors often were forced to take on the yellow hue, and although eventually most newspapers recovered from the disease, modern journalism has exhibited some of the effects of this age of yellow journalism ever since.

WILLIAM RANDOLPH HEARST

The man who more than anyone else brought about the era of yellow journalism was watching with sharp interest while Pulitzer was setting New York journalism on its ear in the mid-eighties. He was William Randolph Hearst, who was to become the most controversial figure in modern journalism before his 64-year publishing career was ended. The youthful Hearst was a calculating witness to Pulitzer's climb to glory, and when eventually he invaded New York to challenge the supremacy of the *World,* he came prepared to dazzle the city with a sensationalized and self-promoted kind of journalism that would put Pulitzer to shame. The resulting struggle brought repercussions whose effects are still being felt.

Hearst was a Californian, born in 1863, the son of a successful pioneer who struck it rich in the silver mines of the Comstock Lode and who later won more riches in Anaconda copper and western and Mexican ranch lands. The only child of George and Phoebe Hearst, he grew up in San Francisco under the guidance of a busy, ambitious father and a schoolteacher mother, who in later years became a noted philanthropist and able manager of the family fortune.

Having achieved wealth, George Hearst aspired to political power. In 1880 he acquired the *San Francisco Examiner,* a debt-ridden morning paper that lagged behind the *Chronicle,* and converted it into a Democratic party organ. Young Hearst showed an interest in the paper, but his father took a low view of the newspapermen who worked for him and packed his heir off to Harvard in 1883.

The Hearst career at Harvard was sensational, if not successful. He was a free-spending westerner who drank too much beer and listened to too much band music and who did his best job as business manager of the humor magazine, the *Lampoon*. He was suspended in his sophomore year for celebrating Grover Cleveland's election to the presidency with a noisy fireworks display and was expelled a few months later for perpetrating a practical joke on Harvard's professors. Distinguished faculty members like William James and Josiah Royce could see no humor, it seemed, in finding their likenesses decorating chamber pots.

But the eastern education had not been entirely wasted. Harvard may not have made its impression on Hearst's mind, but the *Boston Globe* and the *New York World* did. Hearst studied the somewhat sensational techniques of General Charles H. Taylor's successful *Globe* and visited its up-to-date mechanical plant. He was more interested in Pulitzer's *World,* however, and on one of his vacations he worked as a cub reporter for the newspaper he later was to battle. After bowing out at Harvard, Hearst again spent some time in New York studying the *World*'s techniques and then returned to San Francisco.

HEARST'S SAN FRANCISCO EXAMINER

William Randolph Hearst assumed the editorship of the *San Francisco Examiner* in 1887 when George Hearst was named senator from California. He was only 24 but the tall, blue-eyed, shy editor, whose high-pitched voice contrasted with a commanding physical presence, immediately began to staff the paper. Picked as managing editor was Sam S. Chamberlain, who had worked for both Bennett and Pulitzer, edited Bennett's Paris edition of the *Herald,* and in 1884 founded the Paris newspaper *Le Matin.* The brilliant Ambrose Bierce, later famous for his short stories, contributed his "Prattle" column. Star reporters like Edward H. Hamilton signed on, as did Arthur McEwen, an editorial writer who became a key figure in Hearst-style journalism. Homer Davenport began to draw his cartoons, James Swinnerton applied his artist's skill to the new field of comics, and literary flavor was added by Edwin Markham ("The Man With the Hoe," which first appeared in the paper) and E. L. (Phinney) Thayer, whose contribution was "Casey at the Bat."

Chamberlain's grasp of news techniques made him invaluable. He developed the career of Winifred Black—known as "Annie Laurie" to future generations of Hearst readers—who attracted San Francisco women readers with intense stories. Sent to investigate the city hospital's management, she fainted conveniently on the street, was carried to the hospital, and turned in a story "with a sob for the unfortunate in every line." The *Examiner* was ever experimenting with crusades, stunts, and devices to present the news in a yet more luring manner. A stalwart Democrat, Hearst attacked the Southern Pacific railroad, the bulwark of the Republican state machine, and attempted to present other types of serious stories. But news that was important but dull took a back seat as the paper strove for what McEwen called the "Gee-Whiz" emotion.[1]

Hearst's experiments on the mechanical side were important and constructive contributions to the new journalism. Trying many new patterns of makeup, arranging headlines in symmetrical patterns, and using attractive type faces, Hearst eventually arrived at a distinctive formula that many another paper imitated. Hearst himself often worked on the page forms, but his mechanical genius was George Pancoast, who joined the *Examiner* staff in 1888 and for the next 50 years perfected the electric drive for presses, improved color printing, and designed 14 printing plants for the Hearst empire.

The *Examiner,* called by the ambitious Hearst "The Monarch of the Dailies," doubled its circulation in the first year, reaching 30,000, and by 1893 had pushed to 72,000. This was more than M. H. de Young's *Chronicle,* the recognized leading daily. Senator Hearst died in 1891 after watching his son turn a losing proposition into a paper averaging a $350,000 to $500,000 yearly profit.[2] And with that success achieved, young Hearst was ready to tackle the challenge he saw in Joseph Pulitzer's city, New York.

HEARST INVADES NEW YORK   The profits from the *Examiner* now were available for an invasion of New York. But Hearst needed more capital, and eventually he persuaded his mother to sell the family holdings in the Anaconda copper mines for $7.5 million and make the cash available for new publishing ventures.[3] Later, when a friend told Mrs. Hearst that she had heard the *New York Journal* was losing a million dollars a year and expressed fear that the family fortune was being thrown away recklessly, Mrs. Hearst replied that, in such an event, her son could hold out for 30 years more.

Somewhat ironically, Hearst entered the New York field by buying the newspaper that Joseph Pulitzer's brother, Albert, had established in 1882. The *Morning Journal* had been a successful one-cent paper appealing to casual newspaper scanners. In 1894 its price was raised to two cents, and circulation fell off. Albert Pulitzer then sold the *Journal* for a million dollars to John R. McLean, ambitious publisher of the *Cincinnati Enquirer*. McLean was no stranger to sensational methods of publishing newspapers, but he was unable to break into the highly competitive New York field. In the fall of 1895, Hearst picked up the paper from the defeated McLean for $180,000.

PULITZER'S SUNDAY WORLD   Joseph Pulitzer had been busy during the 10 years since Hearst had left New York to launch his career in San Francisco. Particularly he had expanded the mechanical facilities available to his editors, and he had applied the new techniques to the development of the *Sunday World*.

It was Pulitzer who first demonstrated the full potentialities of the Sunday newspaper as a profitable news and entertainment medium. There had been weeklies issued as Sunday papers since 1796. The daily *Boston Globe* put out a Sunday edition briefly in 1833, but James Gordon Bennett's *Herald* was the first daily to print a Sunday edition steadily, starting in 1841. The demand for news during the Civil War stimulated Sunday publication, but even by the time Pulitzer invaded New York in 1883 only about 100 daily newspapers had Sunday editions. Most of them were appearing in eastern cities and a good share were printed in German and other foreign languages. Some carried a four-page supplement filled with entertaining features, fiction, and trivia.

Pulitzer's new *Sunday World* added many more pages of entertainment to the regular news section. Feature material for women, for young readers, and for sports enthusiasts appeared. Humorous drawings and other illustrations were concentrated in the Sunday pages. The offerings of the literary syndicates, such as that developed by S. S. McClure, added to the Sunday paper's appeal. Circulation of the *Sunday World* passed the 250,000 mark in 1887, and by the early 1890s the paper had reached 40 to 48 pages in size as retail advertisers realized the extent of its readership by families and by women. Other newspapers were quick to follow suit, and in 1890 there were 250 dailies with Sunday editions, crowding the metropolitan areas and driving the independent Sunday weeklies out of the picture.

Heading the Sunday staff in the early years was Morrill Goddard, a college graduate who as a young city editor had shown ability to spot the feature angle of news events. But in the Sunday section Goddard jazzed up his page spreads, exaggerating the factual information to the point where serious news sources, particularly men of science and medicine, shied away. Sensationalism and pseudoscientific stories of this era greatly increased the credibility problem of newspapers, but the problem was ignored.

The installation of color presses in 1893 only gave Goddard another medium to exploit. As many as five colors could be used in the Sunday color supplement and included in it were the comic drawings that Goddard knew were most effective in spurring circulation. The *World* had started a regular comic section in 1889 and was the first to use color here (magazines had done so since the 1870s). The most successful of the artists was Richard F. Outcault, whose "Hogan's Alley" depicted life in the tenements. The central figure in each drawing was a toothless, grinning kid attired in a ballooning dress. When the *World*'s printers daubed a blob of yellow on the dress he became the immortal "Yellow Kid."

THE "YELLOW JOURNALISM" WAR

When William Randolph Hearst arrived on the New York scene he immediately set out to buy the men who were making the *Sunday World* a success. Using an office the *Examiner* had rented in the *World* building, he hired away Goddard and most of his staff of writers and artists. Hearst's lavish spending habits made Pulitzer's counteroffers hopeless. Soon even the *World*'s publisher, S. S. Carvalho, was working at the *Journal* building. The battle on, Pulitzer turned to Arthur Brisbane, Socialist Albert Brisbane's brilliant young son who had broken into newspaper work on the *Sun* before joining Pulitzer's staff. As the new Sunday editor, Brisbane drove the circulation to the 600,000 mark, popularizing the news and pushing hard on Pulitzer's social concerns. Goddard had taken Outcault and the "Yellow Kid" with him, but Brisbane used George B. Luks, later a well-known painter, to continue the cartoon.

Circulation men for both papers used posters featuring the happy-go-lucky, grinning kid with his curiously vacant features. To opposition journalists the "Yellow Kid" seemed symbolic of the kind of sensational journalism that was being practiced, and the public agreed. The phrase "yellow journalism" soon became widely used and its techniques the object of hard scrutiny. Unfortunately for Pulitzer, Brisbane moved over to the *Evening Journal* as editor in 1897 and Luks also joined Hearst. At this Outcault moaned:

"When I die don't wear yellow crepe, don't let them put a Yellow Kid on my tombstone and don't let the Yellow Kid himself come to my funeral. Make him stay over on the east side, where he belongs."[4]

Besides raiding Pulitzer's staff, Hearst moved in the best of his San Francisco staffers, including Chamberlain, McEwen, Davenport, and Annie Laurie. Dana's *Sun* lost its star reporters Julian Ralph, Richard Harding Davis, and Edward W. Townsend to Hearst's bankroll. Dorothy Dix joined the women's staff, and writers Stephen Crane, Alfred Henry Lewis, and Rudolph Block (Bruno Lessing) were signed, along with a host of other talented reporters, critics, and artists.

Two other events propelled Hearst into the thick of the fight with Pulitzer. In 1896, when the *Journal* reached the 150,000 mark as a one-cent paper, Pulitzer cut his price to a penny, gaining circulation but allowing speculation that he was afraid of his challenger. More importantly, Pulitzer, while in sympathy with many of William Jennings Bryan's ideas, could not support his inflationary monetary policies. But Hearst, as a silver mine owner, had no problem in arguing against the gold standard.

THE OPEN-AIR SCHOOL IN HOGAN'S ALLEY.

The "Yellow Kid," in his nightshirt, was an 1896 smash hit in the *New York World*.

Political partisans were attracted by Hearst's stand for Bryan in the conservative East where Bryan was looked upon with horror.

Frankly adopting the sins of yellow journalism, the *Journal* continued its surge in circulation figures. One jump of 125,000 came in a single month in the fall of 1896 when the following headlines were typical: "Real American Monsters and Dragons"— over a story of the discovery of fossil remains by an archaeological expedition; "A Marvellous New Way of Giving Medicine: Wonderful Results from Merely Holding Tubes of Drugs Near Entranced Patients"—a headline that horrified medical researchers; and "Henry James' New Novel of Immorality and Crime; The Surprising

Plunge of the Great Novelist in the Field of Sensational Fiction''—the *Journal*'s way of announcing publication of *The Other House*. Other headlines were more routinely sensational: ''The Mysterious Murder of Bessie Little,'' ''One Mad Blow Kills Child,'' ''What Made Him a Burglar? A Story of Real Life in New York by Edgar Saltus,'' ''Startling Confession of a Wholesale Murderer Who Begs to Be Hanged.'' Annie Laurie wrote about ''Why Young Girls Kill Themselves'' and ''Strange Things Women Do for Love.''[5]

The *Journal* was crusading, too, but it went beyond other New York newspapers in a manner that enabled it to shout, ''While Others Talk the Journal Acts.'' The paper obtained a court injunction that balked the granting of a city franchise to a gas company and, pleased by its success, it took similar actions against alleged abuses in government. Hearst then solicited compliments from civic leaders across the country and printed them under such headings as, ''Journalism that Acts; Men of Action in All Walks of Life Heartily Endorse the Journal's Fight in Behalf of the People '' and ''First Employed by the Journal, the Novel Concept Seems Likely to Become an Accepted Part of the Function of the Newspapers of This Country.''[6]

Before his first year in New York had ended, Hearst had installed large color presses at the *Journal,* added an eight-page colored comic section called *The American Humorist* and replaced that with a 16-page color supplement, *The Sunday American Magazine* (later, with Brisbane as editor, this was to become the famous *American Weekly*). In late 1896 the *Journal*'s daily circulation was 437,000 and on Sunday it was 380,000. Within a year the Sunday figures had reached the *World*'s 600,000. Circulation figures moved up and down, depending on the street sale appeal of the moment: on the day following the McKinley-Bryan election the *World* and *Journal* each sold approximately 1.5 million copies to break all records.

It was in this atmosphere that the leading papers scrambled for news around the nation and the world. And it was under these conditions that American papers approached the events that led to an international crisis and the Spanish-American War.

THE SPIRIT OF "MANIFEST DESTINY"   Of all the wars the United States has fought, the Spanish-American War was the most painless. But the results entirely changed the course of American foreign policy. In fewer than four months the Spanish government was forced to request an armistice, at an extraordinarily small cost in American lives, and the American flag floated over an empire stretching from Puerto Rico to the Philippines. Those who have sought to explain the causes of this unwarranted war often have centered the blame on William Randolph Hearst in particular and the newspapers of the country in general. Carefully documented studies made by Marcus M. Wilkerson and Joseph E. Wisan in the early 1930s gave ample proof that Hearst's *Journal*, Pulitzer's *World,* the *Chicago Tribune,* the *Sun,* and the *Herald* in New York (and as usually is ignored, many other American papers) so handled the news of events leading up to the crisis of the sinking of the *Maine* that a war psychosis was developed.[7] It must not be forgotten, however, that the newspapers were cultivating public opinion in a favorable atmosphere.

The policies of expansion being advocated were in line with those pursued throughout the nineteenth century. Americans in general subscribed to the belief in ''Manifest Destiny'' that spurred the westward movement. The War of 1812 was forced on a reluctant New England by western expansionists who viewed the British in Canada as mortal enemies. The Mexican War and cries of ''54-40 or Fight'' brought the completion of the continental United States. Americans liked to buy the territory they wanted, but now, as in the past, they were ready to take it by force if necessary.

When viewed in the long perspective, the Spanish-American War was but one in a series of incidents that marked the arrival of the United States as a world and, in particular, a Pacific power. With newly acquired Alaskan territory protecting one flank, Americans moved to gain a foothold in the Samoan Islands. Agitation began in the 1880s for the annexation of Hawaii. Then, with a new modern navy at his disposal, President Grover Cleveland brought his country to the verge of war with Great Britain over a test of the Monroe Doctrine in the Venezuelan crisis of 1895. This was followed by the annexation of Hawaii, the Philippines, Guam, and Puerto Rico, and the building of the Panama Canal. Interest in the Asian mainland brought about John Hay's Open Door Policy in 1899 and President Roosevelt's negotiation of the peace treaty ending the 1904–5 Russo-Japanese War in a little New Hampshire town. Pan-Americanism became open American intervention in the affairs of Central American countries, and Roosevelt took the United States into European affairs as well by participating in the 1905 Moroccan crisis that had been precipitated by German expansionism.

This desire to be a powerful participant in world affairs was not the only driving force behind the American expansion of interest. There was pride felt by many Americans in the addition of new territories and there was keen interest in the expansion of trade and foreign investments. But Americans also felt they had a role to play in promoting the idea of peace and justice in the world. There was widespread sympathy for those Cubans, Armenians, and Greeks who were fighting for their freedoms in the 1890s. Both idealism and national pride came into play during the Spanish-American War. If later the advocates of imperialism and "dollar diplomacy" won out over the idealists, that was but one phase of America's coming of age in international affairs.

Newspapers reflected this conflict in goals, reporting both atrocities committed by Spanish troops against Cuban insurrectionists and the chance for the new American navy to prove itself against Spain. But mainly there was a strong desire to flex the nation's muscles. As the memory of the Civil War faded, many older Americans wondered if their country's military prowess was still secure. Younger citizens were eager to match the exploits of the boys in Blue and Grey. For them, war, 1898 style, still seemed to be an exciting personal adventure. John D. Hicks, an American historian of first-rank who was not unaware of the role of the newspaper as an organ of public opinion, summed up his discussion of the causes of the Spanish-American War by saying:

> Years later, Theodore Roosevelt recaptured the spirit of 1898 when he mourned apologetically, "It wasn't much of a war, but it was the best war we had." America in the spring of 1898 was ripe for any war, and the country's mood was not to be denied.[8]

COVERING CUBAN NEWS, 1895–98   From March 1895, when the Cuban insurrection began, until April 1898, when Spain and the United States went to war, there were fewer than a score of days in which a story about Cuba did not appear in one of the New York newspapers.[9] This was due partly to the aggressive news policies of the big dailies, partly to the manufacturing of stories by some of the papers (notably the *Journal*), and partly to increasing reader interest in a controversial story. It was also the result of the activities of the Cuban junta that fed information and propaganda to American newsmen in New York and at the Florida news bases nearest the island.

A considerable number of Cubans had emigrated to the United States, settling in

New York, Philadelphia, Baltimore, Boston, and several Florida cities. The junta had its headquarters in New York, where a Cuban newspaper was published. Through the Cuban residents in the eastern cities, a program of mass meetings was established. Money was raised, and several hundred volunteers were obtained in each city for service in running arms and taking part in filibustering expeditions. Cuban agents funneled information on the progress of the fighting in Cuba to the American newspapers. The work was well underway in 1895, and as the crisis intensified, the activities of the junta reached greater heights. Ministers, educators, civic leaders, and politicians were reached by the junta.

The Spanish decision in 1896 to use strong repressive measures in Cuba brought Captain-General Valeriano Weyler into the news. All loyal Cubans were ordered to congregate in small areas adjoining Spanish bases, and those who did not were considered enemies. But those huddled in the camps quickly fell victim to epidemics and many starved to death when food supplies became disrupted. Much of the newspaper copy centered about the effects of famine and pestilence (approximately 110,000 Cubans died in the three years,[10] but newspaper estimates reached 400,000 as part of the exaggeration of these admittedly very serious conditions). Weyler was nicknamed the "Butcher" by American reporters and compared to the "bloodthirsty Cortez and Pizarro" of the days of the Conquistadors.

Competition for news became fierce. The Associated Press provided its own coverage and used information from stories printed by member papers.[11] The *Journal* and *World* led the way as papers with correspondents in Cuba sold their stories to other papers. Papers in competing situations fought to sign up as soon as a rival announced it had obtained *World, Journal, Sun, Herald,* or other "big league" coverage. Striving to keep ahead in every way was Hearst, who persuaded star reporter James Creelman to stop reporting for the *World* in 1896 and sent Richard Harding Davis and artist Frederic Remington to join him in Cuba. The impact of pictorial journalism increased in 1897 when New York papers began to use halftone photographs that sometimes were accurate portrayals of Cuban misery and sometimes were fakes. It also was during this time that Remington, according to Creelman's 1901 reminiscences, cabled Hearst that there would be no war and that he was coming home. Whereupon Hearst was supposed to have cabled back: "Remington, Havana. Please remain. You furnish the pictures, and I'll furnish the war. W. R. Hearst."[12] There is no evidence that Hearst actually sent this cable, so often quoted as conclusive evidence against him, but in a sense it reflected the situation. Of all the American papers, Hearst's *Journal* worked the hardest to create public sentiment for war. Episodes like this did much to tag him with "Hearst's war."

In the summer of 1897, after open advocacy of war for about a year and the sensationalizing of several minor incidents, the *Journal* built the story of Evangelina Cisneros into a daily chant for intervention. Miss Cisneros, a niece of the Cuban revolutionary president, had been sentenced to 20 years in prison for her rebellious activity. The *Journal* devoted an incredible number of news columns, 375, to the details of her condition and to her "rescue" by *Journal* reporter Karl Decker. Many notables congratulated the *Journal* on this achievement and Miss Cisneros was greeted by President McKinley on the White House lawn. Later it was discovered how other New York papers had treated this exciting but out-of-context story: *World,* twelve and one-half columns; *Times,* ten columns; *Tribune,* three and one-half columns; *Sun,* one column; *Herald,* one column.[13] During the incident, when the *World* published Weyler's account of Miss Cisneros' treatment—which had been exaggerated—the *Journal* accused Pulitzer of unpatriotic motives.

The *Journal*'s most significant "scoop" came on February 9, 1898, when Hearst published a private letter written by Dupuy de Lome, the Spanish ambassador to the United States, to a Spanish newspaper editor visiting in Havana. The letter, stolen in Havana by a Cuban junta member, referred to President McKinley as "weak and catering to the rabble, and besides, a low politician." At the same moment Theodore Roosevelt was commenting that his chief had the backbone of a chocolate eclair, but to have the Spanish ambassador say the same thing, even in a private letter, was a different matter. American opinion of the Spanish government hit a new low and six days later the *Maine* blew up in Havana harbor. The impact of the two events proved to be the turning point in the diplomatic crisis.

THE CORRESPONDENTS GO TO WAR

No one has satisfactorily established the cause of the explosion that sank the *Maine*, with the loss of 266 American lives. But some American newspapers set about making it appear that the Spanish were indirectly responsible for the sinking. The *Journal* offered a $50,000 reward for information leading to the arrest and conviction of the criminals, and three days later that paper's streamer read "THE WHOLE COUNTRY THRILLS WITH WAR FEVER." Large headlines and striking illustrations became common in big city papers. Leading the way was Brisbane, who experimented with artist-drawn headlines that virtually filled the front page with two or three words. Later that year Brisbane wrote:

> Before the type size reached its maximum, "War Sure" could be put in one line across a page, and it was put in one line and howled through the streets by patriotic newsboys many and many a time. As war was sure, it did no harm.[14]

Gradually the tide swung toward a declaration of war. Volunteer units such as the Rough Riders were formed, Congress passed a $50 million defense bill for war, and Secretary of State Sherman more than once made statements based on news reports from the *Journal*. In mid-March a leading Republican senator, Proctor of Vermont, made a speech based on his own trip to Cuba. He verified much of what had been published during the previous three years about deaths of Cubans, adding to the pressures on President McKinley to come out for war. The *World* at first urged caution in the handling of the *Maine* matter, but on April 10 Pulitzer published a signed editorial calling for a "short and sharp" war. Most of the nation agreed with this sentiment and Congress passed a war resolution on April 18.

The *New York Sun,* which under Dana's cynical editorship had been extremely jingoistic, stood with the *Journal* and *World* in demanding intervention. The *New York Herald,* while keeping up in sensational news coverage, opposed intervention in its editorial stands—an incongruity also true of the *Chicago Times-Herald, Boston Herald, San Francisco Chronicle,* and *Milwaukee Sentinel.* Strongly interventionist were such papers as the *Chicago Tribune, New Orleans Times-Democrat, Atlanta Constitution,* and *Indianapolis Journal.* Keeping calm were such papers as the *New York Tribune, New York Times, Chicago Daily News, Boston Transcript,* and other papers that reflected the thinking of the business community in their editorial columns. Wilkerson, in his study of the newspapers for the period, ranks the *Journal* as the leader in excessive journalism, and the *Chicago Tribune* and the *World* next in order. Joseph Medill's *Tribune,* strongly nationalistic in its editorial columns, did not originate sensational news stories as did the *Journal* and *World,* but it ran the cream of those collected by both papers.

$50,000 REWARD.—WHO DESTROYED THE MAINE?—$50,000 REWARD.

EDITION FOR GREATER NEW YORK

NEW YORK JOURNAL

AND ADVERTISER.

The Journal will give $50,000 for information, furnished to it exclusively, that will convict the person or persons who sank the Maine.

The Journal will give $50,000 for information, furnished to it exclusively, that will convict the person or persons who sank the Maine.

NO. 5,572. Copyright, 1898, by W. R. Hearst—NEW YORK, THURSDAY, FEBRUARY 17, 1898.—16 PAGES. PRICE ONE CENT In Greater New York, Elsewhere, and Jersey City. TWO CENTS.

DESTRUCTION OF THE WAR SHIP MAINE WAS THE WORK OF AN ENEMY.

$50,000!

$50,000 REWARD!
For the Detection of the
Perpetrator of
the Maine Outrage!

The New York Journal hereby offers a reward of **$50,000 CASH** for information, **FURNISHED TO IT EXCLUSIVELY**, which shall lead to the detection and conviction of the person, persons or government criminally responsible for the explosion which resulted in the destruction, at Havana, of the United States war ship Maine and the loss of 258 lives of American sailors.

The **$50,000 CASH** offered for the above information is on deposit with Wells, Fargo & Co.

No one is barred, be he the humble but misguided seaman, acting out a few miserable dollars by acting as a spy, or the attache of a government secret service, plotting, by any devilish means, to revenge frenzied insults or cripple menacing countries.

This offer has been cabled to Europe and will be made public in every capital of the Continent and in London this morning.

The Journal believes that any man who can be bought to commit murder can also be bought to betray his comrades. **FOR THE PERPETRATOR OF THIS OUTRAGE HAD ACCOMPLICES.**

W. R. HEARST.

Assistant Secretary Roosevelt Convinced the Explosion of the War Ship Was Not an Accident.

The Journal Offers $50,000 Reward for the Conviction of the Criminals Who Sent 258 American Sailors to Their Death. Naval Officers Unanimous That the Ship Was Destroyed on Purpose.

$50,000!

$50,000 REWARD!
For the Detection of the
Perpetrator of
the Maine Outrage!

The New York Journal hereby offers a reward of **$50,000 CASH** for information, **FURNISHED TO IT EXCLUSIVELY**, which shall lead to the detection and conviction of the person, persons or government criminally responsible for the explosion which resulted in the destruction, at Havana, of the United States war ship Maine and the loss of 258 lives of American sailors.

The **$50,000 CASH** offered for the above information is on deposit with Wells, Fargo & Co.

No one is barred, be he the humble, but misguided, seaman, eking out a few miserable dollars by acting as a spy, or the attache of a government secret service, plotting by any devilish means, to revenge fancied insults or cripple menacing countries.

This offer has been cabled to Europe and will be made public in every capital of the Continent and in London this morning.

The Journal believes that any man who can be bought to commit murder can also be bought to betray his comrades. **FOR THE PERPETRATOR OF THIS OUTRAGE HAD ACCOMPLICES.**

W. R. HEARST.

POWDER MAGAZINE

MINE

WIRE

NAVAL OFFICERS THINK THE MAINE WAS DESTROYED BY A SPANISH MINE.

George Eugene Bryson, the Journal's special correspondent at Havana, cables that it is the secret opinion of many Spaniards in the Cuban capital that the Maine was destroyed and 258 of her men killed by means of a submarine mine, or fixed torpedo. This is the opinion of several American naval authorities. The Spaniards, it is believed, arranged to have the Maine anchored over one of the harbor mines. Wires connected the mine with a powder magazine, and it is thought the explosion was caused by sending an electric current through the wire. If this can be proven, the brutal nature of the Spaniards will be shown by the fact that they waited to spring the mine until after all the men had retired for the night. The Maltese cross in the picture shows where the mine may have been fired.

Hidden Mine or a Sunken Torpedo Believed to Have Been the Weapon Used Against the American Man-of-War---Officers and Men Tell Thrilling Stories of Being Blown Into the Air Amid a Mass of Shattered Steel and Exploding Shells---Survivors Brought to Key West Scout the Idea of Accident---Spanish Officials Protest Too Much---Our Cabinet Orders a Searching Inquiry---Journal Sends Divers to Havana to Report Upon the Condition of the Wreck.
Was the Vessel Anchored Over a Mine?

BY CAPTAIN F. L. ZALINSKI, U. S. A.

(Captain Zalinski is the inventor of the famous dynamite gun, which would be the principal factor in our coast defence in case of war.)

Assistant Secretary of the Navy Theodore Roosevelt says he is convinced that the destruction of the Maine in Havana Harbor was not an accident. The Journal offers a reward of $50,000 for exclusive evidence that will convict the person, persons or Government criminally responsible for the destruction of the American battle ship and the death of 258 of its crew.

The suspicion that the Maine was deliberately blown up grows stronger every hour. Not a single fact to the contrary has been produced.

Captain Sigsbee, of the Maine, and Consul-General Lee both urge that public opinion be suspended until they have completed their investigation. They are taking the course of tactful men who are convinced that there has been treachery.

Washington reports very late that Captain Sigsbee had feared some such event as a hidden mine. The English cipher code was used all day yesterday by the naval officers in cabling instead of the usual American code.

Hearst's *Journal* for February 17. The *Maine* sank the night of February 15.

It should be pointed out that the *World* was not a jingo newspaper. Pulitzer had opposed the annexation of Hawaii and did not support President Cleveland in the 1895 Venezuelan crisis, when most major papers warned the United States would fight to uphold Venezuela's boundary claims with British Guiana. During the Cuban crisis the *World* did not stand for the annexation of foreign lands and opposed the taking of the

MAINE EXPLOSION CAUSED BY BOMB OR TORPEDO?

Capt. Sigsbee and Consul-General Lee Are in Doubt---The World Has Sent a Special Tug, With Submarine Divers, to Havana to Find Out---Lee Asks for an Immediate Court of Inquiry---260 Men Dead.

IN A SUPPRESSED DESPATCH TO THE STATE DEPARTMENT, THE CAPTAIN SAYS THE ACCIDENT WAS MADE POSSIBLE BY AN ENEMY.

Dr. E. C. Pendleton, Just Arrived from Havana, Says He Overheard Talk There of a Plot to Blow Up the Ship---Capt. Zalinski, the Dynamite Expert, and Other Experts Report to The World that the Wreck Was Not Accidental---Washington Officials Ready for Vigorous Action if Spanish Responsibility Can Be Shown---Divers to Be Sent Down to Make Careful Examinations.

DRAWN FROM A DESCRIPTION BY EYE-WITNESSES ON THE STEAMSHIP CITY OF WASHINGTON WHO SAW THE EXPLOSION, FOLLOWED BY "A VOLCANO OF FIRE AND SHOWERS OF BOATS, BODIES, IRON AND GUNS," CABLED TO THE WORLD BY ITS OWN CORRESPONDENT IN HAVANA, SYLVESTER SCOVEL.

The *World*'s February 17 front page, somewhat more cautious than that of the *Journal*.

Philippine Islands. The *World* based its call for war on the issue of human liberty and in subsequent actions proved it was not merely jingoistic. Pulitzer later regretted the role the *World* played in preparing public opinion for killing and in 1907, when Theodore Roosevelt ordered the American fleet to the Pacific to impress Japan, Pulitzer requested that his editors ''show that Spain had granted to Cuba all that we had demanded . . . Give further details of jingoism causing Cuban War after Spain had virtually granted everything.''[15]

But in 1898 only Godkin's *Evening Post,* among the New York dailies, held out to the end against yellow journalism and the decision to force Spain from Cuba. Lashing out against Hearst and Pulitzer, he bitterly attacked with statements like this:

A yellow journal office is probably the nearest approach, in atmosphere, to hell, existing in any Christian state. A better place in which to prepare a young man for eternal damnation than a yellow journal office does not exist.[16]

The newspapers fought the war as determinedly as they had fostered it. Some 500 reporters, artists, and photographers flocked to Florida, where the American army was mobilizing, and to the Cuban and Puerto Rican fronts.[17] Small fleets of press boats accompanied the Navy into action. Correspondents sailed with Dewey to Manila and with Schley to Havana. They covered every battle and skirmish in Cuba and more than once took part in the fighting itself. A *Journal* correspondent lost a leg during one fighting charge. Richard Harding Davis, then reporting for the *New York Herald* and the *Times* of London, led another charge and won the praise of Rough Rider Roosevelt.

Leading the *Journal*'s contingent was the publisher himself, who exuded enthusiasm as he directed the work of his staff of 20 men and women reporters, artists, and photographers, including a motion picture man. Creelman, who was wounded in one battle, records a picture of Hearst—wearing a beribboned straw hat on his head and a revolver at his belt—taking the story from his bleeding reporter and then galloping away on horseback to get to a *Journal* press boat.

American correspondents were learning how to use the boats and cables to speed their messages to the news offices. Stories from Cuba had to be brought to Key West for transmission to New York, with leading papers sending several thousand words a day. All this was expensive, but the race for news was an exciting one. The *World* scored the biggest single beat when Edward W. Harden, one of three correspondents to witness Dewey's amazing victory in Manila Bay, got his story off first by paying the "urgent" priority rate of $9.90 a word. Harden's beat arrived in New York too far into the dawn for the *World* to capitalize on it with a full-blown extra, but the *World*'s news client, the *Chicago Tribune*, had time to revamp its final edition and carry the most dramatic story of the war.

While Hearst said he did not care how much all of this cost (his paper spent $500,000 during the four months and put out as many as 40 extras in one day), Pulitzer began to view the situation with dismay. The *Journal* gleefully asked in its front-page ears, "How do you like the *Journal*'s war? " while Pulitzer began to retreat. In the end, Pulitzer withdrew from the competition in sensationalism at the turn of the century, while Hearst continued to exploit the news in a manner that seriously impeded the effectiveness of his role as a people's champion. By 1900, about one-third of metropolitan dailies were following the yellow trend, and it was another ten years before the wave of sensationalism subsided and journalists concentrated on the more intelligent use of headlines, pictures, and color printing.

NOTES

1. Will Irwin, "The Fourth Current," *Collier's,* XLVI (February 18, 1911), 14.
2. Ibid. Estimate by Will Irwin in 1911, for the period up to then.
3. Ferdinand Lundberg, *Imperial Hearst: A Social Biography* (New York: Equinox Cooperative Press, 1936), p. 50. Lundberg presents much information about Hearst's finances but paints the publisher in the blackest possible fashion. For the best balanced accounts see John Tebbel, *The Life and Good Times of William Randolph Hearst* (New York: Dutton, 1952), and W. A. Swanberg, *Citizen Hearst* (New York: Scribner's, 1961).
4. *New York World,* May 1, 1898, p. 7 (supplement).

5. Willard G. Bleyer, *Main Currents in the History of American Journalism* (Boston: Houghton Mifflin, 1927), pp. 357–64. This book documents the case against the *Journal*'s rampant yellow journalism.

6. William Rockhill Nelson, editor of the *Kansas City Star*, also had used his own funds to fight court battles in behalf of the public interest, but not so sensationally.

7. Marcus M. Wilkerson, *Public Opinion and the Spanish-American War* (Baton Rouge: Louisiana State University Press, 1932); Joseph E. Wisan, *The Cuban Crisis as Reflected in the New York Press* (New York: Columbia University Press, 1934).

8. John D. Hicks, *A Short History of American Democracy* (Boston: Houghton Mifflin, 1943), p. 605.

9. Wisan, *The Cuban Crisis*, p. 460.

10. *Public Opinion and the Spanish-American War*, p. 40.

11. There was competition between the Associated Press and the old United Press until 1897. After that time, all the major New York papers except the *Sun* were AP members.

12. James Creelman, *On the Great Highway* (Boston: Lothrop Publishing Company, 1901), p. 178.

13. Wisan, *The Cuban Crisis*, p. 331.

14. Arthur Brisbane, "The Modern Newspaper in War Time," *Cosmopolitan*, XXV (September, 1898), 541.

15. Don C. Seitz, *Joseph Pulitzer* (New York: Simon & Schuster, 1924), p. 312.

16. Wisan, *The Cuban Crisis*, p. 417.

17. Their story is told by Charles H. Brown in *The Correspondents' War* (New York: Scribner's, 1967).

ANNOTATED BIBLIOGRAPHY

Books

BEISNER, ROBERT L., *Twelve Against Empire: The Anti-Imperialists, 1898–1900*. New York: McGraw-Hill, 1968. Two of the twelve were Godkin and Schurz.

BLEYER, WILLARD G., *Main Currents in the History of American Journalism*. Boston: Houghton Mifflin, 1927. The chapter on Hearst admirably documents charges of sensationalism.

BROWN, CHARLES H., *The Correspondents' War*. New York: Scribner's, 1967. All the details of the press corps for the Spanish-American War.

CARLSON, OLIVER, *Brisbane: A Candid Biography*. New York: Stackpole Sons, 1937. A good critical analysis of the famous Hearst editor.

CARLSON, OLIVER, AND ERNEST SUTHERLAND BATES, *Hearst, Lord of San Simeon*. New York: Viking, 1936. Better than other early biographies by John K. Winkler and Mrs. Fremont Older. Still useful for the early Hearst period, but supplanted by Tebbel and Swanberg (see below).

DAVIS, RICHARD HARDING, *Notes of a War Correspondent*. New York: Scribner's, 1910. An American war correspondent in Cuba, Greece, South Africa, and Manchuria, covering four wars.

LUNDBERG, FERDINAND, *Imperial Hearst: A Social Biography*. New York: Equinox Cooperative Press, 1936. A bitter attack on the chain publisher; valuable particularly for financial data.

MERK, FREDERICK, *Manifest Destiny and Mission in American History: A Reinterpretation*. New York: Knopf, 1963. Newspapers document the story of the westward march.

MILLIS, WALTER, *The Martial Spirit; a Study of Our War with Spain*. Boston: Houghton Mifflin, 1931. A readable, critical account.

O'CONNOR, RICHARD, *Pacific Destiny: An Informal History of the U.S. in the Far East*. Boston: Little, Brown, 1969. Thesis is that America moved from Atlantic to Pacific role through deep desires and motives of political, military, and religious leaders at pivotal moments, from Commodore Perry's time to Vietnam. Detailed treatment of Philippine Insurrection.

SWANBERG, W. A., *Citizen Hearst*. New York: Scribner's, 1961. A highly readable study, covering available printed sources in meticulous detail; has some new material.

TEBBEL, JOHN, *The Life and Good Times of William Randolph Hearst*. New York: Dutton, 1952. A well-balanced biography and the best documented study of the Hearst newspaper empire.

WILKERSON, MARCUS M., *Public Opinion and the Spanish-American War*. Baton Rouge: Louisiana State University Press, 1932. A scholarly study of war propaganda and press influence.

WISAN, JOSEPH E., *The Cuban Crisis as Reflected in the New York Press*. New York: Columbia University Press, 1934. A good specialized study.

Periodicals and Monographs

BERG, MEREDITH AND DAVID, "The Rhetoric of War Preparation: The New York Press in 1898," *Journalism Quarterly*, XLV (Winter 1968), 653. Analysis of New York dailies after sinking of the *Maine*.

BRISBANE, ARTHUR, "The Modern Newspaper in War Time," *Cosmopolitan*, XXV (September 1898), 541. The *Journal* editor confesses his sins. See also his "Yellow Journalism," *Bookman*, XIX (June 1904), 400.

BROWN, CHARLES H., "Press Censorship in the Spanish-American War," *Journalism Quarterly*, XLII (Autumn 1965), 581. It was more extensive and effective than believed.

COMMANDER, LYDIA K., "The Significance of Yellow Journalism," *Arena*, XXXIV (August 1905), 150. A contemporary analysis.

DONALD, ROBERT, "Sunday Newspapers in the United States," *Universal Review*, VIII (September 1890), 79. A look at a then-new medium.

HACHTEN, WILLIAM A., "The Metropolitan Sunday Newspaper in the United States: A Study of Trends in Content and Practices," Ph.D. thesis, University of Minnesota, 1960 (Ann Arbor: University Microfilms, 1960). The most complete study of the Sunday paper.

IRWIN, WILL, "The American Newspaper," *Collier's*, XLVI (February 18 and March 4, 1911). The sins of yellow journalism described.

MOTT, FRANK L., "The First Sunday Paper: A Footnote to History," *Journalism Quarterly*, XXXV (Fall 1958), 443. The *Boston Globe*.

PETERS, GLEN W., "The *American Weekly*," *Journalism Quarterly*, XLVIII (Autumn 1971), 466. A review of the Sunday supplements, especially Hearst's.

STEFFENS, LINCOLN, "Hearst, the Man of Mystery," *American Magazine*, LXIII (November 1906), 3. Penetrating study based on interviews of Hearst, rarely obtained.

VANDERBURG, RAY, "The Paradox That Was Arthur Brisbane," *Journalism Quarterly*, XLVII (Summer 1970), 281. Study of the great Hearst editor.

ZOBRIST, BENEDICT KARL, "How Victor Lawson's Newspapers Covered the Cuban War of 1898," *Journalism Quarterly*, XXXVIII (Summer 1961), 323. The non-sensational *Chicago Record* and *Daily News*.

Edward Wyllis Scripps aboard his yacht near the close of his career.

18
The People's Champions

I have only one principle, and that is represented by an effort to make it harder for the rich to grow richer and easier for the poor to keep from growing poorer.

—Edward Wyllis Scripps

The opening of the twentieth century found the United States moving toward a consolidation of its position as an industrial nation. The framework had been completed by 1900: the economic expansion that had begun after the Civil War, the growth in population and the tying together of the country, the rapid development of rich natural resources, the inventive and productive genius, the political and cultural advances—all ensured the future of a new world power.

Vital contests still were in progress, however, that would affect the character of the new America. These contests assumed critical importance at a moment when the economic, political, and social trends of a new era were being shaped. How would the nation conduct itself in the world community? How democratic would it remain? Would there be a balance struck between the advocates of unrestricted economic individualism and the crusaders for social justice? Would the fruits of progress be shared by all the people, in the form of better living conditions, educational and cultural opportunities, higher health standards, and personal security? Would government be responsive to the general welfare? What was to be the role of the press in advancing or retarding necessary adjustments?

Men and women had struggled to obtain affirmative answers to these questions now confronting America since the industrial revolution changed the character of American society. The "consistent rebellion" in the agricultural areas against economic inequities represented one phase of the struggle; the rise of the labor unions in the cities another. The growth of strong political movements that sought to place more power in the hands of the people generally; the efforts of the social scientists to impart knowledge on which wise social and political decisions could be based; the appeals of reformers, agitators, political leaders, and writers for an arousing of the country's social conscience—all these had helped to shape the direction in which the country would turn.

But in the first years of the new century there were major divisions of thought and action that indicated the crucial importance of the struggle to shape public opinion, and to enforce the popular will. Nationalists and internationalists contended in the field of foreign affairs. Economic individualists and social reformers clashed in the domestic arena. The mass media of the times—newspapers, magazines, books—played a most important role in these national debates.

THE TRIUMPH OF "MANIFEST DESTINY"

The generally enthusiastic public response to America's aggressive policy toward Spain in the Caribbean provided the proponents of Manifest Destiny with an excuse for gaining supremacy over as much of Asia as military power could sustain. They included politicians led by Theodore Roosevelt and Henry Cabot Lodge, historian Brooks Adams, evangelist the Reverend Josiah Strong, railroad builder James J. Hill, naval strategist Alfred T. Mahan, entrepreneurs like the American-China Development Company, influential newspaper publishers and editors of rural farm journals, and extremely vocal representatives of the powerful farm bloc, such as Senator William V. Allen of Nebraska.

These leaders, agitating on behalf of Americans of all political faiths, generated the ideas and emotions that resulted in the bloody annexation of the Philippine Islands, the capstone of this nation's relentless drive to be a Pacific rather than an Atlantic power. It also was the propellant for future Asian conflicts. Promises made to insurgent leader Emilio Aguinaldo that American force would guarantee Philippine independence after the overthrow of remaining Spanish troops and friendly Philippine bases would be used for expanded trade with Japan were not kept. Instead, the United States signaled her determination to become a full-fledged colonial power in East Asia, lured on by the mirage of China as a land of vast and lucrative markets where the surplus crops of America's great middlelands could be sold.

This military adventure, which left the United States with an exposed strategic commitment along the axis of Japan's southern expansion, was a colossal blunder that would lead to three more wars in American history. Dewey's victory at Manila had been part of the short but rather exciting 1898 public experience, but the guerrilla war in the Philippines between 1899 and 1902 was, in the words of historian Richard O'Connor, a quickly forgotten "dreary sequel" to the Spanish-American War.[1] At the peak of the fighting approximately 70,000 U.S. troops—fed with notions of racial and religious superiority—were used to brutally crush the insurgency. Horrifying cruelties practiced on Filipino soldiers and massacres of civilians brought the total death count to an estimated 200,000 (American losses were about 10,000). Fighting against the Moros in the southern Philippines continued until World War I, as America strove to subjugate a determined native population. Ironically, as part of this generally confused foreign policy, the United States sent thousands of volunteers to help reconstruct buildings, teach English, and fight disease.

Half a million Americans joined the Anti-Imperialist League that had been founded in Boston. In actions to be repeated years later in protests against the war in Vietnam, they participated in mass meetings, marches, sit-ins, and teach-ins, all the time pressuring their elected representatives against formal annexation of the islands. A bitter Senate debate featured the elderly George F. Hoar of Massachusetts, who tried to awaken his colleagues by telling of concentration camps, burned villages, and the use of the water-cure torture, against Albert J. Beveridge of Indiana, a leader of the Senate expansionists.

Carl Schurz, who in an 1893 *Harper's* article had insisted America could obtain economic objectives "without taking those countries into our national household,"[2] was joined in the anti-imperialist movement by Jane Addams, Andrew Carnegie, William James, Samuel Gompers, Samuel Clemens, and other influential citizens. Clemens wrote that a new American flag should be designed with the white stripes painted black, and the stars replaced by a skull and crossbones. But much of the dissent was drowned out by the thunder of newspapermen like "Marse" Henry Watterson of the *Louisville Courier-Journal*, who bluntly spoke for many when he said, "We escape the menace and peril of socialism and agrarianism, as England has escaped them, by a policy of colonialism and conquest . . . we risk Caesarism, certainly, but Caesarism is preferable to anarchism."[3] Those were not the only choices, but many Americans pursued this all-or-nothing approach in an effort to become dominant in new market areas.

Closer to home and part of this hot-blooded American spirit, the Panama Canal had been built in an occupied zone that Columbia complained had been torn from her by an American-backed revolution. This action, and the extension of American military and economic domination in the Central American and Caribbean areas, dissipated hopes for Pan-American understanding. Cuba and Panama virtually became American protectorates under the Platt amendment. The Dominican Republic, Haiti, and Nicaragua in turn were forced to accept United States intervention in their affairs under the Roosevelt corollary to the Monroe Doctrine, by which the United States undertook to preserve order in those countries and administer their financial affairs to prevent any possible intervention by European powers. The primary intent was to assure American security in a vital area, but American trade and financial interests followed the flag—and many persons complained that they sometimes preceded it.

At the same time, however, there were powerful forces in operation that sought to commit America to a quite different role in world affairs. Cultural and religious ties were made with China after the Boxer Rebellion. The Philippines were promised their eventual independence after a period of tutelage. Roosevelt himself acted as a mediator in helping to end the Russo-Japanese War and in smoothing relations among Germany, France, and Britain at the Algeciras conference. The United States accepted the idea of an international court of arbitration, advanced at The Hague Peace Conference of 1899, and negotiated several arbitration treaties. Americans played a leading part in the unsuccessful attempt to create an international court of justice during the second conference at The Hague in 1907. Out of these movements came American leadership in proposing the League of Nations and the World Court at the close of World War I—proposals most of the other nations of the world adopted only to see the United States slump back into isolationism.

THE CRISIS OF ECONOMIC POWER

Important as was this contest over foreign policy, it was not the major concern of the American people in the years around the turn of the century. Their attention was centered largely on domestic problems created by the industrial revolution: the growth of trusts and centralization of economic power in a few hands; the inadequate incomes of the workingman and farmer; corruption and inadequacies in political and business life. To many Americans it seemed that national wealth and strength, while reflecting basic progress for all the people, actually were mainly benefiting a plundering few who were usurping the freedoms of the many.[4]

Concentration of economic power, which had begun to develop rapidly in the 1880s, was greatly accentuated after 1900. A study made in 1904 listed 318 industrial trusts, three-fourths of which had been incorporated since 1898. These 318 trusts, capitalized at $7 billion, represented the merging of 5,300 individuals' companies. Six big trusts—in steel, oil, copper, sugar, tobacco, and shipping—that had been organized in those six years were capitalized at $2.5 billion. Census figures show that in 1914 one-eighth of American businesses employed more than three-fourths of the wage earners and produced four-fifths of the manufactured products.

The newspaper and magazine editors and the reporters and writers who joined in protesting this economic monopoly were even more concerned with the seemingly insatiable appetite of capitalists for power. Those who won domination in one field promptly reached out into other spheres, until the country's financial power fell largely into the hands of two loosely organized groups, the Morgan and the Rockefeller interests and their satellites. The famous Pujo committee investigation in 1913 reported that four allied financial institutions in New York held 341 directorships in banks, railroads, shipping lines, insurance companies, public utilities, and other businesses with total resources of $22 billion.

Distribution of the wealth being created was heavily one-sided. Two-thirds of the male adult workers failed to earn $600 a year in wages, which was the figure set by sociologists as the minimum needed to maintain decent standards at the current cost of living. There were many material and social advances being made—electricity, gas, and plumbing in homes; better schools and parks; the conveniences of city life; telephones, railroads, and highways. But they did not mean much to the millions in the New York tenements whose plight had been reported on by Jacob Riis.

Labor union membership increased between 1900 and 1910, jumping from 3.5 percent of all workers to 7 percent. The gains were being made by skilled workers: the railway brotherhoods, building trades, machinists, miners, printing trades, and garment workers groups. Unskilled workers, women workers, and immigrants remained victims of the economic order. Immigrants were a major factor in creating the social problem. The flood of immigrants of the period 1880 to 1900 was equaled in the single decade 1900 to 1910. The great bulk of the new immigration was from southern and eastern Europe, and a fourth of those arriving were illiterate. By 1910 one-seventh of the United States population was foreign-born, and in the industrial East more than half the population was foreign-born or of foreign-born parentage. These were the "poor and ill-informed" who were to be championed by such newspaper publishers as Edward Wyllis Scripps.

DEMANDS FOR POLITICAL AND ECONOMIC REFORM
Despite the fact that these conditions inevitably demanded reform, the "quest for social justice" was slow. Eugene V. Debs did see his Socialist party win nearly a million votes in the presidential election of 1912, and some 300 cities and towns elected Socialist officeholders. In the labor movement William D. Haywood and his Industrial Workers of the World sought a radical approach to the plight of the unskilled laborer. But political leadership remained in the hands of the two major political parties,[5] and most labor followed the moderate program of Samuel Gompers and his American Federation of Labor.

The instruments for political action on the national level were Theodore Roosevelt's "Square Deal" and Woodrow Wilson's "New Freedom." But the decisions these two administrations won in the fields of monetary reform, government regulation of business, welfare legislation, and tariff revision stemmed from the spirit of the times. This spirit was reflected in various forms by the agitation of the Populists, the great crusade headed by William Jennings Bryan in 1896, the governmental reforms being proposed by Robert La Follette and his individualistic Wisconsin progressives, the work of the labor union leaders, and the thinking and writing of the intellectuals.

In the Roosevelt years the winning of an antitrust suit against the Northern Securities Company, preventing a monopoly of railroad transportation west of the Mississippi, turned the tide against extreme concentration of economic power. The Hepburn Act brought effective government regulation of transportation rates. And Roosevelt's conservation policies saved a sizable residue of America's natural resources from ruthless exploitation. In the Wilson administration the creation of the Federal Reserve banking system brought a modern currency and credit system to the country for the first time; the Clayton Act struck at the abusive use of court injunctions and contempt citations against striking labor unions; the Federal Trade Commission was given power to regulate unfair business practices; and in other areas government extended its influence to a greater degree than ever before in American history.

But the progress being made, while substantial, was often balked by the supporters of big business. Senators like Nelson Aldrich of Rhode Island were frank spokesmen for the conservative cause and they had great influence. Congressmen like George Norris of Nebraska could clip the wings of House Speaker Joe Cannon, a powerful ally of the big-business forces, but they nevertheless lost many battles to their conservative opposition. William Howard Taft, succeeding Roosevelt as president, was unable to cope with the big-business elements of his Republican party, and an irate Roosevelt launched his third party Progressive movement in 1912. The Bull Moose crusade failed, but it split the Republican party so thoroughly that Woodrow Wilson entered the White House with a minority of the popular vote to inaugurate a Democratic administration.

Many of the gains were made at state and local levels. Popular election of United States senators, presidential primaries, and adoption of the referendum, initiative, and recall were manifestations of the new trend. State laws protecting working women and children, regulating hours of work, providing for workmen's compensation, and advancing social security generally ran the gauntlet of unfavorable court decisions. In the cities, reform movements led by such men as Samuel M. Jones in Toledo, Tom Johnson and Newton D. Baker in Cleveland, Seth Low in New York, and the advocates of commission government in Galveston did yeoman work in restoring governmental decency. Corruption in municipal councils and in state legislatures was a common mark of the times, and newspaper editors who wished to join with the reformers had almost unbelievable instances of bribe-taking and graft to expose.

"THE PEOPLE'S CHAMPIONS"   The crusading spirit is as old as journalism, but never in American history had there been more opportunity for "the people's champions" than in these years following 1900. Voices of protest were raised in colonial days by men like James Franklin and Samuel Adams, in the early years of the republic by Jeffersonian and Jacksonian editors, by the creators of the first mass press before the Civil War, by the leaders of the "new journalism" before the close of the century. The struggle between big business and workers and farmers was as old as the struggle between the Hamiltonians and Jeffersonians for control of the government. The battle for the rights of labor and for a more equitable distribution of wealth was a basic issue of similar standing. And warring on corruption in city governments had been a job for conscientious newspapermen since the rise of urban life. In the ebb and flow of these contests, however, the years following 1900 became critical ones.

Some newspapers were conspicuous in their response to the challenge. So were some of the new popular magazines, which became important vehicles for those whom Teddy Roosevelt eventually termed the "muckrakers." And the school of realistic writers that flowered at the turn of the century added important books to the American literature that dealt with life and problems of the day. Joining hands with politicians and labor leaders, reformers and agitators, professors and ministers, social workers and philanthropists, the men and women of journalism and literature helped to shape the course of the great crusade.

PULITZER'S CRUSADES IN THE *WORLD*

Joseph Pulitzer and his *New York World* became increasingly effective as "people's champions" in the years following the Spanish-American War. In foreign affairs the *World* vigorously opposed the annexation of the Philippines and the imperialism of the Caribbean policy. It continued to support the internationalist movement and the policy of peaceful arbitration of the world's problems, which it had espoused during the Venezuelan crisis. In domestic politics, this stand of the *World* on foreign policy led it to support William Jennings Bryan for president in 1900 on an "anti-imperialism" platform, ignoring Bryan's radical monetary policies, which Pulitzer disliked.

The independent qualities and the crusading spirit of the *World* reached new heights, both on local and national issues. This was not a sudden manifestation of interest in crusading, as in the case of some other newspapers of the period, but a flowering of the Pulitzer editorial-page philosophy. Pulitzer, while agreeing that the *World* was Democrat in political sympathy, argued that his newspaper was independent of party and supported only those elements in a political party whose objectives coincided with those of the *World*. In looking at the major political parties of his day, Pulitzer put little trust in a Republican party with strong elements representing the big-business interests of the country, although he admired and supported Republican insurgents who fought to break the power of Speaker Cannon or Republican candidates of the caliber of Governor Charles Evans Hughes of New York. Pulitzer decided that the Democratic party best represented the political philosophy in which he believed and was most likely to act as the defender of individual liberties, grass-roots government, and progressive democracy.

Part of the *World*'s new strength in its editorial columns was the result of a revamping of its editorial-page staff. In 1904 the ailing Pulitzer, tortured by the acute nervous disorders that made the last few years of his life a nightmare, found a brilliant young editor who was destined to become the central force of the *World*'s editorial page. His name was Frank I. Cobb.

Cobb was then 35, a veteran of 15 years' newspaper experience who had been for four years the chief editorial writer for the *Detroit Free Press*. His somewhat limited formal education had been greatly supplemented by his scholarly interest and wide reading in the fields of history, government, and philosophy, and by his experiences as a newspaper reporter and as a political correspondent. Cobb early had demonstrated the maturity of his judgment and his great intellectual capacity, but he was also a man who understood human nature and who attracted others to him by his friendliness, his eagerness, and his enthusiasm for living.[6] Within a year he had become the recognized chief editorial writer who would succeed to the editorship in 1911 on Pulitzer's death.

The most famous of all the *World*'s crusades began the same year, 1905. A battle had developed for control of the management of the Equitable Life Assurance Society, one of the life insurance companies that had built up great financial resources as Americans took up the purchase of policies and benefits to provide for their personal and family security. Evidence was presented by two *World* reporters, David Ferguson and Louis Seibold, that officials of the company were using funds paid in by policyholders for their own private investments and thereby were building huge personal fortunes—gambling with the people's money, the *World* said. Other editors, like Ervin Wardman of the *New York Press*, joined in the battle and the spotlight was turned on the Mutual Life and New York Life companies as well.

Demand rose for an investigation by a legislative committee. Its counsel was Charles Evans Hughes, a young and forceful attorney who documented the case against the insurance companies. He also substantiated the *World*'s charges that the company had maintained a large fund of money to bribe legislators. The specter of the "money interests" dominating the life insurance companies so aroused public opinion that strict regulatory legislation was enacted in New York State. Hughes rode into the governorship in 1906.

HEARST EXPANDS HIS ROLE

While the *World* was thus rising to greatness, its chief competitor for mass circulation in New York was just as determinedly making a claim to leadership as "the people's champion." William Randolph Hearst, having seen the country start toward annexation of the Philippines and Hawaii, the development of military bases in the Caribbean, and the adoption of other nationalistic policies advocated by the *New York Journal*, turned his attention to domestic affairs. In early 1899 he set forth an editorial platform calling for public ownership of public franchises, the "destruction of criminal trusts," a graduated income tax, election of United States senators by popular vote rather than by state legislatures, and national, state, and local improvement of the public school system. Soon Hearst was urging that the coal mines, railroads, and telegraph lines—the symbols of the new industrial era—all be nationalized. And he gave strong encouragement to labor unions.

Not only was this a more radical program than that of the *World* and other liberal newspapers of the day, but also the impact of Hearst's editorial technique was bitter and extreme. In the presidential campaign of 1900, Homer Davenport's cartoons depicting President McKinley as the stooge of a Mark Hanna wearing a suit made of dollar signs were crude but effective. When President McKinley was fatally wounded by an anarchist with a copy of the *Journal* in his pocket, in September 1901, the Hearst paper's continual assaults on McKinley were recalled. Hearst found it wise to change the name of his morning New York paper to the *American*. But the incident was to haunt him for the rest of his life.

Hearst now sought to advance his political beliefs by seeking office himself. He served two terms in Congress from a Democratic district in New York City, from 1903 to 1907, but his eye was on the White House. His high point came in 1904 when 204 delegates cast votes for him in the Democratic national convention (Judge Alton B. Parker, the successful nominee, received 658). The next year Hearst ran as an independent candidate for mayor of New York and lost by some 3,500 votes as the result of Tammany's counting him out at the ballot boxes.

This was a notable achievement, and Hearst decided to make the race for the New York governorship in 1906 as a stepping-stone to the White House. He won the Democratic nomination in convention but found himself up against Charles Evans Hughes in the November election. Theodore Roosevelt's close associate, Elihu Root, recalled the McKinley assassination episode in a public speech; the *World* and other New York newspapers turned against Hearst, and so did Tammany, which he had challenged the year before. Hughes won by 60,000 votes—the only Republican to be elected that year in the statewide balloting—and Hearst's political star had set.

In his political races and in his newspapers, Hearst was making a heavy play for the support of workers, small businessmen, and other ordinary people. His slashing attacks on the "criminal trusts"—the ice trust, the coal trust, the gas trust—and crooked political bosses found favor with those who had grievances against the established order. His forthright support of the labor unions won him the backing of the American Federation of Labor. And the popularized content of his newspapers appealed to the mass of readers. Emphasis on sensational crime and vice stories, human interest features, pictures and cartoons, and readable typographical display helped draw crowds of new readers to Hearst papers. But despite the following that Hearst had attracted, there was widespread doubting of his journalistic and political motives. Hearst journalism was degrading in its use of techniques to snare the reader, his critics said, and above all, Hearst and his journalism lacked depth: depth of intellectual appeal; depth of sincerity; depth of understanding of social issues. In general, the intellectual leaders of the time spoke out against him.[7]

New publishing ventures brought Hearst to the attention of three more large cities in the first few years of the twentieth century. To his *San Francisco Examiner, New York American,* and *New York Journal,* Hearst added four more papers that put him in the business of chain publishing. In Chicago, the evening *American* was begun in 1900 and the morning *Examiner* in 1902. Boston saw the birth of an evening *American* in 1904. Los Angeles was invaded in 1903 with the founding of the morning *Examiner.* The Los Angeles entry was welcomed with open arms by local labor unions, which had been engaged in a bitter fight with the antilabor *Los Angeles Times.* The *Times,* published by General Harrison Gray Otis, had become an open shop in 1890 after a typographers union strike, and the labor unions cooperated with Hearst in establishing direct competition for the powerful Otis paper. Otis and his son-in-law, Harry Chandler, continued their fight against organized labor until the feud was climaxed in 1910 by the dynamiting of the *Times* building, a crime to which two radically minded union men, the McNamara brothers, eventually confessed.

In the first issue of the *Los Angeles Examiner,* the editors advertised their wares. They listed the Hearst writers: Ella Wheeler Wilcox, "world famous poet and essayist"; Mrs. John A. Logan, wife of a General and writer "on behalf of the American home and American womanhood"; Professor Garrett Serviss, noted astronomer; Dorothy Dix, whose name is the first one recognizable seven decades later; Ambrose Bierce, a truly great writer. The editorial page, the ad said, has "thought-stirring editorials which have done so much to mold public thought in this country." Editorial-page cartoonists listed were Opper, Powers, Davenport, and Howarth; comics included the Katzenjammer Kids and Childe Harold. And, said the editors, "There is nothing in the newspaper world like the magazine section of the Hearst newspapers." Within a month the *Examiner* claimed 32,500 readers, and it remained a strong paper for half a century.[8]

E.W. SCRIPPS AND HIS "PEOPLE'S PAPERS"

Another type of "people's paper" was emerging, meanwhile, under the direction of Edward Wyllis Scripps, the Illinois farm boy who had successfully started the first of his many Scripps newspapers by the time he was 24. Scripps got his start in the Middle West at the moment that Pulitzer was achieving his first success in St. Louis, and when Stone was succeeding in Chicago and Nelson in Kansas City. The *Detroit News,* on which Scripps had served his apprenticeship under his brother James, had been one of the early practitioners of the "new journalism." His own first two papers, the *Cleveland*

Press and the *Cincinnati Post,* were low-priced afternoon dailies appealing to the mass of readers.*

But unlike Pulitzer and Hearst, who sought giant circulations in big cities, Scripps set his sights on the working people in the smaller but growing industrial cities of the country. For them he published brightly written, easily read newspapers, small in size but big in heart. Closely edited news, human interest features, fearless news coverage and local crusades, and hard-fighting independent editorial opinion constituted the Scripps formula.

What made Scripps a distinctive leader as a "people's champion" was his conception of his responsibility to the working man. "The first of my principles," Scripps said, "is that I have constituted myself the advocate of that large majority of people who are not so rich in worldly goods and native intelligence as to make them equal, man for man, in the struggle with individuals of the wealthier and more intellectual class."[9] Scripps viewed his newspapers as the only "schoolroom" the working man had. He believed that nearly all other newspapers were capitalistic and opposed to the working class or else too intellectual in appeal, and he said sadly that the educational system was a failure in its service to his "large majority." So he sought to drive home through his editorial columns the necessity for labor union organization and collective bargaining as the first prerequisite to a better life for the poor and ill-informed. Scripps was the first to admit that his papers did not always maintain the noble objectives he set for them and that they sometimes made mistakes in "always opposing the rich, always supporting the working man." But Scripps believed that if he kept the focus on such a basic policy he would further the long-range pattern of society that he hoped would emerge.

Above all, the Scripps newspapers reflected a "spirit of protest" that was inherent in the character of their owner-editor. Scripps declared that he protested against everything; his motto was "Whatever is, is wrong." He protested against antiquated governmental systems, against undemocratic political actions, against usurpation of power and prestige by the rich and the intellectuals, against inequality of opportunity, against all sorts of authority in religion and law and politics except those exercised for the benefit of mankind, against corruption, against the power of business interests. He pictured himself as a "damned old crank" who was in rebellion against society. But actually he was seeking to build a progressive democracy, and he was enough of a capitalist to urge the worker to better himself or herself by increasing production and thereby adding to the wealth to be distributed.

Scripps started his newspaper career with an investment of $600 in one share of stock in the *Detroit News*. With the help of his sister Ellen and his brothers James and George, he started the *Cleveland Press* in 1878. In 1883, with an income of $10,000 a year, Scripps turned to Cincinnati and took over management of a struggling penny paper that became the *Post.*

These were the formative years of the Scripps newspaper empire. In Cleveland Scripps found an editor, Robert F. Paine, who for more than 30 years was a leader in editorial policy-making. In Cincinnati Scripps found a business manager, Milton A. McRae. Scripps and McRae in 1889 formed the Scripps-McRae League of Newspapers. McRae was to be the speechmaker, the front man, the operations chief. Scripps was to set policy and live as he pleased on a California ranch. And in 1890, at age 36, Scripps did "retire" to a great ranch near San Diego, named Miramar, where he lived

*See pages 209–10 for Scripps's early career.

a burly life, wearing ranch clothes and cowhide boots, playing poker, drinking whiskey, and smoking innumerable cigars. At Miramar, too, he kept in close touch through correspondence and conferences with his principal editors and managers. There he lived to the age of 71 and built himself a fortune of some $50 million.

The Scripps plan for expansion was simple. He and McRae looked for a growing industrial city, usually fairly small and with stodgy newspaper opposition. They put up a few thousand dollars and sent a young, ambitious editor and business manager off to start a paper. If the young journalists succeeded, they could obtain as much as 49 per cent of the stock; if they faltered, new faces replaced them. If the paper failed to make a profit within ten years, it was abandoned as a failure. Scripps papers, as a result of this policy, had a good many employee-stockholders, but they also paid the usual low journalistic salaries of the times to those who were not so blessed. In this respect, Scripps was typically capitalistic in his publishing behavior.

Since the papers were cheap afternoon dailies relying principally on circulation revenue, they had to be edited carefully. Scripps saved newsprint costs by insisting on small headlines and short, concisely edited stories. Saving those extra words so that a Scripps newspaper would be packed with the most news possible became a fine art for Scripps newsmen. Word economy meant also that after the essential news had been told there would be plenty of space for editorial opinion and features.

By 1911 the Scripps-McRae League included 18 papers in Ohio, Indiana, Tennessee, Iowa, Colorado, Oklahoma, and Texas. Scripps himself was building his own chain of West Coast newspapers, meanwhile. He started by buying the *San Diego Sun* in 1893, and in the next 15 years opened up shop in ten other West Coast cities. But here in an only slightly industrialized West, the Scripps record was extremely poor. Only the *San Francisco News* eventually emerged as a strong unit in the Scripps chain. The *Los Angeles Record* and four Pacific Northwest papers seceded from the parent Scripps organization after a quarrel between Scripps and his son James in 1920, and formed the basis for the Scripps League.

Scripps tried another experiment in 1911, when he established an adless tabloid in Chicago, named the *Day Book*. Negley D. Cochran was the editor, and poet Carl Sandburg was chief reporter. The little paper, which represented Scripps's fondest dream, reached a circulation of 25,000 and was within $500 a month of breaking even when the rising newsprint costs of the first war year, 1917, caused its suspension. A second adless paper, the *Philadelphia News-Post,* started in 1912 but also failed.

Through the years the Scripps papers continued to fight for the right of workers to organize. They crusaded for public ownership and against utility abuses. They attacked political bossism and corruption. They supported Theodore Roosevelt's reforms and his third party candidacy. And they backed Woodrow Wilson's "New Freedom" and his reelection campaign. In appearance and in content they were closer to being "labor papers" than any other general circulation newspapers, yet they also won the support of the intellectual liberals whom Scripps sometimes tried to avoid.

OTHER NEWSPAPER CRUSADERS

Pulitzer, Hearst, and Scripps were far from being the only champions of the common man among newspaper publishers and editors of the years around the turn of the century. Nor can all those who opposed the business trusts, who fought against onesided public utilities franchises, who exposed political inadequacy and corruption, be listed. Some idea of the contributions made by newspapermen can be gained by a look across the country, however.[10]

One battle against a tightly run political machine was that waged by Charles H.

Grasty, editor of the *Baltimore Evening News,* and by the *Baltimore Sun.* Grasty, who came to Baltimore from the *Kansas City Star,* was a fighting editor in the Nelson tradition who had exposed the policy racket in Baltimore despite a criminal libel charge brought by his political opponents. When in 1895 the *Sun* broke with its Democratic party traditions and attacked Senator Arthur P. Gorman's state Democratic machine, Grasty pitched in to help oust the Gorman group. Maryland elected its first Republican administration since the Civil War and Gorman lost his senate seat for one term.

Across the country the spectacular but contradictory career of Fremont Older was being unfolded in San Francisco. Older, a typical roving newspaperman in his early years, settled down as managing editor of the *Bulletin* in 1895. He built the struggling evening sheet into a fairly substantial paper by his sensational methods and then decided to join the solid civic leader, the *San Francisco Chronicle,* in its fights against city machine politics. The target was a Union-Labor party headed by Mayor Eugene E. Schmitz and a political boss, Abram Ruef. Older stepped out of his role as a newspaperman to become a civic reform leader, and his dominating personality made him the rallying point for the public-spirited of the city. The reform group brought Schmitz and Ruef to court on indictments for accepting payoffs from houses of prostitution and saw Ruef sent to prison. Others involved escaped conviction, despite the work of prosecutors Francis J. Heney (who was shot and critically wounded in the courtroom) and Hiram W. Johnson. Older's last great crusade was in behalf of Tom Mooney, who Older eventually decided had been unjustly convicted of the Preparedness Day bombing of 1916 in San Francisco. Breaking with the *Bulletin* management on the Mooney issue, Older joined Hearst's *Call* as editor in 1918, saw it become the *Call-Bulletin* in 1929, and died in 1935 before Mooney won his freedom.

Older had been kidnapped and nearly killed during the height of the San Francisco trials. In South Carolina, an editor was assassinated—N.G. Gonzales of the *Columbia State* in 1903. Gonzales was one of three brothers who battled against political boss Ben Tillman with their newspaper, founded in 1893. The paper continued to exert leadership, however, calling for compulsory public education and opposing child labor and "lynch law."

A less spectacular, but solid, champion of decency was Josephus Daniels of North Carolina, who became editor in Raleigh of the *State Chronicle* in 1885. The paper was a weekly, started by Walter Hines Page two years before.

In his first few years in Raleigh, Daniels campaigned against the Southern Railway and its attempt to extend its control over other lines. He advocated a state public school fund as a means of equalizing educational opportunity, urged financial support of the state university, supported establishment of teacher training colleges, and argued for compulsory education as a means of overcoming illiteracy. When the American Tobacco Company was organized by the Duke family in 1890 he began his long campaign against the "tobacco trust."

The established daily in Raleigh was the *News and Observer.* Daniels obtained control of it in 1895 and built it into one of the South's leading newspapers.

Daniels was a fervent supporter of the Democratic party, campaigning for Bryan in his three races for the presidency and supporting Woodrow Wilson with full enthusiasm. Wilson made him his Secretary of the Navy in 1913 and the Daniels political career was under way.

In Chicago, the *Tribune* that Joseph Medill had built enjoyed a varied record. In the last years of Medill's editorship, before his death in 1899, the *Tribune* was strongly nationalistic in foreign policy and generally conservative in its outlook. It fought the liberal Illinois governor, John P. Altgeld, and bitterly attacked the Debs-led Chicago

Josephus Daniels

Joseph Medill

labor unions. But the *Tribune* vigorously crusaded against utility and street-railway franchise grabs and used John T. McCutcheon's front-page cartoons with effectiveness after the artist transferred from the *Record* to the *Tribune* in 1903.

James Keeley, the *Tribune*'s outstanding managing editor, helped develop one of the state's biggest exposés in 1910 when the paper published evidence that William Lorimer had won election to the U.S. Senate by bribing state legislators. Despite the evidence Keeley had obtained, it took two years of campaigning by the *Tribune* and the *Record-Herald* before Lorimer was ousted from the Senate.

THE MAGAZINES: ERA OF MUCKRAKING

Highly important as "people's champions" were the magazines that, in the dozen years after 1900, developed a literature of exposure that Theodore Roosevelt dubbed the work of the "muckrakers." Roosevelt used the expression in a derogatory sense, comparing the more sensational writers to the Man with the Muckrake in *Pilgrim's Progress,* who did not look up to see the celestial crown but continued to rake the filth. The reformers, however, came to accept the designation as a badge of honor, and in the history of American magazines the period is known as "the era of the muckrakers."[11]

When in 1893 three new popular magazines—*McClure's, Cosmopolitan,* and *Munsey's*—cut their prices to a dime, their circulation figures started on an upward climb. After the turn of the century these magazines and such others as the *Ladies' Home Journal, Collier's, Everybody's,* and the *Saturday Evening Post* had circulations running into the hundreds of thousands. Most of them joined with great enthusiasm in the crusade against big business, against corruption, and for social justice. Their writers, who came largely from newspaper ranks, had national audiences for articles that sometimes were original but sometimes were drawn from the stories published by crusading newspapers in various cities. However the articles were obtained, the magazines performed the service of coordinating and interpreting information about social, economic, and political problems for a nationwide audience.

Touching off the muckraking era was S. S. McClure,[12] whose magazine began three significant series of articles in late 1902. McClure, who had founded a newspaper feature syndicate in 1884 and attracted readers and writers to his service, invaded the magazine field in 1893 with a low-priced but unspectacular product filled with interesting and timely articles and literary material. He and his associate editor, John S. Phillips, had selected a staff of talented and responsible writers to handle the nonfiction section of *McClure's*. One was Ida M. Tarbell, whose specialties were biographies and research work. Another was Lincoln Steffens, former reporter for the *Evening Post* and city editor of the *Commercial Advertiser* in New York, who was to become one of the country's most famous crusading liberals. A third was Ray Stannard Baker, who came to *McClure's* from the *Chicago Record* in 1897 and who later was to achieve fame as Woodrow Wilson's biographer. Beginning in late 1902 Miss Tarbell exposed the business practices of John D. Rockefeller and the Standard Oil Company; Steffens opened his attack on corruption in city and state governments; and Baker began discussing the problems of the working man. The circulation of *McClure's* mounted past the half-million mark and the muckraking trend in magazine editing was in full swing.

What McClure was doing was not entirely new to the magazine field. The older magazines of high quality—*Harper's, Scribner's,* the *Century,* and the *Atlantic Monthly*—had paid some attention to current affairs, although they were primarily literary in tone. There were several journals of opinion that had relatively small but influential audiences: Godkin's *Nation,* Albert Shaw's *Review of Reviews,* Lyman Abbott's *Outlook,* the *North American Review,* the *Forum,* and the *Independent.* In the same class but taking an early leadership in crusading for socioeconomic and political reform was Benjamin O. Flower's *Arena.* These magazines and others were giving attention to the rising business trusts, graft, and political machines, but it was *McClure's* that first made a frontal assault of real magnitude.

Miss Tarbell's "History of the Standard Oil Company" ran in *McClure's* until 1904, and her detailed, thoroughly documented account of the unfair business practices used by the company to squeeze out competitors put Rockefeller on the defensive for many years to come. Steffens began his series on "The Shame of the Cities" by recounting the situation in St. Louis that had first been exposed by the *Post-Dispatch* and followed up with reports on corrupt government in Minneapolis, Pittsburgh, Philadelphia, Chicago, New York, and other cities. George Kibbe Turner, an alumnus of the *Springfield Republican,* continued the city series later in the decade. Baker dealt with labor problems, including child labor and the economic status of the Negro. Other contributors to *McClure's* included Burton J. Hendrick, who wrote about the New York life insurance companies, and Kansas editor William Allen White. Newspaperman Will Irwin served as managing editor and editor for a year in 1906–7.

Cosmopolitan joined the muckrakers when the magazine passed from John Brisben Walker to Hearst by running the series "The Treason of the Senate," which appeared in 1906. The author was David Graham Phillips, one of Pulitzer's editorial writers on the *World* staff who retired from newspaper work to write a series of books examining problems of his time. Phillips denounced a score of conservative senators—both Republican and Democrat—as spokesmen of "the interests." Among other prominent muckrakers, Alfred Henry Lewis attacked the International Harvester Company in *Cosmopolitan* and followed up with a series examining the careers of

America's leading millionaires. Charles Edward Russell, who had been managing editor of the *Minneapolis Journal* at 21 and who had worked for several New York and Chicago newspapers, surveyed the weaknesses of state governments in a 1910 series.

Active in the fray, too, was *Everybody's,* founded in 1899 and edited by John O'Hara Cosgrave. When in 1904 it persuaded a colorful Wall Street financier, Thomas W. Lawson, to write "Frenzied Finance," the public appetite for Lawson's inside information drove the magazine's circulation from 200,000 to 735,000 within a year. Less important, but influential, were *Pearson's, Hampton's* (which built a readership of 440,000 in the years 1907 to 1911), and *La Follette's Weekly,* the voice of the Wisconsin progressives.

Taking the lead from *McClure's* in muckraking after 1905 was *Collier's.* Published by Robert J. Collier and edited by Norman Hapgood, the magazine developed an effective editorial voice in national political affairs. Its articles ranged over many social and economic problems, but it caught popular attention for a series of articles by Samuel Hopkins Adams on the patent medicine trade, called "The Great American Fraud," published in 1905 and 1906. Adams exposed the false claims of many of the popular "cure-alls" and demonstrated that some of the patent medicines contained poisonous ingredients. Equally prominent in the attack on the patent medicine business was Edward W. Bok, editor of the *Ladies' Home Journal.* It was Bok who shocked his women readers by proving that Lydia E. Pinkham, to whom American women were supposed to write for advice, had been dead for 22 years.

The attack on the patent medicines coincided with a drive against adulterated foods and unsanitary practices in packing plants. Under the leadership of Dr. Harvey H. Wiley, chief chemist of the Department of Agriculture, federal and state officials had proved widespread adulteration of food and addition of chemicals and artificial dyes by food manufacturers. But the lid was blown off when Upton Sinclair wrote *The Jungle* in 1906, a novel intended to portray the plight of immigrant workers in Chicago's packinghouses, but which was terrifying in its charges of unsanitary practices.

Passage of the Pure Food and Drugs Act of 1906 was the outcome. This regulated the activities of manufacturers, but the problem of "truth in advertising" remained. Some newspapers had obtained testimonials from readers, extolling the virtues of the medicines, and had run them in their news columns. This use of "readers," as they were called, also had been extended to cover publicity stories paid for by the column inch. As the campaign for "truth in advertising" grew, newspapermen cooperated. State laws making untruthful, deceptive, or misleading advertising statements a misdemeanor were adopted after *Printers' Ink* drafted a model statute in 1911, and the federal Newspaper Publicity Law of 1912 required that all matter published for money should be marked "Advertisement."

Other magazines should be noted. One was the *American Magazine,* purchased in 1906 by a group of *McClure's* writers. A disagreement in policy led John S. Phillips, associate editor of *McClure's,* to leave its staff. He took with him Miss Tarbell, Steffens, Baker, William Allen White, and Finley Peter Dunne, America's "Mr. Dooley." These were the leaders of the muckrakers, and for a few years they constituted a distinguished editorial board for the *American.* The high point of muckraking had been reached in 1906, but liberal insurgency continued, climaxed in 1912 by Theodore Roosevelt's third party candidacy and Woodrow Wilson's election as president. The *New Republic* began its career in 1914 under editor Herbert Croly, whose *The Promise of American Life* (1909) became a creed for Wilsonian liberals. Croly and staff member Walter Lippmann supported Wilson in wartime. *The*

McClure's Magazine

VOL. XX   *JANUARY*, *1903*   NO. 3

THE SHAME OF MINNEAPOLIS

The Rescue and Redemption of a City that was Sold Out

BY LINCOLN STEFFENS

FAC-SIMILE OF THE FIRST PAGE OF "THE BIG MITT LEDGER"

An account kept by a swindler of the dealings of his " Joint " with City Officials, showing first payments made to Mayor Ames, his brother, the Chief of Police and Detectives. This book figured in trials and newspaper reports of the exposure, but was " lost "; and its whereabouts was the mystery of the proceedings. This is the first glimpse that any one, except " Cheerful Charlie ' Howard, who kept it, and members of the grand jury, has had of the book

WHENEVER anything extraordinary is done in American municipal politics, whether for good or for evil, you can trace it almost invariably to one man. The people do not do it. Neither do the "gangs," "combines," or political parties. These are but instruments by which bosses (not leaders; we Americans are not led, but driven) rule the people, and commonly sell them out. But there are at least two forms of the autocracy which has supplanted the democracy here as it has everywhere it has been tried. One is that of the organized majority by which, as in Tammany Hall in New York and the Republican machine in Philadelphia, the boss has normal control of more than half the voters. The other is that of the adroitly managed minority. The "good people" are herded into parties and stupefied with convictions and a name, Republican or Democrat; while the "bad people" are so organized or interested by the boss that he can wield their votes to enforce terms with party managers and decide elections. St. Louis is a conspicuous example of this form. Minneapolis is another. Colonel Ed. Butler is the unscrupulous opportunist who handled the non-partisan minority which turned St. Louis into a "boodle town." In Minneapolis "Doc" Ames was the man.

One of the articles that made *McClure's* the leading muckraking magazine.

Masses, edited by Max Eastman and a brilliant voice of protest from 1911 to 1917 when its pacifist-socialist line led to wartime persecution and demise, did not. Among its contributors were Lippmann, Carl Sandburg, Sherwood Anderson, and cartoonist Art Young.

THE AGE OF REALISM   Playing a role, too, in the quest for social justice were a group of America's writers. William Dean Howells and Henry James had pointed the way toward the realistic novel. Joining them in this movement were novelist Stephen Crane and short-story writers Ambrose Bierce and Hamlin Garland. Of the same school were poets Walt Whitman and Emily Dickinson. From this literary heritage, and from the pressure of the times, came a flowering of realism in literature after 1900.

California Frank Norris contributed two volumes of a planned trilogy on the "Epic of Wheat" before his career was cut short by death at 32. His *The Octopus,* appearing in 1901, told the story of the struggle of California farmers against the power of the Southern Pacific Railroad. His protest against Chicago wheat speculators, *The Pit,* made an equally deep impression. Another Californian, Jack London, captured in his stories of adventure and raw, brutal experience a full expression of the rising protest against the capitalistic system. London's *The Iron Heel,* published in 1907, and Upton Sinclair's *The Jungle* were high points in relentless realism. So were Theodore Dreiser's *Sister Carrie,* which was at first suppressed by a frightened publisher, and his later books, *The Financier* and *The Titan.*

More Americans, it is true, were reading historical novels, adventure stories, and popular favorites like *David Harum* and *Mrs. Wiggs of the Cabbage Patch* than were reading the works of Norris, Sinclair, London, and Dreiser. More Americans, too, were reading fiction in *Munsey's* and the *Saturday Evening Post* than were reading the exposés by Lincoln Steffens, Ida M. Tarbell, and Samuel Hopkins Adams. And among newspaper readers, relatively few were absorbing the editorial arguments of Edward Wyllis Scripps, Joseph Pulitzer, and their contemporaries of equal stature. Still, at a critical moment in American history when an arousing of public opinion was needed to ensure economic and political progress and a more equitable social pattern, journalism and literature played their part and produced effective leaders.

NOTES

1. Richard O'Connor, *Pacific Destiny* (Boston: Little, Brown, 1969), p. 256.
2. Carl Schurz, "Manifest Destiny," *Harper's* (October 1893), pp. 737–46, as cited by William Appleman Williams in *The Roots of the Modern American Empire* (New York: Random House, 1969), p. 365, as part of Williams' contention that the agricultural majority played the prime role in forcing the war against Spain in order to open more markets. Also see his *The Contours of American History* (Cleveland: World Publishing, 1961, reissued 1973) for an analysis of the effects of Frederick Jackson Turner's frontier theory on U.S. expansion, and the relationship between expansionism and the reform movement.
3. As cited by Leon Wolff in his *Little Brown Brother* (New York: Doubleday, 1961), p. 270.
4. One documented study of the period is Harold U. Faulkner, *The Quest for Social Justice, 1898–1914* (New York: Macmillan, 1931). A full and fascinating account by a journalistic historian is found in the first three volumes of Mark Sullivan, *Our Times* (New York: Scribner's, 1926 ff.). For a revisionist study with a New Left emphasis, see Gabriel Kolko, *The Triumph of Conservatism: A Reinterpretation of American History, 1900–1916* (Chicago: Quadrangle Books, 1967).
5. Louis Hartz in *The Liberal Tradition in America* (New York: Harcourt Brace Jovanovich, 1955), p. 6, offers this explanation: "It is not accidental that America which has uniquely lacked a feudal tradition has uniquely lacked also a socialist tradition. The hidden origin of socialist thought everywhere in the West is to be found in the feudal ethos."

6. For a sketch of Cobb and a collection of his important editorials, see John L. Heaton, *Cobb of "The World"* (New York: Dutton, 1924).

7. W. A. Swanberg, in *Citizen Hearst* (New York: Scribner's, 1961), contends that the Hearst of 1904 presidential ambitions was not a demagogue but sincerely believed he was the best-fitted Democrat to run. For his estimates of Hearst, see pages 208–19 for this period, and the summation, pages 523–27, in which he concludes Hearst was two men, "a Prospero and a Caliban."

8. *Los Angeles Examiner,* December 12, 1903, p. 4.

9. As quoted in Oliver H. Knight, ed., *I Protest: The Selected Disquisitions of E. W. Scripps* (Madison: University of Wisconsin Press, 1966), p. 270. Knight edited from the Scripps papers a variety of his personal views that establish the publisher as a thinking observer of American affairs.

10. One account, not confined to this period, is Silas Bent, *Newspaper Crusaders* (New York: Whittlesey House, 1939). Another is Jonathan Daniels *They Will Be Heard: America's Crusading Newspaper Editors* (New York: McGraw-Hill, 1965).

11. The full story is told in C. C. Regier, *The Era of the Muckrakers* (Chapel Hill: University of North Carolina Press, 1932). Regier, however, ignores the contribution of newspapers in crusading and thus distorts the picture.

12. Revived interest in muckraking journalism brought two new biographies of McClure: Peter Lyon, *Success Story: The Life and Times of S. S. McClure* (New York: Scribner's, 1963), and Harold S. Wilson, *McClure's Magazine and the Muckrakers* (Princeton, N.J.: Princeton University Press, 1970).

ANNOTATED BIBLIOGRAPHY

For references to the literature about Pulitzer see the bibliography for chapter 16; for the Hearst references see chapter 17. Vol. IV of Mott's *History of American Magazines* covers this period (see chapter 15).

Books

BAKER, RAY STANNARD, *An American Chronicle.* New York: Scribner's, 1945. The autobiography of one of the *McClure's* writers.

BANNISTER, ROBERT C., *Ray Stannard Baker: The Mind and Thought of a Progressive.* New Haven: Yale University Press, 1966. One of the reporters for *McClure's.*

BOK, EDWARD W., *The Americanization of Edward Bok.* New York: Scribner's, 1920. The famous autobiography of the editor of the *Ladies' Home Journal.*

BOWERS, CLAUDE G., *Beveridge and the Progressive Era.* Boston: Houghton Mifflin, 1932. A distinguished study of the Bull Moose progressives, of whom Senator Albert J. Beveridge was one.

BRITT, ALBERT, *Ellen Browning Scripps: Journalist and Idealist.* London: Oxford University Press, 1961. Adds to the Scripps story in early years when Ellen worked with and advised E. W.

CHALMERS, DAVID M., *The Social and Political Ideas of the Muckrakers.* New York: The Citadel Press, 1964. A brief analysis of thirteen muckrakers.

COCHRAN, NEGLEY D., *E. W. Scripps.* New York: Harcourt Brace Jovanovich, 1933. A more factual biography than Gilson Gardner's *Lusty Scripps* (New York: Vanguard, 1932).

DANIELS, JOSEPHUS, *Tar Heel Editor.* Chapel Hill: University of North Carolina Press, 1939. The first volume of the Daniels autobiography, it deals with his early newspaper career.

Editorials from the Hearst Newspapers. New York: Albertson Publishing Company, 1906. Selected reprints of the Hearst editorial-page offerings at the turn of the century.

ELLIS, ELMER, *Mr. Dooley's America.* New York: Knopf, 1941. The life and times of Finley Peter Dunne, humorist and reformer.

FAULKNER, HAROLD U., *The Quest for Social Justice, 1898–1914,* A History of American Life, Vol. XI. New York: Macmillan, 1931. This volume of the series measures up as a work of social history.

FILLER, LOUIS, *Crusaders for American Liberalism.* New York: Harcourt Brace Jovanovich, 1939. A study of the liberals and the muckrakers based on the political problems of the era.

FORCEY, CHARLES, *The Crossroads of Liberalism.* New York: Oxford University Press, 1961. A case study of Herbert Croly, Walter Weyl, Walter Lippmann, and their *New Republic* of 1914.

HAPGOOD, NORMAN, *The Changing Years*. New York: Holt, Rinehart & Winston, 1930. Reflections of the editor of *Collier's*.

HEATON, JOHN L., *Cobb of "The World."* New York: Dutton, 1924. Includes a sketch of Frank I. Cobb and a collection of his *New York World* editorials.

HOFSTADTER, RICHARD, *The Age of Reform*. New York: Knopf, 1955. From Bryan to FDR, the populists, progressives, and liberals wend their way.

KAPLAN, JUSTIN, *Lincoln Steffens: A Biography*. New York: Simon & Schuster, 1974. Points to discrepancy between Steffens' autobiography and real life.

KNIGHT, OLIVER H., ed., *I Protest: Selected Disquisitions of E.W. Scripps*. Madison: University of Wisconsin Press, 1966. An admirable, condensed biography is followed by Scripps' private writings as a "thinker." Best book on Scripps.

KOLKO, GABRIEL, *The Triumph of Conservatism: A Reinterpretation of American History, 1900–1916*. Chicago: Quadrangle, 1967. A revisionist study by a leading New Left historian.

LASCH, CHRISTOPHER, *The New Radicalism in America, 1889–1963*. New York: Knopf, 1965. A New Left historian examines social reform through essays about intellectual writers.

LINK, ARTHUR S., *Woodrow Wilson and the Progressive Era, 1910–1917*. New York: Harper & Row, 1954. A volume in the New American Nation series by the biographer of Wilson.

LINN, JAMES W., *James Keeley, Newspaperman*. Indianapolis: Bobbs-Merrill, 1937. The biography of the *Chicago Tribune*'s crusading managing editor.

LYON, PETER, *Success Story: The Life and Times of S.S. McClure*. New York: Scribner's, 1963. His muckraking magazine provides the climax of this prize-winning biography.

McCLURE, S.S., *My Autobiography*. New York: Frederick A. Stokes & Company, 1914. The story of the magazine publisher.

McRAE, MILTON A., *Forty Years in Newspaperdom*. New York: Brentano's, 1924. Autobiography of E.W. Scripps' partner and business manager.

MARCOSSON, ISAAC F., *David Graham Phillips and His Times*. New York: Dodd, Mead, 1932. The biography of a muckraker.

MAY, HENRY F., *The End of American Innocence*. New York: Knopf, 1969. Intellectual history, 1912–17.

MORRISON, JOSEPH L., *Josephus Daniels Says*. Chapel Hill: University of North Carolina Press, 1962. Detailed biography of editor of Raleigh *News-Observer* 1894–1913; his crusading battles, his white supremacy. See also the political biography, *Josephus Daniels: The Small-d Democrat* (1966).

MOWRY, GEORGE E., *Theodore Roosevelt and the Progressive Movement*. Madison: University of Wisconsin Press, 1946. Traces the relationship of Roosevelt to radicalism.

O'CONNOR, RICHARD, *Pacific Destiny: An Informal History of the U.S. in the Far East*. Boston: Little, Brown, 1969. Traces expansionism from 1854 to 1968.

———, *Jack London*. Boston: Little, Brown, 1964. Best of the author's popular biographies of journalists.

OLDER, FREMONT, *My Own Story*. New York: Macmillan, 1926. The fighting San Francisco editor tells his piece.

PHILLIPS, DAVID GRAHAM, *The Treason of the Senate*, edited by George E. Mowry and Judson A. Grenier. Chicago: Quadrangle, 1964. Excellent discussion by the editors precedes texts of Phillips' famed articles in *Cosmopolitan*.

PRINGLE, HENRY F., *Theodore Roosevelt*. New York: Harcourt Brace Jovanovich, 1931. A Pulitzer Prize biography of the key figure of the muckraking era by a former newspaperman.

REGIER, C. C., *The Era of the Muckrakers*. Chapel Hill: University of North Carolina Press, 1932. An exhaustive study of the crusading magazines and their writers.

SEDGWICK, ELLERY, *The Happy Profession*. Boston: Little, Brown, 1946. Includes a description of the hurly-burly times at *Leslie's*, the *American*, and *McClure's* before Sedgwick became owner and editor of the *Atlantic* in 1909.

STEFFENS, LINCOLN, *The Autobiography of Lincoln Steffens*. New York: Harcourt Brace Jovanovich, 1931. One of the great journalistic autobiographies.

SULLIVAN, MARK, *Our Times*. New York: Scribner's, 1926 ff. Newspaperman Sullivan's six volumes are crowded with the color and the drama of the years 1900 to 1929.

TARBELL, IDA M., *All in the Day's Work*. New York: Macmillan, 1939. The chief woman muckraker reviews her career.

TOMKINS, MARY E., *Ida M. Tarbell*. New York: Twayne, 1974. Brief but scholarly biography; explains how Tarbell made her mark at a time when newswomen were scarce.

VILLARD, OSWALD GARRISON, *Fighting Years*. New York: Harcourt Brace Jovanovich, 1939. The autobiography of the publisher of the *Nation* and *New York Post*.

WEINBERG, ARTHUR AND LILA, eds., *The Muckrakers*. New York: Simon & Schuster, 1961. A compilation of some of the best magazine articles by the muckrakers.

WILLIAMS, WILLIAM APPLEMAN, *The Roots of the Modern American Empire*. New York: Random House, 1969. A leader of New Left historians dissents from United States foreign policy since the 1890s. See also his *The Contours of American History* (Cleveland: World Publishing, 1961, reissued 1973).

WILSON, HAROLD S., *McClure's Magazine and the Muckrakers*. Princeton, N.J.: Princeton University Press, 1970. Solid contribution to the subject.

Periodicals and Monographs

DORWART, JEFFERY M., "James Creelman, the New York *World* and the Port Arthur Massacre," *Journalism Quarterly*, L (Winter 1973), 697. Eyewitness report.

ERICKSON, JOHN E., "Newspapers and Social Values: Chicago Journalism, 1890–1910," Ph.D. thesis, University of Illinois, 1973. Press reported and embodied values marking entry into twentieth century.

FRANCKE, WARREN T., "Investigative Exposure in the Nineteenth Century: The Journalistic Heritage of the Muckrakers," Ph.D. thesis, University of Minnesota, 1974. Muckraking proves to be part of earlier reporting tradition.

GATEWOOD, WILLARD B., JR., "A Negro Editor on Imperialism: John Mitchell, 1898–1901," *Journalism Quarterly*, XLIX (Spring 1972), 43. He saw the claims of liberating peoples from Spain as a mask for American imperialism.

GRENIER, JUDSON A., "Muckraking and the Muckrakers: An Historical Definition," *Journalism Quarterly*, XXXVII (Autumn 1960), 552. A study of the years 1902–14.

HARRISON, JOHN M., "Finley Peter Dunne and the Progressive Movement," *Journalism Quarterly*, XLIV (Autumn 1967), 475. Mr. Dooley's creator was a philosophical anarchist.

HUDSON, ROBERT V., "Will Irwin's Pioneering Criticism of the Press," *Journalism Quarterly*, XLVII (Summer 1970), 263. Based on his biography of Will Irwin, Ph.D. thesis, University of Minnesota, 1970. Authoritative biographical writing.

KNIGHT, OLIVER, "Scripps and His Adless Newspaper, *The Day Book*," *Journalism Quarterly*, XLI (Winter 1964), 51. Full story of the effort to create an adless daily.

PRINGLE, HENRY F., "The Newspaper Man as an Artist," *Scribner's*, XCVII (February 1935), 101. The artist was Frank I. Cobb, editor of the *New York World*.

SARASOHN, DAVID, "Power Without Glory: Hearst in the Progressive Era," *Journalism Quarterly*, LIII (Autumn 1976), 474. Examines Hearst's power and his squandering of political capital.

STARR, LOUIS M., "Joseph Pulitzer and His Most 'Indegoddampendent' Editor," *American Heritage*, XIX (June 1968), 18. The story of Frank Cobb.

STEFFENS, PETE, "The Identity Struggle of Lincoln Steffens—Writer or Reporter?," *Journalism History*, II (Spring 1975), 16. By his son; Lincoln Steffens hesitated to make reporting a career.

STEVENS, GEORGE E., "A History of the Cincinnati *Post*," Ph.D. thesis, University of Minnesota, 1968. Emphasizes local issues and political coverage of a mainstay Scripps daily. See his "Scripps' Cincinnati *Post*: Liberalism at Home," *Journalism Quarterly*, XLVIII (Summer 1971), 231.

WEIGLE, CLIFFORD F., "The Young Scripps Editor: Keystone of E.W.'s 'System'," *Journalism Quarterly*, XLI (Summer 1964), 360. A case study of the founding of the *Houston Press*.

The *New York Times* handles one of the great news stories of the twentieth century.

19

The Great
and the Colorful

*It will be my earnest aim . . . to give the news impartially, without fear
or favor. . . .*

—Adolph S. Ochs

The several preceding chapters have been concerned with the historical development
of patterns of press behavior. A segment of the press was involved successively in
important general trends: the rise of the new journalism, the spread of yellow
journalism, and service as "people's champions." But it is difficult to fit newspapers
into such patterns, because each newspaper has an individuality born of its publishing
environment. In some cases a newspaper's individuality is so pronounced that its story
is best told apart from discussions of trends and patterns.

One conspicuous example is the *New York Times*. The *Times* was rescued from
near oblivion in 1896 and began a rise to greatness as a journalistic institution that
eventually approached the status of a national newspaper. In the same years, fame also
came to a unique and colorful Kansas editor, William Allen White, whose name was
known to more persons than was that of the publisher of the *Times,* even though the
Emporia Gazette was always a small-town paper. Across the country, other
newspapers and newspapermen achieved distinctive notice within and without the
craft, for varying reasons. Some are more colorful than great, but they are a part of
journalistic lore. It is with their stories that this chapter is concerned.

**ADOLPH OCHS
AND THE *NEW YORK TIMES***

The story of the *New York Times* is the story of the man who
rescued it from bankruptcy in 1896 and who guided it until
he died in 1935. He was Adolph S. Ochs, a one-
time printer's devil from Tennessee, who salvaged the glories of the *Times* of Henry J.
Raymond's day and set its course as America's leading newspaper. It was the men and
women he selected to staff the *Times* who made it an institution.

Ochs, like many another great publisher, struggled up from the ranks to win his place. His parents were Germans of Jewish faith, who emigrated to the United States before the Civil War. Adolph, born in 1858 in Cincinnati, was the oldest of six children. The family migrated to Tennessee in a covered wagon, and at 14 Adolph landed a job as printer's devil for the *Knoxville Chronicle*. In 1875 he became assistant composing room foreman for the *Louisville Courier-Journal* and did some reporting for Henry Watterson. But he was judged a colorless and awkward writer; his genius lay in his business ability and in his capacity for developing ideas and journalistic leadership.

Back in Knoxville in 1876, Ochs got his chance. The editor of the rival *Tribune,* Colonel John E. MacGowan, wanted to start a newspaper in Chattanooga. It was a city of 12,000 with no sidewalks, muddy streets, and little interest in newspapers. The city had seen 16 come and go in 40 years, including the *Dispatch* that Ochs and MacGowan first published. The only survivor was the *Times,* with a circulation of 250. Ochs got control for the same amount of dollars. It was July 1878, and he was not yet 21. But he and his 45-year-old editor promised Chattanooga all the local news, the latest news by telegraph, and a strong business and commercial outlook for a booming city. The *Times* boomed with Chattanooga and by 1892 was clearing $25,000 a year. But Ochs owed money on real estate ventures that were imperiled by the approaching depression of 1893. What he needed, Ochs decided, was another newspaper and its profits. He searched the country and in March 1896 he learned there was a chance to buy the *New York Times*.

Ochs was properly impressed by this opportunity. He knew how respected the *Times* had been since its founding by Henry J. Raymond in 1851. After Raymond's death in 1869, the paper had come under the direction of its business manager, George Jones. Jones, editor Louis J. Jennings, and chief assistant John Foord had helped to smash Boss Tweed in the seventies. John C. Reid had served well as managing editor from 1872 to 1889 and the paper had maintained its place until the death of Jones in 1891. By then the impact of the ''new journalism'' was having its effect.

The new guiding spirit on the *Times* became Charles R. Miller, a graduate of Dartmouth and former staff member of the *Springfield Republican,* who assumed the editorship in 1883. With associate editor Edward Cary and other staff members, Miller negotiated purchase of the *Times* from the Jones family heirs in 1893 for approximately a million dollars. But the paper did not prosper. It had the smallest circulation of the city's eight morning dailies, a paltry 9,000 paid circulation concealed in a 21,000 press run. This was not far behind the *Tribune*'s 16,000 but was far below the *Sun*'s 70,000 morning circulation, the *Herald*'s 140,000, and the *World*'s 200,000 morning figure.

OCHS BUYS THE *TIMES*, 1896   Ochs did not have the money to save the *Times,* but he convinced Miller that he had the know-how and the vision that would be needed to put the paper in a sound competitive position. An elaborate refinancing plan was advanced that would give Ochs control of the paper within four years if he succeeded in revitalizing it. Ochs trudged through the Wall Street district for months persuading financiers, even including J.P. Morgan, to buy bonds in the new enterprise. Finally, in August 1896, an agreement was completed, with Ochs putting up $75,000 of his own money and risking his Chattanooga paper on the outcome. The 38-year-old Tennessean, with 24 years of experience since his printer's devil days, now was competing with Pulitzer, Hearst, Dana, Reid, and Bennett in the New York field.

The plan of attack Ochs had devised to save the *New York Times* was simple. He would not attempt to match the sensationalism of Hearst and Pulitzer, nor would he popularize the paper's offerings in a halfway effort to keep up with the mass circulation leaders, as some other New York publishers were attempting to do. Instead he would publish a paper with solid news coverage and editorial opinion that would be designed for readers who did not like overemphasis of entertainment and features. Ochs' declaration of principle contained these lines:

> It will be my earnest aim that the *New York Times* give the news, all the news, in concise and attractive form, in language that is parliamentary in good society, and give it as early, if not earlier, than it can be learned through any other reliable medium; to give the news impartially, without fear or favor, regardless of any party, sect or interest involved; to make the columns of the *New York Times* a forum for the consideration of all questions of public importance, and to that end to invite intelligent discussion from all shades of opinion.[1]

Ochs's first steps were unspectacular, but effective. The *Times* began to publish a guide listing the out-of-town buyers who were in the city. It reported daily real estate transactions. And it expanded its market reports, adding to the daily coverage a weekly financial review. The business and financial community began to find these *Times* features increasingly valuable. Lawyers similarly were attracted by another column listing court cases and records. The class of readers to which Ochs was appealing also liked the emphasis placed on reporting of news of government. It liked Ochs's Sunday magazine, which featured articles of current news significance rather than entertainment. And it liked the *Times* book review section.

Ochs determinedly set his face against the popular features of the new journalism, refusing to run "stunt" stories, banning comics from his columns, and giving pictures short shrift. He sniped at the yellow journalists, advertising the *Times* under the slogan "It Does Not Soil the Breakfast Cloth" before choosing the famous front-page ear, "All the News That's Fit to Print." But circulation in 1898 was still at the 25,000 mark. Ochs decided to make one last gamble. The *Times* was selling for three cents, the *World* and *Journal* for two. Why not cut the price of the *Times* to a penny and thus win the circulation needed to ensure solid advertising support?

Once again the old formula of price adjustment was successful. The *Times* as a penny paper jumped to 75,000 circulation in 1899 and passed the 100,000 mark in 1901. Its advertising linage doubled within two years. The red ink turned to black and Ochs won majority control of the paper's stock under his purchasing agreement. He promptly went into debt again to build the Times Tower on Broadway, in what became Times Square, putting $2,500,000 into what was in 1904 one of New York's most spectacular buildings. The strategic location of the *Times* plant in what became the city's nighttime heart and the later development of its moving electric news bulletins helped to establish the paper as one of the city's institutions.

CARR VAN ANDA,
MANAGING EDITOR
Far more important to the future of the *Times* was another event of 1904, however. That year Carr V. Van Anda, America's foremost managing editor, began his 25-year career as the guiding genius of the *Times* news staff. To single out Van Anda as America's foremost managing editor perhaps seems extraordinary, for comparisons of the accomplishments of men in different eras and different publishing situations are difficult to make. But it is generally agreed that the chief architect of the superior news department of the *New*

Adolph S. Ochs, (*above*) rescued the *New York Times* from bankruptcy in 1896 and made it one of the world's great newspapers before he died in 1935. His longtime managing editor, Carr Van Anda (*left*), achieved fame as the man most instrumental in developing the *Times*'s superb news coverage. It was Ochs, however, whose leadership made possible the achievements of Van Anda and his staff members.

York Times was Van Anda, a man who shunned personal publicity so completely that despite his incredible achievements he became almost a legendary figure even to his own craft.[2]

Alexander Woollcott once remarked that Van Anda "loved the editing of a newspaper more than anything in the world." Apparently he was born with this love, for as a boy of six in an Ohio village in 1870, he was pasting clippings on sheets of paper and selling them for 10 cents a copy. At 10 he made a press out of a wooden frame, an ink roller from a cloth-wrapped broom handle, and printed with type salvaged from the village paper. Next he acquired a small press and did job printing, using the profits to finance his study of chemistry and physics. When he entered Ohio University at 16 he specialized in mathematics and science and had not the lure of journalism been so strong he likely would have become a scholar in the realms of astronomy and physics. As it was, he became a layman who could keep step with the keen minds in those fields.

Van Anda left college at 18 to become foreman for his village paper. Next he set type and reported for the *Cleveland Herald* and other Cleveland papers. When he was 22 he applied for work on the *Baltimore Sun* and was selected for the important post of night editor. Two years later, in 1888, he moved to the *New York Sun,* where after five years he became night editor. When Ochs decided in 1904 that his first managing editor, Henry Loewenthal, should devote full attention to business news, Van Anda's name was suggested to him. The association was to be an ideal one. Ochs was willing to spend money to get the news; Van Anda was more than willing to spend it for him.

Although he was now a managing editor, Van Anda never stopped serving as night editor. His routine at the *Times,* for 20 years, never varied. He appeared in the newsroom at 1 P.M., went home at 6 P.M. for dinner and a rest, and returned at 10 P.M. to stay until the last man departed at 5 A.M. Usually he was the last man. Twelve hours a day, seven days a week, Van Anda was riding the news, giving as much attention to the flow of stories as to the major news breaks. He loved to match his speed and wits against a deadline. He loved to exploit an important but undeveloped story and give it painstaking coverage and significant play. But he never lost sight of the importance of conscientious and intelligent handling of the bulk of the news, and he transmitted this spirit to his staff. He was not a colorful, dynamic leader; rather he was reserved and cold in appearance and his piercing gaze was called the "Van Anda death ray." But those who worked with him found him a modest, sympathetic chief who backed his men completely and who never flew into a rage. His secret was in doing his own job so well that the impress was made both on the newspaper and its staff.

There are many stories of Van Anda's almost legendary ability. Soon after he became managing editor of the *Times,* word arrived that the decisive naval battle of the Russo-Japanese War might be at hand. Van Anda recognized the importance of the event and readied himself to handle the story. When the bulletin came, at 4:30 one morning, that the Japanese admiral, Togo, had smashed the Russian fleet, all of Van Anda's elaborate research and preparation went into play. Within 19 minutes the *Times* had put an extra to press with the bulletin and a half-page of war news on page one, running under headlines written by Van Anda as the page was being remade. Inside was more advance material that Van Anda long before had made ready for this moment. Forty thousand copies were run off and the managing editor rode about the city with a fleet of horse-drawn wagons at dawn seeing personally that his news beat was prominently displayed on the newsstands.

Van Anda's classic achievement was his handling of the story of the sinking of the liner *Titanic* in 1912. Here, as in other situations, it was Van Anda's personal ability and the functioning of a well-trained staff of high caliber that combined to produce superior news coverage.

It was 1:20 A.M. Monday, April 15, 1912, when the first Associated Press bulletin reached the *Times* newsroom reporting that the luxury liner *Titanic* had struck an iceberg on its maiden voyage from Britain to America. An SOS had been picked up by the Marconi wireless station in Newfoundland. The *Titanic* supposedly was unsinkable, but Van Anda's rapid calls to *Times* correspondents in Halifax and Montreal and to the offices of the White Star Line told him that the ship's wireless had fallen silent a half-hour after the first call for help and convinced him that the ship must have gone down.

Before 3:30 A.M. Van Anda and his staff had organized the story. Among the more than 2,200 aboard were many famous persons. A background story was prepared on the passenger list, and a picture of the *Titanic* was prepared for page one. Two other vessels had reported close scrapes with icebergs in the North Atlantic area; this fitted the pattern of the news available about the *Titanic*. The *Times* in several columns of type reported Monday morning that the ship had sunk, while other papers were handling the story in incomplete and inconclusive form.

Tuesday, Wednesday, and Thursday, the story commanded the world's attention, as the liner *Carpathia* sailed toward New York with survivors. Van Anda on Tuesday hired a floor in a hotel a block from the *Carpathia's* pier and installed four telephone lines directly connected to the *Times* city room. The entire staff was mobilized under the direction of Arthur Greaves, city editor, to cover the arrival of the rescue ship Thursday night. Van Anda persuaded Guglielmo Marconi, the wireless inventor, to board the ship to interview the wireless operator—and a *Times* reporter slipped through the police lines with the inventor. He got an exclusive story of the last messages from the *Titanic*.

Within three hours after the arrival of the rescue ship the *Times'* first edition appeared, with 15 of its 24 pages devoted to the story of the loss of 1,500 lives in the *Titanic* disaster. In coverage and in organization of a great news story, that edition of the *Times* remains a masterpiece.[3]

Van Anda and Ochs both loved speed in the gathering of the news and this love had led the *Times* to leadership in the use of correspondents and communications facilities in such instances as the *Titanic* sinking. Both men had watched the work of Marconi, the Italian scientist who between the years of 1895 and 1900 devised a practical system of sending telegraphic messages through space by means of electromagnetic waves. Marconi's "wireless" telegraphy was based on the experiments of others, but it was he who obtained the basic patents and formed the first commercial wireless company in London in 1897.

Ship-to-shore communication and the use of the wireless by English newspapers and the *New York Herald* to cover sporting events soon followed. In December 1901, Marconi successfully transmitted signals from England to Newfoundland. But it was not until 1907 that a headline in the *Times* reported:

"Wireless Joins Two Worlds. Marconi Trans-Atlantic Service Opened With A Dispatch To The *New York Times*."[4]

Ranking above all else in bringing the *Times* to greatness was its coverage of the events of the first World War. It was in this period that the paper began to publish the texts of documents and speeches, a policy that led to its becoming the leading reference newspaper for librarians, scholars, government officials, and other newspaper editors. The compilation of the *New York Times Index* further ensured the paper this position.

Six full pages in an August 1914 issue of the *Times* presented the British White

Paper to American readers. The *Times* had been the first American paper to obtain a copy of the British Foreign Office's correspondence with Germany and Austria and printed it in full. Next day it published the text of the German version of events leading up to the war declaration, brought from Berlin by a *Times* correspondent, for another exclusive.

Van Anda meanwhile was giving his readers minute coverage of the military news, using press association accounts, the reports of his own correspondents with the various armies, and stories obtained from the *London Chronicle*. War pictures were carried in a rotogravure section, added by Ochs in 1914 after Van Anda had investigated rotogravure printing in Germany. Political and economic reporting from European capitals was given proper emphasis with the military news. When the United States entered the war the *Times* expanded its coverage, spending $750,000 a year on cabled news.

THE *TIMES* TO 1935   After 25 years of Ochs' ownership, the *Times* of 1921 had achieved major stature. There was one great reason for this success. The paper had taken in some $100 million in those 25 years and had paid out but 4 percent in dividends. Ochs had poured the millions into the *Times* for buildings and equipment, for staff, and for the tremendous news coverage Van Anda had built. Circulation had reached 330,000 daily and more than 500,000 Sunday, while advertising linage had increased tenfold in the 25 years, passing the 23-million mark. Ochs was a great builder and the *Times* was the symbol of his business success.

Politically the *Times* had been Democratic except during the Bryan campaigns. But it was essentially conservative in tone, particularly in its economic outlook. It was progressive in its social viewpoint but Ochs was not one of the crusaders of the "people's champions" variety. After going down to defeat on the League of Nations issue with the 1920 Democratic ticket of James M. Cox and Franklin D. Roosevelt, the *Times'* favorite Democrat of the early 1920s was John W. Davis, the New York lawyer who was defeated by Calvin Coolidge in the 1924 election. The *Times* supported Alfred E. Smith in 1928 and Franklin D. Roosevelt in 1932 in the final campaigns before Ochs's death.

The 1920s saw one era of *Times* history ending and another beginning. Editor Miller died in 1922 and was succeeded by Rollo Ogden, longtime *New York Post* editor. Van Anda went into semiretirement in 1925 although he continued to hold the title of managing editor until 1932. Frederick T. Birchall, his distinguished associate in the newsroom and also a leading foreign correspondent, continued the Van Anda tradition. Appearing on the staff in the early twenties were such future *Times* luminaries as Anne O'Hare McCormick, who won a Pulitzer Prize for her reporting from Europe as a leading foreign correspondent; Lester Markel, Sunday editor; and Louis Stark, labor reporter. Following them were Waldemar Kaempffert and William L. Laurence in the field of science and Arthur Krock in the Washington bureau. David H. Joseph became city editor in 1927 for a 21-year term, and Edwin L. James became managing editor in 1932 after his European reporting assignments.

While still active in management, Ochs groomed his son-in-law, Arthur Hays Sulzberger, and his nephew, Julius Ochs Adler, to succeed him. The deaths of Ochs and his business manager, Louis Wiley, in 1935 removed the last of the quartet that had been instrumental in building the *Times*. But the organization they had created continued to carry the paper to new heights in the succeeding years. What the newspaper and its staff contributed to recent American journalism becomes a part of a later story.

WILLIAM ALLEN WHITE AND THE *EMPORIA GAZETTE*

While Ochs was guiding the destinies of the *Times* in his comparatively impersonal role as head of a journalistic institution, a small-town Kansas editor was making a highly personal impact on American society. William Allen White was born in Emporia, Kansas, in 1868 and died there in 1944. But between those years he became a citizen of America and a spokesman for its small towns—of which Emporia became the symbol. The editor of the *Emporia Gazette* was anything but a typical representative of his kind of journalism, but nevertheless his newspaper editorship was the foundation for his larger activities.

White worked as a printer and reporter while at the University of Kansas. At 24, he was an editorial writer for William Rockhill Nelson's *Kansas City Star*. He scraped together $3,000 by 1895 and bought the *Emporia Gazette,* a rundown Populist party paper with fewer than 600 subscribers. But William Allen White, age 27, was home in Emporia with his wife, Sallie, to stay.

Kansas had been captured during the 1893 depression by the Populists and the Democrats. White was an active Republican editor and politician—he loved politics all his life and remained a party worker and an intimate of politicians from the time of William McKinley and Theodore Roosevelt to that of Wendell Willkie and Franklin Roosevelt. On August 15, 1896, White exploded with anger at the Populists in an editorial that shot him into national fame. It was "What's the Matter with Kansas?" which White later referred to as representing "conservatism in its full and perfect flower." The editorial cited evidence that Kansas was declining in population and economic standing and placed the blame in fully unrestrained and effective style on the

Emporia Gazette

William Allen White

"shabby, wild-eyed, rattle-brained fanatics" of the reform movement.[5] It was reprinted in virtually every Republican newspaper in the country, as ammunition against the Democratic candidate for president, William Jennings Bryan. William McKinley's campaign manager, Mark Hanna, adopted the young editor. But Bryan and the Democrats won the election in Kansas.

White now moved to the national stage. He became the friend of political leaders and came to know the young New York Republican Theodore Roosevelt, to whom he became deeply attached and who was his lifelong political hero. More importantly, he met S.S. McClure and became a member of the circle that included Lincoln Steffens, Ray Stannard Baker, John Phillips, and Ida M. Tarbell. His articles and stories about Kansas and politics appeared in several magazines. White was now in tune with the times, hobnobbing with the muckrakers and becoming with his wife a frequent visitor at the Oyster Bay home of the Theodore Roosevelts. The *Emporia Gazette* began to demand reforms: conservation of natural resources, railroad rate control, working men's compensation, direct primaries, the initiative and referendum, abolition of child labor.

When Roosevelt split with William Howard

Taft in 1912 and the Progressive party was formed, White was Kansas national committeeman for the new third party. He was a supporter of the League of Nations—an internationalist in isolationist territory—and when World War II came, he was a leader in the Committee to Defend America by Aiding the Allies. He admired the social gains of the New Deal, but he preferred the leadership of Theodore Roosevelt to that of Franklin Roosevelt.

Another of America's distinctive small-town editors also lived and worked in Kansas. He was Ed Howe, who in 1877 at the age of 22 founded the daily *Atchison Globe* with $200 capital. Howe was a superlative reporter. He knew people and how to report their little doings. However, he had none of White's expansiveness and sentimentality but rather an amazing ability to make trouble for himself. He told the people of Kansas that religion was all bosh, and he asserted in a time of agitation for women's rights that a woman's place was strictly in the home. His terse, sardonic editorial paragraphs often reflected a keen understanding of human nature, however, and they were widely requoted in the country's newspapers as the work of the "Sage of Potato Hill." His excellent novel, *The Story of a Country Town,* added to his fame.

THE LAST GREAT YEARS OF THE *NEW YORK WORLD*

Among the great and colorful editors of the years immediately preceding and following World War I were the aging editor of the *Louisville Courier-Journal,* Henry Watterson, and the dynamic editor of the *New York World,* Frank I. Cobb. Watterson, though reaching the close of a career that had started in Civil War days, was vigorously and colorfully attacking Theodore Roosevelt in his columns, expressing his distrust of "Professor" Woodrow Wilson and delighting in an exchange of editorial argument with men like Cobb. Two months after World War I began, Watterson adopted the simple but effective battlecry: "To Hell with the Hohenzollerns and the Hapsburgs!" His more intellectual arguments for American entry into the war won for him the 1918 Pulitzer Prize for editorial writing—a fitting tribute to a great journalistic figure.

Cobb's editorial page represented the realization of Joseph Pulitzer's hopes for the full development of the *New York World.* The editor whom Pulitzer had carefully trained before his own death in 1911 was unexcelled in his forcible expression of logically developed opinions. The *World* commanded deep respect for its intelligent and fair-minded approaches to issues of public importance, for its progressive and hard-hitting crusades that combined the reporting abilities of its news staff and the support of the editorial writers, and for its brilliant, if sometimes erratic, news play. It became one of those favorites of the press world that are called "newspapermen's newspapers."

The *World* helped to "discover" Woodrow Wilson as a presidential candidate, and Cobb and Wilson became close friends. Cobb's often-expressed fear of centralization of authority was in part overcome by his association with Wilson, and the *World* vigorously supported the far-reaching New Freedom program of economic and social reform that gave the federal government vast new powers. Cobb was one of Wilson's advisers at the Versailles peace conference, giving expression to the hopes for international cooperation that the *World* had long held. His battles in the columns of the *World* for American participation in the League of Nations and the World Court were unavailing, but they further established the paper as the leading spokesman of the Democratic party.

Tragedy struck the *World* in 1923 when Cobb died at the height of his powers. For just eight years later the *World* itself succumbed, and many a sorrowing newspaperman muttered, ''If only Cobb had lived. . . .'' Probably there would have been no difference in the fate of the *World* but it was true that after Cobb's death the newspaper lacked the genius of leadership it had enjoyed since its purchase by Pulitzer in 1883.

During the middle twenties the *World* seemed to be continuing its powerful position. Cobb had left behind a distinguished editorial-page staff, headed now by Walter Lippmann. Among the editorial writers were Maxwell Anderson and Laurence Stallings—more famous for their play, ''What Price Glory''—and Charles Merz, later to become editor of the *New York Times*. Appearing on the *World*'s ''op. ed.'' page were Heywood Broun, the liberal-thinking columnist of ''It Seems to Me'' fame, Franklin P. Adams, conductor of the ''Conning Tower,'' and Frank Sullivan, who like Anderson and Stallings moved to other creative fields. Rollin Kirby, the cartoonist, won three Pulitzer Prizes in this period for the *World*.

Despite this brilliance and the distinguished record of the paper, Joseph Pulitzer's creation was losing the battle in New York morning journalism. Pressing it on one side were Ochs's *Times* and the merger-created *Herald Tribune*. Soaking up circulation on the other side were the tabloids that appeared in the early twenties. The *World* failed to keep pace with its orthodox rivals in complete coverage of the news, even though it sometimes performed brilliantly, and it saw some of its subway-riding readers succumbing to the lure of the tabloids. Of the Pulitzer heirs, Joseph Pulitzer, Jr., had shown the most ability but he had assumed control of the *St. Louis Post-Dispatch*. His brothers, Ralph and Herbert, delegated much authority to Herbert Bayard Swope as executive editor, but Swope left the *World* staff in 1928. Already the newspaper was running a deficit, and in the depression year of 1930 Pulitzer losses on the morning, evening, and Sunday editions reached nearly $2 million. Then rumors of an impending sale began to be heard, and staff members made a desperate effort to raise enough cash to buy the *World* themselves. They argued, too, that the Pulitzer will forbade the sale of the paper, but in February 1931, a New York court approved its purchase by Roy W. Howard for the Scripps-Howard interests. The evening *World* was merged with the *Telegram*. The morning *World*—symbol of Pulitzer's journalist genius—was dead, and there was scarcely a newspaperman who did not feel that something peculiarly precious and irreplaceable had been lost to the craft.[6]

There were other newspapers that, like the *World,* were regarded as ''newspapermen's newspapers.'' Very few combined a conception of public responsibility and journalistic brilliance to the degree that made the *World* great. But wherever oldtime newsmen gathered in this period there likely would be mentioned the work of men who wrote for and edited the *New York Sun* and *New York Herald*. Quite likely, too, the name of the *Chicago Inter Ocean* would be mentioned. These papers, now dead, are a part of the colorful story of American journalism, and the alumni of their excellent training grounds were legion. They lagged behind in the journalistic advance into the modern era but they and the people who worked for them had proud traditions and moments of glory.

THE *NEW YORK SUN* GOES DOWN

The *New York Sun* of the days of editor Charles A. Dana and managing editor Amos J. Cummings had emphasized reporting skill, writing style, and human interest techniques to a degree worthy of the admiration of the practitioners of the ''new journalism.'' It was a city editor of the *Sun,* John B. Bogart, who told a young reporter for the first time: ''When a dog bites a man, that is not news; but when a man bites a dog, *that* is news.'' It was an editorial writer for the *Sun,* Francis P. Church, who in 1897 answered the ''Is There a Santa Claus?'' inquiry of a little girl named Virginia with an explanation that was reprinted widely for many years. It was a reporter for the *Sun*, Will Irwin, who in 1906 wrote the journalistic masterpiece, ''The City That Was,'' in memory of San Francisco's destruction by earthquake and fire.[7]

Heading the *Sun* news staff from the eighties to the World War I period were managing editor Chester S. Lord and night city editor Selah M. Clarke, called ''Boss'' by his associates. They helped to train reporters like Irwin, Arthur Brisbane, Julian Ralph, Samuel Hopkins Adams, Richard Harding Davis, and Jacob Riis. From their night desk, too, Carr Van Anda went to his great career on the *Times*. Succeeding Dana as editor was the highly competent and graceful stylist, Edward P. Mitchell. The *Sun* was regarded as a ''school of journalism'' for young journalists, and its graduates formed an alumni association. They were dismayed when control of the *Sun* passed in 1916 to Frank A. Munsey, a business-minded purchaser of newspapers who understood little of the journalistic traditions of the craft. The famous morning edition of the *Sun* disappeared in 1920 and the evening *Sun*, bearing little resemblance to the paper of old, trudged on toward eventual oblivion.

THE *NEW YORK HERALD*, LEADER IN NEWS

The *New York Herald*, under the guidance of founder James Gordon Bennett, had achieved leadership in news enterprise. When James Gordon Bennett, Jr., took control in 1872 the *Herald* ranked first in collecting and presenting the news. Its reporters and correspondents were the best and its insistence on use of the fastest means of communication made it a hard-hitting rival for Pulitzer and Hearst when they invaded New York. Its traditions were still those of its adventurous correspondent of the early seventies, Henry M. Stanley, who spent two years searching in Africa on an assignment from the younger Bennett before he found the missing missionary and inquired, ''Dr. Livingstone, I presume?'' The *Herald* remained a news enterprise paper in the early twentieth century, contesting vigorously for complete and dramatic coverage of the world's events. It had Joseph L. Stickney with Dewey at Manila; Richard Harding Davis covering the Boer War; Oscar King Davis and W.H. Lewis giving it top coverage of the Russo-Japanese War; Dr. Frederick A. Cook reporting on his trip to the North Pole; and a network of political and war correspondents (supplied in part by the *Paris Herald*) that was the equal of any such group in World War I. Its use of art work and photographs embellished its crack coverage of such events as the sinking of the *General Slocum* and the *Titanic* disaster.[8]

In the struggle for survival in New York, however, the *Herald* was handicapped by the personality and practices of its owner, the younger Bennett. He was intelligent and alert, and his driving force dominated the paper. He established the Paris edition of the *Herald* in 1887, now the famed *International Herald Tribune*. But in his 45 years as a publisher he proved to be a dictator who put his personal whims first. He lived in Paris most of his life, rarely visiting the *Herald* office, and his royal manner of living drained an estimated $30 million from the profits of his papers.[9] No other publisher, save William Randolph Hearst, equaled Bennett in irresponsible personal control of a journalistic enterprise.

George Jean Nathan has described Bennett as he appeared in 1909, at the age of 67.[10] He was tall, slender, full of nervous energy, but bearing himself with a military erectness accented by steel-gray hair and moustache. Though he lived in Paris, his editors could neither hire nor fire a reporter without his consent. His editorial committee met at a table with an empty chair at the head—that was Bennett. At his

The *Herald* covers a 1904 ship disaster that had a final death toll of 1,000.

place were set fresh copies of the paper each day, as though he might walk in at any moment.

Bennett's connection with the paper was far from being a psychological one, however. Cabled instructions arrived from Paris each day. Frequently department heads were called to Paris for conferences. Bennett kept close watch on the work of each employee and practiced a policy of seeing to it that no individual achieved personal importance. While he had many good news instincts, he also forced the paper to observe many rules of conduct based on his personal idiosyncrasics and ordered promotion of his personal beliefs. At Bennett's death in 1918, the *Herald* was sold to Frank Munsey, who could not make the leaderless paper profitable and let it disappear into the *Herald Tribune* in 1924. That paper maintained the Bennett news traditions.

CHICAGO'S FAMED
INTER OCEAN

A newspaper in Chicago's past journalism history that for a time attracted a following of newspapermen was the *Inter Ocean*. It started its career in 1865 as the *Chicago Republican,* edited by Charles A. Dana for the first year. It became the *Inter Ocean* in 1872, a staunch Republican spokesman owned by William Penn Nixon. Through its reporting enterprise on the frontier, its religious news, and its agricultural news coverage it built up a midwestern circulation. It also led in introducing mechanical improvements, installing a color press in 1892 in advance of other American newspapers. During the nineties the paper lost money and was sold to Charles T. Yerkes, Chicago's traction line boss. Despite its record for conducting crusades in the public interest, the *Inter Ocean* suffered under Yerkes's ownership until he sold it in 1902 to George W. Hinman, who had come from the *New York Sun* to be the *Inter Ocean*'s editor.

Under Hinman the *Inter Ocean* won notice as a training school for newspapermen. The paper had been one of those that had catered to the "tramp reporters" of the period and by so doing had obtained the services of many young men with journalistic futures. Belonging to the *Inter Ocean* alumni association were Marquis James, William Cuppy, and Ring Lardner, writers; Walter Howey, later a famous Hearst executive; Richard J. Finnegan, later editor of the *Chicago Times* and *Sun-Times;* and a score of other prominent newspapermen. In 1914, however, the *Inter Ocean* fell victim to Chicago's newspaper competition and was added to the list of newspapers that have become reminiscences.[11]

THE *DENVER POST'S*
"BUCKET OF BLOOD"
DAYS

No account of American journalism history is complete without a mention of the *Denver Post* of the days of Harry H. Tammen and Fred G. Bonfils. With its giant bannerlines printed in red ink, its startling and helter-skelter makeup, and its highly sensationalized news play, the *Post* won fame as a dynamic but irresponsible paper. Its owners won fame, too, as ruthless operators of a journalistic gold mine. Tammen, a onetime bartender, and Bonfils, who had come West to make money in real estate and the lottery business, joined forces in 1895 to buy the *Post.* Their yellow journalism tactics succeeded in the rough-and-tumble newspaper warfare of Denver and at the height of their fortunes in the 1920s the paper was making more than a million dollars a year.

The *Post* was filled with features and sensational stories, but it also engaged in stunts and crusades that spread its fame in the Rocky Mountain area, where it advertised itself as "Your Big Brother." The partners operated from an office with red-painted walls, which Denver promptly called "The Bucket of Blood." Victims of the *Post*'s crusades and exposés filed libel suits against Tammen and Bonfils and accusations of blackmailing were leveled against the owners. No such charges were ever proved in court, however, and the *Post* continued in its proclaimed role as ''the people's champion.''

After Tammen's death in 1924, the *Post*'s luck began to change. The conduct of the paper in withholding news of illegal oil leases at Teapot Dome, until Bonfils was in a position to force the lessees to make a contract by which the *Post* would profit by half a million dollars, led the committee on ethics of the American Society of Newspaper Editors to recommend that Bonfils be expelled from membership. Instead, however, he was allowed to resign. His reputation was further darkened just before his death in 1933 when he sued the rival *Rocky Mountain News* for libel and then lost interest when the *News* undertook to document many of the stories about the partners.

Still the *Post* roared on, while the stories about life on Denver newspapers multiplied.[12] Entry of the Scripps-Howard chain into intensified competition with the *Post* in 1926 through purchase of the morning *Rocky Mountain News,* and of the evening *Times* for merger with the Scripps-owned *Express,* brought about one of the country's greatest competitive struggles. No holds were barred by city desks and circulation departments for the next two years, and Denver gorged itself on sensational news and free premium offers. In 1928 a truce was arranged by which the *Times* was killed, leaving the *Post* alone in the evening field, and the *News* in the morning. The journalistic habits of the days when anything went continued to haunt Denver, however, for another two decades, until a change in management at the *Post* brought new policies that pushed memories of the Tammen-Bonfils era into the background.

NOTES

1. *New York Times,* August 19, 1896.

2. See Davis, *History of the New York Times,* p. 274, and Berger, *The Story of the New York Times,* p. 160, for two estimates of Van Anda's role in building the *Times*. Many tributes to Van Anda from leaders in his profession are found in a short biography: Barnett Fine, *A Giant of the Press* (New York: Editor & Publisher Library, 1933). Berger carries the story of Van Anda's achievements through several chapters.

3. For the full story of the ''Titanic'' coverage see Berger, *The Story of the New York Times,* pp. 193–201. A contemporary account by Alexander McD. Stoddart appeared in the *Independent,* LXXII (May 2, 1912), 945.

4. *New York Times,* October 18, 1907.

5. The editorial is reprinted in *The Autobiography of William Allen White* (New York: Macmillan, 1946), pp. 280–83. It also appears in Nevins, *American Press Opinion,* pp. 419–22.

6. The last city editor of the *World* told the story of its death in James W. Barrett, *The World, the Flesh, and Messrs. Pulitzer* (New York: Vanguard, 1931). See also Barrett's *Joseph Pulitzer and His World* (New York: Vanguard, 1941).

7. Some of the color of the *Sun* is found in Frank M. O'Brien, *The Story of The Sun* (New York: George H. Doran Company, 1918). Church's ''Is There a Santa Claus?'' is reprinted on pp. 409–10.

8. See, for example, *Herald* pages in Michael C. Emery *et al., America's Front Page News, 1690–1970* (New York: Doubleday, 1970), pp. 83, 104, 109, 124.

9. Don C. Seitz, *The James Gordon Bennetts* (Indianapolis: Bobbs-Merrill, 1928), p. 377.

10. In *Outing,* LIII (March 1909), 690.

11. The story of the *Inter Ocean* is told in Walter E. Ewert, ''The History of the Chicago Inter Ocean, 1872–1914'' (Master's thesis, Northwestern University, 1940).

12. Many of the colorful stories are found in Gene Fowler, *Timber Line* (New York: Covici-Friede, Inc., 1933).

ANNOTATED BIBLIOGRAPHY

Books

BARRETT, JAMES W., *The World, the Flesh, and Messrs. Pulitzer*. New York: Vanguard, 1931. The best story of the sale of the *World,* by the paper's last city editor.

BERGER, MEYER, *The Story of the New York Times, 1851–1951*. New York: Simon & Schuster, 1951. Mainly the story of the *Times* after Ochs bought it; other books are better for the pre-Ochs period. But reporter Berger gets many reporters into his story, too rare an event in newspaper history-telling, and thus has a lively and interesting book. The *Times* also issued *One Hundred Years of Famous Pages from The New York Times* in its centennial year, and many later reprints.

BOND, F. FRASER, *Mr. Miller of "The Times."* New York: Scribner's, 1931. The biography of *New York Times* editor Charles R. Miller.

BOYLAN, JAMES, ed., *The World and the Twenties: The Golden Years of New York's Legendary Newspaper*. New York: Dial Press, 1973. Captures the flavor and writing skill.

DAVIS, ELMER, *History of the New York Times, 1851–1921*. New York: The New York Times, 1921. Still good for its period.

FINE, BARNETT, *A Giant of the Press*. New York: Editor & Publisher Library, 1933. A short biography of Carr Van Anda, managing editor of the *New York Times*.

FOWLER, GENE, *Timber Line*. New York: Covici-Friede, Inc., 1933. The colorful story of the Bonfils and Tammen era at the *Denver Post*. No tale was too tall for Denver newsmen.

HOSOKAWA, BILL, *Thunder in the Rockies: The Incredible Denver Post*. New York: Morrow, 1976. An update by the executive news editor.

HOWE, E.W., *Plain People*. New York: Dodd, Mead, 1929. The story of an unusual small-town Kansas editor in the usual small town, and of the *Atchison Globe*.

HUTCHENS, JOHN K. AND GEORGE OPPENHEIMER, eds., *The Best in The World*. New York: Viking Press, 1973. Selections from 1921–28.

JOHNSON, GERALD W., *An Honorable Titan*. New York: Harper & Row, 1946. A good, but comparatively uncritical, biographical study of Adolph S. Ochs.

JOHNSON, WALTER, *William Allen White's America*. New York: Holt, Rinehart & Winston, 1947. Important as an interpretation of the swiftly changing half-century in which White was a national figure.

MAHIN, HELEN O., ed., *The Editor and His People*. New York: Macmillan, 1924. An excellent collection of William Allen White's editorials.

MITCHELL, EDWARD P., *Memoirs of an Editor*. New York: Scribner's, 1924. By the distinguished editor of the *New York Sun*.

NEVINS, ALLAN, *American Press Opinion*. New York: Heath, 1928. Nevins' brilliant interpretative essays and selected editorials continue through this period.

PERKIN, ROBERT L., *The First Hundred Years: An Informal History of Denver and the Rocky Mountain News*. New York: Doubleday, 1959. By a staff member of Colorado's first paper.

PICKETT, CALDER M., *Ed Howe: Country Town Philosopher*. Lawrence: University Press of Kansas, 1969. Prize-winning biography of the editor of the *Atchison Globe*.

SEITZ, DON C., *The James Gordon Bennetts*. Indianapolis: Bobbs-Merrill, 1928. The younger Bennett brings the *New York Herald* to its downfall.

WHITE, WILLIAM ALLEN, *The Autobiography of William Allen White*. New York: Macmillan, 1946. No one should miss this autobiography, and few do. See also McKee, John D., *William Allen White: Maverick on Main Street*. Westport, Conn.: Greenwood Press, 1975.

Periodicals and Monographs

EWERT, WALTER E., "The History of the Chicago Inter Ocean, 1872–1914." Master's thesis, Northwestern University. 1940. An excellent account of a famous paper.

FINE, BARNETT, "When 'Boss' Lord Ruled 'The Sun'," *Editor & Publisher,* LXVI (April 22–July 15, 1933). A series of articles about Chester S. Lord, managing editor of the *New York Sun* during 33 of its best years.

HOWE, GENE, "My Father Was the Most Wretchedly Unhappy Man I Ever Knew," *Saturday Evening Post,* October 25, 1941. A dramatic story about E.W. Howe, reprinted in Drewry, *Post Biographies.*

IRWIN, WILL, "The New York Sun," *American Magazine,* LXVII (January 1909), 301. The story of the *Sun's* school of journalism, by one of the pupils.

NATHAN, GEORGE JEAN, "James Gordon Bennett, the Monte Cristo of Modern Journalism," *Outing,* LIII (March 1909), 690. The dramatic critic criticizes an erratic publisher.

STOLBERG, BENJAMIN, "The Man Behind 'The Times'," *Atlantic Monthly,* CXXXVIII (December 1926), 721. A discerning study of Adolph S. Ochs. Reprinted in Ford and Emery, *Highlights in the History of the American Press.*

WHITE, W.L., "The Sage of Emporia," *Nieman Reports,* XXIII (March 1969), 23. Human interest piece by William Allen White's son.

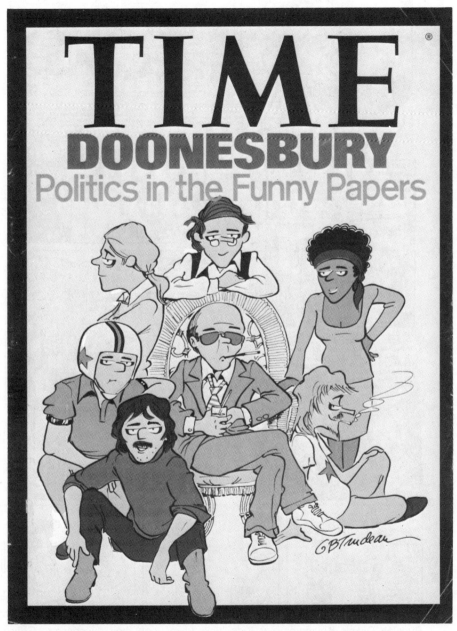

The continued popularity of the comic strips was symbolized by this *Time* cover drawn by Garry Trudeau, the creator of "Doonesbury." From top center, clockwise, are Michael J. Doonesbury, Ginny, Zonker, Duke, Mark, B.D., and Joanie Caucus.

Rudolph Dirks's Katzenjammer Kids look down upon their successors: George McManus's Jiggs of 1926; Frank King's Gasoline Alley of 1923 with Walt adopting Skeezix; Harold Gray's Little Orphan Annie and Sandy, 1936; Chic Young's Blondie and Dagwood, 1936; Milton Caniff's Steve Canyon in 1939 "Terry and the Pirates"; Chester Gould's Dick Tracy as he began in 1931 and again in 1956; and Charlie Brown, Lucy, and Snoopy in a 1956 "Peanuts" strip by Charles M. Schulz (with © permissions for years indicated from United Feature, King Features, and Chicago Tribune-New York Daily News Syndicates).

20

The Common Denominators

. . . when one travels through the country on a Sunday on a fast train and buys . . . Sunday papers . . . one finds the same "comics," the same Sunday magazines, the same special "features" in almost all of them and, of course, in most of them precisely the same Associated Press news . . . The newspaper profession has turned out to be a business and as a result there was bound to be standardization . . .

—Oswald Garrison Villard (1930)

The rise of the American press associations—organizations dedicated to the rapid, thorough, and impartial collection and dissemination of all the news—was an epochal development in the history of journalism. "The right of the people to know" was greatly advanced by the creation of news agencies that utilize journalistic skills and modern communications techniques to find the news, to report it impartially, and to speed it to every corner of the country and of the world. The development in the twentieth century of two strongly competitive press associations, the Associated Press and the United Press International, guaranteed newspaper editors and readers a better kind of national and international news coverage than the world had ever known—despite acknowledged imperfections.

While the press associations have contributed mightily to the excellence of modern newspapers, nevertheless they have become one of the common denominators of a standardized journalism. The news they supply is a vital part of any daily, together with the paper's own local news. Only a few American dailies ever have been able to maintain staff correspondents in leading news centers of the country and world, and the press association logotypes—AP, UPI—have become the symbols of trustworthy service from an outside source. At the same time the influence of the press associations on the character of many daily newspapers has become pronounced. Their usual style of writing—summary lead, inverted pyramid story structure, jampacked facts—affected all newspaper writing, to the detriment of original, individualistic reporting. Their decisions on the relative importance of news events, indicated by the use of "bulletin" slugs and by transmission of news budget summaries to desk editors, became accepted by most papers. In too many newspaper offices the press associations' "flashes of life" and "today's chuckles" replaced local efforts, and entertaining stories of faraway crimes, violence, and romance became too readily available to uninspired and ineffectual news editors. The result was a standardization of content going beyond the beneficial and needed cooperative coverage of significant nonlocal news.

More strikingly emerging as common denominators of journalism were the syndicates and special services. Just as entertaining or exciting news attracts an audience anywhere, so do comic strips, cartoons, Sunday magazine sections, columns, and other features. Again, the syndicates have made available to newspapers of all sizes and localities the work of talented artists and writers whose services could not otherwise be obtained by the average paper. But in more than one city the race to corral the most successful comic strips, the best-read columnists, the most colorful features has at times overshadowed the more serious aspects of journalism. And sadly enough, ability to compete in newspaper publication has been affected by possession or lack of possession of popular syndicated material. Even more sadly, some newspapers ignored the fact that effectively produced local material outdraws most syndicated material in reader interest. Even when syndicated material was used wisely, it had an inevitable standardizing effect, which, combined with the similarity of news display, caused many a reader to refuse to buy more than one paper because "they're all alike." Oswald Garrison Villard, the famous editor of the *Nation* and thoughtful critic of the press whose quotation opens this chapter,[1] saw both the good and the bad in such standardization.

The United States has had three major press associations operating on nationwide and worldwide scales. One is the Associated Press, which arose out of nineteenth-century efforts at cooperative news-gathering. Its twentieth-century competitors were the United Press Associations, founded in 1907 by Edward Wyllis Scripps, and the International News Service, begun in 1909 by William Randolph Hearst. When these two services were merged in 1958 to form the United Press International, the new UPI became quite comparable in strength to the AP. Abroad, the UPI and AP of the 1970s sold their news and picture services to newspapers, radio, and television stations in competition with two other worldwide services. These were Reuters of Great Britain, founded in 1851, and Agence France-Presse, which arose after World War II out of the ruins of the old French Havas agency (1836).

THE ASSOCIATED PRESS: GENESIS

The longest history among the American press associations is that of the Associated Press. The modern cooperative news-gathering association with that name took final form in 1900 after a bitter struggle for control of the press association facilities of the country. The agreement among New York City's leading newspapers in 1849 that brought about the establishment of the Associated Press of New York set the pattern for similar associations. Midwestern dailies formed the Western Associated Press in 1862, and before 1870 a New York Associated Press and the New England Associated Press were organized. Other subsidiary regional groups followed. But always the power of the Associated Press of New York was felt.*

The New York AP had been well-guided by its earliest general agents, Dr. Alexander Jones (1849–51), news-gathering pioneer Daniel H. Craig (1851–66), and former Washington correspondent and San Francisco newspaperman James W.

*See pages 138–42 and 229–30 for earlier accounts.

Simonton (1866–82). Ground was given to restive western AP members when their agent, William Henry Smith, was named general manager (1882–92), and two of five executive committee seats went to westerners. Despite this, the New York AP faced serious competition from rebels who had tried to form a rival since 1869 and who in 1882 created the United Press (no relation to the present-day UPI). Walter Polk Phillips, its general manager, had strong modernized dailies as members and good foreign news. William M. Laffan, business manager of the *New York Sun,* was a UP leader.

The reaction of the ruling groups within the AP and UP was typical of the times. The two executive committees entered into a secret agreement providing for exchange of news between the two associations and a virtual end to competition. There were financial rewards for insiders. When the deal was uncovered in 1891, a new battle in AP ranks was inevitable.[2] The *New York Sun* and *Tribune* bolted to the UP in 1892, to be followed the next year by the remaining members of the Associated Press of New York. Taking control of the AP organization was a new corporation, the Associated Press of Illinois, chartered in late 1892.

Melville E. Stone, new AP general manager, obtained exclusive news exchange contracts with Reuters in Britain, Havas in France, and Wolff in Germany. He thus cut the United Press off from the sources of foreign news long enjoyed by its New York members. A four-year struggle finally ended in early 1897 when all the New York dailies except Dana's *Sun* and Hearst's *Journal* were admitted to the AP, and the United Press went into bankruptcy. Hearst had never been an AP member; Laffan of the *Sun* stubbornly organized his own Laffan News Bureau, which operated successfully until 1916.

Laffan indirectly was to cause the Associated Press more trouble before the association's course was finally set. The *Chicago Inter Ocean* went to court in 1898 to prevent the AP from discontinuing service to it as punishment for the *Inter Ocean's* use of Laffan News Bureau copy. An Illinois court decision, handed down in 1900, found that the incorporation papers of the AP were written so broadly as to make the press association a public utility, bound to provide its service to all newspapers wishing it. For the moment the Illinois ruling seemed to put an end to the exclusive membership character of the AP, but its leaders found a way out. The Associated Press of Illinois was dissolved, and a new Associated Press was formed as a nonprofit membership association under New York State law. Stone continued as general manager of the new AP.

THE NEW ASSOCIATED PRESS OF 1900

The most important fact about the new Associated Press of 1900 was that it was a cooperative. Its members were to supply each other with news originating in individual publication areas. They were to share the cost of this exchange of news, and the cost of maintaining a press association staff that would direct the flow of news and augment it with other coverage. The staff, headed by the general manager, was to be responsible only to the membership, through its officers and directors. The Associated Press thus would be an agency existing only for the benefit of its member newspapers.

There were some faults, however, in the AP organization. Until 1915 its members could not subscribe to other news services. The original members of 1900 owned bonds that carried additional voting rights, keeping control of the board of directors in the hands of older, larger papers. The smaller dailies were given three seats on a board of 18 in 1937. Most serious was the problem of protest rights, by which a member could keep a competitor in its city out of the AP. A four-fifths vote of the entire membership was required to override such a veto and was rarely obtained. The only way into AP in larger cities was to buy an existing membership.

This restriction of AP membership was challenged by the *Chicago Sun,* founded in 1941 by Marshall Field as a competitor in the morning field to the *Tribune.* Court action was begun in 1942, and in 1945 the U.S. Supreme Court held that the AP bylaws concerning protest rights constituted unfair restriction of competition. The AP thereupon amended its membership rules and elected several newspapers previously denied admission.

Another unhappy situation in which the Associated Press found itself stemmed from the news exchange contracts it made in 1893 with European news agencies. This meant that news of the United States that was collected by the Associated Press was distributed abroad by foreign news services. Melville E. Stone, as AP general manager, did his best to open news channels in European countries[3] and the AP established some foreign bureaus before World War I to collect its own news. But lacking the right to sell its foreign news abroad, it could not build the kind of foreign service it eventually achieved. Not until 1934 was this restrictive arrangement finally broken down by the AP management.[4] An AP World Service was begun in 1946.

AP STAFF LEADERS: KENT COOPER

There were many notable names in the AP organization during its formative years under Stone's managership. Charles S. Diehl, a veteran of the Illinois AP regime, became an assistant general manager. So did Jackson S. Elliott, news chief during World War I. Frederick Roy Martin, successful editor of the *Providence Journal,* became assistant general manager in 1912 and succeeded Stone as manager in 1921. Among the noted bureau chiefs were Salvatore Cortesi in Rome, Seymour B. Conger in Berlin, and Edwin M. Hood in Washington. World War I correspondents included Charles T. Thompson, Frederick Palmer, and DeWitt Mackenzie, later an AP news analyst.

The name of Kent Cooper was soon to dominate the history of the Associated Press. An Indianan, he had started reporting for his local paper at 14. His college education was interrupted by the death of his father, and he left school to join the *Indianapolis Press.* From there he went to the Scripps-McRae news service, becoming head of the Indianapolis bureau of what was to become the Associated Press's major rival. There Cooper got the idea that out-of-the-way papers could be better served by a system of telephoning the news report than by telegraphing it. In 1910 he went to General Manager Stone of the AP and so impressed Stone with his knowledge of news communications methods that he was made AP traffic chief. He became an assistant general manager in 1920 and succeeded Martin as general manager in 1925. Through his subsequent career Cooper demonstrated his strong administrative qualities, but he was never a "newspaperman's newspaperman."

Cooper had plans for improving the efficiency and quality of the Associated Press service, and many changes came with his rise to control. The number of bureaus was increased and staffs were expanded. Human interest stories, long frowned on by the AP, gained favor. The transition was marked by the AP's first Pulitzer Prize, won by Kirke L. Simpson in 1922 for a series on the burial of the Unknown Soldier in Arlington Cemetery. State services, permitting exchange of regional news on wires subsidiary to the main AP trunk wires, were expanded. A news photo service was established in 1927, and after a sharp clash between picture-minded publishers and their more conservative colleagues, the AP Wirephoto system was approved in 1935. Automatic news printers, called teletypes, were first used in 1913 and gradually replaced Morse operators.

Kent Cooper (*left*) and Wes Gallagher, general managers of the Associated Press.

The pressures of competition from other news services and of World War II coverage requirements brought further advancès. A leased cable and radio-teletype circuits across the North Atlantic, European leased land circuits, and an overseas radiophoto network were added to the service. The character of the news report was subjected to an increasingly intensive review by members of the Associated Press Managing Editors Association, a group formed in 1931. The managing editors of member papers criticized the AP news coverage and writing style orally until 1947, when the reports of a Continuing Study Committee were put into printed form annually. State memberships began similar analyses of their wires. The AP management hired readability expert Rudolph Flesch to advise its staff, and correspondents like James Marlow of the Washington bureau did excellent work in pointing the way to better writing techniques. After a bitter battle, AP began to sell its news report to radio stations in 1940, five years later than the UP and INS. Radio stations were granted associate membership, without voting rights, in 1946. The Associated Press Radio-Television Association was formed in 1954. And in 1977, three seats were added to the board of directors for the stations, making 21.

RECENT AP MANAGEMENT AND STAFF New faces appeared in the AP management. Two of the men most respected by their colleagues for their capabilities as journalists were Byron Price and Paul Miller. Both served as chiefs of the Washington bureau. Price became the AP's first executive news editor in 1936 before retiring from the news service to become director of the Office of Censorship during World War II and later assistant Secretary General of the United Nations. Miller, after being named an assistant general manager, quit the AP to become an executive of the Gannett newspapers.

Their departures left Frank J. Starzel as the logical successor to Cooper when he retired in 1948. Starzel, a traditional newsman, had joined AP in 1929. Alan J. Gould, sports editor since 1932, served as executive editor from 1941 to

1963. Lloyd Stratton directed AP service abroad until Stanley Swinton was named director of the World Service in 1960.

Wes Gallagher, AP's leading World War II war correspondent and postwar foreign bureau chief, returned to the New York office in 1954 to be groomed as Starzel's 1962 successor. Gallagher, an aggressive AP spokesman, instituted "task force" reporting by a 10-man team based in Washington, opened AP reporting ranks to younger men and also to women, and presided over a massive reorganization of the transmission wires. Keith Fuller replaced him as president and general manager at the close of 1976.

The names of AP staffmen should not be ignored. Serving in Washington were such newsmen as David Lawrence, who left the AP to become a columnist and news magazine publisher, and Stephen T. Early, who became President Franklin D. Roosevelt's press secretary. Pulitzer Prize winners of the 1930s were Francis A. Jamieson, who covered the Lindbergh baby kidnapping story, Howard W. Blakeslee, AP science editor, and Louis P. Lochner, Berlin bureau chief. Other noted byliners were Brian Bell, W.F. Caldwell, foreign correspondent James A. Mills, and Edward J. Neil, killed during the Spanish civil war.

World War II saw AP men distinguish themselves overseas. Hal Boyle, Larry Allen, and Daniel De Luce won Pulitzer Prizes as correspondents. Frank Noel, Frank Filan, and Joe Rosenthal were similarly honored as news photographers—Rosenthal for his famous picture of the Marines raising the flag on Iwo Jima's Mount Suribachi. Lloyd Lehrbas, Wes Gallagher, Don Whitehead, Edward Kennedy, Russell Brines, and C. Yates McDaniel were other leading war correspondents. In the Korean War, correspondents Relman Morin and Don Whitehead and photographer Max Desfor won Pulitzer Prizes. Similar awards for Vietnam war coverage went to correspondents Malcolm W. Browne and Peter Arnett and photographers Horst Faas and Edward T. Adams.

Other major AP figures have included the general news editors Paul Mickelson, Samuel G. Blackman, and Rene Cappon; foreign editors Ben Bassett and Nate Polowetsky; executive editor Louis D. Boccardi and managing editor Robert H. Johnson; Washington bureau chiefs William L. Beale, Jr., and Marvin Arrowsmith; White House correspondents Arrowsmith, Ernest B. Vaccaro, and Frank Cormier; political writers Jack Bell, Douglas Cornell, Relman Morin, and Walter Mears; news analysts John Hightower, J.M. Roberts, Jr., and William L. Ryan; special correspondents Saul Pett and George Cornell; and court trial specialist Linda Deutsch. Some overseas byliners have been Richard O'Regan, Henry Bradsher, Richard K. O'Malley, Eddy Gilmore, and David Mason in Europe; Lynn Heinzerling and son Larry Heinzerling in South Africa; Nick Ludington in the Middle East; Myron Belkind in India; and George Esper in Asia, where he covered the fall of Saigon in 1975.

SCRIPPS AND HEARST CHALLENGE THE AP

Rising alongside the Associated Press as aggressive competing press associations were the United Press Associations of Edward Wyllis Scripps and the International News Service of William Randolph Hearst. This new United Press and the INS were not cooperatives, as was the AP. They were regular business enterprises that sold their news services to clients on a contract basis. Both arose in answer to the Associated Press's closed-membership policy. The chain newspaper publishers who started UP and INS soon found the news they collected could be sold both at home and abroad to others who could not obtain, or did not wish to have, AP service. Serving a variety of clients, as both the UP and INS soon did, their identification with two strong-minded newspaper publishers became only incidental. Their operating staffs were as anxious to cover all the news thoroughly and impartially, for the benefit of their ultimate readers, as were AP men, or any other newsmen.

Edward Wyllis Scripps once said that he founded the United Press Associations because he was suspicious of his fellow publishers who controlled the Associated Press. He did not take his papers into the AP in 1897, when the old United Press folded.

"I knew that at least 90 percent of my fellows in American journalism were capitalistic and conservative," he explained, and went on:

I knew that, at that time at least, unless I came into the field with a new service, it would be impossible for the people of the United States to get correct news through the medium of the Associated Press. . . . I have made it impossible for the men who control the Associated Press to suppress the truth, or successfully to disseminate falsehood.[5]

The rebellious Scripps undoubtedly was too critical of his fellow publishers, but his concept of competing press associations acting as checks on each other proved to be of inestimable value to American journalism.

Scripps had other reasons for establishing his own news service. The AP was most interested in the news report for its big morning paper members, and Scripps published evening papers. The closed-membership character of AP meant that Scripps would have trouble obtaining memberships for the new dailies he was establishing. If he ran his own news service, he could fashion its coverage and writing style to better serve the Scripps type of paper. And finally, he expected to make money running a press association.

THE SECOND UNITED PRESS, 1907, AND ROY HOWARD

After operating two regional news services for his own papers in the Middle West and West for 10 years, Scripps merged them in 1907 with the Publishers' Press Association (begun in 1898 by non-AP eastern papers) to form the United Press Associations. A young Scripps newspaperman named John Vandercook helped create the merger and became head of the United Press, but he died the following year. Succeeding him as general manager was 25-year-old Roy W. Howard, destined eventually to dominate the Scripps publishing empire. Howard had served on the *St. Louis Post-Dispatch* and the Scripps papers in Indianapolis and Cincinnati before getting his big chance with the UP. Scripps described the Roy Howard of this period as

a striking individual, very small of stature, with a large head and speaking countenance, and eyes that appeared to be windows for a rather unusual intellect. His manner was forceful, and the reverse from modest. Gall was written all over his face. It was in every tone and every word he voiced. There was ambition, self-respect and forcefulness oozing out of every pore of his body.[6]

Howard hustled abroad and established bureaus in the major European capitals. He made connections with leading foreign papers and with commercial news agencies not allied with the AP. Howard's biggest break came when the British cut off the cabling of German news service to belligerents and neutrals during World War I. Two leading Argentine newspapers, *La Prensa* and *La Nación,* rebelled against receiving only the one-sided reports of the French Havas agency and requested Associated Press service. The AP, under its contract agreements, could not enter the South American area, and Howard rapidly rushed in to give the Argentine papers the type of war news coverage they wanted. Soon UP was on the way to building up an extensive string of clients in South America and established its own bureaus there.

But Howard and the United Press came a cropper in November 1918, just when the UP was winning attention. Howard was in American naval headquarters at Brest on November 7 when a message arrived from Paris saying the Armistice had been signed at 11 o'clock that morning. Howard flashed the news to the New York UP office, and by an incredible stroke of bad luck for his news service, the message passed the censors. The UP bulletin set off wild celebrations in the United States—until several hours later the AP broke the news that the UP had cabled a false report. Although Howard argued that he did what any newsman would have done when he saw the message at naval headquarters (he decided later that the message had originated with a German secret agent in Paris), some telegraph editors never again fully trusted the United Press. Even when in the 1930s the Associated Press flashed the wrong verdict on the outcome of the trial of Bruno Richard Hauptmann for the kidnapping and murder of the Lindbergh baby, and when in 1944 the AP flashed the news of the D-Day landing in France prematurely, oldtime newsmen still recalled how "Roy Howard ended the first World War four days early."[7]

The United Press survived the false Armistice Day report, however. When Howard left it in 1920 to become a partner in the Scripps newspaper chain, the UP had 780 clients and a fairly good news service. Scripps, who held 51 percent of the controlling common stock, estimated he received $200,000 in dividends during the first 10 years. In the Scripps custom, the remaining 49 percent of the stock went to key United Press men. The intangible "good will" assets were then valued at $2,500,000 by Howard.[8]

A common saying among young, low-paid UP men was, "They pay you with bylines." Early in its career, the UP began giving enthusiastic young staffers some glory and a chance to develop their own writing styles and news specialties. AP men covering World War I were largely anonymous newsgatherers. The UP turned loose young correspondents like Webb Miller, Fred S. Ferguson, William Philip Simms, William G. Shepherd, and Westbrook Pegler. Their vividly written and interpretative copy attracted attention and helped to sell the UP service as a second wire for AP member papers. Miller became European news manager and stayed in command until he was killed in a London blackout early in World War II. Pegler became a widely syndicated columnist, as did three UP Washington staffers of the 1920s—Thomas L. Stokes, Paul Mallon, and Raymond Clapper.

The United Press jumped into several fields ahead of the AP, just as it did in developing its foreign news service. Acme Newspictures began operating in 1925, two years earlier than the AP picture service was established. The United Press pioneered in supplying news to radio stations and, with INS, was first into the television news field in 1951. Acme became United Press Newspictures in 1952 and handled UP Telephoto, rival to AP Wirephoto. In 1954 both services began supplying pictures by facsimile, over the UP Unifax and AP Photofax networks. The teletypesetter, producing a tape that automatically runs a typesetting machine, arrived in 1951 and both UP and AP set up teletypesetter circuits for smaller papers, sports, and financial services.

Howard's successors as president of the United Press all came up
through the ranks. His assistant, William W. Hawkins, held the post
from 1920 to 1923. Then a second strong man of the UP, Karl A. Bickel,
moved into the top command. Bickel became a leader in furthering
freedom of international news coverage, and he did much to advance the UP's own
position in worldwide service.

Hugh Baillie, who succeeded Bickel in 1935, loved nothing better than to whip
his competitors with an exclusive story, preferably a vivid one. He traveled
extensively, impressing his own competitive drive for news on his staff and keeping in
touch by covering some of the big stories personally. He was succeeded as president in
1955 by Frank H. Bartholemew, who presided over the 1958 merger of the UP and
International News Service to form the United Press International. Mims Thomason
became UPI president in 1962, followed by Roderick W. Beaton.

Earl J. Johnson became the working head of the UP news operation in 1935 and
retired as editor in 1965, widely praised for his energetic leadership. Teamed with him
was Roger Tatarian, an outstanding European news chief in the 1950s who succeeded
Johnson as editor. Tatarian became known throughout the news world before a heart
attack forced his early retirement to a professorship. H.L. Stevenson became editor-in-
chief, and Robert E. Page general manager. Frank Tremaine, longtime executive, was
senior vice president.

Merriman Smith, the abrasive dean of White House correspondents and winner of
the Pulitzer Prize for his story of the assassination of President Kennedy, died in 1970
after 30 years covering six presidents. Helen Thomas, his successor, became the head
of the White House correspondents and was showered with honors. Washington bureau
chiefs have been Lyle Wilson, Julius Fransden, and Grant Dillman; political writers

United Press International   *United Press International*

Merriman Smith and Helen Thomas, UPI's White House correspondents.

Raymond Lahr, Arnold Sawislak, and Richard Growald; diplomatic reporter Stewart Hensley; and Supreme Court reporter Charlotte Moulton. Gay Pauley was women's editor. Lucinda Franks and Thomas Powers won the 1971 national Pulitzer Prize.

Among European news chiefs have been Virgil Pinkley, Harry Ferguson, Daniel Gilmore, and Julius B. Humi. Joe Alex Morris, Harrison Salisbury, and Phil Newsome were notable foreign news editors. Reporting abroad in the 1950s and 1960s were A.L. Bradford, W.R. Higginbotham, Joseph W. Morgan, H.R. Ekins, Frederick Kuh, Norman Montellier, Henry Gorrell, Henry Shapiro, Robert Musel, Jack Fox, Joseph W. Grigg, and K.C. Thaler. Shapiro in Moscow and Thaler as diplomatic correspondent became foremost correspondents. Russell Jones won a 1957 Pulitzer Prize for covering the Budapest uprising. In the 1970s, UPI byliners abroad included Peter Uebersex, Arthur Higbee, Wellington Long, and Gerard Loughran in Europe; and Leon Daniel, Alan Dawson, and Joseph Galloway in Asia. UPI opened the first foreign Leningrad bureau in 1977 and was applying for a Peking office.

Reynolds and Eleanor Packard were a colorful World War II team for UP. European war byliners included Frederick C. Oechsner, Ralph Heinzen, Edward W. Beattie, and M.S. Handler. William F. Tyree, Frank Tremaine, William B. Dickinson, and H.D. Quigg were in the Pacific. Three UPI photographers won Pulitzer Prizes in Vietnam: Kyoichi Sawada, Toshio Sakai, and David Kennerly.

THE INTERNATIONAL NEWS SERVICE, 1909–58

The third American press association competitor has been the International News Service. Smaller than its rivals and later in establishing itself as a comprehensive news service, INS nevertheless won prominence for its competitive spirit.

INS was founded in 1909 as an outgrowth of earlier leased wire facilities of the Hearst newspapers. Richard A. Farrelly was its first manager. By 1918 INS was serving 400 clients and had a leased wire system approximately half as extensive as those of the AP and UP. In that year INS and a Hearst morning paper news agency, Universal Service, were put under the direction of Moses Koenigsberg, also head of Hearst's King Features Syndicate. INS developed full 24-hour operations by 1928, but Universal Service was killed in 1937. Executive control of INS passed to Joseph V. Connolly, and on his death in 1945 to Seymour Berkson.

The sparkplug of the INS after 1916 was Barry Faris, editor-in-chief. He established fewer bureaus than the other services, concentrating INS resources on the major news centers. His most successful plan was to offer well-known bylines and special coverage of major news events by talented writers. H.R. Knickerbocker, a Pulitzer Prize winner, and Floyd Gibbons were two longtime INS foreign correspondents. James L. Kilgallen began his roving coverage of major national stories in 1921. Later acquisitions as featured INS writers were Bob Considine and Inez Robb. Other glamor names on the INS wire were Quentin Reynolds, Frank Gervasi, Paul Gallico, Damon Runyon, Arthur "Bugs" Baer, Louella Parsons, and Edwin C. Hill.

The INS foreign service developed stature by the 1930s. Among its leaders were J.C. Oestreicher, foreign editor, Pierre J. Huss, Berlin bureau chief, and J. Kingsbury Smith, who became European general manager. Top World War II correspondents were Howard Handleman, Kenneth Downs, Merrill Mueller, George Lait, Graham Hovey, Frank Conniff, Richard Tregaskis, Lee Van Atta, and Clarke Lee. In Washington were George R. Holmes, William K. Hutchinson, George E. Durno, and Robert G. Nixon. Among the INS women correspondents, Rose McKee achieved prominence for political reporting. In a final burst of glory, the 1956 Pulitzer Prize for international reporting was won for INS and the Hearst newspapers by William Randolph Hearst, Jr., Kingsbury Smith, and Frank Conniff, who conducted interviews with Communist political leaders behind the Iron Curtain.

There were lumps in many throats when the hard-hitting INS staff of 450 saw their agency merged with the UP in May 1958. William Randolph Hearst, Jr., and two of his associates took minority seats on the board of directors of the new United Press International, and some INS staffers joined UPI. A few of the brightest INS stars went to work for the newly formed Hearst Headline Service. Otherwise INS was no more.

UNITED STATES NEWS SERVICES ABROAD

AP and UPI intensified their competition in the wake of the merger. In the late 1970s, both had more than 400,000 miles of leased telephone wires in the United States for transmission of news and pictures. Both used satellite channels, radio teleprinters, and underwater cables to carry their news reports to more than 100 countries in the world. Both had teletype circuits covering more than 20,000 miles in Europe, where their news reports were translated and fed into national wires, and both transmitted pictures worldwide. Both had automated their transmission facilities, using video display terminals and computers to perfect information storage and retrieval systems. The domestic news wire could deliver copy to news offices at 1,200 words a minute, ten times earlier speeds. A news report could be flashed around the world, using the automatic editing system, within a single minute.

Of 1,661 United States dailies listing press association service in the 1976 *Editor & Publisher International Yearbook,* 1,181 were receiving AP news and 823 UPI news (of these, 343 took both, 53 fewer than in 1970). Approximately 47 percent of United States dailies received AP news only, 27 percent UPI news only, 20 percent both services, and nearly 6 percent listed no service. The UPI reported 1977 news service to 3,680 United States radio and television stations, compared to the AP's figure of 3,462 member stations. For both it was big business; their annual budgets were approaching the $75 million level.

United States newspapers also reported 1976 usage of other news services. The long-established New York Times News Service had 134 such clients; the decade-old Los Angeles Times-Washington Post News Service had 114. Next in order were the Chicago Daily News Service, 69; Newspaper Enterprise Association, 64; North American Newspaper Alliance, 41; Copley News Service, 39; Dow-Jones News Service, 33; Reuter's from Britain, 28; and 151 scattered listings. Growth of the Los Angeles Times-Washington Post service undoubtedly cost the UPI most of the duplicate news service contracts it lost in the 1970s.

Only a handful of other United States dailies had their own correspondents abroad to supplement the AP and UPI services (a fact held up by Third World critics of American coverage). Joining the press association and newspaper reporters abroad were those for the broadcast media, magazine groups, and news magazines. A 1975 study for the Overseas Press Club of America painted a depressing picture of American news enterprise abroad. All together, the United States media had only 676 fulltime staff abroad, a 28 percent decline since a 1969 study. Of these, 429 were American citizens, a 23 percent drop. Fifty percent were in Europe, 25 percent in Asia, 15 percent in the western hemisphere, 8 percent in the troubled Middle East, and 2 percent in Africa. Of the United States nationals abroad, 8 percent were women.[9]

Biggest of the newspaper syndicates was the New York Times News Service. Founded in 1917, it was claiming 417 users in 54 countries by 1977. Its leased wire carried its news reports to subscribers from 30 foreign correspondents, 40 Washington bureau staffers, and the city room. The *Times* had won 42 Pulitzer Prizes in 60 years, 14 of them for foreign correspondence. Best known winners were Walter Duranty, 1932; Anne O'Hare McCormick, 1937; Otto D. Tolischus, 1940; Hanson W. Baldwin, 1943; Harrison E. Salisbury, 1955; A.M. Rosenthal, 1960; David Halberstam, 1964, from Vietnam; Max Frankel, 1973, from Peking; Hedrick Smith, 1974, from Moscow; and Sydney Schanberg, 1976, reporting the fall of Cambodia. Arthur Krock and James B. Reston were double winners from the Washington bureau, also represented by Louis Stark and Anthony Lewis. Among other foreign byliners were C.L. Sulzberger, Herbert L. Matthews, Drew Middleton, Flora Lewis, and Malcolm Browne.

Newest on the scene was the Los Angeles Times-Washington Post News Service, begun in 1962 by publishers Otis Chandler and Philip L. Graham. Fifteen years later it had well over 300 users worldwide, who were served by 30 foreign bureaus of the *Times* and the *Post,* their Washington bureaus and local staffs, seven other United States bureaus, and the news services of Agence France-Presse and the *Guardian* of London and Manchester.

Listed among the *Times* foreign correspondents were Robert S. Elegant, Jacques Leslie, and George McArthur in Asia; Jack Foisie in Africa; Sharon Rosenhause in India; Tom Lambert, Stanley Meisler, Donald Cook, William Tuohy, and Joe Alex Morris, Jr., in Europe. Among *Post* byliners were Bernard Nossiter in London, John Goshko in Bonn, Don Oberdorfer in Tokyo, and Joanne Omang in Buenos Aires. Pulitzer Prize winners of the two papers covering Washington were Jack Nelson, Haynes Johnson, Carl Bernstein and Bob Woodward, and David Broder. This was indeed rich fare for the subscribers.

The *Chicago Daily News* foreign service grew out of the coverage begun in 1898 by Victor Lawson for the *Daily News* and *Record-Herald.* It won wide attention during World War I through the work of Edward Price Bell in London, Paul Scott Mowrer in Paris, and Raymond Gram Swing in Berlin. But it hit its most remarkable peak of performance in the 1930s and early 1940s under publisher Frank Knox and the foreign news director, Carroll Binder, himself a noted correspondent before he became head of the service in 1937.

Pulitzer Prizes were won by Paul Scott Mowrer in 1929 and by Edgar Ansel Mowrer in 1933. Ranking with the Mowrer brothers as among the best of American foreign correspondents of the day were John Gunther in London, William Stoneman in Moscow and London, Wallace Deuel in Rome and Berlin, Helen Kirkpatrick in Paris, and David Nichol in Berlin and Moscow. Other leading *Chicago Daily News* foreign correspondents of the World War II period were Leland Stowe, Robert J. Casey, William McGaffin, Paul Ghali, Ernie Hill, Nat A. Barrows, A.T. Steele, and George Weller, a Pulitzer Prize winner for distinguished reporting. Keyes Beech and Fred Sparks won Pulitzer awards for Korean War coverage. Paul Leach, Edwin A. Lahey, and Peter Lisagor were Washington bureau chiefs. Lisagor, ranked as the best of political reporters, died at the close of 1976, just as the *Daily News* was engaged in a staff shakeup. The famed Foreign Service was closed as 1977 opened. Raymond Coffey, London bureau chief since 1971, replaced Lisagor in Washington and survivor Keyes Beech of the foreign staff also joined the reinforced Washington bureau.

The *New York Herald Tribune* foreign service was built on that of the old *Tribune,* which had Frank H. Simonds and Richard Harding Davis as World War I writers. Leland Stowe won a 1930 Pulitzer Prize as a *Herald Tribune* correspondent and Homer Bigart was similarly honored for his World War II work. Other leading *Herald Tribune* correspondents of the war period were Joseph Barnes, Major George

Fielding Eliot, Russell Hill, Joseph Driscoll, and John O'Reilly. Bert Andrews, while Washington bureau chief, won the 1948 Pulitzer Prize for national reporting. Jack Steele was a leading Washington staff member in the early 1950s before becoming Scripps-Howard's chief political writer. Bigart and Marguerite Higgins won Pulitzer Prizes as Korean War correspondents. Columnist Walter Lippmann in 1962 won the paper's final Pulitzer Prize before its death in 1966.

The *Chicago Tribune* foreign service had as World War I stars Floyd Gibbons, Frazier Hunt, John T. McCutcheon, and Sigrid Schultz. Serving the *Tribune* overseas for varying periods were such well-known journalists as Vincent Sheean, William L. Shirer, George Seldes, Jay Allen, and Edmond Taylor. Wilfred C. Barber won the *Tribune* news service's first Pulitzer Prize in 1936. In the following years, the leading correspondents of other foreign and Washington services outshone the *Tribune* men until 1975, when William Mullen, a white reporter, and Ovie Carter, a black photographer, won the Pulitzer Prize for international reporting with a series on famine in Africa and India.

WALTER DURANTY AND THE MOWRER BROTHERS

Of all the foreign correspondents listed in the preceding paragraphs, special attention must be given Walter Duranty of the *New York Times* and the Mowrer brothers of the *Chicago Daily News*. Duranty was a resident correspondent in Russia between 1922–34 and until 1941 was a special traveling writer, spending an average of five months per year studying the land he loved. Even before he began the initial 13-year stint as the leading American reporter in Russia, Duranty had developed a strong philosophy about the rough character of Communist rule. At the outset he hated and feared the Bolsheviks, but as he told H.R. Knickerbocker of INS in 1935, he learned to appreciate the Russian position. "I don't see that I have been any less accurate about Russia because I failed to stress casualties so hard as some of my colleagues . . . I am a reporter, not a humanitarian."[10]

It was during the 1930s that Duranty received some bitter criticism for his open assessments of Stalin's ruthlessness and Soviet goals. Heywood Broun said he wrote "editorials disguised as news dispatches" and others claimed he was far too liberal. Stalin began his purge of the Kulaks, the wealthy peasant class, in 1928, and eventually an estimated 10 million persons were killed in the countryside. But on the other hand, Duranty had accepted one of the toughest individual reporting assignments of the twentieth century. His task was to report the unknown. Stalin consented to talk with Duranty only twice, in the fall of 1930 and at Christmas 1933. Otherwise Duranty depended on his keen knowledge of Russian history and language to overcome physical handicaps. The politically risky business of collectivization was determining many careers within Russia, like that of Leon Trotsky. Duranty sent long interpretative

New York Times

Walter Duranty

dispatches to the *Times* but rarely did these efforts receive prominent display. America was involved with domestic and European problems. During the crucial winter of 1928–29, for example, none of Duranty's nearly 100 stories made page one.[11]

Nevertheless, Duranty's contribution to the field of foreign correspondence was immense. His intellect and analytical ability made him invaluable to the growing *Times'* foreign staff, which at that moment included Wythe Williams in Vienna, Paul Miller in Berlin, Arnaldo Cortesi in Rome, and Allen Raymond in London. Duranty was a confident writer, hardened by scenes of death in World War I. He accepted the brutality of Russian life and wrote from that point. Stalin moved stealthily, the censor was a barrier, the Soviet press did not report internal arguments in any way, official names were rarely mentioned, and travel was restricted. Yet Duranty was able to give detailed and colorful reports of life in that tormented land.

William Henry Chamberlin lived in Russia from 1922–34, writing for the *Manchester Guardian* and then the *Christian Science Monitor* and *Atlantic*. Louis Fischer authored more than 40 articles, most of them for the *Nation,* between 1925–32. And world traveler Maurice Hindus wrote a dozen articles and a best-selling book, *Red Bread*. Along with Duranty these men gave a few Americans their only real look at Russia; the bulk of United States newspapers, including those with prominent foreign staffs, carried only casual mention of Russian affairs. Duranty filed the only regularly published newspaper accounts in the late 1920s, and his fair-minded and sometimes sympathetic portrayal of Bolshevik behavior helped restore the faith of some in the *Times,* which during the "Red Scare" period had confused readers about Russian Communists and American Socialists. In fact, a special *New Republic* supplement of August 1920, edited by Walter Lippmann and Charles Merz, had charged the usually reliable *Times* with irresponsible coverage. Duranty himself had said his paper's early attitude was caused by a fear of the "Red Bogey," which explains why he went to great lengths to provide balanced reports.

Paul Scott Mowrer began his long career in 1905, taking a job with the *Chicago Daily News*. Getting the Midwest out of his system proved to be a problem, as he later admitted.[12] While in Chicago he had shunned Stanley Washburn's dispatches from the Russo-Japanese front. He remembered riding in an elevator with Richard Henry Little, captured by the Japanese at Mukden. But Mowrer cared only for Minnesota, Michigan, and the bustling metropolis, which he considered the heart of journalism. In 1910 he arrived in London, joining men who worked for other papers such as Frederic William Wile, Wythe Williams, and a handful of others who knew Europe before war changed the politics and the boundaries. Writers like Will Irwin occasionally sailed to Europe to write for United States magazines, but the years were dull. Earlier, writers had flocked to the Boer War and Boxer Rebellion. The bitter subjugation of the Philippine rebels under Aguinaldo in the 1899–1901 period had attracted a host of reporters. That first United States experiment with colonial power at one point involved 70,000 American troops. The Russo-Japanese War of 1904–5, where Richard Harding Davis, Jack London, Frederick Palmer, and another 100 American and British reporters had fought Japanese censorship, gained considerable attention in the United States press. But things were quiet in Europe, as Paul Scott Mowrer discovered when he showed up as a 22-year-old assistant to Edward Price Bell. At the outbreak of war nearly four years later he covered the assassination of French Socialist Jean Jaures and broke in his younger brother, Edgar Ansel Mowrer, who thus began his equally distinguished career. Edgar, who had been contributing to United States and British magazines and studying at the Sorbonne, sneaked through enemy lines for an exclusive story. Then Edgar was allowed to accompany mining engineer Herbert Hoover to

Holland, and finally in 1915 was given the job as Rome correspondent. Paul Scott Mowrer headed for the front and ended up reporting the horrors of Verdun.

Following the war, Paul Scott Mowrer was assigned to direct the *Daily News'* bureau at the Versailles conference. Based in Paris, he filed dispatches during the Moroccan campaign of 1924–25 and in 1934–35 became associate editor and chief editorial writer for his paper. The editorship itself was his between 1935 and 1944, until the last year of World War II saw him accept a position as European editor for the *New York Post*. Edgar Ansel Mowrer was bureau chief of the *Daily News* in Berlin and Paris during the "between wars" period. Connected with the Office of War Information after having been forced out of Germany at the start of World War II, he later was a columnist and broadcaster and with his brother contributed several books on foreign affairs. The Mowrer brothers teamed with many famous byliners, like Dorothy Thompson of the *New York Post*, Vincent Sheean of the *Chicago Tribune*, Frederick T. Birchall of the *New York Times*, Reginald Wright Kauffman and Harold Scarborough of the *New York Herald Tribune*, Henry Wales of the *Chicago Tribune*, and the others mentioned earlier to cover the League of Nations, rise of fascism, and coming of another war. They added color and depth to stories at a time when even familiar European situations were in heavy competition with American domestic concerns for space in newspapers.

SPECIAL NEWS
SERVICES

Several special news and feature services were established for American newspapers after 1900. First was the Newspaper Enterprise Association, founded in 1902 by Robert F. Paine, E.W. Scripps's talented editor-in-chief. While NEA by the 1950s offered all types of features to newspaper clients, it also had foreign and Washington correspondence, highlighted by the work of prize-winning Peter Edson and of Fred Sparks, who transferred from the *Chicago Daily News*. A second Scripps contribution was Science Service, begun in 1921 and directed by Watson Davis as an authoritative science news agency. The Scripps-Howard Newspaper Alliance, developed for the chain's own papers, had its share of Pulitzer Prize winners—science editor David Dietz, Washington correspondents Thomas L. Stokes and Vance Trimble, columnist Ernie Pyle, and foreign correspondent Jim G. Lucas.

A major reorganization of the news syndicates took place in 1930 when the North American Newspaper Alliance was founded by a group of metropolitan newspapers under the managership of John N. Wheeler, head of the Bell Syndicate. NANA and Bell absorbed the Associated Newspaper, Consolidated Press, and McClure services and established NANA as the leading specialized news agency. Among its correspondents was military reporter and analyst Ira Wolfert, 1943 Pulitzer Prize winner.[13]

THE FEATURE
SYNDICATES:
ENTERTAINMENT

The impact of the syndicates on newspaper content was heaviest in the non-news field. First to relieve newspaper editors of the necessity of clipping column material, fiction, poetry, and other entertainment features from newspaper and magazine exchanges was Ansel N. Kellogg, the Baraboo, Wisconsin, newsman who founded a ready-print service in Chicago during the Civil War years. One side of the newsprint sheets was left blank for local news and ads. By 1875 stereotyped plates were being supplied to papers by the American Press Association. The giant of the field became the Western Newspaper Union, founded in Des Moines in 1872 and run by George A. Joslyn after 1890. Joslyn eliminated his rivals by 1917 and refined the "patented insides" business, offering editors alternative pre-printed materials. The service, going to nearly 7,000 papers at its peak, gradually declined and was abandoned in 1952.

While Western Newspaper Union was developing in the weekly field, dailies were being offered syndicated literary material by the feature services of Irving Bacheller (1883), S.S. McClure (1884), and Edward W. Bok (1886). McClure and Bok sensed the public demand for entertaining reading, which led to their own more famous careers as magazine publishers. Hearst joined the syndicate movement in 1895, and in 1914 began his King Features Syndicate. George Matthew Adams entered the field in 1907 and John N. Wheeler in 1913.

The early syndicates featured the writings of Robert Louis Stevenson, Rudyard Kipling, Mark Twain, Bret Harte, Henry James, Alfred Henry Lewis, Jack London, and other literary greats. They also could sample the work of a notable group of poetically inclined columnists and humorous writers, which appeared in newspapers throughout the country. Syndication spread the fame of "M. Quad" of the *Detroit Free Press* and *New York Herald;* Bill Nye of Laramie, Wyoming, and the *New York World;* David Ross Locke of the *Toledo Blade,* who created Petroleum V. Nasby; Opie Read of *Arkansaw Traveler* fame; Joel Chandler Harris of the *Atlanta Constitution;* and Finley Peter Dunne, the Chicago newspaperman whose "Mr. Dooley"—a saloon keeper who philosophized on current affairs—became a national institution.

To older newspapermen a column was "a little of everything"—wit, poetry, sentiment, and comment on personalities and events in the news. One such column conductor was Eugene Field, the St. Louis and Kansas City newsman whom Melville E. Stone brought to the *Chicago Daily News* to write his "Sharps and Flats" before 1900. Another was Bert Leston Taylor, who founded the *Chicago Tribune*'s famed "A Line o' Type or Two" column in 1901. A third was Franklin P. Adams, who wrote for the *Chicago Journal* and *New York Mail* before beginning his "Conning Tower" in the *New York Tribune* in 1914. On the *New York Sun* it was Don Marquis with his "Sun Dial" column, inhabited by "archie," the noncapitalizing cockroach.

Walter Winchell set the pace for another kind of column. A New Yorker who entered journalism with the racy tabloids of the 1920s, Winchell promoted the "gossip" column as the Broadway reporter of the tabloid *Graphic*. He shifted to the *Mirror* in 1929 and became a star of Hearst's King Features Syndicate. No other columnist ever approached Winchell's sensationalism and intimate coverage of private lives, but such Hollywood columnists as Louella Parsons and Hedda Hopper did their best. Leonard Lyons and Dorothy Kilgallen were other New York scene columnists of the personal type, while O.O. McIntyre and Mark Hellinger wrote about the metropolis in an older literary style.

THE POLITICAL   The political column began in the early 1920s with the writings of
COLUMNISTS   David Lawrence in his syndicated column and Washington publications,
                 of Mark Sullivan in the *New York Herald Tribune,* and of Frank R. Kent
in the *Baltimore Sun*. Walter Lippmann joined this trio as a *Herald Tribune* columnist when his editorship of the *World* ended in 1931. Their columns were concerned with current politics and issues of the day, as contrasted with Arthur Brisbane's philosophical commentary, which began in 1917 and was front-paged by Hearst newspapers for nearly 20 years. But the coming of the New Deal in 1933 and a consequent revolution in Washington coverage brought a new version of the political column to join the syndicated offerings of Lawrence, Sullivan, Kent, and Lippmann.

The four early leaders in political and current affairs columns were identified as "pundits" who wrote in a sober style and with a serious-minded approach. Sullivan

Dorothy Thompson and Marquis Childs, distinguished political columnists.

Walter Lippmann, longtime dean of commentators, and Mary McGrory, political expert.

Joseph Kraft (*left*) and Art Buchwald were successful columnists of the 1970s.

and Kent were masters of the practical political scene of the 1920s, but they were not responsive to the social and economic shifts that brought the widespread increase in governmental activity in the New Deal era. Sullivan, who had been an enthusiastic interpreter of Theodore Roosevelt's progressive program and an intimate of President Herbert Hoover, became far better known for his superb journalistic history of the 1900–25 period, *Our Times,* than for his later columns. Lawrence continued to hold a place as a commentator on national affairs, as did Lippmann in the international field.

A new kind of political column after 1932 was the personalized or "gossip-type" column. The idea stemmed from the successful book, *Washington Merry-Go-Round,* published anonymously in 1931. The authors were soon identified as Drew Pearson of the *Baltimore Sun* and Robert S. Allen of the *Christian Science Monitor.* These two Washington correspondents quickly left their newspapers to co-author a behind-the-scenes column that Pearson eventually continued alone. Paul Mallon was in the personalized column competition from the start of the New Deal era; joining in as sympathetic commentators on the New Deal's activities were Ernest K. Lindley, Samuel Grafton, and Joseph and Stewart Alsop, writing as a team, then separately. Jack Anderson became prominent in the field after Pearson's death in 1969, uncovering a number of major stories during the "Nixon years." However, Anderson did not escape criticism and his zealousness for the exclusive backfired in 1972 when he mishandled facts about Senator Thomas Eagleton's personal life while Senator George McGovern dropped Eagleton as his running mate.

United Features offered a particularly strong and varied group of columnists and commentators in the 1930s. Raymond Clapper, before his death in a 1944 wartime plane crash, was recognized as perhaps the best-balanced interpreter of the Washington scene. His opinions on national and international problems were widely respected, largely because they were based on reporting ability and Clapper's long experience as a United Press newsman and political writer and as head of the UP Washington bureau and that of the *Washington Post.* Thomas L. Stokes, a hard-working reporter of the Washington scene for United Press and the Scripps-Howard newspapers, developed a large following for his vigorous and crusading columns. Stokes won a Pulitzer Prize for national reporting and a Clapper memorial award for his column before he died in 1958. Carrying on for United Features were Marquis Childs, distinguished Washington correspondent for the *St. Louis Post-Dispatch* who began his column after Clapper's death, and William S. White, from the *New York Times* Washington staff. Childs won a Pulitzer Prize for his column in 1970, the first given for commentary.

Also in the United Features group of columnists were some commentators of the personal variety. One was Westbrook Pegler, the caustic ex-sports writer and United Press and *Chicago Tribune* writer. Pegler had a distinctive, colorful style and won a 1941 Pulitzer Prize for his exposure-type crusading. Unhappily his work degenerated into monotonous and vicious attacks on three small groups—labor unions, New Dealers, and members of the Franklin D. Roosevelt family—and Pegler switched from Scripps-Howard to Hearst sponsorship in the mid-1940s, becoming known as "the stuck whistle of journalism." Balancing Pegler was the witty, warm personality of Heywood Broun. Best described as "looking like an unmade bed," Broun was a deceptive writer who could switch from a gay and easy commentary to a hard-hitting defense of liberal traditions whenever his temper was aroused. His "It Seems to Me" ran first in the *New York Tribune,* then in the *World* during the 1920s, and finally in the Scripps-Howard papers. Broun's leading role in the American Newspaper Guild and his liberal line brought a break with Roy Howard and the column was headed for the *New York Post* when Broun died in 1939. Also writing columns for United Features were Mrs. Eleanor Roosevelt, first signed in 1935 in an unprecedented move for a president's wife, and the lovable Ernie Pyle, whose original cross-country tour columns about little people and things were followed by superb personal glimpses of American fighting men in World War II until he was killed on a Pacific island in 1945.

Well to the right of the United Features columnists in political and social outlooks were the King Features group. Best known were Pegler and the conservative George Sokolsky, both of whom died in the 1960s. Later in the field for King were radio commentator Fulton Lewis, Jr., moral philosopher Bruce Barton, reporter Jim Bishop, and editor William F. Buckley, Jr., of the conservative *National Review*. Buckley was one of the intellectual conservatives who gained favor in the late 1960s and the 1970s. Two others were the former southern newspaper editor, James Jackson Kilpatrick of the *Washington Star* Syndicate, and the young writer for *Esquire* and the *National Review,* Garry Wills.

Three women journalists won high honors in column writing. One was Dorothy Thompson, a European correspondent for the *Philadelphia Public Ledger* and the *New York Post* during the 1920s and early 1930s. Married to Sinclair Lewis, she returned to the United States and wrote a column on international affairs for the *New York Herald Tribune* until she was dropped for endorsing Franklin Roosevelt for a third term in order to meet the threat of Hitler's regime. Her emotion-charged comments were widely syndicated until her career closed in 1961. Doris Fleeson, who came to the columnist field from the *New York Daily News* to write a smooth political commentary until 1970, became in 1954 the first woman to win the Raymond Clapper award for reporting. Taking command in the 1970s as a Pulitzer Prize-winning general political columnist was Mary McGrory of the *Washington Star*. Sylvia Porter became the leading business columnist of the country. Betty Beale, Marianne Means, and Virginia Payette were other syndicated women columnists.

Joseph Kraft was one of a number of liberal-oriented columnists who emerged from the era of Kennedy politics. A speech writer for John Kennedy, he began a political commentary for *Harper's* in 1965 and became one of those syndicated columnists filling the void when Walter Lippmann retired in 1967. A hard-hitting team that gained increasing favor after its 1963 start was that of Rowland Evans and Robert Novak, who had been Washington reporters for the *New York Herald Tribune* and *Wall Street Journal*. Their "Inside Report" became the top political exposure column of the 1970s. Joining the competition in 1977 were Jack W. Germond and Jules Witcover, seasoned Washington newsmen who focused on reporting the political activities of the Carter administration. The country's leading black journalist, Carl T. Rowan, signed with the *Chicago Daily News* after a government career. He was joined as a columnist by William Raspberry of the *Washington Post*.

The *New York Times* contributed political columnists, its serious-minded James Reston and Tom Wicker, and its Washington "funny man," Russell Baker. Baker and Art Buchwald of the *Los Angeles Times* Syndicate used satire to make their political and social points during a period of national frustration that called for such relief.

THE EDITORIAL CARTOONISTS

Syndication also affected the profession of editorial cartooning. As in the field of columning, widespread readership offered fame and financial rewards to the talented. But easy access to their proved reader-drawing copy made it less likely that a newspaper would "bring up" its own cartoonist or columnist. Local columnists always had their field, of course, but serious commentary on national and international affairs by a local staff member became scarcer.

The period after the Civil War saw the development of the political cartoon as an

Rollin Kirby's famous "Two chickens in every garage" barb at Hoover, 1932.

"Halloween 1936"—Jay (Ding) Darling jibed at Wallace, Farley, and FDR.

"You gambled but I paid"—Daniel Fitzpatrick in a 1947 crusade.

"The outstretched hand"—Edmund Duffy's 1939 Pulitzer Prize cartoon.

"Fire!"—Herbert L. Block, in the *Washington Post*, defended freedom during the Joseph McCarthy era.

Bill Mauldin's famous drawing expressing a nation's grief at John Kennedy's death.

editorial device. Until then, the cartoon was more likely to be seen in magazines because of newspaper production difficulties, but the introduction of stereotyping enabled dailies to use illustrations more readily. Thomas Nast, the cartoonist who so savagely attacked the Tweed political ring, drew for the *New York Times* after 1870, as well as for *Harper's Weekly*. In the magazines of the times, Joseph Keppler's work for *Puck* was outstanding. The presidential campaign cartoons of Homer Davenport, drawn for Hearst's *New York Journal* in 1896, scored a new high point, both in prominence and in bluntness.

The first quarter of the twentieth century was a golden age for cartoonists. The issues were simple enough for easy pictorial interpretation, and they were elemental enough for clever satire. These are the ingredients of the political cartoon. One of the famous cartoonists was John T. McCutcheon, who began drawing for the *Chicago Tribune* in 1903 after serving on the *Chicago Record* and who won a Pulitzer Prize before he retired in 1946. Clifford K. Berryman, who first appeared in the *Washington Post* as far back as 1889, was closely identified with the *Washington Star* after 1906. He and his son, James T. Berryman, were the only father and son combination to win Pulitzer Prizes for their work, after the younger Berryman succeeded his father in 1949. Reminiscent of the old school of flowery technique was Jay N. ("Ding") Darling, who began drawing for the *Des Moines Register* in 1906 and who was twice a Pulitzer Prize winner.

Lesser known to the public, but influential among his colleagues, was Arthur Henry Young, who always signed his cartoons "Art Young." He suffered because of his devotion to left-wing causes, especially during the World War I period, but in his day, Young was the cartoonist's cartoonist. He was the first to produce a daily panel, for the *Chicago Inter Ocean,* but the best of his work appeared in *The Masses,* the militantly socialist magazine. Young, unlike earlier cartoonists, strove for simplicity. His technique was to focus attention on a main issue; for example, one of his cartoons showed a ragged child of the slums looking up at the night sky and saying: "Ooh, look at all the stars; they're thick as bedbugs."

Two other great masters of the cartooning art were Rollin Kirby of the *New York World* and Edmund Duffy of the *Baltimore Sun,* both three-time Pulitzer Prize winners. Kirby was a fiercely liberal spirit who began cartooning in 1911 and hit his peak on the old *World* in the 1920s. His "Mr. Dry," a gaunt, black-frocked, blue-nosed caricature of the bigoted prohibitionists, became famous. Duffy exhibited his mastery of satire and caricature for the *Baltimore Sun* for 25 years. In this era, too, was Nelson Harding of the *Brooklyn Eagle,* twice a Pulitzer award winner.

Beginning his work for the *St. Louis Post-Dispatch* in 1913 and continuing until 1958 was Daniel R. ("Fitz") Fitzpatrick, whose devastating cartoon attacks won for him two Pulitzer Prizes. He was succeeded by Bill Mauldin, of Willie and Joe fame in *Stars and Stripes,* who quickly won a second Pulitzer Prize in 1959—and then in 1962 became the syndicated cartoonist of the *Chicago Sun-Times,* which also had the liberal Jacob Burck as a Pulitzer award-winning cartoonist for its editorial page.

The signature "Herblock" became famed in the 1950s and continued to be a solid favorite in the 1970s. Herbert L. Block of the *Washington Post* was widely known through syndication for his distinctive style and extremely effective liberal comment. He was challenged by several other Pulitzer Prize winners who attracted attention for their incisive, independent commentary. Becoming equally popular was Paul Conrad, 1964 and 1971 award winner, who started at the *Denver Post* and became the *Los Angeles Times* editorial cartoonist in 1964. His successor at the *Denver Post,* the Australian-born satirist Patrick Oliphant, was 1967 winner; Don Wright, *Miami News,*

Patrick Oliphant, © 1971 Denver Post

"Mightier Than the Sword"—Patrick Oliphant celebrated the
defeat of Attorney General John Mitchell in the 1971
Pentagon Papers case.

Jeffrey K. MacNelly, © 1977 Chicago Tribune

The *Richmond News Leader*'s syndicated cartoonist
comments on President Jimmy Carter's human
rights crusade, which irritated the Kremlin leaders.

John Fischetti, © 1971 Chicago Daily News

"The Unknown Soldier"—John Fischetti pursued a relentless attack upon
the Nixon "Vietnamization" policy and failure to achieve peace in
Indochina.

won in 1966. John Fischetti, 1969 Pulitzer Prize artist for the *Chicago Daily News,* offered a popular new style, as did young Thomas F. Darcy, 1970 winner from *Newsday,* and Paul Szep, the *Boston Globe's* prize artist, a winner in 1974 and 1977. Garry Trudeau won in 1975 for his "Doonesbury" strip. Vietnam, Nixon, and Watergate gave such cartoonists a field day; other aspects of the era favored the more conservative Jeff MacNelly, 1972 Pulitzer Prize winner from the *Richmond News Leader;* Tony Auth, 1976 winner from the *Philadelphia Inquirer;* and Wayne Stayskal of the *Chicago Tribune.*

Award-winning cartoonists of conventional outlook who won syndication were Vaughan Shoemaker of the *Chicago Daily News,* Frank Miller of the *Des Moines Register,* Reg Manning of the *Arizona Republic,* and the hard-nosed C.D. Batchelor of the *New York Daily News.*

THE WORLD OF COMICS

Highly lucrative for the syndicates was the distribution of the drawings of a different set of artists—the comic strip and humorous panel originators. The battle between Pulitzer and Hearst for possession of Richard F. Outcault's "Yellow Kid" in 1896 set off a fierce competition in Sunday color comic sections and gave the name to yellow journalism. Early favorites like "Foxy Grandpa," "Buster Brown," and "Little Nemo" tickled newspaper readers with portrayals of humorous episodes centering about the same set of characters, but not relating a continuing story. Charles E. Schultze's grandfather who played tricks on boys and Winsor McKay's childish wonderland of Little Nemo both appeared in the *New York Herald* at the turn of the century. But Schultze soon deserted to Hearst's *American.* There "Foxy Grandpa" joined Outcault's "Buster Brown" and other Hearst comics in the same vein.

Paul Conrad, © Los Angeles Times, with permission of The Register and Tribune Syndicate

Paul Conrad selected this drawing as symbolic of his concern for civil rights and the economic plight of minorities.

One was Rudolph Dirks's "Katzenjämmer Kids," longest-lived of all American comics. Dirks began drawing Hans, Fritz, Mama, and the Captain in an 1897 color comic. When he transferred to the *World* in 1912, Hearst successfully sued to retain rights to the title and King Features continued the strip into the 1970s. So did Dirks and his son, for United Features, using the name "The Captain and the Kids."

Other Hearst comic successes before 1910 were James Swinnerton's "Little Jimmy," Frederick Burr Opper's "Alphonse and Gaston" and "Happy Hooligan," and George Herriman's "Krazy Kat." In the *World* were "The Newlyweds," drawn by George McManus of later Jiggs and Maggie fame. The doings of the "Toonerville Folks" were first portrayed by Fontaine Fox in the *Chicago Post* of 1908. H. C. (Bud) Fisher's "Mutt and Jeff" was the first regular daily cartoon strip, appearing in the *San*

Francisco Chronicle in 1907. When John N. Wheeler organized the Bell Syndicate he obtained Fox and Fisher as two of his major drawing cards.

Arising as major competitors in the comic strip business by the end of World War I were the Hearst-owned King Features Syndicate and the *Chicago Tribune-New York Daily News* combine, whose comics were masterminded by Captain Joseph M. Patterson and Colonel Robert R. McCormick. Some of the longtime Hearst favorites, distributed in *Puck* as a Sunday comic section to millions of Hearst readers and also sold separately, were George McManus's "Bringing Up Father," dating from 1912; Cliff Sterrett's "Polly and Her Pals," 1912; James E. Murphy's "Toots and Casper," 1918; Billy De Beck's "Barney Google," 1919; Elzie C. Segar's "Thimble Theatre" featuring Olive Oyl and Popeye, 1919; Russ Westover's "Tillie the Toiler," 1921; Rube Goldberg's "Boob McNutt," 1924; and the most popular of all American comics, Chic Young's "Blondie," 1930. Winning millions of readers, too, for the *Chicago Tribune-New York Daily News* group have been Sidney Smith's "Andy Gump," 1917 (drawn after Smith's death in 1935 by Gus Edson); Frank King's "Gasoline Alley," 1919; Carl Ed's "Harold Teen," 1919; Martin Branner's "Winnie Winkle," 1920; Frank Willard's "Moon Mullins," 1923; and Harold Gray's "Little Orphan Annie," 1924.

People still called them "the funny papers" in this period. But two developments were under way that would change the character of the comics. One was the continuing story strip originating with "Andy Gump" in 1917. Many adults of the 1970s remember how baby Skeezix was abandoned on Uncle Walt's doorstep in the "Gasoline Alley" of 1921 to begin a chronicle of family life now in a third generation. Far less satisfying was the continuity of "Little Orphan Annie," whose waif has been lost from Daddy Warbucks every little while and has never finished school. King died in 1969 and Gray in 1968 but Skeezix and Annie lived on.

The other development was the action story, entering the comic pages with United Features' "Tarzan" in 1929 and soon extending through countless strips involving detectives, cowboys, adventurers, gangsters, and finally supermen. The greatest detective of the comic strip world has been operating in Chester Gould's "Dick Tracy" strip since 1931. Swashbuckling adventure has been most cleverly portrayed by Milton Caniff in "Terry and the Pirates," a 1934 gold mine, and his 1947 "Steve Canyon." Ham Fisher's "Joe Palooka" began fighting in 1931. The first of the superhumans was Buck Rogers, whose twenty-fifth-century era began in 1929. Superman himself, drawn by Jerry Siegel and Joe Schuster, caught on in 1939.

There still was some humor left in the comic pages, despite the invasion of crime, tragedy, death, and lurid action in the 1930s. Harry J. Tuthill's "The Bungle Family," begun in the *New York Evening Mail* in 1918, and Sol Hess's "The Nebbs," dating from 1923, were family favorites. So were Cal Alley's "The Ryatts," Carl Grubert's "The Berrys," and "Hi and Lois," a 1954 entry by Mort Walker and Dik Browne. New heroines were "Ella Cinders," drawn by Charlie Plumb and Bill Conselman since 1925, and "Dixie Dugan," created by J.P. McEvoy and John H. Striebel in 1929. Children and their antics were not ignored; some of the favorites were Edwina Dumm's "Cap Stubbs and Tippie," Ernie Bushmiller's "Fritzi Ritz and Nancy," Robert Brinkerhoff's "Little Mary Mixup," Harry Haenigsen's "Penny," and four King Features offerings—Carl Anderson's "Henry," Percy Crosby's "Skippy," Charles H. Kuhn's "Grandma," and Jimmy Hatlo's "Little Iodine." Sweeping to fame in this field in the 1950s was Hank Ketcham's "Dennis the Menace." Right behind were Charlie Brown, Lucy, Linus, and Snoopy of the "Peanuts" strip by

Charles M. Schulz, for United Features. The little folks of the Schulz drawing board were more popular than ever in the 1970s and made Schulz the wealthiest cartoonist.

Of all the comic characters, none became better known than Al Capp's "Li'l Abner." Capp began his work for United Features in 1935, and by the time Li'l Abner finally married Daisy Mae in 1952 the event was featured as a news item in many papers. Capp's strip sometimes had a social message for its readers going beyond the doings in Dogpatch. Considerably more subtle in its satire was Walt Kelly's "Pogo" sequence dealing with animal characters. Putting Richard Nixon, Henry Kissinger, Jimmy Carter and other persons, real or fictitious, into his comic strip was Garry Trudeau, whose "Doonesbury" satirized not only politics but also women's liberation, rock, and drugs. By 1977, when Capp and "Li'l Abner" retired, the "Doonesbury" strip dominated political cartooning, with B.D., Mark, Mike, Joanie Caucus, Zonker, Duke, and other favorites.

The best humor has been that of the panel artists. Stars of the 1920s were Clare Briggs of the *New York Tribune,* T.A. (Tad) Dorgan of the *American* and *Journal,* and H.T. Webster of the *World* and *Herald Tribune.* Briggs originated "Mr. and Mrs.," a favorite *Herald Tribune* feature. Dorgan's panels were "For Better or Worse" and "Indoor Sports." The master performer was Webster, who invented Caspar Milquetoast for "The Timid Soul" and who drew "The Thrill That Comes Once in a Lifetime," "Life's Darkest Moment," "How to Torture Your Wife," and a humorous series on bridge addicts. Webster's "The Unseen Audience" effectively criticized radio and television until his death in 1952. In a similar tradition were J.R. William's "Out Our Way" and "Born Thirty Years Too Soon," Otto Soglow's "Little King," Clifford McBride's "Napoleon," and Tom Wilson's born loser, "Ziggy."

The impact of the comics is enormous. Chic Young's "Blondie," consistently first in reader preference surveys, runs in 1,600 papers. It and other strips claim from 40 to 80 million readers in up to 50 countries. Mort Walker's "Beetle Bailey" caricature of Army life swept into 1,300 papers in a few years. Today a capable editor must watch the pulling power of his comics, his cartoonists and columnists, and his features (use "Dear Abby" or "Ann Landers"?). The choices are hard ones, for the common denominators of journalism have proved their effectiveness.

NOTES

1. Oswald Garrison Villard, "The Press Today," *Nation,* CXXX (June 1930), 646.
2. Victor Rosewater, *History of Cooperative News-Gathering in the United States* (New York: Appleton-Century-Crofts, 1930), pp. 182–89.
3. For a description of Stone's activities see *"M.E.S."—His Book* (New York: Harper & Row, 1918).
4. The whole story, from the AP's viewpoint, is told in Kent Cooper, *Barriers Down* (New York: Holt, Rinehart & Winston, 1942). Reuters became a cooperative, like the AP, in 1941, and invaded the American market with some success.
5. As quoted in Rosewater, *History of Cooperative News-Gathering,* p. 354.
6. As quoted in Charles R. McCabe, ed., *Damned Old Crank* (New York: Harper & Row, 1951), p. 219.
7. Howard gave his explanation in Webb Miller's *I Found No Peace* (New York: Simon & Schuster, 1936), p. 96. The Associated Press blunder on the Hauptmann verdict stemmed from the setting up of a signal system to get the news out of the courtroom. An overanxious AP man got the wrong signal and flashed news of a life sentence when the verdict was death. The 1944 premature D-Day flash by AP was sent by a girl teletype operator who was "practicing," the AP said. The UP was similarly victimized by an employee who flashed the end of the Japanese war prematurely in 1945.
8. McCabe, *Damned Old Crank,* p. 204.

9. Ralph E. Kliesch, "A Vanishing Species: The American Newsman Abroad," *1975 Directory of the Overseas Press Club of America* (New York: Overseas Press Club, 1975), pp. 18ff.

10. Walter Duranty, *I Write as I Please* (New York: Halcyon House, 1935), p. 166–67.

11. Michael C. Emery, "The American Mass Media and the Coverage of Five Major Foreign Events, 1900–1950," Ph.D. thesis, University of Minnesota, 1968.

12. Paul Scott Mowrer, *The House of Europe* (Boston: Houghton Mifflin, 1945), p. 70. For his brother's personal account, see Edgar Ansel Mowrer, *Triumph and Tragedy* (New York: Weybright and Talley, 1968).

13. Among other special news agencies were the Dow Jones News Service, with some 35 newspaper clients; the Jewish Telegraphic Agency, a world service headquartering in New York, and its Overseas News Agency; Associated Negro Press, largest for Negro papers; Religious News Service, serving 750 clients; and Copley News Service, specializing in Latin American news.

ANNOTATED BIBLIOGRAPHY

Books

ALSOP, JOSEPH AND STEWART, *The Reporter's Trade*. New York: Reynal & Company, 1958. A discussion of Washington reporting and compilation of the Alsop brothers' columns, 1946–58.

BAILLIE, HUGH, *High Tension*. New York: Harper & Row, 1959. Readable autobiography of the former United Press president.

BECKER, STEPHEN, *Comic Art in America*. New York: Simon & Schuster, 1959. Surveys comics, political cartoons, magazine humor.

BLOCK, HERBERT L., *The Herblock Gallery*. New York: Simon & Schuster, 1968. One of several collections of the great cartoonist's work; for his anti-Nixon best, see *Herblock Special Report* (New York: W.W. Norton, 1974).

CATER, DOUGLASS, *The Fourth Branch of Government*. Boston: Houghton Mifflin, 1959. Surveys the Washington press corps.

CHILDS, MARQUIS, *Witness to Power*. New York: McGraw-Hill, 1975. Autobiography.

CHILDS, MARQUIS, AND JAMES B. RESTON, eds., *Walter Lippmann and His Times*. New York: Harcourt Brace Jovanovich, 1959. Twelve essays by admirers.

CLAPPER, RAYMOND, *Watching the World*. New York: Whittlesey House, 1944. A collection of the writings of a great Washington correspondent and columnist.

CONSIDINE, BOB, *It's All News to Me*. New York: Meredith, 1967. Autobiography of a great press association reporter, for INS, and Hearst star.

COOPER, KENT, *Kent Cooper and the Associated Press*. New York: Random House, 1959. Autobiography of the former general manager. For the story of the AP's restrictive news exchange agreements, see his *Barriers Down* (New York: Holt, Rinehart & Winston, 1942).

COUPERIE, PIERRE, AND MAURICE C. HORN, *A History of the Comic Strip*. New York: Crown, 1968. Covers the comic strip worldwide with emphasis upon American.

DAM, HARI N., *The Intellectual Odyssey of Walter Lippmann*. New York: Gordon Press, 1973. The columnist's public philosophy, 1910–60, is analyzed in scholarly, readable style. See also, John Luskin, *Lippmann, Liberty and the Press* (University, Ala.: University of Alabama Press, 1972).

DARLING, JAY N., *Ding's Half Century*, edited by John M. Henry. New York: Duell, Sloan and Pearce, 1962. Ding's best cartoons for the *Des Moines Register*.

DESMOND, ROBERT W., *The Press and World Affairs*. New York: Appleton-Century-Crofts, 1937. Traces early press association developments worldwide. See chapter 1 bibliography for reference to his 1977 study, *The Information Process*.

ELLIS, ELMER, ed., *Mr. Dooley at His Best*. New York: Scribner's, 1938. Writings of Finley Peter Dunne, the famed Chicago columnist.

FARR, FINIS, *Fair Enough: The Life of Westbrook Pegler*. New Rochelle, N.Y.: Arlington House, 1975. Favorable biography of the sportswriter and political columnist.

FISHER, CHARLES, *The Columnists*. New York: Howell, Soskin, Publishers, Inc., 1944. A lively study, outdated but still valuable.

GRAMLING, OLIVER, *AP: The Story of News*. New York: Holt, Rinehart & Winston, 1940. Unreliable in its survey of early period of AP history, on which Rosewater is the authority, the book contains valuable details for the modern era.

HARRISON, JOHN M., *The Man Who Made Nasby, David Ross Locke*. Chapel Hill: University of North Carolina Press, 1969. An excellent biography of the editor of the *Toledo Blade*, who was creator of Petroleum V. Nasby.

HESS, STEPHEN, AND MILTON KAPLAN, *The Ungentlemanly Art: A History of American Political Cartoons*. New York: Macmillan, 1968. A well-done survey from Franklin to Herblock.

HOHENBERG, JOHN, *Foreign Correspondence: The Great Reporters and Their Times*. New York: Columbia University Press, 1964. Foreign correspondence since the French Revolution; best survey of the reporters and the trends.

JOHNSON, GERALD W., *The Lines Are Drawn*. Philadelphia: Lippincott, 1958. A study of Pulitzer Prize cartoons.

KROCK, ARTHUR, *Memoirs: Sixty Years on the Firing Line*. New York: Funk & Wagnalls, 1968. By the longtime Washington chief of the *New York Times*.

McCABE, CHARLES R., ed., *Damned Old Crank*. New York: Harper & Row, 1951. Contains a chapter in which E.W. Scripps explains why he started the United Press, and gives some financial details.

"M.E.S." His Book. New York: Harper & Row, 1918. A book commemorating Melville E. Stone's first 25 years as Associated Press general manager. Much of Stone's own writing and his major speeches are included, along with other historical materials. See also Stone's autobiography, *Fifty Years a Journalist*.

MORRIS, JOE ALEX, *Deadline Every Minute: The Story of the United Press*. New York: Doubleday, 1957. By a UP staff member, observing the press association's fiftieth anniversary. Highly readable; covers both UP executives and newsmen.

MOWRER, EDGAR ANSEL, *Triumph and Turmoil: A Personal History of Our Times*. New York: Weybright and Talley, 1968. Autobiography of one of greatest foreign correspondents, World War I to cold war.

MURRELL, WILLIAM, *A History of American Graphic Humor, 1865–1938*. New York: Macmillan, 1938. The second volume of a work that reproduces many cartoons.

NEVINS, ALLAN, AND GEORGE WEITENKAMPF, *A Century of Political Cartoons*. New York: Scribner's, 1944. The cartoons are presented in historical setting.

O'CONNOR, RICHARD, *Heywood Broun: A Biography*. New York: G.P. Putnam's Sons, 1975. Newest study; well done. See also Dale Kramer, *Heywood Broun* (New York: A.A. Wyn, 1949).

PERRY, GEORGE, AND ALAN ALDRIDGE, *The Penguin Book of Comics*. Harmondsworth, England: Penguin, 1967. History of comics with copious examples.

PILAT, OLIVER, *Drew Pearson: An Unauthorized Biography*. New York: Harper's Magazine Press, 1973. Pearson had questionable news-gathering ethics, but many readers.

READ, WILLIAM H., *America's Mass Media Merchants*. Baltimore, Md.: Johns Hopkins University Press, 1977. Examines overseas impact of ten specific media, including AP, UPI, *Time, Newsweek, Reader's Digest,* and major news syndicates.

RIVERS, WILLIAM L., *The Opinionmakers*. Boston: Beacon Press, 1965. A top-flight study of Washington journalists. See also *The Adversaries* (1970).

ROSEWATER, VICTOR, *History of Cooperative News-Gathering in the United States*. New York: Appleton-Century-Crofts, 1930. The authoritative source for the rise of the press associations.

SANDERS, MARION K., *Dorothy Thompson: A Legend in Her Time*. Boston: Houghton Mifflin, 1973. Prize-winning biography of outstanding foreign correspondent and columnist.

SMITH, MERRIMAN, *A White House Memoir*. New York: W.W. Norton, 1972. How the UPI's great White House correspondent covered the period from FDR to Nixon.

SPENCER, DICK, III, *Pulitzer Prize Cartoons*. Ames: Iowa State College Press, 1953. A history of the winning cartoons since 1922.

STOKES, THOMAS L., *Chip Off My Shoulder*. Princeton: Princeton University Press, 1940. Autobiography of a distinguished reporter-columnist.

SULLIVAN, MARK, *The Education of an American*. New York: Doubleday, 1938. The autobiography of one of the first political columnists.

SULZBERGER, C. L., *A Long Row of Candles*. New York: Macmillan, 1969. Memoirs and diaries of the chief *New York Times* foreign correspondent, 1934–54. His *The Last of the Giants* (1970) carried the story through 1963.

THOMAS, HELEN, *Dateline: White House*. New York: Macmillan, 1975. UPI's top woman.

UNESCO, *World Communications: A 200-Country Survey of Press, Radio, Television, Film*, 5th ed. (New York: Unipub, 1975). Most authoritative report on worldwide media.

————, *News Agencies: Their Structure and Operations*. New York: Columbia University Press, 1953. Includes discussions of AP, UP, and INS and examines their roles in worldwide news distribution. Later information is found in John C. Merrill, Carter R. Bryan, and Marvin Alisky, *The Foreign Press: A Survey of the World's Journalism* (Baton Rouge: Louisiana State University Press, 1970).

WATSON, ELMO SCOTT, *A History of Newspaper Syndicates in the United States, 1865–1935*. Chicago: Publishers' Auxiliary, 1936. Source for the story of Western Newspaper Union and for rise of other early syndicates.

WAUGH, COULTON, *The Comics*. New York: Macmillan, 1947. A first-rate history of the comic pages; detailed but well-written and well-illustrated.

WEBSTER, H.T., *The Best of H.T. Webster*. New York: Simon & Schuster, 1953. One of the best collections of newspaper humorous drawings.

WEINGAST, DAVID E., *Walter Lippmann*. New Brunswick: Rutgers University Press, 1949. An impartial study of the political, social, and economic views of an essentially conservative columnist.

Periodicals and Monographs

ABBOT, WILLIS J., "Melville E. Stone's Own Story," *Collier's*, LXV (February 7, 1920), 51. A well-written portrait of the AP general manager.

ALSOP, JOSEPH AND STEWART, "Our Own Inside Story," *Saturday Evening Post*, CCXXXI (November 8–15, 1958). How the columnists operated, 1946–58.

BARCUS, FRANCIS E., "A Content Analysis of Trends in Sunday Comics, 1900–1959," *Journalism Quarterly*, XXXVIII (Spring 1961), 171. The first report from a major study of comics at Boston University.

BENÉT, STEPHEN VINCENT, "The United Press," *Fortune*, VII (May 1933), 67. A compact treatment of UP history and its 1933 status.

DENNIS, EVERETTE E., "The Regeneration of Political Cartooning," *Journalism Quarterly*, LI (Winter 1974), 664. Focuses on "new wave" debate and three current leaders. See also Everette and Melvin Dennis, "100 Years of Political Cartooning," *Journalism History*, I (Spring 1974), 6, comparing caustic Watergate cartoons with Nast era.

EMERY, MICHAEL C., "The American Mass Media and the Coverage of Five Major Foreign Events, 1900–1950: the Russo-Japanese War, Outbreak of World War I, Rise of Stalin, Munich Crisis, Invasion of South Korea," Ph.D. thesis, University of Minnesota, 1968. The press corps and how the media used their coverage.

ENDRES, KATHLEEN L., "Capitol Hill Newswomen: A Descriptive Study," *Journalism Quarterly*, LIII (Spring 1976), 132. Background material and current research.

HARRISON, RICHARD EDES, "AP," *Fortune*, XV (February 1937), 89. The rise of the AP and a contemporary picture of its operations.

HESTER, ALBERT L., "The Associated Press and News from Latin America: A Gatekeeper and News-Flow Study," Ph.D. thesis, University of Wisconsin, 1972. News becomes more superficial as it flows from Latin America through New York to United States papers.

IRWIN, WILL, "United Press," *Harper's Weekly,* LVIII (April 25, 1914), 6. An estimate by a top-flight newsman of early UP progress.

JOHNSON, CARL E., "A Twentieth Century Seeker: A Biography of James Vincent Sheean," Ph.D. thesis, University of Wisconsin, 1974. Sheean spent 50 years abroad.

KLIESCH, RALPH E., "History and Operations of the McGraw-Hill World News Service," Ph.D. thesis, University of Minnesota, 1968. Describes McGraw-Hill news gathering since 1880s, and the World News Service, 1945–68.

MARBUT, FREDERICK B., "Congress and the Standing Committee of Correspondents," *Journalism Quarterly,* XXXVIII (Winter 1961), 52. The history of the press gallery rules is traced from 1879.

MILLER, MERLE, "Washington, the World, and Joseph Alsop," *Harper's,* CCXXXVI (June 1968), 43. The imperious columnist examined.

ODENDAHL, ERIC M., "The Story and Stories of the Copley News Service," Ph.D. thesis, University of Missouri, 1966. History of the service and analysis of its content.

PEARSON, DREW, "Confessions of 'an S.O.B.'," *Saturday Evening Post,* CCXXIX (November 3–24, 1956). Story of an "inside" columnist.

PEER, ELIZABETH, "Walter Lippmann, 1889–1974," *Newsweek,* LXXXIV (Dec. 23, 1974), 40.

SCHWARZLOSE, RICHARD A., "The American Wire Services: A Study of Their Development as a Social Institution," Ph.D. thesis, University of Illinois, 1965. By a leading student of the press associations.

———, "Trends in U.S. Newspapers' Wire Service Resources, 1934–66," *Journalism Quarterly,* XLIII (Winter 1966), 627. A lessening of competitive service appears in these detailed figures.

SINGLETARY, MICHAEL W., "Newspaper Use of Supplemental Services: 1960–73," *Journalism Quarterly,* LII (Winter 1975), 748. See also Edward J. Trayes, "News/Feature Services by Circulation Group Use," *Journalism Quarterly,* XLIX (Spring 1972), 133.

STROUT, RICHARD L., "Tom Stokes: What He Was Like," *Nieman Reports,* XIII (July 1959), 9. A portrait of a great Washington reporter.

"The Funny Papers," *Fortune,* VII (April 1933), 45. An excellent major study, well-illustrated.

WITCOVER, JULES, "Washington: The News Explosion," *Columbia Journalism Review,* VIII (Spring 1969), 23. A survey of new trends in Washington reporting.

Viet Nam evacuation... the complete story

From Da Nang: Exclusive photos

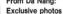

The first pictures from Da Nang to be released by a Western journalist since the Viet Cong took over the city are on page 8. They are by Abbas, a Iranian photojournalist who was accredited after several hundred photographers were refused entry.

Indochina chronology

The 35-year history of the bloody Indochinese conflict, starting with the Japanese occupancy in 1940, is detailed on page 6. Maps showing the Communist expansion and photographs from the battle areas accompany the year-by-year report.

The longest war for U. S.

It cost this country nearly 57,000 lives, 303,659 wounded, and $140 billion. And when it was all over, the other side had won. The war was the longest in the history of the United States. An account of its cost and photographs are on page 7.

Chicago Tribune
THE WORLD'S GREATEST NEWSPAPER

Wednesday, April 30, 1975

Sports **★★★★ Final**

128th Year—No. 120   © 1975 Chicago Tribune

7 Sections   15¢

Saigon surrenders

Americans being evacuated from U. S. Embassy compound in Saigon climb ladder to waiting helicopter.

UPI Telephoto

S. Viet leader gives up 'to avoid bloodshed'

From Tribune Wire Services

SAIGON—The Saigon government surrendered unconditionally to the Viet Cong Wednesday, ending 30 years of warfare.

Columns of South Vietnamese troops pulled out of their defensive positions in the city and marched to central points to turn in their weapons.

President Duong Van [Big] Minh spoke to the nation only hours after an armada of United States Marine helicopters had completed an emergency evacuation of nearly 900 Americans and thousands of Vietnamese from the besieged capital.

WITHIN TWO hours of Minh's broadcast, North Vietnamese and Viet Cong troops began moving into downtown Saigon in tanks and jeeps.

A jeep flying the Viet Cong flag drove along the street a block from the abandoned U. S. Embassy. The eight cheering men in the vehicle were in civilian clothes but carried weapons, including Communist AK-47 rifles.

One of the men was sitting on the fender holding the flag. He beckoned to an American newsman and said in English, "Go home, go home."

THE TANKS and jeeps were greeted by cheering crowds as they pulled into the grounds of Saigon's presidential palace.

People reportedly thronged the streets cheering the green-uniformed troops. The grinning Viet Cong soldiers waved gaily back.

Earlier, the tanks had fired salvos and flares into the air in apparent jubilation.

Some Western newsmen and young missionaries decide to stay in South Viet Nam and take their chances. Tribune reporters Ronald Yates and Philip Caputo are yet to be heard from. Page 16.

THE VIET CONG'S mission to Paris, meanwhile, waited for the fulfillment of one remaining demand before accepting the surrender. That is the withdrawal of American ships waiting off the South Vietnamese coast for flights of refugees.

Minh, a retired general and neutralist, was named president Monday in a desperate and unsuccessful attempt to negotiate a peace with the Communist leaders.

In a five-minute radio address, Minh said, "The Republic of Viet Nam policy is the policy of peace and reconciliation, aimed at saving the blood of our people. I ask all servicemen to stop firing and stay where you are. I also demand that soldiers of the Provisional Revolutionary Government [Viet Cong] stop firing and stay in place.

"WE ARE HERE WAITING for the Provisional Revolution—

Continued on page 9, col. 4

Pained Kissinger turns cautious on nation's future commitments

By Bill Neikirk
Chicago Tribune Press Service

WASHINGTON—With the pain of the Viet Nam disaster showing in his face, Secretary of State Henry Kissinger said Tuesday America must now be more careful about its future commitments and more determined to honor them.

"Obviously this has been a very painful experience," said the man who had seen the triumph of his Paris peace agreement crumble away to a tragic defeat for South Viet Nam.

A somber Kissinger said time is needed to heal the wounds of America's role in Viet Nam and "to concentrate on the problems of the future."

HE SPOKE with more than usual bluntness at a news conference called after the White House announced the last American had been evacuated from Saigon.

If there is any lesson to be learned, he said, it is that the United States "should be careful about the commitments we make and determined to follow those we do make."

Kissinger said that Viet Nam will mean a more mature America when it comes to foreign connections. Now, he said, the nation knows that if foreign policy is going to be effective, it will "have to be sustained over decades."

There was no bitterness in Kissinger's voice as he detailed the last hours of the nation's role in Viet Nam. He refused, however, to give a long analysis of what the war means for the nation and why it was lost.

"I THINK IT will be a long time before anyone will be able to write about it with dispassion," he said. Later, he said this was not the time "to make an assessment of a dec—

Continued on page 2, col. 3

Marines in like heroes, out like foes

EDITORS NOTE—The writer of this dispatch, winner of a Pulitzer Prize for dispatches from Viet Nam, was there when American soldiers first came in force to Indochina. He was there Tuesday when the Americans left, one of several American reporters who elected to remain in Saigon after the evacuation.

By Peter Arnett

SAIGON [AP] — Ten years ago I watched the first United States Marines arrive to help

South Viet Nam. They were greeted on the beaches by pretty Vietnamese girls in white silken robes who draped flower leis around their necks.

A decade has passed.

And on Tuesday I watched the last Americans out of South Viet Nam. They were the same, cleancut-looking young men of a decade ago.

But the Vietnamese were different.

Those who didn't have a place on the last helicopters

out of Saigon—and there were thousands of them left behind —hooted, booed, and scuffled with the Marines guarding the landing zones.

SOME VIETNAMESE threw themselves over walls and wire fences, only to be thrown back by the Marines.

Bloodshed was avoided seemingly only by good luck and bad aim on the part of some angry Vietnamese soldiers who shot at a few buses and departing helicopters.

But the entire, frantic dash from Saigon by the Americans —and the bitter resentment of the thousands of Vietnamese who couldn't go—seemed a sad but accurate reflection of what relations between Americans and Vietnamese had come to in the 10 years since these flowers were gladly given to the Marines.

Americans and the South

Vietnamese used to get along pretty well. That was in the days when the U. S. Marines first arrived in Viet Nam imbued with a determination to see the war thru.

THE SOUTH Vietnamese army, dispirited then, watched with wonder as first the Marines and then the paratroopers and the American infantry came to steaming hot Viet Nam to trudge the coastal plains and mountain valleys in a punishing, unfamiliar environment.

Vietnamese officers began aping the American way. The Americans seemed always to have better pressed uniforms and more detailed maps and diagrams.

Nearly 20,000 Vietnamese officers flew to the United States for education or advanced training, and they returned

Continued on page 19, col. 4

Weather

CHICAGO AND VICINITY: Partly cloudy, Wednesday; high, around 70; southwest to west winds 10 to 20 m. p. h.; low, in upper 40s. Thursday: Mostly cloudy, high, in low to mid 60s. Tuesday's high temperature of 76 degrees at Midway Airport gave Chicago its warmest reading of the year. For map and other reports, see page 13, Sec. 4.

Scene of evacuation

U. S. embassy in Saigon was liftoff point for Americans being evacuated who were unable to reach Tan Son Nhut Air Base because South Vietnamese soldiers refused to let buses enter. Evacuees were transferred to ships in South

China Sea as Bien Hoa fell to Communists and Tan Son Nhut Air Base came under heavy attack. Jim Squires, chief of the Washington bureau, reports on Saigon—"a faraway place that war brought near"—on today's back page.

© 1975, Chicago Tribune

America's Vietnam nightmare ends with dramatic suddenness.

21

The Press
in Modern War

This is a people's war, and to win it the people should know as much about it as they can.

—Elmer Davis

The great war that began in Europe in August 1914 completely altered the pattern of life that a comparatively peaceful nineteenth century had produced. By 1917 it had become a world war, with the embarking of the United States on a "great crusade" to make the world safe for democracy. But men found at war's end that they neither could restore the old order nor build a peaceful new one. Political and social disillusionment, economic depression, and the rise of modern dictatorships brought a second great war in 1939, and the designations World War I and II came into the language. After 1950, when the United States found itself leading a United Nations army into Korea to fight the forces of Communist aggression and ended up in the quagmire of Vietnam, war seemed an unending morass. What happened to the American press in these periods of international war, interrupted by what proved to be only brief interludes of fitful peace, thus becomes a continuing story; equally important is the account of the role played by communication agencies during the periods of conflict.

AMERICAN REACTION
TO EUROPE'S 1914 WAR

No one could foresee in 1914 the ultimate consequences of Germany's transformation of a "Balkan incident" into a general European war. Even though the United States had entered into the world diplomatic arena after the war with Spain, most Americans probably felt secure behind two oceans and were interested only in preserving peace as far as this country was concerned. No doubt the jesting comment of the *Chicago Herald* summarized this attitude: "Peace-loving citizens of this country will now rise up and tender a hearty vote of thanks to Columbus for having discovered America."[1]

Yet underneath this denial of concern by Americans for what was happening in the Old World lay the first instinctive reactions to the shattering of peace. As Americans read the vivid account by Richard Harding Davis of the entry of the German

327

army into Brussels—"one unbroken steel-gray column . . . twenty-four hours later is still coming . . . not men marching, but a force of nature like a tidal wave, an avalanche"—and as they looked almost unbelievingly at pictures of the sacked city of Louvain, they became increasingly uncomfortable.

It is important to record these first American reactions, since in the depths of later disillusionment, when it was evident that our participation in war had failed to bring a lasting peace, a literature appeared that told a different story.[2] British propagandists, American munitions makers, and cynical politicians had led gullible Americans to an unnecessary slaughter, the theme ran, carrying with it the implication that American newspapers were duped by foreign propagandists and by war-mongering capitalists, and thereby misled their readers. A quite convincing case was built on partial evidence for such a thesis, ignoring or overriding such important factors as these: the impact on American public opinion of crisis events, such as the sinking of the *Lusitania*, which were predominantly unfavorable to the German side; the effects of Allied censorships and control of overseas communications in shaping the available news (as distinct from overt propaganda efforts); the effects of socially important pressure groups in shaping American thought; the natural ties between English-speaking peoples, and the distaste of Americans for German "Kultur"; the legitimate pro-Allied decisions of American officials and diplomats based on German-caused events; the feeling that a strong British navy was less hazardous to American interests than a strong German navy; and, most importantly, the basic United States objection to one-nation domination of Europe—an objection that led to two wars with German militarism in defense of the American national interest.[3]

News of military actions was delayed by both sides, and official communiqués often attempted to conceal news of reversals.* Some correspondents managed to obtain beats on news of important battles, but largely as a matter of luck. Front area reporters more often won recognition for their feature stories than for their straight factual accounts, while military analysts in the various European capitals provided the continuing story of the fighting along the sprawling western and eastern fronts. This news, after clearing the military censorships, still had to funnel through the London communications center. This was the result of the British action in cutting the German Atlantic cable on August 5, 1914. Stories written in Berlin, Vienna, and in neutral capitals thereafter had to travel through London to reach the United States.[4]

AMERICA MOVES   The course of events was rapidly bolstering pro-Allied sentiment in
TOWARD WAR   the United States. The *New York Times* printed the various "white
                 papers" giving each belligerent power's version of the events leading
up to the war, but Germany's obvious preparation for war and smashing early victories added reason to believe the Allied versions, imperfectly as they were presented. Natural ties of many Americans to the English traditions, which were particularly strong among social and intellectual leaders, made it fashionable to be pro-British. Yet large segments of the population opposed America's going to war up to the last, for various reasons. The Middle West was more isolationist than the seaboard sections and was suspicious of the pro-Allied easterners. The Irish, a strong minority, were naturally anti-British because of the Irish civil war, although this did not necessarily make them pro-German, it should be pointed out. The large groups of German-

*British journalist Philip Knightley, in his *The First Casualty* (New York: Harcourt Brace Jovanovich, 1975) contended (p. 80) that between 1914 and 1918 "More deliberate lies were told than in any other period of history, and the whole apparatus of the state went into action to suppress the truth." His book is a harsh appraisal of war correspondence and government manipulation from the Crimean War to Vietnam.

Americans who were, on the whole, loyal to the United States, were at the same time naturally sympathetic with the aims of the Fatherland. They regarded Germany's ambitions as no more dangerous or imperialistic than those of Britain, France, and Russia.

One decisive event was the torpedoing of English Cunard line ship *Lusitania,* then the queen of the Atlantic run. When the *Lusitania* went down off the Irish coast on May 7, 1915, with the loss of 1,198 of the 1,924 persons aboard—including 114 of 188 American passengers—Germany celebrated the accomplishment of her U-boat captain. But resentment ran high in the United States, particularly when it was remembered that an Imperial German Embassy advertisement warning travelers on Allied ships that they did so "at their own risk" had appeared in New York newspapers the morning the *Lusitania* left port.

Even though Germany relaxed its submarine warfare after months of diplomatic note-writing by President Wilson, the summer of 1916 was dominated by pro-Allied arguments and by talk of preparedness. Wilson, whose most effective 1916 campaign slogan had been "He kept us out of war," saw his hopes of the United States serving as a neutral arbiter dashed by two final German actions.

One was resumption of unrestricted submarine warfare by the Germans in February 1917. This brought a break in diplomatic relations. Clinching the American decision was the Allied interception of German Foreign Minister Zimmermann's note to the Mexican government, offering Mexico the return of Texas, New Mexico, and Arizona after an American defeat, if Mexico would ally itself with Germany. The text of the note, given to the Associated Press unofficially, created a sensation. The sinking of three American ships by U-boats in March brought Wilson's war call on April 2—"The world must be made safe for democracy"—and the declaration of war on April 6. Wilson's masterful phrases played no small part in the determination of the issue. His denunciation of a group of 11 senators, led by Robert La Follette of Wisconsin, as "a little group of willful men" for filibustering against arming of American merchant ships in early March did much to discredit the opponents of war.

Some periodicals had been pro-Ally almost from the start. Among the most outspoken were the old *Life* magazine, Henry Watterson's *Louisville Courier-Journal,* and the *New York Herald.* The *New York Times* was solidly pro-Ally, along with the *World* and most other New York newspapers. After the sinking of the *Lusitania,* the number of anti-interventionist newspapers dwindled. William Randolph Hearst's chain of papers stood out as bitterly anti-British and was tarred as pro-German because Hearst made special efforts to obtain German-originated news to balance Allied-originated stories. Other holdouts against the war were the *New York Evening Mail* (which had been bought secretly by German agents), *Chicago Tribune, Cincinnati Enquirer, Cleveland Plain Dealer, Washington Post, Milwaukee Sentinel, Los Angeles Times, San Francisco Chronicle,* and *San Francisco Call.*[5] All, of course, supported the war once it was declared. William Jennings Bryan's *Commoner, La Follette's Magazine,* and Oswald G. Villard's *Nation* and *New York Evening Post* were pacifist.

GEORGE CREEL'S
COMMITTEE ON PUBLIC
INFORMATION

Only a week after the declaration of war, Wilson appointed a Committee on Public Information. Its job primarily was one of disseminating facts about the war. It also was to coordinate government propaganda efforts and to serve as the government's liaison with newspapers. It drew up a voluntary censorship code under which editors would agree to refrain from printing material that might aid the enemy. Before it was through, the committee found itself "mobilizing the mind of the world," and Mark Sullivan characterized it as an American contribution to the science of war.

George Creel, the newspaperman who was named by Wilson to direct the committee's work, explained that "it was a plain publicity proposition, a vast enterprise in salesmanship, the world's greatest adventure in advertising."[6]

The opportunity Wilson gave to Creel was a greater one than any other person had enjoyed in the propaganda arena.[7] Creel was a liberal-minded and vigorously competent product of New York, Kansas City, and Denver journalism. He was intensely anxious to achieve every possible task his committee might embrace, and he eventually mobilized 150,000 Americans to carry out its varied and far-flung missions.

Creel's first job was to open up government news channels to the Washington correspondents, insisting that only news of troop movements, ship sailings, and other events of strictly military character should be withheld. He issued a brief explanatory code calling on the newspapers to censor such news themselves, voluntarily. Throughout the war, newspaper editors generally went beyond Creel's minimum requests in their desire to aid the war effort. In May 1917, the CPI began publishing an *Official Bulletin* in which releases were reprinted in newspaper form. Before the war was over this publication reached a daily circulation of 118,000. A weekly newspaperman prepared a digest of the news for rural papers. Still photographs, plates, and mats also were utilized.

A historian who studied the accuracy of CPI news releases years later came to this conclusion: "One of the most remarkable things about the charges against the CPI is that, of the more than 6,000 news stories it issued, so few were called into question at all. It may be doubted that the CPI's record for honesty will ever be equalled in the official war news of a major power."[8]

Creel asked major advertisers and the publications themselves to donate space for various government campaigns, the Red Cross, and other war-related activities. The advertising agencies were organized, and their copy men and artists were used to create newspaper and magazine advertising, streetcar placards, and outdoor posters. The artists in the CPI's division of pictorial publicity, headed by Charles Dana Gibson, contributed stirring posters. The infant motion picture industry produced films of a patriotic and instructive nature. Its stars, including Douglas Fairbanks and Mary Pickford, sparked Liberty bond sales. The college professors served in a division of pamphleteering. It produced a *War Cyclopedia* and 75 million pieces of printed matter. Historian Guy Stanton Ford of the University of Minnesota headed the division, which numbered among its scholars such noted historians as Carl Becker of Cornell University, Evarts B. Greene of the University of Illinois, and Frederic L. Paxson of the University of Wisconsin.[9]

CENSORSHIP OF GERMAN AND SOCIALIST PAPERS

The Espionage Act of June 15, 1917, provided the opening wedge for suppression of those who were considered to be disloyal to the American and Allied war cause. Among the crimes, punishable by heavy fines and imprisonment, the act defined were the willful making of false reports or false statements with the intent to interfere with the successful operation of the military or naval forces, and willful attempts to promote disloyalty in the armed forces or to obstruct recruitments. A section on use of the mails empowered Postmaster General Albert S. Burleson to declare unmailable all letters, circulars, newspapers, pamphlets, books, and other materials violating provisions of the act.

The axe fell most heavily on Socialist organs and German-American newspapers, with a few other pacifist or anti-Ally publications losing their mail privileges. The *American Socialist* was banned from the mails immediately and was soon followed by

Solidarity, journal of the left-wing Industrial Workers of the World—the much-feared anticapitalistic IWW. A vociferous advocate of the Irish independence movement, Jeremiah A. O'Leary, lost mailing privileges for his publication, *Bull,* in July 1917, for opposing wartime cooperation with the British. The magazine *The Masses,* brilliantly edited by Max Eastman, felt the ban in August for publishing an issue containing four antiwar cartoons and a poem defending radical leaders Emma Goldman and Alexander Berkman. An indictment against the editors under the Espionage Act was dismissed in 1919.

Altogether some 75 papers either lost their mailing privileges during the first year of the Espionage Act or retained them only by agreeing to print nothing more concerning the war. The best known were two Socialist dailies, the *New York Call* and Victor Berger's *Milwaukee Leader.* The Austrian-born Berger, in 1910 the first Socialist elected to Congress, was convicted on charges of conspiracy to violate the Espionage Act and sentenced to 20 years imprisonment. The U.S. Supreme Court later overturned the decision due to the prejudicial actions of the presiding judge. Twice the House of Representatives denied him the seat to which he had been reelected. For a time during and after the war, all incoming mail was prevented from reaching the *Leader.* The Supreme Court upheld the Post Office ban on the *Leader* in a 1921 decision, and it was not until June 1921, when Postmaster General Will Hays restored their second-class mailing privileges, that the *Leader* and the *Call* were once again able to reach their numerous out-of-town subscribers. The German-language press likewise was hard hit by mail bans and prosecutions and declined one-half in numbers and in circulation during the war.

Other papers felt the weight of public opinion against those who did not wholeheartedly support the war. The Hearst newspapers, which had bitterly opposed American entry into the war and continued to be clearly anti-Ally even though they supported the American war effort itself, were widely attacked. Hearst was hanged in effigy, his papers were boycotted in some places, and he himself was denounced as disloyal. The *New York Tribune,* itself a strong critic of the way in which the Wilson administration was conducting the war, ran a famous cartoon showing a snake coiled in the flag, with the snake's body spelling the legend "Hears—ss-ss-t." Oswald Garrison Villard's pacifist views and defenses of civil liberties brought such a decline in the fortunes of the *New York Evening Post* that he was forced to sell it in 1918, and one issue of the *Nation* was held up in the New York Post Office because it carried an editorial titled "Civil Liberty Dead."

THE SEDITION ACT OF 1918

The powers of the government to control expression of opinion were strengthened by the passage of two other laws. The Trading-with-the-Enemy Act of October 1917 authorized censorship of all communications moving in or out of the United States and provided that translations of newspaper or magazine articles published in a foreign language could be demanded by the Post Office—a move to keep the German-language papers in line. The Sedition Act of May 1918 amended and broadened the Espionage Act by making it a crime to write or publish "any disloyal, profane, scurrilous or abusive language about the form of government of the United States or the Constitution, military or naval forces, flag, or the uniform" or to use language intended to bring these ideas and institutions "into contempt, scorn, contumely, or disrepute." The application of these broad provisions by the Post Office in banning publications from the mails gave the postmaster general immense powers he hesitated to use. The memory of the blundering Sedition Act of 1798 kept him from using his authority to harass orthodox Republican opponents of the administration, and the brunt of persecution continued to fall on the unpopular radical and pro-German minorities.

Former President Theodore Roosevelt was asking heatedly why the Hearst newspapers had not been denied mail privileges (some Republicans said Hearst escaped because he was a Democrat). Roosevelt also was writing editorials for the *Kansas City Star* criticizing the administration and was speaking strongly against what he called its incompetence and softness in dealing with the enemy. Senator Robert La Follette of Wisconsin, who was politically crucified by an error the Associated Press made in reporting one of his speeches,[10] likewise was a possible candidate for prosecution.

The Department of Justice, however, moved against lesser-known persons like the IWW leaders, who were arrested and imprisoned, and like Mrs. Rose Pastor Stokes, who got a ten-year sentence for writing a letter to the *Kansas City Star* saying "No government which is for the profiteers can also be for the people, and I am for the people, while the government is for the profiteers." The verdict against Mrs. Stokes was reversed in 1920. But not so fortunate was the four-time Socialist party presidential candidate, Eugene V. Debs. When he told a Socialist convention in June 1918 that the Allies were "out for plunder" and defended the Bolshevists in Russia, he was jailed. Debs' conviction for violation of the Espionage and Sedition Acts was upheld unanimously by the Supreme Court. He received the record Socialist party presidential vote total of 920,000 while campaigning in 1920 from a federal prison, however, and was pardoned by President Harding in December 1921.

The wartime atmosphere was favorable to restriction of civil liberties. Generally adopted state laws contained antipacifist, anti-Red, and criminal syndicalism clauses designed to protect business and industry against radical-inspired strikes and violence. Mobs and citizens' committees took care of unpopular persons, including Americans of German ancestry. Many an American was persuaded by community pressure to buy more Liberty bonds than he desired to own. Prosecutors, juries, and judges went beyond the words of the Espionage and Sedition Acts, often because of public pressure. Zechariah Chafee, Jr., the distinguished Harvard law professor, documented the damage done to the spirit of the Constitutional guarantee of free speech in his 1920 work, *Freedom of Speech*.[11] In such circumstances the great bulk of the American press was fortunate to escape not only direct and violent censorship but also the harassments visited on its Socialist and German-language fringe.

Censorship of foreign communications sent by cable, telephone, or telegraph, as provided in the Trading-with-the-Enemy Act, was carried out by a Censorship Board, which Wilson established in October 1917 to coordinate control of communications facilities. The board was mainly concerned with outgoing messages and news dispatches. There were few causes for complaint against the board and it received a "job well done" commendation.[12]

LEADING WAR CORRESPONDENTS

Notable among the early war reporting of Americans was Richard Harding Davis's story of the entry of the German army into Brussels, written for the *New York Tribune* and its syndicate, and Will Irwin's beats on the battle of Ypres and the first German use of poison gas, also printed in the *Tribune*. Irwin was one of several correspondents who represented American magazines in Europe, first writing for *Collier's* and then the *Saturday Evening Post*. However, the brunt of the news coverage responsibility fell on the men

"All the News That's Fit to Print."

The New York Times.

THE WEATHER
Fair today and Tuesday; diminishing northwest winds.

VOL. LXVIII...NO. 22,206.   NEW YORK, MONDAY, NOVEMBER 11, 1918.—TWENTY-FOUR PAGES.   TWO CENTS

ARMISTICE SIGNED, END OF THE WAR!
BERLIN SEIZED BY REVOLUTIONISTS;
NEW CHANCELLOR BEGS FOR ORDER;
OUSTED KAISER FLEES TO HOLLAND

SON FLEES WITH EX-KAISER

Hindenburg Also Believed to be Among Those in His Party.

ALL ARE HEAVILY ARMED

Automobiles Bristle with Rifles as Fugitives Arrive at Dutch Frontier.

ON THEIR WAY TO DE STEEG

Belgians Yell to Them, "Are You On Your Way to Paris?"

LONDON, Nov. 10.—Both the former German Emperor and his eldest son, Frederick William, crossed the Dutch frontier Sunday morning, according to advices from The Hague. His reported destination is De Steeg, near Utrecht.

Kaiser Fought Hindenburg's Call for Abdication; Failed to Get Army's Support in Keeping Throne

By GEORGE RENWICK
Copyright, 1918, by The New York Times Special Cable to The New York Times.

AMSTERDAM, Nov. 10.—I learn on very good authority that the Kaiser made a determined effort to stave off abdication. He went to headquarters with this deliberate intention of bringing the army around to his side.

BERLIN TROOPS JOIN REVOLT

Reds Shell Building in Which Officers Vainly Resist.

THRONGS DEMAND REPUBLIC

Revolutionary Flag on Royal Palace — Crown Prince's Palace Also Seized.

GENERAL STRIKE IS BEGUN

Burgomaster and Police Submit—War Office Now Under Socialist Control.

LONDON, Nov. 10.—The greater part of Berlin is in control of revolutionists, the former Kaiser has fled to Holland and Friedrich Ebert, the new Socialist Chancellor, has taken command of the situation.

Socialist Chancellor Appeals to All Germans To Help Him Save Fatherland from Anarchy

BERNE, Nov. 10.—(Associated Press.)—In an address to the people, the new German Chancellor, Friedrich Ebert, says:

WAR ENDS AT 6 O'CLOCK THIS MORNING

The State Department in Washington Made the Announcement at 2:45 o'Clock.

ARMISTICE WAS SIGNED IN FRANCE AT MIDNIGHT

Terms Include Withdrawal from Alsace-Lorraine, Disarming and Demobilization of Army and Navy, and Occupation of Strategic Naval and Military Points.

By The Associated Press.

WASHINGTON, Monday, Nov. 11, 2:48 A.M.—The armistice between Germany, on the one hand, and the allied Governments and the United States, on the other, has been signed.

The State Department announced at 2:45 o'clock this morning that Germany had signed.

The department's announcement simply said: "The armistice has been signed."

The world war will end this morning at 6 o'clock, Washington time, 11 o'clock Paris time. The armistice was signed by the German representatives at midnight.

GERMAN DYNASTIES BEING WIPED OUT

King of Wuerttemberg Abdicates — Sovereign of Saxony to Follow Suit.

PRINCES MAY BE EXILED

Socialists Are Demanding That Every Sovereign in the Empire Shall be Dethroned.

MORE WARSHIPS JOIN THE REDS

Four Dreadnoughts in Kiel Harbor Espouse the Revolutionary Cause.

GUARDSHIPS ALSO GO OVER

Those Protecting Mines in the Great Belt and the Baltic Abandon Their Posts.

The famous 1918 Armistice Day edition of the *New York Times*.

in the European capital bureaus and those who served as military analysts. Some of the leaders were Karl H. von Wiegand of the United Press, Sigrid Schultz of the *Chicago Tribune,* and Cyril Brown of the *New York Times* in Berlin; Paul Scott Mowrer of the *Chicago Daily News* and Wythe Williams of the *New York Times* in Paris; and Edward Price Bell of the *Chicago Daily News* in London. Frank H. Simonds of the *New York Tribune* did distinguished work as a military critic and Herbert Bayard Swope earned respect for his *New York World* stories.

American war correspondents in France found themselves freer to observe military actions of the American Expeditionary Force than those of the other Allied armies. In General Pershing's area correspondents could go into the front lines without military escorts, they could follow the fighting advances, and they could roam the rear areas, living where they chose. This had not been the case for correspondents with the British, French, and German forces in the early years of the war. But everything the correspondents wrote went through the censorship of the press section of the Military Intelligence Service, headed by Major Frederick Palmer, formerly of the Associated Press. News of general engagements, of casualties suffered, and of troop identifications was releasable only if it had been mentioned in official communiqués. Press officers also were attached to the training camps and cantonments at home.

There were some 500 American correspondents for newspapers, magazines, press associations, and syndicates in Europe by 1915 and the number was augmented when American troops joined the fighting. About 40 actually covered the actions of the AEF. Among the best-known byliners was Fred S. Ferguson of the United Press, who beat his competitors in reporting the battle of Saint-Mihiel by writing an advance story, based on the American battle plan, and having it filed section by section as the battle proceeded. Webb Miller of the United Press and Henry Wales of INS also won prominence, along with Edwin L. James of the *New York Times,* Martin Green of the *New York World,* and Junius Wood of the *Chicago Daily News.* Floyd Gibbons of the *Chicago Tribune* was hit by German machine-gun fire and lost an eye.

A soldiers' journalism also sprouted during wartime, the best-known example being the *Stars and Stripes.* The eight-page paper was established in Paris in February 1918. Harold Ross, later editor of the *New Yorker,* became the chief editor, assisted by such well-known newspapermen as Grantland Rice and Alexander Woollcott. Other overseas units had their publications, as did all of the camps in the United States.

BETWEEN THE WARS:
RED SCARE
AND ISOLATIONISM

With the coming of the Armistice, coverage in Europe turned to the routine of the Army of Occupation in Germany and to the postwar political and economic news, centering about the Versailles peace conference. In the United States a reaction set in against President Wilson's proposed League of Nations. Wilson's physical breakdown while on a nationwide speaking tour in defense of the League left the internationalists leaderless, and the assaults of the Republican Senate leader, Henry Cabot Lodge of Massachusetts, and of the tireless senatorial orators, Hiram W. Johnson of California and William E. Borah of Idaho, had their effect. The peace treaty was loaded with reservations affecting American participation in the League of Nations and the World Court to the point where the ailing Wilson refused to accept a compromise. The United States Senate failed to ratify the treaty, thereby backing out of the international association Wilson had sponsored. As far as the newspapers and magazines were concerned, the League enjoyed a good press on the whole, right up to the end. Republican politics and Wilson's mistakes killed it.

The other major postwar reaction was a gigantic "Red scare," stimulated in part by the events of the Russian Revolution and also by the threat of the IWW movement. Attorney General A. Mitchell Palmer hustled groups of "Reds" to Ellis Island for deportation; the display of red flags was forbidden in New York and other states; the offices of the *New York Call* were raided and wrecked; Socialists were ousted from the New York state legislature and the U.S. Congress; bombings and a dynamite explosion in Wall Street added to the confusion. Many states passed "anti-Red" and criminal syndicalism laws. The conviction of Benjamin Gitlow, an obscure radical, in New York for his writings in the *Left Wing Manifesto* and *Revolutionary Age* was upheld by the Supreme Court despite the arguments of Justices Holmes and Brandeis that Gitlow offered no serious threat to the government. In general, the newspapers failed dismally to defend the civil liberties of those being questionably attacked. One of the worst records on this score was compiled by the usually stable *New York Times*. Civil liberties were best defended by the liberal magazines, led by the *New Republic* and the *Nation,* and by a few newspapers, including the *St. Louis Post-Dispatch, New York Globe,* and *New York World.*

Eventually the turbulence of the wartime period faded into the relatively happy and complacent years of the 1920s. But before that exciting decade had ended, the economic and political storm that had been brewing since the end of the war broke across the world, interrupting America's preoccupation with domestic affairs. Soberly the American people watched the march of new aggressive forces, beginning with the Japanese invasion of Manchuria in 1931. Working outside the crumbling League of Nations, the American government attempted to rally world opinion against the Japanese, Italian, and German militarists, but there was no unity of diplomatic action. Each new episode—Ethiopia, the Rhineland, Austria—brought disturbing headlines and debate in the United States. The disillusionment that had produced the antiwar literature in the 1930s and set the stage for neutrality legislation was slowly passing. Isolationism died hard, however. A Senate committee headed by Gerald P. Nye of North Dakota had advanced the thesis in 1935 that American munitions makers and bankers were almost solely responsible for the country's entrance into the first World War. The neutrality legislation that followed was designed to prevent American loans or sale of war materials to belligerents, on the theory that such a ban would prevent American involvement in "foreign" wars. Even after the Munich crisis of September 1938 and Hitler's occupation of the remainder of unhappy Czechoslovakia in March 1939, the isolationists held the upper hand.[13]

WORLD WAR II BEGINS   The diplomatic bombshell that signaled the opening of World War II was the signing of the German-Russian neutrality pact on August 23, 1939. A week later Hitler marched on Poland and the British and French answered with declarations of war. In November, President Roosevelt obtained a revision of the Neutrality Act as the first step in a reversal of the isolationist trend. Congress repealed the embargo on sale of arms and authorized a cash-and-carry trade with the Allies.

The full nature of Hitler's aggressive designs was revealed in the spring of 1940, when Nazi armies first invaded Denmark and Norway and then on May 10 launched a gigantic offensive against Holland, Belgium, and France. The shock of Dunkirk, the fall of France, and the opening of the Nazi air blitz against Britain in August produced strong pro-Allied sentiment in the United States. In September the Selective Service Act was passed and President Roosevelt announced the trade of 50 destroyers to Britain in return for leases on air-sea bases in the Western Hemisphere. Many American newspapers supported both actions. So did the Republican presidential candidate, Wendell Willkie, who was unsuccessful in stopping Roosevelt's third-term bid.

By now the lines had formed between isolationists and interventionists. On one side was the America First Committee, headed by General Robert E. Wood and championed by Colonel Charles A. Lindbergh, the hero of the first solo New York-to-Paris flight in 1927. Senators Nye and Burton K. Wheeler were on the America First side. Unfortunately for their cause, so were such assorted rabble-rousers as Father Charles E. Coughlin, Gerald L.K. Smith, William Dudley Pelley of the Silver Shirts, Fritz Kuhn of the German-American Bund, and Communists William Z. Foster and Earl Browder. On the other side was the Committee to Defend America by Aiding the Allies, led by Kansas editor William Allen White. The White group attracted many influential newspaper editors and carried out a newspaper advertisement campaign that brought the formation of hundreds of local committees. Among the journalistic leaders were columnist Joseph Alsop, radio commentator Elmer Davis, and playwright Robert E. Sherwood.

The Lend-Lease Act of March 1941, which empowered the president to provide goods and services to those nations whose defense he deemed vital to the defense of the United States, represented a victory for the pro-Allied group. It also served to make America a nonbelligerent ally of the British. In May 1941, President Roosevelt proclaimed an unlimited state of national emergency to facilitate the American mobilization program. In August Roosevelt met Prime Minister Winston Churchill on the high seas and the two announced their peace aims in the Atlantic Charter. The isolationists were far from beaten, however; that same month the House of Representatives continued the military draft by the narrow margin of one vote. Not until December 7, 1941, when Japanese bombs fell on Pearl Harbor, was unity for war achieved. The isolationist minority of the American press, led by the McCormick-Patterson *Chicago Tribune* and *New York Daily News* and the Hearst chain, abruptly subsided in the face of this direct enemy attack.

CENSORSHIP AND PROPAGANDA RENEWED

With organization of the country for war, newspapermen recalled that the Espionage Act and Trading-with-the-Enemy Act of 1917 were still on the statute books. The more sweeping generalities of the Sedition Act had been repealed in 1921, however. Use of these acts to bar publications from the mails and to suppress free speech was more sharply limited than during World War I and mainly affected pro-Fascist and subversive propaganda sheets. The greatest invasion of civil liberties took place when Japanese living in the United States, including many American citizens of Japanese ancestry, were rounded up and kept in what amounted to protective custody in isolated camps during the early years of the war.

Byron Price, executive news editor of the Associated Press and long a Washington newsman, was named director of the Office of Censorship. Probably no other man could have held the respect and confidence of newspapermen everywhere better than Price, who was temperamentally and intellectually equipped to handle the most difficult part of his job—the direction of the voluntary press censorship. He brought into his organization a score of seasoned newspapermen to handle press relationships, headed by John H. Sorrells, executive editor of the Scripps-Howard newspapers, and Nat. R. Howard, editor of the *Cleveland News*.[14]

EXTRA!

San Francisco Chronicle
THE CITY'S ONLY HOME-OWNED NEWSPAPER

FOUNDED 1865—VOL. CLIII, NO. 146 CCCC** SAN FRANCISCO, MONDAY, DECEMBER 8, 1941 DAILY 5 CENTS, SUNDAY 10 CENTS

U.S. AT WAR!

Japan Bombs Hawaii, Manila, Invades Thailand, Malaya; 2 U.S. Battleships Claimed Sunk; FDR Talks to Congress Today!

Without Warning, Bombs Break the Peace
350 Slain--Then Tokyo Declares War on U.S., Britain
Pacific Coast, Electrified, Springs to Wartime Alert

America at War! — EDITORIAL

Air Raid Precautions Taken; Military Leaves Cancelled; Coastal Guns Manned

FDR on Air

Canada, Dutch Indies, Costa Rica Declare War on Japan; Wake Is Reported Taken

Raids Took a Heavy Toll, Hawaii Says

U.S. Faces War: Losses May Be Heavy, Nation Warned

INSIDE

Chronicle News Conference Off Air for Duration

Hoover: Our Decision's Clear

THIS WORLD TODAY — By ROYCE BRIER

Robt. Burns Panatela de Luxe 10¢ — The Sophisticate of Cigars

Big type announced Pearl Harbor and the coming
of World War II to America.

A *Code of Wartime Practices for the American Press* was issued on January 15, 1942. It carefully outlined to those who published newspapers, magazines, books, and other printed materials what would constitute improper handling of news having to do with troops, planes, ships, war production, armaments, military installations, and weather. Similar instructions were given radio stations. The code became a Bible for American newsmen, who usually erred in the direction of oversuppression of news possibly harmful to the war effort.

Most of the 14,462 persons in the Office of Censorship were engaged in the mandatory censorship of mail, cables, and radio communications between the United States and other countries. Price's Office of Censorship in World War II thus combined the World War I operations of the Censorship Board and the voluntary press censorship portion of George Creel's work. Price, however, had nothing to do with the originating of news or with the government's propaganda effort. Those aspects of the work of the World War I Committee on Public Information were handled during World War II by a separate agency.

This was the Office of War Information, established by an executive order of the president in June 1942 to supersede four earlier government agencies. Roosevelt made a wise choice in the person of Elmer Davis as director—a veteran newsman, Davis had served on the *New York Times* staff for 10 years and had been a news analyst and commentator for the Columbia Broadcasting System. "It is the job of OWI," Davis said, "not only to tell the American people how the war is going, but where it is going and where it came from—its nature and origins, how our government is conducting it, and what (besides national survival) our government hopes to get out of victory."[15] This concept of the total function of OWI also was applied to its work abroad.

One function of the OWI was to act as a city desk for the nation's war news. Government departments and war agencies continued to handle approximately 40 percent of government publicity stories without reference to OWI. But those news releases relating significantly to the war effort or dealing with activities affecting more than one government agency had to pass through the OWI News Bureau. The OWI cooperated with the War and Navy Departments in handling military news, and the Army and Navy were required to consult with Davis about withholding of specific military information. The services, however, retained final authority over such withholding of news and Davis did not often win arguments with them. As a result, Davis took a steady drumming of criticism from those suspicious of any information agency.

The News Bureau operated on a million-dollar annual budget with 250 regular employees. Three hundred reporters and correspondents used its facilities, including some 50 reporters working full time in the OWI pressroom. Copy flowed from the general news desk, where policy decisions were made, to the domestic and foreign news desks, the radio news desk, the picture desk, and the feature desk. Cartoons, pictures, features, weekly digests, and fillers became a part of the OWI offering. Background information concerning desired propaganda and informational objectives of the government was given to editorial writers, cartoonists, and columnists.

In all of this work the OWI had the cooperation of the War Advertising Council and the nation's publishers. The government paid for recruiting advertising, but all other war-related newspaper, magazine, radio, and billboard advertising space was donated by the media or by national and local advertisers.

Overseas operations of the OWI were directed by Robert E. Sherwood, with Joseph Barnes, foreign editor of the *New York Herald Tribune,* being deputy director for the important Atlantic area. The overseas news and propaganda programs of the OWI were far more extensive than Creel's work in World War I, particularly because of the availability of radio communication for what became known as the Voice of America. OWI cooperation with the military in the development of psychological warfare techniques also was an advance over World War I methods.

The overseas section received up to 30,000 words a day of teletyped news from the domestic OWI News Bureau. The overseas offices in New York and San Francisco also used the news reports of the press associations, radio networks, and OWI's own regional offices. At its height of activity in 1943, the overseas news and features bureau, headed by Edward Barrett, cabled 65,000 words daily to all parts of the world, mailed hundreds of thousands of words of feature material, and airmailed or radioed 2,500 pictures.[16] OWI was given a $36 million budget in 1943, of which $27 million was allotted for overseas operations. Two-thirds of that sum went for radio operations, mainly the Voice of America.

MILITARY CENSORSHIP

Military censorship for World War II picked up where it had left off at the end of World War I, with the added problem of controlling radio broadcasts. In the early months of the war British censorship was blundering and severe, and it remained tight even after the Ministry of Information became better organized. Nazi Germany was not so badly handicapped by Allied control of cables during World War II, since wireless and radio facilities were available. The Nazis did not censor foreign correspondents before publication, but if they sent stories that Dr. Joseph Goebbels's Ministry of Propaganda did not like, they were subject to expulsion from Germany. Two victims of this policy in the first few months of World War II were Beach Conger of the *New York Herald Tribune* and Otto D. Tolischus of the *New York Times*. Edgar Ansel Mowrer of the *Chicago Daily News* was compelled to leave by reason of threats against his person.

As the war developed, newsmen found the British Admiralty and the U.S. Navy Department most prone to suppressing news of war actions. The American Navy withheld details of the Pearl Harbor disaster, and of the sinkings of ships in the Pacific, for long periods of time on the plea that the Japanese should not be given vital information on a confirmed basis. Newsmen grumbled, however, that evidence of inefficient naval operations also was being kept back. The British censorship in Egypt, conflicting British and American censorships in the India-Burma theater, the Chinese censorship in Chungking, and General Douglas MacArthur's censorship in the Pacific also drew heavy fire from correspondents and editors. Many newsmen said MacArthur's information officers insisted unduly on personal glorification of the commander. Techniques used by General Dwight D. Eisenhower in Europe were, on the other hand, considered generally satisfactory.

PRESS AND RADIO COVER THE WAR

Coverage of World War II by the American press and radio was considered by most observers to be the best and fullest the world had ever seen. A great share of the credit for this achievement went to the overseas and war front correspondents for press associations, newspapers, magazines, and radio. As many as 500 full-time American correspondents were abroad at one time. Altogether the United States armed forces accredited 1,646 different persons. The biggest staffs were those of the press associations and radio networks; the *Times* and *Herald Tribune* in New York; the *Daily News, Tribune,* and *Sun* in Chicago; the *Christian Science Monitor, Baltimore Sun,* and *Time, Life,* and *Newsweek.* Of the 37 American newsmen who lost their lives during the war, 11 were press association correspondents, ten were representing individual newspapers, nine were magazine correspondents, four were photographers, two were syndicated writers, and one was a radio correspondent.

One of the early standouts among American correspondents was the veteran Leland Stowe of the *Chicago Daily News,* who reported the Russo-Finnish War and the Nazi invasion of Norway and who was the first American to reach the Nazi-Soviet front lines after Hitler's invasion of Russia. Webb Miller of the United States covered his eleventh war in Finland, then returned to London to be killed in a blackout accident. Frazier Hunt of International News Service and Marcel W. Fodor of the *Chicago Daily News* filed notable accounts of the French retreat in 1940. On the other side, with Hitler's triumphant army, were Louis P. Lochner of the AP, Pierre J. Huss of INS, and Frederick C. Oechsner of UP.

There were many distinguished examples of war correspondence and many personal stories of performance in the face of danger by reporters. Pulitzer Prizes went to Larry Allen of the AP for his exploits with the British Mediterranean fleet; to Hal Boyle and Daniel De Luce of the AP European staff; to military analyst Hanson W. Baldwin of the *New York Times* and Ira Wolfert of the North American Newspaper Alliance; to Mark S. Watson of the *Baltimore Sun* and Homer Bigart of the *New York Herald Tribune;* to AP war photographers Frank Noel, Frank Filan, and Joe Rosenthal; and to Ernie Pyle of the Scripps-Howard Newspaper Alliance. Clark Lee of the Associated Press and Melville Jacoby of *Time* were among the newsmen who shared the dangers of the Bataan evacuation; Jacoby died later in a plane crash but Lee survived to become an INS byline writer. Among other leading war reporters were Vern Haugland and Wes Gallagher of the AP, Quentin Reynolds of *Collier's,* Edward W. Beattie and Henry T. Gorrell of the UP, James Kilgallen and Richard Tregaskis of INS, Drew Middleton of the *New York Times,* and Russell Hill of the *Herald Tribune.*

World War II had its women correspondents. The INS sent its featured writer, Inez Robb, to North Africa and Europe. Three other INS women war correspondents were Lee Carson, with the U.S. First Army, Dixie Tighe with the British, and Rita Hume in Italy. Among the United Press women correspondents were Eleanor Packard and Dudley Anne Harmon, while the AP had Ruth Cowan and Bonnie Wiley in the field. Other correspondents were Helen Kirkpatrick, *Chicago Daily News;* Peggy Hull (Mrs. Harvey Deuel) of the *Cleveland Plain Dealer,* who served in World War I; Margaret Bourke-White, photographer for *Time* and *Life;* Iris Carpenter, *Boston Globe;* Marguerite Higgins, *New York Herald Tribune,* who became Berlin bureau chief; and Leah Burdette of *PM,* who lost her life in Iran.

Such radio voices as those of William L. Shirer from Berlin and Edward R. Murrow from London for the Columbia Broadcasting System, and that of the National Broadcasting Company's H.V. Kaltenborn, brought the war close to American homes. Bill Henry of CBS and Arthur Mann of Mutual became the first front-line radio reporters in the fall of 1939. Development of mobile units and use of tape recordings soon brought greatly increased radio coverage. Direct reports came from battlefields, from bombers flying over Berlin and Tokyo, and from other action centers. Radiomen covered D-Day brilliantly, with George Hicks of the American Broadcasting Company

Editor & Publisher

Ernie Pyle

doing an outstanding broadcast from a landing barge under German fire. Wright Bryan of the *Atlanta Journal* gave NBC and CBS the first eye-witness account from the cross-channel front by flying over with a planeload of paratroopers.

Perhaps the most well-known reporter of the second World War was the columnist friend of the G.I., Ernest Taylor Pyle. Pyle had won attention before the war for his personal notes on life in the United States, as observed in his wanderings across the country. In 1940 he told his readers what the people of Britain felt as they resisted the Nazi air blitz. Then he attached himself to the American army, writing in a hometown style of the intimate daily life of the G.I. in Ireland, North Africa, Sicily, Italy, and France. His column for Scripps-Howard and his *Here Is Your War* and *Brave Men* won him a national reputation and a Pulitzer Prize. Pyle left Europe in 1944, but after a rest he flew out to cover the final stages of the Pacific war. When a Japanese sniper killed Ernie Pyle on Ie Shima during the Okinawa campaign of April 1945, the saga of a great American war correspondent came to a close.

There was a soldiers' journalism again in World War II. The *Stars and Stripes* reappeared as the leading G.I. newspaper in 1942 and eventually had European and Pacific editions. *Yank,* a magazine with 22 editions, gained a circulation of 2.5 million. The resentments of the enlisted man were portrayed in the *Stars and Stripes* by cartoonist Bill Mauldin, while Sgt. George Baker's "Sad Sack" and Milton Caniff's sexy "Male Call" ran in both publications. Almost every major unit and camp had its own publication. And unlike World War I, the services developed extensive public relations units, of which combat correspondents of the Marine Corps were most effective. Sergeant Jim G. Lucas of the Marines, formerly of the *Tulsa Tribune* staff, wrote one of the outstanding eyewitness stories of the war from a beach at Tarawa.

Coverage of World War II ended in Europe with the confusion of the Edward Kennedy case. Kennedy, Associated Press chief on the western front, was one of 16 Allied newsmen taken to the military headquarters in Reims to witness the German surrender. All were pledged not to release their stories until an officially prescribed time. Kennedy, angered by the news that the German radio was announcing the surrender in advance of the time set by American, British, and Russian political leaders, made an unauthorized telephone call to London and dictated part of his story for transmission. The AP thus had the official story of the German surrender a day in advance of V-E day. But Kennedy's 54 colleagues in Paris charged him with committing "the most disgraceful, deliberate, and unethical double cross in the history of journalism." Kennedy defended his action as necessary to counteract a needless political censorship and won reinstatement as a war correspondent a year after his suspension. But the AP disassociated itself from its stormy petrel, and he left in 1946.

The year 1945 brought hope to the world, with the defeat of the German and Japanese war machines and the founding of the United Nations. But the failure of the Soviet Union and the United States to adjust to each other in the postwar era quickly renewed the feeling of tension and uncertainty the world had endured since the early 1930s. Newsmen found barriers to the collection of news being erected higher than ever before, and the phrase "Iron Curtain" became a familiar one.

Realizing it had to work actively to tell the story of the free democracies to the world, the United States government continued to conduct international propaganda on a worldwide scale as initiated by the Office of War Information in 1942. The first such peacetime operation was the Office of International Information and Cultural Affairs, established within the State Department in 1945 with William Benton as head. In 1948, under the Smith-Mundt Act, the functions were split into an Office of International Information, headed by George V. Allen (later by Edward W. Barrett), and an Office of Cultural Exchange to handle exchange of scholars and students. But the annual budget was a third of OWI's, a mere $12 million.

As the Soviet Union consolidated its grip on the satellite states of eastern Europe and attempted the 1948 Berlin blockade, and with the opening of the Korean War in 1950, Congressional appropriations rose swiftly. By 1952 the revamped International Information Administration, headed by Wilson Compton, had $87 million, 25 percent for the Voice of America.

Creation of an autonomous United States Information Agency in 1953 gave stability to the program. Its annual budget was maintained at well over $100 million. By 1970 the Voice of America was being heard in 40 languages over 92 transmitters by an estimated audience of 43 million. The overseas United States Information Service was operating information libraries and reading rooms in 70 countries, and was distributing news services, motion pictures, magazines, and pamphlets. The policy and planning and the research and assessment sections were involved in the country's foreign policy making, but not enough to satisfy many of the staff. During the 1950s and 1960s there was a running duel between the professionals who viewed USIA and the Voice as agencies for "tell it like it is" journalism, properly interpreting United States involvement in news events, and officials who wished the agencies to reflect their image of how the world should respond to current U.S. policy and who wished to minimize news of conflict with such an image. Increasing White House concern with the war in Indochina polarized the debate after 1965.[17] Late in 1977 President Carter announced a reorganization plan that would combine the USIA and the State Department's educational and cultural affairs activities in a new Agency for International Communication. The Voice of America and overseas USIS would operate as before, with the broadcasters assured of freedom of action.

The news of the Communist North Korean attack on the Republic of South Korea on June 25, 1950, was first flashed to the world by Jack James of the United Press. Headed for a Sunday morning picnic, he stumbled onto the invasion story at the U.S. embassy in Seoul and after confirming it got off his bulletin, which beat the ambassador's cable to Washington by 20 minutes.

Korea had been divided at the 38th parallel for occupation purposes in 1945. Russian troops left North Korea after establishment of a government there in 1948 and

The Korean War opens for U.S. troops; Marguerite Higgins and Homer Bigart report.

Americans left South Korea, save for a small advisory force, early in 1949. No one expected an attack in Korea; State Department representative John Foster Dulles had been in Seoul a week before and had left reassured of the area's stability. The bad news that James and others sent by wireless brought a decision by Secretary of State Dean Acheson and President Truman to seek a United Nations armed intervention, which was voted by the Security Council June 28 after Truman had ordered General Douglas MacArthur to force the North Koreans back.

Walter Simmons of the *Chicago Tribune,* who had traveled to Seoul with Dulles, had stayed on and filed the first action story by a newspaper correspondent. The press associations rushed in Peter Kalischer and Rutherford Poats, UPI; O.H.P. King and photographer Charles P. Gorry, AP; and Ray Richards, INS. Richards was first to fly over the battle area; caught with a lost battalion at Chonan, he was killed ten days after

Marguerite Higgins

his arrival. Eleven American newsmen were killed before the war was over, among a total of 18 from all nations.*

Two of the toughest and most outspoken stars of the Korean news brigade flew to Seoul June 27 from Tokyo under fighter escort. They were Marguerite Higgins of the *New York Herald Tribune* and Keyes Beech of the *Chicago Daily News*.[18] Landing with them at Kimpo airfield were Burton Crane of the *New York Times* and Frank Gibney of *Time.* They were routed from the city during the night as Seoul fell; the men missed death by 25 yards at the River Han and Higgins (she used no "miss") flew back to Tokyo to file her story. She returned June 29 with General MacArthur on his first visit to the front and got an exclusive interview on the return trip. Next day she, Beech, Tom Lambert of the AP, and Gordon Walker of the *Christian Science Monitor* were at the fall of Suwon airfield. With Carl Mydans of *Life* and the bureau chief of Reuters, Ray McCartney, Higgins saw the first U.S. soldier killed in action July 5. David Douglas Duncan of *Life* was taking the first of his great Korean war photographs and *Life*'s July 10 issue brought home the war to a country not yet linked by television.

The South Koreans and their American reinforcements were being forced back on the beachhead port of Pusan. Its outer defense, Taejon, fell in late July and General William P. Dean was captured. By now many more newsmen were risking their lives in the foxholes, rice paddies, and back roads. The *Herald Tribune* sent Homer Bigart to relieve Higgins but she refused to leave Korea and engaged in a give-and-take duel with Bigart for front-page play. The Associated Press sent Relman Morin, Don Whitehead, and Hal Boyle, all veteran war reporters. Fred Sparks came to work with Keyes Beech for the *Chicago Daily News.* When the Pulitzer Prize committee met the following April they honored the *Herald Tribune,* the *Daily News,* and the AP by giving six awards to Bigart and Higgins, Beech and Sparks, Morin and Whitehead. (At that point in time, no one from UP or INS had ever won a Pulitzer Prize.) Behind the correspondents at the front were the bureau chiefs in Tokyo, Earnest Hoberecht of UP, Russell Brines of AP, Howard Handleman of INS, and William H. Lawrence coordinating for the *New York Times.* Edward R. Murrow came to tie CBS coverage together; broadcast coverage essentially was by radio, with film being shot for television and news reels.

Instead of being driven off the Korean beachhead, MacArthur mounted a brilliant amphibious landing with troops from Japan at Inchon September 15 and recaptured Seoul September 26, cutting off the North Koreans to the south. One of the

*Four of the dead were INS–Ray Richards and Frank Emery, correspondents, and Charles D. Rosecrans, Jr., and Ken Inouye, photographers. Nine of the total of 18 died in front-line fighting, nine in air crashes. Among them were Wilson Fielder, *Time-Life;* Charles O. Supple, *Chicago Sun-Times;* Albert Hinton, *Norfolk Journal and Guide,* first black correspondent to lose his life covering a U.S. war; and Ernie Peeler, *Pacific Stars and Stripes.*

correspondents present was Jim G. Lucas, the chronicler of Tarawa, now reporting for Scripps-Howard. Lucas was to win a 1954 Pulitzer Prize for his stories of "Porkchop Hill" during the long stalemate. Another Pulitzer award went to Max Desfor, AP photographer.

General MacArthur, as United Nations commander in Korea, at first left correspondents to their own devices, refusing to institute the field censorship that had prevailed during both World Wars I and II. In the confused situation of the first months of the fighting, the traditional-minded "team-member" reporters found themselves on their own in the thick of battle. Ironically, they also found themselves subject to harsh criticism from MacArthur's staff for stories filed without receiving minimum military assistance. Lambert of AP and Kalischer of UP temporarily lost their accreditations on charges of giving aid and comfort to the enemy. Relations between Colonel Marion P. Echols, MacArthur's press officer, and the newsmen became even more strained than they had been during the years of the occupation of Japan, when dissenting reporters had found their accreditations endangered.

The September 1950 victories following MacArthur's Inchon landing brought an easing of the correspondents' problems. Their interviews with critical and despondent soldiers, which had aroused MacArthur's ire earlier in the summer, were at an end. Nearly 300 correspondents from 19 countries were reporting the advance of United Nations troops to the Yalu. Then came the entry of the Chinese Communist army into the war and a disastrous retreat of the UN's units, best pictured by *Life*'s Duncan, with the Marines at Chosin reservoir. Seoul fell to the Chinese in January but was regained two months later as the UN forces stabilized a line near the 38th parallel. Keyes Beech had reported that at the height of the retreat panic MacArthur had recommended withdrawal from Korea, and other correspondents had criticized MacArthur's tactics in splitting the commands of his forces in northern Korea. The general's answer was the institution of a full and formal censorship, which he claimed had been recommended by the country's top newspaper executives.[19]

Stringent regulations imposed in January 1951 went further, however, than any newsman would have desired.[20] They covered not only censorship of military information but also all statements that would injure the morale of UN forces or would embarrass the United States, its allies, or neutral countries. Correspondents complained that use of the word "retreat" was interpreted by the censors as being embarrassing, and they contended that MacArthur had brought about a political and psychological censorship, as well as a military one. The most dangerous provision of the new censorship was one making correspondents subject to trial by court-martial for serious violations of the rules.

The removal of MacArthur from the Korean command in April for insubordination by President Truman brought another easing of the censorship situation, although his chief intelligence officer, Major General C.A. Willoughby, continued to attack such respected reporters as Hal Boyle, Hanson W. Baldwin, Homer Bigart, and Joseph Alsop as "inaccurate, biased, and petulant." When truce negotiations began in Korea in July 1951, the United Nations Command insisted that newsmen be permitted to cover the truce site. Reporting of the war during the prolonged negotiations became a routine affair, punctuated by excitement over the status of prisoners of war. The Defense Department issued new field censorship instructions in December 1952, which transferred censorship duties from intelligence officers to public relations officers, and put the Army, Navy, and Air Force under a uniform plan. Censorship for reasons other than those involving security was forbidden, but as usual the differing between newsmen and censors about a definition of "security" continued to the end.

Signing of a truce at Panmunjom in July 1953 brought an end to the fighting phase of the Korean War. The repatriated prisoners, whose fate had been such an issue, reappeared at the "Bridge of No Return." In the late 1970s the UN Command, through U.S. troops, still stood guard at Panmunjom. No peace had yet been signed. The war had cost 33,629 U.S. dead, 1,263 other UN allied dead, some 2 million Korean casualties, and several hundred thousand Chinese losses. The principle involved, that the will of the United Nations could not be openly flaunted, had been defended. But one view held it had been defended by the first recapture of Seoul and that MacArthur's advance to the Yalu River boundary of Communist China had changed the character of the war and had polarized Chinese-American relations for decades to come. Whatever the reason, U.S. newsmen did not again see Peking until 1971.

A SERIES OF ALARMS   Disillusionment ran deep in the United States of the early 1950s. A Cold War, rather than eternal peace, had followed World War II and Joseph Stalin had proved to be a treacherous ally by his actions in Hungary, in Czechoslovakia, and in blockading Berlin. The American monopoly of the atom bomb secret had been short-lived, and most Americans believed the Soviets would not have developed atomic capability without the aid of treacherous Americans and Soviet spies (the Rosenbergs were executed on this premise); the astounding proof of Soviet scientific capability, by being first in space, was not to come until their 1957 Sputnik launching. The Korean War had been a frustrating draw, and many viewed it as a defeat. Senator Joseph McCarthy of Wisconsin had been charging treason against various officials since 1950 with unbroken success.

President Eisenhower's election and his ability to get a truce in Korea within six months brought some relaxation. Stalin's death in 1953 brought more. The long French effort in Indochina came to an end at Dienbienphu in 1954 and a Geneva conference made arrangements for peace in Vietnam and Laos. Senator McCarthy overstepped himself by charging the Army with treason and was censured by his colleagues by a vote of 67–22. The Big Four met once again at Geneva in 1955 and Eisenhower and the Russians talked cordially.

But the brief thaw, highlighted by Nikita Khrushchev's "secret" anti-Stalin speech in February 1956, came to an end later that year when Poland and Hungary became restive. Soviet tanks crushed a revolt in Budapest that had won the sympathy of the world but not its active support. Of the newsmen there, Russell Jones won UP's first Pulitzer Prize for his reporting. A team of INS-Hearst stars led by William Randolph Hearst, Jr., had won their first a year earlier for interviews behind the Iron Curtain.

War correspondents rushed to the Middle East in 1956 when Israel, threatened since it became an independent state in 1948, attacked Egypt by land while Britain and France sought to occupy the Suez Canal. Eisenhower and State Secretary Dulles refused to support their allies and forced a UN peacekeeping arrangement. The debacle brought down the government of Anthony Eden and hastened the crisis in France over Algerian independence and the rise of General De Gaulle to power in 1958.

President Johnson's decision in 1965 to intervene in a Dominican Republic dispute and send in U.S. Marines caused 160 journalists to flock to the scene. First to arrive was an old Latin American hand, Jules Dubois of the *Chicago Tribune*. Offering heavy interpretation on the U.S. role were Bernard Collier of the *New York Herald Tribune,* Dan Kurzman of the *Washington Post,* Ted Szulc of the *New York Times*, and Ruben Salazar of the *Los Angeles Times*. CBS's Bert Quint drove to the rebels' section and later reported first-hand observations.

The focus swung back to the Middle East as the standoff between Israel and Egypt resulted in the six-day war of 1967, won by Israeli planes and tanks before correspondents could catch their breaths. Ted Yates, an NBC producer, and Paul Schutzer, *Life* photographer, were U.S. casualties in the blitz war. Egypt and Syria launched a surprise attack in 1973, temporarily pushing the Israelis back and causing concern about that tiny nation's ability to defend itself. The threat of major war was present but Israel regained the lost territory and eventually a United Nations cease-fire agreement was signed. The American audience became used to seeing television scenes from the Suez Canal or Golan Heights areas, as reporters tried to give some meaning to the fast-moving story. The most shocking story broadcast was from Munich during the 1972 Olympic Games when terrorists murdered Israeli athletes in the Olympic village. That plus other raids by various Palestinian guerrilla groups and Israeli retaliation attacks in neighboring countries kept the Middle East in a state of high tension. The Palestinian problem, catalyst for much of the violence, involved setting up a separate nation for those persons who claimed Israel as their home but were pushed back and forth in the various wars. There appeared to be little chance for a solution that would bring a permanent peace.

The war that broke out in the Congo in 1960 was covered by a small band of newsmen. Two, Henry N. Taylor of Scripps-Howard and George Clay of NBC, were shot and killed; Sanche de Gramont of the *New York Herald Tribune* was injured. Lynn Heinzerling of the Associated Press won a Pulitzer Prize for his reporting. Ray Wilson of NBC had to eat his UN press pass to appease some Congolese soldiers.

Premier Khrushchev's visit to the United States in 1959 seemed to follow in the "thaw" pattern, but major confrontations now arose between the United States and the Soviets. The U-2 spy plane incident undermined Khrushchev at home and forced him to break up the Summit Conference held in Paris in May 1960, with more than 3,000 newsmen present for the never-held sessions between Eisenhower, De Gaulle, Macmillan, and Khrushchev. The abortive effort to overthrow the Castro government in Cuba, resulting in the 1961 "Bay of Pigs," put President Kennedy's administration on the defensive. The Berlin Wall crisis later in the year brought a small-scale U.S. mobilization. The air was cleared by the Cuban missile crisis of mid-October 1962, which brought the world to the verge of nuclear war before Khrushchev withdrew Soviet missiles from Cuba on receiving Kennedy's pledge the United States would not again attempt to overthrow the Castro government. In 1963 the nuclear test ban treaty gave the Kennedy administration its first major triumph in forwarding U.S.-Soviet agreements. At that point, President Kennedy was assassinated and Khrushchev was shortly ousted from power.

And at that moment the focus of American attention became Indochina. There a small American press corps was already vainly warning that U.S. policy was leading to war, not peace. But the relentless grinding of the glacier called the Cold War could not be stopped.

THE QUAGMIRE IN VIETNAM

Robert Capa, the Hungarian-born photographer who was world-renowned for his graphic pictures of the Spanish Civil War and the Normandy invasion beaches, was the first American journalist to die in Vietnam. He stepped on a land mine while photographing for Magnum in 1954, the year the French extricated themselves from the Indochina quagmire by surrendering at Dienbienphu. They watched as the Americans then took their places in the quagmire that swallowed up one president and was linked to the resignation of another.[21]

The American phase of the 30-year struggle in Indochina—in Vietnam, in

Cambodia, in Laos—became perhaps the most thoroughly covered war in history. Certainly it caused more moral searching than ever before, and by the time of the U.S. withdrawal in 1975, it seemed possible that it represented the final gasp of the Cold War mentality and an ebbing of the spirit of manifest destiny. Much credit should accrue to the print and broadcast correspondents and photographers covering the war, including the more than 50 who were to die, as well as those few who clarified the issues through their dissent at home.

Vietnam's national hero, Ho Chi Minh, proclaimed a Democratic Republic of Vietnam at Hanoi in 1945, in the wake of the Japanese surrender. But by 1946 the French who had returned to Saigon were engaged in hostilities with Ho's Viet Minh. Ex-emperor Bao Dai was installed in 1948 as chief of state in Saigon by the French, who then obtained financial aid from the United States in 1950 at the time of the Korean crisis. The United States carried up to 80 percent of the cost, but the French were humiliated at Dienbienphu. The Geneva agreements of 1954 ending hostilities provided for a partitioning of Vietnam at the 17th parallel and reunification through national elections in 1956. The Bao Dai government did not sign the agreement or honor it; the United States created the SEATO alliance and included South Vietnam in the protected areas. Premier Ngo Dinh Diem ousted Bao Dai, refused to allow the elections, and obtained the help of the U.S. Military Assistance Advisory Group to train his army beginning in 1955. His opposition in South Vietnam formed the National Liberation Front and its guerrilla force, called by South Vietnamese and Americans the Viet Cong.

By 1960 there were 686 U.S. military advisers, a figure raised to 3,200 at the close of President Kennedy's first year in office (1961) as insurgency grew. Diem, his sister-in-law Mme. Nhu, and the ruling Catholic party became increasingly oppressive. The Buddhist uprisings of 1963 in Saigon and Hue, and countryside insurgency, brought a November coup and the death of Diem. The American supporters, now transformed into a U.S. Military Assistance Command with 16,300 men, took over military affairs as ten Saigon governments came and went in the next 18 months. A new president also was entering the White House three weeks after the Saigon coup.

THE SAIGON PRESS CORPS FORMS
The Saigon press corps already had distinguished itself by the time of Diem's downfall. Three who became the leaders in pointing out the quagmire's dangers were Malcolm Browne, who came to Vietnam in November 1961 for the Associated Press; Neil Sheehan, who came in April 1962 for the United Press International; and David Halberstam, who joined them in May for the *New York Times*. François Sully, the Frenchman who had covered Dienbienphu and who stayed on to interpret the war for *Newsweek* and others until he died in Cambodia in 1971, was expelled by Diem in 1962 and could not return until his overthrow. Among others who appeared in 1962 were Horst Faas, photographer, and Peter Arnett, correspondent, for the AP; Homer Bigart, now with the *New York Times;* Peter Kalischer, now with CBS; Charles Mohr, *Time;* and Beverly Deepe, *Newsweek,* a freelancer who took Sully's place and who later joined the *Christian Science Monitor*.

These and other correspondents had bad news to report about the progress of the war, about the weaknesses of the Diem government, about the very ability of anyone to achieve what the United States government had set out to do in Vietnam. But the spirit of the military command and of the civilians in the embassy and aid missions was most often one of "we have a policy and it has to work if we just try hard enough." Anyone reporting facts that pointed in a contradictory direction was labeled noncooperative.

When Sheehan and Halberstam viewed a military debacle at Ap Bac in January 1963, which proved that the U.S. military advisers had a long way to go to infuse a winning spirit in their allies, they reported the failure of South Vietnamese arms. The U.S. command described it as a victory, and the undermining of the journalistic reputations of the Saigon press corps had begun.[22]

THE SAIGON PRESS CORPS UNDER ATTACK

As Buddhists set themselves afire and the pressures against the Diem dictatorship increased, the Saigon press corps also found conflict within its own ranks. Coming to Saigon for varying amounts of time were Joseph Alsop, the columnist; Marguerite Higgins of the *New York Herald Tribune* and Keyes Beech of the *Chicago Daily News,* veterans of World War II and Korean press corps; and Jim Lucas, Scripps-Howard, who was to win the 1964 Ernie Pyle award for his coverage in Vietnam. These correspondents were typified by Lucas: hard-nosed, ready to fight any attempt at censorship, but more or less ready to accept war as a necessary fact of life and not activists in probing into the humaneness of the military tactics. Indeed, correspondent Higgins was an avowed "hawk" who advocated the use of the atomic bomb if needed to repel the Communists wherever they were; tragically, she was to fall victim to an Asiatic infection on a 1965 trip and die a lingering death in 1966. The criticism by Alsop, Higgins, Beech, and Lucas of the reporting and interpretation given by Browne, Sheehan, Halberstam, and Kalischer left the established Saigon press corps vulnerable to attack by outsiders.

Those attacks mounted in 1963. The correspondents had fought off a State Department "press guidance" issued in 1962 by Carl T. Rowan saying "newsmen should be advised that trifling or thoughtless criticism of the Diem government would make it difficult to maintain proper cooperation between the United States and Diem," only to find in 1963 that Diem's police would beat them over the head and smash their cameras.[23] The pot boiled over in September 1963, when *Time* attacked the Saigon press corps as propagandists plotting to overthrow the Diem government and, through distorted reporting, "helping to compound the very confusion that it should be untangling for its readers at home."[24] *Time* correspondents Charles Mohr and Mert Perry resigned in outraged protest; Mohr joined the *New York Times* and Perry *Newsweek* to stay in Saigon. Mme. Nhu castigated the AP, UPI, *New York Times, Washington Post,* and *Newsweek* as enemies of her brother-in-law, Diem. *Time,* unrepentant, continued to doubt the analyses of the Saigon correspondents until long after their definition of a quagmire had been accepted by all disinterested observers of the Vietnam War.

The attacks on the integrity of the press corps led Halberstam, Sheehan, Browne, and later others to undertake activist roles in writing books and lecturing at home about the nature of the Vietnamese conflict and the danger to the U.S. national interest of a "win at any cost" policy there. Halberstam and Browne shared the 1964 Pulitzer Prize for international reporting. Sheehan joined the *New York Times* staff in 1964 and in 1971 was instrumental in the publishing by the *Times* of the "Pentagon Papers," taken from a secret analysis by Pentagon researchers and validating the 1961–65 reporting of the Saigon press corps. The furor over this, and the problem of the "credibility gap," which came to affect the mass media as well as Presidents Johnson and Nixon, was a polarizing problem affecting all aspects of American life.

In Vietnam the central problem was not only that the military deliberately falsified information, but also that it more often withheld information detrimental to continued belief in the eventual success of U.S. policies and established elaborate statistical counts to justify the policies of the White House and the Pentagon. General William

Westmoreland became the American commander in Saigon in 1964 and remained until Paris peace talks were begun in 1968; it was through him that the twin "search and destroy" and "bomb the North" policies were instituted. The first employed the famed "body count" statistics used by Defense Secretary Robert McNamara to prove the enemy was being exhausted. The second utilized minute reports of "precision bombing" of enemy convoys, roads, factories, and troop concentrations at an unprecedented saturation level. At the daily briefing in Saigon, dubbed "The Five O'Clock Follies" by the correspondents, communiqués on the previous day's action were read; it was folly to attend, the press corps said, because the briefing officer only knew what was in his communiqué. Critics of the press contended that the correspondents nevertheless filed stories filled with body count reports they doubted, as major news events, and created an illusion of conventional battle warfare when none really existed except in calculated situations.

THE WAR ESCALATES, 1964–68

The decision to make the war in Indochina a major U.S. war came in August 1964, when the administration asserted that two American destroyers on patrol in the Gulf of Tonkin had been attacked by North Vietnamese PT boats. Although it developed later that there was common doubt about the incident, President Johnson requested, and Congress quickly approved, a resolution giving him power to repel attacks and to prevent further aggression. It was the contention of Secretary of State Dean Rusk that an aggression from the North was in progress; others contended that the war in Vietnam was a civil war, particularly the actions involving the Viet Cong, guerrilla arm of the South Vietnamese National Liberation Front. The incident of the Gulf of Tonkin seemed to foreclose the issue. Bombings of North Vietnam, secretly planned since the previous August, began in earnest in February 1965, and U.S. advisers went into combat in June, 23,000 strong. By the end of 1965 there were 160,000 more U.S. men in Vietnam. Intensified bombing of the Hanoi-Haiphong area was carried out during 1966. U.S. troops carried out search-and-destroy missions and supported the pacification program aimed at regaining control of the villages.

Two major controversies developed in this period, not between the correspondents and the military, but between the correspondents and the public. In August 1965, Morley Safer of CBS News and two Vietnamese cameramen shot "The Burning of the Village of Cam Ne." U.S. Marines had been fired on in the village area and in retaliation (after the Viet Cong had slipped away) leveled the 150-home village. "This is what the war in Viet Nam is all about," Safer narrated as he stood in front of the burning huts with bullets whizzing about him and his crew. "The Viet Cong were long gone . . . the action wounded three women, killed one baby, wounded one Marine and netted four old men as prisoners."[25] Walter Cronkite used the film; a storm broke. The film was too realistic, its critics contended; U.S. soldiers should not be criticized; the presentation was one-sided and negative. Safer, who had thought to show the inhumanity of war, nearly lost his job.

But a greater sensation came in December 1966, when the respected Harrison Salisbury, a senior editor-correspondent of the *New York Times,* began filing stories from Hanoi. He had been granted a visa since North Vietnam did not consider itself at war with the United States. Salisbury's series of stories, filled with detailed observations, directly contradicted much of the claimed success of the U.S. bombing program. The bombing had not been pinpointed on military targets; many smaller towns had been reduced to ghostly ruins; bombs had been dumped indiscriminately by fliers who needed to lose their payloads; and, worst of all, the unprecedented bombing

Warmer

Tonight — Clear, low in 30s.
Thursday — Sunny, high upper 60s. Friday — Sunny, mild. Chances of rain: Less than 10 per cent.

Map and chart on Page 41.

CHICAGO DAILY NEWS

©1966 by Field Enterprises Inc.

91st Year, Number 252   8 Sections   Wednesday, October 26, 1966   10 Cents   Phone 321-2000

Final Markets
RED STREAK
Stocks Up

Secret 2½-Hour Visit

LBJ Goes to Viet Nam

"I came here today for one good reason: simply because I could not come to this part of the world and not come to see you. "I came here today for one

good purpose, to tell you and through you to tell every soldier, sailor, airman and marine in Viet Nam how proud we are of what you are doing and how proud we

are of the way you are doing it. "I came here today with only one regret: that I could not begin to personally thank every man in Viet Nam for what he is doing."

President Visits GIs At Big Base

By Peter Lisagor
Our Washington Bureau Chief

CAM RANH BAY, South Viet Nam—President Johnson flew to Viet Nam Wednesday for a dramatic 2½-hour visit with American troops and told U.S. commanders to "come home with that coonskin on the wall."

Dressed in light suntan jacket and trousers, with a Presidential seal on the right

Text of President's talk to troops is on Page 2.

Full page of pictures on Back Page.

breast of his jacket, Mr. Johnson stood on a hastily built platform on the airstrip and declared to several hundred troops:

"I give you my pledge: We shall never let you down, nor your fighting comrades, nor the 15,000,000 Vietnamese nor the hundreds of millions of Asians who are counting on us to show here in Viet Nam that aggression doesn't pay and that aggression cannot succeed."

THE PRESIDENT toured the vast base in a jeep with Gen. William C. Westmoreland, commander of U.S. troops in ... the ...

43 Yanks Die in Fire On Carrier

Daily News Wire Services

SAIGON — A searing fire touched off by an explosion of photo flares raged through five decks of the U.S. Aircraft Carrier Oriskany off the coast of North Viet Nam. The blaze killed 43 men and injured 16.

Some men were trapped below decks and died in their bunks. It was the worst naval tragedy of the Viet Nam war.

Firemen, damage control and demolition experts darted into thick, choking smoke and flames so hot it melted steel girders to drag out bombs, rockets and planes.

Other sailors wheeled fighter-bombers out of danger and still

other dived into a nearby officers' quarters and dragged out pilots overcome by heat and smoke.

They were too late for some of the other fliers who had flown through enemy fire over North Viet Nam just a few hours before and died in bed.

THE FIRE broke out shortly after dawn in a locker containing flares on the hangar deck, just below the flight deck, and then spread rapidly to envelop five decks, the Navy said.

Two helicopters were destroyed by the blaze and an undisclosed number of A-4E

Turn to Page 2, Column 1

Closeup Look

President Johnson leans from a jeep to shake hands with servicemen at the U.S. base at Cam Ranh Bay, South Viet Nam. Gen. William Westmoreland, U.S. commander in South Viet Nam, is at his side. (AP)

A confident president exhorted, "Come home with that coonskin on the wall."

attack had scarcely made a dent in the transportation and war supplies capability of the North Vietnamese. Angry attacks were made on Salisbury and the *Times;* he was denied a Pulitzer Prize voted him by a judging committee for what most newsmen conceded was the outstanding news beat of 1966. In some sectors of the American public, the credibility of the press suffered (it should not run material favoring the enemy and derogatory to the armed forces); but in more sectors the credibility of the Pentagon suffered a severe blow. For there were also pictures to back up Salisbury's detailed reporting.

Generals Thieu and Ky were elected president and vice president of South Vietnam in 1967; the next year the runner-up was sentenced to five years in prison for aiding the enemy. U.S. troop strength jumped to 485,000 men by the close of the year and the number of U.S. dead passed the 15,000 mark. The administration claimed it was grinding out a victory and Secretary McNamara could see "a light at the end of the tunnel," a phrase that became a bitter joke for cartoonists. President Johnson, visiting Camranh Bay in late 1966, had urged his soldiers to "come home with that coonskin on the wall,"[26] and his commanders were trying to oblige. Some journalists, including columnists Joseph Alsop and Hanson W. Baldwin, were assessing the North Vietnamese as badly hurt and incapable of winning. But more were foreboding. Peter Arnett of the AP, whose tireless reporting had won him the 1966 Pulitzer Prize, said Westmoreland was "in a critical position." Ward Just, *Washington Post* correspon-

351

dent, said all the statistics reported by the government gave a false picture of conditions; the country was not pacified when you could not travel on the roads. R.W. Apple, Jr., of the *New York Times* said: "Victory is not close at hand. It may be beyond reach." Robert Shaplen, the *New Yorker* magazine's talented correspondent, and Denis Warner of the *Reporter* magazine added their realistic estimates of a stalled effort in Vietnam.[27]

Those who read and believed these leading members of the Saigon press corps were not as badly surprised as most of the public, the U.S. Command in Saigon, and official Washington by the fury of the Tet offensive of late January 1968. The National Liberation Front forces assaulted Saigon and put the U.S. embassy under siege, held Hue for 25 days, and wiped out most of the pacification program in the countryside. General Westmoreland asked President Johnson for another 206,000 men. The answer was a topping off at a total of 538,900 and a reassessment of the Vietnam war policy.

On March 31, the president stunned a vast television audience by withdrawing from the 1968 presidential race, sharply limiting the bombing of North Vietnam, and initiating plans for preliminary peace talks in Paris that got under way in May. General Creighton Abrams replaced General Westmoreland, who came home to be chief of staff. Final details of the bombing halt in the North were not worked out until a few days prior to the election, too late to benefit Hubert H. Humphrey, who had inherited much of the Johnson war mantle. The new president, Richard Nixon, announced a "Vietnamization" policy in November 1969, under which defense of South Vietnam would be turned over to South Vietnamese troops. As U.S. troops were gradually withdrawn, the command ceased placing troops in exposed positions, as had occurred at Con Thien in 1967 and at Khesanh in 1968, in order to draw the enemy out.

One of the biggest stories of the war in Vietnam escaped the Saigon press corps. This was the story of the massacre at My Lai of civilians by U.S. troops, for which Lt. William Calley was convicted of murder in 1971. Despite the taking of military pictures at the massacre scene and floating stories of the "Pinkville" affair, the story did not break until October 1969, when a freelance writer in Washington was tipped to Calley's interrogation. The writer, former AP Pentagon reporter Seymour M. Hersh, won the 1970 Pulitzer Prize for international reporting for a story he had to market through the unknown Dispatch News Service. It was only then that major media outlets began to pick up the story. My Lai was a story Americans did not want to read, just as they had not wanted to hear Morley Safer's anguished broadcast in 1965.

CAMBODIA   It was in the same year that President Nixon began planning his secret bombing campaign against neutral Cambodia. For 14 months, beginning in March 1969, American B-52s pulverized the Cambodian countryside with more than 3,600 sorties and 100,000 tons of bombs. Records of the raids were falsified with the knowledge of the president and high military officers. When the story emerged in July 1973 through the Congressional testimony of an Air Force officer—not from the news media—there was cynical speculation that Nixon's 1968 campaign pledge to use a "secret peace plan" to end the war actually masked a scheme to bomb the opposition into submission. There also were secret bombings in Laos prior to a 1971 American-South Vietnamese invasion that was a complete failure.

Thus the nation was unaware of the full scope of the Asian war when the president appeared on nationwide television April 30, 1970, to announce the ground invasion of Cambodia. Nixon claimed American policy since the Geneva Agreement of 1954 had been to "scrupulously respect the neutrality of the Cambodian people," but that North Vietnamese troops were using Cambodian sanctuaries to attack South Vietnam. News reports of the war's expansion triggered shock and anger throughout the nation. Protests, some violent, broke out on college campuses and there were clashes between students and local police. Peaceful marches were held in many communities. But at Kent State University in Ohio, tired and edgy National Guardsmen fired on a crowd of demonstrating students, killing four persons in the area, one walking to class. Anguish and more anger was the result, with some newspapers and broadcast stations supporting Nixon's criticism of "... these bums ... blowing up the campuses."[28]

Journalist J. Anthony Lukas later wrote that the Cambodian and Kent State experiences, coupled with Senate setbacks, marked a turn as Nixon moved toward a policy of "positive polarization." This meant punishing his enemies and trying to capture the votes of the so-called "silent majority."[29]

In July 1973, Maurey Marder, diplomatic correspondent for the *Washington Post,* added another dimension with his analysis that the Nixon group fought the 1971 disclosure of the Pentagon Papers—and created the "plumbers" unit as part of a system of illegal wiretapping and break-ins—because of the risk of exposure of its Cambodian bombing campaign and other sensitive plans of the president and Secretary of State Henry Kissinger. "Facts now available not only overturn the official version of how the United States entered the Cambodian war," Marder wrote, "they illuminate the kind of thinking that led to Watergate."[30]

DEFEAT AND SURRENDER

The end to 30 years of war came quickly when it finally came. On April 30, 1975, a handful of reporters stood on the roof of the famed Caravelle Hotel in downtown Saigon and watched helicopters carry away the last evacuees from the roof of the American Embassy. They reported that the "Stars and Stripes" no longer flew over the embattled city and that Saigon had surrendered. The final stage of the long battle for national unification was over and the vast American military machine had fallen victim to the persistence of Ho Chi Minh's followers, as had the French 21 years earlier. A demoralized South Vietnamese army, denied further U.S. aid, in turn fell victim to its own corruption, inefficiency, and poor training. The Communists unleashed full scale attacks in January and when Danang fell on March 29 a horrified American television audience saw South Vietnamese troops fighting civilians to board transports leaving the city.

The "peace with honor" that President Nixon and Secretary of State Kissinger had proclaimed in January 1973 was forgotten. So were the formal agreements signed in Paris by the United States, North and South Vietnam, and the Viet Cong. Pressures for negotiations had mounted after the United States mined Haiphong harbor in May 1972 and unloaded the heaviest bombing of the entire war at Christmas time of that year. The last American combat troops had departed in August, along with a good number of journalists who moved on to other breaking stories. In March 1973 the nation watched with mixed emotions the return of American prisoners of war, but the issue of men missing in action added to the debate over how the war should be ended and if America should pay to reconstruct the land it helped destroy. That debate continued in the 1976 election campaign.

More than 50,000 Americans died in combat in Vietnam and several hundred thousand others suffered wounds. There was no estimate of how many millions of Vietnamese, Cambodians, and Laotians were killed or wounded in the 1961–75 period. There seemed to be a consensus that for the most part American journalists had brought the Vietnam dilemma home to the public, but there was continued concern over the failures of the Saigon and Washington press corps to press quickly on stories that would have given some of the fragments greater meaning, such as the Tonkin Gulf incident, My Lai, Cambodian and Laotian bombings and raids, and the truth about the bombing of North Vietnam.

It has been noted that most American journalists—with the exception of those writers and editors for alternative and underground publications—were very slow to truly understand the futility of the Vietnam experience. So were most citizens, while Congress lagged further behind. The most severe criticism of the news media, however, might be its failure to put the war into an historical perspective. With the exception of an occasional "blockbuster" interpretative article or a television documentary, American journalists reported everything about the war except the essence of why it was being fought. David Halberstam had strong feelings about this and undoubtedly spoke for the handful of journalists who tried to explain it in the 1950s and early 1960s:

> The problem was trying to cover something every day as news when in fact the real key was that it was all derivative of the French Indo-China war, which is history. So you really should have had a third paragraph in each story which would have said, ' . . . none of this means anything because we are in the same footsteps as the French and we are prisoners of their experience,' but given the rules of newspaper reporting you can't really do that. This is not usually such a problem for a reporter, but to an incredible degree in Vietnam I think we were haunted and indeed imprisoned by the past.[31]

THE PRESS CORPS: CHANGES AND CASUALTIES   The large number of correspondents who covered a part of the Vietnam story makes it impossible to describe the accomplishments of more than a few. Heading any list, if for no other reason than seniority, would be reporters like Keyes Beech and Peter Arnett. The majority of the journalists, even some of the most well-known, had relatively short stints. Browne shifted to ABC News in 1965, later joining the *New York Times* staff in Moscow. Edwin Q. White took his position with AP. Sheehan also joined the *New York Times,* while Halberstam served briefly as a contributing editor for *Harper's* and then devoted his time to books and articles.

UPI's team included Bryce Miller, Alvin Webb, and Dan Southerland. William Tuohy won a Pulitzer Prize for his reporting for the *Los Angeles Times.* Sydney Schanberg of the *New York Times* won the Pulitzer Prize for his coverage of the surrender in Cambodia. Peter Braestrup divided four years between the *New York Times* and *Washington Post.* Richard Critchfield won distinction for the *Washington Star.* CBS reporters producing field reports and documentaries included Peter Kalischer, Morley Safer, John Laurence, Don Webster, Dan Rather, and Murray Fromson. Among others reporting for NBC were Frank McGee, Ron Nessen, Kenley Jones, and Howard Truckner; for ABC, Dan North, Roger Peterson. In Cambodia were Laurence Stern, *Washington Post;* Henry Kamm, *New York Times;* Raymond Coffey, *Chicago Daily News;* the indefatigable Arnett of AP; and two who were captured and released, Richard Dudman, *St. Louis Post-Dispatch,* and Elizabeth Pond, *Christian Science Monitor.* There were other women correspondents, including the *New York Times'* Gloria Emerson, magazine journalist Frances Fitzgerald, ABC's Marlene Sanders, and Betty Halstead and Kate Webb of UPI.[32] Miss Webb and Michele Ray, a French freelancer, were both captured and released.

Throughout the war the television networks devoted weekly specials to the military, economic, and political aspects of the fighting. Network correspondents took part in special documentaries and year-end roundups, and spoke at various public and

Saigon press corps leaders Neil Sheehan (*left*), UPI, and Malcolm Browne, AP.

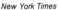

New York Times Vietnam correspondents David Halberstam (*left*) and Harrison Salisbury.

journalistic gatherings. It was, as author Michael Arlen said, America's "living room war" and the television coverage of the killing eventually helped stir protest in the United States. It also added to the divisiveness in the nation and opened the door to harsh criticism of television news by partisans on both sides.

Among photographers who won Pulitzer Prizes for their work in Vietnam was the German-born Horst Faas, 1965 winner, who sparked the Associated Press coverage from the beginning, was wounded in 1967 and met the Tet crisis while still convalescing. Kyoichi Sawada of UPI was the 1966 Pulitzer winner for a picture of a Vietnamese family swimming together in a river current, children's heads bobbing. Sawada won many other prizes, then was killed in 1970 in Cambodia. Toshio Sakai repeated for UPI in 1968. Edward T. Adams of AP swept all 1969 competition with his photo of the Saigon police chief executing a Viet Cong during the Tet offensive. David

Douglas Duncan of *Life* won the 1967 Robert Capa Award, and Catherine Leroy, a freelancer for AP, an Overseas Press Club award.

Death struck heavily in the ranks of photographers. Besides Sawada, two other prize winners died: Larry Burrows of *Life,* in Vietnam since 1962 and twice a Capa award winner, and Henri Huet, who had worked for both UPI and AP and won a Capa award. They died together covering the 1971 Laos invasion. UPI lost three other staff men: Hiromichi Mine, Kent Potter, and Charles Eggleston. Bernard J. Kolenberg of AP and Dickey Chapelle of the *National Observer* died in 1965. Robert J. Ellison of Empire/Black Star was killed at Khesanh. Paul Schutzer of *Life* won a 1965 Capa award in Vietnam, then died in the 1967 Israeli war.

Bernard Fall, the distinguished historian of the Indochina war, was a 1967 casualty. *Look* editor Sam Castan was killed in 1966. Among the dead and missing in the Cambodian invasion were Frank Frosch of UPI, George Syvertsen and Gerald Miller of CBS, and Welles Hangen of NBC.

MILITARY CENSORSHIP IN VIETNAM

To the credit of the U.S. military command in Saigon, only a minimum of censorship was imposed on the Saigon press corps; its principal troubles were with the South Vietnamese government and critics at home. When bombings of North Vietnam were stepped up in 1965, and troop ships flooded in, some correspondents among the 150 Americans and 400 or more other newsmen ran afoul of military police. As casualties mounted, exact numbers were discontinued in daily briefings in favor of weekly totals, another minor complaint. After Tet, and the limiting of U.S. military actions, a simple field censorship was imposed that correspondents readily accepted. Major complaints were heard during news blackouts preceding the Cambodian and Laos invasions of 1970 and 1971. In the latter, restrictions on the use of U.S. helicopters by photographers cost the lives of four in the crash of a Vietnamese substitute craft. Among correspondents, François Sully had been an early victim of expulsion by the Vietnamese; Homer Bigart narrowly missed the same fate, as did Everett Martin of *Newsweek.* Jack Foisie, *Los Angeles Times;* George Esper, AP; and John Carroll, *Baltimore Sun,* had credentials temporarily suspended by the U.S. Command for reporting military actions prematurely.

Major censorship in Vietnam affected the newspaper of the GI, the *Stars and Stripes,* and the Armed Forces Vietnam Network, supplying radio programs and news to the troops. The Armed Forces Network, particularly, fell under the heavy hand of the U.S. Command's Office of Information, which endeavored to eliminate stories that would embarrass the South Vietnamese government or adversely affect morale. The result was a rebellion of staff newsmen, amid charges that the Saigon Command was violating Defense Department regulations and policy. The controversy simmered down with the censors still in control. *Stars and Stripes* weathered charges it was undermining morale by reporting life in Vietnam "like it is." The most sharply censored press in Vietnam was, of course, the local one in Saigon, whose ranks were thinned periodically of political dissenters by charges of aid to the enemy.

OTHER FOREIGN TROUBLE SPOTS

In the 1970s American correspondents were involved with a number of other important foreign stories. The most dramatic was the parting of the bamboo curtain in 1971, when an American ping pong team was invited to play in Peking. China watcher correspondents routinely asked to accompany them and were astounded to be admitted in some cases. John Roderick of the AP visited China again after an absence of 23 years. So did veterans John Rich of NBC and Tillman Durdin of the *New York Times.* A large contingent traveled with President

Nixon on his trip in 1972 and the networks broadcast many of the proceedings live, using satellite transmission. In addition to the China story, civil war in Ireland, unrest in much of Africa, fighting on Cyprus, anti-American feelings in Latin America, continued pressure in the Middle East, and the ever-present power struggle between the United States and the Soviet Union occupied the attention of the foreign press corps as the 1980s approached.

NOTES

1. As quoted in Mark Sullivan, *Our Times,* Vol. V (New York: Scribner's, 1933), p. 32. Sullivan's six-volume journalistic coverage of the years 1900–25 reflects both the life and history of America in an engrossing manner.

2. Edwin Costrell, "Newspaper Attitudes Toward War in Maine, 1914–17," *Journalism Quarterly,* XVI (December 1939), 334. This measurement of an immediate anti-German reaction, before the introduction of concerted propaganda by the belligerents and before the cutting of cable communications with Germany, is significant.

3. Among the more responsible books of the era of disillusionment were C. Hartley Grattan's *Why We Fought* (1929), Walter Millis' *Road to War* (1935), and H.C. Peterson's *Propaganda for War* (1939). For criticism of Peterson's attitude toward newspapers, see Ralph D. Casey, "The Press, Propaganda, and Pressure Groups," *The Annals of the American Academy of Political and Social Science,* CCXIX (January 1942), 68.

4. The best-balanced picture of American press difficulties in covering the war is found in Ralph O. Nafziger's *The American Press and Public Opinion During the World War, 1914 to April, 1917* (Ph.D. thesis, University of Wisconsin, 1936). Nafziger ranks overt propaganda efforts as having less effect on American news presentation than (1) rigid war censorships and (2) limited and controlled communications facilities.

5. Frank Luther Mott, *American Journalism* (New York: Macmillan, 1950), p. 616.

6. George Creel, *How We Advertised America* (New York: Harper & Row, 1920), p. 4.

7. See Harold D. Lasswell, *Propaganda Technique in the World War* (New York: Peter Smith, 1927), p. 20.

8. Walton E. Bean, "The Accuracy of Creel Committee News, 1917–1919: An Examination of Cases," *Journalism Quarterly,* XVIII (September 1941), 272. The major study of the CPI is James R. Mock and Cedric Larson, *Words That Won the War* (Princeton: Princeton University Press, 1939).

9. Paxson eventually wrote a three-volume series titled *American Democracy and the World War*. The war itself is covered in detail in the second volume, *America at War, 1917–1918* (Boston: Houghton Mifflin, 1939).

10. The AP committed a familiar journalistic blunder by adding a "no" to a La Follette statement concerning the American declaration of war, making it read "we had no grievance." An unsuccessful move to oust La Follette from the Senate resulted.

11. Enlarged and brought up to date in his *Free Speech in the United States* (Cambridge, Mass.: Harvard University Press, 1941).

12. James R. Mock, *Censorship 1917* (Princeton: Princeton University Press, 1941), pp. 81, 93.

13. One of the isolationists was historian Charles A. Beard, whose later writings attacking Roosevelt's foreign policy were ably answered in Basil Rauch, *Roosevelt from Munich to Pearl Harbor* (New York: Creative Age Press, Inc., 1950).

14. The activities of the Office of Censorship and the work of other individuals are described by Theodore F. Koop, an Associated Press man and assistant to Price, in *Weapon of Silence* (Chicago: University of Chicago Press, 1946). Sorrells, Howard, managing editor Jack Lockhart of the *Memphis Commercial Appeal,* and Koop were successive heads of the voluntary press censorship division. J. Howard Ryan directed the radio division.

15. Elmer Davis, "OWI Has a Job," *Public Opinion Quarterly,* VII (Spring 1943), 8. For Davis' account of his stewardship, see *Report to the President (Journalism Monographs,* No. 7, August 1968), edited by Ronald T. Farrar. Also see Robert L. Bishop and LaMar S. Mackay, *Government Information in World War II (Journalism Monographs,* No. 19, May 1971).

16. OWI operated everywhere abroad except in Latin America, where Nelson Rockefeller's Office of the Coordinator of Inter-American Affairs held jurisdiction.

17. For an account of USIA from 1948 to 1960 see Wilson P. Dizard, *The Strategy of Truth* (Washington: Public Affairs Press, 1960). Analysis of ups-and-downs is given in Ronald I. Rubin, *The Objectives of the U.S. Information Agency: Controversies and Analysis* (New York: Praeger, 1968).

18. For an evaluation and account of the early weeks of the war coverage see Michael C. Emery, "The American Mass Media and the Coverage of Five Major Foreign Events, 1900–1950," Ph.D. thesis, University of Minnesota, 1968, pp. 316–72.

19. In a letter to *Editor & Publisher*, LXXXIV (January 20, 1951), 7.

20. Text of the censorship code was carried in *Editor & Publisher*, LXXXIV (January 13, 1951), 8.

21. *The Making of a Quagmire*, by David Halberstam (New York: Random House, 1965), sets this tone. Halberstam was the Pulitzer Prize-winning correspondent of the *New York Times* in Vietnam who forecast the tragedy.

22. Dale Minor, *The Information War* (New York: Hawthorn Books and Tower Publications, 1970), pp. 29–34. Minor, who finds both heroes and villains in the Saigon press corps, dismisses the war correspondents of earlier wars as "team players" who accepted the official "line" and the necessity of the war itself. His analysis of the conflict between press and government in Vietnam, and between moral philosophies and concerns for humanity, is perceptive.

23. *Newsweek*, October 7, 1963, pp. 98–99; Malcolm W. Browne, "Viet Nam Reporting: Three Years of Crisis," *Columbia Journalism Review*, III (Fall 1964), p. 4.

24. *Time*, September 20, 1963, p. 62, and October 11, 1963, p. 55.

25. *Time*, October 14, 1966, p. 58.

26. As reported in the *Chicago Daily News*, October 26, 1966, p. 1. For a series of front pages depicting the Indochina war, see Michael C. Emery, et al., *America's Front Page News, 1690–1970* (New York: Doubleday, 1970).

27. Minor, *The Information War*, pp. 95–100; *Newsweek*, November 13, 1967, pp. 68–69.

28. Dan Rather and Gary Paul Gates, *The Palace Guard* (New York: Harper & Row, 1974), p. 182–83. Rather, the former CBS White House correspondent, takes a critical look at the inner workings of Nixon's operations.

29. J. Anthony Lukas, *Nightmare: The Underside of the Nixon Years* (New York: Viking Press, 1976), p. 3. Lukas, whose remarkable Watergate account filled an entire *New York Times Magazine* issue in July 1973, comprehensively documents all of the Watergate-related incidents and the fear that radicals might disclose some "really damaging secrets" or pass them to the Soviets (p. 71).

30. *Los Angeles Times*, July 29, 1973, p. 1, Opinion section. The story originally appeared in the *Post* and was distributed to U.S. and foreign clients by the *Los Angeles Times-Washington Post* News Service.

31. As quoted by Philip Knightley in *The First Casualty*, p. 423.

32. See Frances Fitzgerald, *Fire in the Lake* (Boston: Little, Brown, 1972), and Gloria Emerson, *Winners and Losers* (New York: Random House, 1977), for intimate, personal looks at the effects of war on the Vietnamese people.

ANNOTATED BIBLIOGRAPHY

Books

The literature concerning the journalistic aspects of the two World Wars, Korea, and Vietnam is voluminous. Listed here are the major works in the fields of wartime censorship, propaganda, and informational activity; the most important historical accounts; and a few of the dozens of excellent books by war correspondents.

ARLEN, MICHAEL J., *Living-Room War*. New York: Viking, 1969. Collection of articles from the *New Yorker*, many of television coverage of the Vietnam war.

BLUM, JOHN, *V Was For Victory: Politics and American Culture During World War II*. New York: Harcourt Brace Jovanovich, 1976. Scholarly history, including material on propaganda.

BRAESTRUP, PETER, *Big Story: How the American Press and Television Reported and Interpreted the Crisis of Tet 1968 in Vietnam and Washington*. Boulder, Colo.: Western Press, 1977. A 1,500-page, two-volume analysis by the Saigon bureau chief of the *Washington Post* in 1968.

BROWNE, MALCOLM W., *The New Face of War*. Indianapolis: Bobbs-Merrill, 1968. By AP's Pulitzer Prize winner in Vietnam.

CAPA, ROBERT, *Images of War*. New York: Grossman Publishers, Inc., 1964. Capa's World War II photographs, with text, published after he lost his life in Indochina.

CAPUTO, PHILIP, *A Rumor of War*. New York: Holt, Rinehart & Winston, 1977. The ugliness of the Vietnam experience is described by a former Marine officer who became a newspaper reporter.

CARROLL, WALLACE, *Persuade or Perish*. Boston: Houghton Mifflin, 1948. An excellent account of the World War II propaganda effort.

CHAFEE, ZECHARIAH, JR., *Free Speech in the United States*. Cambridge, Mass.: Harvard University Press, 1941. The major study of the problem, by a Harvard law professor.

CREEL, GEORGE, *How We Advertised America*. New York: Harper & Row, 1920. The chairman of the World War I Committee on Public Information makes his report to the public. See also Creel's autobiography, *Rebel at Large* (New York: G.P. Putnam's Sons, 1947).

CROZIER, EMMET, *American Reporters on the Western Front, 1914–1918*. New York: Oxford University Press, 1959. Much detail about both star reporters and "specials."

EMERSON, GLORIA, *Winners and Losers*. New York: Random House, 1977. A former *New York Times* reporter wrote this so Americans would not forget Vietnam.

FALL, BERNARD B., *The Two Viet-Nams: A Political and Military Analysis*, 2nd rev. ed. New York: Praeger, 1967. The most important study of the historical background and changing nature of the Vietnam War.

FEIS, HERBERT, *From Trust to Terror: The Onset of the Cold War, 1945–1950*. New York: Norton, 1970. A scholarly examination of six fateful years.

FITZGERALD, FRANCES, *Fire in the Lake*. Boston: Little, Brown, 1972. The story of the people of Vietnam by an acclaimed magazine journalist. Hailed as one of the best books on the consequences of the war.

HALBERSTAM, DAVID, *The Making of a Quagmire*. New York: Random House, 1965. By the *New York Times'* Pulitzer Prize winner in Vietnam. Also, *The Best and the Brightest*. New York: Random House, 1972. A thoroughly researched analysis of the Ivy Leaguers and cold war warriors who created the Vietnam strategies.

KALB, MARVIN, AND ELIE ABEL, *Roots of Involvement*. New York: W.W. Norton, 1971. Two distinguished journalists analyze America's role in the Pacific and the beginnings of the Vietnam conflict.

KNIGHTLEY, PHILIP, *The First Casualty*. New York: Harcourt Brace Jovanovich, 1975. A critical study of war correspondence from the Crimean War to Vietnam. Holds that most war coverage has been poor.

KOOP, THEODORE F., *Weapon of Silence*. Chicago: University of Chicago Press, 1946. The story of the World War II Office of Censorship by one of its principal executives.

LANGER, WILLIAM L., AND S. EVERETT GLEASON, *The Challenge to Isolation, 1937–1940;* and *The Undeclared War, 1940–1941*. New York: Harper & Row, 1952–53. An exhaustive, well-documented analysis in two volumes, published for The Council on Foreign Relations under the joint title, "World Crisis and American Foreign Policy." It fairly and objectively traces the story of American entrance into World War II.

LASSWELL, HAROLD D., *Propaganda Technique in the World War*. New York: Peter Smith, 1927. A standard source for World War I propaganda efforts in the major belligerent countries.

LERNER, DANIEL, ed., *Propaganda in War and Crisis*. New York: George W. Stewart, Inc., 1951. A collection of writings in the field of psychological warfare, giving the background of twentieth-century war propaganda efforts.

LUCAS, JIM, *Dateline: Vietnam*. New York: Award Books, 1967. A personal account.

MEYER, ROBERT, JR., *The "Stars and Stripes" Story of World War II*. New York: McKay, 1960. Anthology of stories, with background.

MIDDLETON, DREW, *Where Has Last July Gone? Memoirs*. New York: Quadrangle, 1973. Details his career as a *New York Times* correspondent, with focus on World War II.

MILLER, LEE G., *The Story of Ernie Pyle*. New York: Viking, 1950. Biography of the famed World War II columnist.

MILLER, WEBB, *I Found No Peace*. New York: Simon & Schuster, 1936. One of the best of the foreign correspondents' books, by a longtime United Press correspondent.

MINOR, DALE, *The Information War*. New York: Hawthorn, 1970. Perceptive analysis of press-government conflict in Vietnam.

MOCK, JAMES R., *Censorship 1917*. Princeton: Princeton University Press, 1941. The major work on World War I censorship activities.

MOCK, JAMES R., AND CEDRIC LARSON, *Words That Won the War*. Princeton: Princeton University Press, 1939. Best account of the work of the Committee on Public Information during World War I.

MURPHY, PAUL L., *The Meaning of Freedom of Speech*. Westport, Conn.: Greenwood, 1972. Intensive study from Wilson to Roosevelt.

MURRAY, ROBERT K., *Red Scare: A Study in National Hysteria, 1919–1920*. Minneapolis: University of Minnesota Press, 1955. A well-documented study of a period of violation of civil liberties. Lacks a summary evaluation of newspaper performance.

O'CONNOR, RICHARD, *Pacific Destiny: An Informal History of the U.S. in the Far East*. Boston: Little, Brown, 1969 (See chapter 17).

PALMER, FREDERICK, *With My Own Eyes*. Indianapolis: Bobbs-Merrill, 1933. Biographical account by a leading World War I correspondent who became military field censor.

PAXSON, FREDERIC L., *American Democracy and the World War*. Boston: Houghton Mifflin, 1938 ff. A three-volume study of the 10 years, 1913 to 1923, that ranks at the top for its completeness, balance, and perceptiveness.

PYLE, ERNEST TAYLOR, *Here Is Your War*. New York: Holt, Rinehart & Winston, 1943. A compilation of Pyle's columns.

RAUCH, BASIL, *Roosevelt from Munich to Pearl Harbor*. New York: Creative Age Press, Inc., 1950. An able and spirited answer to the isolationist argument.

SALISBURY, HARRISON, *Behind the Lines*. New York: Harper & Row, 1967. *New York Times* editor's trip to Hanoi opened many eyes to conduct of Vietnamese war, almost won him a Pulitzer Prize.

SCHREINER, GEORGE A., *Cables and Wireless*. Boston: Stratford, 1924. Analyzes effect of World War I on communications.

SHEEHAN, NEIL, ET AL., *The Pentagon Papers*, New York: Quadrangle Books, 1971. The documents showing America's early involvement in Vietnamese affairs, and plans for expansion of this role.

SHERWOOD, ROBERT E., *Roosevelt and Hopkins*. New York: Harper & Row, 1948. An intimate history of the wartime partnership by the writer-confidant of F.D.R.

SHIRER, WILLIAM L., *Berlin Diary*. New York: Knopf, 1941. The years 1934 to 1940 in diary form, by the CBS radio correspondent who covered Hitler's rise to power. Also see his *20th Century Journey*. New York: Simon & Schuster, 1976.

SLOSSON, PRESTON W., *The Great Crusade and After, 1914–1928*, A History of American Life, Vol. XII. New York: Macmillan, 1930. An excellent social history.

SNYDER, LOUIS L., ed., *Masterpieces of War Reporting*. New York: Julian Messner, 1962. Great moments of World War II.

SORENSEN, THOMAS C., *The Word War: The Story of American Propaganda*. New York: Harper & Row, 1968. Focuses on USIA in postwar crises.

STEIN, M.L., *Under Fire: The Story of American War Correspondents*. New York: Julian Messner, 1968. Good popularly written history.

THOMSON, CHARLES A.H., *Overseas Information Service of the United States Government*. Washington: Brookings Institution, 1948. Authoritative account.

TOLAND, JOHN, *The Rising Sun: The Decline and Fall of the Japanese Empire, 1936–1945*, 2 vols. New York: Random House, 1970. A comprehensive account of war in the Pacific.

WILLIAMS, WYTHE, *Passed by the Censor*. New York: Dutton, 1916. A World War I correspondent's story. Twenty years later his *Dusk of Empire* pictured the decline of Europe into another war.

WITTKE, CARL F., *The German-Language Press in America*. Lexington: University of Kentucky Press, 1957. A history from 1732 to 1956; three chapters devoted to World War I period.

Periodicals and Monographs

The files of the *Journalism Quarterly* and *Public Opinion Quarterly* contain many important articles published about World War II censorship and propaganda activities. See particularly the Spring 1943, issue of *Public Opinion Quarterly* and *Journalism Quarterly* from 1942 to 1944. Other important articles include the following:

BAILEY, GEORGE A., AND LAWRENCE W. LICHTY, "Rough Justice on a Saigon Street: A Gatekeeper Study of NBC's Tet Execution Film," *Journalism Quarterly*, XLIX (Summer 1972), p. 221. Step-by-step on decision to use execution episode.

BEAN, WALTON E., "The Accuracy of Creel Committee News, 1917–1919: An Examination of Cases," *Journalism Quarterly*, XVIII (September 1941), 263.

BECK, ELMER A., "Autopsy of a Labor Daily: The Milwaukee Leader," *Journalism Monographs*, No. 16, August 1970.

BISHOP, ROBERT L., AND LAMAR S. MACKAY, "Mysterious Silence, Lyrical Scream: Government Information in World War II," *Journalism Monographs*, No. 19, May 1971. The OWI.

BRAESTRUP, PETER, "Covering the Vietnam War," *Nieman Reports*, XXIII (December 1969), 8. By a Vietnam correspondent for the *New York Times* and *Washington Post*.

BROWNE, DONALD R., "The Voice of America: Policies and Problems," *Journalism Monographs*, No. 43, February 1976. A comprehensive account.

BROWNE, MALCOLM W., "Viet Nam Reporting: Three Years of Crisis," *Columbia Journalism Review*, III (Fall 1964), 4. By the AP senior correspondent in Saigon.

DAVIS, ELMER, "Report to the President," edited by Ronald T. Farrar, *Journalism Monographs*, No. 7, August 1968. On his OWI stewardship.

EPHRON, NORA, "The War Followers," *New York*, XVI (Nov. 12, 1973), p. 49. A report on some of the correspondents covering the Arab-Israeli fighting.

FITZPATRICK, DICK, "America's Campaign of Truth Throughout the World," *Journalism Quarterly*, XXVIII (Winter 1951), 3.

FOUGHT, JOHN P., "News and Editorial Treatment of Alleged Reds and Radicals by Selected Newspapers and Periodicals During 1918–21," Ph.D. thesis, Southern Illinois University, 1970. *New York Times, New York Tribune* had heavy bias.

LARSON, CEDRIC, "Censorship of Army News During the World War, 1917–1918," *Journalism Quarterly*, XVII (December 1940), 313.

———, "OWI's Domestic News Bureau: An Account and Appraisal," *Journalism Quarterly*, XXVI (March 1949), 3.

MCNULTY, THOMAS M., "Network Television Documentary Treatment of the Vietnam War, 1965 to 1969," Ph.D. thesis, Indiana University, 1974. Reaction to spot news, not preconceived notions, determined content.

MILLER, ROBERT C., "Censorship in Korea," *Nieman Reports*, VI (July 1952), 3.

MORRIS, JOHN G., "This We Remember," *Harper's*, 245 (September 1972), 72. The pictures that make Vietnam unforgettable, and portraits of photographers.

PICKETT, CALDER M., "A Paper for the Doughboys: *Stars and Stripes* in World War I," *Journalism Quarterly*, XLII (Winter 1965), 60. The flavor of the soldier's paper is captured.

STEVENS, JOHN D., "Press and Community Toleration: Wisconsin in World War I," *Journalism Quarterly*, XLVI (Summer 1969), 255. Based on Ph.D. thesis, University of Wisconsin, 1967.

———, "From the Back of the Foxhole: Black Correspondents in World War II," *Journalism Monographs*, No. 27, February 1973.

"Vietnam: What Lessons?" A symposium by Jules Witcover, Fred W. Friendly, Robert Shaplen, James McCartney, Edwin Diamond, Don Stillman, and Nathan Blumberg, in *Columbia Journalism Review*, IX (Winter 1970–71). Media plusses and minuses.

Average net paid circulation of THE NEWS, Dec., 1927:
Sunday, 1,357,556
Daily, 1,193,297

DAILY NEWS

FINAL EDITION

NEW YORK'S Copyright, 1928, by News Syndicate Co., Inc. Reg. U.S. Pat. Office PICTURE NEWSPAPER Entered as 2nd class matter Post Office, New York, N.Y.

Vol. 9. No. 174 28 Pages   ***   New York, Saturday, January 14, 1928   2 Cents IN CITY LIMITS | 3 CENTS Elsewhere

FUNERALS HELD For Gray, Mrs. Snyder

Story on Page 3

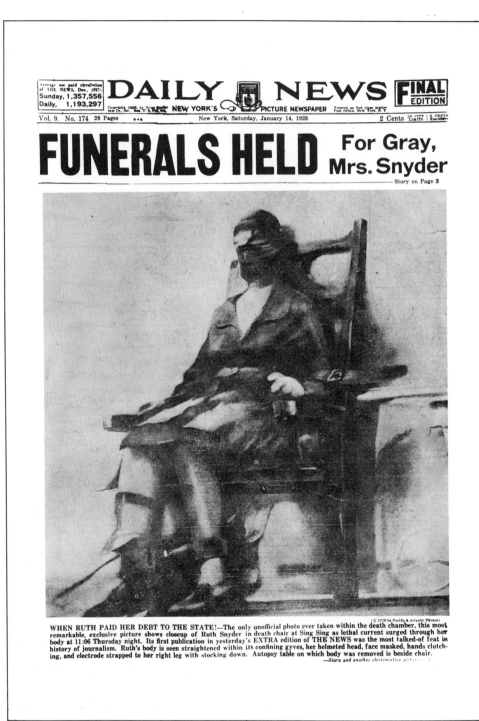

WHEN RUTH PAID HER DEBT TO THE STATE!—The only unofficial photo ever taken within the death chamber, this most remarkable, exclusive picture shows closeup of Ruth Snyder in death chair at Sing Sing as lethal current surged through her body at 11:06 Thursday night. Its first publication in yesterday's EXTRA edition of THE NEWS was the most talked-of feat in history of journalism. Ruth's body is seen straightened within its confining gyves, her helmeted head, face masked, hands clutching, and electrode strapped to her right leg with stocking down. Autopsy table on which body was removed is beside chair.
—*Story and another electrocution picture*

This 1928 front page represented the extreme in New York tabloid sensationalism.

22

From Jazz Journalism to Interpretative Reporting

It is much easier to report a battle or a bombing than it is to do an honest and intelligible job on the Marshall Plan, the Taft-Hartley Law or the Atlantic Pact.

—Edward R. Murrow

A new cycle of sensationalism in journalism began with the close of World War I. Just as in 1833, when the penny press appeared, and in 1897, when the Pulitzer-Hearst duel climaxed the introduction of the new journalism, the times were right for a sensationalized appeal to the people. And there was an untapped audience awaiting such an appeal, just as there had been in 1833 and 1897. In the seven years between 1919 and 1926 three new papers in New York City found more than a million and a half readers without unduly disturbing the circulation balance of the existing dailies. Their sensationalism was accompanied by the use of two techniques that identify the period: the tabloid-style format and the extensive use of photography. As in earlier periods, the wave of sensationalism had its effect on all of the press before it subsided; and, as before, a more substantial journalism followed the era of sensationalized appeal. The 1920s are known as the decade of "jazz journalism,"[1] while the years that followed were marked by a rapid rise in emphasis on the techniques of interpretative reporting, not only in the newspaper field but also in magazine publishing and broadcasting.

The tabloid format introduced so successfully in New York after 1919 was not a stranger to journalism. Before newsprint became relatively plentiful in the middle of the nineteenth century, small-sized pages were common. The *Daily Graphic,* published in New York between 1873 and 1889 and carrying Stephen H. Horgan's early experimental halftone engravings, had a tabloid format. So did Frank A. Munsey's ill-fated *Daily Continent* of 1891, which like the *Daily Graphic* was heavily illustrated but no more sensationalized than other newspapers. It was not these American efforts that stimulated the tabloid era of the 1920s, however. For better or for worse, America owes its tabloids to the cradle of English-language journalism, Great Britain.

Even though English journalistic preoccupation with crime news and court stories played its part in suggesting the advantages of sensationalism to the first American penny press newsmen in 1833, newspapers for the masses lagged in Great Britain because of stamp tax regulations that did not disappear until 1855. The *Daily Telegraph* then became the first penny paper in England, but its appeal was to the middle classes. Not until after the introduction of compulsory education in England in 1870 was there a market for a truly popularized newspaper. Into that market stepped a discerning young man named Alfred C. Harmsworth, who as Lord Northcliffe was to become one of Britain's great press lords. His first project, in 1883, was a human interest weekly magazine named *Answers,* which was modeled after George Newnes' *Tidbits* of 1881. Both publications used the contest idea as a means of enticing working class readers, and Harmsworth had 250,000 of them within 10 years.

Meanwhile Harmsworth was watching the progress of Joseph Pulitzer's *New York World* and of James Gordon Bennett, Jr.'s *Paris Herald* with its short-lived London edition. He first adapted the new American techniques to the *London Evening News,* which he bought in 1894, and then to his far more famous *Daily Mail,* founded in 1896. Soon Pulitzer was taking lessons from Harmsworth, whom the *World*'s publisher admired so greatly that he permitted the Englishman, as guest publisher, to turn the January 1, 1901, issue of the *World* into a tabloid representing "the newspaper of the twentieth century." New York was unimpressed however, and it remained for Harmsworth to do the job in England.

The first widely circulated tabloid was the *Daily Mirror,* which Harmsworth began in London in 1903 as a newspaper for women but soon converted into a "halfpenny illustrated," small, sensational, and amusing. By 1909, its circulation had reached a million copies, and the *Daily Sketch* and *Daily Graphic* jumped into the tabloid field. Harmsworth had become Lord Northcliffe and a leading figure in English journalism by the time of World War I. He still felt that someone should be publishing a tabloid like his *Daily Mirror* in New York, and when he met an American army officer who was overseas from his newspaper desk, Northcliffe told him how lucrative the tabloid could be.

FOUNDING OF THE *NEW YORK DAILY NEWS*

The army officer was Captain Joseph Medill Patterson, partner with Colonel Robert R. McCormick in the publishing of the *Chicago Tribune* since 1914. The two grandsons of Joseph Medill met later in France and agreed to a plan to start a New York tabloid to be called the *Daily News.* The cousins had other reasons than the arguments Northcliffe had advanced for undertaking the New York venture. Colonel McCormick, as will be shown in detail in a later chapter, was a king-sized chip off the conservative Medill block. Captain Patterson was unconventional enough to have written two novels (*A Little Brother of the Rich* and *Rebellion*) that constituted protests against social injustice and economic oppression and was considered socialistic in his thinking by others of his wealthy class. The plan for Patterson to start a tabloid in New York would thus give him an opportunity to reach the many immigrants and least literate native-born, as he wished to do, and at the same time would rid Colonel McCormick of an embarrassing co-publisher arrangement in Chicago.

So the *Illustrated Daily News,* as the paper was called the first few months, made its bow in New York on June 26, 1919. Its half-size front page was covered with a picture of the Prince of Wales (later King Edward VIII and Duke of Windsor), whose forthcoming visit to America already had stirred anticipatory feminine heartthrobs. Its promotion gimmick was the sponsoring of its own beauty contest, which was announced to startled readers of the *New York Times* in a full page ad that read: SEE NEW YORK'S MOST BEAUTIFUL GIRLS EVERY MORNING IN THE ILLUSTRATED DAILY NEWS. New York newsmen of 1919, like those of 1833 who had sniffed at Benjamin Day's newly founded *Sun,* dismissed the tabloid venture without much concern. But one of them, at least, foresaw the effect its sensationalism, its entertainment emphasis, and its reliance on photography would have. He was Carr Van Anda, the astute managing editor of the *Times,* who while hardly in the sensationalized picture paper field himself realized that the *Daily News* would satisfy a widespread postwar public craving and reach a new reading audience. "This paper," he said, "should reach a circulation of 2,000,000."[2] Patterson and his editors did not disappoint Van Anda. In 1924 the *Daily News* circulation of 750,000 was the largest in the country. By 1929 the figure was 1,320,000—gained while the combined circulation of the other New York morning papers stood still. And before World War II it had hit the two million mark.

THE ATMOSPHERE OF THE 1920s

The 1920s were made to order for the extreme sensationalism of the tabloid and for a spreading of its degrading journalistic features to the rest of the press. The great crusade of 1917 was over, and Woodrow Wilson's hopes for American leadership in world affairs were dissolving into a "Red scare" at home and a nationalistic-isolationist outlook toward events abroad. The country's cry was "back to normalcy" insofar as politics were concerned. This did not mean that America wanted to stand still; rather it wanted to forget the troubles of the war years and concentrate on "living."

Political conservatism and laissez-faire policies thus prevailed over rebellious but outvoted progressivism. Occupying the White House were three Republicans, the sincere but scandal-plagued Marion, Ohio, newspaper publisher, Warren G. Harding; the close-mouthed Yankee believer in the status quo, Calvin Coolidge; and the efficient but depression-plagued Quaker, Herbert Hoover. America was a relatively complacent land, and business prosperity and the doings of Wall Street outweighed interest in political and social reform.

The press, preoccupied in many instances with sex, crime, and entertainment, reflected the spirit of the times. The majority of newspapers went with the tide, rather than attempting to give the country leadership either by determined display of significant news or through interpretation. There was good copy in the evidences of political laxity that emerge in all postwar periods, however, and even the tabloids played up the Teapot Dome oil lease scandal and others that issued from the unhappy Harding administration. Dapper Mayor Jimmy Walker's casual handling of New York City affairs was both entertaining and productive of graft exposés. The hue and cry against corruption were valuable, but sober examination of the country's own economic trend and of the world situation went begging in many papers.

And after all, the atmosphere of the 1920s made this inevitable. The national experiment called Prohibition brought rumrunners, speakeasy operators, and gangsters into the spotlight, and they were interesting people. Al Capone, Dutch Schultz, Waxey Gordon, Legs Diamond, and their rivals were sensational copy. Socialites caught in a speakeasy raid made good picture subjects.

Tabloid editors feasted, too, on stories about glamorous and sexy Hollywood and its stars—Rudolph Valentino, Fatty Arbuckle, Clara Bow. They gloried in the love affairs of the great and not-so-great—Daddy Browning and his Peaches, Kip Rhine-lander, the Prince of Wales. They built sordid murder cases into national sensations—Hall-Mills, Ruth Snyder. They glorified celebrities—Charles A. Lindbergh, Queen Marie of Rumania, Channel swimmer Gertrude Ederle. They promoted the country's sports stars—prizefighter Jack Dempsey, golfer Bobby Jones, tennis champion Bill Tilden, football coach Knute Rockne, and homerun hitter Babe Ruth.

The *Daily News* did badly at first. Its initial circulation of 200,000 dropped to 26,000 the second month, and two of its four reporters were fired. But Captain Patterson was discovering that his circulation potential was not among readers of the *Times* but among the immigrant and poorly educated American-born population of New York. The *News* was put on stands where only foreign-language papers had sold before, and its pictures sold the paper. By 1921 it was second in circulation to Hearst's *Evening Journal*. Hearst's morning *American* tried to capture some of the readership going to the *News* by filling its columns with pictures and features but the tabloid won the verdict. The sharp battle between Hearst and McCormick circulation men in Chicago was transferred to New York, with lotteries, coupon prizes, and other inducements for readers. Patterson was the victor again with a limerick contest keyed to the popular taste.

THE *MIRROR* AND THE *GRAPHIC*

Direct competition arrived for the *News* in 1924, the year it became America's most widely circulated newspaper. Hearst had experimented unsuccessfully with the tabloid format in Boston—always a poor town for journalistic innovations—but in despair of the *American*'s ever whipping the *News,* he began his tabloid *Daily Mirror*. Close behind him was Bernarr Macfadden, publisher of *Physical Culture* and *True Story* magazines and a millionaire with a yen to influence the public and hold high office. But as in his successful *True Story* venture, his newspaper aims were unconventional. He wanted a paper, he said, that "will shatter precedent to smithereens."[3] Macfadden selected Emile Gauvreau, up to that time the managing editor of the respectable *Hartford Courant,* as his chief editor, and the two brought out the *Daily Graphic*. The *Mirror* began to challenge the *News* on more or less straight journalistic terms, but the *Graphic* set out to see just how sensational and lurid it could be. The result was the battle of what Oswald Garrison Villard called "gutter journalism."

The *Graphic* quickly became the most notorious of the tabloids. Indeed, Macfadden had no intention of running a newspaper. He did not bother with subscribing to a press association service and played only the "gigantic" general news. He was trying to build a million-reader audience on newsstand sales of a daily that was to be the *True Confessions* of the newspaper world. Reporters wrote first-person stories to be signed by persons in the news, and editors headlined them "I Know Who Killed My Brother," "He Beat Me—I Love Him," and "For 36 Hours I Lived Another Woman's Love Life." Gauvreau's retort to criticism was that the public wanted "hot news,"[4] and the evidence seemed to be on his side, as newsstand sales of the *Graphic* mounted.

Climax year of the war of the tabloids was 1926. First the Broadway producer, Earl Carroll, gave a party at which a nude dancing girl sat in a bathtub full of champagne. Before the furor had died down, the tabloids discovered a wealthy real estate man, Edward Browning, and his 15-year-old shopgirl bride. This was "hot" romance indeed and the pair became Daddy and Peaches to all of America. The *Graphic* portrayed them frolicking on a bed with Daddy saying "Woof! Woof! I'm a Goof!" Gauvreau decided to thrill his shopgirl audience with the details of Peaches' intimate diary, but at that point the law stepped in.

Meanwhile the desperate editors of the *Mirror* had dug up a four-year-old murder story in New Jersey. In 1922 a New Brunswick, New Jersey, minister named Edward Hall and his choir-singer sweetheart, Eleanor Mills, were found dead, apparently suicides. The *Mirror* succeeded in having the minister's widow brought to trial and for months the New Jersey town became one of the most important filing points for press associations and big newspapers in America. One witness became "the pig woman" to the 200 reporters at the trial. Unfortunately for the *Mirror,* Mrs. Hall was acquitted and sued the paper for libel.

A second sensational murder trial was drummed up in the spring of 1927. A corset salesman named Judd Gray and his sweetheart, Mrs. Ruth Snyder, had collaborated in disposing of the unwanted Mr. Snyder. When it came time for Mrs. Snyder's execution in the electric chair at Sing Sing the *Graphic* blared to its readers:

> Don't fail to read tomorrow's *Graphic.* An installment that thrills and stuns! A story that fairly pierces the heart and reveals Ruth Snyder's last thoughts on earth; that pulses the blood as it discloses her final letters. Think of it! A woman's final thoughts just before she is clutched in the deadly snare that sears and burns and FRIES AND KILLS! Her very last words! Exclusively in tomorrow's *Graphic.* [5]

It was the photography-minded *News* that had the last word, however. The *Graphic* might have its "confession" but the *News* proposed to take its readers inside the execution chamber. Pictures were forbidden, but a photographer, Tom Howard, strapped a tiny camera to his ankle and took his picture just after the current was turned on. The *News* put a touched-up shot on its front page, sold 250,000 extra papers, and then had to run off 750,000 additional copies of the front page later.

PATTERSON'S NEWS VALUES CHANGE

Patterson's news and photo enterprise went beyond shocking people. When the steamer *Vestris* sank off the Atlantic coast with the loss of several hundred lives, Patterson sent all his staffers to interview the survivors on the chance that one of them had taken a picture. One had, and for $1,200 the *News* bought one of the greatest action news pictures ever taken, showing the tilted ship's deck and recording the expressions of the victims as they prepared to jump into the water or go down with the ship. Patterson put $750,000 into Associated Press Wirephoto in the early 1930s, when other publishers were balking, and for a while had exclusive New York use of Wirephoto. The *News* developed its own staff of crack photographers and in addition welcomed shots taken by freelancers in the vast New York area. The payoff was consistent.

With 1929 came the Wall Street crash, depression, and deepening years of unemployment. Patterson, with his finger on the pulse of the people, told his editors and reporters that the depression and its effects on the lives of all Americans was now the big story. Not that the *News* and other papers stopped playing crime and sex news and features. But they also gave great space to the serious news of a people in trouble. Patterson's *Daily News* became a firm supporter of Roosevelt's New Deal through the 1930s, to the disgust of the fiercely anti-New Deal Colonel McCormick in the *Chicago Tribune* tower.

The *Daily News* still wisecracked in its editorial columns and still produced its headlines with a twist that caught any reader's eye. But after 1939 it had no gay greetings for the man in the White House. It broke with Roosevelt over involvement in World War II and became bitterly isolationist. Patterson's distrust of the president's foreign policy then led him to fight the administration all down the line. After his death in 1946, the *News* was under the control of Colonel McCormick, although its operations were directed by Patterson's former executives. Despite this political break with the Democratic party the *News* remained a "people's paper," climbing to peak circulations of 2,400,000 daily and 4,500,000 Sunday in 1947, before it felt the effects of a general slackening of metropolitan newspaper circulations and a sharp drop in sales of entertainment-centered papers vulnerable to television's inroads. By 1977 its figures were 1,940,000 daily and 2,760,000 Sunday, easily the country's largest daily. Michael J. O'Neill was editor, seeking to revitalize a paper still sharp enough to produce this 1976 headline on the president's response to the bankrupt city's plea for aid: "FORD TO CITY: DROP DEAD."[6]

THE END OF THE TABLOID ERA

Things did not go so well with the *Mirror* and *Graphic*. Hearst sold the *Mirror* in 1928, had to take it back in 1930, and then bolstered it by stealing columnist Walter Winchell from the *Graphic* and sending Arthur Brisbane in as editor. But the *Mirror* never became a profitable Hearst property and was closed in 1963. The *Graphic* never won any advertising support and died unmourned in 1932, after losing millions of dollars for Macfadden.

Two points should be made clear: very few of the other newspapers that adopted the tabloid format were of the racy character of the New York tabs; and the quest for sensational news did not die with the passing of the *Graphic* and the semi-transformation of the *Daily News*. One hopeful tabloid publisher was Cornelius Vanderbilt, Jr., who started crusading, nonsalacious picture papers in Los Angeles, San Francisco, and Miami in the early 1920s. Vanderbilt won good-sized circulations for his papers, but failed to build up advertiser support, and the chain soon withered. The *Los Angeles Daily News* passed to liberal-minded Manchester Boddy, who built it into a pro-New Deal paper much like orthodox dailies except for a freewheeling style of writing. The *Chicago Times,* founded in 1929, was likewise a liberal, tersely written paper. When Marshall Field combined his *Chicago Sun* with the *Times* in 1947 he kept the tabloid format. The *Daily News* and *Post* in New York and *Newsday* on Long Island were other 1977 tabloid leaders. In addition there were the supermarket-circulated tabloids, led by the *National Enquirer* and the *Star,* which focused on scandals, conspiracies, and celebrities.

Although the newspapers of the 1930s devoted far more space to stories about political and economic events and foreign affairs than those of the 1920s, they did not lose the "big story" complex that characterized postwar journalism. The trial of Bruno Hauptmann in 1934 for the kidnapping and murder of the Lindbergh baby drew more than 300 reporters, who wired more than 11 million words in 28 days. The publicity-seeking judge turned the trial into a newsman's paradise and there was much criticism of "trial by newspaper."

THE RISE OF INTERPRETATIVE REPORTING

The rise of interpretative reporting was the most important development of the 1930s and 1940s, however. Proper back-grounding of news events and covering of major areas of human activity by specialists were not unknown before that time, just as uncritical and sensationalized treatment of news continued in the press after that time. But the impact of the political-social-economic revolution of the New Deal years, the rise of modern scientific technology, the increasing interdependence of economic groups at home, and the shrinking of the world into one vast arena for power politics forced a new approach to the handling of news. "Why" became important, along with the traditional "who did what." Coverage of politics, economics and business, foreign affairs, science, labor, agriculture, and social work was improved by reporter-specialists.[7] Editorial pages also became more interpretative. The news magazines and some specialized newspapers and magazines joined in the movement, together with radio commentators. Old-style objectivity, which consisted in sticking to a factual account of what had been said or done, was challenged by a new concept that was based on the belief that the reader needed to have a given event placed in its proper context if truth really was to be served. Old beliefs that difficult subjects like science and economics could not be made interesting to readers likewise were discarded out of sheer necessity. The Washington and foreign correspondents responded with increasing success to the demands thus made on them by the pressure of the news.

The extreme in interpretation was reached by the New York tabloid, *PM,* founded in 1940 and financed by Marshall Field. *PM,* under the editorship of Ralph Ingersoll, made it a policy to express its liberal point of view in its news columns, to the point where it became a daily journal of opinion. The paper had a notable staff and contributed a fighting spirit to New York journalism. But its hopes that it could exist on the basis of its intelligent writing, excellent pictures, and interpretative appeal—without solicitation of advertising—had faded by 1946. Even when it accepted advertising, *PM* languished financially. Field sold out in 1948; the paper became the *New York Star* and fought for life under the editorship of Joseph Barnes. It backed President Harry S. Truman for reelection before suspending publication in 1949.

LABOR NEWS SPECIALISTS   Specialists were required, however, both in Washington and in newspaper offices across the country. The rise of "big labor" to challenge "big business" under the collective bargaining guarantees of the New Deal brought the labor beat into full prominence. Louis Stark of the *New York Times,* the paper's labor reporter and, with John Leary of the *New York World,* one of the first reporters in the field, transferred his base of operations to Washington in 1933. There Stark became the acknowledged dean of American labor reporters, as writers covered national labor-management bargaining in the steel and coal industries, the activities of the National Labor Relations Board, and legislative contests that culminated in the replacement of the Wagner Act by the Taft-Hartley Law. Coverage of strikes always had been a part of the nation's news report, but fuller interpretation of the problems of labor-management relations now became the good reporter's goal. He also sought to increase direct coverage of organized labor's activities and attitudes. Both Washington and local reporting were improved by numerous labor specialists. Stark thought there should be more full-time labor reporters, but he noted with satisfaction that the list had grown considerably over the years to include such reporters as Edwin A. Lahey of the *Chicago Daily News,* Fred Carr of the *Christian Science Monitor,* John Turcott of the *New York Daily News,* John F. Burns of the *Providence Journal,* A.H. Raskin of the *New York Times,* and a score or more of equally competent associates.

SCIENCE AND AGRICULTURE   The worlds of science and medicine were better covered, too, by reporters who repaired the damage done by the sensationalized science stories of the days of yellow journalism. Science Service, directed by Watson Davis, did much to improve the science coverage of its subscribers after 1921. The *New York Times* again was early in the field. Waldemar Kaempffert, an engineer, joined the paper as a science specialist in 1927, joined by William L. Laurence in 1930. Pulitzer Prizes were given in 1937 to a group of pioneer science writers, including Laurence, David Dietz of the Scripps-Howard newspapers, Howard W. Blakeslee of the Associated Press, John J. O'Neill of the *New York Herald Tribune,* and Gobind Behari Lal of Hearst's Universal Service. The National Association of Science Writers, formed in 1934, had nearly a thousand members four decades later. Top writers included Arthur J. Snider of the *Chicago Daily News,* Victor Cohn of the *Washington Post,* David Perlman of the *San Francisco Chronicle,* Josephine Robertson of the *Cleveland Plain Dealer,* Harry Nelson of the *Los Angeles Times,* Walter Sullivan of the *New York Times,* Christine Russell of the *Washington Star,* John Durham of the *Houston Chronicle,* Earl Ubell of NBC, Delos Smith of UPI, and Alton Blakeslee, Frank J. Carey, and John Barbour of AP. One of their major concerns was space science.

Federal action to stabilize agricultural prices, provide economic security for farmers, and conserve soil resources became major news with the advent of the Agricultural Adjustment Administration. But the agricultural story had been an important one even before the concerted actions of the New Deal. Alfred D. Stedman of the *St. Paul Pioneer Press* and *Dispatch* and Theodore C. Alford of the *Kansas City Star* arrived in Washington in 1929 as the first specialists in agricultural news correspondence. The press associations then left even major stories uncovered or undeveloped. Early in the 1930s, however, the Associated Press selected an agricultural expert, Roy F. Hendrickson. Farm editors like the veteran J.S. Russell of the *Des Moines Register* and *Tribune* and Stedman, returned to St. Paul from a long Washington career, kept their own regional coverage at a high pitch.

URBAN
AND ENVIRONMENT
WRITERS

An Urban Writers' Society was formed in 1968, reflecting the concern of Americans about urban society and the environment. Outstanding among the urban specialists were Ada Louise Huxtable, architecture critic of the *New York Times* since 1963 and winner of the 1970 Pulitzer Prize for criticism; Wolf Von Eckardt, urban and architecture specialist for the *Washington Post* since 1964; George McCue, art and urban-design critic for the *St. Louis Post-Dispatch;* and Allan Temko, the *San Francisco Chronicle's* urban columnist. When *Editor & Publisher* in 1970 asked the nation's dailies to send in names of their writers specializing in environmental news coverage on the ecology beat, 100 did.[8]

Environmental concerns became paramount in the late 1970s and reporters struggled to explain such things as environmental impact reports, nuclear power plants, liquified natural gas, water projects, zoning regulations, and, of course, the economic implications of all this to the tax-paying public. Among the environment and ecology specialists were Gladwin Hill of the *New York Times,* Margaret Freivogel of the *St. Louis Post-Dispatch,* Steve Wynkoop of the *Denver Post,* David Ross Stevens of the *Louisville Courier-Journal,* and Paul Hayes of the *Milwaukee Journal.*

The need for alternative energy sources and conservation of water became acute in 1976–77 when a terrible drought struck the western half of the nation while the eastern half was hit by an unusually severe winter that nearly exhausted fuel supplies. The nation's newspapers and broadcast stations carried the running story with good detail, and the better ones, as usual, offered background stories and editorialized for stringent regulations prohibiting unsafe and wasteful practices. Changing weather patterns also were examined by reporters, who interpreted the divergent viewpoints of leading scientists.

INVESTIGATIVE REPORTING   Digging into the activities of the Pentagon, Central Intelligence Agency, Federal Bureau of Investigation, Teamsters' Union, organized crime syndicates, and corrupt politicians were the so-called investigative journalists of the 1960s and 1970s. Investigative reporting meant developing sufficient sources and documents over a long period of time to offer the public a strong interpretation of the event's meaning. The term "investigative" became extremely popular after Seymour Hersh uncovered the story of the My Lai massacre in Vietnam and joined the *New York Times* staff in time to look into the CIA. Jack Nelson of the *Los Angeles Times* helped demythologize FBI Director J. Edgar Hoover, and Bob Woodward and Carl Bernstein of the *Washington Post* became national heroes. But by its very nature, true investigative reporting could be conducted by only the most wealthy and influential newspapers and hardly at all by the television networks, with the exception of occasional in-depth "Specials" by all three networks and one regular program, CBS News' fine *60 Minutes* show featuring Mike Wallace, Morley Safer, and later Dan Rather.

Investigative journalism did not begin with the 1960s, however. It was a continuation of the muckraking tradition, which never really died. From the 1920s to the present day, small circulation magazines like *Nation* and *New Republic* kept reform ideas alive. Heywood Broun, McAlister Coleman, Lewis Gannett, and Louis Adamic wrote for their pages in earlier days. Matthew Josephson attacked large-scale arms spending in *Nation* in 1956, the same year Fred J. Cook wrote his "The Shame of New York." Editor Carey McWilliams developed special issues on the FBI in 1958 and the CIA in 1962. Ralph Nader's first series, including his "The Safe Car You Can't Buy," appeared in *Nation* in 1959, and as early as 1953 McWilliams was linking cigarettes and lung cancer.

The incomparable I.F. Stone—working only with his wife and an occasional research assistant—began publishing his *I.F. Stone's Weekly* in 1953, biting at the proponents of McCarthyism. He continued the newsletter until 1971, writing of controversies caused by the Korean War, the problems of the black, the early days of Vietnam, and the steady encroachment on private rights in the anti-Vietnam days.[9] Stone and McWilliams emerged as America's most distinguished and consistent independent journalists. Both men had to be content with small circulations but had the satisfaction of knowing that their dedicated readers included some activists and policymakers who eventually made inroads against the status quo in the early 1970s. Stone became a contributing editor for the *New York Review of Books,* where he continued his critical writing.

In addition to magazines, major contributions came from the authors of books. John Steinbeck's *The Grapes of Wrath* and *Factories in the Field* brought the plight of the migrant worker to America's attention in the 1930s. Later, writers like Michael Harrington, Dwight MacDonald, and Herman Miller helped discover the forgotten poor. In the Vietnam and Watergate era a spate of books uncovered governmental deception, white collar and organized crime, and a general neglect of the quality of life. In the broadcasting field CBS led the way, first with Edward R. Murrow's documentaries, and then with *Hunger in America* and *The Selling of the Pentagon*. All three networks and public television looked at the problems of drugs, crime, excessive wealth, and corruption, but for the most part, investigative journalism remained television news' biggest weakness.

Others who made strong efforts in the field of investigative reporting included syndicated columnist Jack Anderson, Denny Walsh, Robert Sherrill, Sanford Watzman, Nick Kotz, Tom Whiteside, Les Whitten, Joseph Goulden, Robert Scheer, George Reasons, and Bob Greene. The controversial Anderson won the 1972 Pulitzer Prize for his exposure of the Nixon administration's deception during the India-Pakistan war; Greene headed a special investigative team at *Newsday* that turned out several important stories, including one on Nixon's Florida connections; and Reasons led the *Los Angeles Times* group that won a Pulitzer Prize for finding corruption in that city's harbor commission. Walsh won a Pulitzer Prize for his *Life* magazine exposé on organized crime. *Life* and *Look* made a number of attempts to investigate problems in America before they fell victim to economic and management problems. Scheer edited *Ramparts,* a leftist magazine of the 1960s, which among other things exposed the CIA's infiltration of the international student movement. After writing one of the first critical books on the war, *How the U.S. Got Into Vietnam,* he became a freelance writer and later reported for the *Los Angeles Times*.

The technique of investigative reporting was also brought to the public's attention in 1976 when Don Bolles of the *Arizona Republic* was murdered in downtown Phoenix. Bolles had been pressing close to uncovering extensive land development scandals when his car was blown up. *Newsday*'s Bob Greene, declaring Bolles' death "the ultimate assault on First Amendment rights," led members of Investigative Reporters and Editors, Inc. (formed in 1975) in "working on the system that killed Bolles—an arrogant system of the mob and the political structure."

It was the largest investigative effort in history: months of work by six permanent staffers and 30 other reporters, assisted by 26 news organizations and several foundations; a compilation of 46,000 index cards boiled down from searches of documentary records, interviews, tape recordings; finally, a 100,000-word series. Twenty of the 26 news organizations ran essentially the entire report. AP, UPI, and a CBS *60 Minutes* broadcast by Morley Safer also helped the IRE to bring nationwide attention to Arizona's crime problem. In late 1977 three men were convicted of Bolles' murder, and others were sought in the conspiracy.

Despite these investigative efforts, the record showed that a number of stories were poorly covered. Blind acceptance of governmental statements led to future public cynicism when the facts of the John Kennedy and Martin Luther King, Jr. assassinations were contradicted. In the Kennedy case, by 1976 most of the public had disavowed the discredited Warren Report, believing instead that Lee Harvey Oswald had not acted alone, if indeed he had acted at all. The killing of Dr. King caused riots and later, when it was revealed that J. Edgar Hoover had conducted a personal vendetta against Dr. King, the public was doubtful that James Earl Ray was singly involved. Other stories that did not receive adequate investigation included the role of major oil companies during energy crises, white collar crime in general, the backgrounds of persons appointed to public office or regulatory commissions on all levels, bribery involving arms sales to both sides in international conflicts, and other subjects involving power and money.

THE *CHRISTIAN SCIENCE* MONITOR

The *Christian Science Monitor* established itself as one of a handful of nationally read dailies and as one of two specialized newspapers of interpretation. The other was the *Wall Street Journal*. Of the regular dailies, only the *New York Times* achieved a fully national circulation, distantly challenged by the *Washington Post* in the 1970s.

The *Monitor* was begun in 1908 by Mary Baker Eddy, founder of the Church of Christ, Scientist, in protest against the sensationalism of other dailies and their emphasis on news of crimes and disasters. It was not intended to be, and did not become, a religious propaganda organ, but rather a serious-minded afternoon daily. Since by Christian Science tenets it avoided or minimized stories involving disasters, crime, or death, it had space in which to develop Washington and foreign correspondence, significant regional stories from around the country, and features dealing with literature, music, and art. Eventually it became noted for its ability to sit back periodically and take a long-view look at major news developments.

In its first ten years the *Monitor* gained 120,000 readers under the editorship of Frederick Dixon, then was temporarily disrupted by a dispute over its management. Editor Willis J. Abbot helped to restore its prestige in the 1920s. But the *Monitor*'s outstanding editor was Erwin D. Canham, who joined the staff in 1925 and served as a Washington and foreign correspondent before becoming managing editor in 1940 and editor in 1945. Canham's voice was often raised in discussions of journalistic problems and his professional associates soon came to regard him as an influential editor of a great newspaper. Paul S. Deland and Saville R. Davis followed Canham as managing editors. In 1964 Canham went into semi-retirement and DeWitt John, a former *Monitor* foreign correspondent, was named editor to help reverse a circulation slump that had touched 185,000. The *Monitor* adopted a five-column front-page makeup, larger type, splashy art work, and more sparkling writing. Before 1970 the staff had won two national reporting Pulitzer Prizes, by Howard James and Robert Cahn, and the international award, by R. John Hughes in Tokyo. In 1970 Hughes succeeded John as editor. During the next decade the *Monitor*'s quality improved but circulation fluctuated from 260,000 to 180,000. Earl W. Froell was managing editor and Charlotte Saikowski edited a superior editorial page. Godfrey Sperling headed Washington coverage, long famed for the reporting of Richard L. Strout. Among foreign correspondents were Elizabeth Pond in Moscow, where Edmund Stevens earlier had won a Pulitzer Prize, Takashi Oka in London, Henry Hayward in Africa, and Daniel Southerland in Asia. Published in Boston, the *Monitor* also printed regional editions in New Jersey, Chicago, and Los Angeles, and an international edition in London.

Harris & Ewing   *Wall Street Journal*

National newspapers were edited by Erwin D. Canham (*left*) and Bernard Kilgore.

THE *WALL STREET* JOURNAL   The *Wall Street Journal* was a solidly edited financial daily like its New York competitor, the *Journal of Commerce,* until Bernard Kilgore became its managing editor in 1940. It had been founded in 1889 by Charles H. Dow as the voice of the Dow Jones and Company financial news service. Clarence W. Barron became owner in 1902. Circulation was at a post-depression level of 30,000 daily when Kilgore took charge. He broadened the paper's coverage to include lucidly written summaries of important national and world news and comprehensive stories interpreting trends in industry. Circulation jumped to 65,000 in 1950, hit 360,000 in 1955, then leaped past 700,000 by 1960 as the *Journal* expanded to eight printing plants across the country, connected to the New York office by electronic typesetting devices. In 1976 the circulation was 1,450,000, second only to the *New York Daily News.* The paper had expanded to 11 printing plants, using facsimile and, after 1976, domestic satellite relays to bring out four essentially similar editions.

When Kilgore died in late 1967 he was company president, with a group of former managing editors of the paper serving in key positions, including William F. Kerby, Buren H. McCormack, and Warren H. Phillips. Pulitzer Prize winner Edward R. Cony became executive editor in 1970. Editors William H. Grimes and Vermont C. Royster both won Pulitzer Prizes for editorial writing. Louis Kohlmeier, Stanley Penn, and Monroe Karmin all won Pulitzer Prizes for national reporting in the 1960s and Peter Kann won the international award in 1972. The paper had a network of domestic news bureaus, plus correspondents in London, Paris, and Hong Kong. Dow Jones launched a general weekly, the *National Observer,* in 1962 and won more than a half-million circulation but closed the paper in 1977 for lack of sufficient advertising. William Giles, Don Carter, and Henry Gemmill served as editors. The company still had its Dow Jones news service and *Barron's,* a business and financial weekly.

MAGAZINES OF OPINION AND INTERPRETATION   Some of the country's magazines became important factors in the trend toward interpretation and news specialization. There was a new element injected into the magazine world, however. The news magazines, as well as the magazines of opinion and general magazines, became important in magazine journalism's contribution to coverage of public affairs. However, by 1977 it was clear that the small circulation publications were being hurt by constant boosts in postal rates, high printing costs, and changing newsstand practices and the "slicks" were becoming dominant. Many other publications were able to concentrate on supermarket sales, further abdicating newsstand space to sex and movie magazines.

In the muckraking era, such general magazines as *Collier's, McClure's, Everybody's,* the *American,* and *Cosmopolitan* served both as entertainment media and as "people's champions," exposing industrial monopolies and political corruption and crusading for a broadening of political and economic democracy. But that phase ended by World War I and the old champions withered. *McClure's* went downhill before 1920 and flickered out in 1933; *Everybody's* died in 1930, and *Collier's* and the *American* in 1956. The *Saturday Evening Post* joined them in 1969, *Look* in 1971, and *Life* in 1972. *Cosmopolitan* remained in the 1970s general magazine field, along with *Reader's Digest* and *Ebony.* These continued to carry significant articles on public affairs. The women's magazines—*Ladies' Home Journal, McCall's,* and *Good Housekeeping*—made some contribution to current affairs coverage. But the influence of the general magazines was far less than at the turn of the century.

Most of the serious magazines that were important as sources of information and as vehicles of opinion before World War I fell by the wayside in the 1920s and 1930s. The *Century* was merged with the *Forum* and then both disappeared into *Current History*. *World's Work,* one of the best, had to combine with *Review of Reviews,* which in turn was sold to the *Literary Digest*. The *Digest,* founded in 1890 and long a highly popular reporter on American newspaper opinion and current affairs, slumped away before the onslaught of newer-type news magazines and abruptly ended its career by publishing the results of a postcard poll that predicted that Alfred M. Landon would defeat Franklin Roosevelt for the presidency in 1936 (Landon carried two states). Of the distinguished literary magazines, *Scribner's* collapsed in 1939.

HARPER'S, ATLANTIC, SATURDAY REVIEW

Harper's, once a leading literary journal, became primarily a public affairs magazine after the mid-twenties and reached its hundredth anniversary in 1950 under the editorship of contemporary historian Frederick Lewis Allen. John Fischer succeeded Allen as editor in 1953 and furthered *Harper's* position among high-grade magazines. His reading audience, he once said, was 85 percent college graduates; more than half had taken some graduate work and had traveled abroad within the calendar year surveyed. But only 6 percent read the more literary-based *Atlantic*. It was this audience that in 1965 attracted John Cowles, Jr., president of the Minneapolis Star and Tribune Company and Harvard graduate, to buy a half-interest from Harper & Row, successor to the House of Harper dating from 1817. Soon Cowles controlled all the stock. He served as chairman, Cass Canfield as vice chairman, and advertising man William S. Blair as publisher.

Willie Morris, liberal young writer who had achieved notice for his muckraking articles for the *Texas Observer,* joined the *Harper's* staff in 1963, and was Cowles' choice at the age of 32 to succeed Fischer in 1967 as *Harper's* eighth editor in 117 years. Morris built a freewheeling staff of Midge Decter, executive editor; Robert Kotlowitz, managing editor; contributing editors David Halberstam, Larry L. King, John Corry, and Marshall Frady. The magazine became unpredictable, imaginative, and a vehicle for personal journalism of social and political concern. Morris ran huge excerpts of William Styron's *The Confessions of Nat Turner* and Norman Mailer's *The Armies of the Night*. But a storm broke at *Harper's* in March 1971, when Mailer's earthy essay on the women's liberation movement, "The Prisoner of Sex," appeared in an effort to bolster declining circulation. When it was over, Cowles had made Robert Shnayerson the ninth editor of *Harper's;* most of the new staff had resigned along with author Mailer.[10] In 1977 the circulation was 300,000; Lewis H. Lapham was editor, and James A. Alcott was publisher.

Things were quieter at the 120-year-old *Atlantic*. It also had shifted toward public affairs articles, but to a lesser degree, after Edward A. Weeks replaced longtime editor Ellery Sedgwick in 1938. But the pages that once carried the contributions of Emerson, Thoreau, and Longfellow continued to present the literary great: Ernest Hemingway, Edwin O'Connor, Saul Bellow, and Lillian Hellman. Public affairs articles gained ground with the appointment in 1964 of Robert Manning as executive editor. An experienced newspaperman and Assistant Secretary of State for Public Affairs in the Kennedy and Johnson administrations. Manning became the *Atlantic*'s tenth editor-in-chief in 1966, with Michael Janeway as managing editor. Elizabeth Drew wrote the Washington commentary. In 1977 *Atlantic* had 340,000 circulation and Janeway had become executive editor. Louise Desaulniers was managing editor.

H.L. Mencken's *American Mercury* was a bright new star of the magazine world in 1924, challenging American complacency, shocking solid citizens, and delighting the young rebels who already had enjoyed the work of Mencken and George Jean

Nathan in *Smart Set* since 1914. But *American Mercury* declined after Mencken and his associates let it pass into other hands in 1933.

Another newcomer of 1924 was the *Saturday Review of Literature,* founded by Henry Seidel Canby (who also was first editor-in-chief of the Book-of-the-Month Club). After Norman Cousins became editor in 1942, the *Saturday Review* (its title was shortened in 1952) expanded its interests beyond literature to include music, science, education, communications, and travel. With circulation mounting to 265,000, the magazine put its business affairs in the hands of the *McCall's* publishing corporation in 1961. Cousins advocated restraint in circulation seeking, yet *SR* had 615,000 by 1970. Ownership changed in 1971 to Nicolas H. Charney and John J. Veronis, who moved the magazine to San Francisco and transformed it into four rotating weeklies. Cousins quit, but two years later he reacquired ownership when the new owners went bankrupt. In 1977 *Saturday Review,* with 520,000 circulation, was sold to a group headed by Carll Tucker, a 25-year-old writer. Cousins remained as editor.

THE LIBERAL LEFT AND RELIGION   Among the struggling magazines of opinion operating at the liberal left, the *Nation* (founded in 1865) and the *New Republic* (founded in 1914) survived into the 1970s. Godkin's *Nation* was owned by the Villard family from 1881 to 1934 and followed Oswald Garrison Villard's liberal, pacifist course. Freda Kirchwey became editor in 1937, and Carey McWilliams in 1955, as the magazine passed through financial crises and intrastaff dissensions over policy toward the Soviet Union. A vigorous liberalism prevailed and by the mid-1960s the *Nation* made perhaps the most passionate attacks on the intensified war in Vietnam. McWilliams and Washington correspondent Robert Sherrill were writers of columns of incisive, fact-supported editorials that accompanied the magazine's articles and sections on books and the arts. Advertising was meager and the unreported circulation was scant, perhaps 25,000. McWilliams retired in 1976 and Blair Clark became editor.

The *New Republic,* founded with money from the Willard D. Straight family in 1914, exerted influence during the Wilsonian era with the writings of editor Herbert Croly and Walter Lippmann. It again had force in the 1930s under editor Bruce Bliven. When Michael Straight took over its direction in 1946 he appointed Henry A. Wallace editor. Circulation touched 100,000, but Wallace's involvement in the ultra-liberal Progressive Party as its 1948 presidential candidate brought his resignation. Sales slumped but were restored after 1956 by editor Gilbert A. Harrison. One bright feature was a column of hard-hitting comment from Washington begun in 1943 and signed merely "TRB," which eventually was identified as the moonlighting activity of Richard L. Strout, mild-mannered *Christian Science Monitor* staff writer. But circulation of the *New Republic* fell to 80,000 by 1977.

Not as fortunate was the *Reporter,* launched in 1949 by Max Ascoli as a fortnightly. It won widespread praise from its liberal and academic audience for its high-grade research articles and sharply pointed opinion pieces, but audience enthusiasm waned when Ascoli supported the escalated war in Vietnam. Despite 200,000 circulation, the disappointed Ascoli sold out in 1968 to *Harper's,* which discontinued it. Douglass Cater had been its star Washington correspondent.

Other opinion magazines with smaller circulations were publishing in the 1960s and 1970s. The *Progressive,* founded in 1909 by the La Follette family in Wisconsin, continued its excellent work under the editorship of Morris H. Rubin. The *New Leader,* socialist but strongly anticommunist in its origins, appeared in 1924 as a tabloid and adopted magazine format in 1950. Samuel M. (Sol) Levitas made it a stronghold of intellectual thought and writing from 1930 until his death in 1961. The

Commonweal, founded in 1924 by a group of Catholics but not connected with the church, won wide respect under the editorship of Edward Skillin. Another leading religious spokesman was the *Christian Century,* a nondenominational Protestant organ dating from 1884 that was given stature by editor Charles Clayton Morrison between 1908 and 1947. His successors were Dr. Paul Hutchison and Harold E. Fey. A rebellious weekly newspaper owned and edited by Catholic laymen made its appearance in Kansas City in 1964; edited by Robert Hoyt until he was forced out in 1971, the *National Catholic Reporter* brought strong support to reform elements within the church, but by 1972 it had greatly lost circulation and influence. Traditional forces dominated, led by the National Catholic News Service and two chains of diocesan newspapers run by *Our Sunday Visitor* and *The Register.*[11] There were other religious publications, such as *Christianity in Crisis* and *Christianity Today,* which appeared as public interest in religion grew steadily during the 1960s, but unfortunately they received little subscriber support and like most other magazines were imperiled by spiraling printing costs of inflation years. Pursuing an unsteady course was a muckraking San Francisco monthly, *Ramparts,* which achieved distinction by exposing CIA incursions into educational and international enterprises. Founded in 1962 as a Catholic journal by wealthy Edward Keating, *Ramparts* nearly died in 1967 when editor Warren Hinckle and his staff supporters ousted publisher Keating and plunged the magazine into bankruptcy. Robert Scheer of the New Left movement replaced Hinckle in 1969 and revived the 250,000-circulation journal. Hinckle went to New York and helped found the scandal-seeking *Scanlan's Monthly* in 1970. Given a better chance to prosper was the *Washington Monthly,* a well-edited muckraking entry of 1969 edited by Charles Peters, who won a national award for uncovering Army intelligence units' surveillance of U.S. civilians. In 1977 former anti-war leader David Dellinger and others started a bi-weekly current events magazine, *Seven Days,* which featured "activist" articles and alternative news sources.

BUCKLEY'S *NATIONAL REVIEW*

The strongest and most intelligent voice of the far right in American political opinion was that of the *National Review.* Founded in 1955 by William F. Buckley, Jr., it had 32,000 readers and an $860,000 deficit by 1960. Buckley and the leaders of political conservatism persisted and by 1977 circulation was 110,000. Election of his brother James, Conservative party candidate, to a United States Senate seat for New York in 1970 stimulated the Buckley family and its publishing enterprise. The editor's wife, Priscilla, was managing editor. Other key staff editors included James Burnham and Russell Kirk. James Jackson Kilpatrick and Ralph de Toledano were contributing editors. Also reaching the American right was *The Alternative,* edited in Bloomington, Indiana by R. Emmett Tyrrell, Jr., who started it as a campus paper in 1966 and began nationwide distribution in 1970. William Buckley, Irving Kristol, Sidney Hook, and Senator Daniel Patrick Moynihan were among an impressive list of article and review contributors. The 1977 circulation was 15,000.

CITY MAGAZINES: NEW YORK

The most spectacular magazine success of the 1960s was that of *New York.* More than a typical city magazine such as those that appeared in other metropolitan centers, *New York* was a continuation of the magazine supplement of the *Herald Tribune.* Editor Clay Felker had developed a style there, printing such "new journalism" writers as Tom Wolfe, Jimmy Breslin, and Peter Maas. In 1967 Felker obtained the right to the name and recruited enough support to launch the magazine in April 1968. He aimed it at the young city dwellers and was rewarded with some 150,000 readers within a year, including a 25,000 newsstand sale that exceeded that of the proud *New Yorker.* His business associate was publisher George Hirsch. Wolfe, Breslin, and Maas continued as contributing editors, along with Judith Crist and George J.W. Goodman ("Adam Smith"). Star writer was Gloria Steinem, whose articles had appeared in other magazines. *New York* did some muckraking, more often carried articles, departments, and tips to better living that served its city audience. It also interested out-of-towners, upping circulation to 375,000.

Felker moved on to assume editorial control of *Village Voice* and then created the splashy *New West,* copying the cover and internal design of *New York.* His empire collapsed in early 1977, however, when Australian press lord Rupert Murdoch outbid Katharine Graham of the *Washington Post* and gained control of three publications by paying $9 million to Felker's fellow stockholders. Murdoch earlier had bought the *New York Post* for $31 million. At this point, he owned more than 80 papers worldwide. James Brady, former editor and publisher of *Harper's Bazaar,* was named editor of *New York,* then was moved to the *Post* executive staff when Murdoch named Joe Armstrong editor-in-chief of *New York* and *New West* and John Berendt of *Esquire*'s staff as editor of *New York. New West* reached 315,000 circulation. Meanwhile political reporter Richard Reeves and other staffers at the three publications resigned and the fate of the New York Magazine Company's valuable holdings was left unclear.

Among other city magazines—some of which resembled Chamber of Commerce sheets—*Philadelphia* magazine twice was honored with National Magazine Awards for its tough reporting. In 1970 the magazine exposed a scandal in the Pearl S. Buck Foundation, and in 1972 it examined the management of the Delaware Port Authority, a case not covered by other media. *Los Angeles* magazine gained attention for its lifestyle coverage and tremendous advertising volume.

ESQUIRE: THE NEW JOURNALISTS

It was in the early 1960s that the term "new journalism" again came into use. Used during the days of Pulitzer and Hearst, it referred to a fresh approach to news gathering.[12] Then in the age of disillusionment, writers like Tom Wolfe, Jimmy Breslin, Gay Talese, Truman Capote, and Norman Mailer began to experiment with what later was called new nonfiction reportage. This took on different forms, but generally it meant using perception and interviewing techniques to obtain a view of a happening from inside the source, instead of relying on the standard information gathering, stock question approach. It meant focusing on writing style and on the quality of description.

The bulk of the so-called New Journalists were newspaper reporters who spent much of their spare time and a good deal of company time trying to sell articles to magazines like *Esquire, New York,* and the *New Yorker.* Wolfe had worked for the *Washington Post* before joining the *New York Herald Tribune* staff, where Breslin already was a newsroom curiosity. Talese wrote for the *New York Times.* It was natural they would approach *Esquire* with their off-beat portraits of people and life styles. For years Arnold Gingrich, who founded the magazine in 1933, had been running the top bylines in American writing, while at the same time dropping away from his habit of filling pages with sexy material. Hemingway, Faulkner, and Steinbeck had preceded the New Journalists. Harold T.P. Hayes and Don Erickson were top editors in the 1960s and Garry Willis and Robert Sherrill were among the contributing editors. *Esquire*'s 1977 circulation was 1,080,000, but its advertising had slumped, and the magazine went up for sale. The New Journalist story came full circle when Clay Felker and graphics designer Milton Glaser, of *New York,* purchased *Esquire* with financial backing from the Harmsworth family. Felker promised to bring other *New York* staffers to *Esquire,* make it a high-level fortnightly, and restore its literary position in New Journalist circles.

Using sights, sounds, and inner thoughts, the New Journalists tackled a wide variety of subjects with their individual styles. In the June 1966 *Atlantic,* writer Dan Wakefield credited Wolfe's *The Kandy-Kolored Tangerine-Flake Streamline Baby* and Capote's *In Cold Blood* with causing the literary world to consider New Journalism as a serious art form. Dozens of articles and several books appeared on the subject but no single definition was agreed on.[13] But whether New Journalism was merely a concentrated use of old feature writing techniques or a genuine breakthrough in gaining "the truth," these journalists made a mark. As early as 1952 Lillian Ross of the *New Yorker* contributed *The Picture,* a factual report of a movie company done in novel form. Later Breslin's looks at the little people were found in *The World of Jimmy Breslin* (1968), Mailer poured out his experiences on a march against the Pentagon in his *Armies of the Night* (1968), Wolfe described the age of drugs in his *Electric Kool-Aid Acid Test* (1969), and Talese tattled on his former bosses at the *Times* with marvelous detail in his *The Kingdom and the Power* (1969).

While examples of new nonfiction reportage appeared in various magazines and books, this writing movement did not spread to newspapers. Of the major writers, only Breslin continued to turn out newspaper columns while doing other forms of writing. Most editors frowned on New Journalism techniques and mistakenly linked them with "advocacy" or "activist" reporting. In addition to this confusion, another group claimed it had the answer to reporting problems, those advocating the use of social science survey techniques in reporting. Called "precision journalists," they learned from the example of Philip Meyer, who covered Washington for the Knight newspapers and authored the book *Precision Journalism.* Of note was his study, *Return to 12th Street,* where a reporting team examined the Detroit riot of 1967 through interviews with hundreds of black residents. Haynes Johnson and a *Washington Post* team used similar tactics in covering national politics. The object was to gather news data that could be used to interpret trends or describe conditions under which people were living.

UNDERGROUND AND ALTERNATIVE JOURNALISM

The roots of the "underground press" movement that swelled to prominence in the mid-1960s can be found in the words of all the radicals of American journalism, starting with James Franklin and including more recently the radical *Guardian* founded in New York City in 1948 and *I.F. Stone's Weekly.* The inspiration for the movement came from men like Allan Ginsberg, Bob Dylan, Jack Kerouac, Lenny Bruce, and Norman Mailer. The immediate stimuli were the four-letter word movement, the sex revolution, the generation and credibility gaps that created the anti-Establishment era, and, above all, the bitter antiwar protest typified by the March on the Pentagon.

Underground papers were printed cheaply by offset, free-swinging in style and content, uninhibited in graphic design, unrestricted in viewpoint, and in many cases, also unprofitable. They reflected a rebellion not only against the national Establishment but also against its conventional mass media. The best of the underground papers did a capable job of criticizing both and of breathing new life into the dead-center American social and political scene of the 1960s. By 1977 much of the spark had left the movement.

One historian of the underground papers, Robert Glessing, listed 457 titles of papers in his 1970 book[14] and commented that they were coming and going almost too rapidly to list. Included in his total were 55 military papers and campus, black, and Chicano publications. He estimated there were 3,000 underground high school papers.

First of the underground papers was *Village Voice,* a sensational weekly when it was founded in Greenwich Village in 1955. Its creators were Daniel Wolf, a freelance writer who became editor; Edward Fancher, a psychologist who became publisher; and novelist Norman Mailer. Its political line was anti-Establishment Democrat, it exhibited the Village interest in books and the arts, and its great coup was to break the four-letter word barrier. It started cartoonist Jules Feiffer on his way, helped Jack Newfield upward, and ran contributions from most of the writers who also appeared in the "new journalism" columns of *Esquire, New York,* and *Harper's.* By 1977 it was a fat 48 pages, with top "underground" circulation of 150,000.

Most successful of the really radical underground publishers of the 1960s was former machinist Art Kunkin, who used $15 to start his *Los Angeles Free Press* in 1964. By 1970 his estimated circulation was 95,000 and Kunkin had not missed a week with his antipolice cartoons, his swinging classified ads, and his put-downs of politicians and society leaders. His paper gained additional attention through serious comment on both national and local issues, however startling the language. A four-year battle between Kunkin and the Los Angeles police over his right to a press pass ended in March 1971 when the U.S. Supreme Court refused to hear the *Free Press's* appeal of an appellate court decision holding that the weekly paper did not automatically qualify for a press pass under the First Amendment. In New York a media council granted press passes to underground papers, but Los Angeles police were adamant about Kunkin, who had published a list of names of narcotics undercover agents in one defiant episode. He lost financial control of the paper late in 1971 and became a free-lance writer and journalism professor.

Best known and most successful of campus-related papers was the *Berkeley Barb,* born in the summer of 1965 out of passionate dislike for the University of California administration and the excitement of the Berkeley "free speech" movement. Its founder, Max Scherr, was in his fifties but still in touch with the alienated people of the streets. The *Barb* produced major Bay area exposés, led the disruptive student protests that split the campus apart, advanced to the sex revolution's frontiers, and grew fat on profits from suggestive classified ads and circulation. In 1969 Scherr and some of his staff split, with the dissidents producing the *Tribe.* The resulting controversies diminished the influence of the *Barb.*

There were other important underground papers of the mid-1960s: Detroit's *Fifth Estate* of 1965, the *Washington Free Press* of 1966, and three products of the climactic year of 1967, *Seed* in Chicago, *Kaleidoscope* in Milwaukee, and *Distant Drummer* in Philadelphia. Praised for their graphic effects were Boston's *Avatar* of 1967 and the *San Francisco Oracle,* a 1966 sensation for its psychedelic effect. Closely connected to rock music were John Bryan's *Open City* of 1967–69 in Los Angeles and San Francisco's later *Rolling Stone.* Breaking down the barriers the *Village Voice* had not tested in New York City were Paul Krassner's *Realist,* founded in 1958, and *East Village Other,* a 1965 protest journal with innovative art forms that grew in influence.

New York's radical political paper, the *Guardian,* became underground in outlook by 1970. The dismal wind-down of the Vietnam War proved I.F. Stone and his *Weekly* to have been right as well as cantankerous. Joining them in the "alternative journalism" category as journals of tough-minded criticism in the 1960s were the *Bay Guardian, Cervi's Rocky Mountain Journal,* and the *Texas Observer.* Each took out after the established press in its area, as well as the political and social establishments, in the best tradition of crusading journalism. The *Bay Guardian*'s editor, Bruce Brugmann, ended up suing the San Francisco dailies for abridging freedom of the press through their joint publishing agreement and won awards for his paper's reporting.

Behind the underground press revolution were its press associations. One, the Liberation News Service, was founded in 1967 during the march on Washington by two graduate students who had been editors of their college papers, Ray Mungo and Marshall Bloom. The Underground Press Syndicate, organized in 1966 and developed by Tom Forcade, became a trade association clearing house and advertising representative for the papers. Forcade later argued for and won the right to cover Congress.

While a number of underground and alternative publications either died or slipped in influence in the 1970s, one early leader became a huge financial success—*Rolling Stone*. Jann Wenner was 21 when his first issue rolled off the presses in 1967, and 10 years later he headed a $10-million-a-year enterprise with circulation approaching 500,000. *Rolling Stone* contributors ranged from the sophisticated Tom Wolfe to the eccentric Hunter Thompson, the proponent of "Gonzo" journalism. By moving his headquarters from San Francisco to New York, Wenner confirmed *Rolling Stone*'s place in the Establishment world. The main focus remained music, although tough stands had been taken during the Vietnam War and political and social commentary continued to be part of the attractive package.

Of the many women's magazines—traditional and feminist—that were born in the 1960s and 1970s, the most successful and influential was *Ms.*, edited by Gloria Steinem. Letty Pogrebin, Patricia Carbine, and a dozen other active writers assisted with the editing chores in this unusually democratic group effort. *Ms.* not only attacked the white male Establishment but also offered a wide range of views on financial, sexual, psychological, and family matters. Its 1977 circulation of 500,000 included a number of males, and it undoubtedly had an effect on many other males in the homes it reached.

ROSS
AND THE *NEW YORKER*

Possibly the most distinctive of American magazines arrived in 1925 when Harold Ross began publication of his *New Yorker*. Ross was editor of the *Stars and Stripes* in World War I days and met Franklin P. Adams and Alexander Woollcott on that distinguished staff. In New York in 1925 they helped him get his magazine venture under way, with the financial backing of Raoul Fleischmann. The magazine, Ross said, would be a humorous one, reflecting metropolitan life and keeping up with the affairs of the day with a gay and satirical vein that would mark it as not "for the old lady in Dubuque." Ross was a demanding, irascible editor who hired and fired about 100 staff members in the first struggling year and a half before he began to find his stars: E.B. White, conductor of "Talk of the Town"; Rea Irvin, art editor who drew Eustace Tilley, the supercilious dandy who is the *New Yorker*'s trademark; writers James Thurber, Ogden Nash, Wolcott Gibbs, S.J. Perelman, A.J. Liebling, Frank Sullivan; artists Peter Arno, Helen Hokinson, Otto Soglow, Charles Addams, and a host of others who contributed the famous *New Yorker* cartoons. But the *New Yorker* was more than cartoons, whimsy, and curiously plotless fiction; it had its penetrating "Profiles," its "Reporter at Large," and other incisive commentaries on public affairs. When Ross died in 1951, his magazine was a solid success, both in circulation and in advertising, and under a new editor, William Shawn, it continued its gains. There was some criticism as bylines inevitably changed (*Time* reported in 1960 that Shawn's *New Yorker* had 97 subscribers in Dubuque, including several old ladies). But in 1977 there were 490,000 subscribers and substantial advertising profits, as well as such newer talent as Washington correspondent Richard Rovere, writer John Updike, public affairs reporters Calvin Trillin and Jonathan Schell, columnist Elizabeth Drew, and critics Penelope Gilliatt and Michael Arlen.

AN ERA ENDS AT THE *POST*   Editing his magazine for the old lady in Dubuque, on the other hand, was George Horace Lorimer of the *Saturday Evening Post*. The solid success of that Cyrus H.K. Curtis enterprise enabled Lorimer to publish the fiction of the leading American writers of the first third of the twentieth century. With the fiction went inspirational biographies, articles stressing the material success of American business, and factual reporting pieces on a variety of current events. The *Post* became the reflection of a middle-of-the-road America, and its influence was spread to all corners of the country. After Lorimer's retirement in 1937 the *Post* had a shakedown, and under the editorship of Ben Hibbs its appearance and contents were modernized and strengthened. By 1961, when Hibbs passed the editorship to Robert Fuoss, the *Post* had 6.5 million circulation. But it was caught in the same downswing of advertising that had caused the deaths of *Collier's* and other general magazines in the era of television, and Fuoss instituted makeup and content changes that would have left Lorimer speechless. Fuoss was replaced by his assistant, Robert Sherrod, when the *Post*'s $4 million loss in 1961 escalated into a $19 million loss by 1962. The *Post* moved to New York late in that same year and Clay Blair became editor. Muckraking tactics and careless editing lost a major libel suit and Blair was dismissed in late 1964 as the two-year loss totaled $17.5 million. William Emerson was named editor and Otto Friedrich managing editor. With the Curtis Publishing Company's business affairs incredibly mishandled by opportunistic businessmen, and $25 million in losses over four years, the *Post* became a biweekly and then ceased publishing in January 1969. It was the last of its kind.*

WALLACE'S *READER'S DIGEST*   Very likely contributing to the demise of the quality magazines was the spectacular success of the *Reader's Digest,* which began in 1922 to print condensed versions of articles of current interest and entertainment value that had appeared in other magazines. The brainchild of DeWitt Wallace and his wife, Lila Acheson Wallace, the *Reader's Digest* slowly won readers during the 1920s, and then mushroomed to a one-million circulation by 1935. The pocket-size style of the magazine, its staff's keen judgment of popular tastes, and skillful editing for condensation continued to make it a national best seller as circulation reached 3 million in 1938, 5 million in 1942, and 9 million in 1946. Wallace now began to develop his own articles, partly because some magazines began to refuse him reprint rights and partly to support his personal outlook on life. Gradually during the 1940s, the magazine, which supposedly was an impartial digest of material in other publications, began to acquire a noticeable and conservative point of view of its own. Critics complained that its "inspirational" tone was unrealistic, if not Pollyanna-like, and offered little help in meeting major national and world problems. Nevertheless the *Reader's Digest* grew in size and influence. In 1977 it had

---

*Otto Friedrich, the *Post*'s last managing editor, tells its sad story best in *Decline and Fall* (New York: Harper & Row, 1970). A revival of the *Post* as a quarterly, using its old-time flavor and material, appeared on newsstands in 1971, succeeded by a monthly in 1977.

won 18.5 million circulation in the United States and an additional 10 or more million for foreign language editions in 60 countries. Wallace reversed an old ban and accepted advertising, beginning in 1955, further adding to the *Digest*'s profits.

HENRY LUCE, *TIME*, AND *LIFE*   The other big new name in magazine journalism was that of Henry R. Luce. He, like Wallace, became extraordinarily successful and therefore a controversial figure. His weekly newsmagazine, *Time*, became dominant in its field, while his picture magazine, *Life*, became a runaway success in circulation and advertising.

The story of Time Inc. began in March 1923. Luce and a fellow Yale man, Briton Hadden, brought out the first issue of *Time* that month. Both had been editors of the *Yale Daily News* and had worked briefly as reporters. The young men looked about them in the era of the 1920s and announced in their prospectus:

Although daily journalism has been more highly developed in the United States than in any other country in the world—

Although foreigners marvel at the excellence of our periodicals, *World's Work, Century, Literary Digest, Outlook,* and the rest—

People in America are, for the most part, poorly informed.

This is not the fault of the daily newspapers; they print all the news.

It is not the fault of the weekly "reviews"; they adequately develop and comment on the news.

To say with the facile cynic that it is the fault of the people themselves is to beg the question.

People are uninformed because no publication has adapted itself to the time which busy men are able to spend on simply keeping informed.

Time, its editors promised, would organize and departmentalize the news of the week. Its slogan became: "*Time* is written as if by one man for one man." Its coverage

Time Inc.—Halsman   *Fabian Bachrach*

Magazine founders Henry R. Luce (*left*) of *Time* and Harold Ross, the *New Yorker*.

of national affairs, foreign news, science, religion, business, education, and other areas was to be written not for people who had expert knowledge of each of the fields, but for *Time*'s "busy man." The editors developed the use of the narrative story in telling the news and injected strong elements of human interest. To accumulate myriads of facts that could be woven into each story, *Time* developed an extensive research and library staff as well as a good-sized news-gathering organization of its own to supplement press association services.

Hadden died in 1929, after seeing *Time* reach a circulation of 200,000, and Luce went on alone. A "March of Time" radio program was begun in 1931 and its motion picture version in 1935. *Fortune,* Luce's lavish magazine for businessmen selling at a dollar a copy, was successful even in the first depression year of 1930. *Life,* hitting the newsstands in 1936, caught the interest of a photography-conscious people and had customers fighting for copies. *Sports Illustrated,* less of a success, was added in 1954. Time Inc. moved to Rockefeller Center in 1938, opened its own 48-story Time & Life building there in 1960, and counted a record-breaking $270 million annual gross. *Time* claimed 3 million circulation for its domestic, Canadian, and three overseas editions. *Life* reached 7 million at the start of 1962. Luce retired as editor-in-chief in 1964 in favor of Hedley W. Donovan, and died in 1967.

Five years later *Life* itself died. The broad approach of television siphoned off both advertisers and readers, while other advertisers began to favor small specialized magazines. *Life*'s brand of photojournalism was no longer appreciated. Circulation was allowed to drop from 8.5 million in 1970 to 5.5 million, but the rate of renewal was not enough. With tears and many a fond remembrance, *Life* staffers headed for other jobs in the media world.[15] By 1977 the empire's circulations were *Time,* 4,365,000; *Fortune,* 625,000; *Sports Illustrated* 2,300,000; and *People,* a gossipy weekly started in 1974, 2,100,000. Donovan remained at the helm and Henry Grun-

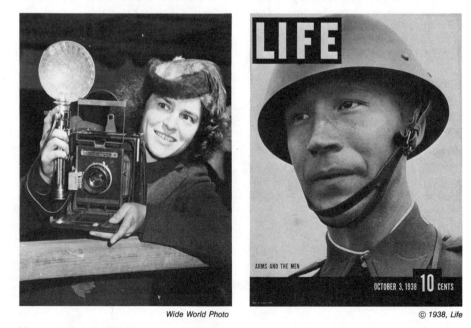

Wide World Photo   © 1938, Life

Margaret Bourke-White captured this and many other *Life* cover shots.

wald was *Time*'s managing editor in charge of ten domestic bureaus and 32 foreign correspondents.

Life was the pioneer of magazine photojournalism in the United States. Its first star reporters in 1936 were Margaret Bourke-White, Alfred Eisenstaedt, Peter Stackpole, and Thomas McAvoy. Wilson Hicks came from the Associated Press within three months to be picture editor, then executive editor. He built a staff of 40 within three years and directed it until 1950. Some of *Life*'s noted photojournalists were Gjon Mili, W. Eugene Smith, Robert Capa, Carl Mydans, David Douglas Duncan, and Gordon Parks. *Life*'s managing editors were John Shaw Billings, Edward K. Thompson, George Hunt, and Ralph Graves.

There were many things about *Time* that aroused criticism. Luce and his editors made no pretense of sticking to the usual concepts of journalistic objectivity, which they considered mythical. Nor did *Time* want to be called impartial, it said; rather, "fairness" was *Time*'s goal. In a historic essay published on its twenty-fifth anniversary *Time* said: "What's the difference between impartiality and fairness? The responsible journalist is 'partial' to that interpretation of the facts which seems to him to fit things as they are. He is fair in not twisting the facts to support his view, in not suppressing the facts that support a different view."[16]

Some critics felt, however, that *Time* sometimes was not fair to its readers since it presented opinion and editorial hypothesis intermingled with the straight news. Later *Newsweek* received the same rebukes. The critics disliked the use of the narrative and human interest techniques. Still, *Time* had widespread influence and it served many readers by summarizing day-by-day news in its weekly digests. Particularly, its specialized departments brought news of science, medicine, religion, business, education, art, radio, the press, and other areas to many who never before had followed happenings in such diverse fields of interest. Its "Essays," begun in the mid-1960s, further enhanced the magazine's appeal for serious readers and its 1976 special Bicentennial editions were outstanding contributions. In that year Time Inc. became the first billion-dollar publishing firm, slightly ahead of the Times-Mirror Company of Los Angeles.

LOOK, THE *SMITHSONIAN*, NATIONAL GEOGRAPHIC

Life's suspension in 1972 had followed on the heels of the death of *Look*, its chief competitor in the world of photojournalism. *Look* was begun by Gardner Cowles in 1937. It at first adopted the rotogravure techniques of the Cowles family newspapers in Des Moines and Minneapolis, but gradually developed major articles on public affairs. A fortnightly, it reached 2 million circulation in 1945, passed 4 million in 1955, and had touched 8 million when it was suspended in 1971, another victim of inflated costs and deflated advertising revenues. Daniel D. Mich was *Look*'s longtime editor, succeeded by William B. Arthur. Arthur Rothstein came from the Farm Security Administration photojournalism group to be director of photography. Achieving distinction with their cameras were John Vachon, Phillip Harrington, and Paul Fusco. The magazine was a national leader in art direction under art directors Allen Hurlburt and William Hopkins.

With only the successful black picture magazine, *Ebony*, left, there was a void to be filled. The venerable *National Geographic*, a travelogue journal begun in 1888, shot upward in circulation as it moved into the general interest level left so short of magazines. It became a center of photojournalism progress with Robert E. Gilka as director of photography. Gilbert Grosvenor was editor of the *Geographic*, which passed the 9 million mark in circulation by 1977.

More exciting, however, was the *Smithsonian,* founded in 1970 by that Society in Washington and turned into a superb example of photojournalism by editor Edward K. Thompson, a refugee from *Life.* Within six years *Smithsonian* was fat with advertising, filled with color photography, and printing 1,575,000 copies monthly.

OTHER NEWS
MAGAZINES:
NEWSWEEK, U.S. NEWS

After *Time* bought the remains of the *Literary Digest* in 1938 its only direct competitor was *Newsweek,* founded in 1933. *Newsweek's* format was almost identical to that of *Time,* but its early editors injected less opinion into its columns. Financed by the wealth of the Astor and Harriman families and directed by Malcolm Muir after 1937, *Newsweek* grew steadily in influence. By 1961 it had 1.5 million circulation, its own New York headquarters building, two overseas editions, and a network of domestic and foreign news bureaus. That year it was sold to the *Washington Post's* publisher, Philip L. Graham, for $9 million. Graham then took control of *Newsweek* as chairman of the board but died in 1963 before his plans for the magazine could be fully developed. Katharine Meyer Graham succeeded her husband as head of the *Post* and *Newsweek.* Osborn Elliott and later Edward Kosner became editors of *Newsweek,* which by 1977 had 3 million circulation and a network of 11 United States bureaus and 20 foreign correspondents.

Devoting itself exclusively to news of national and international importance was *U.S. News & World Report,* a combination of David Lawrence's publishing ventures. Lawrence ran the *United States Daily* in Washington from 1926 to 1933, then changed it to a weekly. In 1946 he launched *World Report,* which he combined with his older journal in 1948. By 1977 the magazine had 2 million readers, a large Washington bureau, and several overseas bureaus. A British weekly of news and comment that attracted American readers was the *Economist,* an incisive interpreter of the United States scene and world affairs.

Specializing in news of business and industry was *Business Week,* founded in 1929 by the McGraw-Hill Publishing Company. Along with 30 other McGraw-Hill magazines, it was served by the McGraw-Hill World News Service. *Business Week's* circulation was 770,000.

New Times, a trendy, outspoken biweekly, appeared in 1973. Under editor George Hirsch's direction, the magazine jabbed at the Establishment, offered sharp commentaries on politics, and in general attracted top writers. The 1977 circulation was 320,000, most of it by subscription. On newsstands and in supermarkets, two feature and picture magazines, the *New York Times'* 1977 entry *US* (1977 circulation of 750,000) and Time Inc.'s *People,* competed as light alternatives to *Time, Newsweek,* or *U.S. News & World Report.*

NOTES

1. The title of a history of the tabloids: Simon M. Bessie, *Jazz Journalism* (New York: Dutton, 1938).
2. As quoted in Bessie, *Jazz Journalism,* p. 82.
3. William H. Taft, "Bernarr Macfadden: One of a Kind," *Journalism Quarterly,* XLV (Winter 1968), 631.
4. Gauvreau used this phrase as the title for a thinly fictionalized account of his editorship of the *Graphic:* Emile Gauvreau, *Hot News* (New York: Macaulay Company, 1931).
5. As quoted in Helen M. Hughes, *News and the Human Interest Story* (Chicago: University of Chicago Press, 1940), p. 235.
6. See Walter E. Schneider, "Fabulous Rise of N.Y. Daily News," *Editor & Publisher,* LXXII (June 24,

1939), 5, for an extensive account of 20 years of the paper's history. Patterson's obituaries appeared in *Editor & Publisher,* LXXIX (June 1, 1946), 9, and in *Time,* LXVII (June 3, 1946), 87.

7. Two books advocating this were Herbert Brucker's *The Changing American Newspaper* (New York: Columbia University Press, 1937) and Sidney Kobre's *Backgrounding the News* (Baltimore: Twentieth Century Press, 1939). Also, Curtis D. MacDougall wrote the first of nine editions of *Interpretative Reporting* in 1932, the pioneer textbook in the reporting field.

8. *Editor & Publisher,* August 8, 1970, p. 45.

9. In addition to numerous articles and books by McWilliams and Stone, see Leonard Downie's *The New Muckrakers* (Washington, D.C.: New Republic, 1977), which examines their work and other leading investigative reporters.

10. Stuart Little, "What Happened at Harper's," *Saturday Review,* LIV (April 10, 1971), 43.

11. Michael R. Real, "Trends and Structure and Policy in the American Catholic Press," *Journalism Quarterly,* LII (Summer 1975).

12. An early use of the term was in Matthew Arnold's attack against a plan for Irish home rule and the British journalists who supported it, found in his "Up to Easter," *Nineteenth Century* (May 1887), pp. 638–39.

13. See Tom Wolfe, "The Birth of 'The New Journalism'; Eyewitness Report by Tom Wolfe," *New York* (February 14, 1972). Also, for a breakdown of different types of New Journalism writing and discussion of leading proponents, see Everette Dennis and William Rivers, *Other Voices: The New Journalism in America* (San Francisco: Canfield, 1974).

14. The *Underground Press in America* (Bloomington, Ind.: Indiana University Press, 1970).

15. Chris Welles, "Lessons from *Life,*" *World* (February 13, 1973).

16. *Time,* LI (March 8, 1948), 66.

ANNOTATED BIBLIOGRAPHY

Books, Background History

ALLEN, FREDERICK LEWIS, *The Big Change.* New York: Harper & Row, 1952. See also Lloyd Morris, *Postscript to Yesterday.* New York: Random House, 1947; Dixon Wecter, *The Age of the Great Depression, 1929–1941,* A History of American Life, Vol. XIII. New York: Macmillan, 1948; Harvey Wish, *Contemporary America: The National Scene Since 1900.* New York: Harper & Row, 1966. Excellent social histories.

BARCK, OSCAR T., AND NELSON M. BLAKE, *Since 1900.* New York: Macmillan, 1965. See also Arthur S. Link, and William B. Catton, *American Epoch.* New York: Knopf, 1963. 20th century histories.

BEARD, CHARLES A. AND MARY R., *America in Midpassage.* New York: Macmillan, 1939. Vol. III of the *Rise of American Civilization,* surveying the 1920s and 1930s.

GOLDMAN, ERIC F., *The Crucial Decade: America, 1945–1955.* New York: Knopf, 1956. A sequel to *Rendezvous with Destiny.* See also Joseph C. Goulden, *The Best Years: 1945–50.* New York: Atheneum, 1976; Peter Joseph, *Good Times: An Oral History of America in the Nineteen Sixties.* New York: Charterhouse, 1973. From the post-war years to the changes of the 1960s.

HOFSTADTER, RICHARD, *The Age of Reform.* New York: Knopf, 1955. A study of reform leaders from Bryan to F.D.R. which won a Pulitzer Prize.

MANCHESTER, WILLIAM, *The Glory and the Dream.* Boston: Little, Brown, 1973. Narrative history, 1932–72.

MURRAY, ROBERT K., *The Harding Era.* Minneapolis: University of Minnesota Press, 1969. A detailed study of the ill-fated Harding administration.

PHILLIPS, CABELL, *From the Crash to the Blitz, 1929–1939, New York Times* Chronicle of American Life Series. New York: Macmillan, 1969. A continuation in spirit of Mark Sullivan's *Our Times* series for 1900–29, newspaper-based.

SCHLESINGER, ARTHUR M., JR., *The Age of Roosevelt.* Boston: Houghton Mifflin, 1957 ff. A multi-volume history of the New Deal years, ranking at the top.

TERKEL, STUDS, *Hard Times.* New York: Pantheon, 1970. An oral history of the Great Depression.

ANDREWS, SIR LINTON, AND H.A. TAYLOR, *Lords and Laborers of the Press*. Carbondale: Southern Illinois University Press, 1970. Presents major figures in British journalism of late 19th and 20th centuries.

AYERST, DAVID, *The Manchester Guardian: Biography of a Newspaper*. Ithaca, N.Y.: Cornell University Press, 1971. Flattering history by a former staff member.

BECKER, STEPHEN, *Marshall Field III: A Biography*. New York: Simon & Schuster, 1964. Good portrait of the founder of *PM* and the *Chicago Sun*.

BESSIE, SIMON M., *Jazz Journalism*. New York: Dutton, 1938. The best story of the tabloids, prefaced with a readable account of the rise of sensationalism.

CANHAM, ERWIN D., *Commitment to Freedom: The Story of the Christian Science Monitor*. Boston: Houghton Mifflin, 1958. By the editor of the *Monitor*.

CHAPMAN, JOHN, *Tell It to Sweeney: The Informal History of the New York Daily News*. New York: Doubleday, 1961. Light touch account.

HUGHES, HELEN M., *News and the Human Interest Story*. Chicago: University of Chicago Press, 1940. A sociological study of the feature story and sensationalism, with some discussion of the tabloid era.

MacDOUGALL, A. KENT, ed., *The Press: A Critical Look from the Inside*. Princeton, N.J.: Dow Jones Books, 1972. Reflections on the press from the columns of the *Wall Street Journal*.

MARTY, MARTIN E., JOHN G. DEEDY, JR., AND DAVID W. SILBERMAN, *The Religious Press in America*. New York: Holt, Rinehart & Winston, 1963. Protestant, Catholic, and Jewish editors combine to analyze their subject.

POUND, REGINALD, AND GEOFFREY HARMSWORTH, *Northcliffe*. London: Cassell, 1959. Based on family papers, most definitive of 15 biographies.

RUCKER, BRYCE W., ed., *Twentieth Century Reporting at Its Best*. Ames: Iowa State University Press, 1964. Good collection.

SNYDER, LOUIS L., AND RICHARD B. MORRIS, *Treasury of Great Reporting*. New York: Simon & Schuster, 1962. Excellent historical work.

TEBBEL, JOHN, *An American Dynasty*. Garden City, N.Y.: Doubleday, 1947. The story of the McCormick and Patterson newspapers, including the *New York Daily News*.

Books, Magazines

BAINBRIDGE, JOHN, *Little Wonder*. New York: Reynal & Hitchcock, 1946. A critical study of the *Reader's Digest,* which originally appeared as a *New Yorker* profile.

BAKER, CARLOS, *Ernest Hemingway: A Life Story*. New York: Scribner's, 1969. By far the best biography of Hemingway.

BUSCH, NOEL F., *Briton Hadden*. New York: Farrar, Straus & Giroux, 1949. The biography of the co-founder of *Time,* covering the magazine's early years.

CHRISTMAN, HENRY M., ed., *One Hundred Years of the "Nation."* New York: Macmillan, 1965. An anthology.

COUSINS, NORMAN, *Present Tense: An American Editor's Odyssey*. New York: McGraw-Hill, 1967. The history of the *Saturday Review* at age 25 by its editor.

ELSON, ROBERT T., *Time Inc.: The Intimate History of a Publishing Enterprise, 1923–1941*. New York: Atheneum, 1968. Successfully done first volume of a two-volume project under company auspices. Also *The World of Time, Inc.,* 1973. Covers 1941–60 period.

FORCEY, CHARLES, *The Crossroads of Liberalism*. New York: Oxford University Press, 1961. Three men who founded the *New Republic*—Croly, Weyl, and Lippmann.

FORD, JAMES L.C., *Magazines for Millions*. Carbondale: Southern Illinois University Press, 1969. An account of specialized publications.

FRIEDRICH, OTTO, *Decline and Fall*. New York: Harper & Row, 1970. About the death of the *Saturday Evening Post*. Also, Joseph C. Goulden, *The Curtis Caper*. New York: G.P. Putnam's Sons, 1965.

GINGRICH, ARNOLD, *Nothing but People: The Early Days at Esquire*. New York: Crown

Publishers, 1971. The founder's account of *Esquire's* pioneering graphics and literary strengths.

HEMINGWAY, ERNEST, *ByLine: Ernest Hemingway,* edited by William White. New York: Scribner's, 1967. His stories in papers and magazines over four decades.

KRAMER, DALE, *Ross and the New Yorker.* Garden City, N.Y.: Doubleday, 1951. See also Brendan Gill, *Here at the New Yorker.* New York: Random House, 1975, and James Thurber, *The Years with Ross.* Boston: Little, Brown, 1957.

Magazine Profiles. Evanston, Ill.: Medill School of Journalism, 1974. Studies by 12 graduate students of nearly 50 current magazines.

MANCHESTER, WILLIAM, *Disturber of the Peace.* New York: Harper & Row, 1950. Best of the biographies of H.L. Mencken, whose autobiography is titled *The Days of H.L. Mencken* (New York: Knopf, 1947). See also Carl Bode, *Mencken.* Carbondale: Southern Illinois University Press, 1969, and M.K. Singleton, *H.L. Mencken and the American Mercury Adventure.* Durham, N.C.: Duke University Press, 1962.

MOTT, FRANK LUTHER, *A History of American Magazines.* Vol. 5, *Sketches of 21 Magazines, 1905–1930.* Cambridge, Mass.: Harvard University Press, 1968. Contains index for all five volumes.

PETERSON, THEODORE, *Magazines in the Twentieth Century.* Urbana: University of Illinois Press, 1964. A gold mine of interpretation and factual detail about the magazine industry and hundreds of publications.

SWANBERG, W.A., *Luce and His Empire.* New York: Scribner's, 1972. Critical study of Luce and his influence on American life.

TEBBEL, JOHN W., *The American Magazine: A Compact History.* New York: Hawthorn, 1969. Main threads of magazine in United States social history.

———, *George Horace Lorimer and The Saturday Evening Post.* Garden City, N.Y.: Doubleday, 1948. Lorimer edited the *Post* from 1899 to 1937.

WOLSELEY, ROLAND E., *The Changing Magazine.* New York: Hastings House, 1973. Trends in readership and management, some individual profiles.

WOOD, JAMES PLAYSTED, *Magazines in the United States.* New York: Ronald Press, 1956. Social background is provided.

———, *Of Lasting Interest: The Story of the Reader's Digest.* Garden City, N.Y.: Doubleday, 1958. Friendly tone.

Books, Investigative Reporting, New Journalism, Radical and Underground Press

AARON, DANIEL, *Writers on the Left: Episodes in American Literary Communism.* New York: Harcourt Brace Jovanovich, 1961. Left-wing writers from 1912 to 1940s in *The Masses, Liberator, New Masses, Daily Worker, Partisan Review.*

CONLIN, JOSEPH R., ed., *The American Radical Press 1880–1960.* 2 vol. Westport, Conn.: Greenwood Press, 1974. 58 authors detail left-wing writing.

DENNIS, EVERETTE E. AND WILLIAM L. RIVERS, *Other Voices: The New Journalism in America.* San Francisco: Canfield, 1974. Identification of types of New Journalism and leading personalities.

DOWNIE, LEONARD, *The New Muckrakers.* Washington, D.C.: New Republic, 1977. Profiles of Stone, Woodward, Bernstein, Anderson, Hersh, McWilliams, others.

HARRISON, JOHN M. AND HARRY H. STEIN, eds., *Muckraking—Past, Present and Future.* University Park, Pa.: Pennsylvania State University Press, 1973. A smorgasbord of inquiries into muckraking, investigative reporting, advocacy journalism, the reform tradition, and sensationalism.

KRIEGHBAUM, HILLIER, *Science and the Mass Media.* New York: New York University Press, 1967. Impact of science and science reporters since Sputnik.

LEAMER, LAURENCE, *The Paper Revolutionaries: The Rise of the Underground Press.* New York: Simon & Schuster, 1972. History of the 1960s with many reproductions. See also Robert J. Glessing, *The Underground Press in America.* Bloomington: Indiana University Press, 1970.

OLSON, MCKINLEY C., ed., *J. W. Gitt's Sweet Land of Liberty*. New York: Jerome S. Ozer, 1975. The writings of the editor-publisher of *The Gazette and Daily* of York, Pennsylvania who crusaded for justice, 1915–70. A small-town I. F. Stone.

STONE, I. F., *Polemics and Prophecies 1967–1970*. New York: Random House, 1970. A collection of some of Stone's significant writings.

————, *In A Time of Torment*. New York: Vintage, 1964. Collections of writings of distinguished independent journalist.

WOLFE, TOM, *The New Journalism*. New York: Harper & Row, 1973. Defends the genre, traces the history, and reprints examples.

Books, Photojournalism

BOURKE-WHITE, MARGARET, *Portrait of Myself*. New York: Simon & Schuster, 1963. Illustrated autobiography of *Life's* great photojournalist.

BROWN, THEODORE M., *Margaret Bourke-White: Photojournalist*. Ithaca, N.Y.: Andrew Dickson Museum of Art, 1972. Biography.

CAPA, CORNELL, *Robert Capa*. New York: Grossman, 1974. A collection of Capa's photographic works.

DUNCAN, DAVID DOUGLAS, *Yankee Nomad*. New York: Holt, Rinehart & Winston, 1966. A photographic autobiography by a great photojournalist who won his spurs with *Life*. See also *I Protest!*, his 1968 collection from Vietnam.

EISENSTAEDT, ALFRED, *Witness to Our Times*. New York: Viking, 1966. Photographs over 40 years by one of *Life's* best.

FABER, JOHN, *Great Moments in News Photography*. New York: Nelson, 1960. From Mathew Brady to Robert Capa in 57 photographs.

GIDAL, TIM N., *Modern Photojournalism Origin and Evolution, 1910–1933*. New York: Macmillan, 1973. Account of photographers and editors who developed the first picture magazines in Germany between 1928–31.

SCHUNEMAN, R. SMITH, ed., *Photographic Communication*. New York: Hastings House, 1972. Trends in photojournalism as seen by its leaders.

Periodicals and Monographs

ALEXANDER, JACK, "Vox Populi," *New Yorker*, XIV (August 6–20, 1938). A profile of Captain Patterson.

ARONSON, JAMES, "A Radical Journalist in the 1950's," *Nieman Reports*, XXIX (Spring and Summer 1975), 34, 16. Two-part recollection of his 19 years with the radical *National Guardian*.

BENNION, SHERILYN COX, "*Saturday Review:* From Literature to Life." Ph.D. thesis. Syracuse, University, 1968. Reviews *SR's* history.

————, "Reform Agitation in the American Periodical Press, 1920–29," *Journalism Quarterly*, XLVIII (Winter 1971), 652. General circulation periodicals largely ignored the reform impulse, reflected public opinion.

BURD, GENE, "Urban Magazine Journalism Thrives During City Crises," *Journalism Quarterly*, L (Spring 1973), 77. Muckraking spirit reborn in 1960's urban magazines. See also Ben L. Moon, "City Magazines, Past and Present," *Journalism Quarterly*, XLVII (Winter 1970).

BURNET, ALASTAIR, "After 10 years," *The Economist*, CCLIII (Oct. 12–26, 1974), 15. Retiring editor of British weekly looks back.

DIAMOND, EDWIN, "The Mid-Life Crisis of the Newsweeklies," *New York*, IX (June 7, 1976), 51. Changes at *Time, Newsweek*. See also Merle Muller, "Why the Editor of *Newsweek* is not the Editor of *Time*, and Vice-Versa," *Esquire*, (June 3, 1973), 169.

GIBBS, WOLCOTT, "Time-Fortune-Life-Luce," *New Yorker*, XII (November 28, 1936), 20. A dissection of the Luce empire.

GOEBBEL, ALFRED R., "*The Christian Century:* Its Editorial Policy and Positions, 1908–1966," Ph.D. thesis, University of Illinois, 1967. Descriptive study.

HENNESSEE, JUDITH, "New York's Budding Beaverbrook," (MORE), V (October 1975), 6. Feature on Clay Felker before his fall.

KOPKIND, ANDREW, "The Importance of Being Izzy," *Ramparts,* XII (May 1974), 39. I. F. Stone's *Weekly* (1953–71) celebrated.

LASCH, ROBERT, "PM Post-Mortem," *Atlantic Monthly,* CLXXXII (July 1948), 44. An excellent analysis of the *PM* experiment and of the reasons for the failure.

LEAMING, DERYL RAY, "A Biography of Ben Hibbs," Ph.D. thesis, Syracuse University, 1969. The editor of the *Saturday Evening Post.*

LEAR, JOHN, "The Trouble with Science Writing," *Columbia Journalism Review,* IX (Summer 1970), 30. By the science editor of *Saturday Review.*

LITTLE, STUART, "What Happened at *Harper's,*" *Saturday Review,* LIV (April 10, 1971), 43. The dismissal of Willie Morris as editor.

McWILLIAMS, CAREY, "One Hundred Years of *The Nation,*" *Journalism Quarterly,* XLII (Spring 1965), 189. By the then-current editor.

MANAGO, B. R., "The *Saturday Evening Post* Under Ben Hibbs, 1942–1961," Ph.D. thesis, Northwestern University, 1968. Decline began in 1950s.

MARTINSON, DAVID L., "News Images of Presidential Candidates, 1920–24: A Survey of Three Major Newspapers," Ph.D. thesis, University of Minnesota, 1974. *Chicago Tribune, St. Louis Post-Dispatch,* and *New York Times.*

MURPHY, JAMES E., "The New Journalism: A Critical Perspective," *Journalism Monographs,* No. 34, May 1974. A careful attempt to define this approach to journalistic writing.

PFAFF, DANIEL W., "The Press and the Scottsboro Rape Cases, 1931–32," *Journalism History,* I (Autumn 1974), 72. Newspaper news and editorial coverage.

RANLY, DONALD P., "The Challengers: Social Pressures on the Press, 1965–75," Ph.D. thesis, University of Missouri, 1975. Exhaustive history of non-governmental pressures brought by individuals, groups, various forms of media review.

SAALBERG, HARVEY, "Don Mellett, Editor of the *Canton News,* Was Slain While Exposing Underworld," *Journalism Quarterly,* LIII (Spring 1976), 88. Details the circumstances surrounding Mellett's attack on crime and his subsequent murder.

TAFT, WILLIAM H., "Bernarr Macfadden: One of a Kind," *Journalism Quarterly,* XLV (Winter 1968), 627. Based on extensive research about the publisher.

"The Story of an Experiment," *Time,* LI (March 8, 1948), 55. *Time* evaluates itself after 25 years.

"The Twenties," articles by Cathy Covert, Garth S. Jowett, James W. Wesolowski, George E. Stevens, Robert V. Hudson, June Adamson and W. Richard Whitaker, in *Journalism History,* II (Autumn 1975).

TOBIAS, ANDREW, "The Hottest Newsweekly in Town," *New York,* VIII (April 21, 1975), 57. Depth study of McGraw-Hill's *Business Week.*

"Tracing the Roots of the New Journalism," a symposium by Warren T. Francke, Jay Jensen, Joseph M. Webb, and Frederick D. Buchstein, in *Journalism History* I (Summer 1974).

WELLES, CHRIS, "The Battle for Control of the *Daily News,*" *New York,* VIII (March 31, 1975), 50. *New York Daily News* becoming subsidiary of *Chicago Tribune;* family ties shown. Also "Lessons from *Life,*" *World* (February 13, 1973).

WHITAKER, W. RICHARD, "The Night Harding Died," *Journalism History,* I (Spring 1974), 16. Based on his "Warren G. Harding and the Press," Ph.D. thesis, Ohio University, 1972.

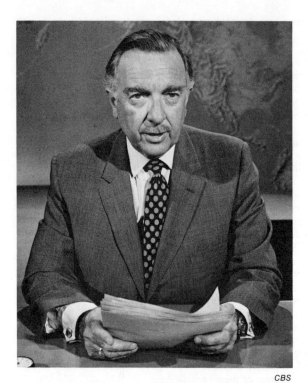

Walter Cronkite of CBS excelled in reporting the Apollo flights to the moon. Below, the NBC team of Chet Huntley and David Brinkley led in election night coverage during the 1960s.

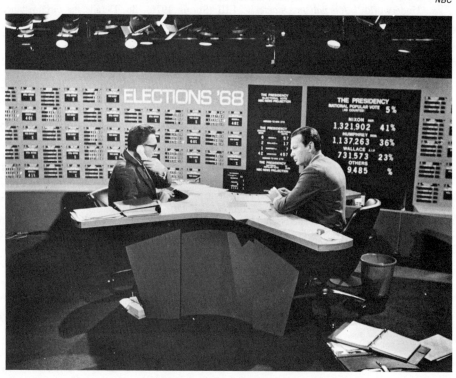

23

Radio and Television: Revolution in Communication

Radio broadcasting is an essential part of the modern press. It shares the same functions and encounters the same problems as the older agencies of mass communication. On the other hand, radio exhibits significant differences. Its ability to draw millions of citizens into close and simultaneous contact with leaders and with events of the moment gives it a reach and an influence of peculiar importance in the management of public affairs.

—Commission on Freedom of the Press

The first American radio stations to seek regular public listenership made their bows in 1920. A half century later, there were four to five times as many radio and television stations as there were daily newspapers in the United States. In the interval the scratchy-sounding crystal sets of radio's headphone days had been transformed into big-screen television whose picture tubes could give home viewers on-the-spot journalistic coverage of history in the making. The reader of the printed page, thus, had also become a listener and a viewer for new communications media competing with newspapers, magazines, and books.

Competition among the media for the attention of the mass audience involved competition to inform as well as to entertain, for radio almost from the first sought to capitalize on the intrinsic drama of news events. And inevitably the growth of broadcasting led to a sharp battle with the print media for advertising revenue. This chapter, and the ones that follow, traces the varying fortunes of the mass media in the years of vast economic and social change that followed the advent of radio.

EARLY BROADCASTING EXPERIMENTS   The name De Forest has the same relationship to the history of radio broadcasting as that of Marconi to wireless telegraphy.* While the Italian scientist was perfecting wireless transmission of messages, other inventors were seeking a way to transform the sounds of the human voice. Radio was the product of many individual efforts, but the improvement made by Dr. Lee De Forest in 1906 in the vacuum tube was essential to

*See page 284 for the story of Marconi's development of wireless.

the development of voice broadcasting. Within the year both De Forest and Reginald A. Fessenden achieved successful voice transmissions. Public attention was attracted in 1910 when De Forest broadcast Enrico Caruso's tenor voice from the stage of the Metropolitan Opera in New York. It was De Forest, too, who did the first newscasting in the United States when he broadcast the 1916 Wilson-Hughes presidential election returns from his Highbridge, New York, experimental station, using bulletins furnished by the *New York American.*

Despite these successes in voice broadcasting, there was no immediate attention paid to the possibilities of mass radio listening. Marconi and other wireless telegraphy pioneers had been interested primarily in point-to-point message communication. The government, too, had an interest in using the new process. The U.S. Navy had 20 wireless stations in operation by 1904 sending code messages, and it was interested in De Forest's success in voice transmission. The Navy had quickly become a rival of the American Marconi Company in developing what the Navy dubbed "radiotelegraph."

Primarily to prevent interference with government broadcasting, Congress enacted in 1912 a law that provided that the Department of Commerce should issue licenses to private broadcasters and assign a wavelength for commercial operators that would not conflict with government wavelengths. During World War I all use of wireless was placed under government control, and experimentation was concentrated on military uses. But by March 1, 1920, private operation of broadcasting facilities was fully restored.

THE FIRST RADIO STATIONS

The radio experimenters now found that they had an audience of some size. It was composed of amateur enthusiasts who had built their own receivers and transmitters to become wireless "hams" and of crystal set owners who could pick up broadcasts on their headphones. When Dr. Frank Conrad, a Westinghouse engineer who operated experimental station 8XK, used music rather than spoken signals to test reception of his 1919 broadcasts in Pittsburgh, he got fan mail from hundreds of radio amateurs. A local department store began advertising Westinghouse crystal sets for sale to hear "Dr. Conrad's popular broadcasts." Westinghouse decided that there was a new sales market awaiting it and applied for the first full commercial license for standard broadcasting. Its station, KDKA, began operating November 2, 1920, with a broadcast of returns from the Harding-Cox presidential election.

KDKA was not the first station on the air with news, despite claims it was. Regular daily programs first began in Detroit, where a De Forest sales organization had obtained a license for experimental station 8MK. On August 20, 1920, that station began daily operations from the *Detroit News* building, under the newspaper's sponsorship. August 31 it broadcast the results of a Michigan primary election and from that time on it carried music, talks, and news for a part of each day. The *News* obtained its full commercial license for what became station WWJ in October 1921.[1]

Radio broadcasting thus began as a means of promoting another enterprise. The *Detroit News* looked on WWJ as a service to the public that would gain goodwill and sell papers. Other newspapers soon followed in establishing stations, among them the *Kansas City Star, Milwaukee Journal, Chicago Tribune, Los Angeles Times, Louisville Courier-Journal, Atlanta Journal, Dallas News,* and *Chicago Daily News.* Department stores also built stations that would promote their names and wares.

THE FOUR "R'S"—READING, 'RITING, 'RITHMETIC AND RADIO
Miss Sara Muller, teacher at the South Haven school, L. I., one of the
smallest schoolhouses in America, instructing her class in calisthenics
with the aid of the radio set on the step.
(Fotograms.)

*Some of the
Manifold Uses
of Radio,
Wonder
Science of the
Century*

GOVERNOR
DONAHEY OF
OHIO
in the studio of The
Cleveland Plain Dealer listening to the rest
of an evening's program to which he had
earlier contributed a speech.
(Times Wide World Photos.)

PRESIDENT'S FATHER LISTENING IN ON "CAL"
Colonel John C. Coolidge at the home of a neighbor at
Plymouth, Vt., hearing over the radio the address deliv-
ered by President Coolidge a. the Associated Press
luncheon in New York.
(International.)

DR. MARX, CHANCELLOR OF GERMANY
and head of the German Democratic Party, using the
radio to expound his political principles during the
recent electoral campaign.
(Times Wide World Photos.)

AN AMBITIOUS
PROGRAM
Reginald Gouraud
of Paris perfect-
ing a radio tele-
phone transmis-
sion set which, he
claims, will be
strong enough to
permit President
Coolidge and
President Mille-
rand of France to
converse with
each other.
(Times Wide World
Photos.)

SWAYING HIS HIDEOUS HEAD IN HARMONY
WITH DULCET STRAINS
The king cobra at the Bronx Zoo, most deadly reptile
in the world, charmed by the "concord of sweet
sounds" that emanates from the loud speaker of a
radio receiving set.
(Times Wide World Photos.)

FASTER THAN ANY PLAYS THEY EVER MADE ON THE DIAMOND
is this radio music transmitted at the rate of 186,000 miles a second to the ears of the
Yankee baseball players, Urban, Roettger and Johnson, when rain caused a postponement of the game.
(Times Wide World Photos.)

Mid-Week Pictorial (1924)

AT&T, WESTINGHOUSE, AND GE

But the most important elements in the growth of national radio broadcasting were the big companies of the communications and electric manufacturing industries: American Telephone & Telegraph, Westinghouse, and General Electric. Radio's growth would mean expansion of outlets for their products and services.

The pioneer Westinghouse station, KDKA, scored many radio firsts as it pointed the way toward achieving public interest in buying radio sets. During 1921 it broadcast a series of public speeches by national figures, an on-the-spot report of a prizefight, and major league baseball games. Westinghouse also opened stations in New York, Chicago, Philadelphia, and Boston. General Electric built WGY, its powerful Schenectady, New York, station, and American Telephone & Telegraph built WEAF (now WNBC) in New York City.

THE RADIO CORPORATION OF AMERICA

More importantly, the three companies had gone together in 1919 to form the Radio Corporation of America. At government urging, stimulated by U.S. Navy officers interested in the new medium, the companies had bought up British-owned Marconi patents on radio equipment, which they pooled with their own patent rights in the new RCA. They thus brought into being the future giant of the radio industry, although at first RCA devoted itself to wireless message service.[2]

In 1922 the big companies began a competitive struggle for control of radio. American Telephone & Telegraph held two trump cards. Under the patent-pooling agreements with its competitors, AT&T held considerable power over many stations' rights to charge fees for broadcasting. And the telephone company observed that KDKA had been successful in using telephone lines to bring church and theater programs into the studio for broadcasting.

So when WEAF went on the air in August 1922, American Telephone & Telegraph announced that it would be an advertising-supported station. Within seven months it had some two dozen sponsors using air time, and the era of commercialization of radio had dawned.[3] At the same time WEAF was experimenting with use of telephone lines to air intercity broadcasts—telephone lines that AT&T now withheld from its competitors.

DAVID SARNOFF, RCA, AND NBC

But despite AT&T's advantage and its withdrawal from the RCA consortium, its rivals were not discouraged. Coming to power in RCA was David Sarnoff, son of a Russian immigrant family who had got his start as a Marconi wireless operator. Sarnoff had been an advocate of mass radio broadcasting since 1916, and long before 1923 he saw that radio could become a major industry.

And indeed it was clear that radio could become a paying proposition for many. The number of stations in the country had increased from 30 in January 1922 to 556 in March 1923. The number of receiving sets jumped from some 50,000 in 1921 to more than 600,000 in 1922. Newspapers found the story of radio's growth one of continuing interest—in June 1922, the *New York Times* was averaging 40 column inches of radio information daily.[4] The public was demonstrating avid interest in radio's newly developing stars—announcers Graham MacNamee and Milton Cross, the vocal duet of Billy Jones and Ernie Hare, and the performers on the Eveready Hour, sponsored by a radio battery company. There were objections to radio's introduction of direct advertising to pay the costs of programming, but they were to prove unavailing in the onward rush of the new medium.

Sarnoff's problem was to break the hold AT&T had won on big-time radio. The outlook appeared grim as long as RCA was hampered in accepting advertising fees or in using telephone lines for intercity programming. WEAF, after broadcasting the 1922 Chicago-Princeton football game from Stagg Field, expanded its experimental circuit to Boston, Washington, Providence, and other cities. In early 1924 the Eveready Hour bought time over a dozen stations—the first use of national radio advertising. A year later the chain headed by WEAF had 26 outlets, reaching as far west as Kansas City. RCA and General Electric set up a competitive network, headed by WJZ, RCA's New York station, and WGY, Schenectady, but it had to use telegraph wires, which proved to be inferior in transmitting voices and music. And only by straining the agreement concerning advertising could RCA accept payment of program costs by sponsors.

Then, at the moment Sarnoff was planning to create an RCA broadcasting subsidiary that could accept unrestricted advertising, the telephone company offered to withdraw from the broadcasting business. WEAF was sold to RCA in 1926. Immediately RCA, General Electric, and Westinghouse incorporated the National Broadcasting Company as an RCA subsidiary, with Merlin H. Aylesworth as president. Networks were extended coast-to-coast in 1927 as the WEAF-led chain became the Red network of NBC and the WJZ-led chain the Blue network. In 1930 a federal antitrust action forced General Electric and Westinghouse to dispose of their holdings in RCA, and the management headed by Sarnoff became supreme. RCA had acquired the Victor phonograph interests and had established the RCA-Victor manufacturing unit to produce phonographs, radio sets, and tubes. RCA Communications, Inc., operated a worldwide radiotelegraph system. And two big coast-to-coast NBC networks were under RCA control.*

CBS AND MUTUAL NETWORKS   NBC's first competition came in 1927 when rival radiomen and the Columbia Phonograph Company formed the Columbia Broadcasting System. William S. Paley, a CBS advertiser, was so delighted with radio's ability to increase sales of his company's cigars that he bought control of CBS in 1928 and began giving it the vigor and enterprise that were to bring it to equal stature with NBC. By 1934, CBS had 97 affiliated stations, to 127 for the two NBC networks. That year four independent stations, headed by WOR, New York, and WGN, the *Chicago Tribune* station, organized the Mutual Broadcasting System, which primarily served to affiliate smaller stations. Chains of a regional nature developed, such as the Yankee network in New England, the Texas and Michigan networks, and the Don Lee network on the West Coast. Networks, radio found, could produce more costly and successful programs because they could draw on the support of national advertising, and their growth made radio a more formidable competitor each year for the advertising dollar.

FEDERAL REGULATION: THE FCC   None of this development of radio would have been possible, however, had not the federal government's power been used to avert chaos on the airwaves. Secretary of Commerce Herbert Hoover had endeavored to regulate the growing number of stations, but he lacked sufficient authority under the 1912 law to prevent one station from interfering with the broadcasts of another. By early 1927, when the number of stations had

---

*Pressure by the Federal Communications Commission brought the sale of the Blue network in 1943 to Edward J. Noble, who renamed it the American Broadcasting Company in 1945.

increased to 733, listeners found stations jumping about on the broadcast band to avoid interference, which in metropolitan areas particularly had reached the point of curtailing sales of radio sets.

National radio conferences held in Washington each year after 1922 urged additional federal regulation of use of the limited number of available broadcast channels, which by common consent were recognized as being in the public domain. Radio manufacturers wanted the government to unscramble the situation. So did the National Association of Broadcasters, which had been formed in 1923. So did the listening public. The American Newspaper Publishers Association, a substantial number of whose members owned stations, also wanted the government to resolve the problem. Walter A. Strong of the *Chicago Daily News* served as chairman of a coordinating committee that sought passage of a new federal radio act. The bill was approved by Congress in February 1927.

The Radio Act of 1927 established a five-man Federal Radio Commission empowered to regulate all forms of radio communication. The federal government maintained control over all channels, with the Commission granting licenses for the use of specific channels for three-year periods. Licenses were to be granted "in the public interest, convenience, or necessity" to provide "fair, efficient, and equitable service" throughout the country.

Under this authority the Federal Radio Commission set about eliminating confusion on the broadcast band. The number of stations fell by approximately 150, and the total remained just above the 600 mark for the next ten years. The commission established a group of "clear channels" on which only one station could operate at night. Of the 57 clear channel stations in 1947, designed to give rural areas unimpeded reception of a powerful metropolitan station's programs, 55 were owned by or affiliated with the networks. They were the lucrative prizes of radio.[5]

Federal authority was broadened by passage of the Communications Act of 1934, which established the seven-man Federal Communications Commission. It took over not only authority to regulate radio broadcasting but also jurisdiction over all telecommunications. The responsibility of the license holders to operate their radio stations in the public interest was more clearly spelled out, with the commission having the power to refuse renewal of a license in cases of flagrant disregard of broadcasting responsibility. The law forbade, however, any attempt at censorship by the commission; no station could be directed to put a particular program on or off the air. The FCC rarely used its power to cancel the licenses of broadcasters; rather it resorted only to indirect pressure in carrying out its supervision of station operations. However, that pressure was to become substantial in later years.

THE CLASH
OVER RADIO NEWS

With the development of widespread network broadcasting, and the unscrambling of the airwaves by exercise of federal authority, radio had come of age. But radio's development ran head-on into the interests of other media, particularly incurring the wrath of the newspaper publishers. The major conflict involved radio's growing income taken from the nation's advertising budget. A second involved radio's broadcasting of the news.

Newspaper reaction to radio in the early days of broadcasting was mixed. Newspapers carried the radio log as a reader service and publicized radio's progress and stars. A report by the American Newspaper Publishers Association's radio committee in 1927 showed that 48 newspapers were owners of stations, that 69 sponsored programs on unowned stations, and that 97 gave news programs over the air. More than half the high-grade stations had some newspaper affiliation. The

ANPA's radio committee took the position that radio reporting of news events stimulated newspaper sales—a belief borne out fully by later experience.[6]

But others took a different view. The Associated Press tried to retain its 1924 presidential election returns for newspaper publication only and fined the Portland *Oregonian* $100 for broadcasting them. But some ten million Americans listened in on three million radio sets to hear of Calvin Coolidge's victory. By 1928, the NBC and CBS networks could reach many of the nation's eight million receiving sets. Both Republican Herbert Hoover and Democrat Alfred E. Smith took to the air, spending a million dollars on campaign talks. That year the press associations—AP, UP, and INS—supplied complete election returns on radio stations.

Stimulated by public interest in radio's coverage of the election, a few stations began to expand their news operations. In December 1928, KFAB in Lincoln, Nebraska, employed the city editor of the *Lincoln Star* to run its newscasts. Stations followed suit in other cities. The most elaborate early news effort was made by KMPC in Beverly Hills, California, which put ten reporters onto Los Angeles news runs in 1930.[7] Some newspaper publishers complained, justifiably, that radio was using public interest in newscasts as one selling point in attracting advertising.

ADVERTISING: NEWSPAPERS VERSUS RADIO   In 1929 newspaper fear of radio seemed unjustified. It was true that radio had advanced spectacularly in advertising revenue, from $4 million in 1927 to $40 million in 1929. But that same year newspapers carried a record $800 million worth of advertising, according to the U.S. Census of Manufactures.

Then came the depression, whose opening phase was recorded with the simplicity that has made *Variety* famous for its headlines: WALL ST. LAYS AN EGG. The financial collapse of October 1929 brought industrial slowdown, decreasing retail sales, growing unemployment, and by 1933, a virtual paralysis of business and banking and ten million unemployed. Newspaper advertising revenue fell 45 percent from the 1929 peak by 1933, while that for magazines was cut in half. But radio advertising revenue doubled in those depression years. It seemed logical for newspaper publishers to eye radio as a source of trouble.

Actually, however, radio was not taking much advertising away from newspapers in those early depression years. Newspapers' loudest complaints were that national advertising was being lost to radio. But out of the total amount spent by national advertisers each year in just the three major media—newspapers, magazines, radio—how much did each of the media receive? According to ANPA Bureau of Advertising estimates, newspapers got 54 percent in 1929, still received 50 percent in 1935. Magazines lost some ground, from 42 percent in 1929 to 35.5 percent in 1935. Radio increased from 4 percent to 14.5 percent. By 1939, however, the figures for this three-way split of national advertising showed a different picture: newspapers, 38 percent; magazines, 35 percent; radio, 27 percent. The publishers' fears had been justified.

Another set of figures—estimates of total expenditures for all forms of advertising by both national and local advertisers—is available for the years after 1935. These estimates, made by McCann-Erickson, Inc., advertising agency, include all types of advertising-connected expense in addition to the direct revenues of the media. Besides the major media, they include direct mail, business papers, farm papers, outdoor, and a large miscellaneous category. Table 23–1 shows the varying fortunes of newspapers, magazines, radio, and beginning in 1950, television.

Again, what hurt most in the 1930s was that among the mass media only radio

Table 23–1   Advertising in the Mass Media as a Percentage of Total Advertising Expenditures

Year	Newspapers	Magazines	Radio	Television	All Other
1935	45.2	8.3	6.5		40.0
1940	39.2	9.6	10.5		40.7
1945	32.0	12.5	14.6		40.9
1950	36.5	9.0	10.7	3.0	40.8
1955	34.0	8.0	6.1	11.2	40.7
1960	31.0	7.9	5.8	13.3	42.0
1965	29.4	7.9	5.9	16.5	41.3
1970	29.7	6.7	6.5	18.6	38.5
1975	29.9	5.2	7.0	18.6	39.3

Source: McCann-Erickson, Inc., estimates. Current estimates appear in *Advertising Age*'s final issue of the year. Originally, they appeared in the now defunct *Printers' Ink.*

was taking in more dollars; newspapers and magazines suffered heavy cuts in actual cash revenue because of declining dollar advertising volume. Some could stand the cuts; some could not. As the depression deepened, newspaper publishers took out after the well-heeled culprit, radio, with new vengeance.

THE RISE OF NETWORK RADIO NEWS   The furnishing of 1932 presidential election returns to the radio networks by the Associated Press, to forestall sale of election coverage by the United Press, precipitated action by the ANPA board of directors in December 1932. The board recommended that press associations should neither sell nor give away news in advance of its publication in the newspapers. Broadcasting of news should be confined to brief bulletins that would encourage newspaper readership. And radio logs should be treated as paid advertising. There were many qualified observers who felt radio was too well established as a news medium to be hobbled in this way.[8] But the ANPA recommendations led to a futile two-year effort to eliminate radio news competition. After a spirited fight, the 1933 AP membership meeting voted not to furnish news to the radio networks and to limit broadcasting of news by AP members to occasional 35-word bulletins. The UP and INS bowed to their newspaper clients' desires and stopped their sale of news to radio stations. The answer of the radio industry was to undertake the job of gathering news.

Columbia Broadcasting System set up the leading network news service under the direction of Paul White, former UP newsman. White staffed bureaus in New York, Washington, Chicago, Los Angeles, and London with other newspapermen, built up an extensive system of correspondents, and imported the British Exchange Telegraph agency's news report for daily CBS newscasts. NBC's rival news service was organized by A.A. Schechter, director of news and special events during the 1930s. Local stations continued to broadcast news regularly, all the while, by the simple expedient of using early editions of newspapers.[9]

THE PRESS-RADIO BUREAU   The networks found the collection of news expensive, while the publishers disliked the new competition. So in December 1933, a new solution was proposed. This was the Press-Radio Bureau, which would present two five-minute unsponsored news broadcasts daily on the networks from news supplied by the press associations. Bulletin coverage of extraordinary events would also be provided. In return, the networks would stop gathering news.

The Press-Radio Bureau began operating in March 1934 and after a year had 245 subscribers. But it was doomed from the start. Not only was it unrealistic, but it left the door open for the founding of new news-gathering agencies not bound by the agreement. Five news services jumped into the field, led by Herbert Moore's Transradio Press Service, which at its peak in 1937 served 230 radio clients and even signed up several newspapers.

Collapse of the effort to curtail news broadcasting came in 1935. The United Press and International News Service obtained releases from the Press-Radio Bureau agreement so that they could meet Transradio's competition by selling full news reports to stations. UP began a wire report especially written for broadcasting, which AP matched after it joined the race for radio clients in 1940. The Press-Radio Bureau suspended in 1940; Transradio slumped away and died in 1951. The United Press International and the Associated Press, which were serving some 3,500 American radio and television stations each by 1977, became dominant in both the newspaper and broadcast news fields.

RADIO NEWS COMES OF AGE

The networks continued to develop their own news staffs and news analysts and commentators. Hans Von Kaltenborn was the first of a long line of radio commentators. A foreign correspondent, managing editor, and associate editor of the *Brooklyn Eagle* in his first journalistic assignments, Kaltenborn started broadcasting in 1922, two years after the first stations went on the air. He became a CBS commentator in 1930, leaving to join NBC in 1940. Radio was building audiences in many ways, but coverage of major news events of the 1930s helped: President Roosevelt's "fireside chats," the presidential nominating conventions and campaigns, King Edward VIII's abdication talk delivered for worldwide shortwave broadcast. Lowell Thomas was the pioneer CBS radio newscaster in 1930, beginning a career that extended to 1976. The voices of Kaltenborn, Boake Carter, Gabriel Heatter, Edwin C. Hill, Walter Winchell, and other pioneers became familiar to millions of Americans, as did those of many regional and local radio newsmen.

The Munich crisis of 1938 and the outbreak of war in 1939 gave radio newsmen an opportunity they fully accepted. Beginning with a patched-together but impact-laden coverage of the Munich crisis, the networks expanded their news reporting and technical facilities tremendously during World War II. At the station level, newscasts won a place of prime importance.

In 1937 CBS sent a then-unknown Edward R. Murrow to London as European news chief. He hired as an assistant William L. Shirer, out of a job after the closing of Hearst's Universal Service. The pattern was to do cultural programs and human-interest stories for shortwave broadcasts that were rebroadcast by U.S. stations. Then came Hitler's invasion of Austria. Murrow hustled to Vienna and on March 12, 1938, improvised the first multiple news broadcast pickup in history. Shirer spoke from London, Murrow from Vienna, and three newspapermen CBS had hired gave their impressions from Berlin, Paris, and Rome. The pattern was thus set for radio coverage of the 20 days of crisis in September, beginning with Hitler's demand that the Czechs give him the Sudetenland and ending with the signing of the Munich Pact.

American radio listeners heard live broadcasts from 14 European cities during the 20-day Munich crisis period. The voices of Hitler, President Benes of Czechoslovakia, Chamberlain, Goebbels, Litvinoff, Mussolini, and Pope Pius XI came in first-hand. In his "Studio Nine" in New York City, Kaltenborn spent the three weeks backstopping the CBS European correspondents, analyzing the news reports, and giving hours of analysis and commentary. It was Kaltenborn who translated Hitler's fiery oratory for American listeners and who predicted the diplomatic steps that would follow given events. He was heard 85 times during the three weeks, catnapping on a cot between his stints. CBS devoted 471 broadcasts to the crisis, nearly 48 hours of air time; of these, 135 were bulletin interruptions, including 98 from European staffers. NBC's two networks logged 443 programs during 59 hours of air time.[10]

NBC's Max Jordan was a worthy competitor for Murrow and Shirer. He had a 46-minute beat on the actual text of the Munich Pact, which he broadcast from Hitler's own radio station. Like CBS, he had a backup crew of top-flight newspaper and press association correspondents to draw on. Mutual had John Steele in London and Louis Huot in Paris. Of the radio men involved in the Munich crisis coverage, CBS had the

RCA   NBC

David Sarnoff (*left*), RCA's head; H. V. Kaltenborn, pioneer radio news commentator.

ABC   CBS

Elmer Davis (*left*), ABC, and Edward R. Murrow, CBS, two great commentators.

most colorful: Kaltenborn went on analyzing the news in his clipped, high-pitched, precisely accentuated tones for another 20 years as NBC's acknowledged dean of political commentators; Murrow became television's best-known and effective commentator and director of the United States Information Agency; Shirer achieved fame as the author of *Berlin Diary* and *The Rise and Fall of the Third Reich*.

Eric Sevareid, a young journalism graduate from Minnesota, was added to Murrow's staff in the summer of 1939; he was to become a leading television commentator for CBS. When the German-Soviet pact signaled the destruction of Poland, Americans tuned in their radios to hear the sad voice of Prime Minister Chamberlain announcing Great Britain was at war. Bill Henry of CBS and Arthur Mann of Mutual gave the first front-line broadcasts; James Bowen of NBC described the scuttling of the "Graf Spee"; Shirer and William C. Kerker of NBC watched the strutting Hitler at the railroad car at Compiègne. Dunkirk, the fall of Paris, and Churchill's stirring oratory followed. But the greatest impact was made on American minds by the "This Is London" broadcasts given by Murrow beginning in August 1940. His graphic reporting of the Battle of Britain in a quiet but compelling voice and his images of a bomb-torn and burning London did much to awaken a still neutral United States to the nature of the war.

The Sunday quiet of December 7, 1941, was shattered for most Americans by radio bulletins announcing the bombing of Pearl Harbor. A record audience heard President Roosevelt's "day of infamy" address to the Congress next day. Radio newsmen used mobile units and wire recorders to report the action: Cecil Brown of CBS describing the fall of Singapore; Murrow riding a plane in the great 1943 air raid on Berlin and living to broadcast about it; George Hicks of ABC winning D-Day honors by broadcasting from a landing barge under German fire. As the war neared its end, radio brought the American people the shocking news of their president's death and solemn music reflecting the sadness of millions of mourners. The figures tell how fully radio news had come of age: in 1937, NBC had devoted 2.8 percent of its total program hours to news; in 1944, 26.4 percent.

Taking Kaltenborn's place at home on CBS was former *New York Times* staff member Elmer Davis. Davis, in his three years with CBS before becoming OWI director and in his work with ABC after the war, won high praise for his clear-eyed reporting, his dry humor and telling barbs, and his ability to cut through conflicting news reports and statements to find the truth. He and Murrow came to represent the best in interpretative broadcasting in the 1940s. Coming to the top, too, was Eric Sevareid, whose analyses from Washington won top professional awards.

RADIO ADJUSTS TO TELEVISION   Radio was now reaching its maturity. As table 23–2 shows, the number of stations on the air more than doubled between 1940 and 1950. Program quality improved, despite increasing emphasis on advertising messages and despite radio's tendency to permit advertising agencies to control the content of their sponsors' entertainment shows.[11] Then came television as the 1950s opened.

Television had written radio's obituary, many observers said. But time proved there was room for both. Network radio withered, as its established stars moved (with the advertising budgets) to network television. The value of time sales for national radio networks was $40 million in 1935, rose to a high of $133 million in 1948, then dropped back to $35 million in 1960, and stood at $60 million by 1975. But the time sales for all of radio increased virtually every year. The "music, news, and sports"

Table 23–2 Numbers of Radio and Television Stations and Sets in Use

Year	AM Stations (on the air)	FM Stations	TV Stations	Radio Sets (millions)	TV Sets
1930	612			13	
1935	605			30	
1940	814			51	
1945	943	53	9	60	(8,000)
1950	2,086	733	97	80	6
1955	2,669	552	439	115	33
1960	3,398	688	573	156	55
1965	4,009	1,270	586	228	61
1970	4,269	2,476	872	303	84
1975	4,463	3,571	962	413	120

Source: Broadcasting Yearbooks. Radios were in 96 percent of all U. S. households in 1950, 98.6 percent in 1970. Television household figures were 13 percent in 1950, 68 percent in 1955, 97 percent in 1975. Of the 425 million radio sets, 310 million were in homes, and 115 million were out of homes. Radio sets were selling at a rate of 44 million a year, television sets at 17 million. The 1977 figures show 4,497 AM stations, 3,743 FM stations, and 984 television stations.

pattern proved successful for the spreading number of smaller stations. Incessant newscasts, rather than longer and more meaningful ones, proved annoying, but radio still produced many excellent network and local news and public affairs broadcasts.

The networks, with the exception of the loosely organized Mutual, moved into television, but they also stayed in radio. American Broadcasting Company (the NBC Blue network until 1943) merged with Paramount Theatres in 1953 in a mutual defense pact against television. ABC had 1,348 radio station affiliates in 1975 in four sub-networks; CBS had 258, and NBC had 232. Mutual, serving 560 stations, went into bankruptcy in 1959 but was reorganized successfully. The number of regional radio networks increased to 81 by 1961, dropped to 53 by 1971, and then jumped to 115 by 1975.

THE BOOM IN FM RADIO   FM (frequency modulation) radio made a bid against the normal AM (amplitude modulation) radio in the 1940s, as table 23–2 shows. FM radio was looked on as the means of providing smaller towns with thousands of radio stations, since FM covers a smaller area with better reception. But only a few hundred FM stations survived in the 1950s, primarily as "better listening" stations, because transistor radio sets produced by mass methods did not tune in FM channels until the mid-1960s. But as the 1970s began, FM had become one of the fastest growing elements in American broadcasting. At the decade year of 1960 there were 688 FM stations; in 1965 there were 1,270; in 1977, the total was 3,743 including 2,873 commercial stations. There were several reasons for this mushrooming of FM broadcasting: (1) a better chance of investors for success than in the network-dominated television area and the badly overcrowded AM station fields; (2) an increased interest in cultural affairs and classical music; (3) the arrival of stereo and the high-fidelity industry, coinciding with this interest in better music; (4) various FCC decisions that helped give FM a separate identity from AM, its longtime subsidizer; (5) driving away by television and radio of some of the audience by poor programming; (6) increasing use of FM by advertisers as the quality and quantity of audience became known; (7) mushrooming sales of FM sets, from 2 million a year in 1960 to 21 million in 1968.[12] By the 1970s, combined AM-FM sets were commonplace.

Appearing on the scene with FM was facsimile broadcasting, also limited in scope of reception. Facsimile broadcasting, begun on a daily basis by KSD, St. Louis, in 1938, was viewed as a possible way of delivering printed newspapers into the home. But the innovation failed to reach mass-production use.

THE RISE OF TELEVISION

Television became the successful competitor, combining the appeals and techniques of film and radio. As early as the 1860s there were efforts to achieve the illusions of depth and movement by projecting pictures on screens. Thomas A. Edison used some of George Eastman's early Kodak film in inventing the Kinetoscope in 1889, and one of his assistants projected *The Great Train Robbery* in 1903, the first motion picture to tell a story. Sound motion pictures were developed by Warner Brothers in 1926; color arrived in 1935. Newsreels had been popular since 1897; in the 1930s documentaries, focusing on a social problem or economic issue, were filmed. By the time of the arrival of commercial television the technological processes and artistic techniques of film making were well established.

Experimental television broadcasting began in the 1920s in the United States. A picture was televised between New York and Philadelphia in 1923, the same year that physicist Vladimir Zworykin, a Russian-born American, applied for a patent on the iconoscope camera tube. Another developer of television's basic principles was San Francisco inventor Philo T. Farnsworth. WGY, the General Electric station in Schenectady, broadcast the first television drama in 1928. By 1937 there were 17 experimental stations on the air. RCA showed its wares at the 1939 New York World's Fair, putting President Franklin D. Roosevelt on television. Baseball, football, and boxing were televised in 1939, and the political conventions in 1940. Commerical broadcasting began in 1941, but World War II put a temporary halt to production of sets and equipment. By 1949, however, 108 stations were broadcasting stimulated by the development of the coaxial cable and the microwave relay, which made possible network television. Some soon failed.[13]

That year the Federal Communications Commission ordered a "freeze" in channel allocations. For three years the FCC replanned and reallocated channels, to permit more than 2,000 channel assignments to nearly 1,300 communities, including 242 channels for noncommercial educational stations. To do this, the FCC extended television broadcasting from the established VHF (very-high-frequency) channels (numbered 2 through 13) to 70 more channels called UHF (ultra-high-frequency). There were more than twice as many UHF as VHF assignments. But different equipment was needed to tune a set to the UHF and VHF stations, and the established patterns of set-making and broadcasting were VHF. By 1977 there were 517 commercial VHF stations, and only 211 commercial UHF stations. There were only 101 VHF and 155 UHF educational stations.

Even if the mechanical problems had been overcome, the FCC's hopes for thousands of television stations probably could not have been realized. For the profits were made by big-time network stations. During the freeze period, the transcontinental relay was completed, and the nation's television viewers saw the Japanese peace treaty conference in San Francisco during September 1951, as their first cross-country program. The networks grew, with stations served numbering 213 for NBC, 197 for CBS, and 183 for ABC in 1975. There were 20 regional chains. The national television networks had just $2.5 million in time sales in 1948; by 1960 the figure was $470 million, and by 1975 it had skyrocketed to $1.7 billion.

The FCC reported that in 1975 commercial television networks made profits of 18 percent before taxes. Their 15 owned-and-operated television stations each earned an average of $7 million before taxes, compared to $1 million for the typical VHF station. Some other big-city network affiliates did nearly as well. Among independent stations, a fourth of VHF stations were losers, as were half of all UHF stations. Heavy productions costs militated against successful small television stations—a factor not true in radio.

Color television was authorized by the FCC in 1953 after a false start in 1950 when the CBS noncompatible color system was given preference over the eventually adopted RCA compatible system—i.e., a system that enables either color or black-and-white sets to receive the same broadcast. The networks expanded telecasting in color, but high prices of color-receiving sets kept their use at only 600,000 in 1961. By 1976, with price declines and quality improvement, there were 55 million color sets in 77 percent of all homes with televisions.

CBS NEWS: MURROW AND CRONKITE   When Edward R. Murrow died in April of 1965, two days after his fifty-seventh birthday, Eric Sevareid said of his mentor—whose skill and imagination set future standards for news and documentary broadcasting—"He was a shooting star. We shall live in his afterglow a very long time . . . we shall not see his like again."[14]

Murrow remains the conscience of responsible broadcast journalists because of his relentless pursuit of the truth, his fondness for the English language, and his deep affection for the best in America's heritage. This, of course, includes the First Amendment guarantees to free and vigorous debate, open assemblies, independent gathering of the news, and critical commentaries about public affairs. This sophisticated man's devotion to hard work and his feeling for the common man's rights were developed by his own tireless Quaker parents who moved from their native North Carolina to the farms and logging mills of Washington when Murrow was a boy.

The 1948 political conventions brought Murrow to the television audience, but it was on November 18, 1951, that he made a full introduction of his style and personality. That first *See It Now* show featured Murrow sitting before two monitors, one showing the Golden Gate Bridge and the San Francisco skyline, and the other the Brooklyn Bridge set into New York's profile. During those 30 minutes the cameras also showed Murrow in New York and Sevareid in Washington talking about the Korean War, and Howard K. Smith in Paris during a pre-filmed telephone conversation with Murrow. Coaxial cable and microwave relays had allowed the first coast-to-coast television broadcast on September 12, when President Truman opened the Japanese Peace Treaty conference in San Francisco. Now Murrow and Fred W. Friendly, his co-producer of radio and television documentaries for the next ten years, were bringing their *Hear It Now* radio show to the new medium.

For the next seven years *See It Now* broke the trail, bringing Americans many moments of hard journalism. Murrow believed that the message was more vital than the medium, and his zeal for fine writing and carefully edited film was contagious. This was the time of live television, and he was able to transmit his sense of honesty and accuracy into the nation's living rooms. His familiar deep voice, rich with conviction, added to the impact of the shows, as did his solemn face and dignified manner.

Gradually the *See It Now* show moved from three or four brief looks at various subjects to occasional longer presentations. One milestone was achieved in late 1952 when Murrow took a large reporting and film crew to Korea for *See It Now*'s first full hour show, the highly acclaimed "Christmas in Korea." It was television's first full-length combat report and it drove home the fact that this war was stalemated.

Then in October 1953, Murrow moved into the most controversial issue of those years, McCarthyism. The tension at CBS was at a peak as Murrow and Friendly prepared the story of a young Air Force reserve officer, Milo Radulovich, who had been classified a security risk because his father and sister read "subversive" newspapers. The frequent abrasive nature of previous shows had caused problems within CBS, and this time the network refused to advertise *See It Now*. Instead Murrow and Friendly paid $1,500 of their own funds to buy a *New York Times* advertisement, while CBS felt strong pressure against the show from its own corporate advertisers.

Murrow and his cameras probed into the Dexter, Michigan, community of the Radulovichs and showed that the paper his father read was a Serbian-language one that supported Marshall Tito in Yugoslavia, five years after Tito had broken from Russian control. Murrow's final words included an offer to the Air Force for a reply and then this:

Whatever happens in this whole area of the relationship between the individual and the state, we will do ourselves; it cannot be blamed upon Malenkov, Mao Tse-tung or even our allies. It seems to us—that is, to Fred Friendly and myself—that this is a subject that should be argued about endlessly. . . .[15]

Lieutenant Radulovich was cleared of being a security risk and the Murrow-Friendly team moved deeper into the emotion of the day. Within a month they produced "An Argument in Indianapolis," which dealt with the local American Legion unit using its influence to stop a newly formed American Civil Liberties Union group from hiring a hall. CBS cameras filmed the Legion and ACLU meetings being held at different locations on the same evening, and the viewer was allowed to judge which speakers were following the dictates of the Constitution.

It also was in 1953 that Murrow began his famed interview show, *Person to Person*. Murrow's distaste for the show business aspects of television already had caused disagreements between him and CBS executives and had strained his longtime relations with CBS president Frank Stanton. But after a shaky start Murrow grew to like the more informal style where he was able to sit in the studio and discuss the lighter side of life with America's personalities.[16]

The *Person to Person* show ran through 500 guests until it ended on June 26, 1959. It was in the "top ten" in the ratings and brought many a thoughtful moment as Murrow, cigarette in hand, quietly probed and tried to make his famous guests at ease. But he reserved his loyalty for *See It Now*.

The March 9, 1954, broadcast of *See It Now* was one of the most controversial in broadcast history. Fully disgusted with the tactics employed by Senator Joseph McCarthy in charging numerous Americans with subversive activities, Murrow pulled out all stops. In his broadcast that night, while showing films of McCarthy in action, Murrow said:

As a nation we have come into our full inheritance at a tender age. We proclaim ourselves—as indeed we are—the defenders of freedom abroad, what's left of it, but we cannot defend freedom abroad by deserting it at home. The actions of the junior Senator from Wisconsin have caused alarm and dismay amongst our allies abroad and given considerable comfort to our enemies, and whose fault is that? Not really his. He didn't create this situation of fear; he merely exploited it, and rather successfully. Cassius was right: "The fault, dear Brutus, is not in our stars but in ourselves" . . . Good night, and good luck.[17]

Murrow had tried to educate the public about the difference between disloyalty and dissent. But the strain of unending work and dissatisfaction with trends in television were taking their toll. Board chairman William S. Paley decided to discontinue *See It Now*, and the last show ran on July 9, 1958.* Throughout this period Murrow had continued his nightly radio news show and often had appeared on television twice a week. He continued his earlier association with *CBS Reports*, in 1960 narrating "Harvest of Shame," which showed the plight of the migrant worker. Then in 1961, greatly disappointed about the commercial nature of television and signs that television news itself would become locked into the ratings scramble, Murrow resigned to take charge of the U.S. Information Agency. Illness forced his retirement in December 1963.

Called the "past master of innuendo, smear, snide implication, and unsupportable accusation"[18] by his enemies, Murrow had the satisfaction of hosting numerous CBS presentations in addition to the more celebrated ones and of being admired by those who realized the true potential of the television invention. Perhaps the most fitting praise came from an executive of rival NBC who after an early *See It Now* broadcast thanked Murrow for offering "a challenge, a target, and an example."[19]

Walter Cronkite, an amiable native of St. Joseph, Missouri, with the stamina of a workhorse became the leading CBS News personality in the 1960s. By the mid-1970s he was hailed as one of the most admired men in America, after having anchored dozens of CBS specials on presidential elections, the Vietnam agony, racial conflicts, assassinations, Watergate, and the many space flights.

Unlike others within CBS News, Cronkite was not one of Murrow's protégés, although Murrow had tried to hire him away from United Press during World War II and eventually did hire him in 1950. Instead of reporting from Korea as planned, Cronkite ended up earning a reputation at CBS's Washington, D.C., station, WTOP-TV. He did not present CBS executives with the outwardly intellectual image of Sevareid or Charles Collingwood but was noted for his devotion to the hard news story. Coming out of the press association tradition, Cronkite went for the bulletin lead or the exclusive interview. But over the years he also became the star of many of CBS's documentary shows, including *Eyewitness to History*, *Twentieth Century*, and *CBS Reports*, and was heard regularly on a CBS radio show.

Cronkite's straight delivery of the news, with a heavy note of seriousness, earned him the evening newscaster spot in 1962. He replaced Douglas Edwards, who had been hired in 1948 to begin a news show. It had been Edwards's fate to be pitted against the popular John Cameron Swayze's *Camel News Caravan* on NBC and later the Huntley-Brinkley team. Cronkite's job was to push CBS up in the ratings.[20]

On Labor Day 1963, Cronkite and the CBS crew, which included the reliable Sevareid in Washington, inaugurated the first 30-minute network news show. Cronkite interviewed President Kennedy at Hyannisport that morning and asked JFK about the growing war in Vietnam, where 47 Americans had been killed. A young field reporter,

---

*John Crosby, television critic for the *New York Herald Tribune*, wrote, *"See It Now . . .* is by every criterion television's most brilliant, most decorated, most imaginative, most courageous and most important program. The fact that CBS cannot afford it but can afford *Beat the Clock* is shocking." Cited by Erik Barnouw, *The Image Empire* (New York: Oxford University Press, 1970), p. 116.

Dan Rather, bluntly described a confrontation between police and blacks in the South, and the veteran Peter Kalischer was in Tokyo. During the next few years, with Cronkite serving as managing editor of the evening news show, CBS's reputation as a no-nonsense news organization grew steadily.

Cronkite suffered a personal setback before the 1964 Democratic National Convention when CBS executives replaced him with veteran Bob Trout and a young reporter named Roger Mudd. Cronkite had been the regular convention anchorman since 1952 and was the backbone of the CBS team originally put together by news chief Sig Mickelson and later Richard Salant. But the Huntley-Brinkley team had run away with the ratings. Trout and Mudd did not fare better, however, and Cronkite was given priority from there on out.

During the American involvement in Vietnam, Cronkite, like most journalists, did not seriously question the nature of the U.S. commitment until the late 1960s. In 1965 he rode in a Canberra jet that divebombed the jungle near Danang, just as he had flown in a bomber over Germany in 1943. But in 1968, after visiting Vietnam for a special on the Tet offensive, Cronkite was sufficiently convinced of the futility of the war to end his broadcast with "to say we are mired in stalemate seems the only realistic, yet unsatisfactory conclusion . . . the only rational way out . . . will be to negotiate [and] not as victors."[21] That was the turning point, and in following years the CBS coverage contained more criticism of American tactics.

The CBS team suffered the wrath of Mayor Richard Daley during the riotous 1968 Democratic National Convention, where Cronkite, watching Rather being slugged by a so-called security guard, called the guards "thugs." With typical fairness, however, he granted Daley a long interview the next day and passed up the chance to criticize Chicago's boss for the tactics used by police on journalists and innocent bystanders. Cronkite in turn was criticized for such politeness, but continually stressed the need for news credibility and insisted the cameras spoke for themselves.

While Lyndon Johnson constantly complained to Cronkite following evening news broadcasts, he had respect for Cronkite's sense of fairness. But the White House of Richard Nixon thought of CBS as a prime enemy. And although television journalists in general did a poor job of analyzing the Watergate-related events in 1972 and 1973—before the open revelations of scandal—Cronkite was credited with the best performance. One study showed that between September 14, 1972, and election day, CBS devoted twice as much air time to the Watergate story as either NBC or ABC.[22]

The tough CBS approach to news, Cronkite's superiority as a space reporter, and Sevareid's voice of reason earned CBS the top spot in the ratings. Speculation grew in the late 1970s as to Cronkite's successor, but in 1977, at age 61, he was still on top of his business. When President Carter held his unprecedented radio talk show with the public in 1977, it was Walter Cronkite who sat in the Oval Office as moderator—the same "Uncle Walter" who babysat Americans through the killing and funeral of John Kennedy, the dangerous re-entry periods of the space missions, and the anxiety of the Watergate crisis. He was counted on to man the fort.

Sevareid, the acknowledged dean of the television news analysts who had logged 38 years with CBS, including 15 political conventions, announced his retirement in 1977. Mudd had become well established as a political reporter, Fred P. Graham offered excellent reports on legal affairs, Charles Kuralt was a favorite for his "On the Road" segments, Bernard and Marvin Kalb covered the State Department, and Lesley Stahl was a leading correspondent. Dan Rather, Mike Wallace, and Morley Safer brought the documentary show *60 Minutes* into the "top 20" with their hard interviewing techniques. With that success, CBS began to experiment, as they had years before with Murrow, by starting a light *Who's Who* show where Rather, socialite Barbara Howar, and Kuralt interviewed personalities in a magazine format.

Other CBS reporters included Bob Schieffer, Bill Henry, Robert Pierpoint, Martin Agronsky, Winston Burdett, Morton Dean, Phil Jones, Michelle Clark, Sylvia Chase, Ed Rabel, Richard Threlkeld, Ed Bradley, Joe Benti, Susan Peterson, Sharon Lovejoy, Heywood Hale Broun, Renee Poussaint and Connie Chung. Harry Reasoner resigned in 1970 to join ABC; Mayra McLaughlin was CBS's first woman reporter in 1965; longtime correspondent Daniel Schorr was forced from his job in 1976 after he gave a controversial report on the CIA to the *Village Voice* and was threatened with contempt of Congress in a much-debated episode.[23] Sylvia Westerman was deputy director of news, and CBS had six women serving as producers in New York.

NBC NEWS: HUNTLEY AND BRINKLEY

For 14 long years, from the benign middle 1950s to the unrest of 1970, NBC News led the nightly ratings because of the unusual team of Chet Huntley and David Brinkley. Huntley, the deep-voiced, rough-hewn Montanan, and Brinkley, the dry, cynically whimsical reporter from Iowa, formed an unlikely match that made millions for NBC.

The Huntley-Brinkley team was conceived for the 1956 political conventions and lasted until Huntley retired in 1970. When Huntley died of cancer in 1974, Brinkley told the television audience of the many times he and his partner had been told by young persons, "I grew up with you guys." Indeed, many Americans did grow to adulthood with Huntley reading the news from New York and Brinkley adding his part from Washington, each time signing off with the somewhat silly and often imitated "Good night, David. Good night, Chet."

NBC's rise to the top of the television news business in the 1950s included John Cameron Swayze's show of 1949–56 and the successful *Today* show, begun in 1952. Two interview-talk shows, the *Tonight* show, which was started in 1954, and the *Tomorrow* show, begun in 1973, added to NBC's luster. In addition, *Weekend,* with a magazine format, joined the lineup in 1974. But the hub of the success was the attention gained by Huntley and Brinkley, whose familiar faces and voices dominated political conventions until 1968, when CBS began to gain ground.

While the industrious *Huntley/Brinkley Report* added much to America's knowledge of itself, the two men were not that close. Huntley was more conservative in outlook, a businessman by nature who retired to his $20 million Big Sky resort complex, defended himself against the protests of conservationists, and did commercials for American Airlines. His many admirers praised his warmth, courage, and strong patriotism. None the less patriotic, Brinkley on the other hand reflected more of the Washington viewpoint. As early as July 1967 he publicly criticized the American involvement in Vietnam and said the air war over North Vietnam should be stopped.[24]

Following Huntley's retirement, Brinkley temporarily found himself in an awkward "troika" arrangement with John Chancellor and Frank McGee. He separated from this to do *David Brinkley's Journal,* a nightly commentary. Chancellor emerged as the sole anchorman and McGee took over the popular *Today* show. Then in 1976 Brinkley returned to co-anchor the evening news when NBC executives decided to intensify the attack against CBS's hold on the ratings. The result was that NBC brought the numbers almost even.

A strong reporter, Chancellor joined NBC in 1950 and worked with Sander Vanocur, Edwin Newman, and McGee at national conventions before heading bureaus in Vienna, London, Moscow, Brussels, and Berlin. His only break in service came

Eric Sevareid, long a CBS commentator, and Lesley Stahl, correspondent.

John Chancellor, NBC anchor, and Marilyn Berger, White House correspondent.

Barbara Walters and Harry Reasoner became the ABC nightly co-anchors.

when he accepted Lyndon Johnson's invitation to head the Voice of America for a brief period. Chancellor went on to special assignments in 1978.

In 1976, with the nature of television news being discussed in dozens of periodicals, Chancellor offered this simple explanation of his confident performance:

What you do is say, "I got up at 10 o'clock this morning, and I worked all day, and read all the wires, and called up a lot of people. Now over there is the news. Let's look at it together. I'll be your guide."[25]

NBC fielded a strong lineup of reporters. McGee was one of the most perceptive, thoughtful persons in the business. As early as December 20, 1965, in an NBC special on the war, he concluded that if the U.S. government could not make a compelling argument why an independent South Vietnam was so vital to American national interests that "it transcends doubts about the legality and morality of the war" then the United States should withdraw.[26] Later he produced the sensitive "Same Mud, Same Blood" documentary about black and white soldiers surviving or dying together. McGee, who also covered the South for NBC during the civil rights battles and anchored the desk for 12 hours on the day of John Kennedy's assassination, himself died of cancer in April 1974, at the age of 52.

Other NBC radio and television reporters and commentators were Tom Brokaw, who covered the White House before sharing the *Today* show with Jane Pauley; Edwin Newman, the veteran who anchored many NBC specials; Joseph C. Harsch, Irving R. Levine, Elie Abel, Hugh Downs, Ray Scherer, Herbert Kaplow, Tom Pettit, Robert Goralski, Peter Hackes, Clifton Utley, Morgan Beatty, Merrill Mueller, and Garrick Utley, Also prominent were Richard Valeriani, Bob Jamieson, Ford Rowan, John Hart, David Burrington, Floyd Kalber, Don Oliver, Jack Reynolds, John Dancy, Douglas Kiker, Richard Hunt, and Frank Blair.

Among women working for NBC were Pauline Frederick, who in 1948 was the first woman to cover a political convention for a network and who stayed until 1974 as UN correspondent; Barbara Walters of *Today* show fame and expert interviewer for NBC before leaving for ABC; Marilyn Berger, appointed White House correspondent in 1976 to replace Brokaw; Catherine Mackin, high-ranking political correspondent and commentator; Aline Saarinen and Esther Tufty, both on the air early; Judy Woodruff, Linda Ellerbee, Carole Simpson, and Betty Rollins. At WNBC, New York, Melba Tolliver, Pia Lindstrom, and consumer reporter Betty Furness awaited network assignments.

NBC compiled an impressive list of documentaries since the 1950s, headed by *NBC White Paper* and the two-hour *First Tuesday*. Chemical and biological warfare, Army intelligence units spying on civilians, migrant labor problems, and the nation's pension plans were among the controversial topics covered. In early 1976 NBC cancelled an entire evening of prime time—something that would have made Edward R. Murrow happy—and offered a three-hour analysis of foreign policy problems.

ABC NEWS: REASONER AND WALTERS   The television news world awoke one morning in 1976 to discover that Barbara Jill Walters, the star of NBC's *Today* show, would be joining ABC with a five-year contract calling for $5 million. But the biggest news was that the highest paid news personality would be co-anchoring the evening news with veteran Harry Reasoner, who immediately began to pout. Cronkite at CBS and Chancellor at NBC were shocked, and critics immediately castigated ABC for its show business approach to the news.

ABC executives came to the defense, though, and pointed out Walters's long record as a writer and interviewer of leading personalities.

It was not the first time ABC had been criticized for its news tactics. The network had been playing catch-up in the ratings race since 1953, when John Daly was the first in a long line of anchormen. Daly lasted until 1960, when John Cameron Swayze had a brief stint. He was followed by Ron Cochran (1963–65), Peter Jennings (1965–68), Bob Young (1968), and Howard K. Smith and Frank Reynolds (1968–70). Smith and Reasoner began a partnership in 1970, but Smith eventually fell into a commentator's slot, leaving Reasoner alone, or so he thought.

In addition to hiring Walters in an effort to put life into the ratings, ABC began experimenting with a heavy use of feature material. The ABC system's encouragement of the so-called "happy talk" format for its local stations in the early 1970s brought strong criticism from traditionalists, who found the joking and exchanges of light comments out of line.

ABC heavily promoted the "marriage" of Walters and Reasoner, but from the beginning there was doubt whether, as one critic put it, "the mix of Manhattan moxie and Iowa wry will chemically click."[27] In addition to the evening news, Walters was scheduled to host a number of special interview shows. Her producer was Lucy Jarvis, who as the first American to receive an invitation from the People's Republic of China to film a news documentary, produced "The Forbidden City" for NBC in January 1973.

The Reasoner-Smith team had brought together two seasoned reporters. Both had worked for CBS for a number of years before moving on. Smith was known for his blunt, crisp phrases, some of which caused his bosses to cringe. Reasoner, with his soft delivery, carried a sense of authority that gave him credibility. Like Cronkite, Sevareid, Huntley, Brinkley, and Chancellor, these men were from the old school of journalism. Reasoner, in fact, was the number two man at CBS when he quit.

With less money, ABC kept pace over the years by offering as news commentators Smith, Quincy Howe of World War II fame, and Frank Reynolds. Reynolds also was one of ABC's top political reporters. Other leading correspondents on the team originally built by James C. Hagerty and later Elmer Lower and William Sheehan included Ted Koppel, Sam Donaldson, Edward P. Morgan, William H. Lawrence, John Scali, Robert Clark, White House reporter Tom Jarriel, Peter Jennings, Peter Clapper, Nancy Dickerson, one of the first women reporters, and until her death, Lisa Howard. A number of other women were involved, including Ann Compton, the first woman assigned by a network to cover the White House. Marlene Sanders, a Vietnam correspondent who became a vice president and director of documentaries, was one of the leaders in that field. In fact, Sanders had anchored the network evening news as a substitute in 1964, when a strike intervened; she later anchored the weekend news for several months in 1971.* In 1977 her main project was the prestigious *ABC Closeups* series, with Smith as the main narrator. Reasoner also had been involved with a number of those shows, as well as *ABC News Reports,* the network's principal documentary efforts outside of special reports. One of Sanders' major productions was "Women's Health: A Question of Survival" in 1976. She was a strong advocate of young women broadcasters and gave much time to that cause. ABC, like the other networks, had talented women at key network stations. Christine Lund of

---

*Dorothy Fuldheim of WEWS-TV, Cleveland, became the first woman to anchor a news show when that station hired her in 1947. In 1976, at 83, she was delivering commentary and had been on the air 29 consecutive years.

Los Angeles's KABC-TV filled in at a weekend anchor position, and John Lunder and Rose Ann Scamardella of WABC-TV's *Eyewitness News* in New York were highly visible.[28]

TELEVISION NEWS: CRITICISMS AND AUDIENCES

The emotions of the 1960s brought the first strong criticisms of television news. Southerners charged that network film crews had distorted the racial picture during the Freedom Rides; blacks and whites alike were angered by coverage of the urban riots; doves and hawks both thought the Vietnam news to be slanted; some veteran broadcasters, like Fred W. Friendly, thought their bosses sought ratings at the expense of public service; conservatives led by former Vice President Agnew thundered against the perceived "liberal bias" of the commentators and reporters covering the Nixon administration.

But in the 1970s, the criticisms began to focus on the very essence of television news, the variables that make it what it is. Edith Efron had written *The News Twisters* in 1971 as an attempt to discredit the major networks, but in 1973 media critic Edward J. Epstein published his scholarly *News From Nowhere,* which simply showed how economic and logistical factors as much as subjective judgments severely hampered the scope and quality of television news.[29] Then followed a rash of criticism in popular publications of the so-called "happy talk" format devised by ABC for its stations; the hiring of non-journalistic consultants to advise on the hiring of anchorpersons, the designing of fancy sets, and the length of story and film segments (the "top 40" concept); the overuse of "pretty faces"; the team approach where several persons sit around a table; and the extensive use of feature material in a magazine format.[30]

Leading newscasters like Cronkite and Brinkley readily admitted the weaknesses of the existing system, but Cronkite for one severely criticized the "pretty faces" on local television shows and pushed for a one-hour evening news show in an effort to avoid some of the superficiality. That extra half-hour would have come from local station time, however, and plans for one-hour news shows were shelved by all three networks in 1977. To the consternation of traditionalists, the major gains in ratings were made by those local stations that pushed ahead with the lighter approach to news, where specialists lined up to report on health tips, consumer news, and legal aid, as well as "people in the news." At the network level the major victim was the documentary of the Murrow-Friendly type.

The economic power of television was startling. So was its coverage of public events. Television had recorded massive audiences for news events since the 1950s. Some 60 million Americans saw President Eisenhower inaugurated in 1953. At least 85 million saw one of the "Great Debates" between John Kennedy and Richard Nixon in 1960. John Glenn's first manned orbital flight drew 135 million persons to the edge of their chairs in 1962. When news of President Kennedy's assassination in 1963 became known, the New York City television audience jumped from 30 percent to 70 percent and rose to 93 percent during the funeral service when for a few moments the nation fell silent.

When men first walked on the moon in 1969 and live television pictures were transmitted to earth, some 125 million Americans saw the climactic broadcast, and a satellite network carried the pictures to an eventual world audience estimated at 500 million. Satellite coverage of the 1970 World Cup matches in Mexico City brought soccer to an estimated 900 million persons. President Nixon's China trip in 1972, the Olympic tragedy in Munich that same year, the signing of the 1973 Vietnam peace accords in Paris, and other international events continued to produce giant audiences. In the United States, 130 million persons watched some part of Nixon's resignation in

Threat to UN Eases; Peking Casts Shadow

By the ASSOCIATED PRESS
New York

President Eisenhower and British Prime Minister Harold Macmillan agreed Sept. 27 to give "full support" to United Nations Secretary - General Dag Hammarskjold in his tasks. Mr. Hammarskjold has been a target of Soviet Premier Nikita S. Khrushchev.

By Joseph C. Harsch
Special Correspondent of The Christian Science Monitor
United Nations, N.Y.

The delicate composure of Indian Prime Minister Jawaharlal Nehru and the phlegmatic urbanity of British Prime Minister Harold Macmillan flowed over the United Nations scene as the General Assembly went into the second week of its extraordinary session here in New York.

Debate Winner? Voters of Nation

By Godfrey Sperling, Jr.
Chief of the Central News Bureau of The Christian Science Monitor
Chicago

The focal point of some 120,000,000 eyes, the presidential candidates squared off in the first of four unprecedented joint appearances before a vast TV audience.

The winner? The American public was the winner.

John F. Kennedy
Resolved . . .

Richard M. Nixon
Resolved . . .

Not One Slip On Banana Peel!

By Richard L. Strout
Staff Correspondent of The Christian Science Monitor
Washington

The first reception of the unprecedented Nixon-Kennedy debate in millions of homes was a gasp of surprise.

State of the Nations
Who Pays for Reform?

By William H. Stringer
Chief, Washington News Bureau, The Christian Science Monitor
Washington

U.S. and U.A.R. Presidents Meet

President Eisenhower (left) and United Arab Republic President Nasser had a show of hands as they met at President Eisenhower's hotel suite in New York. Mr. Eisenhower arrived from Washington earlier and told talks with various foreign dignitaries in New York for the 15th UN General Assembly. President Nasser is reported to have invited Mr. Eisenhower to pay a visit to the U.A.R. as Mr. Nasser's guest of honor.

MDC Probe Hears Political Echoes

By Albert D. Hughes
Staff Writer of The Christian Science Monitor

Political overtones today were injected into the special Massachusetts Senate committee investigation of the Metropolitan District Commission.

Start Identified

Bill Quoted

Goldfine Case To Open in Boston

The World's Day

New England: Tax-Evasion Trial Set for Oct. 3

National: Candidates Back on Campaign Trail

Asia: South Korea Plans to Grant Pardons

Weather: Cloudy Tonight and Wednesday [Page 2]

Arts, Music, Theater: Page 7, Radio, TV, FM: Page 8

Inside Reading

Facts and fireworks over school center managers.
Page 2

Lynn residents take strike threat in stride.
Page 2

Ohio: Ghana keeps up pressure.
Page 9

Glitter gone from golden Prague.
Page 12

Research by NASA disk closes goals for moon probing.
Page 13

Southern Democrats take stand on foreign policy.
Page 14

Just Before the Opening Gavel
Presidential candidates Nixon and Kennedy trade grins

1974, 110 million persons saw a rerun of *Gone with the Wind* in 1976, 120 million saw part or all of the 1976 election returns, and in early 1977 *Roots,* the tracing of black history, became the most watched scheduled show in television history. During the eight consecutive nights that it was aired it was seen by an estimated 85 percent of the potential viewing audience, or about 130 million persons. Four of the episodes landed on the all-time top ten list, and the network, ABC, ended up number one at last.

Some of the illustrious names were gone by 1977, including those of David Sarnoff and his son Robert, of NBC, and Dr. Frank Stanton of CBS. William S. Paley retained his voice in CBS operations and Richard S. Salant was president of the network's news operations. At NBC Julian Goodman was chairman, while Les Crystal was president of news. Leonard H. Goldenson was ABC's chairman, and Roone Arledge, the president of ABC Sports credited with bringing high ratings to that area, was given the additional assignment of heading the news department.

PUBLIC BROADCASTING   A long effort to establish public broadcasting in the United States at the level of other countries was given stability in 1967 by the Congress. The Corporation for Public Broadcasting (CPB) was chartered that year to dispense funds for a unified system of national and local programming. Much of the original programming was done by the well-established National Educational Television (NET). After 1970, the country's noncommercial and educational television stations were connected through the Public Broadcasting Service, which hopefully called itself "the fourth network." In radio, many of these stations were linked by the growing National Public Radio (NPR) system. The future of public financing remained to be determined; the Ford Foundation had given the stations some $200 million, and in 1976 President Ford signed a bill that assured substantial federal funding up to 1981. President Carter then projected $1 billion of support over five years beginning in 1981, still far from enough to assure excellence.

For a few years the CPB, which channels the federal funds, and the PBS, which represents the stations and distributes the programs, fought bitterly. CPB complaints, encouraged by the Nixon White House, centered around the alleged eastern bias of those producing the shows to be distributed. By the late 1970s, a calm was noticeable, but CPB was still accused of bureaucratic interference in the development of public broadcasting's true potential as an imaginative, alternative source of ideas.

Public television's best-known success was *Sesame Street,* which captured the imaginations of the moppets and, aided by the Action for Children's Television group, brought about some reform in children's shows by the commercial networks, which substituted educational fare for violence part of the time. Its successor was *The Electric Company,* for third to fifth graders. Kenneth Clark's series called *Civilisation* was another high-level success; so were *The Forsythe Saga, The First Churchills,* and *The Great American Dream Machine.* There were such innovative programs as the production of an actual courtroom trial and "The Global Village, a shared electronic experience." Two educational stations pioneering in such efforts were WGBH, Boston, and KQED, San Francisco. NET had other staple programs such as another delightful children's hour, *Mister Roger's Neighborhood, NET Playhouse, Nova,* and *NET Festival.* KCET, Los Angeles, was another leader.

The programming, supplemented by the best in British television, continued to improve. Other hit shows included *Upstairs, Downstairs, Shoulder to Shoulder, Monty Python, The Adams Chronicles, The Incredible Machine,* and for news buffs, the *MacNeil-Lehrer Report* and *Washington Week in Review.* Public television provided gavel-to-gavel coverage of the Watergate hearings, and a number of candid documentaries appeared.

ADVANCES
IN BROADCASTING
TECHNOLOGY

Electronic News Gathering, domestic satellites, cable, fibre optical communications, laser beams—these were some of the terms widely discussed in the late 1970s as television moved quickly into the final quarter of the century.

Using lightweight cameras, field reporters had the option of reporting live from city council meetings as well as the scenes of shootouts. Sophisticated videotape recorders allowed instant editing of these transmissions and the days of the motorcycle carrier of film were doomed. Portable videotape recorders and editing machines permitted a field reporter to know at once what the camera had captured, instead of waiting for the film to be developed. How news producers would use the new tool was open to serious question, but the ENG system, developed first by KMOX-TV in St. Louis, was adopted by most other stations.

News by satellites was television's most sensational achievement of the 1960s and 1970s. The ultimate achievement would be broadcasting directly from a satellite to home receivers, or at least to earth stations that would relay the show to private homes. India, Japan, Germany, Canada, and the Soviet Union were at different stages of development of such methods, but U.S. domestic use of the satellite was more conventional.

The FCC in 1972 opened up the nation's skies to all financially responsible firms interested in providing satellite transmission of television, telephone, news, and data services. The first private domestic satellite was Western Union's Westar launched in April 1974. Seven others were launched by RCA, Communications Satellite Corporation (called Cosmat), and Western Union in the next three years as satellite communication became cheaper than land transmission in some cases.

Pay television via cable was begun nationally in 1976 by Time Inc.'s Home Box Office subsidiary, utilizing domestic satellites to beam the programming to earth stations built outside major cities, which then relayed to a million subscribing homes via cable. Plans were under way in 1977 for the servicing of public broadcasting stations in at least 13 cities with several programs delivered simultaneously by Western Union satellite. And there was talk of a "fourth" commercial television network.

The successful launching of AT&T's Telstar on July 10, 1962, permitted the first live transmissions of pictures between the United States and Europe. These were staged shows lasting for the few minutes the signal could be bounced off the moving satellite. RCA's Relay carried pictures to 23 nations at the time of President Kennedy's assassination. The effort to develop continuous service by launching a satellite that would achieve a fully synchronous orbit (an orbit and speed that keep the craft directly over one spot on earth) met success when Howard Hughes launched Syncom III in 1964. Four such satellites, equally spaced around the world, could provide television coverage to all inhabited portions of the planet.

The Communications Satellite Corporation, formed by Congress in 1962 to unify the U.S. effort and to provide international leadership, carried out technical progress well. Early Bird went into synchronous orbit in 1965, followed by successive Intelsat series. By 1977 the Intelsat IV satellites were carrying 4,000 or 6,000 voice circuits and two television channels to 150 antennas in 80 countries using the system to receive simultaneous television broadcasts. In May 1971, a 79-nation Intelsat conference wound up two years of work to develop revised rules for the International Telecommunications Satellite Consortium. Comsat had held control of the group's

The Weather

Today — Showers, thunderstorms, high in 80s. Tuesday—Fair, less humid. Chance of rain, 20% tonight. Winds variable, 10-15 m.p.h. Temperature range: Today, 72-88; Yesterday, 78-68. Details, Page D2.

The Washington Post

Times Herald

Index

56 Pages
4 Sections

Amusements	B 6	Fed. Diary	C 5
Calendar	B 4	Financial	C 8
City Life	D 1	Movie Guide	B 7
Classified	D 4	Obituaries	D 2
Comics	C 4	Sports	C 1
Crossword	B 4	Style	B 1
Editorials	A14	TV-Radio	B 3

92d Year ··· No. 228   © 1969, The Washington Post Co.   MONDAY, JULY 21, 1969   Phone 223-6000 Circulation 223-6100 Classified 223-6200   10¢

'The Eagle Has Landed'—
Two Men Walk on the Moon

'One Small Step For Man ... Giant Leap for Mankind'

By Thomas O'Toole
Washington Post Staff Writer

HOUSTON, July 20—Man stepped out onto the moon tonight for the first time in his two-million-year history.

"That's one small step for man," declared pioneer astronaut Neil Armstrong at 10:56 p.m. EDT, "one giant leap for mankind."

Just after that historic moment in man's quest for his origins, Armstrong walked on the dead satellite and found the surface very powdery, littered with fine grains of black dust.

A few minutes later, Edwin (Buzz) Aldrin joined Armstrong on the lunar surface and in less than an hour they put on a show that will long be remembered by the worldwide television audience.

American Flag Planted

The two men walked easily, talked easily, even ran and jumped happily so it seemed. They picked up rocks, talked at length of what they saw, planted an American flag, saluted it, and talked by radiophone with the President in the White House, and then faced the camera and saluted Mr. Nixon.

"For every American, this has to be the proudest day of our lives," the President told the astronauts. "For one priceless moment in the whole history of man, all the people on this earth are truly one."

At 1:10 a.m.—2 hours and 14 minutes after Armstrong first stepped upon the lunar surface—the astronauts were back in their moon craft and the hatch was closed.

In describing the moon, Armstrong told Houston that it was "fine and powdery. I can kick it up loosely with my toe.

"It adheres like powdered charcoal to the boot," he went on, "but I only go in a small fraction of an inch. I can see my footprint in the moon like fine grainy particles."

Armstrong found he had such little trouble walking on the moon that he began talking almost as if he didn't want to leave it.

"It has a stark beauty all its own," Armstrong said. "It's like the desert in the Southwestern United States. It's very pretty out here."

Amazingly Clear Picture

Armstrong shared his first incredible moments on the moon with the whole world, as a television camera on the outside of the wingless Eagle landing craft sent back an amazingly clear picture of his first steps on the moon.

Armstrong seemed like he was swimming along, taking big and easy steps on the airless moon despite the cumbersome white pressure-suit he wore.

"There seems to be no difficulty walking around," he said. "As we suspected, it's even easier than the one-sixth G that we did in simulations on the ground."

One of the first things he did was to scoop up a small sample of the moon with a long-handled spoon with a bag on its end like a small butterfly net.

"Looks like it's easy," Aldrin said, looking down from the Lem.

"It is," Armstrong told him. "I'm sure I could push it in farther but I can't bend down that far."

Guides Aldrin Down Ladder

At 11:11 p.m., Aldrin started down the landing craft's ten-foot ladder to join Armstrong.

Backing down the nine-step ladder, Aldrin was guided the entire way by Armstrong, who stood at the foot of the ladder looking up at him.

"Okay," Armstrong said, "watch your 'plss' (PLSS, for portable life support system) from underneath. Drop your plss down. You're clear. About an inch clear on your plss."

"Okay," Aldrin said. "You need a little arching of the back to come down."

When he stepped onto the first rung of the ladder, Aldrin went back up to the Lem's "front porch" to partially close the Lem's hatch.

"Making sure not to lock it on my way out," he said in comic fashion. "That's our home for the next couple of hours and I want to make sure we can get back in."

Aldrin reported it was a "very simple matter to hop down from one step to the next." To make the last and longest step, he said he put both hands on the fourth rung up and leaned back with his left foot first.

"Beautiful," said Aldrin when he met Armstrong on the lunar surface.

"Isn't that something," said Armstrong. "It's a magnificent sight out here."

See APOLLO, A8, Col. 1

Neil Armstrong and Edwin Aldrin plant the American flag on the surface of the moon. The flag is kept "flying" on the airless moon by a spring device.

Armstrong takes his first steps on the moon. At left is the Eagle, the lunar landing craft.

Moon Walk Yields Data for Science

By Victor Cohn
Washington Post Staff Writer

HOUSTON, July 20—They landed, eyes open for science, and within minutes became lunar explorers.

Edwin (Buzz) Aldrin was soon making man's first on-the-spot report from another planetary body.

From the spacecraft he saw a rock collection around the lunar lander of "every shape, regularity, irregularity, every variety you'd find." And "quite a few interesting colors."

This promptly led Dr. Harold Masursky, chief of astrogeology for the U.S. Geological Survey — working in one of the science support rooms here — to comment:

"They've hit a good spot to do collecting."

Then Neil Armstrong took the craft for the lunar surface. Fit, eager, apparently healthy — no moon illness on madness — he began the first scientific traverse on earth's oldest satellite.

The mere fact that he did it and did it well immediately answered a vital question:

Man can function on the moon.

One of the first things he reported was: "The MESA came down all right."

That was the "modularized equipment stowage assembly" — a trunk in the skin of the Lem — that held both a television camera and scientific equipment.

He was quickly giving scientists more information about the nature of the lunar surface than they have gained in all their recent years of poking at it with unmanned probes.

"The Lem footpads are only depressed in the surface about one inch or two inches and I only go in a fraction of an inch"—the surface was remarkably firm.

"The surface appears to be very fine ground as you get close to it. It's almost a powder, very fine . . . fine and powdery"—probably because of meteorite bombardment over the ages.

See SCIENCE, A10, Col. 4

'Squared Away and in Good Shape . . .'

The following is a condensed transcript, prepared by UPI, of the conversation during man's first walk on the moon, among astronauts Neil A. Armstrong, Edwin E. (Buzz) Aldrin and Michael Collins; ground commentator Bruce McCandless and Mission Control spokesman John McLeaish:

Armstrong — That's one small step for man, one giant leap for mankind.

...

on the ground. I can see some evidence of rays emanating from the descent engine, but a very insignificant amount.

Armstrong — OK, Buzz, ready to bring down the camera.

Aldrin—All ready. It looks like I'm all squared away and in good shape.

Armstrong—It's quite dark in the shadow and a little hard for me to see but I have good footing. I'll work my way to the sunlight here without looking directly into the sun.

McLeaish — Unofficial time on first step 109:24:20.

Armstrong — Looking at the Lem. I'm standing directly in the shadow now, looking up at Buzz in the windows—and I can see everything quite clearly. The light is sufficiently backlighted in the front of the Lem so that everything is clearly visible.

Aldrin—OK, I'm going to be changing . . .

Armstrong—OK.

McLeaish — The surgeon says the crew is doing well.

Apollo Liftoff Schedule

Apollo 11's key activities slated for today:

1:55 p.m.—Lunar module's ascent engine fires, lifting the module's ascent stage off the moon and leaving the descent stage behind.

5:32 p.m.—Lunar module and command ship dock.

9:25 p.m.—Lunar module is jettisoned.

No live television is scheduled until 9:02 p.m. Tuesday. By this time the Apollo's main engine will have been fired and be out of lunar orbit.

Data is good, the crew is doing well, 35 and a half minutes of PLSS time expended now.

Armstrong—Right.

McCandless — OK, that's good.

Armstrong — It's very interesting. It's a very soft surface but here and there where I plug with the contingency sampler I run into a very hard surface . . .

Aldrin—OK, the handle is off. It pushes about six or eight inches in the surface. It pushes very easy.

See TRANSCRIPT, A11, Col. 4

Millions Follow Moon Landing Around the World, Except in China

By Robert C. Jensen
Washington Post Staff Writer

Man's first journey to the moon was hailed in nearly every part of the world yesterday. The exception was China, where one-fifth of the world's people live.

The Communist rulers in Peking decided to withhold the news that the American astronauts Neil Armstrong and Edwin Aldrin had safely landed on the moon.

In Russia, the news agency Tass announced the moon landing in a 32-word dispatch. And the reports were carried routinely in Soviet television and radio broadcasts. But the Associated Press reported that individual citizens in Moscow cheered and congratulated

said in a dispatch from Peking that no word of the landing or any part of the Apollo mission was mentioned in China.

Americans. "It's a great day," one shouted.

Much the same reaction was voiced by former Vice President Humphrey, who beamed: "What a day to be in Moscow!" Humphrey had returned from a hunting trip with Gen. Sergei I. Sokolov, first deputy defense minister. Humphrey brought back a bear he had shot in a forest near Moscow.

See REACT, A8, Col. 4

policies and technical operations; it agreed to drop U.S. voting power to 40 percent and to give up managerial duties within the decade.

The "hottest" mass communications industry in the United States in the 1970s was cable television, sometimes called CATV for Community Antenna Television system. Cable television started as a means of bringing commercial television signals into isolated communities whose residents could not receive good pictures through their own antennas. It developed rapidly when it became apparent the coaxial cable could be used to bring a variety of programming to smaller communities—including the shows of all three major U.S. networks. It also became apparent that cable has the capability of using large numbers of channels for varying purposes in metropolitan areas. In 1977 there were 3,500 cable systems serving 10.5 million homes, 15 percent of all television homes. The systems took in an estimated $775 million annually from average installation fees of $15 and service charges of $6 to $9 monthly.

Many cable proposals and ideas were still at issue in the late 1970s. High interest rates and a shortage of money aborted some of the "blue sky" proposals early in the decade for this capital intensive industry. However, the regulatory climate became more favorable in Washington by mid-decade as money became more plentiful for completing projects in the large cities that were opened to cable by a comprehensive FCC 1972 order.

FCC policy had been protective of on-the-air broadcasting to the detriment of cable television until the 1972 plan that allowed cable operators to import distant signals to augment off-the-air service. Many systems originated such local programming as game shows, news, public affairs, and sports on extra channels. Other uses were foreseen if costs could be low enough: delivery of news in printed form, informational retrieval hookups with libraries, connections to banks, stores, and other institutions for business purposes. Importation of distant signals to metropolitan markets proved a disappointing plum, because many shows were denied cable operators under previous contractual agreements. Of the top 100 market areas only 17 had attractive marketing potential. Still, some dreamed of the day when satellites and cable would bring up to 80 channels to a community at modest cost.[31]

A new communications tool, the fiber optic, or light wave communications, may open vast new communications capacities. Utilizing a hair-thin glass fiber, the system can transmit intelligence through beams of light. Even though it is much narrower than coaxial cable, it can carry more information cheaper with less signal loss and benefit companies that carry telecommunications signals. In 1976, a number of experiments involving glass fibers were begun by telephone and cable television companies. One thing was clear: the best chance for development of cable systems would come if cable operators were encouraged to develop in partnership with existing technologies.

THE FCC AND THE BROADCASTERS: LICENSING

Radio and television were still under public regulation, through the Federal Communications Commission. The FCC held license control over stations and limited holding of multiple licenses. No person or group could own more than seven television stations (only five of them VHF) plus seven FM and seven AM stations. No one could own more than one radio and one television station in the same city.

For years the FCC looked askance at ownership of broadcast stations by newspaper publishers, whether or not in the same city. In 1944 the FCC commented that licenses would be granted on the merit of individual applications, under the guiding rule of as much diversification of ownership as possible. But in 1970 the FCC began to get deeply involved in cross-channel ownerships. First it voted to prohibit future acquisitions by anyone of both a VHF television station and a radio station in the same market. Then, after a series of hearings and arguments, the FCC in 1975 banned new joint ownership arrangements in the same city but said old ones could stand. However, a federal appeals court decision in 1977 struck this down and appeared to outlaw most of the joint ownership arrangements that had existed since radio began more than 50 years earlier. It was predicted the case could affect at least 80 television-newspaper ownership combinations in 75 cities and perhaps 400 radio-newspaper combinations in about 200 cities.[32]

Two groups appealed the FCC's 1970 decision to the appeals court—newspaper owners and broadcasters upset about the loss of future combinations, and the National Citizens Committee for Broadcasting, led by former FCC commissioner Nicholas Johnson who was angered that old relationships were allowed to stand. One easy alternative, of course, was for the newspaper owners, with their deeper community roots, to trade their broadcasting stocks to each other, whenever possible, to avoid multiple ownerships in the same cities. It was expected to take years to iron out the legal arguments. The FCC also was expected to begin examination of ownership patterns affecting broadcast stations and cable stations.

Existing owners were further disturbed by a federal appeals court ruling in mid-1971 that the FCC was still giving too much preference to license holders in renewal hearings required every three years. The court sought to open the door for serious consideration of license challenges by minority groups and for the shifting of licenses on FCC findings of inferior performance by stations. Such challenges were in progress in various metropolitan areas, so far unsuccessfully.

Television found itself subjected to other regulation in the 1970s. Congress passed legislation banning cigarette advertising from the screens beginning in 1971, for health reasons (magazine cigarette advertising promptly doubled and that in newspapers increased). The immediate loss to the broadcast industry was $225 million in advertising revenues, unless the time were sold to other advertisers. And the FCC voted to limit network-television affiliate stations in the top 50 markets to three hours of network programming in prime time (forcing the stations to scramble around for 30 minutes of fill-in each evening).

THE FCC FAIRNESS DOCTRINE

The problems of editorializing on the air and fairness in presenting all sides of public issues were others involving the stations and the FCC over many decades. In a 1941 ruling, called the "Mayflower decision" because it involved renewal of a Boston station license held by the Mayflower Broadcasting Corporation, the FCC said, "The broadcaster cannot be an advocate." Radiomen presented arguments against this policy, and in 1949 the FCC decided broadcasters could—and should—"editorialize with fairness." Station owners were cautious in taking up the invitation, but by 1967 a survey showed 57 percent of radio and television stations were presenting editorial opinion, one-third of them either daily or weekly, the rest occasionally. This figure steadily increased. Some problems of covering politics were removed in 1959 when bona fide newscasts and news programs were exempted from the FCC's "equal-time" rule, but the basic problem of obtaining "fairness" in access to the air and in presenting all sides of controversial issues remained.

The requirement to be "fair" was based on two arguments: the airwaves are public property, by act of Congress, and the FCC was given power to license broadcasters in the "public interest, convenience, and necessity." The public interest is served, FCC held, if the airwaves are made accessible to many differing viewpoints.

Broadcasters said it was hard to define the "public interest" legally. They also paid such extreme efforts to balance editorial comment and interpretative documentaries mitigated against broadcasters covering important social issues. If, as the FCC implied, a station had to go out and look for at least one other side to any issue it discussed, in order to be fair, it would not go out at all (CBS looking for the other side to the migrant labor problem, or the other side of military propaganda, for example). And if the "other side" came in with program demands by any number of offended or interested groups (as in the case of the Vietnam war and activist resistance to war), the station's time would be filled with programming of little interest to the majority of viewers (any newspaper editor knows a large percentage of citizens is not interested in a given social or political issue, a fact confirmed by opinion polls). To all this, the Supreme Court in a 1969 decision did not agree.

Specifically the court upheld FCC rules requiring notice be given to any person subjected to "personal attack" in an editorial or program, or to candidates for office opposing one endorsed, with right of similar reply. But the decision ranged more widely in the "fairness doctrine" issue, noting "it is the right of the viewers and listeners, not the right of the broadcasters, which is paramount." If broadcasters were not willing to present representative community views on controversial issues, Justice Byron White wrote, the granting or renewal of a license might be challenged within the spirit of the Constitution.[33] Promptly dubbed the *Red Lion* doctrine, this decision created excitement. But when in 1970 Dr. Frank Stanton of CBS decided to afford the Democratic party time to answer President Nixon's unprecedented number of prime time requisitionings to give arguments concerning his foreign policy and the Vietnam war, the FCC emasculated its new power. Yes, it said, CBS was correct in giving the right of reply, but it also had to let the Republican party answer the Democrats, and, presumably, so on and on in an endless circle. CBS cancelled the public discussion it wanted to have and appealed to the courts for relief. The incident served to prove that it is very difficult to legislate "fairness."

In another decision affecting access to the airwaves and public discussion, the FCC reversed a policy that had encouraged anti-smoking, environmentalist, and other groups to seek access. The FCC narrowed previous rulings that held all broadcast advertising was subject to the "fairness doctrine" and had to be balanced with "counter-advertising" whenever controversies were involved. The new ruling was that ads designed merely to sell products did not have to be balanced with opposing viewpoints, but that advertisements dealing with issues were still subject to the provisions calling for balance. However, the FCC and Supreme Court ruled that broadcasters could not be required to sell advertising space to anyone who had the money and were only expected to make a "good faith effort" to ensure balance in their overall programming, as opposed to any one program. The inquiry was intended to settle questions that had arisen during license disputes and was considered to be different from "right of reply" and "equal time" problems.

NOTES

1. The best account of the development of radio newscasting is in Mitchell V. Charnley, *News by Radio* (New York: Macmillan, 1948). For the history of radio to 1933, see Erik Barnouw, *A Tower in Babel* (New York: The Oxford Press, 1966).

2. The full story of RCA's rise and of other concentration of radio control is told in Llewellyn White, *The American Radio* (Chicago: University of Chicago Press, 1947).

3. The *Kansas City Star* offered a combination newspaper-radio rate for advertising users of the *Star* and its station WDAF in 1921, but there were few immediate takers.

4. From testimony by Ralph D. Casey, director of the University of Minnesota School of Journalism, before the Federal Communications Commission, reprinted in part by the Newspaper-Radio Committee in *Freedom of the Press* (booklet, 1942), pp. 5–21.

5. White, *The American Radio,* pp. 144–47.

6. The story of the newspaper-radio struggle and ANPA's part in it is told in Edwin Emery, *History of the American Newspaper Publishers Association* (Minneapolis: University of Minnesota Press, 1950), chap. 13.

7. Charnley, *News by Radio,* p. 9.

8. Including *Editor & Publisher,* which expressed skepticism in its issue of December 10, 1932, p. 5.

9. The AP won suits against KSOO, Sioux Falls, South Dakota, and KVOS, Bellingham, Washington, to stop this practice. Eventually the period of time during which there is a protectible property right in news came to be recognized as a minimum of four to six hours after publication.

10. Michael C. Emery, "The Munich Crisis Broadcasts: Radio News Comes of Age," *Journalism Quarterly,* XLII (Autumn 1965), 576.

11. A policy thoroughly criticized in White, *The American Radio,* and in Charles A. Siepmann, *Radio's Second Chance* (New York: Holt, Rinehart & Winston, 1946).

12. Christopher H. Sterling, "Decade of Development: FM Radio in the 1960s," *Journalism Quarterly,* XLVIII (Summer 1971), 222.

13. For the use of television and radio's adjustment to it, 1933–53, see Erik Barnouw, *The Golden Web* (New York: The Oxford Press, 1968). His *The Image Empire* (1970) continues the story.

14. For a poignant remembrance of Murrow, see Edward Bliss, Jr., "Remembering Edward R. Murrow," *Saturday Review* (May 31, 1975), 17.

15. "The Case Against Milo Radulovich, A0589839," *See It Now,* CBS News, October 20, 1953.

16. Alexander Kendrick, who for 20 years worked with Murrow, provides the full story of Murrow's life, including his many battles with CBS, in *Prime Time* (Boston: Little, Brown, 1969).

17. "Senator Joseph R. McCarthy," *See It Now,* CBS News, March 9, 1954.

18. Charge of National Association of Manufacturers, as cited by Alexander Kendrick in *Prime Time,* p. 418. Also see Fred W. Friendly, *Due to Circumstances Beyond Our Control* (New York: Random House, 1967).

19. Kendrick, *Prime Time,* p. 341. On Murrow's death the Milo Radulovichs wrote: "Wherever men cherish human freedom and dignity, Ed Murrow's spirit will forever stand," p. 513.

20. See David Halberstam's "CBS: The Power & the Profits," *Atlantic,* CCXXXVII (January 1976), 33, and (February 1976), 52 for a critical look at the world of William S. Paley, Frank Stanton, and CBS News from the Murrow years through Cronkite.

21. See Leonard Zeidenberg's "Lessons of a Living Room War," *Broadcasting* (May 19, 1975) for an analysis of reporting achievements.

22. Study conducted by media critic Edwin Diamond, then co-director of the Network News Study Group at the Massachusetts Institute of Technology, and students, in 1973.

23. See Daniel Schorr, *Clearing the Air* (Boston: Houghton Mifflin, 1977), and University of Missouri *Freedom of Information Center Report* No. 361, "The Daniel Schorr Investigation," October 1976.

24. *TV Guide,* July 1, 1967, as cited by Eric Barnouw, *The Image Empire,* p. 301.

25. For a long interview with Chancellor, see Philip Noble's "The Cool and Confident Anchorman," *MORE* (May 1976), p. 7.

26. NBC News, December 20, 1965. McGee, along with CBS's Morley Safer, was one of the first broadcast journalists to openly question the U.S. role.

27. "The New Look of TV News," *Newsweek* (October 11, 1976), p. 76.

28. See Maurine Christopher's "TV News—In the Barbara Walters Era," *Matrix,* LXII (Fall 1976), and "Prime Time for TV Newswomen," *Time* (March 21, 1977).

29. Edith Efron, *The News Twisters* (Los Angeles: Nash, 1971), and Edward J. Epstein, *News From Nowhere.* (New York: Random House, 1973).

30. Eric Sevareid, in his "What's Right with Sight-and-Sound Journalism," *Saturday Review* (October 10, 1976), defended television news against critics who often wrote for print publications that were inferior products.

31. See Anne W. Branscomb, "The Cable Fable: Will It Come True?," *Journal of Communication* (Winter 1975). Contains a thorough look at the economics and technology involved.

32. *Advertising Age,* March 7, 1977, p. 1.

33. *Red Lion Broadcasting Co., Inc.* v. *Federal Communications Commission,* 394 U.S. (1969).

ANNOTATED BIBLIOGRAPHY

Books

BARNOUW, ERIK, *A History of Broadcasting in the United States*. Vol. 1, *A Tower in Babel* (to 1933); Vol. 2, *The Golden Web* (1933–53); Vol. 3, *The Image Empire* (from 1953). New York: The Oxford Press, 1966, 1968, 1970. Best account of radio and television; third volume necessarily becomes less historical in tone.

——, *Tube of Plenty*. New York: Oxford Press, 1975. Condensed updated version of 3 vols.

BARRETT, MARVIN, ed., *Survey of Broadcast Journalism, 1969–1970*. New York: Grosset & Dunlap, 1970. Like its predecessor, a paperback review of major events sponsored by Alfred I. duPont-Columbia University Awards. Issued annually.

BLAKELY, ROBERT J., *The People's Instrument*. Washington: The Public Affairs Press, 1971. Philosophical view of role public television can play.

BLUEM, A. WILLIAM, *The Documentary in American Television*. New York: Hastings House, 1965. Includes historical development and 100 pages of photographs.

BULMAN, DAVID, ed., *Molders of Opinion*. Milwaukee: Bruce Publishing Company, 1945. Includes chapters on H.V. Kaltenborn, Gabriel Heatter, Fulton Lewis, Jr., and Raymond Gram Swing.

BURLINGAME, ROGER, *Don't Let Them Scare You: The Life and Times of Elmer Davis*. Philadelphia: Lippincott, 1961. A good biography of a top-flight news analyst.

CHARNLEY, MITCHELL V., *News by Radio*. New York: Macmillan, 1948. The best source for the growth of radio news.

CHASE, FRANCIS, JR., *Sound and Fury*. New York: Harper & Row, 1942. An informal history of radio with much information, but sometimes inaccurate in precise details.

CULBERT, DAVID HOLBROOK, *News for Everyman*. Westport, Conn.: Greenwood Press, 1976. Account of how American radio affected foreign affairs during 1930s.

DE FOREST, LEE, *Father of Radio: The Autobiography of Lee De Forest*. Chicago: Wilcox & Follett, 1950. The early years.

EMERY, WALTER B., *Broadcasting and Government*. East Lansing: Michigan State University Press, rev. ed., 1971. An encyclopedic survey of all aspects of government interest in, and regulation of, U.S. broadcasting.

EPSTEIN, EDWARD J., *News from Nowhere: Television and the News*. New York: Random House, 1973. The organization and economics of television news.

FANG, IRVING E., *Those Radio Commentators!* Ames: Iowa State University Press, 1977. Study of major commentators of 1930s and 1940s.

FRIENDLY, FRED W., *Due to Circumstances Beyond Our Control...* New York: Random House, 1967. The story of life with Edward R. Murrow, of their controversial CBS documentaries, and of Friendly's break with CBS.

——, *The Good Guys, The Bad Guys and the First Amendment*. New York: Random House, 1975, 1976. Attack on the "fairness doctrine" as it has been applied.

GELFMAN, JUDITH S., *Women in Television News*. New York: Columbia University Press, 1976. Interviews with 30 newswomen including Barbara Walters, Pauline Frederick, Lesley Stahl.

HEAD, SYDNEY W., *Broadcasting in America*, 3rd ed. Boston: Houghton Mifflin, 1976. Excellent survey of the physical bases of broadcasting, its history, economics, and problems of social control.

KAHN, FRANK J., ed., *Documents of American Broadcasting*. New York: Appleton-Century-Crofts, 1968. The pertinent documents, cases to mid-1960s.

KALTENBORN, H. V., *Fifty Fabulous Years, 1900–1950: A Personal Review*. New York: G.P. Putnam's Sons, 1950. Autobiography of a commentator who began on the air in 1922.

KENDRICK, ALEXANDER, *Prime Time: The Life of Edward R. Murrow*. Boston: Little, Brown, 1969. Biography of the great commentator; thorough but misses catching drama of the great events in which Murrow participated.

LeDuc, Don L., *Cable Television and the FCC: A Crisis in Media Control*. Philadelphia: Temple University Press, 1973. Details the history of cable regulation and brings to light various FCC shortcomings.

Lichty, Lawrence W., and Malachi C. Topping, *American Broadcasting: A Sourcebook on the History of Radio and Television*. New York: Hastings House, 1975. Eight-year editing project yields more than 700 pages.

Metz, Robert, *CBS: Reflections in a Bloodshot Eye*. Chicago: Playboy Press, 1975. CBS viewed this critical study with silence. Also, "The Biggest Man in Broadcasting," *New York*, VIII (July 21, 1975), 43. William S. Paley's career.

Murrow, Edward R., *In Search of Light: The Broadcasts of Edward R. Murrow, 1938–1961*. New York: Knopf, 1967. Broadcast history through memorable scripts.

Powers, Ron, *The Newscasters*. New York: St. Martin's Press, 1977. TV critic presents news business as show business.

Rather, Dan, with Mickey Herskowitz, *The Camera Never Blinks*. New York: William Morrow and Company, 1977. The candid autobiography of this CBS reporter who covered the major stories of the 1960s and early 1970s.

Sarnoff, David, *Looking Ahead: The Papers of David Sarnoff*. New York: McGraw-Hill, 1968. Papers of the broadcasting pioneer.

Schechter, A.A., with Edward Anthony, *I Live on Air*. New York: Frederick Stokes, 1941. NBC's first director of news and special events.

Sevareid, Eric, *This Is Eric Sevareid*. New York: McGraw-Hill, 1964. The CBS commentator's thoughts between 1955 and 1964.

Siepmann, Charles A., *Radio, Television, and Society*. New York: Oxford University Press, 1950. Social criticism of the media, by the author of *Radio's Second Chance* (1946).

Skornia, Harry J., and Jack W. Kitson, eds., *Problems and Controversies in Television and Radio*. Palo Alto, Calif.: Pacific Books, 1968. Broadcasting leaders discuss problems of the 1960s.

Smythe, Ted C., and George A. Mastroianni, *Issues in Broadcasting*. Palo Alto, Calif.: Mayfield, 1975. Readings on radio, television, cable.

Tebbel, John W., *David Sarnoff: Putting Electrons to Work*. Chicago: Encyclopaedia Britannica, 1964. A biography of the RCA chairman.

Thomas, Lowell, *Good Evening Everybody*. New York: Morrow, 1976. Autobiography of the pioneer CBS radio newscaster, 1930–76.

White, Llewellyn, *The American Radio*. Chicago: University of Chicago Press, 1947. A publication of the Commission on Freedom of the Press. Best single discussion of radio's growth.

Periodicals and Monographs

Bliss, Edward, Jr., "Remembering Edward R. Murrow," *Saturday Review* (May 31, 1975), 17. CBS radio journalist recalls Murrow's courage and skill.

"Broadcasting at 50," *Broadcasting*, LXXIX (November 2, 1970). A special issue, including a year-by-year review of major events, 1931–70.

"CBS: The First Five Decades," *Broadcasting*, XCIII (September 19, 1977), 45–116. Extensive survey.

Clark, David G., "The Dean of Commentators: A Biography of H.V. Kaltenborn," Ph.D. thesis, University of Wisconsin, 1965. Written from the Kaltenborn papers.

———, "H.V. Kaltenborn's First Year on the Air," *Journalism Quarterly*, XLII (Summer 1965), 373. The *Brooklyn Eagle* editor takes to the air in 1923 on WEAF for a stormy year.

Cranston, Pat, "Political Convention Broadcasts: Their History and Influence," *Journalism Quarterly*, XXXVII (Spring 1960), 186. A survey from 1924 to 1956.

Emery, Michael C., "The Munich Crisis Broadcasts: Radio News Comes of Age," *Journalism Quarterly*, XLII (Autumn 1965), 576. Kaltenborn, Murrow, and Shirer penetrate American minds.

Emery, Walter B., "Nervous Tremors in the Broadcast Industry," *Educational Broadcasting Review*, III (June 1969), 43. A review of FCC rulings and actions affecting license holders.

FEDERAL COMMUNICATIONS COMMISSION, *Annual Report for Fiscal Year 1964*. Washington: Government Printing Office, 1964. Summarizes, as 30th anniversary issue, communication developments since 1934.

FERRETTI, FRED, "The White Captivity of Black Radio," *Columbia Journalism Review*, IX (Summer 1970), 35. Of 310 radio stations serving blacks at least in part, only 16 are owned by blacks—and no TV licenses.

GARVEY, DANIEL E., "Secretary Hoover and the Quest for Broadcast Regulation," *Journalism History*, III (Autumn 1976), 66. Hoover sought stronger regulation than Congress granted.

GUNN, HARTFORD N., JR., "United States Public Broadcasting Goes to Satellite," *European Broadcasting Union Review*, March 1977. An update on PBS' plans for simultaneous broadcasting.

HALBERSTAM, DAVID, "CBS: The Power & the Profits," *Atlantic*, CCXXXVII, (January 1976), 33, and (February 1976), 52. A penetrating two-part study of CBS News.

"How They Do It," *Newsweek*, LXXIII (December 1, 1969), 56. Story of the Huntley-Brinkley broadcast. See also "First Team," *Newsweek*, LVII (March 13, 1961), 53.

LEAMER, LAWRENCE, "The Sunset Ride of a TV Reformer," *Harper's* CCXLVII (December 1973), 22. Personal history of Nicholas Johnson is really a picture of the FCC.

LEWIN, LEONARD C., "Public TV's Corporate Angels," *Nation*, CCXXI (November 22, 1975), 520. Growing corporate influence in public television.

LICHTY, LAWRENCE W., AND THOMAS W. BOHN, "Radio's *March of Time:* Dramatized News," *Journalism Quarterly*, LI (Autumn 1974), 458. The beginning of this technique.

LOWER, ELMER W., "American Television News—Rounding Out a Quarter Century," *European Broadcasting Union Review*, XXVI (May 1975), 49. ABC news chief.

MCKERNS, JOSEPH P., "Industry Skeptics and the Radio Act of 1927," *Journalism History*, III (Winter 1976–77), 128.

MURRAY, MICHAEL D., "Television's Desperate Moment: A Conversation with Fred W. Friendly," *Journalism History*, I (Autumn 1974), 68. Interview about Senator Joseph McCarthy and the media.

"NBC: 50th Anniversary; Spearhead of Broadcast Industry Marks Beginning." *Television/Radio Age*, XXIV (June 21, 1976), special issue. Also, *Broadcasting*, XCI (June 21, 1976).

PEER, ELIZABETH, "Barbara Walters—Star of the Morning," *Newsweek*, LXXXIII (May 6, 1974), 56. Cover story on Today show's co-host. Also see "TV News—The New Look" *Newsweek*, LXXXVIII (October 11, 1976).

"The 'Red Lion' Decision," *Journal of Broadcasting*, XIII (Fall 1969), 145. Text of Supreme Court decision on application of the fairness doctrine.

SEVAREID, ERIC, "What's Right with Sight-and-Sound Journalism," *Saturday Review* (October 10, 1976).

SHAPLEN, ROBERT, "A Farewell to Personal History," *Saturday Review*, XLIII (December 1, 1960), 46. Summarizes radio and television network coverage abroad in the 1950s.

SMITH, RALPH LEE, "The Wired Nation," *Nation*, CCX (May 18, 1970). A pioneering report on CATV in a special issue.

SOMMER, MICHAEL, "A Criticism of News Broadcasting & Regulatory Issues in the Richards Case," Ph.D. thesis, University of Southern California, 1969. Thorough study of celebrated news-slanting case.

STERLING, CHRISTOPHER H., "Newspaper Ownership of Broadcast Stations, 1920–68," *Journalism Quarterly*, XLVI (Summer 1969), 227. Data and discussion of issues.

———, "Decade of Development: FM Radio in the 1960s," *Journalism Quarterly*, XLVIII (Summer 1971), 222. Analysis of reasons for rapid growth.

WERTENBAKER, CHARLES, "Profiles," *New Yorker*, XXIX (December 26, 1953), 28. An excellent profile of Edward R. Murrow.

WILLIAMSON, MARY E., "Judith Cary Waller: Chicago Broadcasting Pioneer," *Journalism History*, III (Winter 1976–77), 111. First station manager of *Daily News'* WMAQ, 1922; 50 years in broadcasting.

Media leaders William S. Paley (*left*), broadcasting; Rupert Murdoch, newspapers.

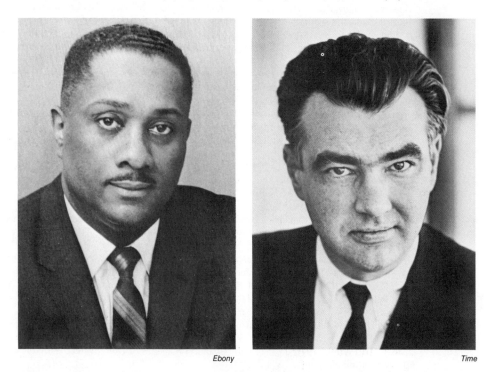

Magazine group owners John H. Johnson (*left*), *Ebony;* Henry Luce III, Time Inc.

24
Economic Pressures Shape the Mass Media

It is often made a matter of boasting, that the United States contain so many public journals. It were wiser to make it a cause of mourning, since the quality, in this instance, diminishes in an inverse ratio to the quantity.

—James Fenimore Cooper (1838)

Competition among the media, in the years after the rise of radio and television, was intense, both for advertising revenues and for attention from the reader, listener, or viewer. But the effects of intermedia competition on the fortunes of any one were less important than were the effects of general changes in the country's economy, fashioned in turn by depressions, world wars, and postwar booms. Deflation, inflation, and war accentuated an already well-developed trend toward newspaper suspensions and mergers and likewise adversely affected magazine publishing. On the other hand, a tremendous expansion of the gross national product and a population explosion beginning in the 1940s served to bulwark the publishing industry's position by providing a wider base for the support of both the old and new media.

At the same time the socioeconomic pressures inherent in modern American society, which had brought about concentration of newspaper ownership throughout the twentieth century, continued to have their effects, both on newspapers and other media. Competition for the mass market encouraged further standardization at the expense of individuality—common denominators for mass readership, listenership, or viewership to win mass advertising. Failure of individual enterprises to keep pace with the requirements of a modern socioeconomic situation also continued to play a part. And increasingly heavy investment costs in both publishing and broadcasting lessened ability to compete. Small radio stations, like small daily and weekly newspapers, could and did spread across the country as community enterprises. But big-time radio and television, like big-time newspaper and magazine publishing, was conducive to concentration of ownership—and radio and television proved to be easily adapted to chain operation. Finally, the natural tendency of publishers to become interested in

427

new communications agencies, and their desire to spread their investments into radio and television, led to extensive interlocking ownership among the media. Alternative media did not flourish, but the nation's black press did survive, joined by those of other minorities.

INTERMEDIA
ADVERTISING
COMPETITION

As explained in chapter 23, only radio made gains in advertising revenue during the 1930s.* During that decade of depression, recovery, and recession, expenditures on radio advertising rose from $40 million in 1929 to $225 million in 1941, last peacetime year. Newspaper advertising revenue, peaking at $800 million in 1929, fell 45 percent by 1933 and was still down 20 percent in 1941, at $650 million. Magazine advertising revenue followed a similar pattern, being cut in half by 1933 from its $240 million 1929 high and recovering to $210 million by 1941. Then came the general advances in the economy of the war years and corresponding gains in advertising revenues.

The story of competition for advertising among the media after 1945—and of the rise of television—can be told in two statistical tables. Table 24–1 shows the total dollar costs of all advertising expenditures by both national and local advertisers, including advertising-related costs. The percentage figures make it clear that television's inroads were made most heavily against radio, with magazines taking the next heaviest percentage drop. Radio's rather steady dollar volume in the 1950s, in contrast to the gains of other media, was due to its substantial cutting of advertising time rates (and parallel cutting of operating costs) and declines in national advertising.

Total advertising expenditures increased from 2 billion, 870 million dollars in 1945 to 28 billion, 230 million dollars in 1975, according to McCann-Erickson, Inc., estimates. But total disposable income in the country was also increasing greatly, and the amount of advertising expenditures stayed at a range between 2 and 3 percent of disposable income. Thus the sizable dollar gains kept the mass media only roughly even in their financial race.

Table 24–2 shows the division among the major mass media of the national and local advertising revenues spent on them alone. In other words, the four major media together were allotted varying amounts of advertising expenditures each year by national and local advertisers. How were these total sums split among the contestants?

*See pages 399–400.

Table 24–1   Dollar Volumes (in Millions) and Percentages of Total Advertising Expenditures Obtained by the Mass Media

Year	Newspapers		Magazines		Radio		Television	
	Dollars	%	Dollars	%	Dollars	%	Dollars	%
1945	920	32.0	360	12.5	420	14.6		
1950	2,080	36.5	510	9.0	610	10.7	170	3.0
1955	3,070	34.0	720	8.0	550	6.1	1,010	11.2
1960	3,700	31.0	940	7.9	690	5.8	1,590	13.3
1965	4,435	29.4	1,200	7.9	890	5.9	2,500	16.5
1970	5,850	29.7	1,320	6.7	1,280	6.5	3,660	18.6
1975	8,440	29.9	1,465	5.2	1,980	7.0	5,265	18.6

Source: McCann-Erickson, Inc., estimates. The percentage for all other advertising expenditures was approximately 40 percent for each period.

Table 24–2 Division of Advertising Expenditures Allotted
Only to the Mass Media (Percentages)

Year	National Advertising in				Local Advertising in		
	Newspapers	Magazines	Radio	Television	Newspapers	Radio	Television
1948	33.5	37.0	29.5		84.1	15.9	
1950	33.6	32.4	24.8	9.2	82.4	14.6	3.0
1952	28.8	31.5	18.9	20.8	80.6	13.6	5.8
1956	28.6	28.8	8.0	34.6	80.3	11.3	8.4
1960	25.0	28.0	7.9	39.1	80.2	12.0	7.8
1965	19.3	26.7	7.1	46.9	78.4	12.6	9.0
1970	18.1	23.0	7.2	51.7	75.6	13.6	10.8
1975	16.8	20.5	7.4	55.3	71.6	14.8	13.6

Source: McCann-Erickson, Inc., estimates.

Table 24–2 shows that television became dominant in this division of national advertising, cutting most sharply into radio but halving newspapers' share and reducing that of magazines (particular victims among the magazines were large general ones appealing to mass audiences, rather than specialized ones).

The changes in divisions of local advertising were small, with television taking a relatively small amount from newspapers. The percentage of total newspaper advertising revenue coming from local advertisers increased from 70 to 85 percent between 1950 and 1975; the percentage of total radio advertising revenue coming from local sources jumped from 41 to 74 percent. Television decreased in percentage of local advertising during the same 25 years, from 27 to 25 percent, as its volume of national advertising revenue increased so dramatically. Radio thus joined newspapers as primarily a local advertising medium. Magazines have no advertising categorized as local, although by the 1970s they offered split-runs so that advertisers could buy space in copies being distributed in restricted areas, with perhaps 15 percent of advertising revenue regional in origin.

NEWSPAPER
CONSOLIDATIONS,
1910–30

The years 1910 to 1914 mark the high point in numbers of newspapers published in the United States. The census of 1910 reported 2,600 daily publications of all types, of which 2,200 were English-language newspapers of general circulation. General-circulation weekly newspapers numbered approximately 14,000. The totals hovered at these peaks until the economic pressures of the World War I were felt by American newspapers.

Wartime pressures, while of marked effect on publishing, only accented trends that were developing as early as 1890. These trends were toward suspension of some competing newspapers, merger of others with their rivals, concentration of newspaper ownership in many cities and towns, and creation of newspaper chains or groups. Before 1930, each of these trends had been clearly developed, to set the pattern for twentieth-century American journalism.

Statistics often can be confusing, and this is true of those concerned with the number of American newspapers published over the years. For example, it might be assumed that if there were 2,200 English-language daily newspapers of general circulation in 1910, and but 1,942 in 1930, then 258 newspapers died in those two decades. Actually, 1,391 daily newspapers suspended publication or shifted to weekly status in those 20 years, and another 362 were merged with rival papers. In the same two decades, 1,495 dailies were being born.[1] The turnover among established dailies was less drastic than these figures might seem to indicate, however, since one-fourth of the newcomers died within the first year of publication, and another one-half eventually joined the suspension list. But some of the newcomers were healthy ventures in the growing small towns and cities of an increasingly urbanized country.

Between 1910 and 1930 the population of the United States increased by 30 million, from 92 to 122 million persons. The number of towns and cities of 8,000 or more persons jumped from 768 to 1,208. Daily newspaper circulation increased at a faster pace, from 22.5 million copies a day in 1910 to 40 million copies in 1930. Sunday newspaper circulation more than doubled in the two decades, moving from 13 million to 27 million copies. Total newspaper advertising revenue tripled in the years 1915 to 1929, increasing from an estimated $275 million to $800 million.[2]

Yet despite this great growth in advertising revenue, in numbers of readers, and in numbers of urban centers that could support daily newspaper publication, there was a net loss of 258 daily newspapers in the 20 years. Reduction of the number of competing dailies in larger cities, elimination of all but one newspaper in smaller towns, and suspension of daily newspaper publishing in some fading communities more than offset the number of new dailies started in growing towns and older publishing centers. The figures given in table 24–3 illustrate daily newspaper

Table 24–3 Growth of One-Daily Cities, 1880–1930

	1880	1900	1910	1920	1930
Number of English-language general circulation dailies	*850*	*1,967*	*2,200*	*2,042*	*1,942*
Number of cities with dailies	*389*	*915*	*1,207*	*1,295*	*1,402*
Number of one-daily cities	*149*	*353*	*509*	*716*	*1,002*
Number of one-combination cities	*1*	*3*	*9*	*27*	*112*
Number of cities with competing dailies	*239*	*559*	*689*	*552*	*288*
Percentage of daily cities with only one daily paper	*38.3*	*38.6*	*42.2*	*55.3*	*71.5*
Percentage of daily cities with competing dailies	*61.4*	*61.1*	*57.1*	*42.6*	*20.6*
Percentage of all dailies published in one-daily cities	*17.5*	*17.9*	*23.1*	*35.1*	*51.6*
Number of one-daily cities above 25,000 population	*4*	*8*	*25*	*47*	*93*
Number of one-daily cities above 100,000 population	*0*	*1*	*1*	*5*	*6*
Total daily circulation (millions)	*3.1*	*15.1*	*22.4*	*27.8*	*39.6*

Sources: For 1880, data tabulated by Edwin Emery from S.N.D. North, *History and Present Condition of the Newspaper and Periodical Press of the United States* (Washington: Government Printing Office, 1884). For 1900–1920, W. Carl Masche, "Factors Involved in the Consolidation and Suspension of Daily and Sunday Newspapers in the United States Since 1900: A Statistical Study in Social Change" (Master's thesis, University of Minnesota, 1932), and Morris Ernst, *The First Freedom* (New York: Macmillan, 1946), p. 284. For 1930, Alfred McClung Lee, "The Basic Newspaper Pattern," *The Annals of the American Academy of Political and Social Science,* CCXIX (January 1942), 46, except figures for one-daily cities of specified population, from Masche.

For numbers of English-language general circulation dailies, 1880, tabulated from North; 1900, from Masche; 1910, from Royal H. Ray (see footnote 1); 1920–30, *Editor & Publisher International Year Book* figures. The census counts of daily publications, which included foreign language, religious, trade, and technical dailies, were 971 dailies in 1880, 2,226 in 1900, 2,600 in 1910, and 2,441 in 1920. But those figures do not compare with the *Editor & Publisher International Year Book* figures available after 1920. Masche, Ernst, and Ray tabulated their data from Ayer directories; Lee used *Editor & Publisher International Year Book* data.

publishing trends from 1880 to 1930, including the steady growth of one-daily cities at all population levels.

Many reasons can be listed for the decline in numbers of newspapers published, for the curtailment of competition in most communities, and for the increasing concentration of ownership. They fall under seven general headings: (1) economic pressures stemming from technological changes in the publishing pattern; (2) pressures resulting from competition for circulation and advertising revenues; (3) standardization of the product, resulting in loss of individuality and reader appeal; (4) lack of economic or social need for some newspapers; (5) managerial faults; (6) effects of wartime inflation and general business depressions; (7) planned consolidation of newspapers for various reasons.

METROPOLITAN DAILIES, 1890–1930: MUNSEY, CURTIS, KOHLSAAT

New York City boasted 15 general-circulation, English-language daily newspapers in 1890. Eight were morning papers and seven were afternoon papers. Twelve owners were represented. By 1932 only three morning papers, four evening papers, and two tabloids remained, representing seven ownerships.

The name of Frank A. Munsey plays a large part in that story. Munsey was a successful New Englander whose career had a Horatio Alger ring. He broke into the New York publishing business with a juvenile magazine, the *Golden Argosy,* then turned to the general magazine field with his *Munsey's.* As a ten-cent monthly, *Munsey's* hit 650,000 circulation by 1900 to lead its competitors by a wide margin. The publisher had a million-dollar-a-year income by 1905. But he dreamt of a great national chain of newspapers, directed from a central headquarters by the most brilliant of American editors and business managers. To Munsey, the successful businessman, the newspaper business was a disorderly, if not chaotic, enterprise. He proposed to bring efficiency to the newspaper world and thereby improve the product.

In 1901 Munsey bought the old *New York Daily News* and the *Washington Times* as the nucleus of his chain. The *Boston Journal* was added in 1902, and in 1908 he invaded two more Eastern cities, buying the *Baltimore Evening News* and founding the *Philadelphia Evening Times.* Munsey set about to improve the papers, installing color presses, featurizing Sunday editions, and seeking to break into higher readership groups. But the public failed to respond, and all the papers were killed or sold to others by 1917.

Munsey still owned one newspaper, the *New York Press,* which he had bought in 1912. The *Press,* under the editorship of Ervin Wardman, had a comfortable circulation. But Munsey eyed the New York field for a newspaper that could be combined with it, and his choice was the *Sun.* The *Sun* was still a proud newspaper, edited after the death of Charles A. Dana in 1897 by Edward P. Mitchell. Munsey paid $2.5 million for the *Sun* and the *Evening Sun* in 1916 and merged the *Press* into the morning edition, making Wardman publisher, Mitchell editor, and the *Press's* renowned Keats Speed, managing editor. But wartime publishing difficulties cost him the profit he hoped to make, and in 1920 he looked about for another prospect for consolidation.

Munsey's first move was to buy the *Herald,* the *Telegram,* and the Paris edition of the *Herald* for $4 million. The younger Bennett had spent lavishly during his long lifetime, and when he died in 1918 his newspapers were in neither a financial nor competitive position to continue. Munsey merged the morning *Sun* into the *Herald* and gave the historical name *Sun* to the evening edition.

The next victim was the *Globe*. Started in 1904, it was considered a healthy, liberal newspaper when Munsey killed it in 1923 for its AP evening membership. The next year Munsey bought the conservative *Mail,* which had survived since 1867, merging it with the *Telegram.*

Munsey's morning paper, the *Herald,* was not faring well. He turned his eyes toward the *Tribune,* lowest in circulation of the morning dailies. But the *Tribune's* owners, Ogden Mills Reid and his able wife, Helen Rogers Reid, refused to sell. Munsey, true to his belief that further consolidation was necessary, thereupon sold the *Herald* and its Paris edition to the Reids for $5 million. Happily, the new *Herald Tribune* successfully added the bulk of the old *Herald's* subscribers to its list and saw its advertising volume expand under the business direction of Mrs. Reid. Of all Munsey's newspaper maneuvering, his part in the creation of the *Herald Tribune* was the happiest, even though it meant the merger of the historic Bennett and Greeley papers.

Death claimed Munsey in 1925. Newspapermen generally were bitterly resentful of the cold and businesslike approach Munsey had toward both them and their profession. William Allen White best expressed the rebels' sentiments in his famed terse obituary published in the *Emporia Gazette:*

Frank A. Munsey contributed to the journalism of his day the talent of a meatpacker, the morals of a money-changer and the manners of an undertaker. He and his kind have about succeeded in transforming a once-noble profession into an eight per cent security. May he rest in trust!

Another magazine publisher played a major role in the consolidation of Philadelphia's newspapers. He was Cyrus H.K. Curtis, who entered the Philadelphia newspaper picture by buying the historic *Public Ledger,* founded by William M. Swain in 1836 in the first wave of penny papers. Ably edited by George W. Childs from 1864 until his death in 1894, the *Public Ledger* had been sold in 1902 to Adolph S. Ochs, who put his brother George in charge. By 1913 Ochs was ready to sell to Curtis at a loss.

Curtis's first move was to give Philadelphia another newspaper, the *Evening Public Ledger,* in 1914. But then, like Munsey, he moved in on the competition. The *Evening Telegraph,* dating back to 1864, was bought for its AP membership in 1918 and killed. The *Press,* founded in 1857, was purchased in 1920 for its newsprint contracts. Newspapermen mourned again in 1925 when the *North American,* on the scene since 1839 and with a reputation as a crusading force under editor E. A. Van Valkenberg, was killed. Curtis poured money into his newspapers, building them a $15 million plant and developing a famous foreign news service that was widely syndicated.

The Curtis newspapers collapsed as the 1929 depression deepened. In a final effort, Curtis bought the rival morning *Inquirer,* but when he died in 1933 the *Public Ledger* was merged into the *Inquirer.* Its evening edition lived until 1942, competing with the *Bulletin* and a tabloid *Daily News* begun in 1925. J. David Stern made the *Record* a liberal morning paper after 1928.

Herman Kohlsaat was the chief figure in Chicago's newspaper consolidations. Enriched by a chain of bakeries and lunch counters and enamored of the newspaper business, Kohlsaat bought into the *Inter Ocean* in 1891. Dissatisfied, he sold out and bought the *Evening Post* and a successful morning Democratic paper, the *Times-Herald.* Kohlsaat was a Republican, and the paper had to compete with the conservative *Tribune*. By 1901 he had to sell out, the *Times-Herald* disappearing into the *Record,* the morning edition of Victor Lawson's *Daily News.*

Chicago in 1902 thus had four morning papers: the *Tribune, Inter Ocean, Record-Herald,* and William Randolph Hearst's newly established *Examiner*. In the evening field were the *Daily News, Post, Journal,* and Hearst's *American*. The highly successful *Tribune* and *Daily News,* and the well-financed Hearst papers, were to squeeze out their competitors in the next 30 years.

One victim was the well-edited *Record-Herald,* which when Lawson brought Frank B. Noyes from the *Washington Star* to run it from 1902 to 1910, ranked as one of the country's best. But by 1914 Kohlsaat, back in the picture, was merging the *Record-Herald* and the *Inter Ocean* as the *Herald* with James Keeley as editor. It failed, and in 1918 the Hearst interests established the *Herald & Examiner* as the *Tribune'*s only competitor. Victor Lawson's *Daily News* developed a distinguished foreign service and passed to Colonel Frank Knox's hands in 1931. Its only evening rivals were Hearst's *American* and the liberal tabloid *Times,* founded in 1929.

The sharp reduction in the number of morning dailies in New York, Philadelphia, and Chicago was part of a nationwide trend. Reader and advertiser preference for afternoon papers, and the time advantage these had in publishing European war news, helped to cut the number of morning papers from 500 in 1910 to 388 by 1930. Early in this period such morning papers as the *Atlanta Constitution, Indianapolis Star, Minneapolis Tribune,* and *St. Paul Pioneer Press* were alone in their fields. They were joined in 1915 by the *Detroit Free Press,* with the death of the old *Tribune*. Cleveland in 1917 saw the *Leader* disappear into the *Plain Dealer,* leaving the latter the only morning paper. Elimination of the *Free Press* in Milwaukee in 1919 left the *Sentinel* without morning competition. The same year the *St. Louis Globe-Democrat* bought its morning rival, the *Republic*. Merger in Buffalo in 1926 of the *Courier* (1831) and the *Express* (1846) ended that city's long morning rivalry. Pittsburgh's morning dailies were reduced to one in 1927, and Kansas City joined the trend in 1928. The *Cincinnati Enquirer* closed out its competition in 1930 by buying the *Commercial Tribune,* successor to Murat Halstead's old *Commercial Gazette*. By 1933 the journalistic historian Willard G. Bleyer could list 40 cities of more than 100,000 population that had only one morning daily.[3]

Morning paper mergers were the most spectacular in the first decades after 1900, but overall consolidation of metropolitan newspapers, and concentration of ownership, continued from coast to coast. Entry of the Hearst papers into Detroit through purchase of the *Times* in 1921 prompted the *News* (founded by James E. Scripps) to buy out the *Journal* in 1922. Thus Detroit, with more than a million population, was left with but three newspapers, the morning *Free Press* and the evening *News* and *Times*. In New Orleans, the *Times-Democrat* and the *Picayune* were merged in 1914, leaving the new *Times-Picayune* alone in the morning field for ten years. The *Times-Picayune,* owned by L.K. Nicholson, bought Colonel Robert Ewing's *States* in 1933 for an evening edition. The other evening paper, the *Item,* published a morning edition, the *Tribune,* from 1924 to 1941.

St. Louis afternoon journalism was dominated by Pulitzer's *Post-Dispatch*. The *Chronicle,* Scripps-McRae entry of 1880, merged with the *Evening Star* (1878) in 1905. The *Times* (1907) joined forces with the *Star* in 1932 as the *Star-Times,* leaving St. Louis with three ownerships. Kansas City rivals of Nelson's *Star* found the going equally difficult. Nelson bought the morning *Times* in 1901. The Scripps-McRae *World,* founded in 1897, faded from the picture. The evening *Post,* started in 1906 and bought by Bonfils and Tammen of *Denver Post* fame in 1909, was sold in 1922 to the owners of the morning *Journal* (1858), and the two papers became the *Journal-Post* in 1928. Kansas City thus dropped to two ownerships.

**HEARST
AND SCRIPPS-HOWARD
1920s CONSOLIDATIONS**

Activities of the country's two biggest group ownerships—Hearst and Scripps-Howard—and of lesser chain aspirants caused newspaper consolidations in still other cities. The Hearst organization, in a buying splurge concentrated in the years 1918 to 1928, put 16 newspapers to death as consolidations were carried out to bulwark the positions of Hearst-owned dailies. The Scripps-Howard group was responsible for the closing of 15 newspapers between 1923 and 1934.

In Boston, where the Hearst-owned evening *American* was founded in 1904, the publisher bought the century-old *Daily Advertiser* in 1917 and the *Record* in 1920. The two papers were juggled in an effort to bring tabloid publication to Boston, with the name *Record* surviving for the morning Hearst paper. Meanwhile the *Boston Herald* was buying the *Traveler* in 1912 for an evening edition and was absorbing the Munsey-owned *Journal* in 1917. Thus Boston, which in 1900 had eleven major newspapers operated by seven ownerships, by 1930 had eight newspapers and five ownerships. The others were Edwin A. Grozier's highly successful morning *Post,* the Taylor family's morning and evening *Globes,* and the limping but traditional *Transcript*.

Washington was one of the few large cities to add newspapers during this period, but Hearst promptly consolidated the ownership of two newcomers. The morning *Post* and the Noyes family's evening *Star* were challenged by the founding of the *Times* in 1894 and the *Herald* in 1906. Munsey bought the *Times* in 1901 and killed its morning edition. When he retired from the Washington field in 1917 the *Times* passed to Arthur Brisbane, who sold it to Hearst two years later. The *Herald* was added to the Hearst group in 1922. Scripps-Howard gave Washington a fourth ownership when it established the tabloid *Daily News* in 1921.

Baltimore was less fortunate. The *Sun,* original penny paper of 1837, took over the *Evening World* in 1910 and made it the *Evening Sun.* The *Herald,* a morning penny paper, died in 1906. The *Evening News,* Grasty's crusading paper that fell into Munsey's control, was consolidated with the *Star* in 1921, and the paper was sold to Hearst in 1922. The *American,* dating from 1799, also passed from Munsey to Hearst and after 1928 was published only as a Sunday paper. A 1922 Scripps-Howard entry, the *Post,* was sold to Hearst in 1934. The Hearst *News-Post* thus opposed the *Sun* papers.

Pittsburgh also saw its newspapers shuffled by the Hearst and Scripps-Howard organizations. The Scripps-Howard group bought the well-established *Press* in 1923 for $6 million, under an agreement with the city's other newspaper owners that the *Dispatch* and *Leader* would be bought out and killed. Four years later Hearst and Paul Block, a Hearst associate and newspaper broker, bought the remaining four Pittsburgh dailies. The morning *Sun* and *Chronicle Telegraph* were transformed into the Hearst-owned *Sun-Telegraph;* the evening *Post* and *Gazette Times* into the Block-owned *Post-Gazette*.

Arthur Brisbane and Hearst teamed up in Milwaukee at the end of World War I, with the result that the *Evening Wisconsin,* the *News,* and the *Telegram* were rolled into the *Wisconsin News,* Hearst-owned after 1919. The morning *Sentinel* joined the Hearst chain in 1924 to give the chain two footholds against the steadily increasing pressure of the *Milwaukee Journal.*[4] Also in the Midwest, the *Omaha News* and *Bee* were bought by Hearst in 1928 and merged as the *News-Bee,* a morning, evening, and Sunday publication.

On the West Coast, Hearst created a strong evening companion for his *San*

Francisco Examiner by combining three papers. He bought the *Call* (1855) in 1913 and combined the *Evening Post* with it to obtain an Associated Press membership. In 1929 the *Bulletin* (1856) was absorbed by Hearst to form the *Call-Bulletin*. The mergers left San Francisco with Hearst morning and evening papers, the locally-owned morning *Chronicle,* and the Scripps-Howard evening *News.* Across the bay in Oakland the *Post-Enquirer* was formed in a 1922 Hearst double purchase and merger as competition for the Knowland family's *Tribune*.

In Los Angeles, Hearst's morning *Examiner* was augmented in 1922 by purchase of the evening *Herald*. The *Express,* founded in 1871, was swallowed up by Hearst in 1931 to form the *Herald & Express.* The *Record,* established by Scripps in 1895, died in the 1920s but was replaced by the *Daily News,* a tabloid that Manchester Boddy developed into a pro-New Deal newspaper. Hearst's solid morning competition in Los Angeles still was Harry Chandler's conservative *Times.*

Among Hearst's other purchases were the *Atlanta Georgian,* 1912; *Detroit Times,* 1921; *Seattle Post-Intelligencer, Rochester Journal,* and *Syracuse Telegram,* 1922; *Albany Times-Union* and *San Antonio Light,* 1924; *Syracuse Journal* (combined with the *Telegram*), 1925.

Strengthening of Scripps-Howard properties by elimination of competitors took place in several cities. Knoxville saw the *News-Sentinel* created by the merger of the *News,* started in 1921, and the *Sentinel,* bought in 1926. The *El Paso Post,* founded in 1922, became the *Herald-Post* with the acquisition of the *Herald* in 1931. The *Akron Press,* begun in 1899 by E. W. Scripps, received a badly needed transfusion in 1925 with the purchase of the *Times,* to form the *Times-Press.* The *Memphis Press,* founded in 1906, became the *Press-Scimitar* by absorbing the *News-Scimitar* in 1926; ten years later Scripps-Howard added the morning *Memphis Commercial Appeal* to the chain. The *New York Telegram,* bought in 1927, became the *World-Telegram* in 1931 when Howard negotiated the purchase of the famous Pulitzer papers. The *Pittsburgh Press* was acquired in 1923 in a deal that eliminated the *Dispatch* and *Leader.*

Denver's newspapers were reshaped by a cutthroat battle between Scripps-Howard and the *Denver Post.* The *Post'* s evening opponents had dwindled over the years. The *Republican,* which had absorbed the *Tribune* in 1884, in turn was merged with the *Times* in 1913. The *Times* and the morning *Rocky Mountain News* came under the same ownership in 1902 and were sold in 1926 to Scripps-Howard. Thereupon the *Express,* in the Scripps fold since 1906, was merged into the *Times.* A truce arranged between the *Post* and the Scripps-Howard newspapers in 1928 brought the demise of the *Times* and left Denver with two newspapers.

On the loss side, Scripps-Howard sold the *Des Moines News, Sacramento Star,* and *Terre Haute Post* to competitors during the 1920s, and the *Baltimore Post* to Hearst in 1934. The *Washington Daily News, Fort Worth Press,* and *Birmingham Post* were founded in 1921. Scripps-Howard purchased the *Indianapolis Times* and *Youngstown Telegram* in 1922 and the *New Mexico State Tribune* in Albuquerque in 1923, while the *Buffalo Times* was acquired in 1929.

STABILIZING
THE DAILIES, 1930–70s

What were the effects on newspapers of intermedia advertising competition and the ups and downs of the economy from 1930 to the 1970s? In broad strokes, the number of dailies decreased, then stabilized near the 1,750 figure; ownership concentration increased as the number of competitive dailies declined; circulation steadily increased; and while financial problems were many, newspaper publishing economy tended to stabilize comfortably.

The sharp drop in advertising revenue in the early 1930s wiped out many newspaper profit margins despite cutbacks in salaries, production costs, and newsprint prices, which fell as low as $40 a ton. There were 145 suspensions of dailies during 1931–33, and 77 more in the recovery years of 1934–36. Then came the business recession of 1937, dropping advertising revenues at a time when labor and production costs had mounted to substantially higher post-depression levels. Some newspaper managements, hit by these new disasters after surviving the great depression, were too tired to struggle any longer. Daily newspaper suspensions and mergers accelerated, totaling 165 in the years 1937 to 1939. These were in many respects the blackest years in the history of American newspapers, with one-third of salaried employees in the newspaper industry losing their jobs, according to census statistics. The war years of 1940 to 1944 brought another 197 newspaper deaths, mostly small dailies pinched by production problems. With 584 suspensions and 386 new starts of dailies since 1931, the number of English language general-circulation daily newspapers dropped from 1,942 in 1930 to a twentieth-century low of 1,744 in 1945.

Postwar expansion brought an excess of new starts over suspensions in the daily field. The mid-1940s and mid-1950s were profitable years for newspapers in general. Despite the loss of 350 dailies between 1945 and 1960, their number rose to 1,786 in 1952, then settled back to 1,763 in 1961. Inflation and recession took a slight toll, to 1,756, by 1976.

Circulation of dailies was approximately 40 million copies in 1930 for a population of 122 million; by 1976 it was 60 million for a population of 210 million. Newspaper circulation stayed even with population expansion to 1960, thanks to a heavy increase in circulation in the 1940s that counterbalanced the population explosion of the 1950s. The number of papers for each household decreased slightly, however, from 1.32 to 1.16 in the period. But the number of papers per household dropped to an even 1.0 by 1970, and circulation trailed the population expansion with its young bulge.

Table 24–4 shows the extent of the decline in competition in cities having daily newspapers, since 1930. The number of one-daily cities steadily increased, and there were more one-combination cities (one owner of two papers) until the 1960s. Joint-printing cities are those in which two owners have merged their printing and business operations and, thus, are not fully competitive.

Table 24-4 Competition in Daily Newspaper Cities, 1940–76

	1940	1945	1954	1961	1971	1976
Number of English language general circulation dailies	1,878	1,744	1,785	1,763	1,748	1,756
Number of cities with dailies	1,426	1,396	1,448	1,461	1,511	1,550
Number of one-daily cities	1,092	1,107	1,188	1,222	1,312	1,369
Number of one-combination cities	149	161	154	160	141	122
Number of joint-printing cities	4	11	19	18	21	20
Number of cities with competing dailies	181	117	87	61	37	39
Percentage of daily cities with competing dailies	12.7	8.4	6.0	4.2	2.4	2.5
Total daily circulation (millions)	41.1	45.9	54.5	58.9	62.1	60.6

Sources: For number of dailies and circulation, *Editor & Publisher International Year Books.* For other data, Raymond B. Nixon and Jean Ward, "Trends in Newspaper Ownership and Inter-Media Competition," *Journalism Quarterly,* XXXVIII (Winter 1961), 3. For 1971, compiled from 1971 *Year Book* data by Nixon; for 1976, compiled from 1976 *Year Book* data by Judith Sobel. See *Journalism Quarterly*'s Spring 1978 volume for an article with more detailed data by Sobel and Emery. In 1977 there were 39 cities with competing dailies and a total of 1,762 dailies with 60.9 million circulation.

Of the 1,550 cities with dailies at the start of 1976, there were competitive dailies in only 24 of 1,370 cities with papers of 100,000 circulation or less and competitors in only four of the cities whose papers had circulations between 100,000 and 500,000. All 11 cities with papers of circulations over 500,000 were competitive. The prevailing pattern was one daily for cities under 100,000 in population, and single ownership or joint printing of a morning-evening combination in cities from 100,000 to 500,000.[5] But if there were only 97 competing voices of daily newspapers in 39 competitive cities in 1976, radio and television obviously added other voices. This was true in all but about 200 of the noncompetitive daily cities.[6]

THE SURVIVING METROPOLITAN DAILIES

Still, there was little direct newspaper competition remaining by 1977. Only New York City had three daily newspapers with three different owners. Only seven other cities supported more than two dailies (all had just two ownerships): Chicago, Philadelphia, Baltimore, Boston, San Antonio, Oklahoma City, and Kingsport, Tennessee (rival small dailies). Twelve of the 25 largest cities had two separately owned dailies: Los Angeles, Detroit, Houston, Dallas, Washington, Cleveland, San Francisco, St. Louis, Columbus (Ohio), Seattle, Pittsburgh, and Denver. Seven of the largest 25 cities had just one owner of their two dailies: Indianapolis, Milwaukee, San Diego, Memphis, New Orleans, Phoenix, and Jacksonville.

Newspaper managements could cite several reasons for these contractions and for continued concern over newspaper financial stability: a steady increase in the price of newsprint, which after leveling off at $135 a ton in 1957 to 1966 jumped to $300 a ton in 1976; increasing supply costs; rising wages and salaries; losses of national advertising to television. Their critics, however, generally agreed that a major difficulty was one of rigidity of advertising rates, which had not been advanced sufficiently in light of circulation increases and rising production costs. Many dailies, however, advanced sale prices to 20 or 25 cent levels. Newspaper profits ranged to 10 percent of gross income as a general picture. *Editor & Publisher* surveys of profits each spring showed that smaller dailies, and noncompetitive larger ones, were likely to be making bigger profit margins than the big-city dailies. Twenty-four major metropolitan dailies were suspended between 1950 and 1976 and eight others were sold to competitors. Some were losing a million dollars a year at the end.

Circulation gains were going to the mid- and smaller-sized dailies, especially in the suburbs. Metropolitan papers generally suffered declines. The largest daily, the tabloid *New York Daily News,* still had 1,925,000 daily circulation and 2,760,000 on Sunday. But it had lost 1,365,000 Sunday circulation and 335,000 daily in 25 years, a reflection in part of the inroads of television on other entertainment-oriented media. The *Mirror* and *Journal-American* in New York disappeared altogether; the *Chicago Tribune* lost 375,000 Sunday and 180,000 daily before changing its appeal. The biggest gainer was the country's second-largest daily in 1976, the *Wall Street Journal,* whose four nationwide editions had 1,408,000 circulation as against 153,000 in 1950. Other major gains since 1950 were by the *Los Angeles Times,* 615,000, and the *New York Times,* 300,000.*

The suburbs offered opportunity for new papers, both daily and weekly. In 1977 there were some 2,000 suburban papers, including 300 dailies, and as many more big-

*The ten largest daily circulations in 1976 were *New York Daily News,* 1,925,643; *Wall Street Journal,* 1,407,985; *Los Angeles Times,* 1,008,995; *New York Times,* 803,123; *Chicago Tribune,* 746,069; *Detroit News,* 627,569; *Detroit Free Press,* 620,651; *Chicago Sun-Times,* 566,127; *Philadelphia Bulletin,* city neighborhood sheets. Major centers for this growing journalism included Los Angeles, Chicago, New York, Philadelphia, and Detroit. Suburban dailies were growing particularly rapidly in the Los Angeles and New York areas. One conspicuous success was *Newsday,* founded in 1940 on Long Island by Alicia Patterson. Its excellence in publishing both local and world news gave it a circulation above 450,000 by 1976 and a standing as one of the top half-dozen evening newspapers in the country. Other new ventures attracting attention were the Gannett group's *Today,* in the Cape Kennedy area of Florida, and the *Los Angeles Times'* satellite paper, the *Orange Coast Daily Pilot.* The existence of growing suburban dailies was a factor in big city journalism's decline.

CHANGES IN MAJOR CITIES   New York City suffered the most severe losses of any U.S. metropolis, dropping from six owners and seven dailies in 1960 to three owners and their three dailies in 1967. The attrition had been steady. Hearst's *American* (his pride and joy as the old morning *Journal* of the 1890s) went in 1937. The evening *Sun* was sold to Scripps-Howard in 1950 for merger with the *World-Telegram.* Hearst's tabloid *Mirror* was next to go in 1963. A 114-day strike in 1963 crippled all the dailies and a second strike in 1965 and management ineptness intensified the crisis. In April 1966, John Hay Whitney of the *Herald Tribune,* the Scripps-Howard interests of the *World-Telegram and Sun,* and the Hearst interests of the *Journal-American* announced plans to publish jointly morning, evening, and Sunday. But strikes again disrupted New York newspapers, and the *Herald Tribune* ceased publication. The new daily, named the *World Journal Tribune,* appeared but died in 1967. With it went the shades of Pulitzer, Greeley, Bennett, Dana, Scripps, Howard, Hearst, and a dash of Munsey. Left to publish were the *Times,* the *Daily News,* and the *Post.* Brooklyn lost its *Citizen* in 1947 and its 114-year-old *Eagle* in 1955. The *Long Island Press* bowed out in 1977. In January 1978, a conservative-oriented daily called *The Trib* made its bow in news magazine format.

Boston lost three historic newspapers: the 111-year-old staid *Transcript* in 1941, the 125-year-old *Post* in 1956, and the 125-year-old *Traveler* (merged in 1967 as the *Herald Traveler*) in 1972. Two Hearst tabloids were combined as the *Record American* in 1961 (renamed *Herald American*). Surviving with it were the two *Globes.*

Washington slipped to two dailies by 1972. Mrs. Eleanor Patterson bought the *Times* and *Herald* from Hearst and merged them in 1939. Ownership passed to her cousin, Robert R. McCormick, in 1949; he in turn sold the *Times-Herald* in 1954 for merger with its morning rival, the *Post.* The Scripps-Howard *News* was merged with the evening *Star* in 1972.

Chicago was cut to McCormick's all-day *Tribune* and Marshall Field's morning *Sun-Times* and evening *Daily News.* After Hearst killed his *Herald & Examiner* in 1939 in the wake of a Newspaper Guild strike, Field launched the *Sun* in 1941 to do battle with McCormick's *Tribune* in the morning field. Finding the going rough, he bought the *Times* in 1947 and made the merged *Sun-Times* a tabloid. The *Tribune* purchased Hearst's *American* as an evening affiliate in 1956 and later renamed it

---

540,851; *Washington Post,* 530,031. Top Sunday circulations were *New York Daily News,* 2,759,182; *New York Times,* 1,406,833; *Los Angeles Times,* 1,265,547; *Chicago Tribune,* 1,113,916. Figures are September 30, 1976, ABC reports. The five leading papers in advertising linage were the *Los Angeles Times, Chicago Tribune, Miami Herald, Houston Chronicle,* and *Washington Post.*

Chicago Today, turning it into a tabloid. The *Sun-Times* countered by buying the *Daily News* from John S. Knight in a record $24-million 1959 transaction. *Chicago Today,* and the ghosts of the legendary newsmen of "The Front Page," disappeared in 1974. In early 1978, it appeared the days of the historic *Daily News* were numbered.

Four other cities had two ownerships but retained three dailies. In Philadelphia, Walter H. Annenberg's *Inquirer* bought the tabloid *Daily News* in 1957, to step up competition with the McLeans' *Bulletin.* The Annenberg papers were then sold to the Knight group in 1969. The liberal *Record* died in 1947 after a Guild strike. Baltimore's survivors were the two *Suns* and the Hearst *News-American.* San Antonio's trio were Hearst's *Light* and the jointly owned *Express* and *News,* purchased by Australian group owner Rupert Murdoch in 1974. Oklahoma City saw the *Oklahoma Journal* started in 1964 to compete with the *Oklahoman* and *Times.*

Los Angeles, the third largest city, dropped to two dailies. The Chandler family's *Times* began the tabloid *Mirror* in 1948 to give it a breezier afternoon entry against two Hearst papers, the morning *Examiner* and evening *Herald-Express.* The competition was fatal for a fifth paper, the liberal tabloid *Daily News,* which suspended in 1954. The *Mirror,* edited drably after a 1957 management shakeup, faltered and was suspended in January 1962. The Hearst group at the same time elected to kill the *Examiner,* naming their evening paper the *Herald-Examiner.*

Scripps-Howard newspapers disappeared in Houston, Fort Worth, and San Francisco. The *Houston Press,* one of the group's liveliest, gave up the struggle against the *Chronicle* and the *Post* in 1964. The *Fort Worth Press* was killed in 1975. In San Francisco, the Hearst and Scripps-Howard evening papers had been combined into the jointly owned *News-Call Bulletin* in 1959; Scripps-Howard bowed out in 1962 and the paper succumbed in 1965 as Hearst's morning *Examiner* moved to the evening field in a joint-business arrangement with the *Chronicle* that saw the two rivals sharing a Sunday edition.

Detroit lost Hearst's *Times* in 1960, victim of a battle with the *News* and *Free Press.* In Cleveland, the *Plain Dealer* disposed of its evening paper, the *News,* to the Scripps-Howard *Press* in 1960. The *St. Louis Star-Times,* published by Elzey Roberts and ably edited by Norman Isaacs, fell before the *Post-Dispatch* and *Globe-Democrat* in 1951. Pittsburgh saw Hearst's *Sun-Telegraph* merged with the Block family's *Post-Gazette* in 1960, with the Scripps-Howard *Press* the remaining rival. Seattle's *Star* blinked out in 1947, leaving the *Times* and Hearst's *Post-Intelligencer.**

*Seven of the 25 largest cities of 1977 had two papers but only one owner. Memphis fell to this status in 1936 when Scripps-Howard bought the *Commercial Appeal* to complement its *Press Scimitar.* In San Diego, James S. Copley's *Union* and *Tribune* eliminated the *Journal* in 1948. The *New Orleans Item* was merged with the *States* in 1958, under the ownership of the *Times-Picayune.* In Milwaukee, Hearst's old *Sentinel* was sold to the *Journal* in 1962. After 78 years, Scripps-Howard's *Indianapolis Times* left the field to Eugene C. Pulliam's *Star* and *News* in 1965. Pulliam also had the field to himself in Phoenix with his *Republic* and *Gazette.* In Jacksonville, the *Florida Times-Union* and the *Journal* came under common ownership in 1959. Among other cities that dropped to one-owner status were Akron and Toledo, through Scripps-Howard withdrawals of the late 1930s, and Omaha (one paper status) and Rochester by 1937 Hearst sales. Other dates for elimination of competition included Louisville, 1936; Providence, 1938; Richmond, 1940; Minneapolis, 1941; Kansas City, 1942; Syracuse, 1943; Harrisburg, 1948; Dayton and Tacoma (one paper), 1949; Oakland (one paper) and Atlanta, 1950; Raleigh, 1955; Tampa and Grand Rapids (one paper), 1958; Charlotte, 1959; Wichita and Albany, 1960; St. Petersburg, 1962; Newark (one paper), 1972; and Hartford (one paper), 1976. Among well-known dailies disappearing and not mentioned in the text above were the *Louisville Herald-Post, Providence Tribune, Kansas City Journal-Post, Newark News,* and *Hartford Times.*

THE GROWTH
OF NEWSPAPER
GROUPS

The daily newspaper followed the American business trend in the twentieth century and increasingly became a group-owned enterprise. In 1900 there were only eight groups of dailies, controlling 27 papers (1.3 percent of the total) and 10 percent of the total circulation.[7] By 1935, 63 groups were counted, with 328 papers (17 percent of the total) and 41 percent of the total circulation.[8] In 1960 the figures were 109 groups with 560 papers (30 percent) and 46 percent of the circulation. By 1977 there were 168 groups listed, with 1,061 papers (60 percent of all dailies) and 71 percent of total daily circulation.[9]

The five largest 1977 groups controlled 25 percent of daily newspaper circulation in the country. But the Knight-Ridder group, largest in circulation, had only 6.1 percent of the total. And the Gannett group, largest in numbers of papers with 73 dailies and 48 Sunday editions, still controlled only 4.8 percent of total circulation. By contrast, William Randolph Hearst alone in 1935 controlled 13.6 percent of daily circulation and 24.2 percent of Sunday. In short, the groups were collectively a problem of media effectiveness, but no one group was a threatening factor in ability to exercise influence. The 168 groups of 1977 averaged 6.3 dailies each. Only 13 had group circulation totals exceeding 750,000. Half the groups were below 50,000 in combined circulation, averaging three dailies each.*

The 1974 merger of the Knight and Ridder newspaper groups created a powerful national publishing organization that in 1977 led in group circulation with 3,725,000 for 34 dailies. John S. Knight, starting with the *Akron Beacon-Journal,* bought the *Miami Herald* in 1937 and with Lee Hills as the chief editorial force made it one of the country's top papers. Knight's other major acquisitions were the *Detroit Free Press,* the *Charlotte Observer* and *News,* and the *Philadelphia Inquirer* and *News.* The Ridder group brought to the merger 11 midwestern dailies led by the *St. Paul Dispatch* and *Pioneer Press* and six California dailies including the *San Jose Mercury* and *News* and the Long Beach and Pasadena papers. Bernard H. Ridder, Jr., represented his family's interests in the new organization.[10]

Largest of the groups in numbers of dailies in 1977 was the Gannett Company, with 73 dailies and 48 Sunday editions. Based in Rochester, New York, the company expanded by buying other groups: Westchester Rockland in 1964; Federated in 1971; the *Honolulu Star-Bulletin* and its satellites in 1971; and in a $173-million stock transaction in 1976, the Speidel western group. Gannett had dailies in 28 states. Allen Neuharth succeeded Paul Miller, the onetime Associated Press executive, as the operating head of Gannett.

Rising rapidly among the group owners was Samuel I. Newhouse. He bought the

*From data supplied by Paul Jess (footnote 9). Figures for 1977 for leading groups are as follows (in thousands):

Group	Total circulation	Percent of daily circulation	Number dailies	Number Sunday
Knight-Ridder	*3,725*	*6.1*	*34*	*23*
S. I. Newhouse	*3,530*	*5.8*	*30*	*21*
Chicago Tribune Co.	*2,995*	*4.9*	*6*	*4*
Gannett	*2,940*	*4.8*	*73*	*48*
Times Mirror Co.	*1,750*	*2.9*	*4*	*4*
Scripps-Howard	*1,750*	*2.9*	*16*	*6*
Hearst	*1,550*	*2.5*	*8*	*7*
Cox	*1,200*	*2.0*	*18*	*8*
New York Times Co.	*1,005*	*1.7*	*11*	*6*
Thomson	*976*	*1.6*	*57*	*21*
Cowles	*925*	*1.5*	*7*	*5*

Newhouse Newspapers

Gannett Newspapers

Group owners Samuel I. Newhouse (*left*); Allen Neuharth, head of Gannett.

Jean Raeburn

Chicago Defender

John S. Knight (*left*); John H. Sengstacke, head of the *Defender* newspaper group.

Minneapolis Tribune

Grinsted Studio

John Cowles, Jr. (*left*), Minneapolis-based; Marshall Field V, of Field Enterprises.

Portland Oregonian in 1950 for $5 million; the *St. Louis Globe-Democrat* in 1955 for $6 million; the *Birmingham News* in 1955 for $18 million; the *Oregon Journal* in Portland in 1961 for $6 million; the *New Orleans Times-Picayune* and *States-Item* in 1962 for $40 million; and the *Cleveland Plain Dealer* in 1967 for $50 million. In a bidding contest for Booth newspaper group stock in 1976, Newhouse spent an estimated $300 million to win control of eight strong Michigan dailies. Newhouse's reputation was that of a successful businessman, but one who permitted local editorial autonomy. His 30 dailies had the second largest total circulation.

The Times Mirror Company joined the largest groups when the youthful publisher of the *Los Angeles Times,* Otis Chandler, bought the *Dallas Times Herald* and the Long Island tabloid, *Newsday,* in 1970 transactions involving $125 million. A long established group with few papers but major size was the Tribune Company, owner of the *Chicago Tribune, New York Daily News,* and the advertising-rich *Orlando Sentinel-Star*, *Fort Lauderdale News,* and *Valley News* (in Los Angeles' San Fernando Valley).

John Cowles, whose family owned the *Des Moines Register* and *Tribune,* invaded Minneapolis in 1935 by buying the evening *Star,* then eliminating the *Journal* in 1939, and buying the morning *Tribune* in 1941. His brother Gardner was unsuccessful in Long Island publishing ventures. James M. Cox started with four Ohio dailies in Dayton and Springfield and built a sizable empire by acquiring the *Miami News* and *Atlanta Journal* in the 1930s and the *Atlanta Constitution* in 1950.

Runner-up in number of dailies was the Thomson Newspapers group, part of a worldwide enterprise built by Lord Thomson of Fleet, a Canadian. His papers, 57 dailies, were predominantly small. At his death in 1976 his son Kenneth assumed the title and control. A flamboyant Australian, Rupert Murdoch, put his News America subsidiary on the map by buying the *New York Post, Village Voice,* and *New York* and *New West* magazines in 1977 after founding the *National Star* in 1974 and buying the *San Antonio News* and *Express* in 1975.

Of the oldest groups, Scripps-Howard dropped from 25 dailies in 1935 to 16 in 1977, with six Sunday editions. Papers were disposed of in Akron, Toledo, Youngstown, Oklahoma City, San Diego, and Buffalo in addition to changes already described. The *San Juan Star* was bought from Gardner Cowles in 1970.

The Hearst chain's 26 dailies of 1935 were cut to eight by 1971 with seven Sunday editions. Sold or killed between 1937 and 1940 were the *Rochester Journal, Syracuse Journal, Omaha News-Bee, Wisconsin News, Washington Times* and *Herald, Chicago Herald & Examiner, Atlanta Georgian,* and *Pittsburgh Post-Gazette.* The *Oakland Post-Enquirer* died in 1950. Then came the 1956–66 withdrawals from Chicago, Pittsburgh, Detroit, Milwaukee, and New York, and contractions in Boston, Los Angeles, and San Francisco. On the plus side, the *Albany Knickerbocker News* was added in 1960.

WEEKLIES AND SPECIALIZED PAPERS

Weekly newspapers followed the same general trends. In 1930 only 13.5 percent of weekly towns had competing newspapers. By 1960 the figure was 5.2 percent, closely paralleling the number of competitive daily cities. The number of weeklies of all types stood at 14,000 in 1910, at 10,000 in 1940, and at 9,400 in 1970. In 1977, according to the *Ayer Directory,* there were 9,127 weeklies; the National Newspaper Association directory counted only 7,579, with the difference depending on a narrower definition of a general interest newspaper. Average weekly newspaper circulation was above 4,900 copies, the National Newspaper Association said, and total circulation was 37.1

million in 1976.[11] Larger county seat weeklies and the fast-growing suburban weeklies were more profitable—some of the suburban press chains were major businesses.

Those who found the country's newspapers too closely conforming in socioeconomic opinion—whether published in one-owner or competitive cities—attempted to publish their own papers, with mediocre success. The Socialist labor press was led by the *New York Evening Call* (1908–23) and the *Milwaukee Leader* (1911–42), both of which achieved substantial circulations before succumbing. However, the Jewish language Socialist paper *Vorwärts (Jewish Daily Forward)*, published in New York with editions in other cities, attained more than 100,000 circulation under editor Abraham Cahan. The Communist *Daily Worker,* founded in 1924, had 100,000 circulation in the late 1930s, but only 5,600 when it dropped to weekly status in 1958.

In other specialized newspaper publishing fields, the foreign-language press steadily declined during the twentieth century. In 1914, peak year for foreign language newspapers, there were approximately 1,000 papers, of which 140 were dailies. By 1977 there were fewer than 40 dailies and perhaps 200 other papers in some two dozen languages. Chinese, Spanish, Polish, Japanese, German, Russian, Yiddish, Italian, and Lithuanian papers were most numerous.

THE MAGAZINE OWNERSHIPS   Variety of reader appeal and diversity of opinion were more possible in the magazine field, where periodicals of every shade of interest could find countrywide audiences. By 1977 there were 9,700 periodicals of all types. Of these, however, no more than 600 were magazines of general interest (a figure that nevertheless was more than double that for 1900). Approximately 50 had circulations of more than a million. The larger of these mass circulation magazines exhibited the same characteristics of bigness and ownership concentration as other media.

Major groups and their leading magazines were Time Inc. (*Time, People, Sports Illustrated, Fortune, Money*); McGraw-Hill (*Business Week* and 30 trade publications); McCall Corporation (*McCall's, Redbook*); Hearst Magazines (14, including *Good Housekeeping, Cosmopolitan, Popular Mechanics, Sports Afield*); Samuel Newhouse (11 Condé Nast and Street & Smith magazines purchased in 1959, including *Vogue* and *Mademoiselle*); Meredith Publishing Company (*Better Homes and Gardens, Successful Farming*); and Walter H. Annenberg's Triangle Publications (three, including *TV Guide* and *Seventeen*).*

Of eight major general interest magazines remaining in 1977, all but *Reader's Digest* and *National Geographic* were group-owned. The others were *Ebony* (monthly picture magazine); *Redbook* and *Cosmopolitan* (general monthlies); and *McCall's, Ladies' Home Journal,* and *Good Housekeeping* (women's monthlies).

Gone were the famous Crowell-Collier magazines—*Collier's,* the *American,* and *Woman's Home Companion*—which dated from the 1870s and 1880s. They suspended in 1956 due to mismanagement, top-heavy costs, and loss of advertising to television. *Collier's* had almost two million circulation, the other two more than four million each. *Coronet,* running mate of *Esquire,* was a 1961 casualty, despite a three million circulation. *Look* vanished in 1971 and *Life* in 1972 despite eight million circulations.

The resilience of the industry was shown, however, in the aftermath of the

*Leading circulations in 1977, in round numbers, were *TV Guide,* 20 million; *Reader's Digest,* 18.5 million; *National Geographic,* 9 million; *Family Circle,* 8.5 million; *Woman's Day* and *Better Homes and Gardens,* 8 million; *McCall's,* 6.5 million; *Ladies' Home Journal,* 6 million; *Playboy* and *Good Housekeeping,* 5.5 million; *Redbook* and *Time,* 4.5 million; *Newsweek,* 3 million. Sunday newspaper supplements: *Parade,* 19 million; *Family Weekly,* 10 million.

crumbling of the great Curtis Publishing Company in 1969. The *Ladies' Home Journal* was sold, but the *Saturday Evening Post* ceased publication. In 1970 Beurt and Cory SerVaas, Indianapolis children's magazine publishers, bought the Curtis remnants to obtain *Jack and Jill* (600,000 circulation in 1977). With it came *Holiday* (387,000 in 1977). The *Saturday Evening Post* was revived as a nostalgic quarterly in 1971 and became a monthly in 1977 with 457,000 circulation. The SerVaas firm located the owner of the title *Country Gentleman* and revived it in 1976 at 330,000 circulation. In the group were *Children's Playmate, Child Life,* and *Young World.*[12]

GROUP OWNERSHIP IN BROADCASTING

Those who complained about a sameness in their newspapers and their mass-circulated magazines fared little better when they turned to television and radio. The major radio networks grew steadily, having 228 station affiliates in 1934, 702 in 1944, and 1,324 (55 percent of all stations) in 1953. The decline in network broadcasting and expansion in number of stations changed the figures to 1,837 affiliates (23 percent of all stations) in 1976. The 962 television stations of 1976 had 593 network affiliations.

Group ownership became strong in radio and television, but not as widespread as in newspapers. A 1949 study arrived at this picture: group ownerships controlled 13 percent of radio stations, 40 percent of television stations, and 21 percent of dailies. Ten years later the figures for group ownership were 23 percent of radio stations, 53 percent of television stations, and 32 percent of dailies.[13] In 1976, only 45 percent of television stations were group owned compared to 60 percent of dailies—testifying to the impact of the FCC ruling limiting groups to seven stations.

CROSS-CHANNEL OWNERSHIP

A final threat to the diversity of communications ownership was the phenomenon of cross-channel ownership of the mass media, which became pronounced in the 1970s.

Even as dedicated a company as that owning the *New York Times* had become a conglomerate by 1977 in its effort to bolster the slipping fortunes of the newspaper itself. The Times Company had 27 subsidiaries, including the magazines *Family Circle, Tennis, Golf Digest* and *US*; ten Florida newspapers; three North Carolina dailies; three publishing houses; and two broadcast stations.

Columbia Broadcasting System, which once owned the New York Yankees, had control of Holt, Rinehart & Winston publishing house; Fawcett Publications, with *Woman's Day, Mechanix Illustrated,* and a paperback publisher; Popular Library paperbacks; *Field & Stream, Road & Track,* and *Cycle World;* Creative Playthings; Steinway pianos; and recording outlets in 20 countries. RCA, which owned NBC, also owned Random House, Ballantine Books, Alfred A. Knopf, Pantheon, Vintage, and Modern Library in the world of books, and the Hertz Corporation.

Otis Chandler's Times Mirror Company was a sprawling business giant that published the *Los Angeles Times, Newsday,* the *Dallas Times Herald,* and the *Sporting News,* as well as telephone directories, Bibles, books, and road maps. It owned two cable television systems and three paperback houses. John Cowles, Jr., controlled four Midwest dailies and bought complete control of *Harper's* magazine along with a portion of Harper & Row publishing house. The Cowles family also owned two other newspapers and interests in other media firms.

The Hearst organization counted eight dailies, 14 magazines, four AM and three FM stations, three television stations, a news service, a photo service, a feature syndicate, and the Avon paperback book firm. Scripps-Howard had 16 dailies, two radio and four television stations, a press association, a photo service, and a feature syndicate. Samuel Newhouse owned 30 dailies, 11 magazines, four AM and three FM stations, and five television stations. He also had invested in cable television systems.

From abroad came Lord Thomson of Fleet, whose worldwide publishing empire numbered about 180 newspapers including the *Times* of London, more than 100 magazines, and a group of broadcast stations. His American holdings ran to 57 dailies, 21 Sunday editions, and seven weeklies. Most spectacular new conglomerate owner was Australian Rupert Murdoch, who set New York on its ear with his 1977 purchase of the *New York Post, Village Voice,* and *New York* and *New West* magazines. That ran his world total of newspapers to 88.

THE BLACK PRESS SURVIVES

One group of Americans who found little to represent their aspirations and interests in the mass media was the Negro population. Not until the 1950s did the average American newspaper or magazine exhibit an understanding interest in the black 10 percent of citizens, and even then few were sensitive to them as readers. There was a clear need for a black press, but little economic support for it from a black community with few socioeconomic resources. Nevertheless, the black press that began in 1827 survived and gained in stature.[14]

More than 3,000 Negro newspapers—owned and edited by blacks for black readers—have appeared since *Freedom's Journal* made its 1827 bow. The best historical statistics were gathered by Professor Armistead Scott Pride of Lincoln University for his 1951 doctoral dissertation. His figures showed that 1,187 black papers were added during the years 1865–1900 to the 40 founded before 1865. Another 1,500 had been added by 1951, but the survivors numbered only 175. The average life span of a Negro newspaper, Pride found, was nine years.[15]

A 1971 survey of black newspapers, verified by telephone calls to all listed offices and personal interviews with a third of the editors, found a total of 196, including two dailies, four semiweeklies, 179 weeklies, and 11 biweeklies or monthlies. Their circulation total (free and paid) was 3,584,000. More than half the papers had been founded since 1950, a third during the 1960s. Of the 196, nearly half (93) had a circulation under 10,000; a quarter (51) exceeded 20,000; only 12 topped 40,000. The researcher, Henry G. La Brie, III, of the University of Iowa, repeated his telephone survey in 1973–74 and found 213 black papers with circulations of 4,300,000.[16] There was tremendous turnover among the papers, La Brie found, and only 38 maintained their own printing facilities. Only 22 had circulations verified by ABC audit. *Editor & Publisher*'s 1976 list, not as exhaustively researched, totaled 162.

Just as the standard daily press grew in numbers, circulation, and stature during the New Journalism era between 1880 and World War I, so did the black press. Among today's leaders that have founding dates in that period are the *Philadelphia Tribune* (1884), Baltimore's *Afro-American* (1892), the *Chicago Defender* (1905), New York's *Amsterdam News* (1909), Norfolk's *Journal and Guide* (1909), and the *Pittsburgh Courier* (1910). Historically important from that period are the *New York Age* (1890), *Boston Guardian* (1901), and *The Crisis* (1910). Founded later, among 1970's leaders, were the *Atlanta World* (1928), *Los Angeles Sentinel* (1934), Detroit's *Michigan Chronicle* (1936), Chicago's *Muhammad Speaks* (1961), and Berkeley's *The Black Panther* (1966), voice of the Black Panther party.

Pride gives several reasons for the increase in black papers beginning in the mid-1880s: increased educational opportunities for Negroes, support of black papers by religious and welfare groups working in the South, establishment of political sheets for enfranchised Negroes, and growth of urban black communities that could support papers. The impact of two world wars and heavy Negro migration to northern industrial cities brought a peak of circulation influence to the leading papers; between 1940 and 1947 the circulations of the *Amsterdam News* rose from 35,000 to 111,000, the *Pittsburgh Courier* from 126,000 to 286,000, and the *Chicago Defender* from 82,000 to 161,000.[17] Black paper circulations then declined, nationally circulating papers lost ground to community-based ones, and the small stable enterprises survived.

THE FOUNDING PUBLISHERS

Ranking in fame with Frederick Douglass and his *North Star* of 1847 are W. E. B. Du Bois and his *The Crisis* of 1910. Other major figures in Negro publishers' ranks to 1910 included John H. Murphy, Sr., of the *Afro-American* papers, T. Thomas Fortune of the *New York Age,* William Monroe Trotter of the *Boston Guardian,* Robert S. Abbott of the *Chicago Defender,* and Robert L. Vann of the *Pittsburgh Courier.* Their stories, and those of other major black papers, follow.

The semiweekly *Philadelphia Tribune,* which celebrated its ninetieth anniversary in 1974, is the oldest continuously published black newspaper in the United States. Founded in 1884 by Chris J. Perry, Sr., it became one of the most substantial and best-edited Negro weeklies. Perry's widow and two daughters continued the *Tribune* after his death in 1921. A son-in-law, E. Washington Rhodes, was publisher and editor until he died in 1970. Rhodes took a moderate view, concentrating on improving the lot of Philadelphia's black citizens. Criticizing the more affluent Negroes for not doing enough to help the poor, the *Tribune* organized charities and scholarship programs as a part of its community responsibility.[18]

John H. Murphy, Sr., is regarded as the founder of the *Afro-American* editions, four regional and one national, centered in Baltimore. Murphy, who did whitewashing for a living, was superintendent of an African Methodist church Sunday school. He began publishing a small paper for it in his basement. When a Baptist minister, Rev. William M. Alexander, began another religious paper, the *Afro-American,* in 1892, Murphy gained control of it; in 1907 he merged it with the *Ledger,* a third religious paper edited by an Episcopal pastor, Rev. George F. Bragg. The paper gained a national reputation before 1920. Murphy wrote a credo that year calling for the *Afro-American* to keep faith with the common people, to fight to get rid of slums and to provide jobs for all, and to "stay out of politics except to expose corruption and condemn injustice, race prejudice and the cowardice of compromise." The credo still appears in his newspapers, which were continued after his death in 1922 by his son, Dr. Carl J. Murphy.

T. Thomas Fortune was one of the best-known Negro editors at the turn of the century, and his *New York Age* won national attention. Born to slave parents, Fortune ran errands for a southern newspaper, learned to set type, and entered New York journalism through the back shops. In 1879 a Negro tabloid named *Rumor* was changed to standard size by George Parker and renamed the *New York Globe;* Fortune and W. Walter Sampson were the printing crew and became Parker's partners. Within a decade Fortune was the principal figure and the paper had become the *Age.* As its editorial writer, Fortune was quoted by the nation's press and was read by political leaders, including Theodore Roosevelt. Booker T. Washington selected the *Age* as national spokesman for the Negro and began to subsidize it. This won the disapproval of W. E. B. Du Bois and other militant black leaders who said Washington was accepting segregation and subservience to whites. Fortune sold his share of the *Age* in 1907 and in the 1920s supported the back-to-Africa movement of Marcus Garvey, writing for Garvey's widely circulating magazine, *Negro World.* The *Age,* under the editorship of Fred R. Moore, remained a major New York black newspaper until it was sold to the expanding *Defender* group of Chicago in 1952.

William Monroe Trotter, another great black leader at the turn of the century, had a background opposite from Fortune's. His father, a Union army officer, became interested in racial equality and married a black slave. He then became a merchant in Boston, where the mulatto son won election to Phi Beta Kappa at Harvard and a master's degree. With George Forbes, an Amherst graduate, Trotter founded the *Boston Guardian* in 1901. It was provocative and militant enough to win the praise of Du Bois. When Booker T. Washington spoke in Boston in 1905 the *Guardian* challenged his conservative leadership, particularly on black education and voting. Trotter later led a protest delegation to the national capital to meet with President Woodrow Wilson and plead the cause of blacks. But in the 1920s his paper languished; Trotter and his wife lost their home and Trotter died in 1934. His sister continued the *Guardian* until her death in 1957.

Robert S. Abbott's *Chicago Defender,* founded in 1905, fared better in the quest for public support than did Trotter's *Guardian.* By 1915 it reached a circulation of 230,000. The figure declined two-thirds by the depression year of 1935 but rose again to 160,000 in post-war 1947. The Chicago paper, with its national edition, then became the cornerstone of the largest American black newspaper group. Abbott was born in 1868 of black parents in Georgia. When his father died, his mother married John H. H. Sengstacke, son of a German merchant who had married a slave. Abbott learned printing at Hampton Institute, worked on his stepfather's small paper, studied law, and in 1905 founded the *Defender* among Chicago's 40,000 black population. It was run on a shoestring from his landlady's house until Abbott developed a familiar black newspaper formula: muckraking on behalf of his race, sensationalizing through ''race-angling'' of headlines and stories, use of crime and scandal stories, and resolute challenges to the Ku Klux Klan, racial rioting, lynchings, and other threats to black Americans' security. By the 1930s Abbott had moderated the *Defender's* tone and had added much more personal, social, cultural, and fashion news. When he died in 1940 his successor was John H. Sengstacke, a nephew.

Robert L. Vann's *Pittsburgh Courier,* founded in 1910, became the largest in circulation of all black newspapers, approaching 300,000 in the late 1940s. Vann was a lawyer who took over a church-sponsored publishing venture and who struck out to fight against racial discrimination and the Jim Crow tradition. The *Courier* backed black athletes, helping Jackie Robinson to break the color barrier. Vann developed a circulation in the South and used his influence to attract capable black journalists.

P. Bernard Young was another black publisher who developed a national newspaper, taking over the *Journal and Guide* in Norfolk in 1910 and running it as a moderate, nonsensational weekly until his death in 1962. By contrast, the various publishers of New York's *Amsterdam News* have concentrated on local circulation since its founding by James H. Anderson in 1909, gradually winning their way to dominance in the competitive Harlem scene.

W. E. B. DU BOIS AND *THE CRISIS*

W. E. B. Du Bois, the militant apostle of protest in the opening decades of the century, became one of the major folk heroes of the black equality movement of the 1960s. His appeal was strong for the radical left of that movement because late in life he became a member of the Communist party and went to live in the new African nation of Ghana, where he died in 1963 at 95.

Du Bois was not a newspaperman, although he was a correspondent or columnist for several. He was primarily a writer and a teacher with a cause to promote—that of rescuing the black race from a crisis that threatened to crush its capability. He is best known for his work between 1910 and 1934 as an executive of the National Association for the Advancement of Colored People and for the founding and editing of its magazine, *The Crisis*. That journal served so well as a combination of a news magazine reporting items of concern to Negroes, a journal of editorial opinion, a review of opinion and literature, and a literary magazine that its entire file for the first 50 years has been reproduced as "A Record of the Darker Races."

Born in New England in 1868, Du Bois was raised by his mother in a white society relatively free of discrimination. He himself was of mixed blood. He edited a high school paper and was correspondent for the *Springfield Republican* and the *New York Age*. At Fisk University he edited the student paper. He studied sociology at Harvard and in Germany and contributed articles to the *Atlantic* and *World's Work*. After attempting two other Negro journals, he succeeded with *The Crisis*. In it he set out to challenge the whole concept of white supremacy, then nationally accepted, and its counterpart of black inferiority. He said his object was to "set forth those facts and arguments which show the danger of race prejudice, particularly as manifested today toward colored people. It takes its name from the fact that the editors believe that this is a critical time in the history of the advancement of men."

"Mentally the negro is inferior to the white," said the 1911 *Britannica*. It was this belief Du Bois set out to destroy. His editorials also attacked immediate ills: wartime discrimination against black soldiers, the widespread race riots and lynchings following World War I, the climax of Ku Klux Klan terrorism, continued white refusal to consider Negro rights in the fields of voting, education, and housing. Circulation of *The Crisis* passed 100,000 in 1918. But dissension within the NAACP and other factors reduced it to fewer than 10,000 when Du Bois retired as editor in 1934, aged 65. Under editor Roy Wilkins until 1949 and then Henry Lee Moon, circulation revived to well above 100,000.

Du Bois became sociology department head at Atlanta University, founded a scholarly journal on world race problems named *Phylon,* and wrote books and countless articles for major publications. Like Frederick Douglass, his writings were being published in the 1970s as a symbol of achievement by a distinguished member of the black race—and, of course, the human race.

CURRENT BLACK PRESS LEADERS

In 1970 John H. Sengstacke, editor and publisher of the *Chicago Daily Defender* and head of the Sengstacke Newspapers group, was elected to the board of directors of the American Society of Newspaper Editors. He was the first black editor to be so honored. This personal recognition also reflected the status of the *Defender* group as the largest in black newspaper publishing, with community and national circulation claims totaling more than 100,000 in 1977. The *Chicago Defender* had 20,000 daily circulation and 21,000 for its national weekly edition. Largest in the Sengstacke group was the *Michigan Chronicle,* founded in 1936 in Detroit, with 35,000 circulation. The *New Pittsburgh Courier,* purchased in 1966 by Sengstacke along with the *Courier* group, had 21,000.

The *Afro-American* group, headed by John H. Murphy, III, had more than 60,000 combined circulation in 1977. Its biggest unit was the semiweekly Baltimore edition, with 25,000 circulation. It also published in Richmond, Washington, and New Jersey, and had a national weekly edition. Mrs. Elizabeth Murphy Moss, vice president of the

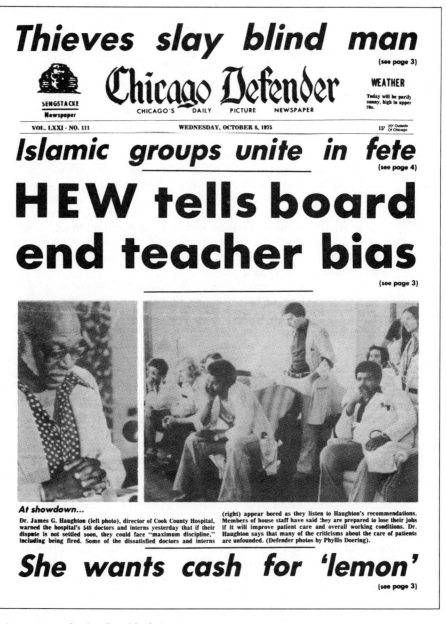

Thieves slay blind man

(see page 3)

Chicago Defender

SENGSTACKE
Newspaper

CHICAGO'S   DAILY   PICTURE   NEWSPAPER

WEATHER

Today will be partly sunny, high in upper 70s.

VOL. LXXI - NO. 111   WEDNESDAY, OCTOBER 8, 1975   15¢   20¢ Outside Of Chicago

Islamic groups unite in fete

(see page 4)

HEW tells board end teacher bias

(see page 3)

At showdown...

Dr. James G. Haughton (left photo), director of Cook County Hospital, warned the hospital's 548 doctors and interns yesterday that if their dispute is not settled soon, they could face "maximum discipline," including being fired. Some of the dissatisfied doctors and interns

(right) appear bored as they listen to Haughton's recommendations. Members of house staff have said they are prepared to lose their jobs if it will improve patient care and overall working conditions. Dr. Haughton says that many of the criticisms about the care of patients are unfounded. (Defender photos by Phyllis Doering).

She wants cash for 'lemon'

(see page 3)

A front page of a leading black paper.

group, was a leading reporter and war correspondent. So was Ethel L. Payne, Washington correspondent for the Sengstacke papers and only black newswoman to cover the Vietnam war.

Dwarfing the other black papers in circulation was *Muhammad Speaks,* the tabloid weekly of the Nation of Islam that was founded in 1961 by Malcolm X. Printed in its own Chicago offset plant, *Muhammad Speaks* claimed 850,000 circulation. The *Black Panther,* begun in 1966 in Berkeley by the Black Panther party, was another militant paper that at its peak had 100,000 sales.

The *Amsterdam News,* largest circulating of standard black community papers, was purchased by Dr. C. B. Powell in 1936 and controlled by him until 1971 when ownership passed to Clarence B. Jones. It concentrated on local items and sensationalized crime and sex news to combat its competition in Harlem from Congressman Adam Clayton Powell's *People's Voice* and the old *New York Age.* Like the *Afro-American* and *Defender* papers, it became moderate in tone, heavily local in news coverage, strong in sports and women's news, and occasionally crusading. Its 1976 circulation was 66,000.

Out of 45 efforts to publish black dailies in the United States, as reported by Pride, only two prevailed. One was the *Chicago Daily Defender,* with daily status since 1956. The other was the *Atlanta Daily World,* founded as a weekly in 1928 and a daily since 1932. Its founder, William A. Scott, was assassinated in 1934; his successor, Cornelius A. Scott, edited a consistently conservative paper in news content, typographical appearance, and editorial direction. World news coverage was good. It supported the Republican party politically and opposed such militant black action as economic boycotts of white merchants who discriminated in hiring blacks. Its 1976 circulation was 23,000.

The *Los Angeles Sentinel,* owned and edited by Ruth Washington, was founded in 1934. Its 34,000 circulation made it the most important black publication in Los Angeles, where it displayed a mildly sensational front page and a liberal-moderate editorial page. The *Philadelphia Tribune* had 33,000 circulation. Other noteworthy black papers were the *Cleveland Call and Post,* 31,000; *Atlanta Inquirer,* 30,000; Norfolk's *Journal and Guide,* 22,000; the semiweekly *Tampa Sentinel-Bulletin,* 22,000; the *Kansas City Call,* founded in 1919, 10,000; and the *Louisiana Weekly,* 9,000. There were large free circulation shopping papers like the Wave Publications in Los Angeles with a distribution of 230,000, and the Berkeley Post Group, 70,000.

La Brie found in his 1971 survey that 80 percent of the black newspapers were printed by the offset method, usually on presses now owned by the publishers. The others owned letterpress equipment. Like the regular weeklies, the black weeklies usually appeared on Thursdays. The reported labor force for 175 papers was 2,500, of whom 200 were white. Advertising occupied about one-third of total space, with two-thirds or more local in origin but national advertising increasing in larger black papers beginning in the 1960s.

Most of the national black papers and largest weeklies subscribed to the United Press International for their state, regional, national, and international news. Best known of specialized press services was the Associated Negro Press, founded in 1919 by Claude A. Barnett. It peaked in 1945 with 112 American subscribers. Barnett made many trips to Africa after World War II and added 100 subscribers there as well as developing African news. But by 1966 ANP had so much competition in coverage of blacks news events that it went out of business.[19] The National Negro Press Association, with Louis Lautier as Washington correspondent, operated between 1947 and 1960 with the support of the larger black papers and began service again in 1974 with John W. Lewis, Jr., as correspondent.

THE BLACK MAGAZINES

John H. Johnson became publisher of one of the country's leading magazines, *Ebony,* and his Johnson Publishing Company in Chicago produced two other important black magazines—*Jet* and *Black World.* The Johnson story is one of imitation: *Ebony* was patterned on *Life; Jet,* a news magazine, succeeded with the format of the ill-fated *Quick* of the Cowles magazines; and *Black World* was called *Negro Digest* until 1970 in honor of its model.

Johnson grew up in Chicago, was befriended by a white businessman, attended the University of Chicago, and eventually borrowed $500 from his widowed mother to found *Negro Digest* in 1942. Its newsstand success enabled him to launch *Ebony* in 1945, as a monthly version of *Life.* Finding sensationalism did not pay, Johnson built a magazine for middle-class Negroes in the 1950s that reached a level of 70 percent home-delivered circulation on 1,300,000 copies in 1976. As black militancy grew in the 1960s, *Ebony* became more concerned with black problems and ran extensive articles in addition to pictures and cartoons. *Jet,* a small-sized news weekly, had 625,000 circulation to rank second among black magazines, a 50 percent increase in five years. *Black World,* published by Johnson as an outlet for black authors, was relatively unsuccessful.

Other major black magazines included *Essence,* a New York-based women's service magazine founded in 1970 that zoomed to 500,000 circulation by 1976; *Players,* men's interest, 240,000; the Good group of Fort Worth, with *Sepia* picture magazine at 160,000, sexy *Jive* at 57,000, and *Soul Teen* at a claimed 550,000; and *Encore,* a biweekly news magazine, with 150,000 circulation.

Tuesday, a magazine supplement edited by blacks but appearing in conventional big dailies, was started in 1965 by W. Leonard Evans, Jr., to reach white readership with a "black leveler," he explained. It won 2,400,000 circulation in five years, with an estimated 20 percent white readership. Among other noteworthy black magazines were *The Crisis,* the literary-styled *Freedomways,* and such scholarly journals as *Negro History Bulletin, Journal of Negro History,* and *Journal of Negro Education.*

BLACK BROADCASTING   No American television station license was held in 1977 by anyone in the black 10 percent of the population. Even so, viewership studies show blacks spent more time watching television than any other identified group. There were 16 radio stations owned by blacks in 1970. Of 13 AM stations, five were in northern cities, three in border cities, and five in the south. Three were college-owned FM stations.

About 180 radio stations devoted ten hours or more of time each week to the black listening audience; of these, 65 were all-black in programming, according to *Broadcasting Yearbook.* Listenership studies showed nearly all blacks tuned in black-oriented radio and 60 percent preferred it to regular stations. In ghetto areas, black radio was the common denominator of communication, followed by television, with print media trailing. Yet a 1970 study of black-oriented radio stations found them so predominantly "rhythm-and-blues"-oriented that little time remained for news, public affairs, even sports. News rarely ran beyond five minutes and was usually headlines; public affairs programs fell far short of the potential if operators were interested in serving the black community.[20]

CHICANO
AND LATINO MEDIA   Nearly 20 million Latinos live in the United States, representing people from South and Central America, the Caribbean, and Mexico. During the 1960s the Chicano movement identified the Mexican-American heritage, but the Latino composite is a major factor in minority life in New York, Florida, Illinois, and New Jersey, as well as in California and the Southwest.

Spanish-language broadcast stations and programs grew rapidly after the civil rights movements of the 1960s, and by the late 1970s Spanish was heard on 60 television stations and nearly 400 radio stations, with Spanish the primary format for 20 television and 80 radio stations. The Spanish International Network serviced television; based in New York it carried Mexican programming by satellite. Radio programs also crossed the border.[21]

Nearly 100 Spanish-language periodicals were listed in the 1977 *Ayer Directory*, and a semiformal Chicano Press Association identified perhaps 50 newspapers that sprang up in that movement, as well as older Latino papers, some of which traced their roots to pre-Civil War days. *El Crepúsculo de la Libertad* ("Dawn of Liberty") was published at Taos in 1835. The frontier days saw considerable activity in the Southwest and California; then a number of papers appeared in the early twentieth century, some of them organs for political movements. Biggest dailies are *El Diario*, New York, 68,000 circulation; *Diario de las Americas*, Miami, 55,000; *La Opinión*, Los Angeles, 25,000; and the *Laredo Times* in Texas, 19,000. Two major magazines are *Agenda*, founded in 1968 in Washington for advocacy and research, and *La Luz*, published from Denver since 1971. *Nuestro*, a four-color monthly focusing on a Latino audience but printed in English, started with a 180,000 press run in April 1977.

The Chicano movement and the Chicano press emerged from the grapeworkers strike in California's San Joaquin Valley under the leadership of Cesar Chavez. *El Malcriado* became the voice of the United Farm Workers union in 1964, published from a shack in Delano. More substantial was *La Raza*, begun in 1967 for Los Angeles' million Chicanos and Latinos. The sheets spread throughout California; *El Rebozo*, published by women, appeared in San Antonio among five Texas papers; others were *El Gallo* in Denver, *La Guardia* in Milwaukee, *Adelante* in Kansas City, and *Lado* in Chicago.[22]

Chicano papers printed their news and opinion in both Spanish and English, used large numbers of pictures, and reflected the cultural stirrings of the Chicano movement in poetry, essays, and interpretive writing. Their aim was to organize Mexican-Americans as sensitive, progressive communities. Much of their support and reportorial skill came from Chicano college students.

NATIVE AMERICAN NEWSPAPERS

The Native American press of the 1970s was almost entirely printed in English, although some papers were used to teach tribal languages. There were 325 newspapers listed by the American Indian Press Association in 34 states; more than 50 school and college papers; 15 prison culture group publications; eight major magazines, four news services, and seven Indian printing firms.[23]

The *Cherokee Phoenix*, first Native American paper, appeared in Georgia from 1828 to 1832. Other early papers were the *Cherokee Advocate*, the Sioux-language *Shawnee Sun (Siwinowe Kesibwi)*, and the *Cherokee Rose Bud*, founded in 1848 by Indian women seminary students in present-day Oklahoma.

Two 1970s national newspapers were *Akwesasne Notes*, a 48-page tabloid published five times annually as the militant publication of the Mohawk nation, and *Wassaja*, a bimonthly of 24–32 pages sponsored by the American Indian Historical Society and devoted to Indian self-determination and education. Both papers claimed more than 80,000 circulation.

Indian papers suffered from limited funding and editorial inexperience. But they were cause-oriented, promoted the welfare and self-pride of Native Americans,

Front page of *Wassaja (left); La Raza* protests the death of a Chicano newsman.

preserved and restored the Indian heritage, and functioned as mirrors of their communities and readerships by presenting their points of view.

NOTES

1. Royal H. Ray, *Concentration of Ownership and Control in the American Daily Newspaper Industry* (Columbia University Microfilms, 1951), pp. 401–8. A summary of this Ph.D. dissertation was published in *Journalism Quarterly,* XXIX (Winter 1952), 31.
2. Census population figures and newspaper circulation totals are conveniently tabulated in the appendices of A.M. Lee's *The Daily Newspaper in America* (New York: Macmillan, 1937). Advertising revenue totals are from figures of the ANPA Bureau of Advertising.
3. Willard G. Bleyer, ''Freedom of the Press and the New Deal,'' *Journalism Quarterly,* XI (March 1934), 29. Those cities with but one morning daily but with two or more evening papers, in addition to the dozen listed above, were Baltimore, Providence, Rochester, Syracuse, Dayton, Columbus (Ohio), Louisville, Richmond, Memphis, Houston, Dallas, Fort Worth, Oklahoma City, Portland (Oregon), and Seattle. Those cities with but one morning and one evening paper were Hartford, New Haven, Tampa, Chattanooga, Knoxville, Grand Rapids, Tulsa, and Denver. One company owned all the dailies published in six cities: New Bedford and Springfield, Massachusetts, Duluth, Des Moines, Wilmington, Delaware, and Charleston, South Carolina. Springfield, however, had two morning and two evening dailies operating under a single ownership headed by Sherman H. Bowles of the historic *Republican* family.
4. Paul Block leased the *Sentinel* from Hearst and operated it from 1929 to 1937.
5. The *Jackson State Times* of Mississippi, founded in 1955 to compete with a morning-evening combination, was the only new daily begun in a city of more than 100,000 in the 1950s. It suspended in 1962. The *Atlanta Times,* founded in 1964 by conservatives, died in 1965. The *Arizona Journal,* liberal Phoenix offset paper, published 1962–64. The *Portland Reporter,* born of a Guild strike in 1960 to become a regular daily,

suspended in 1964. But the *Oklahoma Journal* of Oklahoma City, founded as an offset morning daily in 1964, had a 47,600 circulation in 1976 as against 169,000 for the *Oklahoman*. The 1976 Sobel study shown in table 24–4 records an upturn in competitive cities since 1971. There were seven competitive cities in 1976 not listed in earlier studies; the largest were Hammond, Indiana, Green Bay, Wisconsin, and Kingsport, Tennessee. In Fulton, Missouri, dailies of 5,287 and 3,068 circulation were competing.

6. Raymond B. Nixon, "Trends in U.S. Newspaper Ownership: Concentration with Competition," *Gazette,* XIV (No. 3, 1968), 1–13, gives details.

7. Frank Luther Mott, *American Journalism* (New York: Macmillan, 1950), p. 648.

8. William Weinfeld, "The Growth of Daily Newspaper Chains in the United States: 1923, 1926–1935," *Journalism Quarterly,* XIII (December 1936), 357.

9. A listing of "Groups of Daily Newspapers under Common Ownership" is published annually in *Editor & Publisher International Year Book,* as compiled and updated by Paul Jess, University of Kansas. Papers in each group are identified, and owners named. Jess also prepares statistical data, made available to the authors.

10. The Ridder family founder, Herman Ridder, published the *Staats-Zeitung* in New York City, where his three sons—Bernard H., Joseph E., and Victor F. Ridder—bought the *Journal of Commerce* in 1926. Bernard made the St. Paul papers his center in 1927 and invaded California in 1952. His son Bernard H., Jr., became publisher in St. Paul and Duluth. His other three sons became publishers in California—Joseph B. in San Jose and Herman H. and Daniel as copublishers in Long Beach. Joseph E. Ridder centered his attention on the *Journal of Commerce,* of which one of his sons, Eric, became publisher. The other, Bernard J., published the Pasadena newspapers. Victor F. Ridder's son Walter headed the Ridders' Washington bureau, son Robert the family's radio-TV interests. Grandsons later became active.

11. *Publishers' Auxiliary,* CXII (March 25, 1977), 1.

12. Irene French Clepper, "The Curtis Publishing Company—Born Again in Indianapolis" (research paper, Magazine Division, Association for Education in Journalism, Madison, Wis., August 1977).

13. Warren K. Agee, "Cross-Channel Ownership of Communication Media," *Journalism Quarterly,* XXVI (Fall 1949), 410; Harvey J. Levin, *Broadcast Regulation and Joint Ownership of Media* (New York: New York University Press, 1960), p. 41.

14. See chapter 12, pp. 156–58, for the story of the founding of the black press.

15. Armistead Scott Pride, "Negro Newspapers: Yesterday, Today and Tomorrow," *Journalism Quarterly,* XXVIII (Spring 1951), 179.

16. Henry G. La Brie, III, *Perspectives of the Black Press 1974* (Kennebunkport, Maine: Mercer House Press, 1974), p. ix. La Brie supplied the 1971 information as a revision of his *The Black Press: A Guide* (Iowa City: University of Iowa, 1970).

17. Roland E. Wolseley, *The Black Press, U.S.A.* (Ames, Iowa: Iowa State University Press, 1971), p. 56.

18. Substantial accounts of leading black papers can be found in Wolseley, *The Black Press, U.S.A.* See its bibliography for additional references.

19. Richard L. Beard and Cyril E. Zoerner II, "Associated Negro Press: Its Founding, Ascendency and Demise," *Journalism Quarterly,* XLVI (Spring 1969), 47.

20. Anthony J. Meyer, S.J., *Black Voices and Format Regulations: A Study in Black-Oriented Radio* (Stanford, Calif.: Institute for Communication Research, Stanford University, 1971).

21. From research information supplied by Félix Gutiérrez, California State University, Northridge, and asociado of Southwest Network, Chicano Media Clearinghouse.

22. Frank del Olmo, "Chicano Journalism: New Medium for New Consciousness," in Michael C. Emery and Ted C. Smythe, *Readings in Mass Communication: Concepts and Issues in the Mass Media* (Dubuque, Iowa: Wm. C. Brown, 1972). Also, see Félix Gutiérrez's "Chicanos and the Media" in the 1977 edition; and "Spanish-Language Media Issue," *Journalism History,* IV (Summer 1977).

23. From research information supplied by Sharon Murphy, University of Wisconsin, Milwaukee.

ANNOTATED BIBLIOGRAPHY

Books

BOK, EDWARD W., *A Man from Maine.* New York: Scribner's, 1923. A life of Cyrus H. K. Curtis by his editor.

BRADDON, RUSSELL, *Roy Thomson of Fleet Street.* London: Collins, 1965. A detailed and favorable portrait of a world press lord.

BRITT, GEORGE, *Forty Years—Forty Millions; The Career of Frank A. Munsey.* New York: Holt, Rinehart & Winston, 1935. A critical biography.

BUNI, ANDREW, *Robert L. Vann of the Pittsburgh Courier: Politics and Black Journalism*. Pittsburgh, Pa.: University of Pittsburgh Press, 1974.

CLARKE, JOHN H., ET AL., *Black Titan W. E. B. Du Bois: An Anthology by the Editors of Freedomways*. Boston: Beacon Press, 1970. Writings about Du Bois, first editor of *The Crisis* and legendary black leader.

DENNIS, CHARLES H., *Victor Lawson: His Time and His Work*. Chicago: University of Chicago Press, 1935. The authorized story of Lawson and the *Daily News*.

DETWEILER, FREDERICK G., *The Negro Press in the United States*. Chicago: University of Chicago Press, 1922. Basic historical study together with Vishnu V. Oak, *The Negro Press* (Yellow Springs, Ohio: Antioch Press, 1948).

DU BOIS, W. E. B., *The Autobiography of W. E. Burghardt Du Bois*. New York: International Publishers, 1968. Written at age 90 by the editor of *The Crisis* as volume three of his autobiography.

ELLIS, L. ETHAN, *Newsprint: Producers, Publishers and Political Pressures*. New Brunswick: Rutgers University Press, 1960. Study of costs, 1940–60.

FINKLE, LEE, *Forum for Protest: The Black Press During World War II*. Cranbury, N.J.: Fairleigh Dickinson University Press, 1975. Study of editorial policies and campaigns of the major black newspapers in the war years.

FOX, STEPHEN R., *The Guardian of Boston: William Monroe Trotter*. New York: Atheneum, 1971. Trotter's *Guardian* was one of the leading black papers of 1900–20.

LA BRIE, HENRY G., III, ed., *Perspectives of the Black Press: 1974*. Kennebunkport, Me.: Mercer House Press, 1974. Current summary of La Brie's research and a collection of significant thoughts of black editors.

LENT, JOHN A., *Newhouse, Newspapers, Nuisances*. New York: Exposition Press, 1966. Story of the building of a media empire, with business details.

LEVIN, HARVEY J., *Broadcast Regulation and Joint Ownership of Media*. New York: New York University Press, 1960. Contains a wealth of statistical information.

PETERSON, THEODORE, *Magazines in the Twentieth Century*. Urbana: University of Illinois Press, rev. ed. 1964. The most comprehensive discussion of magazine industry economics.

RUCKER, BRYCE W., *The First Freedom*. Carbondale: Southern Illinois University Press, 1968. Prize-winning analysis of position of mass media, designed as updating of Morris Ernst's *The First Freedom* (1946).

SAGE, JOSEPH, *Three to Zero: The Story of the Birth and Death of the World Journal Tribune*. New York: American Newspaper Publishers Association, 1967. A brief analysis placing most blame for the fiasco on labor unions.

SIM, JOHN CAMERON, *The Grass Roots Press: America's Community Newspapers*. Ames: Iowa State University Press, 1969. The most recent and penetrating study of weeklies, rural and suburban, and their community roles.

THORNBROUGH, EMMA L., *T. Thomas Fortune: Militant Journalist*. Chicago: University of Chicago Press, 1972. Black editor of the *People's Advocate*.

VILLARD, OSWALD GARRISON, *The Disappearing Daily*. New York: Knopf, 1944. Criticism of the trend toward consolidation and bigness.

———, *Some Newspapers and Newspaper-Men*. New York: Knopf, 1923. Like *The Disappearing Daily*, this book discusses newspapers in major cities as well as major publishers: New York, Boston, Philadelphia, Washington, among others.

WOLSELEY, ROLAND E., *The Black Press, U.S.A.* Ames: Iowa State University Press, 1971. A comprehensive survey, with substantial historical material for black newspapers, magazines, and broadcasting.

Periodicals and Monographs

AGEE, WARREN K., "Cross-Channel Ownership of Communication Media," *Journalism Quarterly*, XXVI (Fall 1949), 410. Summary of Master's thesis, 1949, University of Minnesota. First detailed study of the problem.

BAGDIKIAN, BEN H., "Newspaper Mergers—the Final Phase," *Columbia Journalism Review,* XV (March/April 1977), 17. A gloomy picture, well-researched.

BLEYER, WILLARD G., "Freedom of the Press and the New Deal," *Journalism Quarterly,* XI (March 1934), 22. Report on trend toward newspaper combinations.

BOGART, LEO, "Magazines Since the Rise of Television," *Journalism Quarterly,* XXXIII (Spring 1956), 153. A study of magazine readership and economics from 1946–55.

BRADSHAW, JON, AND RICHARD NEVILLE, "Killer Bee Reaches New York," *More,* VII (February 1977), 12. The career of Rupert Murdoch, newest press lord.

CLICK, J. W., "Comparison of Editorial Content of Ebony Magazine, 1967 and 1974," *Journalism Quarterly,* LII (Winter 1975), 716. Significant editorial content is down.

DUFFUS, ROBERT L., "Mr. Munsey," *American Mercury,* II (July 1924), 297. A gently critical rejection of Munsey as a newspaper owner. Reprinted in Ford and Emery, *Highlights in the History of the American Press.*

EBERHARD, WALLACE B., "Circulation and Population: 1940 and 1970," *Journalism Quarterly,* LI (Autumn 1974), 503. Most U.S. papers held onto their readers.

———, "Daily Newspaper Starts and Suspensions, 1960–69," *Journalism Quarterly,* LII (Spring 1975), 117. Best chance is in small community.

EVANS, JAMES P., "Clover Leaf: The Good Luck Chain, 1899–1933," *Journalism Quarterly,* XLVI (Autumn 1969), 482. The chain had a *Daily News* in Omaha, St. Paul, and Des Moines and a Kansas City *World.*

FURLONG, WILLIAM B., "The Midwest's Nice Monopolists, John and Mike Cowles," *Harper's,* CCXXVI (June 1963), 64. A sketch of responsible monopoly publishers.

GOTHBERG, JOHN A., "The Local Influence of J. R. Knowland's Oakland *Tribune,*" *Journalism Quarterly,* XLV (Autumn 1968), 487. Knowland's half-century.

GROSE, CHARLES W., "A Century of Black Newspapers in Texas, 1868–1969," Ph.D. thesis, University of Texas, 1972. Depression broke GOP's hold on them.

GROTTA, GERALD L., "Changes in the Ownership Structure of Daily Newspapers and Selected Performance Characteristics, 1950–1968," Ph.D. thesis, Southern Illinois University, 1970. Data and analysis.

GUIMARY, DONALD, "The Decline and Death of Portland's *Daily Reporter,*" *Journalism Quarterly,* XLV (Spring 1968), 91. A strike-born daily lived on a shoestring.

GUTIÉRREZ, FÉLIX F., "Spanish-Language Radio and Chicano Internal Colonialism," Ph.D. thesis, Stanford University, 1976. Non-Chicanos largely in charge.

———, ed., "Spanish-Language Media Issue," *Journalism History,* IV (Summer 1977).

HENSHER, ALAN, "No News Today: How Los Angeles Lost a Daily," *Journalism Quarterly,* XLVII (Winter 1970), 684. Death of the *Daily News* in 1954.

HIRSCH, PAUL M., "An Analysis of *Ebony*: The Magazine and Its Readers," *Journalism Quarterly,* XLV (Summer 1968), 261. Covers 1945–66.

HOWARD, HERBERT H., "Broadcast Station Group Ownership: A 20th Century Phenomenon," *Journalism History,* II (Autumn 1975), 68. Study of top 100 markets.

———, "Cross-Media Ownership of Newspapers and TV Stations," *Journalism Quarterly,* LI (Winter 1974), 715. Legal status. See also, "The Contemporary Status of Television Group Ownership," *Journalism Quarterly,* LIII (Autumn 1976), 399. Background and current data in top 100 markets.

"John H. Johnson of *Ebony,*" *Nation's Business,* LXII (April 1974), 45.

KIMBROUGH, MARVIN G., "W. E. B. Du Bois as Editor of the *Crisis,*" Ph.D. thesis, University of Texas, 1974. Study of NAACP's paper, 1910–34.

KREILING, ALBERT L., "The Making of Racial Identities in the Black Press: A Cultural Analysis of Race Journalism in Chicago, 1878–1929," Ph.D. thesis, University of Illinois, 1973. Differing cultural groups find expression.

KROMPACK, FRANK J., "Socio-Economic Influences Affecting Texas Press in the Great Depression," Ph.D. thesis, University of Texas, 1975. Most papers survived declining revenues and circulation by economizing.

LA BRIE, HENRY G., III, "A Profile of the Black Newspaper Old Guard," Ph.D. thesis, University of Iowa, 1972. Based on 93 interviews.

LA BRIE, HENRY G., III, AND WILLIAM J. ZIMA, "Directional Quandaries of the Black Press in the United States," *Journalism Quarterly*, XLVIII (Winter 1971), 640. Black editors re-examine function of their press in depth survey.

LARSON, CARL M., "The Struggle of Paddock Publications Versus Field Enterprises, Inc.," *Journalism Quarterly*, XLVIII (Winter 1971), 700. Field lost.

MARZOLF, MARION T., "The Danish-Language Press in America," Ph.D. thesis, University of Michigan, 1972. Small ethnic press grew from 1872 to 1914.

MURPHY, SHARON, *Other Voices: Black, Chicano, and American Indian Press*. Dayton, Ohio: Pflaum/Standard, 1974. A monograph using survey findings.

NELSON, HAROLD L., "The Political Reform Press: A Case Study," *Journalism Quarterly*, XXIX (Summer 1952), 294. An analysis of an almost successful farmer-labor newspaper, the *Minnesota Daily Star* (1920–24).

NIXON, RAYMOND B., "Trends in U.S. Newspaper Ownership: Concentration with Competition," *Gazette*, XIV (No. 3, 1968), 181. A review with comprehensive data. See also Nixon, Raymond B., and Jean Ward, "Trends in Newspaper Ownership and Inter-Media Competition," *Journalism Quarterly*, XXXVIII (Winter 1961), 3. See also Nixon's "Trends in Daily Newspaper Ownership Since 1945," *Journalism Quarterly*, XXXI (Winter 1954), 3, and "Concentration and Absenteeism in Daily Newspaper Ownership," *Journalism Quarterly*, XXII (June 1945), 97.

PALMER, L. F., JR., "The Black Press in Transition," *Columbia Journalism Review*, IX (Spring 1970), 31. A survey, 1945–70.

PETERSON, PAUL V., "The Omaha *Daily World* and *World-Herald*, 1885–1964," Ph.D. thesis, University of Minnesota, 1965. Story of a major midwest daily.

PETERSON, WILBUR, "Is Daily Circulation Keeping Pace with the Nation's Growth?" *Journalism Quarterly*, XXXVI (Winter 1959), 12. Covers the period 1929–57.

———, "Loss in Country Weekly Newspapers Heavy in 1950s," *Journalism Quarterly*, XXXVIII (Winter 1961), 15. An evaluation with full data.

PRIDE, ARMISTEAD, *The Black Press: A Bibliography*. Jefferson City, Mo.: Lincoln University Department of Journalism, 1968. Sponsored by AEJ.

RASKIN, A. H., "The New York Newspaper Strike," *Columbia Journalism Review*, II (Spring 1963), 13. Text of the *New York Times'* labor reporter's story.

RAY, ROYAL H., "Economic Forces as Factors in Daily Newspaper Concentration," *Journalism Quarterly*, XXIX (Winter 1952), 31. An excellent summary.

REICHLEY, A. JAMES, "How John Johnson Made It," *Fortune*, LXXVIII (January 1968), 152. Profile of Negro publisher.

RILEY, SAM G., "The Cherokee Phoenix: The Short Unhappy Life of the First American Indian Newspaper," *Journalism Quarterly*, LIII (Winter 1976), 666. The 1834 *Phoenix* succumbed to tribal problems, white harassment.

ROBB, ARTHUR, "Chain Journalism in the Sixth Decade," *Editor & Publisher* golden jubilee number, July 21, 1934. A descriptive essay summarizing developments.

RUPP, CARLA MARIE, "Lee Hills: A Reporter in the Executive Suite," *Editor & Publisher*, CIX (March 13, 1976), 12. Portrait of Knight-Ridder executive.

SHAPIRO, FRED C., "The Life and Death of a Great Newspaper," *American Heritage*, XVIII (October 1967), 97. Extensive portrait of the *New York Tribune* and *Herald Tribune*.

SHAPLEN, ROBERT, "The Newhouse Phenomenon," *Saturday Review*, XLIII (October 8, 1960), 55. Analysis of the rise of Samuel Newhouse, group owner of newspapers, magazines, and broadcasting stations.

SIM, JOHN CAMERON, "19th Century Applications of Suburban Newspaper Concepts," *Journalism Quarterly*, LII (Winter 1975), 627. How they did it then.

"S. I. Newhouse and Sons: America's Most Profitable Publisher," *Business Week*, XLVIII (January 26, 1976), 56. Major article on a multi-media group.

SMYTHE, TED C., "A History of the *Minneapolis Journal*, 1878–1939," Ph.D. thesis, University of Minnesota, 1967. Leading Minneapolis afternoon daily.

STERLING, CHRISTOPHER, H., "Trends in Daily Newspaper and Broadcast Ownership, 1922–70," *Journalism Quarterly*, LII (Summer 1975), 247. More concentration.

"The Thomson Organization: How to Raise £40 Million," *The Economist,* CCLIII (October 12, 1974), 90. Financial view of Lord Thomson's newspapers.

THORNBROUGH, EMMA LOU, "American Negro Newspapers, 1880–1914," *Business History Review,* XL (Winter 1966), 467. Of hundreds of papers, only a few subsidized ones survived any length of time.

UDELL, JON G., "Economic Trends in the Daily Newspaper Business 1946 to 1970." A research report of the Bureau of Business Research and Service, University of Wisconsin, Madison, 1970. Data-laden; sponsored by ANPA.

WACKMAN, DANIEL B., ET AL., "Chain Newspaper Autonomy as Reflected in Presidential Campaign Endorsements," *Journalism Quarterly,* LII (Autumn 1975), 411. Analysis of 1960–72 period shows group papers endorse more.

WEINFELD, WILLIAM, "The Growth of Daily Newspaper Chains in the United States: 1923, 1926–1935," *Journalism Quarterly,* XIII (December 1936), 357. The first important study of the problem.

WEISSBERGER, S.J., "The Rise and Decline of the Yiddish-American Press," Ph.D. thesis, Syracuse University, 1972. Yiddish papers' fortunes since 1870.

WERTHEIMER, JERROLD L., "The Community Press of Suburbia," Ph.D. dissertation, Northwestern University, 1960. Chicago case study.

WILSON, NOEL AVON, "The *Kansas City Call:* An Inside View of the Negro Market," Ph.D. thesis, University of Illinois, 1968. History and influence of the *Call.*

It seemed a good place for a miracle—Saint Peter's Basilica in Rome, and in the winter of 1965 after Vatican Council II closed there were many Roman Catholics who thought a miracle of sorts had happened in the vaulting central shrine of their faith. Twenty-four hundred bishops who had gathered there from all over the world, men whose skill at business administration was certain but whose ardor for theological change was faint, had somehow moved an ancient church with medieval ways into the modern world. Not all of them had helped, of course. There were resisters and obstructors, bishops who smelled heresy in the house and cardinals who felt God-summoned to save their Church from its popes. Still, as the bishops went back to their chanceries after the Council, a Catholic looking about could not help but be astonished at what God—or was it the bishops?—or was it a small band of willful men behind the scenes?—had wrought.

Even those outside Rome's fold were impressed. One was Ignazio Silone, the rugged old Italian who had been a devout Catholic, then a devout Communist, and is now a devout Christian without a church. "In the effort made to bring herself up to date and to overcome internal resistance," he wrote, "the Church has shown a spiritual vitality of which many believed her incapable. How can one fail to rejoice?" So a creed that had claimed its ways timeless had found the time right to change its ways. It would be a true *aggiornamento*, a renewal, an opening out. From then on it would worship in vernaculars and forgo a dead Latin. It would retire cultic pietisms and accent the dignity of prayer. It would look to the rights of other faiths in officially Catholic states. In no state would it countenance oppression in this life with allusions to a good life after death. It would search for ecumenical reunion with all sects calling themselves Christian. It would lift the charge of deicide from the Jews, and even foresee divine mercy for those who deny divine order. And it would do an amazing thing to its governing structure: Its popes, instead of carrying on as absolute monarchs long after the age of kings had passed, would share their power with the universal college of bishops, the same twenty-four hundred very mortal men with their vanities and virtues about them in Saint Peter's. The bishops' new power was called "collegiality," and those who inquired about it were told to regard collegiality as the needed counterbalance to the primacy and infallibility of the pope, attributes of his office that few bishops had even thought to contest.

In prospect, collegiality was the Vatican Council's greatest accomplishment. In practice, it was to evaporate without a trace the first chance it had to work. That was only a few months after the Council. At an audience with Italian gynecologists, Pope Paul VI re-proclaimed his faith's old stand against contraception. The theological, medical and population experts whose advice he sought advised him not to do it, and the laity had plainly been disregarding it. Long before the bishops defined their collegial function with him, Paul had said he would hear all the advice but decide the birth-control issue himself. That he still decided it himself after collegiality became Church law was only a maladroit reminder of papal power. Had he accepted the counsel of his advisers to change birth-control teaching, and then invited the bishops to join with him in changing it, the Pope would have set col-

The Vatican

The Power and the Glory are passing

Jailed or married priests, and bishops who gave up hope, are only signs of the crisis in Roman Catholicism. At its center is the question of the infallibility of the Pope.

BY JOSEPH RODDY
LOOK SENIOR EDITOR

legiality off to a good start. But to reject the counsel and then bypass the bishops was an act of desperation. The Roman Catholic Church has been in disorder ever since.

The prospect now is that the Vatican Council the Catholics were so proud of may have accomplished little more than the trivialization of their beliefs. The liturgy of the Mass, shorn of its Latin, has degenerated in places into speech and song at its most primitive, crying out for the noble cadence of a *Dominus vobiscum*. In no country has the religious liberty of other creeds improved through the efforts of the Catholics. No non-Communist government has had its moves called immoral even when they were at the edge of, or into, genocide. The momentum has gone, and with it the heart, from the ecumenical movement toward Christian unity. Jews the world over felt Rome turn remote at the start of the Six Day War. And the unbelieving who looked for a few years with some interest at the faith because it gave the world such a good and true man as Pope John, have mostly turned from it now as just one more light that failed. Apart from their obliterating effect on collegiality, the Pope's long-awaited words on contraception included the stunning claim that his Church's teaching on birth control had at no time been in any question. But if it had never been in any question, then why had the Pope gathered around him banks of experts to draft the cases for and against changing it? That question drove Father Charles Davis, the leading young Catholic theologian in England, to answer that the Pope lied, and that under Paul, the Church was hopelessly irreformable. Davis then made his own exit from Roman Catholicism with regrets. There has been a steady flood of defections from the clergy since then, including two U.S. bishops, at least 11,000 priests by the Vatican's count, and an incalculable number of laymen and laywomen who may never be counted among those who have given up their faith—for, in fact, most haven't given it up at all. What they have given up is their allegiance to a besieged institution—that once-august, ecclesiastic principality whose temporal strength was reckoned at all the parliaments of great power "A noble, a venerable superstructure," Silone wrote. "But what happens to poor Christ in such a superstructure?"

There are now two irreconcilable Roman Catholic churches and an array of others between them, sharing one ancient foundation. There is the Pope's fortress church behind the Vatican walls, with outposts in most dioceses where bishops minister to comfortable flocks unaffected by the suffering about them. And there is the servant church of the Christ-ridden, some of them baptized Catholics, some not, but all ill at ease in their skins because they care deeply about the suffering they combat. Ignored by the servant church with no center, the Pope's fortress church is what remains of a once-solid structure now cracked in many places, its foundation not yet fragmented perhaps, but not very far from it either. There are Roman Catholics uncertain that God exists, who believe the Word just became semantics. Once a Mass was the same, sound for sound, sign for sign, whether in the center of Brazil or the hamlets of the Great Plains. Now there may well be drumbeaters at one, folk-rock singing at the other, and at neither can a worshiper be sure that the priest isn't planning to marry—if he doesn't already have a wife.

continued

Page from final issue of *Look* (1971).

WEATHER

Today: Sunny and cool.
Tomorrow: Cloudy, milder.

TEMPERATURE RANGE
Yesterday 45-60; Today 32-48.

HUMIDITY
Yesterday 3 p. m. 36%; Today 48-42.

Reports and Maps—Page 36

NEW YORK
Herald ✦ Tribune

Established 123 Years Ago. A European Edition Is Published Daily in Paris

VOL. CXXIII No. 42,613

230 West 41st Street, New York 18164, N. Y.
Telephone PEnnsylvania 6-4000

MONDAY, NOVEMBER 25, 1963

© 1963, New York
Herald Tribune Inc.

THE CITY

TEN CENTS

A Nation Appalled

BULLET STRIKES VITALS of accused assassin Lee Oswald as night club owner Jack Ruby pulls the trigger, detective recoils, in crowded corridor of city hall basement.

UPI telephoto by BOB JACKSON, copyright, 1963 The Dallas Times-Herald

IN THE NEWS THIS MORNING

[FROM THE HERALD TRIBUNE'S WORLD-WIDE SOURCES]

Monday, Nov. 25, 1963

TOPIC A—

❦The body of John Fitzgerald Kennedy was borne from the White House to the Capitol Rotunda yesterday. An estimated 300,000 watched the mournful procession along Pennsylvania Avenue when the flag-covered coffin was lifted from the black caisson and placed inside the Rotunda. Mrs. Jacqueline Kennedy, dressed in black and wearing a black veil, knelt and kissed it. In a brief ceremony, government leaders mixed their eulogies with pleas for an end to bitterness, violence and hatred in the land. And then the people began to file past. (Page 1)

IN DALLAS—

❦In the same Dallas Hospital under the hands of the same doctors who had labored to save President Kennedy, Lee Harvey Oswald, the accused assassin, died at 1:07 p. m. One bullet fired point-blank from the nickel-plated revolver of nightclub owner Jack (Ruby) Rubenstein cut down Oswald as an army of Dallas detectives ushered him out of City Hall jail for transfer to County Jail. Within an hour, Rubenstein was charged with Oswald's murder and Dallas homicide chief Will Fritz said the case of the assassination of the 35th President was "closed." (Page 1)

❦Rubenstein was not regarded as a criminal type although he was arrested six times for minor incidents. Un-married, he lived with a roommate who said he showed "a terrible grievance" over the President's assassination and lamented: "That poor family." He was a physical-fitness enthusiast reportedly well acquainted with Dallas police and newspapermen. (Page 3)

IN WASHINGTON—

❦Fresh from the melancholy experience of the cortege, President Johnson turned immediately to the country's No. 1 foreign policy problem—the shooting war in Viet Nam. In a conference with top security officials and Henry Cabot Lodge, his Ambassador in Saigon, President Johnson heard a "hopeful" report on a bold Communist move against a training center 20 miles from Saigon. (Stories on Page 5)

❦The late President's widow and two young children followed directly behind the horse-drawn caisson that brought Mr. Kennedy's flag-draped coffin from the White House to the Capitol. Caroline, nearly six, occasionally looked up at her mother's tear-stained face as if to comfort her. John Jr., who will be three today, waved a small American flag. Other members of the Kennedy family followed. The President's father, Joseph, was unable to travel to Washington because of illness. (Full story, Page 9)

❦Leaders from all parts of the world began to assemble in Washington to pay last respects to the late President Kennedy. Sixty-seven nations indicated they were sending representatives. The U. S. told foreign governments the presence of regular envoys would suffice, did not encourage the mass influx of heads of state. President Johnson will receive heads of state and other dignitaries at 5:30 p. m. today on the eighth floor of the State Department Building. (Reports on Page 7)

IN THE NATION—

❦The single shot that cracked in the basement of the Dallas City Hall yesterday closed forever the story of the man who the police believe committed one of the century's most incredible crimes. His motives, his preparations, his reasoning will never be known exactly. The bizarre shooting bewildered and angered people across the nation. (Story on Page 4)

❦Unprecedented radio and television coverage of the events in Dallas and Washington continued into a third day. It appeared there would be no return to normal broadcasting schedules until tomorrow morning. While millions of Americans considered the coverage the medium's finest hour, both the White House and the networks reported receiving calls from people around the country annoyed that their favorite programs had been deleted. (Page 13)

❦Of the problems suddenly placed on Lyndon Johnson's shoulders, one of the first he must deal with will be the threatened national rail strike. Tomorrow, a board set up by Congress to avoid the strike by compulsory arbitration of two key issues will deliver its decision to the new President. (Details, Page 20)

IN THE CITY—

❦Clergymen of all faiths eulogized the late President Kennedy, and church attendance increased throughout the city yesterday. A typical response: the Rev. Peter Chase, canon pastor of the Cathedral of St. John the Divine, told his congregation: "This is a great country with a great mission to lead us on." (Story on Page 13)

Nightclub Owner Silences Assassin

By Maurice C. Carroll
Of The Herald Tribune Staff

DALLAS.

Lee Harvey Oswald met an assassin's death yesterday just 48 hours and seven minutes after the bullets he was accused of firing killed the President of the United States. With much of the nation watching on television, Oswald was shot down amid a crowd of reporters, photographers and policemen as he was to be taken from the Dallas police station to the county jail. He was rushed to Parkland Hospital and gasped out his final breath in the same emergency ward, just 10 feet from the room where John F. Kennedy died Friday.

At the Dallas police station, detectives were mounting guard again over their newest killer, nightclub owner Jack Rubinstein, alias Jack Ruby. Dallas District Attorney Henry Wade, who had vowed to seek the death penalty for Oswald, said he would seek it for Oswald's killer.

Last night police barricaded parts of downtown Dallas to help control the crowds which have been increasing at the scene of the President's assassination and the Oswald shooting.

The chief of the Texas Highway Patrol ordered 20 extra men into Dallas to guard Gov. John Connally, still recuperating in Parkland Hospital after being wounded in the fusillade that killed Mr. Kennedy.

"We have complete respect for the Dallas Police Department and we do not mean to imply that we do not," said Col. Homer Garrison Jr., head of the State Department of Public Safety.

The 20 troopers were brought in from Tyler, 98 miles east of Dallas. Col. Garrison refused to say whether more had been ordered in from other areas of the state.

Dallas was exceptionally tense as wild rumors of telephone threats of new shootings floated through the city. Dallas and Texas as a whole have free-and-easy laws concerning the possession of firearms, and many citizens ap-

parently feel that the violence of the last three days has disgraced the city's good name. No one is sure the violence is over yet.

Oswald died without ever having changed his statements that he was innocent of the murder of President Kennedy. Authorities had said that they had an overwhelming case prepared against him.

The bullet that killed the admitted Communist sympathizer pierced Oswald's spleen, pancreas, aorta, kidney and liver.

The same physicians who had treated President Kennedy at Parkland were unable to save Oswald, even though they administered repeated transfusions and used an electronic Pacemaker to attempt to bring his heart back into action.

He died in Emergency Room Two, the same room where physicians had worked over his second victim, Texas Gov. John Connally, who is recovering from his wounds. The room is across the corridor from the room where President Kennedy died.

The shooting was witnessed by millions of Americans on all three television networks which had set up cameras to view the President's accused assassin as he was transferred from the police station to the county jail.

This reporter was within eight feet of Oswald when he was shot. I may have shouted the last words he was ever to hear.

The prisoner, hands cuffed in front of him, was led into the cavernous garage under the station. Seconds before the shooting there was a

More on MILLIONS—P 3

ON THE WHITE HOUSE STEPS, the woman the slain assassin widowed, Jacqueline Kennedy, appears with her children, John jr. and Caroline, to escort the President's body to the Capitol where it lay in state in the Rotunda.

Associated Press wirephoto

MOURNING IN CAPITAL

By David Wise
Washington Bureau Chief

WASHINGTON.

Under an American flag and a bright autumn sun, to the roll of muffled drums, the body of John F. Kennedy, 35th President of the United States, was borne along Pennsylvania Ave. to the Capitol rotunda yesterday, and rested there overnight. Pleas for an end to bitterness, violence and hatred in the land were voiced in eulogies.

In an unforgettable scene, Mrs. Jacqueline Kennedy, in black and veiled, stood in the rotunda in sorrowful dignity, holding the hands of her two children, Caroline and John jr. Then she and her daughter knelt and Mrs. Kennedy kissed the flag-draped casket.

At the very moment that Sen. Mike Mansfield, the Democratic leader of the Senate, stood at the bier and decried "the hatred, prejudice and the arrogance which converged in that moment of horror to strike him down," there was new horror in Dallas, Texas. At 2:07 p. m. as Sen. Mansfield spoke, Lee Harvey Oswald, accused of assassinating the President, died in an emergency room of Parkland Hospital in Dallas.

He had been shot with a single bullet fired point-blank by a man police identified as Jack Ruby, the owner of a dance hall and a strip-tease club.

All day and into the night, thousands of people filed past the bier of the dead President as the nation and the world paid tribute to his passing. Today, he will be buried in Arlington National Cemetery after a requiem mass.

The leaders of the world converged on Washington to attend the funeral today.

President Lyndon B. Johnson rode in the cortege from the White House to the Capitol, but then sped back to the Executive Office Building to deal with a new crisis in Viet Nam.

Thousands of spectators, with tears in their eyes, watched as seven white horses carried the body of the President to the Capitol on the same caisson that once bore the body of President Franklin D. Roosevelt 18 years ago.

The rain that had poured for hours in Washington Saturday was gone. Yesterday dawned bright, cloudless and crisp. The sun glinted off the black wooden wheels of the caisson, accompanied by a military honor guard, as it moved slowly to the capitol, to the mournful rhythm of the muffled drums. The procession took just 40 minutes.

As it began, word spread among the throngs that the man charged with the assassination of President Kennedy had been killed. It added a new nightmarish twist to the horror of the past 48 hours.

In the brief, moving ceremony in the rotunda, pleas for unity and an end to violence were voiced by Sen.

More on MOURNING—P 6

25

The Surviving
Newspaper Press

*. . . it is as difficult to apply objective standards to newspapers as it is
to people, and the greatest newspaper is as difficult to identify as the
greatest man. It all depends upon what you require.*
                                                                    —Gerald W. Johnson

The obligations of any newspaper to its community are to strive for honest and
comprehensive coverage of the news and for courageous expression of editorial
opinion in support of basic principles of human liberty and social progress. Those
newspapers that have been most consistent in fulfilling these obligations have been
rewarded with public and professional acclaim. Other factors that have operated to give
some newspapers greater professional recognition are brilliance of individual leadership on the staff and the maintenance of a steady and sound publishing tradition. No
one, however, can with any certainty rank America's leading papers in numerical
order. But the results of three opinion polls on the subject, taken in 1960 and 1961,
offer some at least interesting results. One was of 335 editors, one of 311 publishers,
and the third of 125 journalism professors.

The *New York Times, Christian Science Monitor, St. Louis Post-Dispatch,
Washington Post,* and *Milwaukee Journal* were rated among the top six dailies in all
three polls. The *Louisville Courier-Journal* was in the first eight of all three polls. The
Chicago Daily News, Wall Street Journal, New York Herald Tribune, and *Chicago
Tribune* were in the first ten of two of the polls. Included in the top 15 dailies by one or
more polls were the *Baltimore Sun, Atlanta Constitution, Minneapolis Tribune,
Kansas City Star, Los Angeles Times, Miami Herald, Detroit Free Press,* and *Des
Moines Register.*[1]

A mail poll taken in 1970 by veteran public opinion expert Edward L. Bernays
showed 130 publishers confirming most of the selections of the previous decade. The
New York Times again ranked a clear first, with 60 percent of the ballots listing it. A
clear second was the *Los Angeles Times,* with a 50 percent rating, up sharply during the

462 The Surviving Newspaper Press

1960s. Clustered at 40 percent were three dailies with distinguished editorial pages—the *Louisville Courier-Journal, St. Louis Post-Dispatch,* and *Washington Post.* At the 30 percent level were the *Christian Science Monitor, Milwaukee Journal,* and moving upward, the *Miami Herald.* Ninth and tenth, at the 20 percent level, were the *Chicago Tribune* and *Wall Street Journal.* A consensus later in the decade, after Watergate, would put the *Washington Post* in a "big three" ranking with the *New York Times* and *Los Angeles Times,* and add the *Boston Globe* to the list. Threads of journalistic achievement can be woven together by examining the current status of these and some other representative daily newspapers whose accounts were not completed in earlier chapters of this volume.*

THE *NEW YORK TIMES*   The *New York Times* ranked first in all four polls, continuing to hold its place in the forefront of American journalism by maintaining the tradition of telling the news with completeness and integrity. Arthur Hays Sulzberger, who became publisher when his father-in-law, Adolph S. Ochs, died in 1935, lived up to his responsibilities as the head of the country's "newspaper of record." Throughout the 1930s and 1940s, the news staff was led by the team of Edwin L. James, managing editor, and David H. Joseph, city editor. Responsibility for the editorial page, which rested briefly with John H. Finley after the death of Rollo Ogden in 1937, passed in 1938 to Charles Merz. Merz had been managing editor of *Harper's Weekly* and an associate editor of the *New York World.*

Turner Catledge, well-tested as a Washington correspondent, became managing editor in 1951, the *Times'* centennial year. Catledge named two *Times* veterans, Theodore Bernstein and Robert E. Garst, as assistant managing editors with responsibility for enlivening the paper's writing and news presentation. Frank S. Adams became city editor, presiding over a block-long city room in the $18-million Times building down 43rd Street from the old Times Square location (the Times Tower was sold in 1961). Major changes came in 1961 when Sulzberger turned over the publisher's chair to his son-in-law, Orvil E. Dryfoos, and Merz retired as editorial page chief in favor of John B. Oakes (a nephew of Adolph Ochs), who had won distinction as an editorial writer. Lester Markel remained as editor of the Sunday edition, a post he had held for 40 years. In 1962 the *Times* began a Western edition printed in Los Angeles but lost heavily and killed it in 1964.

The management struggle described by Gay Talese in *The Kingdom and the Power* began with the sudden death of Dryfoos in June 1963. The family turned to Arthur Ochs (Punch) Sulzberger, 37, as publisher. Strong man Amory Bradford, chief negotiator for the publishers in the disastrous 1963 New York strike, quit as business manager. In September young Sulzberger named Turner Catledge executive editor for both daily and Sunday editions, relegating Markel to retirement. Clifton Daniel was named managing editor and Tom Wicker replaced columnist James B. Reston as head of the Washington bureau.

A crisis arose over control of the Washington bureau early in 1968 when a non-*Times* man, James L. Greenfield, was nominated to head it. Wicker and Reston reversed the decision, and the struggle undermined Catledge, who was soon moved up to a vice-presidency in favor of Reston as executive editor. The elder Sulzberger died at the close of 1968, and his son then took full command. Reston was made a vice

*The stories of the *Christian Science Monitor* and *Wall Street Journal* are told on pages 372–74 of chapter 22, and that of the *Chicago Tribune* on pages 488–91 of chapter 26.

president in August 1969 and returned to column writing in Washington, where Wicker was also a columnist and Max Frankel the bureau chief. Clifton Daniel was shunted to control of the New York Times Service and Abe Rosenthal, a loser in the 1968 crisis, became Sulzberger's managing editor. He brought Greenfield to the staff as foreign editor.

By 1977 Sulzberger had promoted Rosenthal to executive editor and replaced John Oakes with Max Frankel as editorial page chief. Frankel shrank the 14-member editorial board, to the dismay of some of its senior members. Associate editors were now Clifton Daniel, Tom Wicker, and Charlotte Curtis, who edited the "op-ed" page. Seymour Topping was managing editor, and Arthur Gelb metropolitan editor. Hedrick Smith, winner of a Pulitzer Prize covering Moscow, headed the Washington bureau, and Greenfield remained foreign editor. The *Times* streamlined its makeup and added "Weekend" and "Living" sections.

Editorially the *Times* was staunchly internationalist in world outlook, progressive-conservative in domestic affairs. It supported Democrat Franklin D. Roosevelt in 1936 and 1944 and backed Republicans Wendell Willkie in 1940, Thomas E. Dewey in 1948, and Dwight D. Eisenhower in 1952 and 1956. Beginning in 1960, it supported Democrats in five consecutive elections. Like other responsible papers it vigorously defended individual freedoms against reactionary attacks and illegal use of power. By 1977 the *Times* and its staff had won a record number of 42 Pulitzer Prizes, including three gold medals.

THE *INTERNATIONAL* HERALD TRIBUNE   After 1966 the legend *"Herald Tribune"* could be found only on a paper circulating throughout Western Europe: "The *International Herald Tribune*. Published with the New York Times and the Washington Post." For reasons of both quality and tradition, the paper should be included among the surviving greats.

The *New York Herald Tribune* was for 42 years a distinguished morning rival of the *Times*. Ogden M. Reid and his wife, Helen Rogers Reid, succeeded to control of the *Tribune* when editor Whitelaw Reid died in 1912. With the purchase of the *Herald* from Frank Munsey in 1924, and the creation of the *Herald Tribune,* a distinctive newspaper emerged. Ogden Reid was content to have his wife assume the major responsibilities of the publisher's office.

Like the *Times,* the *Herald Tribune* became known for its foreign and Washington correspondence and for its coverage of cultural news. Its syndicated columnists included Mark Sullivan, Walter Lippmann, Joseph Alsop, and Roscoe Drummond. Geoffrey Parsons, a Pulitzer Prize winner, served as chief editorial writer from 1924 to 1952. Stanley Walker became one of New York's best known city editors, and assistant editor Wilbur Forrest was an important journalistic figure. When Ogden Reid died in 1947 his sons, another Whitelaw Reid and Ogden R. Reid, joined their mother in directing the paper's affairs. But difficulties piled up, and in 1958 the Reids reluctantly sold the *Herald Tribune* to millionaire John Hay Whitney.

The paper adopted a magazine-style format under editors John Denson and James G. Bellows. Crippled by a 114-day 1963 strike, the "Trib" still presented some of the best designed front pages and most literate writing in American journalism. But most New York newspapers were losing money, and in early 1966 Whitney, the Hearst group, and Scripps-Howard planned a merger in which the *Herald Tribune* would become the morning edition of a World Journal Tribune Company. The final edition of the *Herald Tribune* appeared April 24; agreement could not be reached with the printing unions and Whitney announced its death August 15. A *World Journal Tribune* appeared evenings and Sundays from September 1966 to May 1967. Mrs. Helen Rogers Reid died in 1970, and an era was no more.

Left from the wreckage was the *International Herald Tribune,* successor to the Bennetts' old *Paris Herald.* In 1967 the *New York Times* gave up its European edition and Whitney, Katharine Graham of the *Washington Post,* and Sulzberger became joint owners of the Paris-based "Trib." It ran editorials from all three ownership sources.

Consistently conservative in its outlook, the old *Herald Tribune* won wide respect for fairness and for high quality interpretative writing. It supported the internationalist wing of the Republican party and early promoted the presidential bids of Willkie and Eisenhower, as against that of Senator Robert A. Taft. In its final campaign in New York the *Herald Tribune* rejected Goldwater for Lyndon Johnson.

THE *LOS ANGELES*   Bursting out almost as dramatically as California's population in
TIMES   the 1960s, the *Los Angeles Times* became a major force in national
and international journalism. It had led all the nation's dailies in total advertising linage by a wide margin and also led in space allotted to editorial material. Now in the 1970s it reached the million mark in circulation and became something more than the fat, dullish paper that the *New York Times* had thought could be challenged on its home grounds.

The heritage of the *Los Angeles Times* was strictly conservative. Harrison Gray Otis assumed control in 1882 and became a civic booster and Republican stalwart. When his plant was dynamited in 1910 by union radicals, his support of antiunion forces in the city was intensified. His son-in-law, Harry Chandler, was an equally conservative publisher engaged in a circulation struggle with the Hearst papers in Los Angeles. The *Times'* political editor, Kyle Palmer, so slanted his news stories that the Washington correspondents in 1937 voted the paper next to Hearst and McCormick papers as "least fair and reliable." Norman Chandler, publisher from 1944 to 1960, was more middle-of-the-road, but the paper lacked drive. It did win Pulitzer Prizes for public service in 1942, for fighting a contempt of court charge to the Supreme Court, and in 1960 for an exposure of narcotics traffic.

Changes in the *Times* were being planned even before Norman Chandler's retirement. His wife, Dorothy, and son, Otis, were working with Nick B. Williams, appointed editor in 1958, to revitalize the paper. Otis Chandler, 32 when he became publisher, proved to be one of the most effective American publishers of his time. Two new Sunday sections were created, "Opinion" and "Outlook," and two Sunday magazines, *Home* and *Calendar.* Acres of local and regional news releases were replaced with significant national and foreign news. Otis Chandler struck a bargain with youthful Philip L. Graham of the *Washington Post* to form the Los Angeles Times-Washington Post News Service. Within a decade it was one of the most important interpretative news services in the world and the *Times* had seven domestic bureaus and 18 foreign bureaus of its own as well as the resources of the *Post.* At home, Williams doubled the number of staff members to 516 in his years of control. Chandler moved further onto the national stage by purchasing control of both *Newsday* and the *Dallas Times Herald* in 1970.

Williams retired to a consultant's post in 1971, and Chandler named as the new editor William F. Thomas, formerly metropolitan editor. Robert J. Donovan, *New York Herald Tribune* bureau chief in Washington, was lured to a similar position with the *Los Angeles Times* in 1963, becoming an associate editor and Washington columnist after 1970. James G. Bellows, last editor of the *Herald Tribune,* joined the *Times* in 1966 as an associate editor but left in 1974 to resuscitate the *Washington Star.* James Bassett and Jean Sharley Taylor became associate editors. Frank P. Haven was managing editor, and Mark Murphy metropolitan editor. Dennis A. Britton was named national editor, and Pulitzer Prize winner Jack Nelson headed the Washington bureau. Anthony Day was in charge of the progressive, skillfully edited editorial pages.

Richard Nixon noted the *Times'* changing outlook during his ill-fated gubernatorial campaign in 1962, attacking the paper among others in his postelection "blowup." In 1964 the *Times* backed Nelson Rockefeller for the Republican nomination but, failing, endorsed Goldwater for election. That year Paul Conrad joined the paper as editorial cartoonist, and his liberal line drawings won Pulitzer Prizes in 1964 and 1971. The paper also won the 1966 local coverage award for reporting the Watts riot; the 1969 international reporting and public service awards, the latter for an exposure in city government; and the 1976 editorial writing prize. The *Times* bitterly fought Mayor Sam Yorty and joined a coalition successfully electing his black opponent, Tom Bradley. Early in 1971 it called on President Nixon for an immediate withdrawal of troops from Vietnam. Lacking faith in McGovern's foreign and defense plans, it supported Nixon in 1972, but printed Jack Nelson's Watergate exposure stories and denounced Nixon in 1974.

Its forthright, thoughtful editorials seemed to some to lack "zip," in keeping with the generally cautious attitude of the paper's management and staff. Still, the *Times* had moved into an independent-minded editorial position. It was doing a good, if not outstanding, job of covering its huge metropolitan area. Reporters were given time to develop lengthy, in-depth investigative stories featured on page one and filling inside pages. Another asset was the highly read "View" section, carrying articles on city life, personalities, changing values, health, and consumer issues, some quite interpretative.

THE *WASHINGTON POST*

Other than the *Los Angeles Times,* no American newspaper rose more rapidly in esteem in recent decades than did the *Washington Post* after Eugene Meyer, a civic-minded financier, rescued it from a receivership in 1933. Meyer's object in buying the *Post* from the McLean family heirs was to give Washington a newspaper with a sound and intelligent editorial page. This he achieved with two editors who won Pulitzer Prizes for editorial writing: Felix Morley, editor until 1940, and Herbert Elliston, who served until 1953. Robert H. Estabrook then became editor of the editorial page. Giving the page added distinction were the cartoons of Herbert L. Block, better known as Herblock. Through its editorial page and its interpretative coverage of national news, the *Post* won recognition as the most independent paper in the capital. It also carried a large volume of foreign news.

When Meyer became president of the International Bank in 1946, he named Philip L. Graham, his son-in-law, as publisher, but he and his wife, Agnes E. Meyer, remained influential in the newspaper's continued progress. Purchase of the *Post's* morning competition, the *Times-Herald,* in 1954, ensured the *Post's* economic stability. With James Russell Wiggins as editor and Alfred Friendly as managing editor, the paper had effective news-side leaders. They joined Graham in raising voices in behalf of improved journalistic practices and in defense of fundamental press freedoms. Editorially the *Post* avoided direct endorsements, but it favored the Dewey, Eisenhower, and Kennedy candidacies. It was strongly internationalist in outlook and became known for its outspoken and early criticism of Wisconsin Senator Joseph R. McCarthy's political movement of the early 1950s, which became known as

"McCarthyism." Herblock, who had won a 1942 Pulitzer Prize, repeated in 1954 with his dramatically liberal cartoons, which had McCarthy as a particular target. Another was Vice President Nixon, whom the *Post* continued to oppose in future years.

Graham's tragic suicide in 1963 brought his wife Katharine to control of the Washington Post Company, including its television stations and *Newsweek,* purchased in 1961. Mrs. Graham was a friend of both President Kennedy and Johnson and a firm supporter of their reform policies. In 1965 she moved Benjamin C. Bradlee to the *Post* from *Newsweek* and made him managing editor in 1966. Friendly became a roving reporter and won the Pulitzer Prize for covering the war in Israel. Wiggins retired to become UN ambassador in 1968. Bradlee, then 47, became executive editor and Howard Simons managing editor.

The *Post* vigorously favored Hubert Humphrey in 1968, sympathized with dissent movements, and supported the black population of its area, employing more blacks than any other American paper. When activist-philanthropist Agnes Meyer died in 1970, she had seen her daughter's paper pass the half-million mark in circulation and take a position as the most influential of the country's liberal-intellectual newspapers.

During the 1970s the *Washington Post* took center stage in the Watergate crisis through the courage of its publisher and chief editors in supporting the investigative reporting of Carl Bernstein and Bob Woodward, despite reprisal threats from the Nixon administration. The paper won a Pulitzer gold medal and much prestige. Editorial page editor Philip Geyelin, himself a Pulitzer Prize winner, and his associate, Meg Greenfield, also played roles. Columnist David Broder won the 1973 award for commentary; other columnists included Nicholas Von Hoffman, Hobart Rowen on economics, and William Raspberry. Charles B. Seib served as ombudsman and press critic.

THE *ST. LOUIS POST-DISPATCH*

The revolution of the 1870s and 1880s known as the "new journalism" gave the Midwest nationally known newspapers that continued to demonstrate their leadership in the 1970s. None was more consistently in the foremost rank of American newspapers than the *St. Louis Post-Dispatch,* founded in 1878 by the first Joseph Pulitzer, edited from 1911 to 1955 by the second Joseph Pulitzer, and since then by the third of the line, Joseph Pulitzer III, who began assuming authority in the late 1940s.

Continuity, both of Pulitzer family ownership and of the *Post-Dispatch* editorial policies, proved to be the key to greatness. Hammering away consistently to make the editorial page an independent, liberal voice were six editorial page editors: George S. Johns, who served from 1897 to 1928, Clark McAdams, Charles G. Ross, Ralph Coghlan, Irving Dilliard, and Robert Lasch. Daniel R. Fitzpatrick's incisive cartoons dramatized *Post-Dispatch* crusades from 1913 until 1958.

O. K. Bovard, one of America's great newsmen, provided the necessary complement of leadership during his 30 years as *Post-Dispatch* managing editor, from 1908 to 1938. Under his tutelage, such brilliant reporters as Paul Y. Anderson, Charles G. Ross, Marquis Childs, and Raymond P. Brandt advanced from St. Louis to the Washington scene to help win a national reputation for the paper. Anderson proved to be the mainspring of Bovard's effort after World War I to expand *Post-Dispatch* coverage of the national scene. Through his efforts the paper successfully led a campaign in 1923 to obtain the release of 52 Americans still imprisoned five years after the war's end for expression of radical antiwar opinion. Anderson and his paper were the first to realize the significance of the Teapot Dome scandal. And as a Washington correspondent, Anderson aided in the impeachment, for improper conduct, of federal

Arthur Hays Sulzberger, *New York Times;* Mrs. Helen Rogers Reid, the *Herald Tribune.*

Katharine Graham, *Washington Post;* Otis Chandler, *Los Angeles Times* and *Newsday.*

Barry Bingham, *Louisville Courier-Journal;* Joseph Pulitzer III, the *Post-Dispatch.*

judge George W. English of East St. Louis in 1926. English resigned before his impeachment trial.

What *Post-Dispatch* men called the "dignity page"—the opening page of the editorial section—was developed by Bovard to carry special articles on political, economic, scientific, and cultural subjects. When Bovard resigned in 1938 after differences with his publisher, Benjamin H. Reese became managing editor. Raymond L. Crowley succeeded Reese in 1951.

During the 15 years beginning in 1937 the *Post-Dispatch* won five Pulitzer Prize gold medals for meritorious public service. Politically, *Post-Dispatch* support had usually been given to Democratic presidential candidates, although it deserted Roosevelt once, in 1936, and supported Dewey in 1948. It opposed Richard Nixon in his three presidential races, giving George McGovern positive support in 1972.

Crowley's retirement in 1962 brought Arthur R. Bertelson to the managing editorship; when he advanced to executive editor, Evarts A. Graham, Jr., succeeded him. Raymond P. Brandt retired in 1967 after 44 years in the Washington bureau; Marquis Childs, his successor as bureau chief, won the 1970 Pulitzer Prize for commentary before retirement. Richard Dudman replaced him to become another outstanding Washington bureau chief for the *Post-Dispatch*.

THE *MILWAUKEE JOURNAL*

The *Milwaukee Journal* stood in the uppermost level of the country's newspapers in the 1970s as a conscientiously edited, well-written, community-conscious daily blessed with one of the nation's largest volumes of advertising and space for comprehensive news coverage. Its editorial page ranked in stature with those of the *St. Louis Post-Dispatch* and *Washington Post*.

The *Journal,* founded in 1882, faced strong competition through all its early years. Publisher Lucius W. Nieman set the trend for its community leadership. Under Nieman's guidance the *Journal* developed an international outlook, supporting the League of Nations and the United Nations. The paper clashed with the isolationist-minded La Follette family and Milwaukee's Socialist leader, Victor Berger, on foreign policy. But as a middle-of-the-road, independent paper it tended to support progressive-minded politicians of whatever party. Nationally, it supported Roosevelt in 1932, 1936, and mildly in 1944; Willkie in 1940, Dewey in 1948, and then the Stevenson candidacies. Its fiercest battle was with Senator Joseph R. McCarthy on his home ground; when McCarthy won reelection in 1952 he failed to carry Milwaukee. It refused to support either Nixon or Goldwater in the 1960s, endorsing Kennedy, Johnson, Humphrey, and Carter.

A dominant personality appeared on the *Journal* staff in 1916 when Harry J. Grant became business manager. Grant acquired 20 percent of the stock and the title of publisher in 1919. He imported Marvin H. Creager from the *Kansas City Star,* and Creager, as managing editor and later as editor and company president, reinforced the *Journal*'s local coverage and writing qualities with an insistence born of his *Star* experience.

Nieman died in 1935 and his wife in 1936. Part of the Nieman fortune was left to Harvard University, which used it to establish the Nieman Fellowships for newspapermen. The Nieman stock holdings in the paper were up for sale, but Grant saved the situation by organizing an employee-ownership plan similar to that of the *Star* in Kansas City. Grant, as board chairman and a substantial stockholder, remained in firm control. J. Donald Ferguson succeeded Creager as editor in 1943, giving way to Lindsay Hoben in 1961.

Richard H. Leonard became managing editor in 1962 and moved up to the

Chicago Tribune

Milwaukee Journal

Clayton Kirkpatrick, *Chicago Tribune;* Richard H. Leonard, *Milwaukee Journal.*

New York Times

Los Angeles Times

A. M. Rosenthal, *New York Times;* William F. Thomas, *Los Angeles Times.*

Washington Post

Knight Newspapers

Benjamin C. Bradlee, *Washington Post;* Lee Hills, the Knight Newspapers.

editorship in 1967 on the death of Hoben. John Reddin edited the editorial pages and Joseph W. Shoquist became managing editor. The *Journal* won the 1967 Pulitzer Prize for public service, repeating its 1918 award. Its employees owned 80 percent of the stock in the Journal Company, which also owned the *Milwaukee Sentinel* and the city's major television station.

THE *LOUISVILLE COURIER-JOURNAL*

The South, with a more slowly developing industrial economy, smaller population, and fewer major cities, did not match the East and Midwest in producing newspapers that could win the highest possible rankings in the estimate of the craft. But as early as the 1950s at least one—the *Louisville Courier-Journal* from the border state of Kentucky—became a newspaper that ranked among the nation's best.[2]

The retirement in 1919 of Henry Watterson, editor of the *Courier-Journal* since 1868, brought the Bingham family to the fore. Judge Robert Worth Bingham bought the *Courier-Journal* and the afternoon *Times* in 1917. Before he died in 1937 he saw his son, Barry Bingham, well established as directing owner of the newspapers. At his right hand was Mark Ethridge, former associate editor of the *Washington Post* and publisher of the *Richmond Times-Dispatch,* who came to Louisville as general manager in 1936 and became publisher in 1942. Bingham took the title, and writing responsibilities, of editor of the *Courier-Journal.*

Events moved rapidly at Louisville under the Bingham-Ethridge regime. James S. Pope became executive editor of the two papers. Norman E. Isaacs, managing editor of the *St. Louis Star-Times* when it closed down in 1951, came to Louisville as managing editor of the *Times.* Bingham, Ethridge, Pope, and Isaacs all were recognized as vocal, intelligent leaders in the journalistic profession. Russell Briney became editor of the *Courier-Journal* editorial pages, and George Burt editor of those for the *Times.*

Steadily Democratic in its political preferences, the *Courier-Journal* exerted a strong influence as a progressive, fair-minded newspaper dedicated to defending basic democratic principles. In news play, it excelled in international and national coverage, but it also paid close attention to Louisville, where it did effective work in behalf of the Negro, union labor, education, music, and art.

The deaths of two of Bingham's sons in accidents left Barry Bingham, Jr., who preferred a broadcasting career, with the family newspaper responsibility. He became editor and publisher in 1971, with his father remaining as board chairman. Ethridge and Pope had retired; Isaacs left the executive editorship in 1970 to teach at Columbia University. Robert P. Clark succeeded him. Ben F. Reeves was managing editor of the *Courier-Journal.* Molly Clowes succeeded Briney as head of the editorial pages in 1966, giving way in 1970 to Robert T. Barnard. Carol Sutton replaced Reeves as managing editor in 1974, first woman to hold that post on a major daily. Two years later she was named assistant to young Bingham. Michael J. Davies became managing editor. The *Courier-Journal* won the 1967 Pulitzer Prize for public service, the judges citing a successful campaign to control the Kentucky strip mining industry and thus preserve the environment.

THE *MIAMI HERALD*

The most progressive newspaper in the South, winning its way to a top place nationally by 1970, was the *Miami Herald,* a member of the Knight newspaper group. In 1977 it was the sixteenth largest American daily in circulation and third in advertising volume, despite Miami's rank in city size—42 by population, 26 by market area.

John S. Knight began his career in the 1920s on the family's *Akron Beacon-*

Journal. Their first expansion outside Ohio was to the *Miami Herald* in 1937. Purchase of the *Detroit Free Press* in 1940 gave the Knights a major group, to which they added the Charlotte and Macon newspapers and the *Philadelphia Inquirer* and *Daily News*. James L. Knight, a brother, concentrated his interest on the Miami and Charlotte operations, while John Knight focused on Detroit. But the management was integrated.

Lee Hills joined the *Herald* in 1942, coming from the Scripps-Howard papers. As managing editor, he built up the Latin American coverage of the *Herald* and began an international air express edition. In 1951 the *Herald* won a Pulitzer public service award for a drive on organized crime. The same year Hills was named executive editor of the *Detroit Free Press,* where he won a 1955 Pulitzer Prize for spot news. He became executive editor of all Knight newspapers in 1959. Directing the *Herald*'s news operations in 1977, and helping win a 1976 Pulitzer Prize for local reporting, were George Beebe, associate publisher; Don Shoemaker, editor; and Larry Jinks, executive editor.

John S. Knight had written his famed column, "The Editor's Notebook," for 32 years before he won the Pulitzer Prize for editorial writing in 1968. Both he and Hills served as president of the American Society of Newspaper Editors, Knight twice. Knight helped found and was president of the Inter American Press Association, which Hills later headed. Among American publishers of the 1970s, Knight was one of the most outspoken. Against participation in the Indochina war since 1954, he had a loud and clear position on that issue. Knight and his group of papers generally supported Republicans for the presidency but deserted Senator Goldwater in 1964.

OTHER EASTERN LEADERS
Coming into contention for top national ranking in the 1970s was the *Boston Globe,* founded in 1872 and published by the Charles H. Taylor family since 1877. Survivors with the Hearst *Herald American* after 1972, the morning and evening *Globes* won attention for joining the *New York Times* and the *Washington Post* in publishing the Pentagon Papers until stopped by court order. The *Globe* continued investigative reporting in the Watergate years and developed stars: Washington bureau chief Martin Nolan, columnist Ellen Goodman, and cartoonist Paul Szep. The paper won the 1975 Pulitzer gold medal for its coverage of the Boston school desegregation controversy and antibusing riots. Davis Taylor, grandson of the builder, was publisher. Thomas Winship became editor in 1965, succeeding his father Laurence, and won national notice.

Vying with the *Washington Post* and the *New York Times* for position on important Washington breakfast tables was the *Baltimore Sun*. The *Sun,* giving special attention to Washington coverage since its founding in 1837, had developed one of the strongest capital bureaus as well as a notable foreign service. Rejuvenated in the decade preceding World War I by Charles H. Grasty and Van-Lear Black, the *Sun* prospered under the effective leadership of Paul C. Patterson, publisher from 1918 to 1950. Hamilton Owens directed an aggressive editorial page. Washington columnist Frank R. Kent, H. L. Mencken, and Gerald W. Johnson were well-known staff members, followed by four Pulitzer Prize winners of the 1940s—Dewey L. Fleming, Paul W. Ward, Mark S. Watson, and Price Day. Philip Potter continued the *Sun* tradition of excellence in foreign and Washington correspondence. In the 1970s W. F. Schmick, Jr., was publisher and Philip Heisler managing editor.

Among other leading newspapers of the East was the *New York Post,* which completed 175 years of continuous daily publication in 1976, a record for currently published American dailies. The *Post* entered a new phase when Dorothy Schiff bought it in 1939. With editor Ted O. Thackrey, she made the paper a streamlined tabloid, departmentalized the news, and added feature content. Its columnists, led by Max Lerner, were prominently displayed. James A. Wechsler, from the staff of *PM*, became editor in 1949. The *Post* was the only New York City daily supporting Democratic candidate Adlai Stevenson in 1952 and 1956 and backed Democrats continuously thereafter. When metropolitan New York journalism collapsed in the mid-1960s, the *Post* emerged as the only afternoon daily and increased its circulation by two-thirds. Still, publisher Schiff found the struggle hard and sold the *Post* in January 1977 to the newest press lord, Australian Rupert Murdoch. Edwin Bolwell was named editor as Paul Sann elected to retire.

Long Island's *Newsday,* founded by Alicia Patterson in 1940 and controlled by her until she died in 1963, won its spurs as one of the top evening papers by combining local area coverage with substantial national and world news. It won the Pulitzer Prize for public service in 1964 and 1970 for uncovering Long Island governmental scandals and won a third prize in 1974. Tom Darcy won the 1970 award for cartooning. Alicia Patterson and her husband, Harry F. Guggenheim, differed on politics, he being the more conservative. In presidential races the paper supported Democrats in 1956, 1960, and 1964 and Republicans in 1952 and 1968. The switch to Nixon in 1968 came after Guggenheim took control in 1963. His editors were Mark Ethridge, from Louisville, followed by Bill D. Moyers, President Johnson's press secretary, in 1966. Guggenheim apparently intended to put Moyers in control of *Newsday* but became fearful of his policies and sold his 51 percent stock interest to Otis Chandler of the *Los Angeles Times* in 1970. Moyers resigned and William Attwood came from the Cowles magazines to head *Newsday* as publisher. David Laventhol was editor.

The *Washington Star,* solid if unspectacular, celebrated its centennial in 1952, still in the possession of the Noyes and Kauffmann families that took control of it in 1867. Its editors had been Crosby Noyes, 1867 to 1908; Theodore Noyes, to 1946; an outsider, Benjamin McKelway, to 1963; and then Newbold Noyes. Frank B. Noyes, longtime AP president, was president of the *Star* from 1909 to 1948. Samuel H. Kauffmann followed him to 1963 and was succeeded by his son, John. But during the 1960s the *Star*'s fortunes dwindled. It vainly bought out the rival *News* to bolster itself and in 1974 was sold to Joe L. Allbritton of Texas. He installed James G. Bellows as editor, and circulation was held even by a rejuvenated staff including three Pulitzer Prize winners—columnist Mary McGrory, reporter James R. Polk, and cartoonist Patrick Oliphant. Bellows resigned and Time Inc. bought the *Star* in 1978.

In Philadelphia, the solid *Bulletin* was being published by William L. McLean III, grandson of the founder, with B. Dale Davis as executive editor. The *Inquirer,* a Knight-owned paper after 1970, won the 1975 Pulitzer Prize for national reporting, and Tony Auth the 1976 cartooning award. Eugene Roberts was executive editor and Edwin O. Guthman ran the editorial page.

In Ohio, publisher Paul Block, Jr.'s *Toledo Blade* advanced steadily after 1950 in comprehensive news coverage, community leadership, and independence of opinion. With its morning edition, the *Times,* it was allied in ownership with the *Pittsburgh Post-Gazette,* published by William Block. The *Blade* also was one of the few American dailies to have a European correspondent. The *Cleveland Press,* long edited by Louis B. Seltzer, remained the best of the Scripps-Howard group and a strong civic leader. John S. Knight's *Detroit Free Press,* survivor with the *News* in that city's circulation battle, won the Pulitzer Prize for public service in 1945, and editor Royce Howes won for editorial writing in 1955. The prize for local reporting followed in 1968. But the *Free Press* and rival *News* were crippled by long strikes and major racial disturbances in the 1960s. The *Free Press* in 1977 was led by publisher Lee Hills, executive editor Kurt Luedtke, and his associate, Frank Angelo. It responded to Watergate and Detroit's dilemmas by endorsing Jimmy Carter in 1976.

MIDWEST JOURNALISTIC LEADERS   The *Chicago Daily News* retained a high place among newspaper leaders despite a series of ownership changes after the deaths of owners Victor F. Lawson in 1925 and Walter A. Strong in 1931. Colonel Frank Knox, former general manager of the Hearst newspapers and a leading Republican political figure, then became publisher. Knox kept the *Daily News* operating in its old traditions until his death in 1944. Its famous foreign and Washington news service reached brilliant heights. Henry Justin Smith, a news executive from 1901 to 1936, ran a "school for reporters."

Sale of the *Daily News* to John S. Knight in 1944 brought in Basil L. Walters as executive editor. Walters introduced new typographical and readership techniques he had learned while with the Cowles newspapers in Des Moines and Minneapolis. The paper emphasized local news and developed crusades on local issues. As a result, the *Daily News* printed the stories of its own foreign staff in less depth, although the service remained a strong one. The paper won two Pulitzer Prizes for public service, in 1950 and 1957, and gained in circulation and financial position.

Chicago newspaper ownership was streamlined in 1959, when Knight sold the *Daily News* to Marshall Field IV, owner of the morning *Sun-Times*. Field's father, founder of the *Sun* in 1941, had died in 1956. The *Daily News* became the evening affiliate of the *Sun-Times* in Chicago's circulation battle, and Field named himself its editor when Walters retired in 1961. His death at 49 in 1965 left control to the Field Enterprises executives until Marshall Field V was ready to assume command in 1969 at age 28. He eventually designated James F. Hoge as editor-in-chief of the papers, with Daryle M. Feldmeir as editor of the *News* and Ralph Otwell as managing editor of the *Sun-Times*. Hoge took direct charge of the *News* in 1977.

The *Daily News* won a Pulitzer Prize for public service once again in 1963. Reporter William J. Eaton received the 1970 national reporting prize for exposing the inadequacies of Supreme Court nominee Clement Haynsworth after his paper had endorsed President Nixon's selection. Cartoonist John Fischetti won a Pulitzer Prize in 1969, and columnist Mike Royko one in 1972. Both Field papers usually endorsed Republican presidential candidates but backed Jimmy Carter in 1976. Both were internationalist in outlook.

When journalism educators were asked in a 1961 poll to select the best combinations of morning and evening newspapers published by the same organization, they placed the Cowles-owned *Minneapolis Star* and *Tribune* and *Des Moines Register* and *Tribune* second and third, close behind the *Louisville Courier-Journal* and *Times*. Of the four papers owned by John and Gardner Cowles, the *Minneapolis Tribune* ranked highest as an individual daily.

Under publisher John Cowles the morning *Tribune* and evening *Star* developed wide upper Midwest circulations from their Minneapolis base. Gideon Seymour, after a successful career with the Associated Press, joined the papers in 1939 and was named executive editor in 1944. Carroll Binder, *Chicago Daily News* foreign editor, became editorial page editor of the *Tribune* in 1945.

Cowles, Seymour, and Binder teamed together to give the papers broadened news coverage, strong interpretative qualities, and independent-minded editorial pages strongly internationalist in outlook. Seymour died in 1954 and Binder in 1956. William P. Steven became executive editor, and Wilbur E. Elston editorial pages editor. Both left when John Cowles, Jr., took direct control of the news and editorial pages after 1960. Republican in national politics through 1960, the papers endorsed Democrats thereafter and were vigorously opposed to the Vietnam war early. In the 1970s they won a reputation for independent editorial endorsements from both parties for local and state offices and for a crusading opposition to right-wing movements.

In Des Moines, editorial editors W. W. Waymack, Forrest W. Seymour, and Lauren K. Soth all won Pulitzer Prizes for editorial writing. The Cowles Washington bureau won four Pulitzer awards for national reporting, and the 1976 national reporting award went to James Risser of Des Moines. Kenneth MacDonald became chief operating officer for Gardner Cowles.

While other leading dailies were expanding staff reporting of national news, the *Kansas City Star* was sticking principally to the local and regional area coverage William Rockhill Nelson had emphasized from the time he founded the *Star* in 1880 until his death in 1915. Fine writing of news and features, and vigorous crusading in the community interest, were special ingredients that kept the *Star* high in newspaper ratings. Continuity was ensured for the paper when the staff bought stock control in 1926, with some 90 employees raising $2.5 million in cash and assuming an $8.5 million mortgage that was paid off by 1939.

Two men became particularly prominent in *Star* affairs. One was Henry J. Haskell, named editorial page director in 1910 and editor from 1928 to 1952. The *Star* won two Pulitzer Prizes for editorial writing during his tenure. Overshadowing him, however, was the bulky, jovial Roy A. Roberts, who came to be Kansas City's leading citizen. Roberts joined the staff in 1908, served as the paper's Washington correspondent for 15 years, and then became managing editor in 1928. He was elected president and general manager of the *Star* and its morning edition, the *Times,* in 1947. Roberts loved politics as well as newspapering, and he became an important, if unofficial, figure in Republican party affairs. He retired in 1965 and William W. Baker became editor. In 1977 the employees sold their stock to Capital City Communications, a small publishing group, for $125 million, making some 20 of them millionaires.

The morning *St. Louis Globe-Democrat* was the *Post-Dispatch*'s only rival after the closing of the *Star-Times* in 1951. The *Globe-Democrat,* built to prominence by Joseph B. McCullagh before 1900, also worked vigorously for civic progress, although less dramatically and in a conservative political atmosphere. E. Lansing Ray was publisher from 1925 to 1955, when the paper was sold to Samuel I. Newhouse. Editorial editor Louis LaCoss won the Pulitzer Prize for editorial writing in 1952, the paper's centennial year.

OTHER TOP PAPERS OF THE SOUTH

Affiliated with the *Miami Herald* through the Knight newspapers group, the *Charlotte Observer* rose to prominence in southern journalism during the 1960s. Purchased by the Knight family in 1954, it was given the personal attention of James L. Knight, who became publisher. Named editor in 1955 was C. A. (Pete) McKnight, who had been editor of the small evening *News* (later bought by Knight). McKnight had just served as editor of the *Southern School News,* an objective reporter of school desegregation developments, and took the *Observer* along a conciliatory road on civil rights. Cartoonist Eugene Payne won a 1968 Pulitzer Prize. Other rising North Carolina papers were the *Winston-Salem Journal* and *Twin City Sentinel,* winners of the 1971 Pulitzer Prize for public service for blocking a strip mining operation that would have defaced the Carolina hill country.

Atlanta gave the South two strong newspapers, the *Constitution* and the *Journal*. Clark Howell, Sr., who succeeded Henry Grady at the *Constitution* in 1889, became the paper's owner and served as editor until 1936. His son, Clark Howell, Jr., named Ralph McGill as editor in 1938. McGill opposed the Ku Klux Klan and the Talmadge political machine in Georgia and won a Pulitzer Prize for editorial writing in 1959. James M. Cox, owner of the *Journal,* obtained control of the *Constitution* in 1950, but the papers continued to have separate editorial policies. The *Constitution* won a Pulitzer Prize for public service in 1931, and both papers won Sigma Delta Chi awards for public service in the 1950s. When McGill became a syndicated columnist and publisher of the *Constitution* in 1960, Eugene C. Patterson was named editor. He won the Pulitzer Prize in 1967 for his daily column and editorials attacking racism and political demagoguery. Then, declaring he lacked support by his management, he left. In 1977 Ann Cox Chambers was board chairman, Jack Tarver was publisher, and William H. Fields was executive editor.

Long known for its liberalism and stubborn fight against the conservative *Nashville Banner,* the paper developed by Silliman Evans, the *Nashville Tennessean* also won respect for its civil rights attitudes. The paper's fortunes declined after Evans's death in 1955, but they rose again when his younger son Amon Carter Evans became publisher at age 29 in 1962. With liberal John Seigenthaler as editor, the *Tennessean* supported the Kennedy-Johnson-Humphrey program for domestic reform. It also resumed the local crusading for which the elder Evans was famous.

Nelson Poynter's *St. Petersburg Times* won the 1964 Pulitzer Prize for public service for uncovering frauds in the state turnpike authority. The paper won a reputation for good reporting and news display based in part on Poynter's national journalistic reputation. In Memphis, the Scripps-Howard group had one of its best representatives in the *Commercial Appeal,* which developed its coverage and influence across state lines.

There were other famous names in southern journalism. Josephus Daniels continued his interest in the *Raleigh News and Observer* until his death in 1948 and passed on his editorship to his son, Jonathan, who also exerted influence in community and political affairs. Editor Virginius Dabney of the *Richmond Times-Dispatch* eyed traditional attitudes skeptically and jarred complacent conservatives with his editorials from 1928 into the 1960s. He won a Pulitzer Prize in 1948. Dr. Douglas Southall Freeman, editor of the *Richmond News Leader* from 1915 to 1949, won Pulitzer Prizes for his biographies of Robert E. Lee and George Washington. In Little Rock, J. N. Heiskell completed 60 years as editor of the respected *Arkansas Gazette* in 1961. His paper won the Pulitzer Prize for public service, and executive editor Harry S. Ashmore the award for editorial writing, for leadership during the 1957 school desegregation crisis in Little Rock. The stand cost the paper some of its public support, and Ashmore left to join the Ford Foundation.

Rapidly growing Texas fostered a journalism in keeping with the state's free enterprise economic atmosphere. Vigorous competition existed in many cities but among dailies essentially conservative in their editorial outlooks. The *Dallas News,* inherited by E. M. (Ted) Dealey in 1946 from his father, George, became an arch-conservative voice in Republican-voting Dallas. Houston's two largest papers, the morning *Post* and evening *Chronicle,* were carefully conservative. The *Post* was built into prominence by William P. Hobby and his editor-wife, Oveta Culp Hobby. The *Chronicle,* owned by financier Jesse Jones until his death in 1956, obtained William P. Steven as editor in 1960 but discharged him in 1965 for moving too rapidly. Another financier, Amon G. Carter, and his son firmly established the *Fort Worth Star-*

Telegram as a leading Texas daily. Noteworthy for taking a strong liberal stand on the integration issue were the *San Antonio Express* and *News.* Among Texas editors who achieved national prominence professionally were Felix R. McKnight of the *Dallas Times Herald* and Walter R. Humphrey of the Scripps-Howard *Fort Worth Press.* A vigorous smaller daily was published in Corpus Christi by the Harte-Hanks group. The morning *Caller* and the evening *Times,* joined on Sunday as the *Caller-Times,* typified the excellence of growing small dailies in various parts of the country.

VOICES OF THE WEST   Palmer Hoyt's entry into Denver journalism as publisher of the *Post* signaled a definite end of the Tammen-Bonfils type of newspapering. Hoyt gradually modified the *Post*'s gaudy makeup, increased its interpretative news coverage, and gave the paper a better editorial balance. The *Post* developed a strong internationalist point of view and an independent editorial page that swung the usually Republican paper to the Kennedy camp in 1960. It continued to support Democratic candidates Johnson, Humphrey, and Carter. Some of the paper's energy was expended in fighting lengthy court battles over attempts by the S. I. Newhouse group to add enough stock to their minority interest to control the *Post.* Hoyt retired in 1970 and was succeeded as editor and publisher by the *Post*'s general manager, Charles R. Buxton. William H. Hornby was executive editor, and William Hosokawa associate editor. The paper ranked after the *Los Angeles Times* among western dailies of national reputation.

The *San Francisco Chronicle* was famed under publisher George T. Cameron, editor Chester Rowell, and general manager Paul C. Smith in the 1930s and 1940s for its comprehensive national and foreign news coverage. But in the 1950s, under new direction, the *Chronicle* turned heavily toward features, columnists, and circulation-getting news. It passed the Hearst-owned *Examiner* in readers, but saw the *Examiner* surpass it in solid news. The *Chronicle* was always an interesting paper, however, under the editorship of Scott Newhall, who resigned in 1971 to protest what he felt was an increasing managerial conservatism in sociopolitical outlook. Charles deYoung Thieriot long carried the paper's historic family names and the titles of editor and publisher. Gordon Pates became executive editor in 1977.

In Portland, the long respected *Oregonian* ran into difficulties. Its famous editor, Harvey W. Scott, died in 1910, and manager Henry L. Pittock in 1919. Their heirs found a strong editor in Palmer Hoyt, from 1933 until he left to become publisher of the *Denver Post* in 1946. Control of the *Oregonian* passed to Samuel Newhouse in 1950, as did ownership of the rival *Oregon Journal* in 1961. The papers were badly hurt by a prolonged strike beginning in 1959 that sharply reduced their staff morale. Robert C. Notson, a longtime *Oregonian* editor, was named publisher in 1967. J. Richard Nokes edited the *Oregonian,* and Donald J. Sterling, Jr., the *Journal.*

The McClatchy-owned *Bee* newspapers in California, published in Sacramento, Fresno, and Modesto, won a reputation as fiercely independent dailies. The *Sacramento Bee,* founded in 1857, became well known under its publisher-editor, C. K. McClatchy, who served from 1883 to 1936. The *Bee* crusaded for public power, spoke out for individual liberties, and won a Pulitzer Prize for public service in 1935 for exposing political corruption. Eleanor McClatchy succeeded her father as publisher and kept to his usually pro-Democratic political beliefs. Another C. K. McClatchy became editor of the McClatchy papers, and Frank McCulloch managing editor of the *Bee.*

When Helen Copley inherited James S. Copley's newspaper empire in 1973, she became one of the most powerful women in publishing. The paper she knew best was the *San Diego Union,* whose stolid conservatism discouraged newcomers to the booming city. With editor Gerald L. Warren, she shook up the staff, encouraged aggressive reporting, and brought the *Union* toward a more conventional conservative position. The *Santa Barbara News-Press,* long owned by Thomas M. Storke and sold to the *Philadelphia Bulletin* in the 1960s, was another noteworthy western paper. It won the 1962 Pulitzer Prize for editorial writing by exposing the character of the John Birch Society.

Few of the present-day newspapers whose stories have been told date back more than 100 years. Indeed, fewer than three centuries separate the crudely printed sheets produced in Boston by Benjamin Harris and John Campbell from the modern dailies of the late twentieth century. But vast changes have been recorded. The story of the growth of newspapers—and the addition of magazines, books, radio, and television to create the mass media—is the story of both the development of communications and the maturing of a nation. It is the story of journalism in American life—of the press and America.

NOTES

1. For the poll of editors, see *Editor & Publisher,* XCIII (April 2, 1960), 12. For the poll of publishers, see *Editor & Publisher,* XCIII (April 9, 1960), 66. For the poll of journalism professors, see John Tebbel, "Rating the American Newspaper," *Saturday Review,* XLIV (May 13 and June 10, 1961).
2. It is interesting to note that Baltimore, Washington, Louisville, St. Louis, and Kansas City all border state cities and developed outstanding newspapers.

ANNOTATED BIBLIOGRAPHY

Books

BERGER, MEYER, *The Story of the New York Times, 1851–1951.* New York: Simon & Schuster, 1951. The best history of the *Times.*

CATLEDGE, TURNER, *My Life and The Times.* New York: Harper & Row, 1971. A readable autobiography of a capable newspaperman, reaching a climax with the struggle for "the kingdom and the power." Candid evidence given.

CONRAD, WILL C., KATHLEEN F. WILSON, AND DALE WILSON, *The Milwaukee Journal: The First Eighty Years.* Madison: University of Wisconsin Press, 1964. A good newspaper history of a great daily.

GOTTLIEB, ROBERT, AND IRENE WOLT, *Thinking Big: The Story of the Los Angeles Times, Its Publishers and Their Influence on Southern California.* New York: G.P. Putnam's Sons, 1977. Unauthorized work; relates development of the paper and city; takes a critical look at General Harrison Gray Otis, Chandlers.

GRIFFIN, DICK, AND ROB WARDEN, eds., *Done in a Day: 100 Years of Great Writing from the Chicago Daily News.* Chicago: Swallow Press, 1977.

HART, JIM ALLEE, *A History of the St. Louis Globe-Democrat.* Columbia: University of Missouri Press, 1961. Tells the story of St. Louis's "other paper" in a social and political framework.

HOHENBERG, JOHN, *The Pulitzer Prizes.* New York: Columbia University Press, 1974. A meticulous accounting of the first 714 awards.

JOHNSON, GERALD W., ET AL., *The Sunpapers of Baltimore.* New York: Knopf, 1937. An outstanding newspaper history over a 100-year span.

KOBRE, SIDNEY, *Development of American Journalism*. Dubuque, Iowa: Wm. C. Brown Company, 1969. Traces in detail the twentieth-century histories of many leading newspapers.

LYLE, JACK, *The News in Megalopolis*. San Francisco: Chandler, 1967. Los Angeles area news media analyzed.

LYONS, LOUIS M., *Newspaper Story: One Hundred Years of the Boston Globe*. Cambridge, Mass.: Harvard University Press, 1971. Much internal detail.

McNULTY, JOHN B., *Older than the Nation*. Stonington, Conn.: Pequot Press, 1964. A well-presented, scholarly history of the *Hartford Courant* on its 200th birthday.

MARKHAM, JAMES W., *Bovard of the Post-Dispatch*. Baton Rouge: Louisiana State University Press, 1954. A discerning biography.

MERRILL, JOHN C., *The Elite Press: Great Newspapers of the World*. New York: Pitman, 1968. Forty great newspapers in terms of performance and influence include, from the U.S., the *Baltimore Sun, Christian Science Monitor, St. Louis Post-Dispatch, Los Angeles Times,* and *New York Times*. An excellent worldwide survey.

PRICE, WARREN C., *The Eugene Register-Guard*. Portland, Ore.: Binford & Mort, 1976. A leading journalism scholar tells the story of a distinguished smaller daily as citizen of its community and state.

PUSEY, MERLO J., *Eugene Meyer*. New York: Knopf, 1974. A prize-winning biography of the *Washington Post* publisher, father of Katharine Graham.

RIVERS, WILLIAM L., AND DAVID M. RUBIN, *A Region's Press: Anatomy of Newspapers in the San Francisco Bay Area*. Berkeley: Institute of Governmental Studies, University of California, 1971. Contemporary study with some historical material.

ROBERTS, CHALMERS M., *The Washington Post: The First 100 Years*. Boston: Houghton Mifflin, 1977. Centennial history by a retired staff member.

STEWART, KENNETH, AND JOHN TEBBEL, *Makers of Modern Journalism*. Englewood Cliffs, N.J.: Prentice-Hall, 1952. Contains extensive comment on many of the newspapers and men covered in this chapter; see index.

TALESE, GAY, *The Kingdom and the Power*. New York: New American Library, 1969. Penetrating, informative recent history of the *New York Times* and study of its publishers and editors as they struggled for power.

Periodicals and Monographs

Bibliographies in the *Journalism Quarterly* annotate articles in the academic journals, in *Editor & Publisher, Time, Newsweek,* and in other periodicals. See the bibliography for chapter 24 for references to Knight, Cowles, Newhouse.

BAGDIKIAN, BEN H., "What Makes a Newspaper Nearly Great?," *Columbia Journalism Review,* VI (Fall 1967), 30. The paper is the *Washington Post*.

BRIDGES, LAMAR W., AND ALAN BUSSEL, "The Fight Against Boss Crump," *Journalism Quarterly,* XLIV (Summer 1967), 240, 245. Two articles recording battles of Memphis editors Mooney and Meeman against bossism.

BRINTON, JAMES E., "Failure of the Western Edition of the *New York Times,*" *Journalism Quarterly,* XLI (Spring 1964), 170. The famed eastern paper loses out to the *Los Angeles Times*.

CHU, CHI-YING, "Henry Justin Smith (1875–1936), Managing Editor of the *Chicago Daily News,*" Ph.D. thesis, Southern Illinois University, 1970. A teacher of writing.

CORRY, JOHN, "The *Los Angeles Times,*" *Harper's,* CCXXXIX (December 1969), 74. An analysis of America's biggest paper, one of its best.

DeVOTO, BERNARD, "Always Be Drastically Independent," *Harper's,* CCVII (December 1953), 42. The *St. Louis Post-Dispatch* is nominated as the "finest practitioner of liberal journalism."

DUNCAN, CHARLES T., "The *International Herald Tribune:* Unique (World) Newspaper," *Journalism Quarterly,* L (Summer 1973), 348. Contemporary status.

"The Fair Lady of Milwaukee," *Time,* LXIII (February 1, 1954), 44. An extensive report on the *Journal.*

HART, JACK R., "The Information Empire: A History of the *Los Angeles Times* from the Era of Personal Journalism to the Advent of the Multi-Media Communications Corporation," Ph.D. thesis, University of Wisconsin, 1975. Times-Mirror Co. profits enable paper to devote more resources to news.

HELLMAN, GEOFFREY T., "Profiles: Publisher," *New Yorker,* XLIV (August 10, 1968), 37. Dorothy Schiff, owner-publisher of the *New York Post.*

MAYER, MARTIN, "The Lady as Publisher," *Harper's,* CCXXXVII (December 1968), 90. Profile of Katharine Graham, head of the *Washington Post* and *Newsweek.*

NORWOOD, CHRISTOPHER, "The Last Puritans," *New York,* VIII (November 3, 1975), 58. Depth study of *New York Times* editorial board in John Oakes era.

PATTERSON, ALICIA, "This Is the Life I Love," *Saturday Evening Post,* CCXXXII (February 21, 1959), 19. *Newsday's* early story.

RIVERS, WILLIAM L., AND DAVID M. RUBIN, "The *Chronicle:* Schizophrenia on the Bay," *Columbia Journalism Review,* VIII (Fall 1969), 37. Analysis of an interesting paper.

ROSENBAUM, LEE, "Charlotte Curtis: Opting for Op-Ed," *Quill,* LXII (February 1974), 22. Woman editor of the *New York Times* opposite-editorials page.

SHEEHY, GAIL, "The Life of the Most Powerful Woman in New York," *New York,* VI (December 10, 1973), 51. Extensive feature on then *New York Post* publisher Dorothy Schiff. See also, Nora Ephron's "Media" column in *Esquire,* LXXXIII (April 1975), 8.

SMITH, LEE, "The Battle for Sunday," *New York,* IV (October 25, 1971), 34. A depth analysis of a challenge by Otis Chandler and *Newsday* to downtown.

STERN, MORT P., "Palmer Hoyt and the *Denver Post,*" Ph.D. thesis, University of Denver, 1969. A field study of organizational change.

TAIT, SAMUEL W., JR., "The St. Louis Post-Dispatch," *American Mercury,* XXII (April 1931), 403. An analysis of editorial policy.

TEBBEL, JOHN, "Rating the American Newspaper," *Saturday Review,* XLIV (May 13 and June 10, 1961). Ratings by 125 journalism educators.

WALDROP, A. GAYLE, "A Chinook Blows on Champa Street," *Journalism Quarterly,* XXIV (June 1947), 109, and "Reborn Denver 'Post' Has Prestige and Power," XXVIII (Summer 1951), 327.

WHITE, LLEWELLYN, "Papers of Paradox," *Reporter,* II (January 31, 1950), 22. *Louisville Courier-Journal* and *Times* analyzed.

————, "A Good Paper Pays Off," *Reporter,* III (August 29 and September 12, 1950). Excellent reports on the *Milwaukee Journal.*

WILLIAMS, ROGER M., "Newspapers of the South," *Columbia Journalism Review,* VI (Summer 1967), 26. Qualitative judgments on leading dailies.

WINTER, WILLIS L., JR., "The Metamorphosis of a Newspaper: The *San Francisco Chronicle,* 1935–1965,*" Ph.D. thesis, University of Illinois, 1968. The editorships of Paul C. Smith and Scott Newhall.

Nixon to Visit China

President Nixon
He Will . . .

Chou En-lai
. . . Visit Him

Kissinger, Chou Hold Secret Talks

BY ALDO BECKMAN
(Chicago Tribune Press Service)

SAN CLEMENTE, Cal., July 15—President Nixon will visit mainland China sometime before next May, he told the nation tonight in a live television and radio broadcast.

The groundwork for the historic meeting was laid by Henry Kissinger, Nixon's assistant for national security, when he met secretly with Chinese Premier Chou En-lai from July 9 to July 11, Nixon said. At that time, it was announced that Kissinger was in Asia to visit Saigon, Pakistan, and India.

Chou extended the invitation for the Nixon visit during his talks with Kissinger, Nixon said. A statement that Nixon read and which was released simultaneously in Peking, said:

"President Nixon has accepted this invitation with pleasure.

"The meeting between the leaders of China and the United States is to seek the normalization of relations between the two countries and also to exchange views on questions of concern to the two sides."

Acts to Mute Criticism

Nixon emphasized, in an obvious effort to mute criticism from supporters of Nationalist China and Chiang Kai-shek, that "our action in seeking a new relationship with the People's Republic of China will not be at the expense of our old friends.

"It is not directed against any other nation. We seek friendly relations with all nations. Any nation can be our friend without being any other nation's friend."

White House officials explained that Nixon was trying to indicate that America's old friendships and alliances will not be discarded because of the new friendlier relations with China.

The President, without giving any hint about when before May he will make the trip, said that he will undertake it "deeply [hoping] that it will

become a journey for peace, not just for our generation but for future generations on this earth we share together."

As Nixon began his three-minute statement, he noted that he had pointed out on a number of occasions that "no stable and enduring peace [is possible] without the participation of the People's Republic of China and its 750 million people."

Kissinger Secret Well Kept

Then, he revealed Kissinger's visit, which was one of the best kept secrets in the history of international diplomacy.

Midway during Kissinger's journey, it was announced that he had departed from his prepared

Text of Speech on Page 2

itinerary because of an upset stomach. That, apparently, was when he flew to Peking for his meeting with Chou En-lai.

Nixon said he decided to accept the visit to China "because of my profound conviction that all nations will gain from a reduction of tensions and a better relationship between the United States and the People's Republic of China."

Calls Security Council

Several hours before his statement, the Western White House announced that Nixon had called a meeting of the National Security Council for tomorrow. At that time, there was no agenda given for the session.

Kissinger returned from his nine-day trip, which included a stop in Paris to meet with American peace negotiators, on Tuesday, and has spent most of the time since then meeting with Nixon and Secretary of State William Rogers at the Western White House.

While it was assumed that their talks revolved around the Viet Nam War, White House officials said repeatedly that the discussions covered a wide range of foreign policy matters.

Ford Sees Indochina Peace Talks Resulting from Visit

(From Tribune Wire Service)

WASHINGTON, July 15—Republican House Leader Gerald R. Ford said tonight President Nixon's impending visit to mainland China could lead toward the convening of an Indochina peace conference.

"I would expect . . . that one subject that the President and Premier Chou En-lai would discuss would be the convening of an Indochina peace conference," the Michigan congressman and close supporter of Nixon said.

Mansfield Delighted

Democratic congressional leaders also reacted positively to Nixon's announcement on a brief televised address that he had been invited to visit China. Senate Democratic leader Mike Mansfield said he was "flabbergasted" and "delighted."

Sen. Hubert H. Humphrey [D., Minn.] said he thought such a journey could be of "immense importance in bringing

to attend a revived Geneva conference on Indochina.

Thant Welcomes Action

United Nations Secretary General U Thant said arrangements for President Nixon to visit China "has opened a new chapter in the history of international relations."

"The Secretary General warmly welcomes Nixon's announcement of his acceptance of Premier Chou En-lai's invitation to visit the People's Republic of China in the course of the next few months," Thant's spokesman said.

"This development has opened a new chapter in the history of international relations and it augurs well not only for relations between two great countries, but also for the future of the United Nations."

Gough Whitlam said yesterday in Hong Kong after returning from Peking that Premier Chou had told him China was willing

normal relations with the people of China."

He said he hoped Nixon's announcement that Premier Chou had invited him to visit Peking and the President had accepted would "mark the end of a long period of innocence in our relations with China and the beginning of a new era of common sense."

Sen. Harold Hughes [D., Ia.] who only 12 hours earlier had ruled himself out of the 1972 Democratic Presidential sweepstakes, said he, too, was delighted. He said he saw in the move a chance to wind down the Viet Nam war at a faster pace.

Senate Republican leader Hugh Scott of Pennsylvania said Nixon's decision "is bound to have worldwide impact and is an extremely important step in producing world peace."

"I join with all Americans in wishing the President Godspeed and good fortune in his journey for peace."

McGovern Applauds Nixon

Sen. George McGovern [D., S. D.] commented: "I applaud the President's imagination and judgment in accepting this opportunity to open up more

Already a Swinger

Kissinger Sure to Be a Legend

(Chicago Tribune Press Service)

SAN CLEMENTE, Cal., July 15—Henry Kissinger's secret trip behind the Bamboo Curtain to Peking is certain to make a living legend of the man already romanticized as the swinger of the Nixon administration.

Kissinger, the former Harvard professor who was foreign policy adviser to Gov. Nelson Rockefeller when Rockefeller

was running for President, is a divorced father of two who delights in being seen with beautiful women, such as movie star Jill St. John. During his recent stop in Paris, Kissinger was seen leaving a night spot with a pretty girl who turned out to be a CBS television producer.

A German Jew who was driven out of Germany with his parents in the late 1930s, Kiss-

inger still has a heavy German accent, a sharp wit, and is a favorite among White House reporters.

His own accent and his well-publicized foreign policy briefings, complete with ground rules which forbid quoting him or even using his name, are favorite targets of his wit.

The President obviously has great trust in Kissinger's intellect, and White House ob-

servers smiled knowingly when "it is not directed against any other nation," this dramatic development was certain to cause a deep reassessment of foreign policy within a Kremlin already actively seeking to mend its Western fences for reasons among which concern over China must be one.

The announcement also represented a personal victory of colossal proportions for the foreign policy of a President who deliberately set out to reverse what has been a firm policy not only of his nation but of his party for more than 21 years.

Formosa Protests, Others Approve Visit

(From Tribune Wire Service)

Nationalist China announced today in Taipei that it has lodged a strong protest with Washington over President Nixon's projected visit to mainland China.

Formosa was electrified by the joint statement by Nixon and officials in Peking and observers saw the visit as one of the biggest blows to Generalissimo Chiang Kai-shek since the Communists took over the mainland in 1949.

One Nationalist Chinese Government spokesman James Wei had only a one-sentence comment to newsmen who surrounded him here.

"The Chinese government has lodged a strong protest

Why? He Likes the Food

LOS ANGELES, July 15 [Reuters]—President Nixon said tonight after the announcement of his planned visit to the People's Republic of China that his reasons for going were purely gastronomic.

In his only reference to the trip when he spoke to reporters after his television broadcast, he quipped, "I like the food."

with the U. S. government," he announced.

He made the statement after being summoned by Nationalist Premier C. K. Yen this morning.

The foreign ministry was holding an emergency meeting, apparently studying the impli-

There was a tense atmosphere in government circles and some officials appeared visibly perturbed by the announcement.

In Manila earlier, Foreman Foreign Minister Chow Sho-kai commented when asked about the announcement of the visit, "If it is true then it will be part of their [China's] psychological warfare."

The surprise announcement also jolted other officials of America's Asian allies attending the Asia and Pacific Council [ASPAC] ministerial meeting in Manila.

Vincente Singian, secretary general of the organization said he would announce the visit

cations of Nixon's projected visit.

Another, more detailed statement was expected later today. Formosa has lodged several protests with Washington in recent months, mainly over the Communist takeover of the mainland in 1949, but had been the

What China Visit Means

BY FRANK STARR
(Washington Bureau Chief)
(Chicago Tribune Press Service)

WASHINGTON, July 15 — President Nixon's bombshell announcement that he would visit Peking within the next 10 months carried with it an implicit recognition of China as the third corner in a new triangle of superpowers.

Despite his assurance that "it is not directed against any other nation," this dramatic development was certain to cause a deep reassessment of foreign policy within a Kremlin already actively seeking to mend its Western fences for reasons among which concern over China must be one.

The announcement also represented a personal victory of colossal proportions for the foreign policy of a President who deliberately set out to reverse what has been a firm policy not only of his nation but of his party for more than 21 years.

Blow to Nationalists

Also implicit in the announcement is the severe blow to the Nationalist Chinese government of Generalissimo Chiang Kai-shek, which, since the Communist takeover of the mainland in 1949, had been the

News Analysis

beneficiary of such a policy.

Less clear but certainly at issue is the strengthening of the U. S. hand in newly developing war talks with the Communist Vietnamese, whose unqualified support from Red China until recently has included Peking's uncompromising rejection in public pronouncements of everything American.

Among the areas of speculation that were raised by the development was the possibility that China could play a new role in the efforts to reach an Indochina settlement thru multilateral negotiation.

Interest in Conference

Yesterday it was reported by an Australian diplomat in Hong Kong that China had expressed an interest in participating in a new Geneva conference on Indochina, an idea which appeared to sit, nonetheless fit into a pattern of emerging participation in world diplomacy by the Communist Chinese that goes back about two years when Chinese diplomats, recalled from their foreign posts during the turmoil of the Cultural Revolution, gradually began reap-

pearing at international functions in the world's major capitals.

The pattern really began to develop, however, with the positive response of Nixon, who unilaterally took several steps, beginning in July, 1969, to ease the isolation the United States

[Continued on page 2, col. 2]

How Kissinger's Peking Parley Was Kept Secret

A visit to Red China was masterfully hidden from the press.

On the days he was talking to Chinese officials, the government was releasing stories to the press placing him thousands of miles away, in Pakistan, India, and Paris.

Reported 'Indisposed'

On July 9, apparently the day the Presidential adviser made his trip into China, stories datelined from Islamabad, Pakistan, placed him as arriving that day in that country from India.

A story from Pakistan by United Press International said Kissinger had arrived to take several days with officials there, but until last night, nobody except a small group of high echelon government officials knew Kissinger was visiting Red China during his trip.

Last night, during his dramatic televised announcement to the nation of his upcoming trip to Communist China, Nixon said Kissinger had made the arrangements in Peking. The President said Kissinger spent three days, from July 9 thru 11, in the Chinese capital talking with Premier Chou En-lai.

Kissinger's mission to main-

[Continued on page 2, col. 1]

Features

Weather

FRIDAY, JULY 16, 1971
CHICAGO AND VICINITY: Mostly sunny and pleasant today; high in lower 80s; partly cloudy tonight with chance of thundershowers; low in lower 60s; warm to northwest winds 8 to 18 m. p. h. Tomorrow: Fair with little temperature change; high in lower 80s. Map and other reports on page 12.

© 1971 Chicago Tribune

26

The Challenge of Criticism

Partisanship, in editorial comment which knowingly departs from the truth, does violence to the best spirit of American journalism; in the news columns it is subversive of a fundamental principle of the profession.

—ASNE Canons of Journalism

Criticism of the performance of America's mass media became particularly pointed during the liberal resurgence of the 1930s known as the New Deal. Driven by the impact of the great depression, the nation established new patterns of social justice and economic security under the leadership of Franklin D. Roosevelt. In doing so, it vastly expanded governmental participation in socioeconomic affairs. A roll call of 1933–35 legislation includes the establishment of the Federal Deposit Insurance Corporation to insure bank deposits; the Works Progress Administration to aid the one-sixth of the population on relief; the National Recovery Administration to stimulate industrial production; the Agricultural Adjustment Administration to stabilize farm prices; and the Securities Exchange Commission to regulate financial markets. The Social Security Act of 1935 and the Wagner Labor Relations Act of 1935 were cornerstones of personal and job security.

That there was criticism of newspapers during these years of swift change was nothing new; press critics had been having their say since the dawn of newspaper publishing. But while much of the earlier criticism had dealt with the cultural and social values of the press, the emphasis in the 1930s was on its political power. The press as an institution thus came under challenge more directly than at any time since the Federalist attacks on press freedom in the 1790s. Supporters of Franklin Roosevelt and the New Deal charged that much of the press was opposed to socioeconomic reforms, sometimes in ways viewed as bitterly partisan. To the liberals who won sweeping ballot box victories, it seemed that the press too often was unresponsive to change and democratic decisions.

The favorite targets for the critics were those publishers dubbed "the press lords''—notably William Randolph Hearst, Robert R. McCormick, and Roy W. Howard. Their prominence kept them at the center of an upsurge of criticism that affected newspapers generally, in a time when America was engaging in a searching reexamination of all its social, political, and economic institutions. Their actions exposed the journalistic profession to the danger of loss of public confidence by providing a vast amount of ammunition to those who used their newspapers as proof that the press was irresponsible.

From the 1940s onward, two factors operated to widen the base of the challenge of criticism to the mass media. One, of course, was the rise of television and the attending revolution in mass communication patterns. The other was an increasing recognition of Robert E. Park's observation—''The press, as it exists, is not, as our moralists sometimes seem to assume, the willful product of any little group of living men. On the contrary, it is the outcome of a historic process. . . .''[1] This does not mean that the Hearsts and McCormicks, the Pulitzers and Ochses, the Greeleys and Bennetts did not exert powerful and lasting influences on the newspaper press, or the Sarnoffs and the Murrows on the electronic media. It does mean—as the theme of this book has stated—that social and economic forces shaping our system of values and our culture have been at least as important in shaping the mass media and in affecting their performance. In many respects, this is more true of the broadcast media than of the print media because of broadcasting's organizational structure and semipublic character.

This chapter, after examining political-based criticism of the newspapers and the roles of their ''press lords'' who adversely affected their images, will shift—as did public attention—to criticisms of television program content and of television's involvement in controversial issues. These criticisms came to a swelling climax in the 1960s and brought a crisis of credibility involving government, press, and people. That crisis exploded into the Watergate era of the 1970s. Parallel to this story is one of the growth of a professional spirit in journalism, involving extensive self-analysis and efforts to improve media performance, as a counterbalancing response to the challenge of criticism. This story of media responses and counterattacks will appear in the succeeding chapter, followed by that of the crisis of credibility.

**THE PRESS
IN PRESIDENTIAL
ELECTIONS**

Criticism of newspapers since the 1930s centered about, more than anything else, their editorial positions in political campaigns. Historically, a small but definite majority of daily newspapers giving editorial-page support to a presidential candidate was to be found on the side of the Republican party. As Franklin Roosevelt entered the first of his four presidential campaigns in 1932, he had the support of 38 percent of the nation's dailies, compared to 55 percent for President Hoover. In 1936, Roosevelt was backed by 34 percent of the dailies, Republican Alfred M. Landon by 60 percent. These figures are approximations gathered by *Editor & Publisher* when it launched, beginning in 1940, a comprehensive preelection poll of dailies concerning editorial page support. Approximately three-fourths of all dailies, with 90 percent of total daily newspaper circulation, responded to the polls until the 1960s, when the character of the contests caused the responses to drop to 60 percent of the dailies with 80 percent of total circulation. Table 26–1 shows the percentages of the responding newspapers giving editorial page support to the Republican or Democratic candidate each four years and the percentages of circulation they represented.

The figures show that the number of dailies supporting Roosevelt declined for his

Table 26-1 Editorial Page Support of Presidential Candidates

	Republican		Democratic		Uncommitted	
Year	Percent of Dailies	Percent of Circulation	Percent of Dailies	Percent of Circulation	Percent of Dailies	Percent of Circulation
1940	63.9	69.2	22.7	25.2	13.4	5.6
1944	60.1	68.5	22.0	17.7	17.9	13.8
1948	65.1	78.5	15.3	10.0	15.6	10.0
1952	67.3	80.2	14.5	10.8	18.2	9.0
1956	62.3	72.3	15.1	12.8	22.6	14.9
1960	57.7	70.9	16.4	15.8	25.9	13.3
1964	35.1	21.5	42.3	61.5	22.6	17.0
1968	60.8	69.9	14.0	19.3	24.0	10.5
1972	71.4	77.4	5.3	7.7	23.3	14.9
1976	62.3	62.2	12.1	22.8	25.6	15.0

Source: *Editor & Publisher* polls. In 1948, Progressive party candidate Henry A. Wallace had the support of 4 percent of the dailies with 1.5 percent of circulation. See *Editor and Publisher*, XCIII (November 5, 1960), 9. In 1968, American Independent party candidate George C. Wallace had the support of 12 dailies (1.2 percent) with 159,000 circulation (0.3 percent).

1940 and 1944 races with Wendell Willkie and Thomas E. Dewey, as did the circulation they represented. Harry S. Truman reached a low point of support in his successful 1948 contest with Dewey. Dwight D. Eisenhower enjoyed the most support in 1952, for his first race against Adlai E. Stevenson. John F. Kennedy's position was improved as he defeated Richard M. Nixon in 1960. Kennedy was endorsed by 22 dailies above 100,000 circulation, while 12 endorsed no candidate. This represented more large pro-Democratic papers, with a better geographic spread, than at any time since 1944.[2]

Then came political upheaval stemming from the assassination of President Kennedy. His successor, Lyndon Johnson of Texas, became the first southerner to win the Democratic nomination in modern times. His opponent, Senator Barry M. Goldwater, represented the frustrated right wing of the Republican party. Given such a choice, newspaper publishers and editors chose to endorse President Johnson for reelection. The scales were essentially turned. Among dailies over 100,000 in circulation, Nixon had enjoyed the support of 87 to 22 for Kennedy in 1960. Johnson won 82 to his side four years later, and Goldwater only 12.[3]

Four years later came more upheaval—the assassination of Senator Robert Kennedy, the forced withdrawal of President Johnson from the Democratic race by the Eugene McCarthy crusade—and the nominations in vacuums of Hubert Humphrey and Richard M. Nixon. The scales tilted back, and the big dailies divided 78 for Nixon and 28 for Humphrey. Humphrey's percentage of the reporting circulation was better than any since Roosevelt's in 1940 on the Democratic side, save for the 1964 aberration.[4]

It was the Democrats' turn in 1972 to nominate a candidate from an extreme wing of their party, Senator George McGovern, who won only one state. Dailies representing only two-thirds of the total circulation responded to the poll, and the big dailies split 66 for President Nixon and 9 for McGovern, with 40 uncommitted or unreported.[5]

Participation in the poll was even more dispirited in 1976, with dailies representing only 55 percent of the total circulation responding. Among 114 dailies with more than 100,000 circulation, 50 backed President Gerald Ford and 21 Democratic candidate Jimmy Carter of Georgia, while 43 were blank.[6] The *Los Angeles Times, Philadelphia Bulletin, Washington Star,* and *Kansas City Star* were among normally Republican papers avoiding an endorsement in the wake of the forced resignations of President Nixon and Vice President Agnew. The Hearst newspapers also did not endorse. Carter bettered Humphrey's 1968 performance in attracting press support, after McGovern's all-time low.

OTHER OPINION-   Adlai Stevenson called it "a one-party press in a two-party country."
MAKING FORCES   But partisan critics did not acknowledge the impact day-by-day
                      coverage of the news has on voter decisions, and available studies of campaign news coverage indicate at least larger dailies were essentially fair in their news columns. Research shows, too, that voters are often strongly affected by social pressures, group associations, and "opinion leaders." Radio and television can become highly important factors.[7]

A classic study of how news came to Paducah, Kentucky, made by *Fortune* magazine (August 1947) also illustrates the point that it is impossible for a single newspaper to exercise a monopoly in the realm of opinion making. Paducah's one daily newspaper had a circulation of 12,000 copies within the city. There was also a small weekly, and the city had two radio stations, one owned by the daily paper. Outside publications came into Paducah in the following numbers: *Louisville Courier-Journal,* 1,400 copies daily and 2,400 on Sunday; New York, Chicago, St. Louis, and Memphis newspapers, 428 daily and 2,770 Sunday; weekly news magazines, 429 copies; picture weeklies, 1,968 copies; other general weeklies, 1,769 copies; monthly magazines, 13,037 copies. The public library had 110 magazines on file and circulated about 10,000 books a month. Motion pictures, public meetings, and club and luncheon gatherings also brought information to Paducah's 33,000 citizens.

CRITICISM   Political tension, and accompanying criticism of the news-
OF THE "PRESS LORDS"   paper's role in elections, made for extensive public accept-
                             ance of a literature of criticism of the press. Upton Sinclair's bitter book, *The Brass Check* (1919), unrealistically painted a picture of a false, cowardly press dominated by its business offices and its advertisers. While there were newspaper situations that fitted these patterns, in isolated instances of time and place, the Sinclair thesis did not ring true generally. Suspicious individuals, however, continued to quote the book as evidence of advertiser domination of the press long after that bugaboo had been exploded as a serious charge.

Caustic surveys of the "press lords" began in earnest with Oswald Garrison Villard's *Some Newspapers and Newspaper-Men* (1923). They flourished in the 1930s, which saw the publication of such books as George Seldes' *Lords of the Press* (1938), Harold L. Ickes' *America's House of Lords* (1939), and individual studies such as Ferdinand Lundberg's *Imperial Hearst* (1936). These books were valuable as exposés, but their influence was undue in that they enjoyed wider public circulation than such counterbalancing and more constructive discussions as Casper S. Yost's *Principles of Journalism* (1924), Villard's brief *The Press Today* (1930), Herbert Brucker's *The Changing American Newspaper* (1937), Silas Bent's *Newspaper Crusaders* (1939), and such products of the growing journalism schools as Leon N. Flint's *The Conscience of the Newspaper* (1925), Willard G. Bleyer's *Main Currents in the*

History of American Journalism (1927), and *Interpretations of Journalism* (1937), edited by Frank L. Mott and Ralph D. Casey.

In any event, the dynamic and intriguing personalities of some of the "press lords" provided more interesting fare for the American reading public than any other material about newspapermen and newspaper problems. To understand, therefore, the bitterness and extent of criticisms of the press since the 1930s, it is necessary to examine the roles played by the most often discussed newspaper publishers of the times.

WILLIAM RANDOLPH HEARST   William Randolph Hearst, as has been suggested in previous chapters, is one of the most difficult men of journalism to study and to estimate, considering the complex nature of his personality, the variegated social and political impact of his many ventures, and the length and extent of his career.* Those who wrote about Hearst were never permitted access to the publisher's private papers or the records of the Hearst empire. As a result, the official Hearst biography released by International News Service when the publisher's 64-year newspaper career closed in 1951 noted in its second paragraph: "And as he fashioned his vast enterprises, there grew progressively in the public mind a picture of the builder himself. It was a strange portrait, obscured by myth and legend, confused by controversy and distortion."

When Hearst had lived out his 88 years, the question became, Did he deserve the criticism that had been heaped upon him, more vehemently than on any other publisher? The points most often made in support of a thesis that Hearst made positive contributions to American journalism are these:

1. Hearst built the world's biggest publishing empire in terms of newspapers and their combined circulations. At the peak, in 1935, Hearst printed 26 dailies and 17 Sunday editions in 19 cities. The papers had 13.6 percent of the total daily circulation in the country and 24.2 percent of Sunday circulation. In addition, he controlled the King Features Syndicate, largest of its kind; the money-coining *American Weekly;* International News Service, Universal Service, and International News Photos; 13 magazines, eight radio stations, and two motion picture companies. This, it is argued, spells a success that must be recognized.

2. Hearst's methods and innovations in newswriting and news-handling—particularly in makeup and headline and picture display—and his utilization of new mechanical processes were highly important. Hearst newspapers were edited to appeal to the mass of readers and encouraged millions to increase their reading habits. Because of this, and because of Hearst's editorial policies and his own political activities, Hearst newspapers exercised a powerful influence in American life that must be recognized.

3. Hearst was in many ways a constructive force: stalwart in his Americanism; a believer in popular education and in the extension of the power of the people; and during different phases of his long career an advocate of many progressive solutions to national problems. These included early advocacy of popular election of senators, of the initiative and referendum, of a graduated income tax, of widespread public ownership of utilities, of breaking up of monopolies and trusts, and of the rights of labor unions.

---

*Chapters 17 and 18 deal with Hearst's earlier career. See also pages 434–35 in chapter 24 for the extent of his newspaper operations.

These points, the argument runs, are in the record for all to see. Hearst's critics, and the public record, provided counterarguments:

1. The Hearst empire, for all its one-time size, was not the roaring success a recital of figures would indicate. Its finances were shaky in the 1920s. The crash came for Hearst in 1937, when he was forced to abdicate temporarily and watch a group of trustees liquidate a portion of his empire. Nine dailies and five Sunday editions were dropped by 1940; Universal Service was consolidated with INS; movie companies, radio stations, and some magazines were sold. The trustees began liquidating $40 million worth of New York City real estate. Many of the $40 million in art treasures that were Hearst's pride and joy were auctioned off at Gimbels and Macy's. Eventually even many of San Simeon's 275,000 acres were sold to reclaim some of the $36 million spent there.

Through it all, however, Hearst continued to live in regal style. The man who had bought a castle in Wales, Egyptian mummies, Tibetan yaks, and a Spanish abbey (which was dismantled stone by stone and shipped to a New York warehouse, after which Hearst never saw it again), had a truly precapitalistic attitude toward money as such. His guests at San Simeon, who were legion, continued to dive into an indoor pool from a sixteenth century Italian marble balcony, to pick flowers in a mile-long pergola stretching along Hearst's private mountain range, and to eat from kingly silver plate. Before World War II had ended, the trimming down of his empire and wartime publishing profits had accomplished the desired miracle, and the Hearst once thought to be broke was back in full command again.

When death had claimed its founder, the Hearst organization had 16 dailies and 13 Sunday editions appearing in a dozen cities. They had 9.1 percent of the country's total daily circulation and 16.1 percent of the Sunday total, a substantial decline in Hearst influence from the 1935 figures of 13.6 percent daily and 24.2 percent Sunday. The Hearst estate was valued at some $56 million, based on estimated stock values, but the profit margins of the Hearst enterprises were below those of other newspapers of their size for which financial reports are available, forecasting further contraction.

2. Undoubtedly, Hearst drew many new readers of newspapers to his fold and held more than 5 million daily and 8 million Sunday to the day of his death. But what was the end result? Pulitzer defended the use of sensationalism in his *World* by arguing that it attracted readers who then would be exposed to the columns of his carefully planned, high-quality editorial page. The same could never be said of a Hearst newspaper. Nor did Hearst ever exercise the powerful influence in American life his great circulations might indicate. Among the men whom he wanted to see become president of the United States were William Jennings Bryan, Champ Clark, Hiram W. Johnson, William Gibbs McAdoo, John Nance Garner, Alfred M. Landon, General Douglas MacArthur, and William Randolph Hearst. Among the men whom he fought while they were in the White House were William McKinley, Theodore Roosevelt, William Howard Taft, Woodrow Wilson, Herbert Hoover, Franklin D. Roosevelt, and Harry S. Truman.

3. What then of Hearst as a constructive social force? Certainly he was an advocate of Americanism. But to many his continued espousal of nationalistic policies bordering on jingoism, in a time that demanded American cooperation in international security efforts, was the most distressing feature of his newspapers. And the "Red hunts" his newspapers fostered in the 1930s among the ranks of political leaders, educators, YMCA secretaries, labor leaders, and other citizens were based on the familiar tactics of the demagogue: those who disagreed with Hearst were "Communists." A nationalist-isolationist to the end, Hearst opposed the basic foreign policy adopted by the American people during and after World War II and distrusted the United Nations as thoroughly as he had distrusted the League of Nations.

In domestic affairs, Hearst newspapers continued to give stalwart support to public education and to the idea of public ownership of utilities. But they backslid during the 1920s and 1930s on many of the other progressive features of the Hearst editorial program as written before World War I. Hearst had helped to elect Franklin Roosevelt and in the spring of 1933 his newspapers applauded vigorously as Roosevelt undertook unemployment relief, suspended exports of gold, and proposed the National Recovery Act—which, a Hearst editorial said, "embodies several basic policies long advocated by the Hearst newspapers."[8] By 1935 the tune had changed. It was the "Raw Deal" and the "National Run Around" in both news and editorial columns. The unanimous Supreme Court decision outlawing the NRA, which the Hearst papers had once proudly claimed for their own, was greeted with an American flag and the headline: "Thank God for the Supreme Court!"

There are other examples in the columns of the Hearst papers of 1935 that illustrate the extent to which the earlier beliefs of Hearst had changed. The publisher who before World War I had been perhaps the most aggressive in supporting the power of labor unions now said "the Wagner Labor Bill . . . is one of the most vicious pieces of class legislation that could be conceived—un-American to the core, violative of every constitutional principle and contrary to the whole spirit of American life. Congress in passing it is betraying the country."[9]

The publisher who had fought so long against monopolies and trusts now said "the Wheeler-Rayburn Bill, decreeing death to the holding companies, is PURE VENOM distilled by a PERSONAL and MALIGNANT OBSESSION, without a pretense of economic or legal justification."[10]

The publisher who always believed that he understood the common people, and was understood by them, sparked an extensive front-page coverage of WPA activities in 1936 with headlines like this one: "Taxpayers Feed 20,000 Reds on N.Y. Relief Rolls." And his newspapers warned that the Social Security Act was "A Pay Cut for You! . . . Governor Landon, when elected, will repeal this so-called security act."[11]

Hearst newspapers threw every resource of the editorial and news pages into the campaign to elect Governor Alfred M. Landon of Kansas president in 1936. When President Roosevelt was reelected by the greatest majority in history, carrying all the states but two, Hearst's enemies cried for his scalp. But the triumphant liberals overreached themselves in launching the Supreme Court reorganization bill of 1937, called the "court packing bill" by those who defeated it. The New Deal reform period came to an abrupt halt. Just as the Hearst papers weathered their economic difficulties in the next few years, they weathered public attacks against them and moved into a different political climate in which they once more could go on the offensive.

THE HEARST PAPERS CHANGE

With Hearst's death came some changes in the empire. His longtime friend, at whose home he died, Marion Davies, no longer found her wishes carried out by Hearst editors (it had been she who sponsored the Hearst papers' antivivisection campaign which harassed American medical schools). William Randolph Hearst, Jr., one of five brothers, took the lead as editor-in-chief. Local editors were given greater autonomy; they were told to "use the greatest care to avoid bias or lack of objectivity in the handling of the news."

The Hearst family reappeared in the center of the news during 1974–76, when granddaughter Patricia (whose father Randolph was publisher of the *San Francisco Examiner*) was kidnapped by radical terrorists, emerged herself as the radical "Tania," and eventually was convicted of bank robbery. The *Examiner* played a key role in early ransom negotiations, which included a $4 million gift of food from the Hearsts to the Bay Area's needy. The fiery death of most of the radical group in a Los Angeles police ambush, Patricia's long flight, and her sensational trial created another Hearstian myth full of contradictions and controversy.

Even so, the Hearst image improved with better editing, more independent political judgments, and better balanced news choices. The Hearst Foundation gave substantial scholarships to college journalists annually in a move to uncover new talent. Still, in 1977, the Hearst empire was down to 8 dailies and 7 Sunday editions with 2.5 percent of daily circulation and 4.5 percent of Sunday. The *American Weekly* was no more. Fabulous San Simeon became a California Historical Monument in 1958, open to bus loads of tourists. Hearst, Jr., had one major triumph: the Pulitzer Prize for international reporting went to him, J. Kingsbury Smith, and Frank Conniff in 1956 for stories from the Soviet Union. "I have a feeling that Pop and Joe Pulitzer are getting almost as big a kick out of it as we are," he told his readers.

COLONEL McCORMICK AND THE *CHICAGO TRIBUNE*

Second only to Hearst in stirring up the wrath of critics was Colonel Robert R. McCormick, publisher of the *Chicago Tribune*. The quarrel with McCormick was not so much that his *Tribune* clung to an outmoded and dangerous nationalist-isolationist point of view in the face of overwhelming public support of efforts to find peace and security through international cooperation. Nor was it so much that his *Tribune* became the principal spokesman for the ultraconservative right wing in American politics and rejected a President Eisenhower as violently as it had rejected a President Truman. The real quarrel McCormick's critics had with him was that as he tried so hard to prove that the *Tribune* was right, and most everybody else was wrong, editorial columns became bitter personal proclamations whose prejudiced approaches to matters of public interest spilled over into the news columns. McCormick's answer, until death stilled his voice in 1955, was that his *Tribune* was the "World's Greatest Newspaper."

This claim would have had merit if newspaper greatness were measured only in terms of financial success, circulation, and mechanical excellence. In the mid-1950s the *Tribune* carried as much advertising as its three Chicago rivals combined. Its circulation, while down to 900,000 daily from a 1946 high of 1,075,000, was still the largest of any standard-sized American newspaper and was spread through five states in an area McCormick called "Chicago-land." Its 450-man news staff, operating from the 36-story Tribune Tower, provided blanket coverage of local and area news events that was the despair of rival city editors. For a venture that rated as the most often criticized single American newspaper, the *Tribune* was doing all right, and Colonel McCormick frequently reminded his critics of that fact.

Not all of this success was due to McCormick. The *Tribune* has a long history, beginning in 1847. The builder was Joseph Medill, who from 1855 to 1899 devoted his energies to the creation of a powerful conservative newspaper. Medill left a financial trust that provided for the families of his two daughters—the McCormicks and the Pattersons. The Robert R. McCormick era began in 1914, the year his brother Medill

San Francisco Examiner   Chicago Tribune

Newspaper owners William Randolph Hearst, Jr. (*left*), and Robert R. McCormick.

retired from the paper to become a senator. Sharing responsibility for the *Tribune* with the future colonel was his cousin, Joseph Medill Patterson, founder in 1919 of the *New York Daily News*. The fourth Medill grandchild, Eleanor Medill Patterson, was to become owner of the *Washington Times-Herald*. The young cousins doubled *Tribune* circulation and advertising during the World War I period. Patterson had a particular brilliance for spotting the best comic strips and other features; McCormick proved to be an able businessman.

The success of the *New York Daily News,* and the disappearance of Captain Patterson into that venture, further entrenched McCormick's position. The two papers made as much as $13 million a year. The *Tribune-Daily News* feature syndicate, radio station WGN, and Canadian paper and power investments followed. When Captain Patterson died in 1946, McCormick became the head of the *New York Daily News,* although he preferred to exercise influence by remote control. When Eleanor Patterson died in 1948, she willed the *Washington Times-Herald* to seven of her executives, but they sold it to McCormick in 1949 for $4.5 million. The *Tribune* formula did not work in Washington, and in 1954, ill and weary of a paper that was losing $500,000 a year, McCormick sold the *Times-Herald* for $8.5 million to Eugene Meyer's *Washington Post*. But despite this retreat, no one except the Hearst heirs had more readers than McCormick had, with his two big dailies.

The memos signed "R.R.Mc." were law in the *Tribune* empire. The six-foot four-inch colonel turned eyes of ice-water blue on all aspects of the business. His private domains were the Tribune Tower and his 1,000-acre farm and estate outside Chicago, named Cantigny for the World War I battle in which McCormick participated. McCormick made a deep study of military history, but his opinions about international affairs were based on a belief that foreigners, especially Englishmen, were dangerous. Almost as dangerous, the *Tribune* said, were New York financiers, Eastern internationalists, and educators.

Among the men who helped to build the *Tribune* as McCormick's aides were Edward Scott Beck, managing editor from 1910 to 1937; J. Loy Maloney, managing editor from 1939 to 1951, when he became executive editor; W. D. Maxwell, city editor who became managing editor in 1951; and sports editor Arch Ward. Heading the Washington bureau were Arthur Sears Henning and his successor, Walter Trohan, who learned to shape their coverage to back up the Colonel's opinions.

McCormick opposed President Franklin Roosevelt and the domestic policies of the New Deal with every resource. As a result the *Tribune* was voted in a 1936 poll of Washington correspondents as runner-up to the Hearst papers for the title "least fair and reliable." When the World War II crisis began to develop, the *Tribune* bitterly denounced cooperation with Great Britain, the ancient enemy; a typical eight-column banner when the lend-lease bill was under debate read: "HOUSE PASSES DICTATOR BILL." It was this combination of extreme conservatism and nationalism that incited Marshall Field to start the *Chicago Sun* as a rival morning paper (the *Tribune* having inherited the field alone when Hearst retired from it in 1939).

But McCormick's luck held. Three days after the *Sun* appeared, its principal issue of isolationism versus interventionism was exploded by the bombs at Pearl Harbor. McCormick supported the American war effort, although the *Tribune* called American entrance an "FDR war plot." The Washington correspondents again estimated the *Tribune*'s standing in 1944, voting it "the newspaper . . . most flagrant in angling or weighting the news."[12]

How much the *Tribune*'s activities could embarrass all American newspapers was driven home the morning after the presidential election of 1948, when reelected Harry Truman was photographed gleefully holding a home edition of the *Tribune* whose banner line read, "DEWEY DEFEATS TRUMAN." An overconfident *Tribune* Washington bureau had let its hopes override the facts, to the delight of press critics and to the dismay of newspapermen who had conscientiously tried to maintain news page objectivity.

CHANGES AT   Key McCormick executives took over his *Tribune* in 1955, in the absence
THE *TRIBUNE*   of direct family heirs, and unswervingly continued its policies for more
than a decade. The *Chicago American* was purchased from Hearst in 1956 and renamed *Chicago Today,* afternoon rival for the *Daily News.* Under editor W. D. Maxwell the *Tribune* viewed the social and racial crises of the 1960s with uncompromising law-and-order stances that perpetuated the image of the doughty Colonel. As a result, its circulation lead was eroded by its morning rival, the *Sun-Times*.

The *Tribune*'s turning point came with the assumption of the editorship by Clayton Kirkpatrick in 1969. He had the necessary credentials of one who had been a part of the McCormick era, so he was able to achieve changes any less-established editor would have found impossible. The slogan "The American paper for Americans" was dropped, editorializing in the news columns was curbed, and the strident editorial voice was restrained. As the older generation of *Tribune* editors and policy makers retired, Kirkpatrick gave increasing authority to younger minds. The paper's news staff was expanded. And from 1971 to 1976 the *Tribune* won three Pulitzer Prizes for local investigative reporting and an international award. Some of the paper's most unrelenting critics of the past began to talk about the "new *Chicago Tribune*." Its managing editor was former *Today* editor Maxwell McCrohon, whose paper had been closed down by the *Tribune* in 1974 to consolidate circulation in one paper. The *Sun-Times* had come within 100,000 copies of the *Tribune* in 1974, but two years later the gap was 180,000 when the *Tribune* leveled off at 750,000. As 1977 opened it dropped the Colonel's slogan, "World's Greatest Newspaper."

ROY W. HOWARD
AND THE SCRIPPS
IMAGE

Receiving special attention, too, was Roy W. Howard, the man who by the 1930s had come to dominate the newspapers founded by E. W. Scripps. Howard was held responsible by his critics for a rightward shift in the outlook of the 20 surviving Scripps-Howard dailies, which ranked third behind Hearst and McCormick-Patterson papers in circulation. The complaints were not of the same character as those made against Hearst and McCormick; they reflected rather the disappointment and dismay of the liberals that the "people's papers" of Edward Wyllis Scripps had become in many respects conventionally conservative in tone.*

Robert Paine Scripps, the founder's youngest son, inherited the controlling interest in the newspapers, the United Press, Acme Newsphotos, Newspaper Enterprise Association, and United Feature Syndicate when his father died in 1926. Robert Scripps had been at the editorial helm as family representative since 1918, while Roy Howard, the architect of the United Press, had taken over business management of the newspaper chain in 1922, the year the Scripps-McRae newspapers were renamed Scripps-Howard.

The son was imbued with the philosophy of the father, although his quiet and sensitive nature kept him from exercising a firm control over policy. When editor Carl Magee of Albuquerque, New Mexico, was persecuted and driven from business in 1922 because of his efforts to expose the political machine headed by Secretary of the Interior Albert B. Fall (later convicted of bribe-taking in the Teapot Dome scandal), Robert Scripps bought the paper, the *Tribune,* and restored Magee to its editorship. In 1924 the Scripps-Howard papers supported Robert M. La Follette, Progressive party candidate for the presidency. The Scripps-Howard editors, called into session periodically to decide matters of national policy, backed Herbert Hoover for the presidency in 1928 but swung back to Franklin D. Roosevelt in 1932 and 1936.

Howard's ascendancy in Scripps-Howard affairs became apparent in 1937, when the chain's papers broke with Roosevelt over the Supreme Court reorganization bill. Lowell Mellett, editor of the *Washington News,* and other old Scripps men left the organization. Robert Paine Scripps, who had been in virtual retirement, died aboard his yacht in 1938. The Scripps wills provided for Howard, William W. Hawkins of the United Press, and George B. Parker, editor-in-chief of the newspapers, to serve as trustees until the sons of Robert Scripps reached the age of 25. Under this regime the Scripps-Howard papers opposed a third term for President Roosevelt in 1940 and supported Republican presidential candidates every four years through 1960. Organized labor no longer found the papers to be stalwart champions. They still reflected variety in outlook and reader appeal, however, and won particular recognition in Memphis and Cleveland. After World War II, Scripps heirs inherited the trustee positions, and Charles E. Scripps became chairman. The eventual leadership in editorial matters fell to Edward W. Scripps II, a Nevadan with traits similar to those of his grandfather.

Howard remained powerful, however, as head of the *New York World-Telegram and Sun* until he died in 1964—just three years before his favorite paper succumbed.

*See chapter 18 and page 435 in chapter 24 for the earlier Scripps story.

Roy W. Howard (*left*) and the grandson of E. W. Scripps, Edward W. Scripps II.

His son Jack was high in the councils as president and general editorial manager of the Scripps-Howard Newspapers and president of the parent E. W. Scripps Company that controls far-flung interests in broadcasting, syndicates, and United Press International. In the Far West, the family of James Scripps, eldest son of the founder, who quarreled with his father in 1920, was successfully rebuilding the once nearly defunct Scripps League by developing small daily newspapers in Utah, Idaho, Montana, and Oregon. Another Scripps grandson, John P. Scripps, had built a chain of small California dailies. The name Scripps seemed certain to remain an important one.

SPOTLIGHT ON BROADCASTING As television became a dominant mass medium in the 1960s, the public attention earlier given to faults of newspapers shifted to the sins of the image-makers. Two major areas of public activity were an ever-growing preoccupation with sex in all conceivable forms and continuing eruptions of violence—urban, racial, campus, radical, and military. What television did or did not do relative to sex and violence became a focus of public debate. Predictably, the medium was blamed for the problem in many quarters, even though sex is as old as creation and violence has been a national characteristic of American life.

Like newspapers and magazines, television had built up a list of achievements that stood it in good stead as attacks on broadcasters mounted in the 1960s. Its ability to project viewers into an event, and let them judge for themselves, had been demonstrated during the Army-McCarthy hearings in 1954 when attorney Joseph Welch turned on Senator Joseph McCarthy for attacking a young lawyer on his staff and again in 1960 during the Great Debates between John Kennedy and Richard Nixon. It had afforded Nixon the opportunity to defend himself when his place on the 1952 Republican ticket was threatened; it had afforded Edward R. Murrow the opportunity to unmask Joseph McCarthy in his famed 1954 documentary. It had reported magnificently the national sorrow at the assassination of President Kennedy. It had reported the onset of the Black Revolution in the 1960s and the climactic march on Washington led by Dr. Martin Luther King in 1963: "I have a dream," King said. In documentaries, ABC had offered "Walk In My Shoes," a brilliant examination of the Negro's problems; NBC had produced "Same Mud, Same Blood," one of the finest documentaries from Vietnam; CBS had screened "Harvest of Shame" and "Hunger in America" as studies of economic and social inequality.

But for all this, television became the most sharply criticized of the media in the 1960s. Some thought the coverage was slanted; some thought television was creating the events; some thought that material they disliked should be suppressed. And some were justifiably criticizing television for its imperfections and shortcomings.

PROGRAMMED VIOLENCE   Violence has been a central theme of countless plays, novels, movies, comic books, and television scripts, from the times of the Greek dramatists to those of Matt Dillon. Television, which in the 1960s had a full quota of real violence to report from battlefields and urban riots, also loaded its programming with fantasy violence. The assassinations of John and Robert Kennedy and Martin Luther King, coupled with urban rioting and campus disorders, gave the opponents of programmed violence an opportunity.

They had the statistics in abundance. The *Christian Science Monitor* had counted 210 violent incidents and 81 killings in 78 hours of 1967 prime time; a year later the counts for 75 hours were 254 incidents and 71 killings despite network promises of reduced violence in the wake of the shootings of Robert Kennedy and Dr. King. The National Commission on the Causes and Prevention of Violence, appointed following those assassinations, logged violent incidents an average of every 15 minutes on NBC and every 10 minutes on ABC. The latter network had some incident of violence in 91 percent of its evening programming in 1968. The Saturday morning children's cartoons had a violent incident every 3.5 minutes.[13]

Senator Thomas Dodd's Juvenile Delinquency Subcommittee focused on television throughout the 1960s as a contributor to the increase in crime among the young. It pointed out that an impression was created that violence is a satisfying outlet for frustrations, that the fist and the gun are both manly and romantic. Most authorities agreed that seeing violence on the screen rarely directly caused criminal behavior, but they pointed out it was a needless and dehumanizing experience to watch endless destruction of human life on television. At least at the children's level, marked improvement had occurred by 1971, with the success of such educational fare as *Sesame Street* encouraging the major networks to program similar material and markedly reduce violence.

By contrast, a study of print media in the early 1960s showed a lower percentage of content portraying sex and violence than readers might suppose. An analysis of the stories in 55 newsstand magazines (family, intellectual, detective, men's, romance) showed an average of 46 incidents of violence per issue and 23 incidents dealing with sexual themes. The family magazines carried only 12 violence items and 4 involving sex. A study of ten metropolitan newspapers showed 5 percent of the total news space devoted to violence, less than 1 percent to sex (except for the *New York Daily News,* which devoted a third of its space to news of violence and 3 percent to sex).[14] Violence was defined as news of crime, war, accidents. It is apparent that prominent display of stories of sex and violence in newspapers distorts the public image of the volume of such material. The data also shows why the spotlight of public concern shifted to television during the 1960s. It had loaded its entertainment time with common denominator material—violence spiced with sex. These programs drew good ratings, but the Violence Commission reported that a 1968 Harris poll showed 63 percent of women and 59 percent of men felt there was too much violence on television.

Part of that 1968 public reaction to violence on television screens undoubtedly stemmed from reporting on news and public affairs shows of turbulence in cities and on campuses, of disorders and riots in black communities, of the tragedies of assassination cutting down such public figures as Robert Kennedy and Martin Luther King.

Watts was the scene of one great explosion in August 1965. It cost 34 lives, 898 injured, 4,000 arrested, and $45 million in property damage. "Burn, Baby, Burn" was the cry of frustrated blacks angered by what they considered to be police brutality and tortured by years of racial discrimination and white indifference. Two years later, in July 1967, the scenes of destruction were Newark and Detroit. At this juncture President Johnson appointed the National Advisory Commission on Civil Disorders with Governor Otto Kerner of Illinois as chairman. Chapter 15 of its March 1968 report dealt with the mass media and the president's question, "What effect do the mass media have on the riots?"[15]

The Kerner Commission said that the media on the whole had tried hard to give a balanced factual account of the 1967 disorders. There had been some evidence of sensationalism, distortion, and inaccuracy: most of the shooting had been done by national guardsmen and policemen, not blacks; there was no organized conspiracy spurring the rioting, but mainly hostile young ghetto blacks; property damage was exaggerated, by as much as ten times by one AP dispatch from Detroit. In many cases of error, the media had relied on police authorities for their information. This observation by the commission was graphically reinforced in 1971 when false official statements were made that the prison guards who died at Attica in New York state had had their throats slashed. In reality they had been shot by their would-be rescuers. A courageous coroner and determined media reporters forced a prompt retraction of the false statements in fairness to the black convicts.

Television fared well in its riot coverage. The commission staff looked at 955 sequences of news and classified 494 as "calm" treatment to 262 as "emotional." Moderate black leaders were shown three times as often as militants. Because the soldiers and police were white, television scenes of actual rioting tended to make viewers think they were witnessing a black-white confrontation; actually the riots were in Negro slum areas. Overall, both network and local television coverage was cautious and restrained, the Kerner report said.

But the commission had a ringing indictment of the mass media, which was also an indictment of American society since the performance of the media largely reflected the public attitude of the times. The communications media, the commission said,

have not communicated to the majority of their audience—which is white—a sense of the degradation, misery, and hopelessness of living in the ghetto. They have not communicated to whites a feeling for the difficulties and frustrations of being a Negro in the United States. They have not shown understanding or appreciation of—and thus have not communicated—a sense of Negro culture, thought, or history . . . When the white press does refer to Negroes and Negro problems it frequently does so as if Negroes were not part of the audience . . . such attitudes, in an area as sensitive and inflammatory as this, feed Negro alienation and intensify white prejudices.

There has been no serious reporting of the Negro community, the commission said, with few black reporters and fewer race experts. "Tokenism—the hiring of one Negro reporter, or even two or three—is no longer enough. Negro reporters are essential, but so are Negro editors, writers, and commentators," the report declared.

The commission also recognized the problem conscientious journalists face when it commented:

Fear and apprehension of racial unrest and violence are deeply rooted in American society. They color and intensify reactions to news of racial trouble and threats of racial conflict. Those who report and disseminate news must be conscious of the background of anxieties and apprehension against which their stories are projected.

A CBS News survey in 1968 pointed up this public fear: 70 percent of whites responding thought the police should have been tougher in putting down riots.[16] In Watts's case, the white community later denied the area badly needed hospital facilities, even though the *Los Angeles Times* had won a Pulitzer Prize for its analysis of the Watts problem—after the riot was over.

Other studies bore out the Kerner Commission's statements about lack of black participation in the mass media. A 1969 study covering 32 of 48 major newspapers in 16 of the 20 largest cities showed that of 4,095 news executives, deskpersons, reporters, and photographers, 108, or 2.6 percent, were black, including only one news executive and six on desks.[17] A 1970 survey by *Time* listed the *Washington Post* as the most integrated newspaper, with 19 black editorial staffers, or 8.5 percent. In 1977 the *Post* reported 34 black professionals, or 10 percent. A 1977 ASNE survey obtained responses from 28 percent of dailies with 16,000 employees; they reported 563 black newsroom employees, or 3.5 percent.[18] Among them were Carl T. Rowan, syndicated columnist; William Raspberry, *Washington Post* columnist; Charlayne Hunter, *New York Times;* L.F. Palmer, Jr., *Chicago Daily News* columnist; and William A. Hilliard, appointed city editor of the *Portland Oregonian* in 1971.

CHICAGO 1968 AND THE WALKER REPORT   Late in 1968, after the presidential hopes of Hubert Humphrey had been wrecked by the image created during the turbulent Democratic convention in Chicago, a study of that convention, known as the Walker Report, was issued. Chicago attorney Daniel Walker made it for the National Commission on the Causes and Prevention of Violence. His staff took statements from 1,410 eyewitnesses and participants and had access to over 2,000 interviews conducted by the FBI. The Walker Report, referring to "a police riot," said that conditions were worse than the media had described them. Quoting from that summary:

During the week of the Democratic National Convention, the Chicago police were the targets of mounting provocation by both word and act. It took the form of obscene epithets, and of rocks, sticks, bathroom tiles and even human feces hurled at police by demonstrators. Some of the acts had been planned; others were spontaneous or were themselves provoked by police action. Furthermore, the police had been put on edge by widely-published threats of attempts to disrupt both the city and the Convention.

That was the nature of the provocation. The nature of the response was unrestrained and indiscriminate police violence on many occasions, particularly at night.

That violence was made all the more shocking by the fact that it was often inflicted upon persons who had broken no law, disobeyed no order, made no threat. These included peaceful demonstrators, onlookers, and large numbers of residents who were simply passing through, or happened to live in, the areas where confrontations were occurring.

Newsmen and photographers were singled out for assault, and their equipment deliberately damaged. Fundamental police training was ignored; and officers, when on the scene, were often unable to control their men. As one police officer put it: "What happened didn't have anything to do with police work."[19]

The final report of the commission, made in December 1969, said that in Chicago police used "excessive force not only against the provocateurs but also against the peaceful demonstrators and passive bystanders. Their conduct, while it won the support of the majority, polarized substantial and previously neutral segments of the population against the authorities and in favor of the demonstrators."

If these were the documented conclusions of a distinguished national commission appointed by President Johnson—the man against whom much of the bitterness at Chicago 1968 was directed—how did the media come out with tarnished public images?

Here best operated William Small's warning—the public, rather than accept reality, will prefer "to kill a messenger." The messenger was primarily television. CBS anchor man Walter Cronkite found himself exploding with wrath when he saw (as did the audience) floor guards slug CBS correspondent Dan Rather to the floor—but Cronkite later found himself virtually apologizing to Chicago's political boss, Mayor Richard J. Daley, on whom primary responsibility for using "law and order" to create disorder rested. NBC correspondent Sander Vanocur never recovered professionally from the public disfavor he incurred while covering the convention and retired from NBC in 1971. The flow of antimedia letters was so intense that the Federal Communications Commission felt compelled to conduct an investigation of the news coverage of the affair by the networks. The networks agreed to cooperate, reluctantly; in September 1969, the FCC reported that the networks had been fair.

Most Americans saw a 17-minute television sequence reporting the police-crowd confrontation on Wednesday night of convention week in front of the Conrad Hilton Hotel. There, and on the side streets, police brutality reached its peak, the Walker Report said. What most viewers would scarcely believe is the fact that those 17 minutes comprised half of the time CBS used to cover the demonstrations—32 minutes out of 38 hours of network time devoted to covering the week's activities. NBC devoted 36 minutes to violence on the floor out of 35 hours of coverage, 28 minutes to demonstrations outside the hall. ABC devoted 14 minutes to the disorders. Thus only a little more than 1 percent of network time was devoted to violence during the turbulent week, 99 percent to events on the floor, discussions, and the boredom of political convention coverage.[20]

The public, however, criticized the media for paying too much attention to the demonstrators and for reporting too much violence. A study reported by *Broadcasting* magazine put the Wednesday night audience at 90 millions, of whom 21.3 percent thought the police used excessive force and 56.8 percent thought they did not. Only 13 percent thought the tight security measures on the convention floor were unjustified— even though one critic commented that Humphrey was nominated "in a stockade."

In Chicago that week Del Hall of CBS News was clubbed from behind as he filmed. Jim Strickland of NBC News was clubbed in the mouth when he tried to assist Hall. Claude Lewis of the *Philadelphia Bulletin* was clubbed when he refused to give his notebook to a policeman. Jim Jones of *Newsweek* was kicked in the ribs and clubbed over the head while trying to show his press credentials. Robert Jackson of the *Chicago American* suffered the same fate. Altogether the news media suffered some 70 injuries at the hands of the police, equally divided between the electronic and print media.

But scant attention was paid to them. Eric Sevareid summed up the dilemma:

The explanation seems obvious. Over the years the pressure of public resentment against screaming militants, foul mouthed demonstrators, arsonists, and looters had built

JIMMY BRESLIN
Kids Take A Pounding—From Police, Delegates

By Jimmy Breslin

He was running with his body too far over and he had no control of himself, so he kept stumbling into the cops in the street and the cops chopped down on his head with their clubs.

Here was this young kid running with his legs out of control and his eyes closing and hair flying each time a club came onto his head—all the way from the front entrance of the Conrad Hilton Hotel to the corner. Running, stumbling, running, staggering and then going down on his face in the middle of Michigan Av. in the city of Chicago.

The cops ran up and kicked him. A few steps away, in the

Lines of policemen are strung across Michigan Av. outside the Conrad Hilton Hotel to block demonstrators trying to reach the International Amphitheatre. (Sun-Times Photo by Tom Kneebone)

gutter under the streetlight, doctors leaned over somebody who seemed badly hurt.

The crowd in the street stood with handkerchiefs over faces in the tear gas and they screamed at the cops.

The police gathered into groups and then ran into the kids and swung their clubs, cops in blue helmets and short-sleeve blue shirts. Cops with bare arms swinging in the television lights while they went for the head with their clubs, or for any place below the belt they could reach. Chicago cops who had been misdirected all day and now were completely without supervision. They were running into young kids and beating them.

They gather in groups under the lights.

"Get these bastards over there," one of them says.

"Let's get 'em."

"No, no, now wait a minute, wait a minute. Over there. There."

The Worst—In 20 Years

And they ran with their clubs into the kids who are unarmed and had, for hours, infuriated the cops with their youth and their dress and their manner of talking.

In 20 years of being policemen, having policemen in the family, riding with policemen in cars, drinking with them, watching them work in demonstrations and crowds in cities all over the world, the performance of the police of Chicago on Michigan Av. last night was the one worst I ever have seen.

"My head, my head, my head, my head," a girl in a gray sweater keeps saying as she falls against the building. Her hands go to her brown head of hair, where she has just been hit by a cop.

"Get out of here," the cop shouts. He aims his club for below your midsection. He misses, changes direction and goes for somebody else.

The tear gas was everywhere and people ran into buildings with their hands over their mouths. An Ohio delegate came out of his hotel to ride to the convention and the gas hit him. He stumbled into an office building with tears streaming. The tear gas went up, and it got through the open windows of Hubert Humphrey suite.

It began in the afternoon when the kids sat on the grass in the park across the street from the hotel.

"It was a very together thing last night," a kid was saying. "We had an apartment set up and we brought in anybody who got zonked with tear gas."

A girl was on her back, blowing smoke up. "I'd tell you my name," she said. "But I can't give it. Like my parents."

Machineguns At The Ready

The National Guard had machineguns up on the bridges that cross the railroad tracks that run through the park—machineguns, machineguns on tripods. One on each sidewalk of the bridge. The cops had the kids blocked off in the park where they had gone into them with tear gas and clubs earlier.

Now the kids sat on the grass and waited for word from their leader, Sidney Peck, the professor from Case-Western Reserve who is in the militant peace movment with such people as Dave Dellinger.

As Peck is far superior to the police at the simple art of crowd movements, he waited while his kids taunted the National Guardsmen.

"Wouldn't you rather hold a girl than a rifle?" a kid said, his arms around a girl who stood inches away from the line of rifles pointed at them.

Then Peck got on the loud-speaker and told the crowd of perhaps 4,000 to break up into small groups and just walk out of the park. And the kids broke up and walked away from the police and the National Guard. Walked away and left the police and National Guard motionless. And the kids went into Michigan Av. and captured the whole street and began shouting slogans at the hotel.

To the police, however, a kid shouting a political slogan is a thing to be feared and beaten. There was no way to control them. The police of Chicago have been out of hand since April, when Mayor Daley said they should shoot young looters. Daley went over the head of his police chief when he did this. When you deal with the intelligence of the average policeman you must be very careful. Mayor Daley was not.

Voice At Convention Headquarters

So Wednesday night, rather than watch the nomination of a candidate for the office of the President of the United States, you came, crying and choking and burning from tear gas, into the lobby of the Conrad Hilton Hotel, the headquarters for the convention, and the hotel speaker called out," all guests of the hotel please go to your room immediately and stay there." And out in the street, moving through the lights, national guardsmen in gas masks pointed rifles and moved at the crowd.

There were only 4,000 kids in the streets and the treatment given them by police created a national scandal, the effect of which will be felt through the days and the weeks that they try to conduct a campaign for the Presidency. For 4,000 kids is a very small number, compared to what surely will

Turn to Page 22

The *Chicago Sun-Times* covers the climactic "police riot" in picture and story.

up in the national boiler. With Chicago it exploded. The feelings that millions of people released were formed long before Chicago. Enough was enough: the police *must* be right. Therefore, the reporting *must* be wrong.[21]

It was a sobering experience for the media. It was a disastrous week for the Democratic party and Hubert Humphrey, whose campaign fell apart fatally in Chicago. The image of violence and radicalism projected from Chicago alienated one group of voters; Humphrey's defense of the Vietnamese war turned off the liberal left that once had supported him. Republican Richard Nixon adroitly used telecasts, and won the White House that had eluded him in 1960 by a hairline decision, despite Humphrey's valiant closing rush.

THE "BOYS   The long, grueling presidential contests of the 1970s were marred by
ON THE BUS": the lavish spending of advertising monies designed to package the candi-
1972 and 1976 dates for television and the preoccupation of many press corps members
              with the contenders' personal styles rather than the substance of ideas.
At times the storytellers became the story, as hordes of tired journalists chased the equally exhausted politicians from dawn to midnight, through state after state.

The tendency of the journalists to report basically the same things gave rise to the terms "pack" and "herd" journalism, while the soft content of much of the reporting led to comments about "news trivia" and "junk news." Coverage devoted to the latest public opinion poll was called "horserace" reporting. Feeding the American public a steady diet of news were the well-known national political reporters and columnists who joined the circuit for the pivotal moments; the regular reporters for prestige newspapers and magazines and a few smaller papers; the network television and radio correspondents; and the handful of press association reporters.

It was clear that the whistle-stop technique was still a basic part of political campaigning even if candidate appearances were arranged in part to entice coverage by the ever-present network television cameras. While research indicated most voters cast their ballots following traditional lines and did not make up or change their minds during actual campaigns, the number of close elections (1948, 1960, 1968, 1976) showed media influences to be crucially important.

The newspaper reporter with the most personal influence on the coverage by the traveling press corps was R. W. ("Johnny") Apple, Jr., of the *New York Times,* who had been with the paper since 1963. Because the *Times* was the only paper regularly available on the many stops, Apple's stories provided continuity for the group. An industrious, aggressive man, Apple worked around the clock to provide the *Times* with updated information and fresh insights.

Other regulars included Jules Witcover who left the *Los Angeles Times* to join the *Washington Post,* a veteran of more than 25 years; Haynes Johnson of the *Washington Post,* a leader in reporting voter preferences; Jack Germond, another 25-year veteran who headed Gannett's coverage before becoming chief political writer for the *Washington Star;* the old reliable of the *Baltimore Sun,* Phil Potter; James McCartney of the Knight newspapers; Curtis Wilkie, who made his mark in 1972 with Wilmington's *News Journal* and later became the *Boston Globe*'s White House correspondent; Kenneth Reich of the *Los Angeles Times,* who gained attention during the 1976 campaign; and Jim Perry of the *National Observer.* Eleanor Randolph of the *Chicago Tribune* and Roger Simon of the *Chicago Sun-Times* were cited for 1976 stories.

Pounding out their columns and background pieces were David Broder of the *Washington Post,* considered by many the most influential political columnist; Peter Lisagor of the *Chicago Daily News;* Rowland Evans and Robert Novak of the *Chicago Sun-Times,* whose column was syndicated in hundreds of papers; the syndicated George Will, a relative newcomer hailed for his fresh writing style and balanced thought; and Robert Donovan of the *Los Angeles Times,* another veteran of the Truman days, a distinguished political writer. Some of the most astute commentaries were by the *New Yorker'*s Elizabeth Drew, who turned her diaries into a book.

Dozens of correspondents reported for the press associations and television networks. Walter Mears, Saul Pett, and Karl Lcubsdorf of the Associated Press and Arnold Sawislak, Clay Richards, and Steve Gerstel of United Press International had leading bylines. On television in 1976, CBS's Ed Bradley, ABC's Sam Donaldson, and NBC's Judy Woodruff and Don Oliver led in covering Carter. Tom Jarriel, ABC, Phil Jones, CBS, and Bob Jamieson, NBC, followed Ford. Cassie Mackin, NBC, Ann Compton, ABC, and Sharon Lovejoy, CBS, were active on camera.

The "Boys on the Bus," as they were called by Timothy Crouse in his classic description of the 1972 campaign,[22] came in for a great amount of criticism after both elections. They were accused of following the lead of a Johnny Apple or a Walter Mears and not developing their own story angles, partly because of laziness and partly because their editors also followed what the *New York Times,* AP, or UPI said. Some writers were said to be partial to a particular candidate; some were said to be rude, arrogant, and too ambitious; others were said to be easily manipulated by candidates or their campaign aides. Suggestions were made for more pool reporting and less emphasis on routine speeches.

The 1972 campaign was marked by rough attacks on Senator Edmund Muskie in New Hampshire (later attributed in part to the White House "dirty tricks" campaign); Senator George McGovern's fumbles near the end of an otherwise well-organized

NBC

Pauline Frederick (*left*), at PBS after an NBC career, and Elizabeth Drew, *New Yorker* political writer, were two of the panelists at the Ford-Carter debates.

campaign, including his agony in dropping Senator Thomas Eagleton as his running mate after Eagleton's previous history of nervous disorder was revealed; McGovern's charges, largely ignored, that Nixon's White House was the most corrupt in the nation's history; Nixon's skillful use of the media in an effort to avoid public contact; Nixon's massive war chest of political contributions.

In 1976 Jimmy Carter of Georgia had an advantage. Not only had he and his staff read Crouse's book, but they had also begun their campaign early, as had McGovern. As early as October 1975, Apple of the *New York Times* was writing that Carter had a chance. The snowball grew (some cynics said because the news media have a way of making predictions come true), and Carter entered every one of 26 statewide Democratic primaries, the most ever held. However, the campaign coverage was criticized as much as before. "Never was so much that meant so little presented in such technologically perfect fashion to such a widely yawning public," one critic wrote.[23]

The campaign began in August with President Ford 13 poll points behind. It ended with Jimmy Carter winning the presidency by 2 poll points and 297 electoral votes, a squeak-through majority. Carter was hurt by media overexposure and repeated charges that he was "fuzzy" on the main issues, despite the issuance of dozens of position papers by his staff. He also was attacked for granting a candid interview with *Playboy* magazine. Ford was belittled for a generally dull performance, and the "trivialization of the news" included accounts of his hitting his head on plane doors and slipping several times. Also hurtful was his association with Earl Butz, the secretary of agriculture, whose antiblack comment was reported by former Nixon aide John Dean in *Rolling Stone* and explained more fully by *New Times*. Media critics said events like this distracted from major foreign policy and domestic issues that needed further amplification.[24]

Three nationally televised debates between Carter and Ford, and one between vice presidential candidates Walter Mondale and Robert Dole, gave millions of Americans the chance to judge the candidates for themselves. Sponsored by the League of Women Voters, the debates (called press conferences by critics who wanted point by point challenges by the men) allowed Carter the opportunity to demonstrate his knowledge of foreign policy issues and his capacity to handle himself under pressure against the more experienced Ford. After a shaky start in the first debate, Carter came on strong in the final two and headed into election day with a slight buildup in poll points, which he held.

TELEVISION IN THE 1970s

The biggest problem for television was that a great bulk of its audience was becoming increasingly uncomfortable with the violence, sex, seminudity, vulgarity, smoking, and drinking heard and seen on prime time television shows. In 1975 the FCC encouraged the networks and National Association of Broadcasters to adopt a "family viewing time," known later as the "family hour." The idea was to keep shows with high amounts of sex and violence like *Kojak, Hawaii Five-O,* and *Charlie's Angels* off the air until young children were in bed.

Writers and directors guilds immediately challenged the broadcasters' action and charged FCC pressure was involved in a violation of their First Amendment rights. The National Citizens Committee for Broadcasting, led by former FCC commissioner Nicholas Johnson, joined the fight against the networks. The public was not in sympathy, though. The specter of murders and beatings led to increased talk in Congress of revamping the FCC Act of 1934. From the White House, President Carter joined in the criticism, saying "I think the President has the right or obligation to express to the public displeasure or criticism of programming content."[25]

Coupled with the high degree of violence was the increasing abandonment of entertainment taboos, as demonstrated by the hit of 1975–76, *Mary Hartman, Mary Hartman.* Public awareness of the problem was heightened by the movie *Network,* the Academy Award winner of 1977 that bitterly satirized the ratings system.

Johnson's NCCB group encouraged a boycott of the advertisers of the highest rated violent shows, claiming the real power was in the hands of the consumer audience. Other changes were effected by Action for Children's Television, formed by a Newton, Massachusetts, housewife Peggy Charren who was perturbed about programming and advertisements shown to children. In 1975, following a number of improvements, Senator Frank Moss said:

ACT represents the most significant grass roots effort at consumer protection that exists today... ACT was born out of the great promise of television that has been perverted into mind-rotting commercial exploitation of our nation's children.[26]

Then, in 1976, the American Medical Association, the American Psychiatric Association, and the national Parent-Teacher Association pushed national campaigns against televised violence. The J. Walter Thompson and other advertising companies started to disassociate themselves from violent programming, but the battle was far from over.[27]

Coming to the defense of the American television system, while citing its fine achievements and acknowledging its faults, was CBS News commentator Eric Sevareid. Noting the adversary relationship between print and electronic journalism, Sevareid challenged print journalists who criticize television to look at their own products:

Don't publish lofty editorials and critiques berating the culturally low common denominator of TV entertainment programming and then feature on the cover of your weekly TV supplements, most weeks of the year, the latest TV rock star or gang-buster character. Or be honest enough to admit that you do this, that you play to mass tastes for the same reason the networks do—because it is profitable. Don't lecture the networks for the excess of violence—and it is excessive—on the screen and then publish huge ads for the most violent motion pictures in town, ads for the most pornographic films and plays, as broadcasting does not.[28]

NOTES

1. Made in 1925 in his "The Natural History of the Newspaper," a chapter in Robert E. Park, Ernest W. Burgess, and Roderick D. McKenzie, *The City* (Chicago: University of Chicago Press), pp. 80–98.

2. Among major dailies supporting Kennedy in 1960 outside the South were the *New York Times, St. Louis Post-Dispatch, Milwaukee Journal, Louisville Courier-Journal, New York Post, Newsday, Long Island Press, Pittsburgh Post-Gazette, Toledo Blade, Hartford Times, Denver Post,* and *Sacramento Bee.* The *Washington Post* did not endorse, but favored, Kennedy.

3. The 12 major dailies supporting Goldwater in 1964 were the *Chicago Tribune* and *American, Los Angeles Times, Oakland Tribune, Cincinnati Enquirer, Columbus Dispatch, Milwaukee Sentinel, Richmond Times-Dispatch* and *News Leader, Nashville Banner, Tulsa World,* and *Birmingham News.*

4. Nine major dailies that had supported Nixon in 1960 swung to Humphrey: Hearst's *San Francisco Examiner* and *Boston Record-American,* the Cowles's *Minneapolis Star* and *Tribune* and *Des Moines Register* and *Tribune,* the Ridders' *St. Paul Dispatch* and *Pioneer Press,* and Newhouse's *Newark Star-Ledger.* Four that had backed Kennedy in 1960 now endorsed Nixon: *Newsday,* the *Toledo Blade,* Gannett's *Hartford Times,* and the Ridders' *Long Beach Press-Telegram.*

5. The nine major dailies supporting McGovern in 1972 were the *New York Times, New York Post, Louisville Courier-Journal, Minneapolis Tribune, St. Louis Post-Dispatch, Portland Oregon Journal, Arkansas Gazette, Bergen County* (N.J.) *Record,* and *St. Petersburg Independent.*

6. Switching to the Democrats with Carter were the *Chicago Sun-Times* and *Daily News* and the *Detroit Free Press*. Although he carried virtually the entire South, Carter had the backing of only six major southern dailies: *Atlanta Journal* and *Constitution, Charlotte Observer, St. Petersburg Independent, Nashville Tennessean,* and Little Rock's *Arkansas Gazette.* Other Carter supporters, in addition to McGovern's 1972 list, included the *Des Moines Register, Denver Post, Dayton News, Long Island Press, Milwaukee Journal,* and *Minneapolis Star.*

7. See Bernard Berelson, Paul F. Lazarsfeld, and William N. McPhee, *Voting* (Chicago: University of Chicago Press, 1954). For studies of campaign news coverage in large cities, see the bibliography for this chapter. In his three studies of the news coverage of the presidential campaigns of the 1960s in 15 "prestige papers," as selected by the nation's editors and educators (see chapter 25 for the polls), Guido H. Stempel found that only one deviated by more than 5 percent from 50-50 division of space in both the 1960 and 1964 campaigns. That was the *Chicago Tribune,* whose news of the campaigns was 59.2 percent Republican in 1960 and 65.6 in 1964. But in 1972, a follow-up study showed, the *Tribune* was most favorable to the Democrats in news coverage (62.9 percent) of six papers analyzed, all favoring McGovern.

8. *San Francisco Examiner,* May 6, 1933.

9. Ibid., May 29, 1935.

10. Ibid., June 21, 1935.

11. Ibid., October 30, 1936.

12. *Time,* XLIX (June 9, 1947), 68. The 1936 survey of Washington correspondents, cited here, was taken by Leo C. Rosten for his book, *The Washington Correspondents* (New York: Harcourt Brace Jovanovich, 1937). Cited most often as "least fair and reliable" by 93 correspondents were, in order, the Hearst newspapers, the *Chicago Tribune,* the *Los Angeles Times,* and the Scripps-Howard newspapers. Cited most often as "most fair and reliable" by 99 correspondents were, in order, the *New York Times, Baltimore Sun, Christian Science Monitor,* the Scripps-Howard papers, and the *St. Louis Post-Dispatch.*

13. William Small, *To Kill a Messenger* (New York: Hastings House, 1970), pp. 80–81.

14. Herbert A. Otto, "Sex and Violence on the American Newsstand," *Journalism Quarterly,* XL (Spring 1963), 19–26.

15. *Report of the National Advisory Commission on Civil Disorders* (New York: Bantam Books, 1968).

16. Small, *To Kill a Messenger,* p. 60.

17. Edward J. Trayes, "The Negro in Journalism," *Journalism Quarterly,* XLVI (Spring 1969), 5.

18. *Time,* April 6, 1970, p. 89; *ASNE Bulletin,* November 1977, p. 18. Figures for other minorities in the 1977 report: 94 Chicanos, 83 Latinos, 88 Orientals, 23 American Indians. Of minorities, 38 were serving as news executives, 130 as deskpersons.

19. As quoted in Small, *To Kill a Messenger,* p. 211.

20. Ibid., p. 214.

21. Ibid., p. 216.

22. Timothy Crouse, *The Boys on the Bus* (New York: Random House, 1973).

23. See the *Columbia Journalism Review*'s special report, "Reporting the 1976 Campaign," (January–February 1977), with articles by Sanford J. Ungar, Walter Mears, James McCartney, Philip Meyer, and others.

24. Roger Morris, "Foreign Policy Reporting: Quarantined for the Campaign," *Columbia Journalism Review* (November–December 1976), p. 19.

25. "Television: A Gold Mine That's Coming Under Heavy Attack," *U.S. News and World Report.* (February 7, 1977), p. 29.

26. Cited by Donald P. Ranly in "Action for Children's Television," *Freedom of Information Center Report,* No. 364 (December 1976), p. 10.

27. See George Comstock, "The Role of Social and Behavioral Science in Policymaking for Television," The Rand Corporation (January 1977).

28. Eric Sevareid, "What's Right with Sight-and-Sound Journalism," *Saturday Review* (October 10, 1976), p. 19.

ANNOTATED BIBLIOGRAPHY

Books

AGEE, WARREN K., ed., *The Press and the Public Interest.* Washington: Public Affairs Press, 1968. Collection of 18 William Allen White lectures at the University of Kansas by leading journalists.

BLUMBERG, NATHAN B., *One Party Press?* Lincoln: University of Nebraska Press, 1954. How 35 large dailies covered the 1952 campaign; news columns found to be essentially fair.

CASEY, RALPH D., ed., *The Press in Perspective*. Baton Rouge: Louisiana State University Press, 1963. Seventeen addresses in critical vein by leading journalists and writers, in Guild Lecture series at University of Minnesota.

COMMISSION ON FREEDOM OF THE PRESS, *A Free and Responsible Press*. Chicago: University of Chicago Press, 1947. A penetrating summary.

CROUSE, TIMOTHY, *The Boys on the Bus: Riding with the Campaign Press Corps*. New York: Random House, 1973. The reporters' wolf-pack and their presidential quarries. See also Hunter S. Thompson, *Fear and Loathing: On the Campaign Trail '72* (San Francisco: Straight Arrow Books, 1973). By the national affairs editor of *Rolling Stone*.

DREWRY, JOHN E., ed., *Post Biographies of Famous Journalists*. Athens: University of Georgia Press, 1942. Contains articles about Hearst, Roy Howard, McCormick.

EMERY, MICHAEL C., AND TED CURTIS SMYTHE, eds., *Readings in Mass Communication: Concepts and Issues in the Mass Media*, 3rd ed. Dubuque, Iowa: Wm. C. Brown, 1977. Articles examining current changes and debates.

FORD, EDWIN H., AND EDWIN EMERY, eds., *Highlights in the History of the American Press*. Minneapolis: University of Minnesota Press, 1954. Contains articles about Hearst, Scripps-Howard, and McCormick.

HOFSTETTER, C. RICHARD, *Bias in the News: Network Television Coverage of the 1972 Election Campaign*. Columbus: Ohio State University Press, 1976. Detailed study of 213-page length involving 17-week content analysis finds no bias in political way.

HULTENG, JOHN L., *The Messenger's Motives*. Englewood Cliffs, N.J.: Prentice-Hall, 1976. Criticisms of the mass media are summarized and evaluated.

HYNDS, ERNEST C., *American Newspapers in the 1970s*. New York: Hastings House, 1975. A critical survey of the contemporary press.

LEUCHTENBERG, WILLIAM E., *Franklin D. Roosevelt and the New Deal*. New York: Harper & Row, 1963. Study of domestic policy.

LINDSTROM, CARL E., *The Fading American Newspaper*. New York: Doubleday, 1960. A strong critique of trends and methods by a 40-year newspaperman (*Hartford Times*).

MOTT, FRANK LUTHER, *The News in America*. Cambridge, Mass.: Harvard University Press, 1952. An excellent discussion of news-gathering and news-distribution and of sociopolitical responsibilities.

MOTT, FRANK LUTHER, AND RALPH D. CASEY, eds., *Interpretations of Journalism*. New York: Appleton-Century-Crofts, 1937. The most important historical collection of statements on press problems.

Report of the National Advisory Commission on Civil Disorders. New York: Bantam Books, 1968. Chapter 15 discusses the mass media.

RESTON, JAMES B., *The Artillery of the Press*. New York: Harper & Row, 1967. Essays discussing press influence on foreign policy.

RIVERS, WILLIAM L., AND WILBUR SCHRAMM, *Responsibility in Mass Communication*. New York: Harper & Row, 1969. An examination of the social problem, also done by J. Edward Gerald in *The Social Responsibility of the Press* (Minneapolis: University of Minnesota Press, 1963) and by John Hohenberg in *The News Media* (New York: Holt, Rinehart & Winston, 1968).

RIVERS, WILLIAM L., THEODORE PETERSON, AND JAY JENSEN, *The Mass Media and Modern Society*. San Francisco: Rinehart Press, 1971. Relationships between media and government; social, economic, intellectual environments of the media.

ROWSE, ARTHUR E., *Slanted News*. Boston: Beacon Press, 1957. Analysis of how 31 large dailies reported the "Nixon fund" episode in 1952.

SCHLESINGER, ARTHUR, JR., *The Age of Roosevelt*. Boston: Houghton Mifflin, 1957–60. Vol. 1, *The Crisis of the Old Order* (1957), covers 1919–33; Vol. 2, *The Coming of the New Deal* (1958), covers 1933–34; Vol. 3, *The Politics of Upheaval* (1960), covers 1935–36. No further volumes appeared.

SCHRAMM, WILBUR, ed., *Communications in Modern Society*. Urbana: University of Illinois Press, 1948. Contains essays on press responsibility by Paul F. Lazarsfeld, Ralph D. Casey, and Robert J. Blakely.

SKORNIA, HARRY J., AND JACK W. KITSON, eds., *Problems and Controversies in Television and Radio*. Palo Alto, Calif.: Pacific Books, 1968. Basic readings for the 1960s.

SMALL, WILLIAM, *To Kill A Messenger*. New York: Hastings House, 1970. A prize-winning study of "television news and the real world" by the CBS Washington news manager, excellent coverage of crises of the 1960s.

SMYTHE, TED C., AND GEORGE A. MASTROIANNI, eds., *Issues in Broadcasting: Radio, Television and Cable*. Palo Alto, Calif.: Mayfield Publishing, 1975. Readings.

SWANBERG, W. A., *Citizen Hearst*. New York: Scribner's, 1961. A highly readable, detailed biography.

TEBBEL, JOHN, *An American Dynasty*. New York: Doubleday, 1947. An analysis of the McCormick-Patterson publishing empire.

————, *The Life and Good Times of William Randolph Hearst*. New York: Dutton, 1952. Best single book about both Hearst and his publishing empire.

WALDROP, FRANK C., *McCormick of Chicago*. Englewood Cliffs, N.J.: Prentice-Hall, 1966. Best biography of the *Chicago Tribune* publisher. See also Jerome E. Edwards, *The Foreign Policy of Col. McCormick's Tribune, 1929–1941* (Reno: University of Nevada Press, 1971), a carefully researched analysis.

WHITE, THEODORE H., *The Making of the President—1960. —1964. —1968. —1972*. New York: Atheneum, 1961, 1965, 1969, 1973. The campaigns and their journalistic developments. For a revised version of 1972, see his *Breach of Faith: The Fall of Richard Nixon*. New York: Atheneum, 1975.

WITCOVER, JULES, *Marathon: The Pursuit of the Presidency, 1972–1976*. New York: The Viking Press, 1977. Detailed report of events by *Washington Post* reporter.

Periodicals and Monographs

BARTNESS, GAROLD L., "Hearst in Milwaukee," Ph.D. thesis, University of Minnesota, 1968. Study of *Wisconsin News, 1918–39*, "a real Hearst newspaper."

BIGMAN, STANLEY K., "Public Reactions to the Death of a Daily," *Journalism Quarterly,* XXXII (Summer 1955), 267. Little public concern found after merger of *Washington Post* and *Times-Herald*.

"The Broadcast Media and the Political Process: 1976," *Broadcasting,* XCII (Jan. 3, 1977), 33–76. A special issue on all aspects of the Ford-Carter campaign.

BROD, DONALD F., "Church, State, and Press: Twentieth Century Episodes in the United States," Ph.D. thesis, University of Minnesota, 1968. Examines newspaper coverage of Scopes trial, Vatican relations, 1928 and 1960 elections.

CARLISLE, RODNEY P., "William Randolph Hearst: a Fascist Reputation Reconsidered," *Journalism Quarterly,* L (Spring 1973), 125. Hearst supported early New Deal.

"The Chicago Tribune," *Fortune,* IX (May 1934), 101. Detailed study.

COLUMBIA JOURNALISM REVIEW, "Campaign Coverage: An Appraisal of 1960—and Implications for 1964," *Columbia Journalism Review* (Fall 1961), 6. A 14-page report on 25 metropolitan areas.

————, "Reporting the 1976 Campaign," (January–February, 1977). Articles by participants and observers in Carter-Ford campaign.

COMSTOCK, GEORGE, ET AL., "The Role of Social and Behavioral Science in Policymaking for Television," Santa Monica, Calif.: Rand Corporation, report, 1977.

COPE, NEIL B., "A History of the *Memphis Commercial Appeal*," Ph.D. thesis, University of Missouri, 1969. Story of a leading Scripps-Howard paper.

DANIELSON, WAYNE A., AND JOHN B. ADAMS, "Completeness of Press Coverage of the 1960 Campaign," *Journalism Quarterly,* XXXVIII (Autumn 1961), 441. A report on a sample of 90 dailies, based on completeness of coverage of 23 campaign events.

EVARTS, DRU, AND GUIDO H. STEMPEL III, "Coverage of the 1972 Campaign by TV, News Magazines and Major Newspapers," *Journalism Quarterly,* LI (Winter 1974), 645. The study indicates that in the 1972 campaign the media generally showed no news bias.

FLANERY, JAMES A., "Chicago Newspapers' Coverage of the City's Major Civil Disorders of

1968," Ph.D. thesis, Northwestern University, 1971. Violence by police minimized in stories.

GERBNER, GEORGE, ET AL., *Violence Profile No. 7: Trends in Network Drama and Viewer Conceptions of Social Reality, 1967–1975.* Philadelphia: Annenberg School of Communication, 1976. Violence diminished little, "family hour" proved ineffective.

GRABER, DORIS A., "Press Coverage and Voter Reaction in the 1968 Presidential Election," *Political Science Quarterly,* LXXXIX (March 1974), 68. A major study of 16 dailies found candidates' personalities covered more than issues, and voters ignoring data.

HAUSMAN, LINDA WEINER, "Criticism of the Press in U.S. Periodicals, 1900–1939: An Annotated Bibliography," *Journalism Monographs,* No. 4, August 1967. What the magazines said about newspapers.

"Journalism and the Kerner Report," a special section in *Columbia Journalism Review,* VII (Fall 1968), 42. An analysis of the report's chapter 15.

LIEBLING, A.J., "Publisher," *New Yorker,* XVII (August 2–23, 1941). Critical profile of Roy W. Howard.

LOWRY, DENNIS T., "Measures of Network News Bias in the 1972 Presidential Campaign," *Journal of Broadcasting,* XVIII (Fall 1975), 387. Content analysis shows anti-GOP.

MARTINSON, DAVID L., "Coverage of La Follette Offers Insights for 1972 Campaign," *Journalism Quarterly,* LII (Autumn 1975), 539. How the press stereotypes in campaigns.

MEADOW, ROBERT G., "Cross-Media Comparison of Coverage of the 1972 Presidential Campaign," *Journalism Quarterly,* L (Autumn 1973), 482. Uniform coverage in the media.

MEYERS, W. CAMERON, "The Chicago Newspaper Hoax in the '36 Election Campaign," *Journalism Quarterly,* XXXVII (Summer 1960), 356. Criticism of *Chicago Tribune* by the biographer of *Chicago Times* editor Richard J. Finnegan (Ph.D. dissertation, Northwestern University, 1959).

NIXON, RAYMOND B., AND ROBERT L. JONES, "The Content of Non-Competitive vs. Competitive Newspapers," *Journalism Quarterly,* XXXIII (Summer 1956), 299. No major differences were found.

NOBILE, PHILIP, "What Makes the Apple Machine Run?," *More,* VI (July–August 1976), 23. Interview with R. W. Apple, *New York Times,* rated ablest of the 1976 boys-on-bus.

"The Press and Chicago," a group of articles on the 1968 Democratic convention, by Jules Witcover; the metropolitan Chicago press and the *Chicago Journalism Review,* by Edwin Diamond; and the Chicago suburbs by Gene Gilmore and David Beal, in *Columbia Journalism Review,* VII (Fall 1968), 5.

"The Press in the 1972 Campaign," *Nieman Reports,* XXVII (Autumn 1973), 3. Report of a Harvard conference on campaign decision-making.

ROBINSON, JOHN P., "The Press as King-Maker: What Surveys from Last Five Campaigns Show," *Journalism Quarterly,* LI (Winter 1974), 587. Excellent summary from Michigan Survey Center showing a relationship between newspaper endorsements and voters' choices.

STEMPEL, GUIDO H., III, "The Prestige Press in Two Presidential Elections," *Journalism Quarterly,* XLII (Winter 1965), 15. Study of 15 leading papers' news coverage in 1960 and 1964.

———, "The Prestige Press Meets the Third-Party Challenge," *Journalism Quarterly,* XLVI (Winter 1969), 685. Coverage of 1968 campaign by 15 major dailies.

TAYLOR, FRANK J., "The Incredible House That Hearst Built," *Saturday Evening Post,* CCXXXII (May 9, 1959), 38. Hearst's San Simeon estate becomes a California Historical Monument.

The *New York Times* reports its victory; inset, Frank Stanton and CBS avoid censure.

27

Media Responses and Counterattacks

There can be no such thing as a free press and no such thing as the integrity of the news if the men and women who write the news live in fear of the security of their jobs.

—Heywood Broun

Through all the years of external criticism of the media, increasing in the 1930s and escalating in the 1960s and 1970s, those within the profession were responding to pressures for improvement of the press and broadcasting. They also were creating some pressures of their own.

Those responses took the forms of improvement of professional working conditions, establishing of effective media associations, writing of voluntary codes of conduct, development of professional organizations devoted to the highest purposes of journalism, encouragement of education for journalism, support of studies of the press, sponsorship of press councils and journalism reviews, and taking advantage of improvements in technology.

In the crisis year of 1933, the gaining of adequate income and job security by newspaper men and women was the first prerequisite. While other workers in newspaper plants had long ago unionized, the editorial employees remained unorganized and relatively underpaid. Section 7-a of the National Industrial Recovery Act of 1933 offered them their chance, since it guaranteed the right of collective bargaining. The NRA also contained licensing provisions that alienated conservative leaders of the American Newspaper Publishers Association. This made the writing of a daily newspaper code under the "Blue Eagle" provisions a grueling duel. It provided for a 40-hour week in bigger cities, minimum salaries, and carried an open-shop provision.

Newspapermen received the wage and hour provisions of the daily newspaper code with little enthusiasm. The $11 to $15 weekly salary minimums did nothing to further the professional status of journalism or the economic security of its workers—an obvious conclusion to which thoughtful leaders of the profession agreed.

The code provisions were far from the $40 a week minimum for those with two years or more experience, which New York reporters considered equitable at the time.

THE NEWSPAPER GUILD   Reporters and deskmen around the country began talking about formation of collective bargaining units in the summer of 1933 when the trend of the code negotiations became apparent. Heywood Broun, the liberal and combative columnist for the *New York World-Telegram,* sounded a call for action in his syndicated column for August 7, 1933, which sparked the translation of talk into deeds. Broun deftly chastised his fellow newspaper workers for not having formed a union like those of the better-paid printers and gently chided those who feared "the romance of the game" would be lost if they organized. Then in typical Broun style he concluded:

> But the fact that newspaper editors and owners are genial folk should hardly stand in the way of the organization of a newspaper writers' union. There should be one. Beginning at nine o'clock in the morning of October 1, I am going to do the best I can in helping get one up. I think I could die happy on the opening day of the general strike if I had the privilege of watching Walter Lippmann heave a brick through a *Tribune* window at a nonunion operative who had been called in to write the current "Today and Tomorrow" column on the gold standard.[1]

The cautious Lippmann ignored Broun's call to arms, but the newspaper people across the country who read his column did not, nor did they wait until October 1. Cleveland's reporters were the first to respond, forming what became the first local of

Heywood Broun

the Newspaper Guild on August 20. The Twin Cities, Minneapolis and St. Paul, were second in line. New York, Rockford, Newark, Akron, Duluth–Superior, Cincinnati, Philadelphia, and Youngstown locals followed in rapid order. There had been newswriters' locals chartered by the American Federation of Labor and its affiliated International Typographical Union as early as the 1890s, but few had lived for any length of time. Broun himself had headed a New York effort in 1923.[2]

New York newsmen, headed by Broun, issued the first number of the *Guild Reporter* on November 23, 1933, and called for a national convention to be held in Washington December 15. Delegates from 30 cities responded. Broun was elected president, a post he held until his death in 1939, and Jonathan Eddy became the first executive secretary. The newspapermen and women were seeking, they said, "to preserve the vocational interests of the members and to improve the conditions under which they work by collective bargaining, and to raise the standards of journalism."

By the time the first annual convention met in St. Paul in June 1934 the Guild had 8,000 members. But only one of its local units had a contract with a publisher. The 1934 Guild convention called for more contracts covering minimum wages and maximum hours, paid holidays and vacations, overtime pay, sick leave, severance pay, and other usual trade union contract provisions—goals that remained to be gained by the average newspaper staff. Publishers who disliked seeing the Guild take on the form of a trade union organization were further antagonized when the convention approved a code of ethics that listed what the Guild regarded to be harmful practices of newspapers. The Guild, rebuffed in its effort "to raise the standards of journalism" on a philosophical plane and realizing that it faced a hard fight to win union contracts, thereafter stuck closely to problems of salaries and working conditions when dealing with employers. Local units sponsored Guild discussions and competitions designed to improve journalistic practices.

Head-on clashes became unavoidable. The Guild did not shrink from using the strike and picket line and was involved in 20 strikes during its first five years. Bitterest was a 508-day strike against Hearst newspapers in Chicago; the longest in Guild history was the strike called in 1967 against Hearst's *Los Angeles Herald-Examiner* that millions of dollars and ten years later remained unwon. But in the main the Guild negotiated peacefully. It developed Guild shop provisions to ensure 80 percent membership, joined the CIO in 1937, and broadened the membership base to office employees. All this aroused controversy, but by 1938 the Guild had 75 newspaper contracts and its first with a press association, the United Press.[3]

But the biggest early Guild victory was gained in a court case involving one Associated Press staffman, Morris Watson. Watson, who had been discharged by the Associated Press in 1935, asserted he had been dismissed for Guild activities. He appealed to the National Labor Relations Board for an order compelling his reinstatement under the provisions of the Wagner Labor Relations Act of 1935, whose collective bargaining guarantees had replaced those of the NRA codes outlawed by the Supreme Court that year. When the NLRB ruled in favor of Watson in 1936, the AP carried the case to the Supreme Court, contending that the Wagner Act was unconstitutional and that in any event it did not apply to newspapers or press associations.

The Supreme Court, which had ruled adversely on key New Deal legislation in 1935 and 1936, announced a series of decisions in April 1937 upholding the constitutionality of the Wagner Act. Among the cases decided was that of Morris Watson. Justices Hughes and Roberts swung to the liberal side to join Justices Brandeis, Stone, and Cardozo in ordering the Associated Press to reinstate Watson in his job. The five justices ruled that Watson had been illegally discharged for union activity, and it was on that point that the case turned.[4] But the majority also observed that "the publisher of a newspaper has no special immunity from the application of general laws."

Upholding of the Wagner Act was a great Guild victory. It assured it a permanent place in newspaper life. Gradually contracts were won in larger cities, including one with the *New York Times,* whose staff had long been skeptical of the Guild. But the road was still a rocky one. The recession years of 1937–39 brought widespread newspaper closings and staff prunings that left thousands of newspapermen and women unemployed and made contract negotiation difficult.

The Guild, after the tragic death of Heywood Broun at age 51 from pneumonia, became engaged in a bitter fight between conservative or "pro-Guild" members and left-wing elements who were strongest in the New York City locals. Forcing an election of officers by nationwide referendum, however, brought victory to the "pro-Guild" group whose anti-Communist slate was managed by Wilbur Bade, early editor of the *Guild Reporter*. The Guild was the first CIO union to throw out its Communist national officers. New York's locals did the same in 1947. Under the leadership of presidents Milton M. Murray and Harry Martin, and executive vice-presidents Sam Eubanks and Ralph B. Novak, the Guild remained vigorously liberal but continued its anti-Communist policy in following years to include material and moral aid to journalists' groups in other countries.[5]

World War II brought a general "freezing" of labor relations activities. As the war ended, the Guild's goal was a $65 a week top minimum for all contracts. Then in 1946 the goal was set at a seemingly impossible $100 level. When it was reached with ease by 1954, new goals were set. Founders would have been amazed by the breaking of the $500 a week level at the *Washington Post* in 1977 and an average top reporter salary nationally of $321. The average starting salary for reporters in Guild shops reached the $200 a week level. Membership, concentrated in larger dailies and press associations, passed 33,000. Guild leaders since 1950 have included Joseph F. Collis, Arthur Rosenstock, William J. Farson, and Charles A. Perlik, Jr.

Although its original hopes for influencing journalistic standards had been shelved, the Guild revived such interests in the 1960s. It established the Mellett Fund for a Free and Responsible Press to finance press councils in local communities. It encouraged establishment of critical media reviews, and Guildsmen cautiously sought more voice in advising newspaper management on institutional policy. Race discrimination, reporters' privilege, restrictions on the press, and physical harassment of reporters were other issues occupying Guild attention. Remembering their founder, the Guild in 1941 established an annual award for newspaper work "in the spirit of Heywood Broun."

THE AMERICAN NEWSPAPER PUBLISHERS ASSOCIATION

The American Newspaper Publishers Association, founded in 1887 as the trade association of the dailies, had grown to 850 members by the 1930s. In contrast to its position on the Guild, the ANPA had sponsored an imaginative policy of voluntary arbitration with the printing unions after 1900. Its Bureau of Advertising was involved in the *Continuing Study of Newspaper Reading*. It had sponsored research in printing processes and had defended newspaper owners' interests in newsprint tariffs and postage rates.

But in the 1930s its leadership proved unresponsive to changing social and economic conditions. Its manager, Lincoln B. Palmer, and counsel, Elisha Hanson, put the ANPA in full opposition to the major legislation of the New Deal. Exemptions for the newspaper business were asked when reform legislation was before the Congress. After Cranston Williams became general manager in 1939, the uncompromising conservative stance was altered. By the time Stanford Smith took charge in 1960, the ANPA was a typical trade association with a progressive flair. Membership rose to 1,200 dailies.

The publishers long had supported a mechanical department devoted to the study of improvements in the printing processes. After World War II they felt the growing pressures of a "cold type revolution" brought about by the introduction of the photographic process into printing. In 1947 a research director was named and funds were voted to establish a research center in Easton, Pennsylvania, which formally opened in 1951. It was incorporated as the ANPA Research Institute in 1954, with its own board of publisher-directors. A 1958 evaluation by a six-man committee headed by Otto A. Silha of the *Minneapolis Star* and *Tribune* gave the Institute new direction, toward experimental work in utilizing the fruits of technological innovations in printing newspapers. An annual mechanical conference for members emphasized photocomposition, offset printing, run-of-paper color printing, computerized typesetting and editing, and other advances.

The establishment of a Newspaper Information Service in 1960 was another step forward. Through it ANPA headquarters could work with educators, students, other media, and the public. Objectives included promotion of journalism as a career; giving of awards to college and high school newspaper staffs; publication of newsletters, brochures, and booklets; and interpretation of the newspaper industry. Already ANPA had worked with other media organizations to support accreditation of journalism schools and departments.

ANPA's biggest legislative victory was the passage of the Newspaper Preservation Act, after three years of debate in the Congress. The act exempted from antitrust suits the joint printing operations of 44 newspapers in 22 cities and overturned a Supreme Court decision dissolving a pooled business operation in Tucson. Opponents said the new law, signed by President Nixon in 1970, would perpetuate the status quo.

ASNE, NAB, AND CODES OF CONDUCT

The American Society of Newspaper Editors was organized in 1922, under the leadership of Casper S. Yost of the *St. Louis Globe-Democrat,* to fill a long-felt need. As the group's constitution pointed out, "Although the art of journalism has flourished in America for more than two hundred years, the editors of the greater American newspapers have not hitherto banded themselves together in association for the consideration of their common problems and the promotion of their professional ideals." State and regional newspaper associations had considered news and editorial problems, but the American Newspaper Publishers Association had virtually excluded all but business topics from its agendas.

Membership in the ASNE was limited to editors in chief, editorial page editors, and managing editors of dailies published in cities of more than 100,000 population, a figure soon reduced to 50,000. Limited numbers of editors of smaller dailies were admitted to membership in later years.

Early meetings of the society were enlivened by a bitter dispute over the power of the group to expel a member, Fred G. Bonfils of the *Denver Post,* who stood accused of blackmailing oil millionaire Harry Sinclair in connection with the Teapot Dome scandal. At one point a vote of expulsion was taken, but the action was rescinded and the Denver editor was permitted to resign. Later the ASNE clarified its power to expel a member for due cause, but the Bonfils incident made it clear that the group did not propose to serve as a policing organization. Willis J. Abbot of the *Christian Science Monitor* and Tom Wallace of the *Louisville Times* were leaders in the fight for a stern policy, but Yost and others held to a middle course.

A code of ethics, called the "Canons of Journalism," was presented to the first annual meeting in 1923. Chief author was H.J. Wright, founder of the *New York Globe.* Some of the key paragraphs read as follows:

The right of a newspaper to attract and hold readers is restricted by nothing but considerations of public welfare. The use a newspaper makes of the share of public attention it gains serves to determine its sense of responsibility, which it shares with every member of its staff. A journalist who uses his power for any selfish or otherwise unworthy purpose is faithless to a high trust.

Freedom of the press is to be guarded as a vital right of mankind. It is the unquestionable right to discuss whatever is not explicitly forbidden by law, including the wisdom of any restrictive statute.

Freedom from all obligations except that of fidelity to the public interest is vital.

Partisanship, in editorial comment which knowingly departs from the truth, does violence to the best spirit of American journalism; in the news columns it is subversive of a fundamental principle in the profession.

Annual meetings of the ASNE are held each April, usually in Washington. Proceedings are reported in a series of books, dating from 1923, titled *Problems of Journalism,* which offer in their pages some significant discussions of professional matters.[6] Lively debate is found in the monthly *ASNE Bulletin.*

Codes of conduct for the broadcasting industry were developed by its trade association, the National Association of Broadcasters. The NAB was founded in 1923 during a skirmish between the radio station owners and ASCAP over fees the latter insisted be paid for broadcasting music of ASCAP members. Paul Klugh was first NAB managing director. The role of the trade association expanded to include relationships with advertising and then, increasingly, its relationships with the Federal Communications Commission.

The NAB Code of Ethics and the NAB Standards of Commercial Practice were adopted in March 1929 as the first voluntarily-imposed regulations on broadcasters. More detailed documents, the NAB Radio Code and the NAB Television Code, were added. About half of all commercial radio and television stations subscribed to the codes. There were other major codes and statements, particularly those of the Radio-Television News Directors Association and the programming standards of the networks and many individual stations.

Headquarters of the NAB are in Washington, with a large staff for administration, legal problems, station services, broadcast management, government affairs, public relations, and research. The NAB Code Authority staff hears complaints concerning violations by those subscribing to the codes. There are also review boards for the Television Code and Radio Code.

NCEW, APME, AND RTNDA

Editorial-page editors and editorial writers who wanted a smaller and more vigorous "working" organization than the 450-member ASNE formed the National Conference of Editorial Writers in 1947. The idea came from a group attending an American Press Institute session at Columbia University[7] and was promoted by Leslie Moore of the *Worcester Telegram* and *Gazette,* Ralph Coghlan of the *St. Louis Post-Dispatch,* John H. Cline of the *Washington Star,* Robert H. Estabrook of the *Washington Post,* and Forrest W. Seymour of the *Des Moines Register* and *Tribune,* among others. Annual sessions were held beginning in 1947 that featured small-group critique panels in which members appraised the editorial-page efforts of their colleagues. A quarterly magazine, the *Masthead,* and convention proceedings were published. A code of principles was adopted in 1949 "to stimulate the conscience and the quality of the American editorial page."[8]

Another important national group, the Associated Press Managing Editors Association, was formed in 1931 by news executives who found the annual meetings of the ANPA and the Associated Press too little concerned with improvement of the news columns' content. The organizers in this case included Oliver O. Kuhn of the *Washington Star,* Roy Roberts of the *Kansas City Star,* Sevellon Brown of the *Providence Journal* and *Bulletin,* W.C. Stouffer of the *Roanoke World-News,* and Roy Dunlap of the *St. Paul Pioneer Press* and *Dispatch.* The AP news report was analyzed and criticized orally in annual meetings until 1947 when a printed report was prepared by a Continuing Study Committee. Although the studies of the different portions of the

Associated Press news report were penetrating enough to arouse replies from the AP management, they were made public as the *APME Red Book* beginning in 1948.[9] Setting the pattern for the Continuing Study reports were the first chairmen, William P. Steven of the *Minneapolis Tribune* and Lee Hills of the *Miami Herald*.

The equivalent newsmen's organization in broadcasting is the Radio-Television News Directors Association. It was founded in 1946 as the National Association of Radio News Directors. First leaders were John Hogan, WCSH, Portland, Maine; John Murphy, WCKY, Cincinnati; Sig Mickelson, WCCO, Minneapolis; Jack Shelley, WHO, Des Moines; and Edward Wallace, WTAM, Cleveland. Its publication is the *RTNDA Bulletin*. The group set broadcast news standards and worked closely with journalism schools.

OTHER PROFESSIONAL GROUPS

Other professional groups were concerned with varying aspects of journalistic problems: the National Newspaper Association, representing weeklies and some smaller dailies; the Magazine Publishers Association; the National Association of Educational Broadcasters; the National Press Photographers Association; the United Press International editors; and many regional organizations. Some schools of journalism joined with newsmen in sponsoring various professional conferences dealing with journalistic problems. Awards for outstanding achievement were inaugurated by Sigma Delta Chi, the professional journalism society begun in 1909 at DePauw University and expanded to include professional chapters and both men and women, under the name Society of Professional Journalists. Research about journalism was encouraged by annual awards of both Sigma Delta Chi and Kappa Tau Alpha, journalism scholastic society founded in 1910 at the University of Missouri. Theta Sigma Phi, women's journalism society founded in 1909 at the University of Washington, stimulated interest through its annual Matrix table gatherings; it became Women in Communications, Inc.

EDUCATION FOR JOURNALISM BEGINS

The ties between campus and city room were strengthened greatly in the second quarter of the twentieth century. The famous cartoon showing a city editor asking a young hopeful, "And what, may I ask, is a school of journalism?" no longer held true. It was likely that the city editor was a journalism school graduate also—or at least a college graduate with an appreciation of the necessity for sound educational training for newspapermen.

Talk about education for journalism began seriously after the Civil War, but little action resulted until the turn of the century. General Robert E. Lee, president of Washington College (later Washington and Lee University), attempted to establish training in printing in 1869, but the program languished, as did another effort at Cornell University in 1875. Kansas State College instruction in printing dates from 1873, and courses in history and materials of journalism were given at the University of Missouri from 1878 to 1884. The first definitely organized curriculum in journalism was offered at the University of Pennsylvania from 1893 to 1901 by Joseph French Johnson, a former financial editor of the *Chicago Tribune*. The University of Illinois organized the first four year curriculum in journalism in 1904 under the direction of Frank W. Scott. The first separate school of journalism, with newspaperman Walter Williams as dean, opened in 1908 at the University of Missouri.[10]

In this first period of journalism education, emphasis was placed on establishment of technical courses. But journalism teachers, often getting their starts in English departments, had to win academic recognition as well as the confidence of the newspaper profession. Their most successful early leader in this regard was Willard G. Bleyer, who began his journalism teaching at the University of Wisconsin in 1904. Bleyer advocated integration of journalism education with the social sciences and, through his development of this concept and his own journalism history research, established Wisconsin as a center for graduate study by future journalism teachers. Other early leaders were Eric W. Allen of the University of Oregon, H. F. Harrington of Northwestern University, Leon N. Flint of the University of Kansas, Arthur L. Stone of Montana State University, J. W. Piercy of Indiana University, Merle H. Thorpe of the University of Washington, Everett W. Smith of Stanford University, and Talcott Williams and John W. Cunliffe of Columbia University, the first two men to head the Pulitzer School of Journalism, opened in 1912 with a $2 million endowment from the *New York World* publisher.

JOURNALISM AS A SOCIAL INSTITUTION   The second phase of journalism education saw emphasis placed on the study of journalism history and of the press as a social institution, as well as a widening of instruction to areas other than that of the daily and weekly newspapers. Pioneer textbooks had been written by Bleyer, Harrington, James Melvin Lee of New York University, Grant M. Hyde of Wisconsin, and M. Lyle Spencer of Syracuse. In the early 1920s the books of Bleyer in journalism history and of Flint and Nelson Antrim Crawford of Kansas State College in newspaper ethics pointed the way toward integration of technical training with analysis of the social responsibilities of the journalist. Coming into importance were the American Association of Teachers of Journalism, founded in 1912, and the American Association of Schools and Departments of Journalism, established in 1917.

Other newspapermen than Pulitzer aided in the establishment of journalism schools. Second in size to the Pulitzer gift to Columbia University was the endowment fund provided in 1918 by William J. Murphy, publisher of the *Minneapolis Tribune,* for journalism education at the University of Minnesota. The fund's value by the 1970s was $800,000.* The owners of the *Chicago Tribune* established the Medill School of Journalism at Northwestern University in 1921 and continued to assist the school financially in subsequent years. State press associations and individual newspapermen played parts in the establishment of other schools and departments of journalism.

The 1920s saw the founding of the *Journalism Quarterly,* devoted to research studies in the field of mass communications. It began as the *Journalism Bulletin* in 1924, taking the title *Quarterly* in 1930 with Frank Luther Mott of the University of Iowa (later Missouri) as editor. His successors were Ralph D. Casey, Raymond B. Nixon, and Edwin Emery of the University of Minnesota, and Guido H. Stempel III of Ohio University. The educators successively founded *Journalism Educator, Journalism Monographs, Journalism Abstracts,* and *Journalism History.* Other research journals included the *Journal of Broadcasting* and the *Journal of Communication.*

JOURNALISM AS A SOCIAL SCIENCE   A third phase of journalism education was developing by the 1930s. Fuller integration of journalism education with the social sciences was the goal, and the leading schools and departments undertook research and teaching in the field of communications as a whole. Journalism students, it was recognized, should receive a broad liberal arts education, sound journalistic technical training, and an understanding of the social implications of their

---

*In 1977 John Cowles of the *Minneapolis Star* and *Tribune* established a $2 million endowment for journalism education at the University of Minnesota.

chosen profession. Northwestern University developed a five-year plan for professional training in 1938; the Pulitzer School at Columbia had restricted its year's course to holders of a bachelor's degree in 1935. Graduate level instruction was expanded at other institutions, along with research in mass communications. In 1944 the Minnesota School of Journalism set up a journalism research division, the first of its kind. Among early leaders in mass communications research based on the social and behavioral sciences were Chilton R. Bush of Stanford University, Ralph O. Nafziger of Minnesota (later at Wisconsin), Wilbur Schramm of Iowa (later at Illinois and Stanford), Paul F. Lazarsfeld of Columbia University's Bureau of Applied Social Research, and Douglas Waples of the University of Chicago.

MEDIA SUPPORT FOR EDUCATION   Closer ties between newspapermen and the schools were established during the 1930s. The idea of a joint committee that would include representatives of the principal newspaper associations and the schools and departments of journalism was suggested by Fred Fuller Shedd, editor of the *Philadelphia Bulletin* who had been instrumental in the founding of the department at Pennsylvania State College (later University). Journalism educators, led by Bleyer of Wisconsin, Allen of Oregon, and Frank L. Martin of Missouri, joined in the plan in 1931. The project lapsed during the depression years but was brought into full operation in 1939 through the efforts of Kenneth E. Olson of Northwestern University. The American Council on Education for Journalism was formed by journalism educators and five major newspaper organizations—the American Society of Newspaper Editors, the American Newspaper Publishers Association, the National Newspaper Association, the Inland Daily Press Association, and the Southern Newspaper Publishers Association. The professional associations in broadcasting, magazine publishing, advertising, business communication, and public relations later joined those and other newspaper groups in the council's work. The ACEJ established an accrediting program and approved studies in one or more areas of journalism at 40 schools and departments in the late 1940s. The number of accredited institutions increased to 65 by 1977.

In 1949 the American Association of Teachers of Journalism reorganized as the Association for Education in Journalism. Accepting coordinate roles within the AEJ structure were the American Association of Schools and Departments of Journalism (now composed of the accredited schools) and the American Society of Journalism School Administrators, founded in 1944.

Journalism schools in the 1970s were thus well established in the fields of teaching, research, and service. They had close ties with the profession and their scope of interests included daily and weekly newspapers, magazines, radio and television, photojournalism, advertising, the graphic arts, industrial editing, and public relations. The doctorate in mass communications was offered at more than a dozen universities in the fields of communication theory, mass communications history, law and social institutions, and international communication.

A million-dollar endowment left to Harvard University in 1936 by the widow of Lucius W. Nieman, founder of the *Milwaukee Journal,* was used for a different type of educational opportunity. The Nieman Foundation, beginning in 1937, annually selected a dozen highly qualified working newspapermen for a year of study at Harvard as Nieman Fellows, on leave from their newspapers or press associations. Louis M. Lyons, first curator of the foundation, established a thoughtful quarterly magazine, *Nieman Reports,* in 1947.

EFFORTS TO IMPROVE:
STUDIES OF THE PRESS

Other attempts to study the responsibilities and the character of the American press were made in the years after World War II. Magazine publisher Henry R. Luce financed an important private study by the Commission on Freedom of the Press. The commission was headed by Chancellor Robert M. Hutchins of the University of Chicago and was composed chiefly of social science professors outside the field of journalism. Its summary report, *A Free and Responsible Press* (1947), covered newspapers, radio, motion pictures, magazines, and books, and consisted of a general statement of principles. The commission itself conducted only a limited research program in the making of its report, but it sponsored the publication of a number of books, including Zechariah Chafee, Jr.'s *Government and Mass Communications,* William E. Hocking's *Freedom of the Press,* and Llewellyn White's *The American Radio.*

The presidential elections of 1948 and 1952 brought flurries of activity in the analysis of press behavior in relation to public questions. *Editor & Publisher,* trade journal for the daily newspapers, sponsored a meeting in March 1949 of a panel on the press, composed of ten newspapermen and educators. The panel suggested studies for press self-improvement, but an ASNE committee appointed to consider the problem came to no specific conclusions. Before the 1956 election journalism educators and Sigma Delta Chi urged a major study of press election coverage, but a group of hesitant publishers and editors vetoed action. However, effective voices were raised within the profession and among educators in analysis of media performance, and major research studies resulted.

EFFORTS TO IMPROVE:
PRESS COUNCILS

The example of the successful British Press Council, established in 1953 to hear complaints against newspapers under rules carefully drawn to protect the rights of both editors and citizens, led to movements to create press councils in the United States. The first to appear were local press councils organized in the late 1960s under the auspices of the Newspaper Guild's Mellett Fund.

One effort was made on the West Coast under the direction of William L. Rivers and his associates from Stanford University; another in Sparta and Cairo, Illinois, by Kenneth Starck and others from Southern Illinois University. A media-black council, to develop a better understanding between media executives and the black community, was directed by Lawrence Schneider of the University of Washington for 19 months in Seattle. In 1971, the first statewide press council was established in Minnesota through the efforts of the Minnesota Newspaper Association, the Newspaper Guild, Sigma Delta Chi, other media leaders, and public officials. The council membership was divided between representatives of the media and the public, under the chairmanship of a state supreme court judge. The same year Hawaii's council was formed. The two state councils and local ones in Littleton, Colorado, and Peoria, Illinois, survived in 1977.

Efforts to establish a national press council bore fruit in 1973 with the establishment of the National News Council. A task force supported by the Twentieth Century Fund set as its goals "to examine and report on complaints concerning the accuracy and fairness of news reporting in the United States, as well as to initiate studies and report on issues involving the freedom of the press." At first shunned by major media leaders, the National News Council gained support through its handling of issues presented to it for consideration of ten public members and eight professional members. William B. Arthur was executive director, and Norman E. Isaacs chairman.

Beginning in 1977 its reports were printed in the *Columbia Journalism Review,* published by Columbia University's journalism school.

EFFORTS TO IMPROVE: Another phenomenon was the journalism review. Prior to
JOURNALISM REVIEWS 1968 only three existed: the *Montana Journalism Review* (1958), *Columbia Journalism Review* (1961), and *Seminar,* a review of sorts published by Copley Newspapers (1966). The *Chicago Journalism Review* (1968–75) inspired a number of local and journalism department reviews but of the approximately 40 established between 1968 and 1976, fewer than a dozen survived in 1977, including the Columbia and Montana reviews; *MORE,* a national review published in New York; *Accuracy in Media* (AIM), a conservative newsletter; *Media Report to Women; feed/back,* published in San Francisco; the *St. Louis Journalism Review;* the *Twin Cities Journalism Review; Pretentious Idea* in Tucson; and *Lexington Media Review* (Kentucky).[11] *Washington Journalism Review* appeared in 1977.

The *Chicago Journalism Review* appeared in the wake of the riots at the time of the 1968 Democratic convention. Edited by Ron Dorfman, the monthly afforded an aggressive criticism of the city's press and a forum for issues of press criticism and self-improvement among young newsmen. It inspired not only local imitators but also the springing up of informal "reporter power" groups in city rooms, where young staff members met to seek improvements in their professional contributions. In some cities regular meetings of journalists and management resulted. The *Columbia Journalism Review* and *MORE* kept the spirit of self-criticism alive.

EFFORTS TO IMPROVE: Criticism of newspapers' technical performance has taken
PRINTING TECHNOLOGY two forms: lack of sufficient research about their product and audience and failure to keep pace in technological progress. Both criticisms are valid, but recent efforts to meet them should be recognized. Since the 1930s newspapermen—as well as magazine, broadcasting, and advertising men—have paid ever-increasing attention to audience and motivational research, readership and listenership studies, readability formulas, and design and layout.

In technological progress, the major result has been to produce a "cold type" revolution, involving the introduction of photography into the printing process. Such machines of the 1950s as the Fotosetter, Linofilm, and Photon produced words on film and transferred them directly to a printing plate. Widely used in advertisement composition, they proceeded to make steady inroads on "hot metal" typesetting.

Offset printing, based on the age-old lithography process, avoids both typesetting and photoengraving by use of pasteups photographed onto flexible printing plates. The *Opelousas Daily World* in Louisiana, begun in 1939, was the first successful daily to print by offset. The Phoenix *Arizona Journal,* founded in 1962 as a rival to the jointly owned *Arizona Republic* and *Gazette,* was the first attempt at producing an offset daily in a metropolitan competitive situation. It died in 1964, but the *Oklahoma Journal* founded that year was still printing by offset in 1977 against two established rivals. *Publishers' Auxiliary* reported in 1975 that about 1,000 of 1,750 dailies and 88 percent of weeklies were printing by offset, using 23 different models of web offset newspaper presses.

But a far greater electronic revolution was underway in printing. By 1970 newspapers were using computers to set type, to store factual information, and to sort out the day's news and abstract it at the central news desks of the press associations. As electronic tube typesetting became feasible, editors attended seminars to learn the language of the "new technology" and how to change headlines with a light pencil. In the new system, reporters typed at video display terminals on electronic keyboards that reproduced their stories on small video screens. A story was then stored in a computer's memory bank until an editor called it up on his or her video screen for review and possible changes. The final version went to a computer-run composing room. Newspapers still used their expensive printing presses by conversion to the DiLitho system, but the long rows of Linotypes and other typesetting machines were a thing of the past. By 1977, the industry reported, 94 percent of dailies had converted from hot type to photo composition, 65 percent used computers, and 57 percent used video display terminals.[12]

Improvements in digital newspaper page transmission systems, as used by the *Wall Street Journal* and other publishers, pointed the way toward unlimited satellite-printing of a publication at different points inside one country or, indeed, throughout the world. Truly national or international newspapers could emerge. Another predicted development for printing out in the home through facsimile or electrostatic technique seemed less likely to be in the newspaper's immediate future, for cost reasons if nothing else. Delivering newspapers on film for exposure on an electronic video device and subsequent printout might be more likely as the video revolution progresses in the world of electronics. At the same time, some observers worried about the effects of new technology on the number and types of media jobs and whether or not this would lead to a cheapening of the final product.

LANDMARK LEGAL DECISIONS: THE FIRST AMENDMENT

Significant episodes involving freedom of the press and the right of the people to know became a part of the record beginning in the 1930s. There were landmark cases in which newspapers appealed to the courts to uphold the historic right under the First Amendment to freedom of expression without prior restraint and without punitive action by government or courts.

An obscure Minnesota publisher provided a case in which the Supreme Court, in 1931 for the first time, applied the freedom of the press guarantees of the First Amendment against the states through the due process clause of the Fourteenth Amendment. The case of *Near* v. *Minnesota* thus served as a turning point in the battle to hold states as strictly accountable for invasions of liberty as the federal government. What was known as the Minnesota "gag law" of 1925, permitting the suppression of malicious and scandalous publications, had been applied by a court to the *Saturday Press* of Minneapolis in order to stop its smear attacks on public officials. Calling the law a threat to all newspapers, no matter how unworthy the *Saturday Press* might be, chairman Robert R. McCormick of the ANPA committee on freedom of the press retained counsel to carry the case to the Supreme Court. There Chief Justice Hughes, speaking for the majority in a 5-4 decision, held the Minnesota law unconstitutional because it permitted prior restraint on publication.[13] Suppression, the court said, was a greater danger than an irresponsible attack on public officials, who in any event had proper recourse through libel action.

Huey Long, the Louisiana political boss, provided the next major case in 1934. The Long machine obtained passage by the state legislature of a special 2 percent tax on the gross advertising income of Louisiana papers with a circulation of 20,000 or more. Twelve of the 13 papers affected were opposed to the Long regime. They appealed to the courts, again with the assistance of Colonel McCormick's ANPA committee, and in 1936 the Supreme Court found the punitive tax unconstitutional. Justice Sutherland wrote a unanimous decision, holding that Long's bill was "a deliberate and calculated device . . . to limit the circulation of information to which the public is entitled by virtue of the constitutional guarantees.''[14]

Although the press may not be singled out for discriminatory taxation, it is subject to taxes and other government regulation of general applicability. The Supreme Court in *Associated Press* v. *NLRB*[15] said ''the publisher of a newspaper has no special immunity from the application of general laws,'' thus defining the limits of First Amendment protection the press can expect from government regulation of business.

In another case determined partly on the basis of this doctrine, the Supreme Court in *Branzburg* v. *Hayes* ruled that reporters had the same obligation as other citizens to respond to legitimate grand jury subpoenas and answer questions relevant to an investigation into the commission of a crime. Three reporters had refused to testify about information they had received in confidence, but the Court said the ''First Amendment does not invalidate every incidental burdening of the press that may result from the enforcement of civil or criminal statutes of general applicability.''[16] At least 25 states have passed shield laws allowing reporters to protect the confidentiality of their sources, but courts since *Branzburg* have not lightly granted this protection, especially when security of the judicial process was at stake.*

Newspapers do have latitude in commenting on judges' activities, but they often have had to appeal to higher courts for relief after being held in contempt by lower courts. A landmark case in this area was decided by the Supreme Court in 1941. This was *Bridges* v. *California,*[17] a companion case to another involving the *Los Angeles Times*. Harry Bridges, the longshoreman labor leader, had been cited for contempt because newspapers had published the text of a telegram he had sent the Labor Department threatening to call a strike if a court decision went against him. The *Times* was cited for publishing editorials deemed threatening by a court. The California Bar Association asked the Supreme Court to declare the two contempt citations unconstitutional. This the court did by applying the sanctions of the First Amendment against the state court under the due process clause of the Fourteenth Amendment and by utilizing the clear and present danger test first applied in the Schenck case. Newspapers henceforth in theory could comment on a court action not yet closed, without fear of punishment, unless a judge could hold that press comment created so great and immediate a danger that his court could not continue to function. But state courts continued to resist this trend in thinking, and hard battles were fought by the *Miami Herald* and the *Corpus Christi Caller-Times* in 1946 and 1947 to avoid the penalties of contempt charges.[18]

PRIOR RESTRAINT:
THE PENTAGON
PAPERS CASE

The United States government attempted in June 1971 to impose prior restraint on American newspapers. And for 15 days it successfully stopped one of the country's most influential dailies from publishing a vital news story. For those 15 days the clock was turned back to the time of Henry VIII, who in 1534 imposed prior restraint on the English press. Prior restraint ended in England in 1694 and in the colonies in 1721, to be temporarily revived exactly 250 years later.

That the Supreme Court came to the rescue of press freedom and the First Amendment guarantee on June 30, by vacating its own temporary stay order of June 25

---

*The Branzburg ruling also included *In re Pappas* and *U.S.* v. *Caldwell*. Paul Branzburg of the *Louisville Courier-Journal* refused to tell a grand jury about drug law violations he had observed. Earl Caldwell of the *New York Times* and Paul Pappas, a Massachusetts television reporter, refused to give grand juries information about Black Panther members they had interviewed.

and earlier lower court orders, afforded some reassurance. But the fact that President Nixon had ever instructed Attorney General John Mitchell to go to court to seek imposition of a prior restraint on publication did great damage to the concept of liberty of the press so painstakingly developed through historical evolution and legal decisions since 1694. In the history of the Republic, no other president had so acted.

In the judgment of legal scholars, the Pentagon Papers case left little legal residue and will be remembered far longer for its political implications than for its legal stature.[19] In that respect it perhaps paralleled the Zenger case of 1735; there was no guarantee after Zenger's acquittal that another editor would not be charged in another government effort to muzzle the press—but it never seemed politically feasible for colonial administrators to try in the same manner. Possibly the next president faced with circumstances similar to those involved in the Pentagon Papers case will seek a postpublication criminal prosecution, if one seems warranted, rather than attempt again to impose prior restraint on publication. In that sense, the case is worth detailed examination.

Sometime in March 1971, the *New York Times* came into possession of a 47-volume study entitled "History of the U.S. Decision-Making Process on Vietnam Policy," compiled for the Pentagon at the order of former Secretary McNamara. Many copies of the study were circulating. Its contents were historical and nonmilitary in character but highly explosive in terms of political and diplomatic interest. All documents were classified "Top Secret" under a 1953 executive order. *Times* correspondent Neil Sheehan, who had represented UPI in the original Saigon press corps and who in 1971 covered the Pentagon, was a key figure in the development of the Pentagon Papers series for the paper. Managing editor Abe Rosenthal assigned several leading *Times* staffers to weeks of painstaking work in a hotel room hideaway. June 13 the *Times* printed the first installment.

Attorney General Mitchell asked the *Times* to stop the series; it refused. The government then went to a federal district judge just appointed by President Nixon and serving the first day on his new bench with its unprecedented prior restraint order request. Judge Murray Gurfein issued a temporary restraining order June 15, forcing the *Times* to stop after the third installment. June 19 Judge Gurfein refused to grant a permanent restraining order, saying the government had failed to prove its case other than to plead a "general framework of embarrassment." But he let the temporary order stand. June 23 the U.S. Court of Appeals in New York reversed Gurfein's decision. In the meantime, the *Washington Post* had started a series of its own and had won a clear-cut victory when Judge Gerhard A. Gesell ruled the government could not "impose a prior restraint on essentially historical data." The U.S. Court of Appeals for the District of Columbia upheld Gesell and the two cases reached the U.S. Supreme Court June 25. There, with Justices Black, Douglas, Brennan, and Marshall dissenting, the court voted 5–4 to hear testimony and continue the temporary order of prior restraint.

At this point the case collapsed as a legal landmark. The newspaper attorneys, shaken by the adverse 5–4 vote of the Supreme Court continuing a temporary prior restraint, refused to gamble on a plea that the First Amendment prohibited prior restraint under any and all circumstances. Instead, they preferred to win the immediate

---

In another action, California state courts and the U.S. Supreme Court ruled against reporter William Farr of the *Los Angeles Herald-Examiner* (later *Los Angeles Times*) in a five-year battle with a judge who jailed Farr 46 days for contempt after he refused to disclose case-related information. Justice Douglas freed Farr, and his rejailing was forbidden.

case on the grounds the government could not prove that national security was involved. This they did, on a 6–3 *per curiam* decision.[20] It was based on *Near* v. *Minnesota* and two more recent press freedom decisions. There were then nine individual decisions, with Justices Black and Douglas, both of whom have since left the Court, arguing that freedom of the press is absolute; Justices Brennan and Stewart declaring the government had not proved its case; Justice Marshall rejecting the contention the president had inherent power to declare a document nonpublishable in the national interest; Justice White joining the majority but inviting a criminal prosecution of the newspapermen; Chief Justice Burger and Justice Blackmun objecting to the haste shown in the case and requesting an exhaustive review of the documents; and Justice Harlan indicating he believed the president should have the power to foreclose publication of any document whose disclosure would in his judgment be harmful.

The anonymous writer of the *per curiam* decision did cite *Near* v. *Minnesota,* the landmark case of 1931 defending liberty of the press and extending the protection of the First Amendment against acts of Congress to include a ban on state action. Also cited were two quotations:

Any system of prior restraints of expression comes to this court bearing a heavy presumption against its constitutional validity.[21]

The Government thus carries a heavy burden of showing justification for the enforcement of such a restraint.[22]

The first of these quotations indicates strongly that the Supreme Court's majority stood by the landmark case of *Near* v. *Minnesota* and its basic concepts. The second reminds society that there is a loophole in the legal concept of liberty of the press—a loophole that at least Justice Harlan would have allowed the president to use unrestrainedly.

Chief Justice Hughes, in giving the 5–4 verdict in the 1931 *Near* case, had quoted from Blackstone on prior restraint and postpublication punishment:

The liberty of the press is indeed essential to the nature of a free state; but this consists in laying no *previous* restraints upon publications, and not in freedom from censure for criminal matter when published. Every freeman has an undoubted right to lay what sentiments he pleases before the public; to forbid this is to destroy the freedom of the press; but if he publishes what is improper, mischievous or illegal, he must take the consequences of his own temerity.

Hughes went on to include a dicta, or observation, that weakened the case for absolute protection against prior restraint:

The objection has also been made that the principle as to immunity from previous restraint is stated too broadly, if every such restraint is deemed to be prohibited. That is undoubtedly true; the protection even as to previous restraint is not absolutely unlimited. But the limitation has been recognized only in exceptional cases.

The Chief Justice then cited examples of military secrets, overthrow of the government, and obscenity as areas where prior restraint might apply. But he drew the line, in the following passage from *Near,* on the kind of situation the Pentagon Papers case represented—disclosure of activities of public officers deemed by many citizens to be censurable:

The exceptional nature of its limitations places in a strong light the general conception that liberty of the press, historically considered and taken up in the Federal Constitution, has meant, principally although not exclusively, immunity from previous restraints or censorship. The conception of the liberty of the press in this country had broadened with the exigencies of the colonial period and with the efforts to secure freedom from oppressive administration. That liberty was especially cherished for the immunity it afforded from previous restraint of the publication of censure of public officers and charges of official misconduct.

The question of postpublication punishment was raised in the Pentagon Papers case by Justice White and also by Chief Justice Burger, who chastised the *Times* and *Post* for not turning over the papers to the government. Here the freedom of speech cases would apply, involving the concept of "clear and present danger" evolved by Justices Holmes and Brandeis and the opposing "balancing" theory. The landmark cases include four stemming from the World War I period "red scare" and one from the post-World War II anti-Communist period.

Justice Holmes first advanced the theory that punishment be limited to political expression that constituted a clear and present danger to the governmental action at issue in the 1919 case of Schenck, a Socialist who issued a pamphlet urging resistance to the draft. Even so, Holmes concurred in upholding the conviction under the Espionage Act. In the case of Abrams, who issued pamphlets opposing an expeditionary force being sent to the Soviet Union in 1918, Holmes dissented. In this dissent, Holmes talked of the "competition of the market" of ideas.[23] In the 1925 case of Gitlow, convicted under a New York state criminal anarchy law of issuing Socialist manifestoes, the majority advanced the theory of balancing by the courts of the competing private and public interests represented in First Amendment cases. Brandeis and Holmes dissented.[24] *Gitlow* forecast extension of First Amendment protection to state action through the Fourteenth Amendment, which was applied in the *Near* v. *Minnesota* case six years later. In 1927, while concurring in the conviction of Anita Whitney under California law outlawing the Communist party, Brandeis brilliantly restated the clear and present danger theory.[25] Cold comfort, perhaps, to the convicted that progressive legal theory was being advanced. In the 1951 case of Dennis, convicted of conspiracy under the Smith Act, the majority used the clear and present danger argument to convict Communist party members, citing the world tensions of 1948.[26] Whatever the outcomes, such postpublication trials were preferable to prior restraint mandates, for Schenck and his successors at least had their say.

A NEW "PUBLIC LAW OF LIBEL"

The historic law providing citizens recourse against defamation of character in the press always provided for fair comment on, and criticism of, those who were in the public eye when they became involved in the news. But in the 1960s the Supreme Court so clarified and extended the media's protections against libel that a new theory emerged, called the "public law of libel." Under this theory, public officials and public figures cannot recover for libel unless they can prove deliberate lying or extreme recklessness in publishing without ascertaining truth.[27]

The landmark case was *New York Times Co.* v. *Sullivan,* decided in 1964. The *Times* had published an advertisement in 1960 protesting police actions in Montgomery, Alabama, against followers of Rev. Martin Luther King, Jr. Sullivan, a police commissioner, sued for libel and was awarded $500,000 damages in a state court. Reversing the judgment, the Supreme Court held that errors contained in the advertisement were not malicious and that the First Amendment protects "uninhibited, robust and wide-open" debate of public issues without any test of truth.[28]

In 1967 the Supreme Court extended this theory to cover "public figures" as well as "public officials" but drew a line concerning recklessness in not following professional precautions in checking truth when time permits. The Court reversed a $500,000 judgment a right-wing spokesman, General Edwin A. Walker, had obtained against the Associated Press, ruling that Walker was a public figure subject to criticism. But it upheld a $460,000 judgment given University of Georgia football coach Wallace Butts for a story in the *Saturday Evening Post* accusing Butts of throwing games. The court said handling of the story "involved highly unreasonable conduct constituting an extreme departure from the standards of investigation and reporting ordinarily adhered to by responsible publishers."[29]

In *Time Inc.* v. *Hill* in 1967, the Court restricted the theory of right of privacy in favor of the theory of public law of libel by ruling newsworthy persons may not seek damages for invasion of privacy without proving deliberately false publication.[30] The Supreme Court in a 1974 case sustained an invasion of privacy judgment against an Ohio newspaper in which the plaintiffs had been placed in a "false light," but in 1975 the Court rejected an invasion of privacy suit against an Atlanta radio station that had broadcast, contrary to state law, the name of a rape victim who had been identified in open court.[31]

And in 1971, the Supreme Court, which had "buried the common law crime of seditious libel" in *Sullivan,* extended its "actual malice" requirement from public officials and public persons to include even private individuals who had been projected into the public interest area. The case, *Rosenbloom* v. *Metromedia,* involved a broadcaster's references to a book dealer's "obscene" literature.[32]

By a 5–4 majority in 1974, however, the Court held in *Gertz* v. *Robert Welch, Inc.* that private citizens, even if involved in events of public interest, were entitled to recover damages without having to prove the *New York Times* malice test, but only if they could prove actual damages. The *Times* malice rule still applied to a plaintiff who sought punitive damages. The range of the public law of libel appeared to be lessening.*

OBSCENITY AND CENSORSHIP   The Post Office Department, with its power to exclude publications from the mails under certain conditions, also has at times been a threat to freedom of the press. Over the years, court decisions, administrative actions, and the sweeping use of the postmaster's power during World War I to throw Socialist publications out of the mails built up a spirit of censorship in the Post Office. Matters came to a head in 1943 when the postmaster general proposed to withdraw use of the second-class mailing rate from *Esquire* magazine. The second-class rate, it was contended, was a privilege the government could withdraw if the publication using it was not making a "special contribution to the public welfare." The Post Office thought *Esquire* was not worthy of the use of the second-class rate. The magazine's publishers, who were faced with paying a half-million-dollars a year in additional postal charges, carried the case to the Supreme Court. There *Esquire* was upheld, with Justice Douglas commenting, "But to withdraw the second-class rate from this publication today because its contents seemed to one official not good for the

---

Gertz v. *Robert Welch, Inc.,* 418 U.S. 323 (1974). In 1976 the court, in *Time Inc.* v. *Firestone,* narrowed its definition of "public figures" to only those who have roles to play in the resolution of public issues, while giving a prominent socialite libel damages against *Time.*

public would sanction withdrawal of the second-class rate tomorrow from another periodical whose social or economic views seemed harmful to another official."[33] The decision put the Post Office Department back into its normal role of excluding publications for reasons of obscenity.

It was not an easy task to determine what was obscene, however, and society's standards on that subject, as they affected newspapers, magazines, and films, were to change dramatically in the 1960s and 1970s. This was particularly true in the areas of four-letter words and nudity. But the Supreme Court was slow to find clear-cut guides. A landmark case came in 1957 with *Roth* v. *United States*. Roth, who sold distasteful material, had been convicted under the federal obscenity statute. The court upheld his conviction but set a new standard for testing obscenity: "Whether to the average person, applying contemporary community standards, the dominant theme of the material taken as a whole appeals to prurient interests."[34] To this the court in later decisions added a test of "redeeming social importance"; if this were present, the law need not apply. Under this interpretation, *Fanny Hill* was cleared. But Ralph Ginzburg, publisher of *Eros,* was not. The court ruled he had flaunted this test and had exploited erotic materials solely on prurient appeal.[35] How to define these terms remained a puzzle.

A 5–4 majority of the Supreme Court revised the *Roth* standard in *Miller* v. *California,* a 1973 case.[36] The Court held that to be judged obscene the work only must lack "serious literary, artistic, political or scientific value" and added that the contemporary community standards against which the jury is to measure prurient appeal are to be the standards of the state or local community. This ruling leaving standards of taste to individual communities posed serious problems for products distributed nationwide for audiences of diverse sophistication, and the courts were left grappling with the problem of how to define these terms.*

PUBLIC ACCESS TO THE MEDIA

The concept of "fairness," involving right of access to the broadcast media by persons or ideas, has already been discussed in chapter 23. The theory of a public right of access to the print media was advanced by law professor Jerome A. Barron in a 1967 *Harvard Law Review* article that envisioned a two-dimensional First Amendment that not only forbade the inhibiting of expression by the government but also, in some circumstances, mandated government affirmative action to provide for public access to the media.[37] Barron later saw the *Red Lion* decision as a media case, not just a broadcast case, and unsuccessfully tried to have a right of access rider attached to the Newspaper Preservation Act.[38]

Barron's concept was unanimously rejected by the Supreme Court in a constitutional test of a 1913 Florida law granting a political candidate the right to equal space to reply to criticism and attacks on his record by a newspaper. Chief Justice Burger ruled for the Court in the 1974 *Tornillo* case that mandatory access was unconstitutional:

A responsible press is an undoubtedly desirable goal, but press responsibility is not mandated by the Constitution and like many other virtues it cannot be legislated.[39]

*Two 1977 cases involved Larry C. Flynt, editor and publisher of *Hustler,* convicted in an Ohio city other than where he published under the community standards concept and an Illinois storekeeper whose conviction was accepted for review by the Supreme Court in a case hinging on the *Miller* decision. Flynt had wide media support for an eventual Supreme Court appeal.

Media spokesmen, while agreeing efforts should be made to open more time and white space to individuals, minority groups, unpopular ideas, and simply nonconsensus thinking, quail at the idea of compulsory acceptance of everything offered a station, newspaper, or magazine.

ECONOMIC THREATS TO FREEDOM   Freedom of the press can of course be jeopardized by a newspaper publisher. This was found true by the Supreme Court in the case of the *Lorain Journal,* an Ohio daily. When a radio station was established in the nearby town of Elyria in 1948, the *Journal's* management refused to carry the advertising of any merchant who also bought time on the radio station. The radio station obtained an injunction against the newspaper, under the antitrust laws, that the *Journal* insisted was unconstitutional. But the Supreme Court held that the First Amendment was not intended to protect monopolistic practices that would destroy a competing medium and in a unanimous decision forced the *Journal* to recant.[40]

This was a clear-cut case involving the use of boycott to destroy a competitor. Less clear-cut was the government's subsequent contention that the selling of advertising in jointly owned morning and evening papers under a unit rate plan also constituted an illegal action. A complaint brought by the *New Orleans Item* against the jointly owned *Times-Picayune* and *States* reached the Supreme Court in 1953. The court held, in a 5–4 decision, that the *Times-Picayune* and *States* were not violating the antitrust laws, but the decision was limited to the New Orleans situation alone.[41] The *Item* sold out to its rivals in 1958.

The government's next case was stronger. In 1955 it obtained a jury conviction of the *Kansas City Star* and its advertising manager on charges of monopolizing dissemination of news and advertising in the Kansas City area. The *Star,* together with its morning edition, the *Times,* and its broadcasting stations, WDAF and WDAF-TV, accounted for 85 percent of mass media advertising income in the metropolitan area. The government charged that forced and tied-in sales of advertising and of newspaper subscriptions had brought about the death of the competing *Journal-Post* in 1942. The Supreme Court declined to review the case in 1957, and the *Star* agreed to end its combination sales and to sell the two stations, which in both instances had been pioneering efforts.[42] The *Wichita Eagle's* advertising and circulation price policies for morning, evening, and Sunday editions were brought under regulation in a 1959 antitrust suit, but the action did not save the rival *Beacon* from being forced to sell out in 1960.

FREE PRESS, FAIR TRIAL   The weighing of the rights of a free press and its readers against the rights of an accused to a fair trial became a major problem of the 1960s. In this case, the courts clearly had their way, and in the end the press generally agreed that the placing of restrictions on reporters, photographers, and broadcasters was warranted—provided that they stemmed from cooperative agreements and not from judicial fiat.

Early action centered about the presence of photographers in the courtroom. The American Society of Newspaper Editors, the National Press Photographers Association, and the National Association of Broadcasters waged a battle through the 1950s to gain access to courtrooms for newspaper and television photographers. Their argument that the photographers need not be interrupting the trials had merit, for pictures could be made without noise or light. But lawyers said the publicity stemming from photographs served to frighten witnesses and accused persons, affected juries, and offended the judicial feeling. In 1959 the American Bar Association did agree to review its Canon 35 regulating such activity in the courtroom. But no action resulted and admission of cameras remained a local decision of a judge.

Other events meanwhile vastly broadened the "free press, fair trial" debate. The assassination of President Kennedy and the haphazard conditions surrounding the killing of the accused by Jack Ruby in a press-filled area brought a plea for reform from the Warren Commission. When a Texas judge permitted television cameras into the trial of financier Billy Sol Estes, the Supreme Court reversed his conviction.[43] That 1965 decision was followed by one in 1966 ruling that Dr. Sam Sheppard had been deprived of a fair trial in Cleveland on a charge of murdering his wife because the trial judge failed to protect him from massive prejudicial "trial by newspaper" before and during his prosecution.[44]

The Reardon Report of the American Bar Association came out of the debate. Issued in October 1966 by a ten-man committee of lawyers and judges headed by Justice Paul C. Reardon of Massachusetts, the report favored putting the responsibility on judges to curtail pretrial publicity generated either by the prosecution or the defense. The commission recommended the withholding of such information as the prior criminal record of the accused, existence of a confession, names of prospective witnesses, speculation on a possible plea, and interviews or photographs obtained without the consent of the accused. The American Bar Association adopted the Reardon Report in 1968, leaving the spelling out of specific provisions to negotiations with media representatives. By the fall of 1969 the press-bar committees of the Bar and the ASNE had found common ground for the imposition of the "fair trial" provisions without endangering the "free press." The media, in major trials of the late 1960s and 1970s, resorted to using artists to make sketches of courtroom scenes for both print and television use, thus reverting to the artists' skills of the late nineteenth century in catching the drama of an event.

Reporters were placed in the position of having either to face contempt charges or obey a judicial ruling, even if unconstitutional, after the ruling in a 1972 Louisiana case, *United States* v. *Dickenson*.[45] A judge ordered the press not to report a hearing held in open court, and two reporters who wrote stories despite the warning were then convicted of contempt. The Appeals Court said the order was unconstitutional, but upheld the conviction, saying the reporters should have obeyed the order and appealed it. The Supreme Court declined to review the case, letting the decision stand.

A Nebraska murder trial in 1976 brought another press–bar confrontation when the trial judge entered an order that, as modified by the state supreme court, restrained the news media from reporting (1) the existence of any confession or admissions made by the defendant to law enforcement officers or third parties, except members of the press, (2) the substance of these confessions or statements, and (3) other facts "strongly implicative" of the defendant. The order, designed to follow *Sheppard* guidelines concerning pretrial publicity, expired when the jury was impaneled.

Chief Justice Burger, speaking for the Supreme Court, struck down this order, commenting that the media can report evidence presented at an open preliminary hearing and also that the prohibition on "implicative" information was "too vague and too broad" to survive scrutiny given restraints on First Amendment rights. The press victory was somewhat diluted in that the Supreme Court denied a motion to expedite the appeal, which was not heard until it was moot, and by wording of the opinion that did not preclude future "gag" orders.

"We need not rule out the possibility of showing the kind of threat to fair trial rights that would possess the requisite degree of certainty to justify restraint," Burger wrote, but "the barriers to prior restraint remain high and the presumption against its use remains intact."[46]

THE RIGHT TO KNOW   The battles for freedom to print and freedom to criticize, carried on in the courtrooms, were important ones. But just as important were the fights put up for the right to have access to the news—for the right to publish news is worthless if the sources of information have been dried up.

Freedom of information campaigns were carried on beginning in the late 1940s by the American Society of Newspaper Editors, the Associated Press Managing Editors Association, the Radio-Television News Directors Association, and Sigma Delta Chi, professional journalism society. Through their efforts, and those of others, all but five states by 1970 had some sort of laws requiring open public records and open meetings for conduct of public business. Leaders of the fight included James S. Pope, *Louisville Courier-Journal;* J. R. Wiggins, *Washington Post;* V. M. Newton, Jr., *Tampa Tribune;* and Harold L. Cross, ASNE legal counsel.

Creation of the House Subcommittee on Government Information in 1955, headed by Congressman John E. Moss of California, brought a campaign against secrecy at the federal level. Aided by the newsmen's groups, the Moss committee won revision of the 1789 "housekeeping statute" in 1958 to stop its use in denying access to records. It also won some ground in opposing the claim of executive privilege by the president and his subordinates and reported success in 95 of 173 cases exposing undue federal censorship of information during 1958–60. Controversy between the Kennedy administration and the press flared up during the Cuban crisis and gave impetus to an effort to adopt the Freedom of Information bill, which was passed and signed by President Johnson on July 4, 1966. It provided that after one year a citizen could go to court if a federal official arbitrarily withheld information of a public transaction other than in the areas specifically exempted under the law. These areas were nine in number including the all-important "national defense or foreign policy" one. Nevertheless, Representative Moss and others said a victory had been scored. The effect was as much to aid businessmen seeking information in federal offices as to aid reporters.

In an effort to speed up the search process, the Freedom of Information Act was amended in 1974, requiring each federal agency to promulgate detailed regulations implementing the substance of the amendments and outlining information request procedures, appeal procedures, and search and duplicating costs. The amendments sought to eliminate agency stalling by shortening the allowable response time by agencies, providing for judicial review of denial decisions, and authorizing fines for officials who arbitrarily refused to release information.

Another encouraging sign in the battle for the right to know was enactment by Congress of a Government in the Sunshine Law that took effect early in 1977. This law requires open meetings of more than 50 federal boards and agencies with two or more members. The Sunshine Law allows meetings to be closed for certain specified reasons but requires that the reasons for any closed meetings be certified by the chief legal officer or general counsel of the agency.

NOTES

1. Broun's column is reprinted in the *Guild Reporter*, XVI (December 9, 1949), which contains several pages reviewing early Guild history and Broun's career. The early years of the Guild are examined in Daniel

J. Leab, *A Union of Individuals: The Formation of the American Newspaper Guild 1933–1936* (New York: Columbia University Press, 1970).

2. The early AFL efforts are summarized in National Labor Relations Board, *Collective Bargaining in the Newspaper Industry* (Washington: Government Printing Office, 1939), and in Alfred McClung Lee, *The Daily Newspaper in America* (New York: Macmillan, 1937). The most successful locals were in Scranton, Milwaukee, Boston, New York, Philadelphia, and Columbus, Ohio.

3. The details can be followed in the *Guild Reporter* and *Editor & Publisher,* and are summarized in the NLRB's *Collective Bargaining in the Newspaper Industry* and in the special issue of the *Guild Reporter,* XVI (December 9, 1949).

4. *Associated Press* v. *NLRB,* 301 U.S. 103 (1937).

5. This subject is explored in detail in Sam Kuczun, "History of the American Newspaper Guild," Ph.D. thesis, University of Minnesota, 1970. Some other data in this account is taken from Kuczun's research in Guild archives and other documentary sources.

6. The proceedings of the twenty-fifth annual ASNE meeting, in 1947, contain on pages 39–53 historical reminiscences of three early members, Grove Patterson of the *Toledo Blade,* Marvin H. Creager of the *Milwaukee Journal,* and Donald J. Sterling of the *Oregon Journal.*

7. The American Press Institute was founded in 1946 through the efforts of Sevellon Brown of the *Providence Journal* and *Bulletin.*

8. The NCEW code of principles appears in *Editor & Publisher,* LXXXII (October 29, 1949), 7.

9. The *APME Red Book* for 1948 opens with a history of the organization and its Continuing Study activities to that time.

10. See Albert A. Sutton, *Education for Journalism in the United States* (Evanston: Northwestern University Press, 1945), for an historical treatment. For a current picture see Warren K. Agee, Phillip H. Ault, and Edwin Emery, *Introduction to Mass Communications* (New York: Harper & Row, 1977), chap. 20.

11. Unpublished report of Claude-Jean Bertrand, University of Paris—Nanterre, studying American media, 1976–77. Scheduled for 1978 publication in *Journalism Quarterly.*

12. *Editor & Publisher,* CX (January 29, 1977), 9.

13. *Near* v. *Minnesota ex rel. Olson,* 283 U.S. 697 (1931).

14. *Grosjean* v. *American Press Co.,* 297 U.S. 233 (1936).

15. *Associated Press* v. *NLRB,* 301 U.S. 103 (1937).

16. *Branzburg* v. *Hayes,* 408 U.S. 665 (1972). For further discussion, see Fred P. Graham and Jack C. Landau, "The Federal Shield Law We Need," *Columbia Journalism Review,* XII (March–April 1972), reprinted in Michael C. Emery and Ted. C. Smythe, *Readings in Mass Communication* (Dubuque, Iowa: Wm. C. Brown, 1977). Washington newsmen Graham and Landau were members of The Reporters Committee for Freedom of the Press, whose *Press Censorship Newsletter/Media Law Reports* contains hundreds of summaries of press freedom matters.

17. *Bridges* v. *California,* 314 U.S. 252 (1941).

18. *Pennekamp* v. *Florida,* 328 U.S. 331 (1946); *Craig* v. *Harney,* 331 U.S. 367 (1947).

19. See Don R. Pember, "The 'Pentagon Papers' Decision: More Questions Than Answers," *Journalism Quarterly,* XLVIII (Autumn 1971), 403, whose conclusions were endorsed by other mass communications law scholars.

20. *New York Times Company* v. *United States* and *United States* v. *The Washington Post Company,* 403 U.S. 713 (1971). The government soon admitted its error by selling 43 volumes of the Pentagon Papers from its Printing Office to all comers.

21. *Bantam Books, Inc.* v. *Sullivan,* 372 U.S. 58 (1963).

22. *Organization for a Better Austin* v. *Keefe,* 402 U.S. 215 (1971).

23. *Schenck* v. *United States,* 249 U.S. 47 (1919); *Abrams* v. *United States,* 250 U.S. 616 (1919).

24. *Gitlow* v. *People of State of New York,* 268 U.S. 652 (1925).

25. *Whitney* v. *California,* 274 U.S. 357 (1927).

26. *Dennis* v. *United States,* 341 U.S. 494 (1951). A subsequent decision of 1957 in the Yates case narrowed the grounds for Smith Act convictions and freed five defendants.

27. See Donald M. Gillmor and Jerome A. Barron, *Mass Communication Law: Cases and Comment* (St. Paul: West Publishing Company, 1969), 250 ff.

28. *New York Times Co.* v. *Sullivan,* 376 U.S. 245 (1964).

29. *Curtis Publishing Co.* v. *Butts* and *Associated Press* v. *Walker,* 388 U.S. 130 (1967).

30. *Time Inc.* v. *Hill,* 385 U.S. 374 (1967).

31. *Cantrell* v. *Forest City Publishing Co.,* 419 U.S. 245 (1974); *Cox Broadcasting Corp.* v. *Cohn,* 420 U.S. 469 (1975).

32. *Rosenbloom* v. *Metromedia,* 403 U.S. 29 (1971).

33. *Hannegan* v. *Esquire,* 327 U.S. 146 (1946).

34. *Roth* v. *United States,* 354 U.S. 476 (1957).
35. *Ginzburg* v. *United States,* 383 U.S. 463 (1966).
36. *Miller* v. *California,* 413 U.S. 15 (1973).
37. Jerome A. Barron, ''Access to the Press—A New First Amendment Right,'' 80. *Harvard Law Review* 1641 (1967).
38. Jerome A. Barron, *Freedom of the Press for Whom? The Right of Access to Mass Media* (Bloomington: Indiana University Press, 1973). For the *Red Lion* case, see p. 421.
39. *Miami Herald Publishing Co.* v. *Tornillo,* 418 U.S. 241 (1974).
40. *Lorain Journal* v. *United States,* 342 U.S. 143 (1951).
41. *Times-Picayune Publishing Co.* v. *United States,* 345 U.S. 594 (1953).
42. *Kansas City Star Co.* v. *United States; Emil A. Sees* v. *United States* (8th Circuit) 240 Fed. 2d 643 (1957).
43. *Estes* v. *State of Texas,* 381 U.S. 532 (1965).
44. *Sheppard* v. *Maxwell,* 384 U.S. 333 (1966).
45. *United States* v. *Dickenson,* 46496 (5th Cir. 1972).
46. *Nebraska Press Association* v. *Stuart,* 427 U.S. 539 (1976).

ANNOTATED BIBLIOGRAPHY

Discussions involving press problems are to be found in the American Society of Newspaper Editors' *Problems of Journalism* series, in the Associated Press Managing Editors' *APME Red Book* series, and in the periodicals *Journalism Quarterly, Journal of Broadcasting, Columbia Journalism Review, Masthead, Nieman Reports, Grassroots Editor, Editor & Publisher, Broadcasting, Guild Reporter, Publishers' Auxiliary, Quill, Matrix, ASNE Bulletin, MORE,* and *RTNDA Bulletin.*

Books

AGEE, WARREN K., PHILLIP H. AULT, AND EDWIN EMERY, *Introduction to Mass Communications,* 5th ed. New York: Harper & Row, 1976. Current status of mass media, research, journalism schools.

BAGDIKIAN, BEN H., *The Information Machines.* New York: Harper & Row, 1971. Based on report financed by the RAND Corporation dealing with news communication methods presently and for next three decades; much data.

BRUCKER, HERBERT, *Freedom of Information.* New York: Macmillan, 1949. Able defense of press by *Hartford Courant* editor.

CHAFEE, ZECHARIAH, JR., *Government and Mass Communications.* Chicago: University of Chicago Press, 1947. A two-volume specific study of areas involving government and press, for the Commission on Freedom of the Press.

CLARK, DAVID G., AND EARL R. HUTCHISON, eds., *Mass Media and the Law: Freedom and Restraint.* New York: Wiley-Interscience, 1970. Good collection of essays in major areas of concern.

CROSS, HAROLD L., *The People's Right to Know.* New York: Columbia University Press, 1953. Scholarly, detailed study of problems of access to news.

DEVOL, KENNETH S., ed., *Mass Media and the Supreme Court: The Legacy of the Warren Years,* 2nd ed. New York: Hastings House, 1976. Fifty selected Supreme Court cases, 17 interpretative articles, and editor's comments.

EMERY, EDWIN, *History of the American Newspaper Publishers Association.* Minneapolis: University of Minnesota Press, 1949. Updated in 1962 in 75th anniversary booklet (New York: ANPA). ANPA's history covered in detail; ANPA-Guild relationships explored.

GERALD, J. EDWARD, *The Press and the Constitution.* Minneapolis: University of Minnesota Press, 1948. The best source for freedom of the press cases, 1931–47.

GILLMOR, DONALD M., *Free Press and Fair Trial.* Washington: Public Affairs Press, 1966. Scholarly survey and analysis of critical cases, best of the literature. See also John Lofton, *Justice and the Press* (Boston: Beacon Press, 1966).

GILLMOR, DONALD M., AND JEROME A. BARRON, *Mass Communication Law: Cases and Comments,* 2nd ed. St. Paul, Minn.: West Publishing, 1974. Comprehensive casebook, comments.

HACHTEN, WILLIAM A., ed., *The Supreme Court on Freedom of the Press: Decisions and Dissents.* Ames: Iowa State University Press, 1968. The main historical story, with commentaries.

HOCKING, WILLIAM E., *Freedom of the Press: A Framework of Principle.* Chicago: University of Chicago Press, 1947. Discusses philosophical problems; written for the Commission on Freedom of the Press.

KRAMER, DALE, *Heywood Broun.* New York: A.A. Wyn, Inc., 1949. Biography of the Guild's founder, a famous columnist.

LEAB, DANIEL J., *A Union of Individuals: The Formation of the American Newspaper Guild 1933–1936.* New York: Columbia University Press, 1970. Scholarly detail.

LEVY, H. PHILLIP, *The Press Council: History, Procedure and Cases.* London: Macmillan, 1967. The British Press Council examined in detail 1953–67. For U.S. examples, see Kenneth Starck, "What Community Press Councils Talk About," *Journalism Quarterly,* XLVII (Spring 1970), 20; William B. Blankenburg, "Local Press Councils," *Columbia Journalism Review,* VIII (Spring 1969), 14; Lawrence Schneider, "A Media–Black Council: Seattle's 19-Month Experiment," *Journalism Quarterly,* XLVII (Autumn 1970), 439; and Rivers and Rampal (below).

NATIONAL LABOR RELATIONS BOARD, *Collective Bargaining in the Newspaper Industry.* Washington: Government Printing Office, 1938. Studies both the Guild and printing union movements.

NELSON, HAROLD L., *Libel in News of Congressional Investigating Committees.* Minneapolis: University of Minnesota Press, 1961. Scholarly study of problems faced in reporting attacks on individuals.

NELSON, HAROLD L., AND DWIGHT L. TEETER, JR., *Law of Mass Communications: Freedom and Control of Print and Broadcast Media,* 2nd ed. Mineola, N.Y.: Foundation Press, 1973. A leading casebook exploring communications law in the United States.

The Pentagon Papers. New York: Bantam, 1971. Publication in paperback of the decisions and documents, edited by the *New York Times.*

PITTS, ALICE FOX, *Read All About It—Fifty Years of the ASNE.* Reston, Va.: American Society of Newspaper Editors, 1974. The ASNE's own story.

RIVERS, WILLIAM L., WILLIAM B. BLANKENBURG, KENNETH STARCK, AND EARL REEVES, *Backtalk: Press Councils in America.* San Francisco: Canfield Press, 1971. By men who operated several local press councils.

SCHMIDT, BENNO C., *Freedom of the Press Versus Public Access.* New York: Praeger Publishers, Inc., 1975. A comprehensive review of the background and constitutional implications of access.

WHALEN, CHARLES W., JR., *Your Right to Know.* New York: Random House, 1973. A congressman argues for shield law by examining cases.

WIGGINS, JAMES RUSSELL, *Freedom or Secrecy.* New York: Oxford University Press, 1964. A summation of access-to-news problems by an ASNE leader.

Periodicals and Monographs

BLANCHARD, ROBERT O., "Present at the Creation: The Media and the Moss Committee," *Journalism Quarterly,* XLIX (Summer 1972), 271. Story of the information crusade. See also his "A Watchdog in Decline," *Columbia Journalism Review,* V (Summer 1966), 17, and "The Freedom of Information Act—Disappointment and Hope," *Columbia Journalism Review,* VI (Fall 1967), 16.

BROUN, HEYWOOD, "An Army with Banners," *Nation,* CXL (February 13, 1935), 154. The Guild president's own account.

CONN, EARL L., "The American Council on Education for Journalism: An Accrediting History," Ed.D. thesis, Indiana University, 1970. Traces the growth of accrediting standards.

DEARMAN, MARION, AND JOHN HOWELLS, "Computer Technology and the Return of the Printer-Journalist," *Journalism History*, II (Winter 1975), 133. New technology's outcome.

DENNIS, EVERETTE E., "Purloined Information as Property: A New First Amendment Challenge," *Journalism Quarterly*, L (Autumn 1973), 456. Based on his Ph.D. thesis, University of Minnesota, 1974, which covers episodes in 1795, 1848, and 1970s.

DONAGHUE, PETER, "Reconsideration of Mandatory Public Access to the Print Media," 21 *St. Louis University Law Journal* 91 (1977). Newspapers urged to adopt a voluntary code.

"The First Amendment on Trial," a special issue containing 13 articles on the Pentagon Papers case, *Columbia Journalism Review*, X (September–October 1971).

GERALD, J. EDWARD, "Press-Bar Relationships: Progress Since *Sheppard* and Reardon," *Journalism Quarterly*, XLVII (Summer 1970), 223. Outcome of free press vs. fair trial debate summarized.

GILLMOR, DONALD M., "The Puzzle of Pornography," *Journalism Quarterly*, XLII (Summer 1965), 363. Traces court decisions in area of obscenity including Roth. For *Ginzburg* case and aftermath, see Kenneth S. Devol, "The Ginzburg Decision: Reactions in California," *Journalism Quarterly*, XLV (Summer 1968), 271.

GORDON, A. DAVID, "Protection of News Sources: The History and Legal Status of the Newsman's Privilege," Ph.D. thesis, University of Wisconsin, 1971. Cases from 1848.

GRANATO, LEONARD A., "Prior Restraint: Resurgent Enemy of Freedom of Expression," Ph.D. thesis, Southern Illinois University, 1973. From 14th century England to now.

HUDSON, ROBERT V., "FoI Crusade in Perspective: Three Victories for the Press," *Journalism Quarterly*, L (Spring 1973), 118. Breakthrough in congressional action.

KEATING, ISABELLE, "Reporters Become of Age," *Harper's*, CLXX (April 1935), 601. One of the best early articles about the Guild.

KOEHLER, MARY A., "Facsimile Newspapers: Foolishness or Foresight?," *Journalism Quarterly*, XLVI (Spring 1969), 29. History of a disappointment.

KUCZUN, SAM, "History of the American Newspaper Guild," Ph.D. thesis, University of Minnesota, 1970. Comprehensive overview based on access to Guild archives.

PEMBER, DON R., "The 'Pentagon Papers' Decision: More Questions than Answers," *Journalism Quarterly*, XLVIII (Autumn 1971), 403. A scholarly analysis.

PETRICK, MICHAEL J., "Inspection of Public Records in the States: The Law and the News Media," Ph.D. thesis, University of Wisconsin, 1970. Covers the period 1824–1969.

PFAFF, DANIEL W., "The First Amendment and Symbolic Speech: Toward a Rationale of the Public Forum," Ph.D. thesis, University of Minnesota, 1972. Sit-ins, flag burnings.

———, "Race, Libel, and the Supreme Court," *Columbia Journalism Review*, VIII (Summer 1969), 23. Surveys Supreme Court decisions of 1960s in libel area that involved press freedom, points out connection to racial decisions.

PRINGLE, HENRY F., "The Newspaper Guild," *Scribner's*, CV (January 1939), 21. A review at a turning-point time in Guild affairs.

RAMPAL, KULDIP, "The Concept of the Press Council," Freedom of Information Center Report No. 350 (March 1976). A review of the importance of press councils.

SAALBERG, HARVEY, "The Canons of Journalism: A 50-Year Perspective," *Journalism Quarterly*, L (Winter 1973), 731. History of the ASNE's code of ethics.

SCHER, JACOB, "Access to Information: Recent Legal Problems," *Journalism Quarterly*, XXXVII (Winter 1960), 41. An authoritative summary for the 1950s by a Northwestern journalism professor who was special counsel for the Moss committee.

SINICHAK, STEVEN, "The Chicago Journalism Review," *Grassroots Editor*, XI (July–August 1970), 10. Story of the journal's first two years.

STONECIPHER, HARRY, AND ROBERT TRAGER, "The Impact of Gertz on the Law of Libel," *Journalism Quarterly*, LIII (Winter 1976), 609. Case of *Gertz* v. *Robert Welch, Inc.*

SWINDLER, WILLIAM F., "The AP Antitrust Case in Historical Perspective," *Journalism Quarterly*, XXIII (March 1946), 40. Scholarly analysis.

WATKINS, JOHN J., "Newsgathering and the First Amendment," *Journalism Quarterly*, LIII (Autumn 1976), 406. Right of newsgathering not yet adequately dealt with in courts.

The Weather

Today—Rain, high in the low to mid 80s, low in the upper 60s. Chance of rain in 40 per cent today, 60 per cent tonight. Saturday— Cloudy, high around 80. Yesterday's temp. range, 77-68. Details, Page D19.

The Washington Post

Index 112 Pages 4 Sections

Amusements D 1	Metro D12
Classified C14	Obituaries D19
Comics D20	Outdoors C 8
Editorials A30	Sports C 1
Fed. Diary D21	Style D 1
Financial C 9	TV-Radio D 8

97th Year · · · No. 247   © 1974 The Washington Post Co.   FRIDAY, AUGUST 9, 1974   Phone (202) 223-6000   Classified 223-6200   15¢

Nixon Resigns

By Carroll Kilpatrick
Washington Post Staff Writer

Richard Milhous Nixon announced last night that he will resign as the 37th President of the United States at noon today.

Vice President Gerald R. Ford of Michigan will take the oath as the new President at noon to complete the remaining 2½ years of Mr. Nixon's term.

After two years of bitter public debate over the Watergate scandals, President Nixon bowed to pressures from the public and leaders of his party to become the first President in American history to resign.

"By taking this action," he said in a subdued yet dramatic television address from the Oval Office, "I hope that I will have hastened the start of the process of healing which is so desperately needed in America."

Vice President Ford, who spoke a short time later in

front of his Alexandria home, announced that Secretary of State Henry A. Kissinger will remain in his Cabinet.

The President-to-be praised Mr. Nixon's sacrifice for the country and called it "one of the very saddest incidents that I've ever witnessed."

Mr. Nixon said he decided he must resign when he concluded that he no longer had "a strong enough political base in the Congress" to make it possible for him to complete his term of office.

Declaring that he has never been a quitter, Mr. Nixon said that to leave office before the end of his term "is abhorrent to every instinct in my body."

But "as President, I must put the interests of America first," he said.

While the President acknowledged that some of his judgments "were wrong," he made no confession of the "high crimes and misdemeanors" with which the House

Judiciary Committee charged him in its bill of impeachment.

Specifically, he did not refer to Judiciary Committee charges that in the cover-up of Watergate crimes he misused government agencies such as the FBI, the Central Intelligence Agency and the Internal Revenue Service.

After the President's address, Special Prosecutor Leon Jaworski issued a statement declaring that "there has been no agreement or understanding of any sort between the President or his representatives and the special prosecutor relating in any way to the President's resignation."

Jaworski said that his office "was not asked for any such agreement or understanding and offered none."

His office was informed yesterday afternoon of the President's decision, Jaworski said, but "my office did not participate in any way in the President's decision to resign."

Mr. Nixon's brief speech was delivered in firm tones and

he appeared to be in complete control of his emotions. The absence of rancor contrasted sharply with the "fare-well" he delivered in 1962 after being defeated for the governorship of California.

An hour before the speech, however, the President broke down during a meeting with old congressional friends and had to leave the room.

He had invited 20 senators and 26 representatives for a farewell meeting in the Cabinet room. Later, Sen. Barry M. Goldwater (R-Ariz.), one of those present, said Mr. Nixon said to them very much what he said in his speech.

"He just told us that the country couldn't operate with a half-time President," Goldwater reported. "Then he broke down and cried and he had to leave the room. Then the rest of us broke down and cried."

In his televised resignation, after thanking his friends for their support, the President concluded by saying he was leaving office "with this prayer: may God's grace be with you in all the days ahead."

As for his sharpest critics, the President said, "I leave with no bitterness toward those who have opposed me." He called on all Americans to "join together . . . in helping our new President succeed."

The President said he had thought it was his duty to persevere in office in face of the Watergate charges and to complete his term.

"I the past days, however, it has become evident to me that I no longer have a strong enough political base in the Congress to justify continuing that effort," Mr. Nixon said.

His family "unanimously urged" him to stay in office and fight the charges against him, he said. But he came to realize that he would not have the support needed to carry out the duties of his office in difficult times.

"America needs a full-time President and a full-time Congress," Mr. Nixon said. The resignation came with "a great sadness that I will not be here in office" to complete work on the programs started, he said.

But praising Vice President Ford, Mr. Nixon said that "the leadership of America will be in good hands."

In his admission of error, the outgoing President said: "I deeply regret any injuries that may have been done in the course of the events that led to this decision."

He emphasized that world peace had been the overriding concern of his years in the White House.

When he first took the oath, he said, he made a "sacred commitment" to "consecrate my office and wisdom to the cause of peace among nations."

"I have done my very best in all the days since to be true to that pledge," he said, adding that he is now confident that the world is a safer place for all peoples.

"Thus more than anything is what I hoped to achieve when I sought the presidency," Mr. Nixon said. "This more than anything is what I hope will be my legacy to you, to our country, as I leave the presidency."

Noting that he had lived through a turbulent period, he recalled a statement of Theodore Roosevelt about the man "in the arena whose face is marred by dust and sweat and blood" and who, if he fails "at least fails while daring greatly."

Mr. Nixon placed great emphasis on his successes in foreign affairs. He said his administration had "unlocked the doors that for a quarter of a century stood between the United States and the People's Republic of China."

In the Mideast, he said, the United States went again to build on the peace in that area. And with the Soviet Union, he said, the administration had begun the process of ending the nuclear arms race. The goal now, he said, is to reduce and finally destroy those arms "so that the threat of nuclear war will no longer hang over the world." The two countries, he added, "must live together in cooperation rather than in confrontation."

Mr. Nixon has served 2,026 days as the 37th President of the United States. He leaves office with 2½ years of his second term remaining to be carried out by the man he nominated to be Vice President last year.

Yesterday morning, the President conferred with his successor. He spent much of the day in his Executive Office Building hideaway working on his speech and attending to last-minute business.

At 7:30 p.m., Mr. Nixon again left the White House for the short walk to the Executive Office Building. The crowd outside the gates waved U.S. flags and sang "America" as he walked slowly up the steps, his head bowed, alone.

At the EOB, Mr. Nixon met for a little over 20 minutes with the leaders of Congress—James O. Eastland (D-Miss.), president pro tem to the Senate; Mike Mansfield (D-Mont.), Senate majority leader; Hugh Scott (R-Pa.), Senate minor-

See RESIGN, A3, Col. 1

Ford Assumes Presidency Today

By Jules Witcover
Washington Post Staff Writer

Gerald Rudolph Ford Jr., a Grand Rapids, Mich., lawyer who never aspired to national office but had it thrust upon him as a result of two of the greatest political scandals in American history, will become the 38th President of the United States at noon today.

He will be the first American President not elected to national office by the people, having been nominated Vice President by President Nixon last Oct. 12 under provisions of the new 25th Amendment to the Constitution.

Last night, immediately after watching Mr. Nixon's televised announcement that he is resigning, Ford walked onto the lawn of his Alexandria home, praised the President for deciding to step aside and pledged to continue Mr. Nixon's foreign policy "that has achieved peace and built the future more secure."

Ford announced that he had asked Secretary of State Henry A. Kissinger, whom he called "a very great man," to stay on in the new administration and that Kissinger had accepted. "He and I will be working together in the pursuit of peace in the future, as we have achieved it in the past," he said.

Ford is expected to keep on and have the support of the entire Nixon Cabinet, which promises to give him an initial period of stability. But even before he is sworn in, he faces some squabbling within his own party over the question of the Vice President he will choose. Some conservatives were openly advocating yesterday that former New York Gov. Nelson A. Rockefeller be dropped from consideration.

Ford, speaking calmly before a battery of microphones and under hot TV lights in the summer night, also pledged to address himself to domestic problems by working in a "spirit of cooperation" with Congress, where he served in the House for 25 years.

"I've been very fortunate in my lifetime in public office to have a good many adversaries in the political arena in Congress," he said, "but I don't think I have a single enemy in the Congress. And the net result is that I think tomorrow I can start out working with Democrats and Republicans, in the House as well as in the Senate, to work on the problems, serious ones, which we have at home."

The Vice President called the turn of events that has brought him to the presidency "one of the most difficult and very saddest periods, and one of the very saddest incidents, that I've ever witnessed."

He said President Nixon "has made one of the greatest personal sacrifices for the country, and one of the finest personal decisions on behalf of all of us as Americans, by his decision to resign as President of the United States."

"I pledge to you tonight," he concluded, "as I will pledge tomorrow and in the future, my best efforts and cooperation and leadership and dedication to do what's good for America and good for the world."

The swearing in of the new President is to take place at noon at the White House. The ceremony will be held in the Rose Garden if the weather is good and in the East Room if it is not. The U.S. Weather Service said last night there was a 60 per cent chance of rain today.

Ford is to speak briefly to the nationwide television audience after being sworn in, and according to congres-

See FORD, A11, Col. 1

Era of Good Feeling

Congress Expects Harmony

By Spencer Rich and Richard L. Lyons
Washington Post Staff Writers

From one end of Capitol Hill to the other, members of Congress predicted last night that the presidency of Gerald R. Ford will start with a new era of good feeling between Congress and the White House, helping to heal the deep and wrenching blows the nation's government has suffered in the past two years.

The tone was set by the Democratic leaders of the House and the Senate, both of whom have served with Ford on terms of close cooperation during his 25 years in Congress before he became Vice President.

"Jerry Ford is a personal friend," said House Speaker Carl Albert (D-Okla.). "I am sure our relationship will be good."

Senate Majority Leader Mike Mansfield (D-Mont.) said, "He's a decent man. He's conservative but you

know where he stands. He'd give consideration to congressional views. He would get exceptional cooperation."

The predominant reaction to President Nixon's resignation was enormous relief that Congress and the nation have been spared the agony of a House vote and Senate trial that would force each member to be counted and divide the nation.

House leaders of both parties and the tone of the President's r e s i g n a t i o n speech satisfied them and they didn't see any need to go ahead with a floor vote on impeachment. Albert said, "The manner of his leaving was a vast relief to me. I think, one of his best efforts. I believe that bitterness was averted by the tone of his speech. . . he went out not trying to say he was framed."

See CONGRESS, A8, Col. 1

President Nixon and daughter Julie embracing Wednesday after the President's decision to resign.

(Official White House Photo)

The Washington Post — THE NIXON YEARS

A 24-page special section on the Nixon presidency—inside today.

A Solemn Change

Power Is Passed Quietly

By Richard Harwood and Haynes Johnson
Washington Post Staff Writers

When the day finally came, the anger and tensions and recriminations that had so enveloped this capital for weeks had been subdued in the solemnity of change. A sense of calm and a tenuous spirit of conciliation began to emerge.

There was no chorus of jubilation in Washington and no cries for vengeance or retribution. There was an absence of turmoil, mobs, violence, massive protests.

The crowds that began gathering at the White House on Tuesday remained quiet, solemn and patient. They were witnesses to history, yes, and someday they would tell their grandchildren about it. But now on this Thursday, Aug. 8, 1974, they seemed more preoccupied by personal feelings of sorrow and sadness.

"Think of it," said a tourist from Wheaton, Ill. "The most beautiful building in the country, right across the street, and the man that lives there, that has worked all his life to get there, has to give it up. . . It's a sad terrible thing, but he brought it all on himself. But it makes me sad that he has to be humiliated like this."

Another visitor who had driven up from Myrtle Beach, S.C., was philosophical: "Our country will survive. In a way, this is like the Kennedy assassination. It is a sad time for everyone but we'll pull through."

By nightfall, the crowd had swelled to large proportions, blocking traffic on historic Pennsylvania Avenue, filling beautiful Lafayette Park with its flower beds, benches and statues.

See DAY, A7, Col. 1

The climax of two years of persistent investigative reporting.

28

A Crisis
of Credibility

The press was to serve the governed, not the governors.
—Justice Hugo L. Black

The credibility gap as an institution became painfully apparent in American life. There were gaps between president and people, president and press, press and people. To these were added gaps between old and young, black and white, intellectuals and silent majority.

One reason for the difficulties of the presidents was the growth of a cult of disbelief. At his height, Senator Joseph McCarthy had half of the American people believing in him, which meant they believed their government was a combination of Communism and corruption—even the Army harbored treason, McCarthy said. The senator was unable to bring down war hero Eisenhower, who was less affected than were his successors by the credibility gap. John F. Kennedy inherited a Cuban crisis; news was managed, and many disbelieved their government's explanations. The Warren Commission hearings failed to keep Americans from doubting accounts of President Kennedy's assassination; that doubt increased over the years. Senator Barry Goldwater could offer rueful testimony about the depth of disbelief he encountered in his disastrous 1964 presidential campaign. Senator Eugene McCarthy found in the winter of 1967–68 that President Johnson's public support was a hollow shell; his "children's crusade" and the reality of the Tet attacks in Vietnam shattered belief in the war effort there. The credibility gap that had been attributed to the Lyndon Johnson personality persisted for Richard Nixon as his problems multiplied, partially for the same reason but also because it was a part of the American way of life.

Another reason for the difficulties of both presidents and press was the steady diet of bad news that characterized the 1950s and 1960s, despite many years of prosperity and notable accomplishments. Americans did not want to hear they had to settle for a stalemate in Korea—"Communism, Corruption, and Korea" was a 1952 election

533

slogan to explain the bad news, not the hard facts of a capable Chinese army opponent. A recession in the late 1950s; antagonistic receptions abroad of Vice President Nixon and even President Eisenhower; and a challenge to American prestige by Charles de Gaulle were all unwanted subjects. They piled up in the 1960s: the Bay of Pigs, the Berlin Wall, the assassination of a president, the Vietnam war, racial riots in big cities, college campus riots, the assassinations of Senator Kennedy and Martin Luther King, the collapse of the promise of victory in Vietnam, long hair, sex and four-letter words in the open, drug addiction, Kent State, My Lai, a near-depression, and Watergate. Traditionally a president pays politically for adverse news, particularly of an economic nature. But as William Small of CBS put it in a book title, the public seemed willing like the kings of old "to kill a messenger"—in this case, CBS and other networks, the *Washington Post* and other liberal newspapers, even the objectivity-seeking press associations that brought them the bad news.

The situation was ripe for demagogues. There was much bad news people did not want to believe, much reality they did not want to have exist. One group did not believe the president; another did not believe the press. And both president and press encouraged people not to believe the other. It was easy to argue, then, that reporting bad news was unpatriotic; to say that those who made bad news—as at Kent State or in the streets of Chicago—were un-American and deserving of their fates. The only solace defenders of freedom had was that such credibility gaps had existed before in history and that with determination this one also could be overcome.

In seeking to understand the development of this era of the credibility gap, one starts with the record of the relationships between the presidents and the press, examines the overt attacks on the press, estimates the extent of the gap between the press and the people, and also records the frictions between government and press that resulted in legislation and court decisions involving freedom of the press.

THE PRESIDENTS AND THE PRESS: FDR

No president had more effective relationships with the press than did Franklin D. Roosevelt. He met the White House correspondents informally, often in his office. He was at ease, communicative, gay, or serious as the news might dictate. Like all presidents he came to be irritated by his critics in the press, who were assigned dunce caps or iron crosses. But he met the press 998 times during his 12 years in office, an average of 83 times a year. He was known for his Fireside Chats on the radio, but in his first term he gave only eight; the same four years he communicated with the American people and won 46 states in the next election by holding 340 press conferences, most of which made solid news. FDR had capable press secretaries, of whom Steve Early was the most effective, and built a tradition of presidential press conferences that would be hard to follow. To look ahead, President Truman dropped the average number of press conferences yearly from 83 to 42; the yearly averages later were Eisenhower 24, Kennedy 22, Johnson 25, Nixon 7, Ford 16, and Carter 26.

TRUMAN AND THE PRESS

The relationship of the president and the news media underwent drastic changes during the tenure of Harry S. Truman. The Truman style, the complexity of events after World War II, and the growth of the news-gathering apparatus—particularly broadcasting—during and after the war contributed to the metamorphosis.

While Truman and the newsmen around him enjoyed a cordial personal relationship—they generally liked each other—professionally, they remained sharp adversaries throughout his 93 months in office. As president, he held 324 news conferences, averaging three to four a month. The president's abrupt and sometimes unpredictable comments at these sessions often appeared strangely contradictory to a period dominated by the realities of atomic energy and cold war politics.

If reporters relished the Truman news conferences for the possibility of an unexpected and sensational utterance, they also came to realize that the structure of the conferences was changing to give the administration more control over them. Truman began meeting with press secretary Charles G. Ross and others of his staff for preconference briefings and greatly increased the use of carefully prepared opening statements to which he would refer a questioning reporter when he chose not to elaborate on a matter.[1]

In the spring of 1950, the location of presidential news conferences was moved from the intimate atmosphere of the Oval Room of the White House to a 230-seat room in the Executive Office Building. While the change was brought about because of the growth in the number of Washington correspondents, its effect was to further formalize the presidential press conference. The move also ushered in the use of microphones and, by 1951, presidential authorization to use excerpts of recordings for broadcast news programs. As news conferences thereby became increasingly public during the Truman years, the president was obliged to exercise greater control over them, to come to them better prepared, and to respond during them with greater care. Truman's tendency to speak his mind, or "shoot from the hip" as some critics termed it, was not obscured entirely by the new overlay of safeguards. Salty, sometimes embarrassing slips continued despite preparation to prevent them. But the groundwork of control was laid for his successors.

Apart from the news conference, another effort at control of information created a furor among publishers and newsmen during the Korean War. Convinced that magazines and newspapers were guilty of leaking most of America's military secrets, Truman ordered all government agencies handling military information to classify it at their discretion and to restrict its use by the media. Despite a wave of criticism, the order stood.[2]

Truman responded to harsh and continuing criticism of himself and his administration by the news media with strong denunciations of the media. Particularly after his stunning election in 1948 in the face of overwhelming editorial opposition and daily news stories predicting his defeat did the president lash out at "the kept press and the paid radio." He attacked what he called the "confusion of fact with mere speculation by which readers and listeners were undoubtedly misguided and intentionally deceived."

Only when he prepared to leave office in January 1953 did some media opponents relent. Some even saluted him affectionately. It was an unexpected pleasure for the retiring Truman who later recalled that "some editors ate crow and left the feathers on."[3]

EISENHOWER AND HAGERTY

President Eisenhower was an American hero when he assumed office and a five-star general who maintained a reserve and a dignity in his relations with others, even though they called him Ike. He enjoyed the services of a talented press secretary, James C. Hagerty, who held office longer than any of his predecessors and who tauntingly was called by some of the newsmen he bested in professional duels "the best Republican president who was never elected." This was unfair to both Hagerty and Eisenhower, for Hagerty prided himself on knowing how best to use the press to serve his boss, and Eisenhower exercised a basic command of the responsibilities of his office.

Eisenhower continued the large formal news conferences that had begun with Truman, having 250 correspondents at his first session and 309 at his final one, eight years and 190 press conferences later. He permitted direct quotations and taping for later television release, new gains for the press corps. Hagerty, however, had to check the material. Eisenhower made many slips of the tongue, thought faster than he talked, and skipped parts of sentences so that press conference transcripts had to be reworded to be intelligible. A penetrating personal question might bring a display of the famed Eisenhower controlled anger. But generally he was not too concerned with the press. He told one conference he went over the important sections of the Sunday papers that reviewed world events and studied them carefully—"but the kind of things you talk of, cartoons and unfriendly quips, I just can't be bothered with."[4] The president had a few bad incidents: Hagerty was mobbed by left-wing demonstrators at the Tokyo airport, forcing cancellation of a presidential visit, and the U-2 spy plane controversy in 1960 brought about a debacle at the Paris Summit conference.

KENNEDY AND TELEVISION

John F. Kennedy introduced live televising and broadcasting of presidential press conferences, an innovation with mixed blessings. The White House correspondents found that their home offices heard and saw the presidential responses long before the news stories clattered into their news desks. The mystique of the White House press conference in the oval room was gone. A skillful president could use the correspondents as foils or actors, and a few correspondents became actors by choice. On the positive side, millions of Americans could see the press conferences for themselves, live at the moment or digested in the evening news. Most of Kennedy's press conferences were in the afternoons in time for Walter Cronkite and Huntley-Brinkley to feature their highlights. Kennedy handled the star role far better than any of the presidents of his period; he was young, charming, stylish, and as disarmingly humorous or severely grave as circumstances dictated. In short, he put on a good show.

Behind this Kennedy the public knew was a president who was anxious for his administration's image, who gave frequent individual interviews and had correspondents as personal friends, who read a half-dozen leading papers daily and resented their criticisms so much he once banned the *Herald Tribune* temporarily. His press secretary, Pierre Salinger, took a hard line with the correspondents, as did Pentagon spokesman Arthur Sylvester, who uttered the ill-fated comment about "the government's inherent right to lie" (to save itself when faced with nuclear disaster). The press was upset about the clouded information given it about the Bay of Pigs; the administration was insisting there was a crisis between the United States and the Soviet Union so severe as to require self-control and censorship on the part of the press. The government unified its news sources, sought to manage the contacts between officials and the press, and was accused of seeking to manage the news itself. Publication of the Pentagon Papers in 1971 proved a far deeper involvement in Vietnam affairs by 1963 than the Kennedy administration ever acknowledged, including a share of responsibility for the assassination of President Diem, and showed the Saigon press corps had been essentially correct in vainly protesting the deepening involvement in a "quagmire." While public opinion supported the president, there was enough doubt to indicate a credibility gap existed.

LYNDON JOHNSON AND THE GAP   No president worked harder in trying to make himself available to the White House "regulars" than Lyndon Johnson. He did not care to undertake immediately the televised conferences so expertly run by Kennedy, so he called the two dozen or so regular correspondents into his office, plied them with food, and answered their questions. He took them with him to the LBJ ranch and held barbeques; he argued with them on walks in the White House rose garden; he swam with them in the pool; he even subjected himself to 135 regular press conferences, a slightly better average than Eisenhower or Kennedy. In 1964 Johnson was elected president in his own right with a record popular majority and the support of all but a dozen of the country's major newspapers. The next year his Great Society legislation consolidated the gains the country wanted to make in civil rights, aid to education, medical aid, and other social gains. Yet, for all this, the credibility gap grew as the war in Vietnam grew, until in March 1968 the president was to use live television to announce his retirement and the start of peace negotiations.

The war in Vietnam was not the war the president and the Pentagon planned. But as chapter 21 suggests, the newspaper and television reporters in Vietnam found not only the administration but also many of the public and sometimes their own home offices disbelieving their stories that the war was not going as Secretary McNamara had blueprinted it.

Not until the tragedy of Tet did the extent of the quagmire in Vietnam become clear to either the president or the public. And by that time Senator Eugene McCarthy's antiwar movement was sweeping Johnson out of the presidential race. But combinations of public disbelief, disillusionment, and distaste for violence led to a stalemate in public opinion. The assassination of Senator Robert Kennedy tore the heart out of the Democratic political campaign and opened the way for a fatal compromise in the welter of Chicago's street demonstrations and riots. The public, already recoiling from rioting and racial violence in the cities, rejected violence on its campuses and in its politics. It also rejected the "free speech" movement with its four-letter words. The Republicans, with Richard Nixon and Spiro T. Agnew, were a calm refuge for just enough voters to give them victory.

NIXON AND AGNEW   Richard Nixon had spent years studying his mistakes in the 1960 presidential race, with its "great debates" on television, and in his 1962 failure in California, which ended with an ill-tempered attack on the press. In 1968 he used television skillfully, appearing before controlled audiences with filtered questions rather than giving set speeches. But he held standard press conferences only rarely, at one-third the rate of recent presidents. Instead he relied on a technique Johnson had developed when he had dramatic news from the war to announce: request prime time network television for a brief appearance. He did this 37 times while in office, appearing at a higher frequency than any other president. Nixon averaged 11 regular press conferences a year his first two years in the White House but then trailed off and ended with a total of 38. A committee of the Associated Press Managing Editors, made up of executives of three conservative papers that had supported Nixon (the *Christian Science Monitor, Washington Star,* and *Philadelphia Bulletin*), criticized him for using press conferences to "raise questions about the credibility of the press."

Agnew aroused a stormy debate late in 1969 when, in speeches at Des Moines and later, he declared that the networks and newspapers with multiple media holdings

Paul Conrad, © 1971 *Los Angeles Times,* with permission of the *Register* and *Tribune* Syndicate.

Cartoonist Paul Conrad expresses American disillusionment with the Vietnam War.

(favorite target: *Washington Post, Newsweek,* Mrs. Graham's TV stations) exercised such powerful influence over public opinion that they should vigorously endeavor to be impartial and fair in reporting and commenting on national affairs. Specifically, Agnew criticized network managements for using commentators with a preponderant "Eastern Establishment bias" and for failing to provide a "wall of separation" between news and comment.

Also dominated by the "Establishment," he said, were such antiwar papers as the *Washington Post* and *New York Times* (others equally well staffed from similar social backgrounds, but conservative in tone, went unmentioned). Agnew made specific references to the dependence of broadcasting stations on licenses, and no amount of disclaimer by him or the administration that he was threatening a censorship could calm those who assumed they would be the victims. It was indisputably true that never before had such a high federal official made such direct attacks on those reporting and commenting on the news. Their defenders contended that the mere making of the statements by Agnew inhibited the freedom of the broadcasters suffering tongue lashes. A research study comparing random samples of newscast items reporting administration activities for one week periods in 1969 and 1970 bore out the contention that the Agnew-generated criticism had significantly affected the newscasts in the direction of "safe" handling.[5]

The vice president went into eclipse after the Republican setbacks in the 1970 congressional elections, but CBS gave him another opening when it screened "The Selling of the Pentagon" early in 1971. A congressional committee attempted to subpoena all records and unused film CBS had filed in making the Pentagon film; Rep. Harley O. Staggers, West Virginia Democrat, obtained the support of the Commerce Committee in requesting the House of Representatives to try CBS and CBS President Frank Stanton on charges of contempt of Congress. This the House refused to do, voting 226 to 181 in July 1971 to return the request to the committee. The refusal, while encouraging to free press advocates, was more politically shocking (such turndowns by the House have been rare) than legally reassuring.

THE WATERGATE STORY   The most widespread political corruption in the nation's history, more than a dozen major events conveniently listed under the headline word Watergate, forced the resignation of Richard Nixon and deepened the cynicism of a public already battered by the endless Vietnam fighting, partisan politics, and economic chaos. The scope and magnitude of the illegal activities and deceptions revealed during Nixon's desperate fight to save his presidency between 1972 and 1974 shocked Republicans and Democrats alike, most of whom were loath to believe that men who had entered the White House on a strict "law and order" platform had misused their power, money, and public trust.

Watergate was not an aberration. As previously discussed, its roots lay deep in the misdeeds of other administrations. But these events were unprecedented because of the

IN CAMBODIA—American soldiers try to spot enemy through rubber trees in the Fishhook region.

IN KENT, OHIO—National guardsmen advance during clash in which four students were killed.

Los Angeles Times

LARGEST CIRCULATION IN THE WEST, 982,075 DAILY, 1,317,220 SUNDAY.

VOL. LXXXIX 2† SEVEN PARTS—PART ONE   CC) F   TUESDAY MORNING, MAY 5, 1970   110 PAGES   Copyright 1970 Los Angeles Times   DAILY 10c

DEATH ON THE CAMPUS—A girl screams over the body of a student shot at Kent State University.

Troops Kill Four Students in Antiwar Riot at Ohio College

Large S. Viet-U.S. Force Opens Third Cambodia Offensive

SAIGON ⒰—Thousands of American and South Vietnamese troops launched a third offensive into northeast Cambodia today, seeking to smash more North Vietnamese base camps and sanctuaries, the U.S. command announced.

The American command said the operation was kicked off early this afternoon in the Se San base area, about 50 miles west of Pleiku, in the Central Highlands.

A spokesman said troops of the U.S. 4th Infantry Division and the South Vietnamese 22nd Infantry Division were participating in the operation.

(Their target is a highlands bivouac area that long has served as an entry point for the Ho Chi Minh Trail into Vietnam, United Press International said. It lies just south of the point where the borders of Laos, Cambodia and South Vietnam meet.

(Communist troops operating from this area have besieged several border Green Beret camps in the course of the war.

Defense Secretary Melvin R. Laird said in Washington Saturday that all North Vietnamese and Viet Cong sanctuaries along the full length of the border would be attacked by the allies.

There are numerous enemy base camp areas in Cambodia from the western Mekong Delta to the area north of Saigon which are outside the areas attacked last week by allied troops.

The two earlier allied drives, one into an area known as the Parrot's Beak and the other into an area called the Fishhook, have accounted for 2,711 North Vietnamese and Viet Cong killed. U.S. losses were given as 16 killed and South Vietnamese deaths were put at 131.

My Lai Disclosure Wins Pulitzer Prize

BY RICHARD DOUGHERTY
Times Staff Writer

NEW YORK—Seymour M. Hersh, the reporter who broke the story of the alleged My Lai massacre in Vietnam, won the 1970 Pulitzer Prize for international reporting Monday.

President Andrew W. Cordier of Columbia University announced the award on behalf of Columbia's trustees who make the annual selections for excellence in journalism and letters under terms of the will of the late Publisher Joseph Pulitzer.

Recognition of the 33-year-old Hersh's exposé of the alleged killing of nearly all the residents of a Vietnamese hamlet—including women and children—was not unexpected. The story was written by Hersh for Dispatch News Service. It was syndicated in 36 papers in this country

Please Turn to Page 10, Col. 1

WAR SITUATION AT A GLANCE

The stock market took a heavy beating Monday, reacting to concern over U.S. action in Cambodia. The Dow Jones industrial average dropped 19.07. Part 3, Page 9.

The Vietnam peace talks in Paris hung in the balance as the result of the U.S. Cambodia action. Page 1a.

The Senate Foreign Relations Committee said the Cambodian invasion was "constitutionally unauthorized." Page 11.

U.S. troops swept through Cambodia's Fishhook toward what was believed to be a major Communist headquarters base. Page 22.

Soviet Premier Alexei N. Kosygin railed for "vigorous measures" to get the U.S. out of Indochina. Page 19.

Official Washington, however, noted that Kosygin gave no indication of any Russian action to counter the United States. Page 19.

For Red China, U.S. action was "frantic provocation." Page 16.

Guards' Gunfire Wounds 11 at Kent University

KENT, Ohio (UPI)—Four students were shot to death on the Kent State University campus Monday when national guardsmen, believing a sniper had attacked them, fired into a crowd of rioting antiwar protesters.

At least 11 persons were wounded, three critically, before order was restored. The university was shut down for at least a week.

The town of 10,000 was sealed off and a judge ordered the university's

California student protesters disrupt campuses. See Page 3, Part 1.

20,000 students to leave the campus by noon Tuesday.

By late Monday night only 300 students, most of them foreign students, remained as 800 guardsmen patrolled in convoys of jeeps and personnel carriers armed with .30-caliber machine guns.

Students and National Guard officials gave different versions of what triggered the gunfire, but the guard admitted no warning was given that the troops would begin firing their M-1 semiautomatic rifles.

In one of the most violent campus confrontation since the antiwar movement began. The trouble started when about 1,000 demonstrators, defying an order not to assemble, rallied on the commons at the center of the tree-lined campus.

Guardsmen moved in and fired tear gas grenades at the mob, which broke and ran.

The protesters then regrouped and confronted about 300 guardsmen on a practice football field. The students, now numbering 1,500, charged down a hill and pelted the troops with rocks. Guardsmen exhausted their supply of tear gas. Students, who tossed back the canisters, surrounded the troops on three sides.

Believes Sniper Fired

Then, according to S. T. Del Corso, state adjutant general, "a sniper opened fire against the guardsmen from a nearby rooftop."

Del Corso, who was in Columbus, the state capital, maintained contact with the troops through Brig. Gen. Robert Canterbury, who commanded the guard force on campus. Canterbury said the students were given no warning before the shooting started.

Student eyewitnesses said they did not hear any shots before the guardsmen began shooting.

"All of a sudden," said one male student," some of them turned around and fired."

Please Turn to Page 6, Col. 1

THE WEATHER

U.S. Weather Bureau forecast: Night and morning low clouds with local drizzles but heavy afternoon sunshine today and Wednesday. High today, 70. High Monday, 82; low, 55.

Smog report and complete weather information in Part 2, Page 4.

New U.S. Air Raids Halted Over North, but Option Remains

BY TED SELL
Times Staff Writer

WASHINGTON—A new bombing campaign against North Vietnam was publicly declared ended Monday but defense sources said privately that a new policy giving field commanders increased authority to launching air strikes remained in effect.

The formal announcement, by Daniel Z. Henkin, assistant secretary of defense for public affairs, was that three heavy strikes against Communist supply areas just north of the border with South Vietnam was "all that were planned." Henkin said that with the strong attacks, the operation had "terminated."

Henkin, chief spokesman for the Defense Department, said there had been no change in the U.S. policy of protecting American reconnaissance flights.

But on Sunday, equally well-informed Pentagon officials said the policy had in fact been changed, permitting far more massive retaliatory bombing of North Vietnam.

Under the old policy, fighter escorts could attack only whatever single antiaircraft positions fired on reconnaissance planes.

Under the new policy, fighters no longer hold. If antiaircraft positions in any military base area fired, escorts could attack both that position and any military targets associated with it.

That expansion of authority, Pentagon sources said Monday, has not been revoked. White House officials,

Please Turn to Page 15, Col. 1

ALABAMA ELECTION

Wallace's Drive for Presidency at Stake Today

BY KENNETH REICH
Times Staff Writer

MONTGOMERY, Ala.—In the 1968 presidential election, George C. Wallace received 65% of the Alabama vote.

In 1966, his late wife Lurleen—a political amateur running in his stead for governor because he could not legally succeed himself—drew 54% of the vote in the Democratic primary and became the nominee without a runoff.

In today's primary election, if there is agreement on anything among the political factions in this state, it is that Wallace won't do as well as his wife did in 1966.

Wallace may still win this election. If he does, victory will likely come after a runoff against his long-time protege, incumbent Gov. Albert P. Brewer. (There are five minor candidates in today's race.)

But Wallace's basic strength in the state he claimed to personify so long has seemingly eroded.

A charismatic man whose political fortune was bred on crisis, he may be in trouble in today's election because Alabama is not in the midst of crisis.

He may be in trouble because at least the state's mind, if not its heart, has changed on the vital racial issue.

He has certainly found trouble because his tactics in challenging Brewer left a bad taste in many people's mouths and some of them had previously been strong supporters.

"Albert doesn't deserve Wallace opposition," was the way one man put it in Birmingham. And in Mont

Please Turn to Page 12, Col. 1

Hopes Rise for Teacher Strike Settlement by End of the Week

BY HARRY BERNSTEIN
Times Labor Writer

The Los Angeles teachers' strike started its fourth week Monday amid rising hopes that the walkout will be over by this weekend.

A possible delaying effect on the hoped-for settlement was avoided Monday when Superior Judge Stevens Fargo agreed with another Superior Court judge that the strike is illegal and issued a preliminary injunction to that effect, but delayed action at least until May 18 on contempt of court charges against strike leaders.

This means United Teachers of Los Angeles President Robert Ransom, Vice President Larry Sibelman, Executive Secretary Don Baer and Assistant Executive Secretary Roger Segure can devote full time to seeking a settlement instead of to the court proceedings.

A UTLA spokesman said the preliminary injunction issued Monday against the strike will be appealed on constitutional grounds.

The hopes for a quick end to the strike are based on the belief that

UCLA law Prof. Benjamin Aaron will come up Thursday with a contract proposal acceptable both to the striking teachers and the Board of Education.

Neither side is obligated to accept his recommendations, but public pressure for both to do so will be great.

Some of the more militant teachers are unhappy about the procedure proposed by Aaron and accepted by both sides because they feel it means, in effect, that the outcome of the entire strike rests on one man.

If Aaron recommends any significant concessions to the teachers, it will be difficult for the strike to continue because the already divided teachers will be further divided on their next move.

Equally heavy pressure will be felt by the Board of Education to accept the recommendations even if Aaron makes concessions to the teachers that the board majority would not have approved before the strike.

Please Turn to Page 26, Col. 1

Index to The Times

Newsweek

Bob Woodward and Carl Bernstein of the *Washington Post*.

scope and magnitude of the totalitarian methods used by Nixon and his closest advisers to discredit their foes and maintain their long-sought control over America's destiny.

Crucial to the following developments was Nixon's decision to begin a secret bombing campaign against neutral Cambodia in March 1969. Enmity and distrust between the White House and Congress grew when the Senate twice rejected his nominations to the Supreme Court. Then came massive public demonstrations against an open invasion of Cambodia and the killing of four Kent State University students. The White House atmosphere became one of tenseness, and a number of news leaks added to the pressure.

In June 1970, Nixon agreed to a plan advanced by White House aide Tom Huston that called for a domestic security group to be formed from representatives of the White House, FBI, CIA, and other government agencies. It was to be authorized to wiretap, commit burglary, and violate other laws, if necessary, in the interest of providing intelligence information on persons disloyal to the administration. FBI Director J. Edgar Hoover, jealously protecting his hold over domestic intelligence gathering, refused to cooperate. Nixon then recalled his memos to the other organizations. The White House learned a lesson here. In the future, if sensitive missions needed to be carried out, they would have to be conducted by persons not connected to any official agency.

In the absence of any such secret group, however, Nixon authorized FBI wiretaps on four newsmen and 13 government officials between May 1969 and February 1971. Secretary of State Henry Kissinger, fearful of possible leaks from members of his staff, encouraged some of the wiretaps. A turning point came in June 1971, with the publication of the Pentagon Papers. Worried that his own secret foreign maneuverings, including the Cambodian bombing,* might be revealed, Nixon authorized the establishment of a White House surveillance team—later to be called the "Plumbers." Their chief assignment was to plug leaks of classified information. On September 3, 1971, several of the unit's members broke into the office of Daniel Ellsberg's psychia-

---

*The recipient of one news leak was William Beecher of the *New York Times* who reported on May 9, 1969, that secret B-52 raids were being conducted in Cambodia. The full story did not emerge until 1973. See the journalism review *MORE* (October 1973, p. 17). Beecher's "offhand disclosure" may have been meant to help Nixon signal a new get-tough policy; if so, he went too far. First his phone was one of those tapped; then, after being judged loyal, he was named Deputy Assistant Secretary of Defense for Public Affairs. Other reporters claimed they knew of the Cambodian bombings but did not consider them major news. After the one *Times* story, only *Newsweek,* once in its news briefs section, mentioned the bombing during the 14-month period.

trist in an effort to find personal information that might discredit the man who brought the Pentagon Papers to the *New York Times*.

That same week White House aide Charles Colson, one of Nixon's closest personal confidants, gave John Dean, the president's counsel, a "priority list" of 20 "political enemies." The list, later expanded, contained the names of journalists, politicians, movie stars, and other prominent Americans. From this time until June 1972, operatives hired by persons with White House contacts attempted to disrupt the campaigns of Democratic candidates, especially the acknowledged frontrunner, Senator Edmund Muskie. Their object was to destroy Muskie's candidacy in the hopes that a more vulnerable candidate, Senator George McGovern, might emerge as Nixon's opponent in the 1972 elections. Nixon's White House chief of staff, H. R. ("Bob") Haldeman, was kept advised of these activities, known later as the "dirty tricks" campaign.

It was the White House "Plumbers" who on June 17, 1972, entered the Washington headquarters of the Democratic National Committee, located in the Watergate apartment complex. Washington police caught five men redhanded, planting listening devices in the office of Lawrence F. O'Brien, chairman of the Democratic party. It later was determined this was part of a large-scale plan to spy on Democratic leaders* and was financed by contributions (some of them illegal) to the Committee to Re-elect the President, called CREEP.

The *Washington Post* ran as its second lead on June 18 an 83-inch story that linked Watergate burglar James McCord to the CIA. The *New York Times* ran a 13-inch story on an inside page, as did most newspapers. Since this broke as a local story, the *Post* assigned several metropolitan reporters to it, including Bob Woodward and Carl Bernstein. It was Woodward who traced the name of E. Howard Hunt, found in one burglar's address book, to a White House office.

The pattern of media coverage quickly developed. As the *Post* pushed onward with its stories by Woodward and Bernstein, assisted by the mysterious contact "Deep Throat," White House spokesmen branded them as being false or misleading. These official rebuttals received more attention than the original stories. On June 19 Ronald Ziegler, Nixon's press secretary, called Watergate a "third-rate burglary attempt" and said "certain elements" would attempt to blow the event out of proportion.

A few papers were disturbed, such as the *St. Louis Post-Dispatch,* which said, "the whole episode has a distasteful aura which cannot be dispelled by bland and unelaborated disclaimers from top Republican strategists."[6] But majority sentiment was reflected in this *Chicago Tribune* editorial: "It is hard to believe that it had the participation, approval, or knowledge of any official Republican organization, let alone the White House . . . it is Mr. O'Brien who is guilty of gutter politics and of sharing guilt by association."[7]

In an impromptu news conference on June 22, Nixon denied White House involvement in any break-in and said attempted surveillance "has no place in our electoral process or in our governmental process."[8] But the very next day Haldeman brought Nixon up to date on a plan to sidetrack any FBI investigation of the break-in, by telling the FBI that certain CIA operations in Mexico would be endangered. The cover-up was underway and had been since the morning of June 17. The White House knew the Watergate burglars and their chiefs, E. Howard Hunt and G. Gordon Liddy,

*O'Brien was a likely target because of his friendship with Edward Kennedy, his demands for investigation of the ITT case, and his possible knowledge of a $100,000 contribution given Nixon friend Charles ("Bebe") Rebozo by billionaire Howard Hughes that was not passed on to CREEP.

had knowledge of other break-ins. If Hunt and Liddy were caught, the entire "dirty tricks" campaign, wiretapping, and other scandals might come to light.[9]

The *Post's* team of Woodward and Bernstein came up with a major breakthrough in an August 1 story that claimed a $25,000 check deposited in the account of Watergate burglar Bernard L. Barker had been written by Kenneth H. Dahlberg, Nixon's Midwest finance chairman, and given to Maurice Stans, in charge of finances for the Republican campaign. Senator McGovern and O'Brien pressed their attack against the Nixon White House, but Republican National Chairman Robert Dole and other GOP spokesmen continued to receive good coverage of their countercharges.

On August 29, Nixon said at a news conference that the FBI, Department of Justice, and General Accounting Office had, at his direction, been given total cooperation by the White House staff. On October 5 he said, "The FBI assigned 133 agents to this investigation. It followed out 1800 leads. It conducted 1500 interviews. . . . I wanted to make sure that no member of the White House staff and no man or woman in a position of major responsibility in the Committee for Re-election had anything to do with this reprehensible activity." Eventually eighteen of those persons pleaded guilty or were convicted despite such efforts to shield them.

The *Post* struck again in October. Courageous decisions by Katharine Graham, the publisher, and Benjamin Bradlee, executive editor, allowed Woodward and Bernstein to publish on October 10 that Watergate had been only part of a White House plan for massive spying and political espionage. But the next time they came out with a major story, they almost made a fatal error. On October 25 they wrote that Hugh Sloan, White House aide, had testified before a Washington grand jury that Haldeman was one of the individuals authorized to disburse payments from a secret cash fund used for political intelligence. Sloan immediately denied that exact testimony, and the *Post* reeled from attacks by Republicans and other newspapers. Ziegler called it the "shoddiest type of journalism," and the *New York Times* gave the rebuttals strong coverage. Even when the *Post* was awarded the gold Pulitzer Prize medal for meritorious public service in 1973, Senators William Proxmire, Mike Mansfield, Hugh Scott, and others continued to denounce the paper for printing what they called "rumor and innuendo."

As with the great bulk of the early accusations, this one also proved to be essentially correct. Six months later it was learned that Sloan had said, if asked by the grand jury about Haldeman, he would have testified to that effect. That same month intensive lobbying by Republicans, including Rep. Gerald R. Ford, kept the House Banking Committee of Rep. Wright Patman from opening its own investigation.

Studies of press performance during the fall of 1972 revealed that for the most part the Watergate story got little attention. The *Post* had been the leader, and the *New York Times* had tried to keep up. In August, *Time* magazine had broken a major story identifying the "Plumbers" as a group run from the White House by Hunt and Liddy. Leads like that were not followed up, however. One press critic calculated that of 433 Washington-based reporters who could in theory have been assigned to the Watergate story, only 15 actually were. Of some 500 political columns written by Washington pundits between June and election day, fewer than two dozen concerned Watergate.

Regarding television coverage, it was discovered that during the seven-week period beginning September 14, the networks treated the story in a routine way. CBS devoted almost twice as many air time minutes (71) as did NBC and ABC (42 and 41). More than one-third of NBC's coverage came on two broadcasts, the September 15 news of the indictments of the Watergate burglars and the October 10 sabotage story broken by the *Post*. Many of the stories were less than a minute in length. CBS made

"I KNOW WHAT IS BEST FOR VIETNAM ... I HAVE MORE FACTS."

"I KNOW WHAT IS BEST FOR THE ECONOMY... I HAVE MORE FACTS."

"I KNOW WHAT IS BEST TO STOP INFLATION... I HAVE MORE FACTS."

"I KNOW WHAT IS BEST FOR CAMBODIA ... I HAVE MORE FACTS."

"I KNOW WHAT IS BEST FOR AMERICA ... I HAVE MORE FACTS."

"HOW COULD I HAVE KNOWN ABOUT WATERGATE?.. I'M JUST THE PRESIDENT!"

Paul Conrad, © 1973 Los Angeles Times, with permission of The Register and Tribune Syndicate

In 1973, cartoonist Conrad points to the logical chief Watergate conspirator.

its strongest efforts with two special reports, 15 and 8 minutes in length, the week preceding the election.[10] It was no wonder that an October Gallup Poll showed only 52 percent of Americans recognized the word Watergate. McGovern's charges of the worst corruption in American history were openly scoffed at.

It was in this atmosphere that Nixon was reelected. While the *Washington Post, New York Times, Louisville Courier-Journal, St. Louis Post-Dispatch,* and *Minneapolis Tribune* clamored against Nixon's policies, the bulk of the press gave him its blessing, including the *Los Angeles Times,* which lived to regret its decision.

Watergate became the biggest story in 1973 but not merely because of investigative reporting. The trial of the burglars began in Judge John J. Sirica's courtroom in January, and in February the Senate Select Committee on Presidential

Campaign Activities, headed by Senator Sam J. Ervin, Jr., of North Carolina, began hearing testimony. The American public began hundreds of hours of television viewing. But behind all of this was a growing revolt against Nixon by persons in the FBI and Department of Justice and finally by Republican congressmen and papers that had endorsed him.

The lid could not be kept on the cover-up. In March, McCord wrote Judge Sirica a letter charging that he and other defendants were under pressure to plead guilty and remain silent, that perjury had been committed at their trial, and that higher-ups were involved. Nixon's response to the allegations was to accept responsibility for Watergate, along with the resignations of top aides H. R. Haldeman and John Erlichman. But in a televised speech the president denied any personal knowledge of the break-in or any cover-up. Nixon also fired White House counsel John Dean, who later provided damaging testimony against the president.

Media pressure intensified. The *New York Times* put its top investigative reporter, Seymour Hersh, onto the story. Jack Nelson of the *Los Angeles Times* and other writers began to dig. *Time* and *Newsweek* ran numerous stories containing serious allegations. CBS's Dan Rather and Nixon engaged in combat at several news conferences. Then came perhaps the most startling discovery of all. On July 16 a presidential aide, Alexander Butterfield, testified before the Senate committee that since 1970 Nixon had secretly taped all conversations in his offices, in the Lincoln Room, and at Camp David.

From this point until July 24, 1974, the president and his lawyers dueled the Senate committee, special prosecutors Archibald Cox and Leon Jaworski, and the local grand jury for possession of the tapes. The issue was decided on that day by an 8–0 vote of the Supreme Court, which held Nixon had to turn over to Judge Sirica 64 recordings that might contain evidence of wrongdoing by his aides. Otherwise, it was clear, the president would be openly guilty of obstruction of justice.

Throughout this same period Nixon suffered a series of other defeats but remained on the defensive in claiming no knowledge of a cover-up. On October 1, 1973, the transcript of a Los Angeles grand jury investigating the Ellsberg break-in revealed Erlichman's testimony that Nixon had supervised the "Plumbers" unit. On October 10 Vice President Agnew resigned, after pleading no contest on charges of income tax evasion. Nixon picked Gerald Ford to replace him. And on October 20 Nixon fired the original special prosecutor, Cox, in a dispute over subpoenas of the tape recordings. Attorney General Elliot Richardson and his deputy, William Ruckelshaus, resigned in protest of what was immediately called "the Saturday night massacre." Within days, calls for impeachment were heard that would not be quieted.

Nixon raged at an October 26, 1973, televised news conference that he had never seen such "outrageous, vicious, distorted . . . frantic, hysterical reporting." A few days later he felt compelled to tell an Associated Press Managing Editors con-

CBS

Dan Rather

vention, "I am not a crook." But in early 1974 the dam broke. A panel of experts appointed by Judge Sirica ruled that a strange 18.5 minute gap in a tape recording of a June 20, 1972, Nixon-Haldeman talk (released earlier by the president) was caused by manual erasure. The House voted 410–4 to begin impeachment hearings. Nixon attempted to stem the tide on April 30 by releasing edited transcripts of some White House conversations, but he refused to give up other tapes demanded by Jaworski. The plan failed. The language used and behavior described in the widely published transcripts only caused more of his former supporters, notably the *Chicago Tribune* and *Los Angeles Times,* to call for his impeachment. In June the *Los Angeles Times* reported that Nixon, saved from formal indictment only because of his office, was named an "unindicted co-conspirator" by a 19–0 vote of the Washington grand jury, which indicted Attorney General John Mitchell, Haldeman, and Erlichman (all later convicted and sent to prison).

The bipartisan House Judiciary Committee voted three articles of impeachment in late July, charging the president with obstruction of justice, abuse of power, and contempt of Congress for failure to turn over the tapes. Several hold-out Republicans on the Judiciary Committee dropped their staunch support on August 5 when Nixon, complying with the Supreme Court order, released the transcript of his June 23, 1972, talk with Haldeman. It was the "smoking gun" that proved Nixon had been lying for two years to the public, his supporters, and even his lawyers about his lack of knowledge of the break-in.

The end came on the evening of August 8 when Nixon, defending his overall record as he had on so many other occasions during the 26-month ordeal, told a stunned nation he would resign effective the following noon. The next morning he gathered his cabinet and staff for an emotional farewell, which also was televised. A few minutes later Gerald Ford took the oath of office and attempted to reassure the country, saying "Our long national nightmare is over. Our Constitution works."

FORD AND CARTER: ATTEMPTS TO RESTORE CREDIBILITY   President Ford was the only person to serve either as vice president or as president without being elected by the people. A friendly, down-to-earth man, Ford quickly earned the praise of a press corps tired of the daily battles with the administration. He had inherited the disengagement from Vietnam, a high inflation rate, and a higher degree of public cynicism about politicians. But Ford's honeymoon ended only a month after it began, at the moment he appeared on television, September 8, 1974, to announce he was giving Richard Nixon a full presidential pardon for any offenses he may have committed, before all investigations had been completed. J. F. terHorst, Ford's press secretary, resigned in protest and the president was subjected to criticism from all quarters. Former NBC newsman Ron Nessen was named press secretary and served with mixed success, frequently butting heads with a press corps whose skepticism had been quickly revived. It was during Ford's tenure that the nation's institutions, including the news media, would undergo a wholesale reappraisal of basic values. In this post-Watergate era, Ford was credited with bringing to the White House a humility it had lacked for some time.

Ford held 39 regular press conferences during his busy two and one-half years in office: 5 in the balance of 1974, 19 in 1975, and 15 more in 1976. A stubborn man, he spoke bluntly and plainly, maintaining his conservative credentials. The Nixon pardon hurt his credibility, as did his link to the Nixon years in general. His selection of Nelson A. Rockefeller as vice president was one move toward unity in his party and the nation, and Ford gave the country some reassurance in that respect.

Jimmy Carter's close victory over Ford in the 1976 election brought a new style to the White House. Publicly dedicating himself to total honesty with the public, the religious-minded Carter lost no time in trying to continue where Ford left off in encouraging faith in the nation's cherished institutions. He began holding regular news conferences every two weeks, trying to avoid frequent charges of the campaign days that he was less than precise in his answers. As a further step in communicating with the public, in March of 1977 he conducted a two-hour "phone-in" from the Oval Office. Persons lucky enough to have their calls get through the jammed circuits found themselves talking first to Walter Cronkite and then the president. Only time would tell how long Carter could maintain his White House policy of access and candid talk.

The great importance of a period of "crisis of credibility" is that people learn anew the lesson that all freedoms are dependent on freedom of speech and press. These are never secure, never certain, always capable of being lost. In 1971 the United States government tried to deny its people the right to read a report prepared by their own government about a war in which they had fought and died. The rights of citizens are only as strong as their will to defend them and their willingness to defend those who bring them news and opinion with no other interest than their own. From James Franklin the printer to Edward R. Murrow the broadcaster, men and women have so tried.

NOTES

1. Elmer E. Cornwell, Jr., *Presidential Leadership of Public Opinion* (Bloomington: Indiana University Press, 1965), p. 170.
2. James E. Pollard, *The Presidents and the Press: Truman to Johnson* (Washington: Public Affairs Press, 1964), p. 45.
3. See Randall L. Murray, "Harry S. Truman and Press Opinion, 1945–53," Ph.D. thesis, University of Minnesota, 1973.
4. *New York Herald Tribune*, May 12, 1960, as quoted in Pollard, *The Presidents and the Press.*
5. Dennis T. Lowry, "Agnew and the Network TV News: A Before/After Content Analysis," *Journalism Quarterly*, XLVIII (Summer 1971), 205.
6. *St. Louis Post-Dispatch*, June 20, 1972.
7. *Chicago Tribune*, June 22, 1972.
8. The public record is found in *Watergate: Chronology of a Crisis* (Washington, D.C.: Congressional Quarterly, 1975), a documentary review by the impartial and authoritative research organization.
9. For background on the Nixon years, see the bibliographies for this chapter and chapter 21.
10. Edwin Diamond's 1973 study was part of an effort by the Network News Study Group at MIT, of which he was co-director. Also see, Edward J. Epstein, "How the Press Handled the Watergate Scandal," *Los Angeles Times*, September 14, 1973.

ANNOTATED BIBLIOGRAPHY

Books

ARCHER, JULES, *Watergate: America in Crisis*. New York: Thomas Y. Crowell, 1975. Retraces the tales of political espionage and dirty tricks.
ASSOCIATED PRESS, *Triumph and Tragedy: The Story of the Kennedys*. New York: William Morrow, 1968. Assassinations of JFK and RFK. See also United Press International, *Assassination: Robert F. Kennedy* (New York: Cowles, 1968).
BARRETT, MARVIN, ed., *The Politics of Broadcasting*. New York: Thomas Y. Crowell, 1973. This fourth duPont-Columbia University survey finds Nixon intimidated press.
———, ed., *Moments of Truth*. New York: Thomas Y. Crowell, 1975. Fifth duPont-Columbia survey of broadcast journalism compresses story of 1973–75 confrontation.

BERNSTEIN, CARL, AND BOB WOODWARD, *All the President's Men*. New York: Simon & Schuster, 1974. The *Washington Post's* reporters tell how they laid the groundwork for toppling Nixon; transformed into top-ranking motion picture. See also Bob Woodward and Carl Bernstein, *The Final Days* (New York: Simon & Schuster, 1976).

BRESLIN, JIMMY, *How the Good Guys Finally Won*. New York: Viking, 1975. A great reporter produces one of the best step-by-step accounts of the Nixon impeachment.

CORNWELL, ELMER E., JR., *Presidential Leadership of Public Opinion*. Bloomington: Indiana University Press, 1965. The press conference from Theodore Roosevelt to John Kennedy.

DREW, ELIZABETH, *Washington Journal: The Events of 1973–1974*. New York: Random House, 1975. The *New Yorker's* political writer details the final year of Watergate.

FARRAR, RONALD T., *The Reluctant Servant: The Story of Charles G. Ross*. Columbia: University of Missouri Press, 1969. Ross was a longtime *St. Louis Post-Dispatch* star before serving as President Truman's press secretary, 1945–50.

HALBERSTAM, DAVID, *The Best and the Brightest*. New York: Random House, 1972. *New York Times* Saigon correspondent analyzes sad effect of Vietnam era on America's leaders.

HOFSTADTER, RICHARD, *Anti-intellectualism in American Life*. New York: Knopf, 1963. A Pulitzer Prize-winning study of the anti-intellectual climate of the 1950s, with historical antecedents.

KEARNS, DORIS, *Lyndon Johnson and the American Dream*. New York: Harper & Row, 1976. Best study of LBJ, by a scholar and confidante; portrays strengths and weaknesses.

LUKAS, J. ANTHONY, *Nightmare: The Underside of the Nixon Years*. New York: Viking, 1976. Comprehensive analysis.

MILLER, MERLE, *Plain Speaking*. New York: G.P. Putnam's Sons, 1973. An oral biography of Harry S Truman that gives, among many other opinions, ex-President's views on the press.

New York Times, The End of a Presidency. New York: Bantam Books, 1974. Day-by-day listing of Watergate-related events, with documents.

POLLARD, JAMES E., *The Presidents and the Press: Truman to Johnson*. Washington: Public Affairs Press, 1964. Continues his earlier study.

PORTER, WILLIAM E., *Assault on the Media: The Nixon Years*. Ann Arbor: University of Michigan Press, 1976. Penetrating analysis of 1969–72 Nixon-Agnew assault on media.

SMALL, WILLIAM, *To Kill a Messenger*. New York: Hastings House, 1970. A prize-winning study by a CBS executive of television's troubles in the 1960s.

SORENSEN, THEODORE C., *Kennedy*. New York: Harper & Row, 1965. One of the best of the studies of President John F. Kennedy and his administration.

UNITED PRESS INTERNATIONAL, *Four Days: The Historical Record of the Death of President Kennedy*. New York: Simon & Schuster, 1964. An *American Heritage* volume, includes journalistic coverage. See also The Associated Press, *The Torch Is Passed* (New York: The Associated Press, 1964).

Watergate: Chronology of a Crisis. Washington: Congressional Quarterly, 1975. A thousand page documentary study of 1972–74 events on a week-by-week basis; factual presentation but draws conclusions from evidence in documents, hearings, tapes, press.

WISE, DAVID, *The Politics of Lying*. New York: Vintage Books, 1973. A veteran journalist traces the credibility gap, from the U-2 to Watergate.

Periodicals and Monographs

CORNWELL, ELMER E., JR., "The Johnson Press Relations Style," *Journalism Quarterly*, XLIII (Spring 1966), 3. The press got much attention from LBJ.

DIAMOND, EDWIN, "How the White House Keeps Its Eye on the Network News Shows," *New York*, IV (May 10, 1971), 45. President Nixon had television monitors, 7 a.m. to midnight.

FURLONG, WILLIAM B., "Dan ('Killer') Schorr, The Great Abrasive," *New York*, VIII (June 16, 1975), 41. How the controversial CBS correspondent faced his critics.

HALBERSTAM, DAVID, "Press and Prejudice," *Esquire*, LXXXI (April 1974), 109. Subtitle: "How our last three Presidents got the newsmen they deserved," by one of them.

HUTCHISON, EARL R., "Kennedy and the Press: the First Six Months," *Journalism Quarterly*, XXXVIII (Autumn 1961), 453.

KWONG, CHAN YING, AND KENNETH STARCK, "The *New York Times* Stance on Nixon and Public Opinion," *Journalism Quarterly,* LIII (Winter 1976), 723. Paper was ahead of public.

LATHAM, AARON, "The Reporter the President Hates," *New York,* VII (Jan. 21, 1974), 34. The Nixon duel with Dan Rather, CBS White House correspondent. See also Philip Nobile, "Dan Rather Is Going Fishing," *Esquire,* LXXXI (April 1974), 106.

LOWRY, DENNIS T., "Agnew and the Network TV News: A Before/After Content Analysis," *Journalism Quarterly,* XLVIII (Summer 1971), 205. Networks played it somewhat safer post-Agnew.

MARTIN, L. JOHN, ed., *Role of the Mass Media in American Politics. Annals* of the American Academy of Political and Social Science, No. 427, September 1976. A special issue with 13 articles on media coverage, effects, image building, perspectives.

MURRAY, RANDALL L., "Harry S. Truman and Press Opinion: 1945–1953," Ph.D. thesis, University of Minnesota, 1973. Documented analysis of influence of press opinion on the President; also excellent for details of Truman's press relations.

NOBILE, PHILIP, "How the *New York Times* Became Second Banana," *Esquire,* LXXXIII (May 1975), 185. Good report on how the *Washington Post* took honors on Watergate.

PAYNE, DARWIN, *The Press Corps and the Kennedy Assassination. Journalism Monographs,* No. 15, February 1970. Newspaper and broadcast performance at Dallas.

OIL MUSCLE

Saudis Wield Clout Beyond Arab World

BY JOE ALEX MORRIS JR.
Times Staff Writer

RIYADH, Saudi Arabia—At times during the past fortnight, this desert capital has been a Grand Central Station for visiting statesmen.

President Carter was here, preceded by the president of Algeria and followed by the Shah of Iran and U.S. Energy Secretary James R. Schlesinger. Delegations of five U.S. senators and 15 congressmen, the French minister of industry, former British Prime Minister Edward Heath and a host of lesser luminaries visited Riyadh during the same period.

All were drawn by Saudi Arabia's rapid rise to a position of influence and power in the world, particularly in the Middle East.

Financed by massive oil revenues that totaled about $38 billion last year, this remote nation of 7 million people has become a strong moderating influence on the Arab political scene and beyond.

It is not a role the Saudis particularly welcomed. But they are becoming used to it, and they accept the responsibility their immense wealth has given them. Most Western observers here believe they are playing their new role wisely.

For aiding King Khaled, it has meant tedious trips to Riyadh from his desert encampment southward hundred miles to the north where he prefers to be—surrounded by loyal Bedouin tribes and his falcons, far from the clang, dust and bustle of the construction boom in the capital.

He comes into Riyadh to greet each visiting leader, then turns the business over to Crown Prince Fahd, the prime minister.

Saudi Arabia's new political power is a direct outgrowth of the post-1973 quadrupling of crude oil prices, which made it overnight a financial power on Wall Street and in international monetary circles. The money made it possible for the kingdom to emerge from the wings to center stage in the Arab sphere and the Third World.

Today, when the Saudis demand a bigger vote in the International Monetary Fund, they get it. When they agree to gradually shift their short-term U.S. Treasury notes into medium-term investments, as they are now doing, the U.S. government breathes more easily.

And in the Arab world, their influence is omnipresent.

As a former Jordanian ambassador to the United Nations and Egypt put it, "The Saudis hold the key to the Arab world now. If you have their support, you don't need anyone else's."

And a top Syrian official close to President Hafez Assad added, "Prince

Please Turn to Page 14, Col. 1

DALLAS WINS 27-10 IN SUPER BOWL XII

The Dallas Cowboys took advantage of costly mistakes by the Denver Broncos to win Super Bowl XII 27-10 Sunday in New Orleans' Superdome. The Cowboys, winning their second Super Bowl in four appearances, gained a 13-0 lead in the first half when they intercepted four Denver passes. Details in Sports Section.

Carter Aides Back Changes in Party's Nominating Rules

BY ROBERT SHOGAN
Times Political Writer

WASHINGTON—Of all the people who phoned Mark Siegel, White House political trouble shooter, last week, none was treated with more elaborate courtesy than Morley Winograd, chairman of the Democratic Party's Commission on Presidential Nomination and Party Structure.

"I quiver at the thought of what you could do to us," Siegel told Winograd. "You have the President's renomination in your hands."

Siegel was joshing with Winograd, an old friend generally regarded as a Jimmy Carter loyalist. But underneath the facetiousness was a serious point.

It is generally agreed that the relatively wide-open Democratic delegate selection system—with 31 primaries and proportional representation—contributed to unseating Jimmy Carter's victory in the race for the 1976 nomination.

Now, however, the Winograd commission, with White House backing, is considering some changes in the rules. These revisions, critics say, would discourage Democrats who might have been inspired by Carter's example from challenging the President for the 1980 nomination.

The commission, which has been conducting hearings and studies for months under a mandate from the 1976 convention, will meet in Washington next weekend to draft its final recommendations to the Democratic National Committee.

Please Turn to Page 8, Col. 1

THE WEATHER

National Weather Service forecast: Partly cloudy with showers likely today, becoming heavy at about mid-afternoon and tonight. Partly cloudy with chance of showers decreasing Tuesday. Highs both days in the low 60s. High Sunday 62; low 55.

Complete weather information and smog report in Part 2, Page 2.

FINAL TRIBUTE—Muriel Humphrey stands at right during memorial service for her late husband, Sen. Hubert H. Humphrey, in the Capitol Rotunda. At her right are President and Mrs. Carter; behind the Carters are former President Gerald R. Ford and former Vice President Nelson A. Rockefeller. Happy Rockefeller is to her husband's left; former President Richard M. Nixon is also at far left.
AP Wirephoto

Egyptians, Israelis Resolve Impasse, Reschedule Talks

BY DIAL TORGERSON
Times Staff Writer

JERUSALEM—Israeli-Egyptian peace talks, on the brink of failure over the weekend, were saved Sunday by a compromise agreement and rescheduled for Tuesday.

And U.S. Secretary of State Cyrus R. Vance, who on Saturday had abruptly postponed his departure from Washington because the two sides had failed to agree on an agenda, left for the Jerusalem talks Sunday night.

The cause of the near-impasse was the agenda for what will be the first meeting of a joint political committee of the Israeli and Egyptian foreign ministers. On one agenda item, the one dealing with the Israeli-occupied territories and the Palestinians, the two sides apparently had not been able even to agree on how the item should be worded.

It was after a meeting of the Israeli cabinet—which Prime Minister Menahem Begin said had decided in favor of a compromise on the agenda—that events shifted and a crisis was averted.

Although it was not disclosed how the differences were resolved, it appeared that the major compromise was by Israel. An Israeli Foreign Ministry spokesman said, "The agenda has been sufficiently discussed so that the meeting can open on Tuesday."

According to Israeli officials, there was some compromise on both sides.

Please Turn to Page 12, Col. 1

Giscard Indirectly Warns Carter

Says He'll Let No One Interfere in Elections

YAMOUSSOUKRO, Ivory Coast (AP)—French President Valery Giscard d'Estaing, in an oblique warning to the Carter Administration, declared Sunday he will allow nobody to interfere in upcoming French elections.

The French leader's comments, in a news conference closing his five-day visit to the Ivory Coast, expressed concerns of concern Thursday by the U.S. State Department over "Eurocommunism" and the possibility of Communist participation in a new Italian government.

"I have always made it a rule never to accept that anybody—and I mean anybody—interfere in French political life," he said. "That is our business."

Giscard d'Estaing's deliberate tone—and his hesitation before saying "I mean anybody"—made it clear he was seeking to deliver a warning. His statement was tacked onto the an-

Please Turn to Page 11, Col. 4

Two-Day Storm Dumps 1.6 Inches of Rain on L.A.

Slides, Flooding, Blackouts Plague Wide Area; 2 Motorists Drown in Raging San Diego River

BY TED THACKREY JR.
Times Staff Writer

Morning clouds turned to sunny skies for most of Southern California Sunday, but the latest storm left a legacy of death, mudslides, flash flooding, power outages and at least one tornado report.

San Diego police said two motorists drowned when their car was swept into the rampaging San Diego River near Mission San Diego. Lifeguards said 17 other persons were rescued from flooded homes and automobiles during the morning hours.

Ski and resort areas reported massive traffic jams as weekend motorists found access highways blocked in the vicinity of Mt. Baldy and Big Bear.

There were other mudslides and traffic tieups in canyons of the Malibu area and traffic was down to a crawl at times along Pacific Coast Highway.

Both the Los Angeles Department of Water and Power and Southern California Edison Co. reported several thousands of their customers without electric power for varying periods during the night and into the morning because of weather-related problems.

And what residents of the Willow-brook area said was a tornado tore off a garage door, blew out several windows, damaged two roofs and knocked down numerous power lines nearby.

The storm, which began Saturday, dropped 1.60 inches of rain at Los Angeles Civic Center, bringing the season's total to 12.48 inches—and private weather statistician Ken Levitt said this was more than double the statistical norm of 6.06 inches for Jan. 15.

It is also, he said, .17 of an inch more than the 12.31 inches of rain that fell during the whole of last season.

Elsewhere, the storm left 5.05 inches of rain at Lake Arrowhead in the 24 hours preceding 4 p.m. Sunday; Mt. Wilson got 4.99 inches in the

Please Turn to Page 3, Col. 3

Nixon Attracts Little Notice on Return to Capital

BY RUDY ABRAMSON
Times Staff Writer

WASHINGTON—Richard M. Nixon, who left Washington in the biggest political convulsion of modern times, returned Sunday after 3½ years, barely noticed.

On a bright, cold day, with a raw and whipping down from the Blue Ridge Mountains, Nixon crossed the Potomac River from Virginia half an hour before memorial services for Sen. Hubert H. Humphrey, a lifelong political adversary. Nixon had spent Saturday night in seclusion in a residence in suburban Virginia.

Washington's streets were half empty Sunday morning as the former President's dark limousine, followed by a carload of security men, zipped down Pennsylvania Ave. to the Capitol.

On the wind-swept plaza in front of the Capitol, shivering crowds watched the arrival of an unusual gathering of political leaders. It was in stark contrast to the steamy August day on which Nixon had resigned and the U.S. government had come almost to a standstill.

Before the crowd realized it, Nixon's car had slipped beneath a covered archway and the former President entered the Senate wing of the Capitol unobserved.

He went directly to the Senate minority leader's office, already occu-

Please Turn to Page 9, Col. 5

U.S. Leaders Say Farewell to Humphrey

Carter and Mondale Deliver Eulogies at Services in Capitol

BY JOHN AVERILL
and DON IRWIN
Times Staff Writers

WASHINGTON—With eulogies by President Carter and Vice President Mondale, America's leadership, present and past, said farewell Sunday to Hubert Horatio Humphrey in majestic memorial services under the Capitol's Great Dome.

"Hubert Humphrey was the most beloved of all Americans," the President said in a soft-spoken eight-minute eulogy. "We and our families are here today to testify that Hubert Humphrey may well have blessed our country more than any of us."

Mondale said of Humphrey: "He taught us all how to hope and how to love, how to win and how to lose. He taught us how to live and, finally, he taught us how to die."

That Humphrey commanded the deep affection of his fellow men was evident from the hundreds of dignitaries who joined the Capitol's huge Rotunda, where the bodies of nine Presidents, beginning with that of Abraham Lincoln in 1865, have lain in state.

Joining in the tribute to the 66-year-old Minnesota senator and former Vice President, who died Friday of cancer, were former Presidents Gerald R. Ford and Richard M. Nixon, Lady Bird Johnson, widow of President Lyndon B. Johnson, and former Secretary of State Henry A. Kissinger.

It was Nixon's first visit to Washington since he resigned from the Presidency in August, 1974, who was accompanied by his daughter Tricia.

Seated in a circle around the flag-draped coffin were members of the Cabinet, the Supreme Court, foreign ambassadors, members of the Senate and House and the Joint Chiefs of Staff.

After the 36-minute memorial service, eight servicemen in dress uniform slowly lifted the coffin from the catafalque and carried it down the steep steps of the East Front of the Capitol to a waiting motorcade.

At Carter's direction, the body was flown aboard Air Force One to St. Paul, Minn., where it was to lie in state in the Minnesota Capitol before funeral services in St. Paul. Burial will be in Minneapolis this afternoon, in services to be attended by Carter and other dignitaries, including Gov. Brown.

Before the massive bronze doors of the Rotunda were closed to the public prior to Sunday morning's service, an estimated 65,000 persons had walked through the Capitol to view Humphrey's coffin. The Rotunda was open to the public throughout the night.

Five servicemen with fixed bayonets provided an honor guard for the closed coffin. During the memorial service, several thousand persons filled the plaza outside the Capitol.

In his eulogy Carter followed earlier private amends with a public apology for some unkind remarks he had made about Humphrey during the 1976 campaign, when the Minnesotan was considering challenging Carter for the Democratic nomination.

Please Turn to Page 6, Col. 4

THREE CHIEFS—President Carter, with former Presidents Gerald R. Ford and Richard M. Nixon.
AP Wirephoto

Another time of transition.

Index